Western Society: A Brief History

WESTERN SOCIETY:
A Brief History

VOLUME II:
From Absolutism to the Present

John P. McKay
University of Illinois at Urbana-Champaign

Bennett D. Hill
Late of *Georgetown University*

John Buckler
University of Illinois at Urbana-Champaign

Clare Haru Crowston
University of Illinois at Urbana-Champaign

Merry E. Wiesner-Hanks
University of Wisconsin–Milwaukee

Bedford/St. Martin's
Boston   New York

For Bedford/St. Martin's

Publisher for History: Mary Dougherty
Director of Development for History: Jane Knetzger
Executive Editor for History: Traci Mueller
Senior Production Editor: Rosemary R. Jaffe
Senior Production Supervisor: Joe Ford
Executive Marketing Manager: Jenna Bookin Barry
Associate Editor for History: Lynn Sternberger
Production Assistants: David Ayers and Lidia MacDonald-Carr
Copyeditor: Peggy Flanagan
Text Design: Cia Boynton
Photo Research: Carole Frohlich
Indexer: Jake Kawatski
Cover Design: Donna Lee Dennison
Cover Art: Alois Schonn, *Fruit Market in Vienna, near Maria Theresien Brücke,* 1826–1827.
    Watercolor, Museum der Stadt, Vienna. Alfredo Dagli Orti/The Art Archive.
Cartography: Charlotte Miller/GeoNova
Composition: NK Graphics
Printing and Binding: RR Donnelley and Sons

President: Joan E. Feinberg
Editorial Director: Denise B. Wydra
Director of Marketing: Karen R. Soeltz
Director of Editing, Design, and Production: Marcia Cohen
Assistant Director of Editing, Design, and Production: Elise S. Kaiser
Managing Editor: Elizabeth M. Schaaf

Library of Congress Control Number: 2008928070

Manufactured in the United States of America.
4   3   2   1   0   9
f   e   d   c   b   a

For information, write: Bedford/St. Martin's, 75 Arlington Street, Boston, MA 02116
(617-399-4000)

ISBN-10: 0–312–68299–9 ISBN-13: 978–0–312–68299–6 (combined edition)
ISBN-10: 0–312–68300–6 ISBN-13: 978–0–312–68300–9 (Vol. I)
ISBN-10: 0–312–68301–4 ISBN-13: 978–0–312–68301–6 (Vol. II)

Preface

The first edition of *A History of Western Society* grew out of our desire to infuse new life into the study of Western civilization. We knew that historians were using imaginative questions and innovative research to open up vast new areas of historical interest and knowledge. We also recognized that these advances had dramatically affected the subject of European economic, cultural, and, especially, social history, while new scholarship and fresh interpretations were also revitalizing the study of the traditional mainstream of political, diplomatic, and religious developments. Our goal was to write a textbook that reflected these dynamic changes, and we have been gratified by the tremendous response to this book on the part of both instructors and students.

This version of the textbook—*Western Society: A Brief History*—reflects the same goals and approach of its full-length counterpart. But its brevity addresses the needs of a growing number of instructors whose students need a less comprehensive text, either because of increased supplemental reading in the course or because their students benefit from less detail in order to grasp key developments. It also suits courses that cover the entire history of Western civilization in one semester. Finally, its lower price makes it an affordable alternative to larger texts, and the retention of a particularly strong illustration and map program and a full program of pedagogical support make the book a particularly good value.

In developing *Western Society: A Brief History*, we shortened our full-length narrative by thirty percent. We began by judiciously reducing coverage of subjects of secondary importance. We also condensed and combined thematically related sections and aimed throughout the text to tighten our exposition while working hard to retain our topical balance, up-to-date scholarship, and lively, accessible writing style. The result, we believe, is a concise edition that preserves the narrative flow, balance, and power of the full-length work.

Central Themes and Approach

It was our conviction, based on considerable experience introducing large numbers of students to the broad sweep of Western civilization, that a book in which social history was the core element could excite readers and inspire a renewed interest in history. Therefore we incorporated recent research by social historians as we sought to re-create the life of ordinary people in appealing human terms. At the same time, we were determined to give great economic, political, cultural, and intellectual developments the attention they unquestionably deserve. We wanted to give individual readers a balanced, integrated perspective so that they could pursue—on their own or in the classroom—those themes and questions that they found particularly exciting and significant.

In an effort to realize fully the potential of our innovative yet balanced approach, we made many changes, large and small, in the editions that followed the original publication of *A History of Western Society*. In particular, we approached the history of the West as part of the history of the world, devoting more attention throughout the book to Europe's interactions with other cultures and societies. Too, we took advantage of the exciting recent scholarship on women's and gender history to provide even fuller discussion of the role of gender in the shaping of human experience. Producing this briefer edition gave us the opportunity to bring even more clarity and focus to our core themes and approach.

Pedagogy and Features

We know from our own teaching that students need and welcome help in assimilating information and acquiring critical-thinking skills. Thus we retained the class-tested learning and teaching aids of the parent text while adding more such features. Each chapter opens by posing four or five historical questions keyed to its main sections in a clearly defined *chapter preview* that accompanies the chapter introduction. The relevant questions appear at the start of the chapter's main sections, all of which conclude with a *section review* that encapsulates the material presented and provides an answer to the question. Then a carefully crafted *chapter review* at the close of each chapter reprises the chapter questions and summary answers.

In other measures to promote clarity and comprehension, bolded *key terms* in the text are defined in the margin next to their appearance and repeated at the end of the chapter, and confidence-building *phonetic spellings* are located directly after terms that readers are likely to find hard to pronounce. *Chapter chronologies* alert students to the major developments discussed in the chapter and *topic-specific chronologies* appear at key points throughout the book.

We are particularly proud of the illustrative component of our work, its *art and map programs*. Over 340 illustrations, many of them in full color and all contemporaneous with the subject matter—reveal to today's visually attuned students how the past speaks in pictures as well as in words. Recognizing students' difficulties with geography, we also offer over 65 full-color maps and the popular *"Mapping the Past"* chapter feature, which provides questions that encourage students' close investigation of one map in each chapter, often with prompts to compare it to other maps in order to appreciate change over time. Substantive captions for all our illustrations help students to make the most of these informative materials.

We are proud as well of the biographical and primary-source special features that appear in each chapter to spotlight our focus on social history. These were so well received by readers of the full-length edition that we determined to keep them in our concise account.

Each chapter features *"Individuals in Society,"* an illustrated biographical essay of a woman, man, or group intended to extend the chapter narrative while showing students the similarities and differences between these former lives and their own. This special feature evidences our focus on people, both famous and obscure, and we believe that student readers will empathize with these human beings as they themselves seek to define their own identities. Examples include Bithus, a typical Roman soldier (Chapter 6), the German abbess and mystic Hildegard of Bingen (Chapter 10), freed slave and abolitionist Olaudah Equiano (Chapter 19), and Tariq Ramadan, the controversial European-Muslim intellectual (Chapter 31). "Questions for Analysis" guide students' consideration of the historical significance of these figures. For a complete list of the individuals highlighted, see page xxiii.

Each chapter also includes a one- or two-page feature titled *"Listening to the Past,"* chosen to extend and illuminate a major historical issue raised in the chapter through the presentation of a single original source or several voices on the subject. Each "Listening to the Past" selection opens with a problem-setting introduction and closes with "Questions for Analysis" that invite students to evaluate the evidence as historians would. Selected for their interest and importance and carefully fitted into their historical context, these sources, we hope, do indeed allow students to "listen to the past" and to observe how history has been shaped by individual men and women, some of them great aristocrats, others ordinary folk. Sources include Gilgamesh's quest for immortality (Chapter 1), an Arab view of the Crusades (Chapter 9), parliamentary testimony of young British mine workers (Chapter 22), and Simone de Beauvoir's critique of marriage (Chapter 30). A full list of these features appears on page xxiii.

The complete volume presents eight photo essays entitled *"Images in Society."* Each consists of a short narrative with questions, accompanied by several pictures. The goal of the feature is to encourage students to think critically: to view and compare visual illustrations and draw conclusions about the societies and cultures that produced those objects. Thus, in Chapter 1 appears the discovery of the "Iceman," the frozen remains of an unknown herdsman. "The Roman Villa at Chedworth" in Britain mirrors Roman provincial culture (Chapter 6). The essay "From Romanesque to Gothic" treats the architectural shift in medieval church building and aims to show how the Gothic cathedral reflected the ideals and values of medieval society (Chapter 11). "Art in the Reformation" (Chapter 14) examines both the Protestant and Catholic views of religious art. Chapter 17 presents the way monarchs displayed their authority visually in "Absolutist Palace Building." Moving to modern times, the focus in Chapter 19 changes to "London: The Remaking of a Great City," which depicts how Londoners rebuilt their city after a great catastrophe. "Class and Gender Boundaries in Women's Fashion, 1850–1914" studies women's clothing in relationship to women's evolving position in society and gender relations (Chapter 24). Finally, "Pablo Picasso and Modern Art" looks at some of Picasso's greatest paintings to gain insight into his principles and the modernist revolution in art (Chapter 28).

Supplements

To aid in the teaching and learning processes, a wide array of print and electronic supplements for students and instructors accompanies *Western Society: A Brief History.* Some of the materials are available for the first time with our new publisher, Bedford/St. Martin's. For more information on popular value packages and available materials, please visit bedfordstmartins.com/mckaywestbrief/catalog or contact your local Bedford/St. Martin's representative.

For Students
Print Resources

The Bedford Series in History and Culture.   Over 100 titles in this highly praised series combine first-rate scholarship, historical narrative, and important primary documents for undergraduate courses. Each book is brief, inexpensive, and focuses on a specific topic or period. Package discounts are available.

Rand McNally Atlas of Western Civilization.   This collection of over fifty full-color maps highlights social, political, and cross-cultural change and interaction from classical Greece and Rome to the post-industrial Western world. Each map is thoroughly indexed for fast reference.

The Bedford Glossary for European History.   This handy supplement for the survey course gives students historically contextualized definitions for hundreds of terms—from Abbasids to Zionism—that students will encounter in lectures, reading, and exams. Available free when packaged with the text.

Trade Books.   Titles published by sister companies Farrar, Straus and Giroux; Henry Holt and Company; Hill and Wang; Picador; St. Martin's Press; and Palgrave are available at a 50 percent discount when packaged with Bedford/St. Martin's textbooks. For more information, visit bedfordstmartins.com/tradeup.

New Media Resources

WESTERN SOCIETY: A BRIEF HISTORY e-Book. This electronic version of *Western Society: A Brief History* offers students unmatched value—the complete text of the print book, with easy-to-use highlighting, searching, and note-taking tools, at a significantly reduced price.

Online Study Guide at bedfordstmartins.com/mckaywestbrief. The popular Online Study Guide for *Western Society: A Brief History* is a free and uniquely personalized learning tool to help students master themes and information presented in the textbook and improve their critical-thinking skills. Assessment quizzes let students evaluate their comprehension, a flashcard activity tests students' knowledge of key terms, and learning objectives help students focus on key points of each chapter. Instructors can monitor students' progress through the online Quiz Gradebook or receive e-mail updates.

Benjamin, A Student's Online Guide to History Reference Sources at bedfordstmartins .com/mckaywestbrief.** This Web site provides links to history-related databases, indexes, and journals, plus contact information for state, provincial, local, and professional history organizations.

The Bedford Bibliographer at bedfordstmartins.com/mckaywestbrief.** *The Bedford Bibliographer*, a simple but powerful Web-based tool, assists students with the process of collecting sources and generates bibliographies in four commonly used documentation styles.

The Bedford Research Room at bedfordstmartins.com/mckaywestbrief.** *The Research Room*, drawn from Mike Palmquist's *The Bedford Researcher*, offers a wealth of resources— including interactive tutorials, research activities, student writing samples, and links to hundreds of other places online—to support students in courses across the disciplines. The site also offers instructors a library of helpful instructional tools.

Diana Hacker's Research and Documentation Online at bedfordstmartins.com/ mckaywestbrief.** This Web site provides clear advice on how to integrate primary and secondary sources into research papers, how to cite sources correctly, and how to format in MLA, APA, *Chicago*, or CBE style.

The St. Martin's Tutorial on Avoiding Plagiarism at bedfordstmartins.com/ mckaywestbrief.** This online tutorial reviews the consequences of plagiarism and explains what sources to acknowledge, how to keep good notes, how to organize research, and how to integrate sources appropriately. The tutorial includes exercises to help students practice integrating sources and recognizing acceptable summaries.

For Instructors

Print Resources

Instructor's Resource Manual. This helpful manual offers both first-time and experienced teachers a wealth of tools for structuring and customizing Western civilization history courses of different sizes. For each chapter in the textbook, the manual includes a set of instructional objectives; a chapter outline; lecture suggestions; suggestions on using primary sources in the classroom; a list of classroom activities; a suggested map activity; an audiovisual bibliography; a list of internet resources; and an annotated list of suggested reading.

New Media Resources

Instructor's Resource CD-ROM.   This disc provides instructors with ready-made and customizable PowerPoint multimedia presentations built around chapter outlines, maps, figures, and selected images from the textbook, plus jpeg versions of all maps, figures, and selected images suitable for printing onto transparency acetates. Also included are chapter questions formatted in PowerPoint for use with i>clicker, a classroom response system, as well as outline maps.

Computerized Test Bank.   This test bank CD-ROM offers instructors a flexible and powerful tool for test generation and test management. The test bank offers key term identification, essay questions, multiple choice questions with page references and feedback, map questions that refer to maps in the text, and a sample final exam. Instructors can customize quizzes, add or edit both questions and answers, and export questions and answers into a variety of formats, including WebCT and Blackboard.

Book Companion Site at bedfordstmartins.com/mckaywestbrief.   The companion Web site gathers all the electronic resources for the text, including the Online Study Guide and related Quiz Gradebook, at a single Web address. Convenient links to PowerPoint chapter outlines and maps, an online version of the Instructor's Resource Manual, the digital libraries at Make History, and PowerPoint chapter questions for i>clicker, a classroom response system, are also available from this site.

***Make History* at bedfordstmartins.com/mckaywestbrief.**   Comprising the content of Bedford/St. Martin's acclaimed online libraries—*Map Central*, the Bedford History Image Library, DocLinks, and HistoryLinks—*Make History* provides one-stop access to relevant digital content including maps, images, documents, and Web links. Students and instructors alike can search this free, easy-to-use database by keyword, topic, date, or specific chapter of *Western Society: A Brief History*. Instructors can create collections of content and post their collections to the Web to share with students.

Content for Course Management Systems.   A variety of student and instructor resources developed for this textbook are ready to use in course management systems such as WebCT, Blackboard, and other platforms. This e-content includes nearly all of the offerings from the book's Online Study Guide as well as the book's test bank.

Videos and Multimedia.   A wide assortment of videos and multimedia CD-ROMs on various topics in European history is available to qualified adopters.

Acknowledgments

It is a pleasure to thank the many instructors who read and critiqued the manuscript for the ninth edition of the parent text, from which this version is derived:

Hugh Agnew, George Washington University
Melanie Bailey, Centenary College of Louisiana
Rachael Ball, Ohio State University
Eugene Boia, Cleveland State University
Robert Brown, State University of New York, Finger Lakes Community College
Richard Eichman, Sauk Valley Community College
David Fisher, Texas Technical University
Wayne Hanley, West Chester University of Pennsylvania
Michael Leggiere, Louisiana State University, Shreveport
John Mauer, Tri-County Technical College
Nick Miller, Boise State University
Wyatt Moulds, Jones County Junior College
Elsa Rapp, Montgomery County Community College
Anne Rodrick, Wofford College
Sonia Sorrell, Pepperdine University
Lee Shai Weissbach, University of Louisville

It is also a pleasure to thank our many editors for their efforts on this edition. To Carol Newman and Rosemary Jaffe, who guided production, and to Tonya Lobato, our development editor, we express our special appreciation. And we thank Carole Frohlich for her contributions in photo research and selection as well as Doug McGetchin of Florida Atlantic University and Cynthia Ward for their editorial contributions.

Many of our colleagues at the University of Illinois and the University of Wisconsin–Milwaukee continue to provide information and stimulation, often without even knowing it. We thank them for it. In addition, John McKay thanks JoAnn McKay for her unfailing support and encouragement. John Buckler thanks Professor Jack Cargill for his advice on topics in Chapter 2. He also thanks Professor Nicholas Yalouris, former General Inspector of Antiquities, for his kind permission to publish the mosaic from Elis, Greece in Chapter 3. He is likewise grateful to Dr. Amy C. Smith, Curator of the Ure Museum of Archaeology of the University of Reading, for her permission to publish the vase also in Chapter 3. His sincerest thanks go also to Professor Paul Cartledge of Clare College, Cambridge University, for his kind permission to publish his photograph of the statue of Leonidas in Chapter 3. Clare Crowston thanks Ali Banihashem, Max Edelson, Tara Fallon, John Lynn, Dana Rabin, and John Randolph. Merry Wiesner-Hanks thanks Jeffrey Merrick, Carlos Galvao-Sobrinho, and Gwynne Kennedy.

Each of us has benefited from the criticism of his or her coauthors, although each of us assumes responsibility for what he or she has written. Originally, John Buckler wrote the first six chapters; Bennett Hill continued the narrative through Chapter 16; and John McKay wrote Chapters 17 through 31. Beginning with the ninth edition of the parent text and continuing with this brief edition, Merry Wiesner-Hanks assumed primary responsibility for Chapters 7 through 14, and Clare Crowston took responsibility for Chapters 15 through 21.

Finally, we continue to welcome the many comments and suggestions that have come from our readers, for they have helped us greatly in this ongoing endeavor.

J. P. M.   J. B.   C. H. C.   M. E. W.

Brief Contents

Contents

18

Toward a New Worldview, 1540–1789   458

19

The Expansion of Europe in the Eighteenth Century   484

20

The Changing Life of the People   510

21

The Revolution in Politics, 1775–1815   535

26
The West and the World, 1815–1914

27
The Great Break: War and Revolution, 1914–1919

28

The Age of Anxiety, ca. 1900–1940　　726

29

Dictatorships and the Second World War, 1919–1945　　752

Maps, Figures, and Tables

Features

About the Authors

John P. McKay   Born in St. Louis, John P. McKay received his B.A. from Wesleyan University (1961), his M.A. from the Fletcher School of Law and Diplomacy (1962), and his Ph.D. from the University of California, Berkeley (1968). He began teaching history at the University of Illinois in 1966 and became a Professor there in 1976. John won the Herbert Baxter Adams Prize for his book *Pioneers for Profit: Foreign Entrepreneurship and Russian Industrialization, 1885–1913* (1970). He has also written *Tramways and Trolleys: The Rise of Urban Mass Transport in Europe* (1976) and has translated Jules Michelet's *The People* (1973). His research has been supported by fellowships from the Ford Foundation, the Guggenheim Foundation, the National Endowment for the Humanities, and IREX. He has written well over a hundred articles, book chapters, and reviews, which have appeared in numerous publications, including *The American Historical Review, Business History Review, The Journal of Economic History*, and *Slavic Review*. He contributed extensively to C. Stewart and P. Fritzsche, eds., *Imagining the Twentieth Century* (1997).

Bennett D. Hill   A native of Philadelphia, Bennett D. Hill earned an A.B. from Princeton (1956) and advanced degrees from Harvard (A.M., 1958) and Princeton (Ph.D., 1963). He taught history at the University of Illinois, where he was department chair from 1978 to 1981. He published *English Cistercian Monasteries and Their Patrons in the Twelfth Century* (1968), *Church and State in the Middle Ages* (1970), and articles in *Analecta Cisterciensia, The New Catholic Encyclopaedia, The American Benedictine Review*, and *The Dictionary of the Middle Ages*. His reviews appeared in *The American Historical Review, Speculum, The Historian*, the *Journal of World History*, and *Library Journal*. He was one of the contributing editors to *The Encyclopedia of World History* (2001). He was a Fellow of the American Council of Learned Societies and served on the editorial board of *The American Benedictine Review*, on committees of the National Endowment for the Humanities, and as vice president of the American Catholic Historical Association (1995–1996). A Benedictine monk of St. Anselm's Abbey in Washington, D.C., he was also a Visiting Professor at Georgetown University.

John Buckler   Born in Louisville, Kentucky, John Buckler received his Ph.D. from Harvard University in 1973. In 1980 Harvard University Press published his *Theban Hegemony, 371–362* B.C. He published *Philip II and the Sacred War* (Leiden 1989) and also edited *BOIOTIKA: Vorträge vom 5. Internationalen Böotien-Kolloquium* (Munich 1989). In 2003 he published *Aegean Greece in the Fourth Century* B.C. In the following year appeared his editions of W. M. Leake, *Travels in the Morea* (three volumes), and Leake's *Peloponnesiaca*. Cambridge University Press published his *Central Greece and the Politics of Power in the Fourth Century*, edited by Hans Beck, in 2008.

Clare Haru Crowston   Born in Cambridge, Massachusetts, and raised in Toronto, Clare Haru Crowston received her B.A. in 1985 from McGill University and her Ph.D. in 1996 from Cornell University. Since 1996, she has taught at the University of Illinois, where she has served as associate chair and Director of Graduate Studies, and is currently Associate Professor of history. She is the author of *Fabricating Women: The Seamstresses of Old Regime France, 1675–1791* (Duke University Press, 2001), which won two awards, the Berkshire Prize and the Hagley Prize. She edited two special issues of the *Journal of Women's History* (vol. 18, nos. 3 and 4) and has published numerous articles and reviews in journals such as *Annales: Histoire, Sciences Sociales, French Historical Studies, Gender and History,* and the *Journal of Economic History.* Her research has been supported with grants from the National Endowment for the Humanities, the Mellon Foundation, and the Bourse Châteaubriand of the French government. She is a past president of the Society for French Historical Studies and a former chair of the Pinkney Prize Committee.

Merry E. Wiesner-Hanks   Having grown up in Minneapolis, Merry E. Wiesner-Hanks received her B.A. from Grinnell College in 1973 (as well as an honorary doctorate some years later), and her Ph.D. from the University of Wisconsin–Madison in 1979. She taught first at Augustana College in Illinois, and since 1985 at the University of Wisconsin–Milwaukee, where she is currently UWM Distinguished Professor in the department of history. She is the co-editor of the *Sixteenth Century Journal* and the author or editor of nineteen books and many articles that have appeared in English, German, Italian, Spanish, and Chinese. These include *Early Modern Europe, 1450–1789* (Cambridge, 2006), *Women and Gender in Early Modern Europe* (Cambridge, 3d ed., 2008), and *Gender in History* (Blackwell, 2001). She currently serves as the Chief Reader for Advanced Placement World History and has also written a number of source books for use in the college classroom, including *Discovering the Western Past* (Houghton Mifflin, 6th ed, 2007) and *Discovering the Global Past* (Houghton Mifflin, 3d. ed., 2006), and a book for young adults, *An Age of Voyages, 1350–1600* (Oxford 2005).

Western Society: A Brief History

Absolutism and Constitutionalism in Western Europe

ca. 1589–1715

Hyacinthe Rigaud, *Louis XIV, King of France and Navarre* (1701).
Louis XIV is surrounded by the symbols of his power: the sword of
justice, the scepter of power, and the crown. The vigor and strength
of the king's stocking-covered legs contrast with the age and wisdom
of his lined face. (Scala/Art Resource, NY)

Chapter Preview

Seventeenth-Century Crisis and Rebuilding
What were the common crises and
achievements of seventeenth-century
states?

Absolutism in France and Spain
To what extent did French and Spanish
monarchs succeed in creating absolute
monarchies?

The Culture of Absolutism
What cultural forms flourished under
absolutist governments?

Constitutionalism
What is constitutionalism, and how did
this form of government emerge in
England and the Dutch Republic?

INDIVIDUALS IN SOCIETY: Glückel of Hameln
LISTENING TO THE PAST: The Court at Versailles

The seventeenth century was a period of crisis and transformation. Agricultural and manufacturing slumps meant that many people struggled to feed themselves and their families. After a long period of growth in the sixteenth century, population rates stagnated or even fell. Religious and dynastic conflicts led to almost constant war, visiting violence and destruction on ordinary people.

The demands of war reshaped European states. Armies grew larger than they had been since the time of the Roman Empire. To pay for these armies, governments greatly increased taxes. They also created new bureaucracies to collect the taxes and to foster economic activity that might increase state revenue. Despite numerous obstacles, European states succeeded in gathering more power during this period. What one historian described as the long European "struggle for stability" that originated with the Reformation in the early sixteenth century was largely resolved by 1680.[1]

Important differences existed, however, in terms of *which* authority within the state possessed sovereignty—the Crown or privileged groups. Between roughly 1589 and 1715 two basic patterns of government emerged in Europe: absolute monarchy and the constitutional state. Almost all subsequent European governments have been modeled on one of these patterns.

Seventeenth-Century Crisis and Rebuilding

What were the common crises and achievements of seventeenth-century states?

Historians often refer to the seventeenth century as an "age of crisis." After the economic and demographic growth of the sixteenth century, Europe faltered into stagnation and retrenchment. This was partially due to climate changes beyond anyone's control, but it also resulted from the bitterness of religious divides, the increased pressures exerted by governments, and the violence and dislocation of war. Overburdened peasants and city dwellers took action to defend themselves, sometimes profiting from elite conflicts to obtain redress of their grievances. In the long run, however, governments proved increasingly able to impose their will on the populace. This period witnessed a spectacular growth in army size as well as new forms of taxation, government bureaucracies, and increased state sovereignty.

Economic and Demographic Crisis

In the seventeenth century the vast majority of western Europeans lived in villages centered on a church and a manor. A small number of peasants in each village owned enough land to feed themselves and the livestock necessary to work their land. These independent farmers were leaders of the peasant village. They employed the landless poor, rented out livestock and tools, and served as agents for the noble lord. Below them were small landowners and tenant farmers who did not have enough land to be self-sufficient. These families sold their best produce on the market to earn cash for taxes, rent, and food. At the bottom were the rural proletariat who worked as dependent laborers and servants.

Rich or poor, bread was the primary element of the diet. Peasants paid stiff fees to the local miller for grinding grain into flour and sometimes to the lord for the right to bake bread in his oven. Bread was most often accompanied with a soup made of roots, herbs, beans, and perhaps a small piece of salt pork. One of the biggest annual festivals in the rural village was the killing of the family pig. The whole family gathered to help, sharing a rare abundance of meat with neighbors and carefully salting the extra and putting down the lard.

Rural society lived on the edge of subsistence. Because of the crude technology and low crop yield, peasants were constantly threatened by scarcity and famine. In the seventeenth century a period of colder and wetter climate, dubbed by historians as a "little ice age," meant a shorter farming season. A bad harvest created dearth; a series of bad harvests could lead to famine. Recurrent famines significantly reduced the population of early modern Europe. Most people did not die of outright starvation, but rather of diseases brought on by malnutrition and exhaustion. Facilitated by the weakened population, outbreaks of bubonic plague continued in Europe until the 1720s.

Industry also suffered. While the evidence does not permit broad generalizations, it appears that the output of woolen textiles, one of the most important European manufactures, declined sharply in the first half of the seventeenth century. Food prices were high, wages stagnated, and unemployment soared. This economic crisis was not universal: it struck various regions at different times and to different degrees. In the middle decades of the century, Spain, France, Germany, and England all experienced great economic difficulties; but these years were the golden age of the Netherlands.

The urban poor and peasants were the hardest hit. When the price of bread rose beyond their capacity to pay, they frequently took action. In towns they invaded the bakers' shop to seize bread and resell it at a "just price." In rural areas they attacked convoys taking grain away to the cities and also redistributed it. Women often led these actions, since their role as mothers gave them some impunity in authorities' eyes. Historians have labeled this vision of a world in which community needs predominate over competition and profit a **moral economy**.

1589–1610	Henry IV in France
1598	Edict of Nantes
1602	Dutch East India Company founded
1605–1715	Food riots common across Europe
1618–1648	Thirty Years' War
1635	Birth of French Academy
1640–1680	Golden age of Dutch art (Vermeer, Van Steen, Rembrandt)
1642–1649	English civil war ends with execution of Charles I
1643–1715	Louis XIV in France
1648–1653	The Fronde
1653–1658	Military rule in England under Oliver Cromwell
1659	Treaty of the Pyrenees marks end of Spanish imperial dominance
1660	Restoration of English monarchy under Charles II
1665–1683	Jean-Baptiste Colbert applies mercantilism to France
1685	Edict of Nantes revoked
1688–1689	Glorious Revolution in England
1701–1713	War of the Spanish Succession
1713	Peace of Utrecht

moral economy A historian's term for an economic perspective in which the needs of a community take precedence over competition and profit.

Seventeenth-Century State-Building: Common Obstacles and Achievements

In this context of economic and demographic depression, monarchs began to make new demands on their people. Traditionally, historians have distinguished sharply between the "absolutist" governments of France, Spain, Central Europe, and Russia and the constitutional monarchies of England and the Dutch Republic. Whereas absolutist monarchs gathered all power under their personal control, constitutional monarchs were obliged to respect laws passed by representative institutions. More recently, historians have emphasized commonalities among these powers. Despite their political differences, absolutist and constitutional monarchs shared common projects of protecting and expanding their frontiers, raising new taxes, and consolidating state control.

Rulers who wished to increase their authority encountered formidable obstacles. Some obstacles were purely material. Without paved roads, telephones, or

An English Food Riot

Nothing infuriated ordinary women and men more than the idea that merchants and landowners were withholding grain from the market in order to push high prices even higher. In this cartoon an angry crowd hands out rough justice to a rich farmer accused of hoarding. (Courtesy of the Trustees of the British Museum)

other modern technology, it took weeks to convey orders from the central government to the provinces. Rulers also suffered from a lack of information about their realms, due to the limited size of their bureaucracies. Without accurate knowledge of the number of inhabitants and the wealth they possessed, it was impossible to police and tax the population effectively. Cultural and linguistic differences presented their own obstacles. In some kingdoms the people spoke a language different from the Crown's, diminishing their willingness to obey its commands.

Local power structures presented another serious obstacle to a monarch's attempts to centralize power. Across Europe, nobles retained great legal, military, political, and financial powers, in addition to their traditional social prestige. Moreover, the church, legislative corps, town councils, guilds, and other bodies had acquired autonomy during the course of the Middle Ages. In some countries whole provinces held separate privileges granted when they became part of the kingdom.

While some monarchs succeeded in breaking the power of these institutions and others were forced to concede political power to elected representatives, the situation was nuanced. Absolutist monarchs did not crush the power of nobles and other groups but rather had to compromise with them. Louis XIV, the model of absolutist power, succeeded because he co-opted and convinced nobles. And in England and the Netherlands constitutional government did not mean democracy, the rule of the people.

Both absolutist and constitutional monarchs were able to overcome obstacles and achieve new levels of central control. They exercised greater power in four areas in particular: greater taxation, growth in armed forces, larger and more efficient bureaucracies, and the increased ability to compel obedience from their subjects. Over time, centralized power added up to something close to **sovereignty.** A state may be termed sovereign when it possesses a monopoly over the instruments of justice and the use of force within clearly defined boundaries. In a sovereign state, no system of courts, such as ecclesiastical tribunals, competes with state courts in the dispensation of justice; and private armies, such as those of feudal lords, present no threat to central authority because the state's army is stronger. State law touches all persons in the country. While seventeenth-century states did not acquire total sovereignty, they made important strides toward that goal.

sovereignty The supreme authority in a political community; a modern state is said to be sovereign when it controls the instruments of justice (the courts) and the use of force (military and police powers) within geographical boundaries recognized by other states.

Popular Political Action

In the seventeenth century bread riots turned into **popular revolts** in England, France, Spain, Portugal, and Italy.[2] In 1640 Philip IV of Spain faced revolt on three fronts simultaneously: Catalonia, the economic center of his realm; Portugal; and the northern provinces of the Netherlands. In 1647 the city of Palermo, in Spanish-occupied Sicily, exploded in protest over food shortages caused by a series of bad harvests. The city government responded by subsidizing the price of bread, but Madrid ordered an end to subsidies. Local women led a bread riot, shouting, "Long live the king and down with the taxes and the bad government!" Apart from affordable food, rebels demanded the suppression of extraordinary taxes, participation in municipal government, and the end to noble tax exemptions. Lacking unity and strong leadership, the revolt was squelched.[3] The Spanish were equally successful in the Netherlands, at first; by the early 1570s, however, a new wave of revolt broke out, resulting in the independent Dutch Republic (see page 424).

popular revolts Uprisings that were extremely common in the seventeenth century across Europe, due to the increasing pressures of taxation and warfare.

In France, uprisings became "a distinctive feature of life"[4] in the cities, where resentment at taxes fostered violence. Major insurrections occurred at Dijon in 1630 and 1668, at Bordeaux (bor-DOH) in 1635 and 1675, at Montpellier in 1645, at Lyons from 1667 through 1668 and again in 1692, and at Amiens in 1685, 1695, 1704, and 1711. All were characterized by deep popular anger, a vocabulary of violence, and what a recent historian calls "the culture of retribution"—that is, the punishment of royal "outsiders," officials who attempted to announce or collect taxes.[5] Royal officials were sometimes seized, beaten, and hacked to death. The limitations of royal authority gave some leverage to rebels. Royal edicts were sometimes suspended, prisoners released, and discussions initiated. By the end of the seventeenth century, this leverage had largely disappeared. Municipal governments were better integrated into the national structure, and local authorities had prompt military support from the central government. People who publicly opposed royal policies and taxes received swift and severe punishment.[6]

Section Review

- Rural society was dependent on crops, especially grain, so when a period of colder weather came, crop yields fell, bringing famine, malnutrition, and disease.

- Economic crisis hit the urban poor and peasants hardest and often led to "moral economy" tactics: when bread prices were too high, the peasants seized the grain or bread to resell or redistribute at "just" prices.

- Absolutist monarchs had full personal control, while constitutional monarchs followed laws representative institutions passed.

- In the seventeenth century, both absolutist and constitutional monarchs confronted—and partially overcame—limitations on their sovereignty, produced by poor infrastructure, weak bureaucracies, cultural differences, and local power structures.

- Popular revolts arose as peasants protested food shortages and tax increases, but the rise of central authority by the end of the period allowed governments to repress them severely.

Absolutism in France and Spain

To what extent did French and Spanish monarchs succeed in creating absolute monarchies?

In the Middle Ages monarchs were said to rule "by the grace of God." Law was given by God; kings discovered or "found" the law and acknowledged that they must respect and obey it. In the seventeenth century absolutist state, kings amplified these claims, asserting that, because they were chosen by God, they were responsible to God alone. They claimed exclusive power to make and enforce laws, denying any other institution or group the authority to check their power.

Philosophers and theologians supported the kings' position with arguments for the necessity of absolute power for the public good. In *Leviathan* (li-VYE-uh-thuhn) (1651), the English philosopher Thomas Hobbes argued that any limits on or divisions of government power would lead only to paralysis or civil war. At the court of Louis XIV the French theologian Bossuet (baw-SWAY) proclaimed that without "absolute authority the king could neither do good nor repress evil."

The Foundations of Absolutism: Henry IV, Sully, and Richelieu

Louis XIV's absolutism had long roots. In 1589 his grandfather Henry IV (r. 1589–1610), the founder of the Bourbon dynasty, acquired a devastated country. As we saw in Chapter 14, civil wars between Protestants and Catholics wracked France in the last decades of the sixteenth century. Catastrophically poor harvests meant that peasants across France lived on the verge of starvation. Commercial activity had fallen to one-third its 1580 level. Nobles, officials, merchants, and peasants wanted peace, order, and stability. "Henri le Grand" (Henry the Great), as the king was called, promised "a chicken in every pot" and inaugurated a remarkable recovery. He was beloved because of the belief that he cared about the people; his was the only royal statue the Paris crowd did not tear down two hundred years later in the French Revolution.

Aside from a short war in 1601, Henry kept France at peace. He had converted to Catholicism but also issued the Edict of Nantes (see page 362), allowing Protestants the right to worship in 150 traditionally Protestant towns throughout France. Along with his able chief minister, the Protestant Maximilien de Béthune (mak-suh-MIL-yuhn duh bay-TOON), duke of Sully, Henry IV laid the foundations for the growth of state power. He sharply lowered direct taxes on the overburdened peasants and focused instead on increasing income from indirect taxes on salt, sales, and transit. He also instituted an annual fee on royal officials to guarantee heredity in their offices. (Although effective at the time, the long-term effect of this tax was to reduce royal control over officeholders.)

Alongside fiscal reform, Henry sponsored new industries and trade and improved the infrastructure of the country, building new roads, bridges, and canals to repair the ravages of years of civil war. In only twelve years he significantly raised royal revenues and restored public order.[7] Yet despite his efforts at peace, Henry was murdered in 1610 by François Ravaillac, a Catholic zealot, setting off a national crisis.

After the death of Henry IV his wife, the queen-regent Marie de' Medici (MED-ih-chee), headed the government for the child-king Louis XIII (r. 1610–1643). In 1624 Marie de' Medici secured the appointment of Armand Jean du Plessis—Cardinal Richelieu (ree-shuh-LYOO) (1585–1642)—to the council of ministers. Richelieu's maneuvers would allow the monarchy to maintain power within Europe and within its own borders despite the turmoil of the Thirty Years' War (see pages 435–436).

Richelieu's goal was to subordinate competing groups and institutions to the French monarchy. The nobility constituted the foremost threat. Nobles sat in royal councils, ran the army, controlled large provinces of France, and were immune from direct taxation. Richelieu sought to curb their power. In 1624 he succeeded in reshuffling the royal council, eliminating nobles who were potential power brokers and dominating the council as its president. In 1628 he became the first minister of the French crown.

Cardinal Richelieu's political genius is best reflected in the administrative system he established to strengthen royal control. He extended the use of **intendants,** commissioners for each of France's thirty-two districts who were appointed directly by the monarch, to whom they were solely responsible. Intendants could not be natives of the districts where they held authority; thus they had no vested interest in their localities. They recruited men for the army, supervised the collection of taxes, presided over the administration of local law, checked up on the local nobility, and regulated economic activities—commerce, trade, the guilds, marketplaces— in their districts. They were to use their power for three related purposes: to inform the central government about their districts, to enforce royal orders, and to undermine the influence of the regional nobility. As the intendants' power increased under Richelieu, so did the power of the centralized French state.

Under Richelieu the French monarchy also reasserted the principle of one people united by one faith. In 1627 Louis XIII decided to end Protestant military and political independence because, he said, it constituted "a state within a state." According to Louis, Huguenots were politically disobedient because they did not allow Catholics to worship in their cities.[8] Attention focused on La Rochelle, fourth largest of the French Atlantic ports and a major commercial center with strong ties to the northern Protestant states of Holland and England. Louis personally supervised the siege of La Rochelle. After the city fell in October 1628, its municipal government was suppressed and its walled fortifications were destroyed. Although Protestants retained the right of public worship, the king reinstated the Catholic liturgy, and Cardinal Richelieu himself celebrated the first Mass. The fall of La Rochelle weakened the influence of aristocratic Huguenots and was one step in the removal of Protestantism as a strong force in French life. Richelieu did not aim to wipe out Protestantism in the rest of Europe, however. His main foreign policy goal was to destroy the Catholic Habsburgs' grip on territories that surrounded France. Consequently, Richelieu supported the Habsburgs' enemies, including Protestants. In 1631 he signed a treaty with the Lutheran king Gustavus Adolphus promising French support against the Habsburgs in what has been called the Swedish phase of the Thirty Years' War (see page 436). French influence became an important factor in the political future of the German Empire. Richelieu acquired for France extensive rights in Alsace in the east and Arras in the north.

In building the French state, Richelieu knew that his approach sometimes seemed to contradict traditional Christian teaching. As a priest and bishop, how did he justify his policies? He developed his own *raison d'état* (reason of state): "Where the interests of the state are concerned, God absolves actions which, if privately committed, would be a crime."[9] Richelieu's successor as chief minister for the next boy-king, Louis XIV, was Cardinal Jules Mazarin (1602–1661). Along with the regent, Queen Mother Anne of Austria, Mazarin continued Richelieu's centralizing policies. His struggle to increase royal revenues to meet the costs of war with Spain led to the uprisings of 1648–1653 known as the **Fronde.** A *frondeur* was originally a street urchin who threw mud at the passing carriages of the rich, but the word came to be applied to the many individuals and groups who opposed the policies of the government. The most influential of these groups were the robe nobility—court judges—and the sword nobility—the aristocracy—both of whom resented growing centralized control. During the first of several riots, the queen mother fled Paris with Louis XIV. As the rebellion continued, civil order broke down completely. In 1651 Anne's regency ended with the declaration of Louis as king in his own right. Much of the rebellion died away, and its leaders came to terms with the government.

intendants Royal commissioners. Appointed by and answering directly to the monarch, they were key elements in Richelieu's plan to centralize the French state.

Fronde A series of violent uprisings during the minority of Louis XIV triggered by oppressive taxation and growing royal authority; the last attempt of the French nobility to resist the king by arms.

The conflicts of the Fronde had significant results for the future. The twin evils of noble factionalism and popular riots left the French wishing for peace and for a strong monarch to re-impose order. This was the legacy that Louis XIV inherited when he assumed personal rule in 1661. Humiliated by his flight from Paris, he was determined to avoid any recurrence of rebellion.

Louis XIV and Absolutism

The reign of Louis XIV (r. 1643–1715) was the longest in European history, and the French monarchy reached the peak of absolutist development. In the magnificence of his court and the brilliance of the culture that he presided over, the "Sun King" dominated his age.

Religion, Anne, and Mazarin all taught Louis the doctrine of the **divine right of kings:** God had established kings as his rulers on earth, and they were answerable ultimately to God alone. Though kings were divinely anointed and shared in the sacred nature of divinity, they could not simply do as they pleased. They had to obey God's laws and rule for the good of the people.

Louis worked very hard at the business of governing. He ruled his realm through several councils of state, and insisted on taking a personal role in many of the councils' decisions. He selected councilors from the recently ennobled or the upper middle class because he wanted "people to know by the rank of the men who served him that he had no intention of sharing power with them."[10] Despite increasing financial problems, Louis never called a meeting of the Estates General. The nobility therefore had no means of united expression or action. Nor did Louis have a first minister; he kept himself free from worry about the inordinate power of a Richelieu. Louis also used spying and terror—a secret police force, a system of informers, and the practice of opening private letters—to eliminate potential threats.

Religion was also a tool of national unity under Louis. In 1685 he revoked the Edict of Nantes, by which his grandfather Henry IV had granted liberty of conscience to French Huguenots. The new law ordered the destruction of Huguenot churches, the closing of schools, the Catholic baptism of Huguenots, and the exile of Huguenot pastors who refused to renounce their faith. The result was the departure of some of his most loyal and industrially skilled subjects.

Richelieu had already deprived French Calvinists of political rights and many had converted to Catholicism. Why, then, did Louis XIV undertake such an apparently unnecessary, cruel, and self-destructive measure? First, Louis considered religion primarily a political question. Although he was personally tolerant, he hated division within the realm and insisted that religious unity was essential to his royal dignity and to the security of the state. Second, aristocrats had long petitioned Louis to crack down on Protestants. His decision to do so won him enormous praise.

Louis's personal hold on power, his exclusion of great nobles from his councils, and his ruthless pursuit of religious unity persuaded many earlier historians that his reign witnessed the creation of an **absolute monarchy.** Louis supposedly crushed the political pretensions of the nobility, leaving them with social grandeur and court posing but no real power. A later generation of historians has revised that view, showing the multiple constraints on Louis's power and his need to cooperate with the nobles. Louis may have declared his absolute power, but in practice he governed through collaboration with nobles, who maintained tremendous prestige and authority in their ancestral lands. Scholars also underline the traditional nature of Louis's motivations. Like his predecessors, Louis XIV sought to enhance

divine right of kings The belief that God had established kings as his rulers on earth and that they were answerable ultimately to God alone.

absolute monarchy A form of government in which sovereignty is vested in a single person, the king or queen; absolute monarchs in the sixteenth and seventeenth centuries based their authority on the theory of the divine right of kings.

Rubens: The Death of Henri IV and The Proclamation of the Regency (1622–1625)
In 1622 the regent Marie de' Medici commissioned Peter Paul Rubens to paint a cycle of paintings depicting her life. This one portrays two distinct moments: the assassination of Henry IV (shown on the left ascending to Heaven), and Marie's subsequent proclamation as regent. The other twenty-three canvasses in the cycle similarly glorify Marie, a tricky undertaking given her unhappy marriage to Henry IV and her tumultuous relationship with her son Louis XIII, who removed her from the regency in 1617. As in this image, Rubens frequently resorted to allegory and classical imagery to elevate the events of Marie's life. (Réunion des Musées Nationaux/ Art Resource, NY)

the glory of his dynasty and his country, mostly through war. The creation of a new state apparatus was a means to that goal, not an end in itself.

Financial and Economic Management Under Louis XIV: Colbert

France's ability to build armies and fight wars depended on a strong economy. The king named Jean-Baptiste Colbert (1619–1683), the son of a wealthy merchant-financier of Reims, as controller general of finances. Colbert came to manage the entire royal administration and proved himself a financial genius. His central principle was that the wealth and the economy of France should serve the state. He did not invent the system called "mercantilism," but he rigorously applied it to France.

Mercantilism is a collection of governmental policies for the regulation of economic activities, especially commercial activities, by and for the state. In seventeenth- and eighteenth-century economic theory, a nation's international power was thought to be based on its wealth, specifically its gold supply. Because resources were limited, mercantilist theory held, state intervention was needed to secure the largest part of a limited resource. To accumulate gold, a country always had to sell more goods abroad than it bought. Colbert thus insisted that France should be self-sufficient, able to produce within its borders everything French subjects needed. Consequently, the outflow of gold would be halted; debtor states would pay in bullion; unemployment and poverty would greatly diminish; and with the wealth of the nation increased, its power and prestige would be enhanced.

mercantilism A system of economic regulations aimed at increasing the power of the state.

Colbert supported old industries and created new ones so that France would be self-sufficient. He focused especially on textiles, the most important sector of the economy, reinforcing the system of state inspection and regulation and forming guilds. Colbert encouraged foreign craftsmen to immigrate to France by giving them special privileges, and he worked to bring more female workers into the labor force. To encourage the people to buy French goods, he abolished many domestic tariffs and raised tariffs on foreign products. One of Colbert's most ambitious projects was the creation of a merchant marine to transport French goods. In 1661 France possessed 18 unseaworthy vessels; by 1681 it had 276 working ships manned by trained sailors. In 1664 Colbert founded the Company of the East Indies with (unfulfilled) hopes of competing with the Dutch for Asian trade.

Colbert also hoped to make Canada—rich in untapped minerals and some of the best agricultural land in the world—part of a vast French empire. He sent four thousand peasants from western France to the province of Quebec. (In 1608, one year after the English arrived at Jamestown, Virginia, Sully had established the city of Quebec, which became the capital of French Canada.) Subsequently, the Jesuit Jacques Marquette and the merchant Louis Joliet sailed down the Mississippi River and claimed possession of the land on both sides as far south as present-day Arkansas. In 1684 the French explorer Robert La Salle continued down the Mississippi to its mouth and claimed vast territories and the rich delta for Louis XIV. The area was called, naturally, "Louisiana."

During Colbert's tenure as controller general, Louis was able to pursue his goals without massive tax increases and without creating a stream of new offices. Colbert managed to raise revenues significantly by cracking down on inefficiences and corruption in the tax collection system. The constant pressure of warfare after Colbert's death, however, undid many of his economic achievements.

Louis XIV's Wars

Louis XIV wrote that "the character of a conqueror is regarded as the noblest and highest of titles." In pursuit of the title of conqueror, he kept France at war for thirty-three of the fifty-four years of his personal rule. In 1666 Louis appointed François le Tellier (later, marquis de Louvois) as secretary of state for war. Under the king's watchful eye, Louvois created a professional army that was modern in the sense that the French state, rather than private nobles, employed the soldiers. Louvois utilized several methods in recruiting troops: dragooning, in which press gangs seized men off the streets; conscription; and, after 1688, lottery. With these techniques, the French army grew from roughly 125,000 men in the Thirty Years' War (1618–1648) to 250,000 during the Dutch War (1672–1678) and 340,000 during the War of the League of Augsburg (1688–1697).[11] Uniforms and weapons were standardized and rational systems of training and promotion devised. Many historians believe that the new loyalty, professionalism, and size of the French army is the best case for the success of absolutism under Louis XIV. Whatever his compromises elsewhere, the French monarch had firm control of his armed forces. As in so many other matters, Louis's model was followed across Europe.

Louis's supreme goal was to expand France to what he considered its "natural" borders and to secure those lands from any threat of invasion. His armies managed to expand French borders to include important commercial centers in the Spanish Netherlands and Flanders, as well as all of Franche-Comté between 1667 and 1678. In 1681 Louis seized the city of Strasbourg, and three years later he sent armies into the province of Lorraine. At that moment the king seemed invincible.

In fact, Louis had reached the limit of his expansion. The wars of the 1680s and 1690s brought no additional territories.

Louis understood his wars largely as defensive undertakings, but his neighbors naturally viewed French expansion with great alarm. Louis's wars inspired the formation of Europe-wide coalitions against him. As a result, he was obliged to support a huge army in several different theaters of war. This task placed unbearable strains on French resources, especially given the inequitable system of taxation.

Colbert's successors as minister of finance resorted to the devaluation of the currency and the old device of selling offices and tax exemptions. They also created new direct taxes in 1695 and 1710, which nobles and clergymen had to pay for the first time. In exchange for this money, the king reaffirmed the traditional social hierarchies by granting honors, pensions, and titles to the nobility. Commoners had to pay the new taxes as well as the old ones.

A series of bad harvests between 1688 and 1694 added social to fiscal catastrophe. The price of wheat skyrocketed. The result was widespread starvation, and in many provinces the death rate rose to several times the normal figure. Parish registers reveal that France buried at least one-tenth of its population in those years, perhaps 2 million in 1693 and 1694 alone. Rising grain prices, new taxes for war, a slump in manufacturing, and the constant nuisance of pillaging troops all meant great suffering for the French people. France wanted peace at any price and won a respite for five years, which was shattered by the War of the Spanish Succession (1701–1713).

In 1700 the childless Spanish king Charles II (r. 1665–1700) died, opening a struggle for control of Spain and its colonies. His will bequeathed the Spanish crown and its empire to Philip of Anjou, Louis XIV's grandson (Louis's wife, Maria-Theresa, had been Charles's sister). This testament violated a prior treaty by which the European powers had agreed to divide the Spanish possessions between the king of France and the Holy Roman emperor, both brothers-in-law of Charles II. Claiming that he was following both Spanish and French national interests, Louis broke with the treaty and accepted the will.

In 1701 the English, Dutch, Austrians, and Prussians formed the Grand Alliance against Louis XIV. The allied powers united to prevent France from becoming too strong in Europe and to check France's expanding commercial power in North America, Asia, and Africa. The war dragged on until 1713. The **Peace of Utrecht,** which ended the war, applied the principle of partition. Louis's grandson Philip remained the first Bourbon king of Spain on the understanding that the French and Spanish crowns would never be united. France surrendered Newfoundland, Nova Scotia, and the Hudson Bay territory to England, which also acquired Gibraltar, Minorca, and control of the African slave trade from Spain. The Dutch gained little because Austria received the former Spanish Netherlands (see Map 16.1).

The Peace of Utrecht had important international consequences. It represented the balance-of-power principle in operation, setting limits on the extent to which any one power—in this case, France—could expand. The treaty completed the decline of Spain as a great power. It vastly expanded the British Empire, and it gave European powers experience in international cooperation. The Peace of Utrecht also marked the end of French expansion. Thirty-five years of war had brought rights to all of Alsace and the gain of important cities in the north such as Lille, as well as Strasbourg. But at what price? In 1714 an exhausted France hovered on the brink of bankruptcy. It is no wonder that when Louis XIV died on September 1, 1715, many subjects felt as much relief as they did sorrow.

Peace of Utrecht A series of treaties, from 1713 to 1715, that ended the War of the Spanish Succession, ended French expansion in Europe, and marked the rise of the British Empire.

French Bourbon lands
Spanish Bourbon lands
Austrian Habsburg lands
Prussian lands
Great Britain
Boundary of the
Holy Roman Empire
Russian Empire
Russian gains, by 1725
Ottoman Empire, 1722

RUSSIAN EMPIRE

• Moscow

• Smolensk

• St. Petersburg
INGRIA
ESTONIA
LIVONIA
• Riga
LITHUANIA

SWEDEN

NORWAY
• Oslo

Baltic Sea

KINGDOM OF DENMARK
DENMARK

North Sea

POLAND

• Warsaw
EAST PRUSSIA

BRANDENBURG-PRUSSIA
• Berlin
Elbe R.
SAXONY
Oder R.
SILESIA

HANOVER

UNITED NETHERLANDS
Utrecht •

HOLY ROMAN EMPIRE
BOHEMIA
Rhine R.
PALATINATE
Danube R.
BAVARIA
AUSTRIA
• Vienna
LORRAINE
Strasbourg •
SWITZERLAND
SAVOY
MILAN
GENOA
MODENA
Po R.
Rhône R.

Vistula R.

Dnieper R.

Dniester R.
UKRAINE
• Kiev

CRIMEA

Black Sea

MOLDAVIA
TRANSYLVANIA
WALLACHIA
Danube R.
BULGARIA
SERBIA
• Belgrade
BOSNIA
HERZEGOVINA
MONTENEGRO
ALBANIA

OTTOMAN EMPIRE
• Constantinople

Aegean Sea

GREECE

HUNGARY
Buda • • Pest
SLAVONIA
CROATIA

REPUBLIC OF VENICE
Adriatic Sea

TUSCANY
PAPAL STATES
• Rome
KINGDOM OF NAPLES
• Naples

Corsica (Genoa)
Sardinia (Austria)
Sicily (Savoy)

Mediterranean Sea

Paris •
Seine R.
Loire R.
FRANCE
Garonne R.
Toulouse •
Marseilles •
CATALONIA
Ebro R.

GREAT BRITAIN
SCOTLAND
Edinburgh •
ENGLAND
London •
Thames R.
IRELAND
Dublin •

ATLANTIC OCEAN

PORTUGAL
Lisbon •

SPAIN
• Madrid
Duero R.
Tagus R.

GIBRALTAR (Gr. Br.)

Minorca (Gr. Br.)
Balearic Is.

300 Mi.
150
0
300 Km.
150
0

40°E
30°E
20°E
10°E
0°
10°W

50°N
60°N

MAPPING THE PAST

MAP 16.1   Europe in 1715

The series of treaties commonly called the Peace of Utrecht (April 1713–November 1715) ended the War of the Spanish Succession and redrew the map of Europe. A French Bourbon king succeeded to the Spanish throne. France surrendered to Austria the Spanish Netherlands (later Belgium), then in French hands, and France recognized the Hohenzollern (HOH-uhn-zol-urn) rulers of Prussia. Spain ceded Gibraltar to Great Britain, for which it has been a strategic naval station ever since. Spain also granted to Britain the *asiento,* the contract for supplying African slaves to America. **[1]** Identify the areas on the map that changed hands as a result of the Peace of Utrecht. How did these changes affect the balance of power in Europe? **[2]** How and why did so many European countries possess scattered or discontiguous territories? What does this suggest about European politics in this period? **[3]** Does this map suggest potential for future conflict?

The Decline of Absolutist Spain in the Seventeenth Century

As French power was growing, Spanish power was diminishing. By the early seventeenth century the seeds of disaster were sprouting. Between 1610 and 1650 Spanish trade with the colonies fell 60 percent, due to competition from local industries in the colonies and from Dutch and English traders. At the same time, the native Indians and African slaves who toiled in the South American silver mines suffered frightful epidemics of disease. Ultimately, the lodes started to run dry, and the quantity of metal produced steadily declined after 1620.

In Madrid, however, royal expenditures constantly exceeded income. To meet mountainous state debt and declining revenues, the Crown repeatedly devalued the coinage and declared bankruptcy. In 1596, 1607, 1627, 1647, and 1680, Spanish kings found no solution to the problem of an empty treasury other than to cancel the national debt. Given the frequency of cancellation, national credit plummeted.

Seventeenth-century Spain was the victim of its past. It could not forget the grandeur of the sixteenth century and respond to changing circumstances. Although Spain lacked the finances to fight expensive wars, the imperial tradition demanded the revival of war with the Dutch at the expiration of a twelve-year truce in 1622 and a long war with France over Mantua (1628–1659). Spain thus became embroiled in the Thirty Years' War. These conflicts, on top of an empty treasury, brought disaster.

In 1640 Spain faced serious revolts in Catalonia and Portugal. The Portuguese succeeded in regaining independence from Habsburg rule under their new king, John IV (r. 1640–1656). In 1643 the French inflicted a crushing defeat on a Spanish army at Rocroi in what is now Belgium. By the Treaty of the Pyrenees of 1659, which ended the French-Spanish conflict, Spain was compelled to surrender extensive territories to France. This treaty marked the decline of Spain as a great military power.

Spain's decline can also be traced to a failure to invest in productive enterprises. In contrast to the other countries of western Europe, Spain had only a tiny middle class. Public opinion, taking its cue from the aristocracy, condemned moneymaking as vulgar and undignified. Thousands entered economically unproductive professions: there were said to be nine thousand monasteries in the province of Castile alone. Some three hundred thousand people who had once been Muslims were expelled by Philip III in 1609, significantly reducing the pool

Peeter Snayers: Spanish Troops (detail)
The long wars that Spain fought over Dutch independence, in support of Habsburg interests in Germany, and against France left the country militarily exhausted and financially drained by the mid-1600s. Here, Spanish troops—thin, emaciated, and probably unpaid—straggle away from battle. (Museo Nacional del Prado, Madrid. Photo: José Baztan y Alberto Otero)

of skilled workers and merchants. Those working in the textile industry were forced out of business when the flood of gold and silver produced severe inflation, pushing their production costs to the point where they could not compete in colonial and international markets. Other businessmen found so many obstacles in the way of profitable enterprise that they simply gave up.[12] Spanish aristocrats, attempting to maintain an extravagant lifestyle they could no longer afford, increased the rents on their estates. High rents and heavy taxes in turn drove the peasants from the land. Agricultural production suffered, and peasants departed for the large cities, where they swelled the ranks of unemployed beggars.

Spanish leaders seemed to lack the will to reform. If one can discern personality from pictures, the portraits of Philip III (r. 1598–1622), Philip IV (r. 1622–1665), and Charles II (r. 1665–1700) hanging in the Prado, the Spanish national museum in Madrid, reflect the increasing weakness of the dynasty. Pessimism and fatalism permeated national life. In the reign of Philip IV, a royal council was appointed to plan the construction of a canal linking the Tagus and Manzanares Rivers in Spain. After interminable debate, the committee decided that "if God had intended the rivers to be navigable, He would have made them so." Spain ignored new scientific methods because they came from heretical nations, Holland and England.

Don Quixote A novel authored by Miguel de Cervantes that is perhaps the greatest work of Spanish literature. It is a survey of the entire fabric of Spanish society that can be read on several levels: as a burlesque of chivalric romances and as an exploration of conflicting views (idealistic vs. realistic) of life and of the world.

In the brilliant novel **Don Quixote** (dohn kee-HOH-tee), Spanish writer Miguel de Cervantes (1547–1616) produced one of the great masterpieces of world literature. The main character, Don Quixote, lives in a world of dreams, traveling about the countryside seeking military glory. From the title of the book, the English language has borrowed the word *quixotic*. Meaning "idealistic but impractical," the term characterizes seventeenth-century Spain. As a leading scholar has written, "The Spaniard convinced himself that reality was what he felt, believed, imagined. He filled the world with heroic reverberations. Don Quixote was born and grew."[13]

The Culture of Absolutism

What cultural forms flourished under absolutist governments?

Under absolutist monarchs, culture became an instrument of state power. The **baroque style** in art and music flourished in Spain, Italy, and Central Europe. Baroque masters like Rubens painted portraits celebrating the glory of European monarchs. Architecture became an important tool for the French monarch Louis XIV, who made the magnificent palace of Versailles (vehr-SIGH) the center of his kingdom, inspiring imitators across Europe (see Chapter 17). Even language reflected the growing power of the French crown. Within France Richelieu established an academy to oversee French literature and language. Outside its borders French became the common language of the European elite.

Baroque Art and Music

Rome and the revitalized Catholic church of the later sixteenth century played an important role in the early development of the baroque. As we have seen (pages 539–540), the papacy and the Jesuits encouraged the growth of an intensely emotional, exuberant art aimed at kindling the faith of ordinary churchgoers. In addition to this underlying religious emotionalism, the baroque drew its sense of drama, motion, and ceaseless striving from the art and architecture of the Catholic Reformation. Yet baroque art was more than just "Catholic art" in the seventeenth century and the first half of the eighteenth. True, neither Protestant England nor the Netherlands ever came fully under the spell of the baroque, but neither did Catholic France. And Protestants accounted for some of the finest examples of baroque style, especially in music. The baroque style spread partly because its tension and bombast spoke to an agitated age that was experiencing great violence and controversy in politics and religion.

In painting, the baroque reached maturity early with the painter Peter Paul Rubens (1577–1640). Rubens studied the masters of the High Renaissance such as Michelangelo but developed his own style, which was characterized by animated figures, melodramatic contrasts, and monumental size. Rubens excelled in glorifying monarchs such as Queen Mother Marie de' Medici of France (see the painting on page 409). He was also a devout Catholic; nearly half of his pictures treat Christian subjects. Yet one of Rubens's trademarks was fleshy, sensual nudes who populate his canvases as Roman goddesses, water nymphs, and remarkably voluptuous saints and angels.

In music, the baroque style reached its culmination almost a century later in the dynamic, soaring lines of Johann Sebastian Bach (1685–1750), an organist and choirmaster of several Lutheran churches across Germany. Bach's organ music combined the baroque spirit of invention, tension, and emotion in both secular concertos and sublime religious cantatas. Unlike Rubens, Bach was not fully appreciated in his lifetime, but since the early nineteenth century his reputation has grown steadily.

Section Review

- Henry IV of France restored order and prosperity but his premature death left queen-regent Marie de' Medici and Cardinal Richelieu to rule for the boy Louis XIII; Richelieu led France into the Thirty Years' War and continued Henry IV's work of increasing the power of the centralized state.

- After the death of Louis XIII, Cardinal Mazarin and the regent, Queen Mother Anne of Austria, ruled for the boy-king Louis XIV; the Fronde uprisings during this time protested growing royal power and war-related tax increases.

- The "Sun King" Louis XIV created an "absolute monarchy," ruling according to the doctrine of the "divine right of kings" in which a king answered to God alone.

- Jean-Baptiste Colbert, Louis XIV's brilliant finance minister, adopted mercantilist policies intended to foster economic self-sufficiency so that everything French subjects needed would be produced internally—therefore halting the external flow of gold and increasing the wealth of the nation.

- Louis XIV built a large, loyal, professional army that expanded French borders but required expensive maintenance, taxing French resources.

- The Peace of Utrecht ended the War of the Spanish Succession and redrew the map of Europe, marking the end of French expansion, an increase in the British Empire, and the decline of Spain.

- Spain's power declined due to a loss of trade with the colonies, diminished production of South American silver, bankruptcy from fighting wars, a failure to invest in productive enterprises, the deportation of formerly Muslim workers, and high rents and heavy taxes that drove peasants from the land.

baroque style An intensely emotional and exuberant style of art, practiced by artists such as Rubens and associated with the late-sixteenth-century Catholic Reformation; in music, it reached maturity almost a century later with the compositions of Bach.

Juan de Pareja: The Calling of Saint Matthew

Using rich but subdued colors, Pareja depicts the biblical text (Mark 2:13–17), with Jesus in traditional first-century dress and the other figures, arranged around a table covered with an oriental carpet, in seventeenth-century apparel. Matthew, at Jesus's right hand, seems surprised by the "call." Pareja, following a long tradition, includes himself (*standing, far left*). (Museo Nacional del Prado, Madrid/The Bridgeman Art Library)

Court Culture

In 1682 Louis formally established his court at Versailles, which became the center of the kingdom: a model of rational order and the perfect symbol of the king's power. The art and architecture of Versailles were tools of Louis's policy, used to overawe his subjects and foreign visitors. The Russian tsar Peter the Great imitated Versailles in the construction of his palace, Peterhof, as did the Prussian emperor Frederick the Great in his palace at Potsdam outside Berlin and the Habsburgs at Schonbrunn outside Vienna. (See the feature "Images in Society: Absolutist Palace Building" on pages 440–441.)

The palace was the summit of political, social, and cultural life. The king required all great nobles to spend at least part of the year in attendance on him at Versailles. Between three thousand and ten thousand people occupied the palace each day. Given the demand for space, even high nobles had to make do with cramped and uncomfortable living quarters. The palace gardens, and the palace itself on some occasions, were open to the public, allowing even local peasants a glimpse of their sovereign. More than a royal residence or administrative center, Versailles was a mirror of French greatness to the world.

Much has been made of the "domestication" of the nobility at Versailles. Nobles had to follow a tortuous system of court etiquette, and they vied for the honor of serving the monarch, with the highest in rank claiming the privilege to hand the king his shirt when he dressed. These rituals were far from meaningless or trivial. The king controlled immense resources and privileges; access to him meant favored treatment for pensions, military and religious posts, honorary titles, and a host of other benefits. Courtiers sought these rewards for themselves and for their family members and followers. As in ancient Rome, a patronage system—in which higher-ranked individuals protected lower-ranked ones in return for loyalty and services—dominated political life. Patronage flowed from the court to the provinces; it was the mechanism through which Louis gained cooperation from social elites.

Although they were denied public offices and posts, women played a central role in the patronage system. At court, the king's wife, mistresses, and other female relatives used their high rank to establish their own patronage relations. They recommended individuals for honors, advocated policy decisions, and brokered alliances between noble factions. Noblewomen played a similar role, bringing their family connections to marriage to form powerful social networks. Onlookers sometimes resented the influence of powerful women at court. The Duke of Saint-Simon said of Madame de Maintenon, Louis XIV's mistress and secret second wife:

> The power of Madame de Maintenon was, as may be imagined, immense. She had everybody in her hands, from the highest and most favored ministers to the meanest subject of the realm. Many people have been ruined by her, without having been able to discover the author of the ruin, search as they might.

French Classicism

To this day, culture is a central element of French national pride and identity. French emphasis on culture dates back to Cardinal Richelieu, whose efforts at state centralization embraced cultural activities. In 1635 he gave official recognition to a group of scholars interested in grammar and rhetoric. Thus was born the French Academy, which prepared a dictionary to standardize the French language; the dictionary was completed in 1694 and has been updated in many successive editions. The Academy survives today as a prestigious society and retains authority over correct usage in the French language.

Scholars characterize the art and literature of the age of Louis XIV as **French classicism.** By this they mean that the artists and writers of the late seventeenth century imitated the subject matter and style of classical antiquity, that their work resembled that of Renaissance Italy, and that French art possessed the classical qualities of discipline, balance, and restraint. This was a movement away from the perceived excesses of baroque style.

French classicism A style of French art, architecture, and literature (ca. 1600–1750), based on admiration and imitation of Greek and Roman models but with greater exuberance and complexity.

Louis XIV was an enthusiastic patron of the arts. Music and theater frequently served as backdrops for court ceremonials. Louis favored Jean-Baptiste Lully (1632–1687), whose orchestral works combined lively animation with the restrained austerity typical of French classicism. Louis also supported François Couperin (1668–1733), whose harpsichord and organ works possessed the regal grandeur the king loved, and Marc-Antoine Charpentier (1634–1704), whose solemn religious music entertained him at meals.

Louis XIV loved the stage, and in the plays of Molière (mohl-YAIR) (1622–1673) and Racine (ra-SEEN) (1639–1699) his court witnessed the finest achievements in the history of the French theater. As playwright, stage manager, director, and actor, Molière (born Jean-Baptiste Poquelin) produced comedies that exposed the hypocrisies and follies of polite society through brilliant caricature. *Tartuffe* (tahr-TOOF) satirized the religious hypocrite; his plays *Le Bourgeois Gentilhomme* (The Bourgeois Gentleman) and *Les Précieuses ridicules* (The Pretentious Young Ladies) mocked the social pretensions of the bourgeoisie, stopping short of criticizing the high nobility.

- The baroque style, practiced by artists such as Rubens, was intensely emotional and exuberant; it was particularly associated with the late sixteenth century Catholic Reformation, but appeared in both religious and secular themes and in Protestant artists.
- Baroque composers such as Bach combined invention, tension, and emotion in their music, much of which was organ music played in church.
- The palace at Versailles was the showpiece and center of the French kingdom, crowded with nobles vying for the king's favor and patronage
- French classicism, a movement reviving classical antiquity in art and literature, was popular during the reign of Louis XIV; theater also gained popularity with playwrights such as the comic Molière and the tragedian Racine.
- The French language was adopted by elites across Europe for diplomacy, scholarship, and polite conversation.

constitutionalism A form of government in which power is limited by law and balanced between the authority and power of the government on the one hand, and the rights and liberties of the subject or citizen on the other hand.

Molière's contemporary Jean Racine based his tragic dramas on Greek and Roman legends. His persistent theme was the conflict of good and evil. Several plays—*Andromaque* (ahn-dro-MAK), Bérénice (bear-ay-NEES), Iphigénie (if-ee-jay-NEE), and *Phèdre* (FAY-druh)—bear the names of women and deal with the power of female passion. For simplicity of language, symmetrical structure, and calm restraint, the plays of Racine represent the finest examples of French classicism.

Louis XIV's reign inaugurated the use of French as the language of polite society, international diplomacy, and, gradually, scholarship and learning. The royal courts of Sweden, Russia, Poland, and Germany all spoke French. France inspired a cosmopolitan European culture in the late seventeenth century, which looked to Versailles as its center.

Constitutionalism

What is constitutionalism, and how did this form of government emerge in England and the Dutch Republic?

While France and later Prussia, Russia, and Austria (see Chapter 17) developed the absolutist state, England and Holland evolved toward **constitutionalism,** which is the limitation of government by law. Constitutionalism also implies a balance between the authority and power of the government, on the one hand, and the rights and liberties of the subjects, on the other.

A nation's constitution may be written or unwritten. It may be embodied in one basic document, occasionally revised by amendment, like the Constitution of the United States. Or it may be only partly formalized and include parliamentary statutes, judicial decisions, and a body of traditional procedures and practices, like the English and Dutch constitutions. Whether written or unwritten, a constitution gets its binding force from the government's acknowledgment that it must respect that constitution—that is, that the state must govern according to the laws.

Absolutist Claims in England (1603–1649)

In 1588 Queen Elizabeth I of England exercised very great personal power; by 1689 the English monarchy was severely circumscribed. Change in England was anything but orderly. Seventeenth-century England executed one king and experienced a bloody civil war; experimented with military dictatorship, then restored the son of the murdered king; and finally, after a bloodless revolution, established constitutional monarchy. Political stability came only in the 1690s. After such a violent and tumultuous century, how did England produce a constitutional monarchy?

A rare and politically astute female monarch, Elizabeth was able to maintain control over her realm in part by refusing to marry and submit to a husband. The problem with this strategy was that it left the queen with no immediate heir to continue her legacy.

In 1603 Elizabeth's Scottish cousin James Stuart succeeded her as James I (r. 1603–1625). King James was well educated and had thirty-five years' experience as king of Scotland. But he was not as interested in displaying the majesty of monarchy as Elizabeth had been. Urged to wave at the crowds who waited to greet their new ruler, James complained that he was tired and threatened to drop his breeches "so they can cheer at my arse." Moreover, in contrast to Elizabeth, James was a poor judge of character, and in a society already hostile to the Scots, James's

Scottish accent was a disadvantage.[14] James's greatest problem, however, stemmed from his belief that a monarch has a divine (or God-given) right to his authority and is responsible only to God. James went so far as to lecture the House of Commons: "There are no privileges and immunities which can stand against a divinely appointed King." This notion, implying total royal jurisdiction over the liberties, persons, and properties of English men and women, formed the basis of the Stuart concept of absolutism. Such a view ran directly counter to the long-standing English idea that a person's property could not be taken away without due process of law. James's expression of such views before the English House of Commons was a grave political mistake, especially given the royal debt that he had inherited from Elizabeth. The House of Commons guarded the state's pocketbook.

In England, unlike France, there was no social stigma attached to paying taxes. Members of the wealthy House of Commons were willing to assess and pay taxes to ease the royal debt provided they had some say in the formulation of state policies. James I and his son Charles I, however, considered such ambitions intolerable and a threat to their divine-right prerogative. Consequently, at every Parliament between 1603 and 1640, bitter squabbles erupted between the Crown and the articulate and legally minded Commons. Charles I's attempt to govern without Parliament (1629–1640) and to finance his government by arbitrary nonparliamentary levies brought the country to a crisis.

Religious Divides

Religious issues also embittered relations between the king and the House of Commons. In the early seventeenth century increasing numbers of English people felt dissatisfied with the Church of England established by Henry VIII and reformed by Elizabeth. Many **Puritans** believed that the Reformation had not gone far enough. They wanted to "purify" the Anglican church of Roman Catholic elements—elaborate vestments and ceremonials, bishops, and even the giving and wearing of wedding rings.

It is difficult to establish what proportion of the English population was Puritan. According to present scholarly consensus, the dominant religious groups in the early seventeenth century were Calvinist; their more zealous members were Puritans. It also seems clear that many English people were attracted by Calvinism's emphasis on hard work, sobriety, thrift, competition, and postponement of pleasure. These values, which have frequently been called the "Protestant ethic" or "capitalist ethic," fit in precisely with the economic approaches and practices of many successful business people and farmers. While it is hazardous to identify capitalism with Protestantism—there were many successful Catholic capitalists, for example—the "Protestant virtues" represented the prevailing values of members of the House of Commons.

Puritans wanted to abolish bishops in the Church of England, and when James I said, "No bishop, no king," he meant that the bishops were among the chief supporters of the throne. Under Charles I, people believed that the country was being led back to Roman Catholicism. Not only did he marry a French Catholic princess, but he also supported the policies of the Archbishop of Canterbury William Laud (1573–1645), who tried to impose elaborate ritual on all churches.

In 1637 Laud attempted to impose two new elements on church organization in Scotland: a new prayer book, modeled on the Anglican *Book of Common Prayer*, and bishoprics, which the Presbyterian Scots firmly rejected. The Scots therefore revolted. To finance an army to put down the Scots, King Charles was compelled to summon Parliament in November 1640.

Puritans Members of a sixteenth- and seventeenth-century reform movement within the Church of England that advocated "purifying" it of Roman Catholic elements, such as bishops, elaborate ceremonials, and the wedding ring.

a Confectioner   a Smith   a Sho=maker   a Taylor

a Sadler   a Porter   a Box-maker   a Sope-boyler

a Glover   a meal-man   a Chitken-man   a Button-maker

Puritan Occupations
These twelve engravings depict typical Puritan occupations and show that the Puritans came primarily from the artisan and lower middle classes. The governing classes and peasants adhered to the traditions of the Church of England. (Visual Connection Archive)

Charles I was an intelligent man, but contemporaries found him deceitful and treacherous. After quarreling with Parliament over his right to collect customs duties on wine and wool and over what the Commons perceived as religious innovations, Charles had dissolved Parliament in 1629. From 1629 to 1640, he ruled without Parliament, financing his government through extraordinary stopgap levies considered illegal by most English people. For example, the king revived a medieval law requiring coastal districts to help pay the cost of ships for defense, but he levied the tax, called "ship money," on inland as well as coastal counties. Most members of Parliament believed that such taxation without out consent amounted to despotism. Consequently, they were not willing to trust the king with an army. Moreover, many supported the Scots' resistance to Charles's religious innovations and had little wish for military action against them. Accordingly, this Parliament, called the "Long Parliament" because it sat from 1640 to 1660, enacted legislation that limited the power of the monarch and made arbitrary government impossible.

In 1641 the Commons passed the Triennial Act, which compelled the king to summon Parliament every three years. The Commons impeached Archbishop Laud and then went further and threatened to abolish bishops. King Charles, fearful of a Scottish invasion—the original reason for summoning Parliament—accepted these measures. Understanding and peace were not achieved, however, partly because radical members of the Commons pushed increasingly revolutionary propositions, and partly because Charles maneuvered to rescind those he had already approved.

The next act in the conflict was precipitated by the outbreak of rebellion in Ireland, where English governors and landlords had long exploited the people. In 1641 the Catholic gentry of Ireland led an uprising in response to a feared invasion by anti-Catholic forces of the British Long Parliament.

Without an army, Charles I could neither come to terms with the Scots nor respond to the Irish rebellion. After a failed attempt to arrest parliamentary leaders who remained unwilling to grant him an army, Charles left London for the north of England. There, he recruited an army drawn from the nobility and its cavalry staff, the rural gentry, and mercenaries. The parliamentary army was composed of the militia of the city of London, country squires with business connections, and men with a firm belief in the spiritual duty of serving.

The English civil war (1642–1649) pitted the power of the king against that of the Parliament. After three years of fighting, Parliament's **New Model Army** defeated the king's armies at the battles of Naseby and Langport in the summer of 1645. Charles, though, refused to concede defeat and accept restrictions on royal authority and church reform. Both sides jockeyed for position, waiting for a decisive event. This arrived in the form of the army under the leadership of Oliver Cromwell, a member of the House of Commons. In 1647 Cromwell's forces captured the king and dismissed members of the Parliament who opposed his actions. In 1649 the remaining representatives, known as the "Rump Parliament," put Charles on trial for high treason, a severe blow to the theory of divine-right monarchy. Charles was found guilty and beheaded on January 30, 1649, an act that sent shock waves around Europe.

New Model Army The parliamentary army, under the command of Oliver Cromwell, that fought the army of Charles I in the English civil war.

Puritanical Absolutism in England: Cromwell and the Protectorate

With the execution of Charles, kingship was abolished. A *commonwealth*, or republican government, was proclaimed. Theoretically, legislative power rested in the surviving members of Parliament, and executive power was lodged in a council of state. In fact, the army that had defeated the king controlled the government, and Oliver Cromwell controlled the army. Though called the **Protectorate,** the rule of Cromwell (1653–1658) constituted military dictatorship.

The army prepared a constitution, the Instrument of Government (1653), that invested executive power in a lord protector (Cromwell) and a council of state. The instrument provided for triennial parliaments and gave Parliament the sole power to raise taxes. But after repeated disputes, Cromwell dismissed Parliament in 1655 and the instrument was never formally endorsed. Cromwell continued the standing army and proclaimed quasi-martial law. He divided England into twelve military districts, each governed by a major general. Reflecting Puritan ideas of morality, Cromwell's state forbade sports, kept the theaters closed, and rigorously censored the press.

Protectorate The military dictatorship established by Oliver Cromwell following the execution of Charles I in 1649.

On the issue of religion, Cromwell favored some degree of toleration, and the Instrument of Government gave all Christians except Roman Catholics the right to practice their faith. Cromwell had long associated Catholicism in Ireland with sedition and heresy. In September of the year that his army came to power, it crushed a rebellion at Drogheda and massacred the garrison. Another massacre followed in October. These brutal acts left a legacy of Irish hatred for England. After Cromwell's departure for England, the atrocities worsened. The English banned Catholicism in Ireland, executed priests, and confiscated land from Catholics for English and Scottish settlers.

Cromwell adopted mercantilist policies similar to those of absolutist France. He enforced a Navigation Act (1651) requiring that English goods be transported on English ships. The Navigation Act was a great boost to the development of an English merchant marine and brought about a short but successful war with the commercially threatened Dutch. Cromwell also welcomed the immigration of Jews because of their skills, and they began to return to England after four centuries of absence.

The Protectorate collapsed when Cromwell died in 1658 and his ineffectual son, Richard, succeeded him. Having lost support of the army, Richard was forced to abdicate. Fed up with military rule, the English longed for a return to civilian government and, with it, common law and social stability. By 1660 they were ready to restore the monarchy.

Cartoon of 1649: "The Royall Oake of Brittayne"

Chopping down this tree signifies the end of royal authority, stability, Magna Carta (see page 205), and the rule of law. As pigs graze (representing the unconcerned common people), being fattened for slaughter, Oliver Cromwell, with his feet in Hell, quotes Scripture. This is a royalist view of the collapse of Charles I's government and the rule of Cromwell. (Courtesy of the Trustees of the British Museum)

Test Act Written in 1673, this act stated that those who refused to receive the Eucharist of the Church of England could not vote, hold public office, preach, teach, attend the universities, or even assemble for meetings.

The Restoration of the English Monarchy

The Restoration of 1660 brought Charles II (r. 1660–1685) to the throne at the invitation of a special session of Parliament called for that purpose. He was the eldest son of Charles I and had been living on the European continent. Both houses of Parliament were also restored, together with the established Anglican church, the courts of law, and the system of local government through justices of the peace. The Restoration failed to resolve two serious problems, however. What was to be the attitude of the state toward Puritans, Catholics, and dissenters from the established church? And what was to be the relationship between the king and Parliament?

Charles II, an easygoing and sensual man, was not interested in imposing religious uniformity on the English, but members of Parliament were. They enacted the **Test Act** of 1673 against those who refused to receive the Eucharist of the Church of England, denying them the right to vote, hold public office, preach, teach, attend the universities, or even assemble for meetings. But these restrictions could not be enforced. When the Quaker William Penn held a meeting of his Friends and was arrested, the jury refused to convict him.

In politics Charles II was determined "not to set out in his travels again," which meant that he intended to avoid exile by working well with Parliament. Therefore he appointed a council of five men to serve both as his major advisers and as members of Parliament, thus acting as liaison agents between the executive and the legislature. This body—known as the "Cabal" from the names of its five members (Clifford, Arlington, Buckingham, Ashley-Cooper, and Lauderdale)—was an ancestor of the later cabinet system. It gradually came to be accepted that the Cabal was answerable in Parliament for the decisions of the king. This development gave rise to the concept of ministerial responsibility: royal ministers must answer to the Commons.

Harmony between the Crown and Parliament was upset in 1670, however. When Parliament did not grant Charles an adequate income, he entered into a secret agreement with his cousin Louis XIV. The French king would give Charles two hundred thousand pounds annually, and in return Charles would relax the laws against Catholics, gradually re-Catholicize England, support French policy against the Dutch, and convert to Catholicism himself. When the details of this treaty leaked out, a great wave of anti-Catholic fear swept England. This fear was compounded by a crucial fact: with no legitimate heir, Charles would be succeeded by his Catholic brother, James, duke of York. A combination of hatred for French absolutism and hostility to Catholicism produced virtual hysteria. The Commons passed an exclusion bill denying the succession to a Roman Catholic, but Charles quickly dissolved Parliament, and the bill never became law.

When James II (r. 1685–1688) succeeded his brother, the worst English anti-Catholic fears, already aroused by Louis XIV's revocation of the Edict of Nantes, were realized. In violation of the Test Act, James appointed Roman Catholics to positions in the army, the universities, and local government. When these actions were challenged in the courts, the judges, whom James had appointed, decided for the king. The king was suspending the law at will and appeared to be reviving the absolutism of his father and grandfather. He went further. Attempting to broaden his base of support with Protestant dissenters and nonconformists, James issued a declaration of indulgence granting religious freedom to all.

Two events gave the signals for revolution. First, seven bishops of the Church of England were imprisoned in the Tower of London for protesting the declaration of indulgence but were subsequently acquitted amid great public enthusiasm. Second, in June 1688 James's second wife produced a male heir. The fear of a Roman Catholic dynasty supported by France and ruling outside the law prompted a group of eminent persons to offer the English throne to James's Protestant daughter Mary and her Dutch husband, Prince William of Orange. In December 1688 James II, his queen, and their infant son fled to France and became pensioners of Louis XIV. Early in 1689 William and Mary were crowned king and queen of England.

The Triumph of England's Parliament: Constitutional Monarchy and Cabinet Government

The English call the events of 1688 and 1689 the "Glorious Revolution" because it replaced one king with another with a minimum of bloodshed. It also represented the destruction, once and for all, of the idea of divine-right monarchy. William and Mary accepted the English throne from Parliament and in so doing explicitly recognized the supremacy of Parliament. The revolution of 1688 established the principle that sovereignty, the ultimate power in the state, was divided between king and Parliament and that the king ruled with the consent of the governed.

The men who brought about the revolution quickly framed their intentions in the Bill of Rights, the cornerstone of the modern British constitution. The principles of the Bill of Rights were formulated in direct response to Stuart absolutism. Law was to be made in Parliament; once made, it could not be suspended by the Crown. Parliament had to be called at least once every three years. Both elections to and debate in Parliament were to be free in the sense that the Crown was not to interfere in them (this aspect of the bill was widely disregarded in the eighteenth century). The independence of the judiciary was established, and there was to be no standing army in peacetime. And while Protestants could possess arms, the feared Catholic minority could not. Additional legislation granted freedom of worship to Protestant dissenters and nonconformists and required that the English monarch always be Protestant.

Second Treatise of Civil Government
A work of political philosophy published by John Locke in 1690 that argued government's only purpose was to defend the natural rights of life, liberty, and property. A justification of the Glorious Revolution of 1688 to 1689.

The Glorious Revolution and the concept of representative government found its best defense in political philosopher John Locke's **Second Treatise of Civil Government** (1690). Locke (1632–1704) maintained that a government that oversteps its proper function—protecting the natural rights of life, liberty, and property—becomes a tyranny. By "natural" rights Locke meant rights basic to all men because all have the ability to reason. Under a tyrannical government, the people have the natural right to rebellion. Such rebellion can be avoided if the government carefully respects the rights of citizens and if people zealously defend their liberty. Locke linked economic liberty and private property with political freedom. On the basis of this link, he justified limiting the vote to property owners.

The events of 1688 and 1689 did not constitute a *democratic* revolution. The revolution placed sovereignty in Parliament, and Parliament represented the upper classes. The great majority of English people acquired no say in their government. The English revolution established a constitutional monarchy; it also inaugurated an age of aristocratic government that lasted at least until 1832 and in many ways until 1928, when women received full voting rights.

The Dutch Republic in the Seventeenth Century

In the late sixteenth century the seven northern provinces of the Netherlands fought for and won their independence from Spain. The independence of the Republic of the United Provinces of the Netherlands was recognized in 1648, in the treaty that ended the Thirty Years' War. The seventeenth century witnessed an unparalleled flowering of Dutch scientific, artistic, and literary achievement. In this period, often called the "golden age of the Netherlands," Dutch ideas and attitudes played a profound role in shaping a new and modern worldview. At the same time, the United Provinces was another model of the development of the modern constitutional state.

The government of the United Provinces had none of the standard categories of seventeenth-century political organization. The Dutch were not monarchical but rather fiercely republican. Within each province, an oligarchy of wealthy merchants and financiers called "regents" handled domestic affairs in the local Estates (assemblies). The provincial Estates held virtually all the power. A federal assembly, or **States General,** handled matters of foreign affairs, such as war. But the States General did not possess sovereign authority; all issues had to be referred back to the local Estates for approval. In each province, the Estate appointed an executive officer, known as the **stadtholder** (STAT-hohl-der), who carried out ceremonial functions and was responsible for military defense. Although in theory freely chosen by the Estates and answerable to them, in practice the Princes of Orange were almost always chosen as stadtholders. Tensions persisted between supporters of the staunchly republican Estates and those of the aristocratic House of Orange. Holland, which had the largest navy and the most wealth, dominated the seven provinces of the republic and the States General.

States General   The national assembly of the United Provinces of the Netherlands; because many issues had to be refereed back to the provinces, the United Provinces was a confederation, or weak union of strong states.

stadtholder   The chief executive officer in each province of the United Provinces; in the seventeenth century these positions were often held by the princes of the House of Orange.

The political success of the Dutch rested on the phenomenal commercial prosperity of the Netherlands. The moral and ethical bases of that commercial wealth were thrift, frugality, and religious toleration. As long as business people conducted their religion in private, the government did not interfere with them. Although there is scattered evidence of anti-Semitism, Jews enjoyed a level of acceptance and assimilation in Dutch business and general culture unique in early modern Europe. (See the feature "Individuals in Society: Glückel of Hameln.") For example, Benedict Spinoza (1632–1677), a descendant of Spanish Jews who fled the Inquisition, passed his entire life in Amsterdam, supporting himself as a

Individuals in Society

Glückel of Hameln

In 1690 a Jewish widow in the small German town of Hameln* in Lower Saxony sat down to write her autobiography. She wanted to distract her mind from the terrible grief she felt over the death of her husband and to provide her twelve children with a record "so you will know from what sort of people you have sprung, lest today or tomorrow your beloved children or grandchildren came and know naught of their family." Out of her pain and heightened consciousness, Glückel (1646–1724) produced an invaluable source for scholars.

She was born in Hamburg two years before the end of the Thirty Years' War. In 1649 the merchants of Hamburg expelled the Jews, who moved to nearby Altona, then under Danish rule. When the Swedes overran Altona (1657–1658), the Jews returned to Hamburg "purely at the mercy of the Town Council." Glückel's narrative proceeds against a background of the constant harassment to which Jews were subjected—special papers, permits, bribes—and in Hameln she wrote, "And so it has been to this day and, I fear, will continue in like fashion."

When Glückel was "barely twelve," her father betrothed her to Chayim Hameln (HI-um HAH-muhln). She married at age fourteen. She describes him as "the perfect pattern of the pious Jew," a man who stopped his work every day for study and prayer, fasted, and was scrupulously honest in his business dealings. Only a few years older than Glückel, Chayim earned his living dealing in precious metals and in making small loans on pledges (articles held on security). This work required his constant travel to larger cities, markets, and fairs, often in bad weather, always over dangerous roads. Chayim consulted his wife about all his business dealings. As he lay dying, a friend asked if he had any last wishes. "None," he replied. "My wife knows everything. She shall do as she has always done." For thirty years Glückel had been his friend, full business partner, and wife. They had thirteen children, twelve of whom survived their father, eight then unmarried. As Chayim had foretold, Glückel succeeded in launching the boys in careers and in providing dowries for the girls.

Glückel's world was her family, the Jewish community of Hameln, and the Jewish communities into which her children married. Social and business activities took her to Amsterdam, Baiersdorf, Bamberg, Berlin, Cleves, Danzig, Metz, and Vienna, so her world was not narrow or provincial. She took great pride that Prince Frederick of Cleves, later the king of Prussia, danced at the wedding of her eldest daughter. The rising prosperity of Chayim's businesses allowed the couple to maintain up to six servants.

Glückel was deeply religious, and her culture was steeped in Jewish literature, legends, and mystical and secular works. Above all, she relied on the Bible. Her language, heavily sprinkled with scriptural references, testifies to a rare familiarity with the basic book of Western civilization. The Scriptures were her consolation, the source of her great strength in a hostile world.

Gentleness and deep mutual devotion seem to pervade Rembrandt's *The Jewish Bride*. (Rijksmuseum-Stichting Amsterdam)

Students who would learn about business practices, the importance of the dowry in marriage, childbirth, the ceremony of bris, birthrates, family celebrations, and even the meaning of life can gain a good deal from the memoirs of this extraordinary woman who was, in the words of one of her descendants, the poet Heinrich Heine, "the gift of a world to me."

Questions for Analysis

1. Consider the ways in which Glückel of Hameln was both an ordinary and an extraordinary woman of her times. Would you call her a marginal or a central person in her society?

2. How was Glückel's life affected by the broad events and issues of the seventeenth century?

Source: The Memoirs of Glückel of Hameln (New York: Schocken Books, 1977).

---

* A town immortalized by the Brothers Grimm. In 1284 the town contracted with the Pied Piper to rid it of rats and mice; he lured them away by playing his flute. When the citizens refused to pay, he charmed away their children in revenge.

Jan Steen: The Christening Feast
As the mother, surrounded by midwives, rests in bed *(rear left)* and the father proudly displays the swaddled child, thirteen other people, united by gestures and gazes, prepare the celebratory meal. Very prolific, Steen was a master of warm-hearted domestic scenes. In contrast to the order and cleanliness of many seventeenth-century Dutch genre paintings, Steen's more disorderly portrayals gave rise to the epithet "a Jan Steen household," meaning an untidy house. (Wallace Collection, London/The Bridgeman Art Library)

lens grinder while producing important philosophical treatises. In the Dutch Republic, toleration paid off: it attracted a great deal of foreign capital and investment. People of all races and creeds traded in Amsterdam, at whose docks on the Amstel River five thousand ships were berthed.

The Dutch came to dominate the shipping business by putting profits from their original industry—herring fishing—into shipbuilding. They boasted the lowest shipping rates and largest merchant marine in Europe. Their shipping power allowed them to control the Baltic grain trade, buying entire crops in Poland, eastern Prussia, and Swedish Pomerania. Because the Dutch dealt in bulk, nobody could undersell them. Foreign merchants coming to Amsterdam could buy anything from precision lenses for the microscope (recently invented by Dutchman Anton van Leeuwenhoek) to muskets for an army of five thousand. Although Dutch cities became famous for their exports—diamonds and linens from Haarlem, pottery from Delft—Dutch wealth depended less on exports than on transport.

Dutch East India Company A joint stock company chartered by the States General of the Netherlands to expand trade and promote relations between the Dutch government and its colonial ventures. It established a colony at the Cape of Good Hope (1652), and in the 1630s it paid a return of 35 percent on investments.

In 1602 leaders of the Estate of Holland formed the **Dutch East India Company,** a joint stock company. The investors each received a percentage of the profits proportional to the amount of money they had put in. Within half a century the Dutch East India Company had cut heavily into Portuguese trading in East Asia. The Dutch seized the Cape of Good Hope, Ceylon, and Malacca and established trading posts in each place. In the 1630s the Dutch East India Company was paying its investors about a 35 percent annual return on their investments. The Dutch West India Company, founded in 1621, traded extensively with Latin America and Africa (see Map 16.2). Ultimately both companies would move beyond trading to imperialist exploitation.

Trade and commerce brought the Dutch the highest standard of living in Europe, and perhaps in the world. Salaries were high for all workers except women, but even women's wages were high when compared with those of women in other parts of Europe. All classes of society, including unskilled laborers, ate well. Massive granaries held surplus supplies so that the price of bread remained low. A higher percentage of the worker's income could therefore be spent on fish, cheese, butter, vegetables, and even meat. A scholar has described the Netherlands as "an island of plenty in a sea of want." Consequently, the Netherlands experienced very few of the food riots that characterized the rest of Europe.[15] The Dutch republic was not a federation but a confederation—that is, a weak union of strong provinces. Wealthy and lacking a monarch, the provinces were a temptation to other European powers. Nonetheless, the Dutch resisted the long Spanish effort at reconquest and withstood both French and English attacks in the second half of the century. They were severely weakened, however, by the long War of the Spanish Succession, which was a costly drain on Dutch labor and financial resources. The peace signed in 1713 to end the war brought the republic few gains to compensate for its expenses and marked the beginning of Dutch economic decline.

Section Review

- In England, King James I's belief that he was subject only to God led to tension with the House of Commons as he tried to govern without Parliament.

- Financial and religious disputes between King Charles I and the House of Commons led to civil war, and even though the king allied himself with northern nobles, Parliament won out, tried Charles for treason, and beheaded him in 1649.

- After Charles's death, Cromwell came to power, proclaiming a commonwealth that was actually a military dictatorship, holding Puritanical ideals of morality, earning the ire of the Irish by outlawing Catholicism in Ireland, but also boosting the English sea trade and allowing Jewish immigration.

- After Cromwell's death, the 1660 Restoration brought Charles to the throne, who alienated the English by favoring Catholics; Protestant fears intensified when the Catholic James II succeeded his brother, ending in the Glorious Revolution of 1688, whereby James was exiled to France while his Protestant daughter Mary and her Dutch husband William of Orange were crowned as the monarchs.

- The government of William and Mary was a constitutional monarchy that provided freedom of religion, but economic and political liberty came only with property ownership, so the masses still had no political rights.

- The Dutch republic in the seventeenth century found political success and prosperity by providing religious tolerance, attracting foreign capital, and promoting trade.

MAP 16.2   Seventeenth-Century Dutch Commerce

Dutch wealth rested on commerce, and commerce depended on the huge Dutch merchant marine, manned by perhaps forty-eight thousand sailors. The fleet carried goods from all parts of the globe to the port of Amsterdam.

Chapter Review

What were the common crises and achievements of seventeenth-century states? (page 402)

Most parts of Europe experienced the seventeenth century as a period of severe economic, social, and military crisis. Across the continent, rulers faced popular rebellions from their desperate subjects, who were pushed to the brink by poor harvests, high taxes, and decades of war. Many forces, including powerful noblemen, the church, and regional and local loyalties, constrained the state's authority. Despite these obstacles, most European states emerged from the seventeenth century with increased powers and more centralized control. Whether they ruled through monarchical fiat or parliamentary negotiation, European governments strengthened their bureaucracies, raised more taxes, and significantly expanded their armies.

According to Thomas Hobbes, the central drive in every human is "a perpetual and restless desire of Power, after Power, that ceaseth only in Death." The seventeenth century solved the problem of sovereign power in two fundamental ways: absolutism and constitutionalism.

To what extent did French and Spanish monarchs succeed in creating absolute monarchies? (page 405)

Under Louis XIV France witnessed the high point of absolutist ambition in western Europe. The king saw himself as the representative of God on earth, and it has been said that "to the seventeenth century imagination God was a sort of image of Louis XIV."[16] Under Louis's rule, France developed a centralized bureaucracy, a professional army, and a state-directed economy, all of which he personally supervised.

Despite his claims to absolute power, Louis XIV ruled, in practice, by securing the collaboration of high nobles. In exchange for confirmation of their ancient privileges, the nobles were willing to cooperate with the expansion of state power. This was a common pattern in attempts at absolutism across Europe. In Spain, where monarchs made similar claims to absolute power, the seventeenth century witnessed economic catastrophe and a decline in royal capacities.

What cultural forms flourished under absolutist governments? (page 415)

France's dominant political role in Europe elevated its cultural influence as well. French became the common language of the European elite, as all heads turned to Versailles and the radiant aristocratic culture emanating from it. Within France, the Bourbon monarchy pursued culture as one more aspect of absolutist policy, creating cultural academies, sponsoring playwrights and musicians, and repressing Protestantism with a bloody hand.

What is constitutionalism, and how did this form of government emerge in England and the Dutch Republic? (page 418)

As Louis XIV personified absolutist ambitions, so Stuart England exemplified the evolution of the constitutional state. The conflicts between Parliament and the first two Stuart rulers, James I and Charles I, tested where sovereign power would reside. The resulting civil war did not solve the problem. The Instrument of Government provided for a balance of government authority and recognition of popular rights; as such, the Instrument has been called the first modern constitution. Unfortunately, it

Key Terms

moral economy (p. 403)

sovereignty (p. 405)

popular revolts (p. 405)

intendants (p. 407)

Fronde (p. 407)

divine right of kings (p. 408)

absolute monarchy (p. 408)

mercantilism (p. 409)

Peace of Utrecht (p. 411)

Don Quixote (p. 414)

baroque style (p. 415)

French classicism (p. 417)

constitutionalism (p. 418)

Puritans (p. 419)

New Model Army (p. 421)

Protectorate (p. 421)

Test Act (p. 422)

Second Treatise of Civil Government (p. 424)

States General (p. 424)

stadtholder (p. 424)

Dutch East India Company (p. 426)

did not survive the Protectorate. James II's absolutist tendencies brought on the Glorious Revolution of 1688 and 1689, and the people who made that revolution settled three basic issues: sovereign power was divided between king and Parliament, with Parliament enjoying the greater share; government was to be based on the rule of law; and the liberties of English people were made explicit in written form in the Bill of Rights.

Having won independence from Spain, the United Provinces of the Netherlands provided another model of constitutional government, one dominated by wealthy urban merchants rather than the landed gentry who controlled the English system. The federal constitution of the Netherlands invested power in the Estates General, but diluted their authority by giving veto power to provincial assemblies. Dominated by Holland, the Netherlands provided a shining example of industriousness, prosperity, and relative tolerance for the rest of Europe.

Notes

1. The classic study is by Theodore K. Rabb, *The Struggle for Stability in Early Modern Europe* (Oxford: Oxford University Press, 1975).
2. G. Parker and L. M. Smith, "Introduction," and N. Steensgaard, "The Seventeenth Century Crisis," in *The General Crisis of the Seventeenth Century*, ed. G. Parker and L. M. Smith (London: Routledge & Kegan Paul, 1985), pp. 1–53, esp. p. 12.
3. H. G. Koenigsberger, "The Revolt of Palermo in 1647," *Cambridge Historical Journal* 8 (1944–1946): 129–144.
4. See W. Beik, *Urban Protest in Seventeenth-Century France: The Culture of Retribution* (New York: Cambridge University Press, 1997), p. 1.
5. Ibid.
6. See ibid., chaps. 1, 2, 3, and 11.
7. Ibid., pp. 22–26.
8. See M. Turchetti, "The Edict of Nantes," in *The Oxford Encyclopedia of the Reformation*, ed. H. J. Hillerbrand, vol. 3 (New York: Oxford University Press, 1996), pp. 126–128.
9. Quoted in J. H. Elliott, *Richelieu and Olivares* (Cambridge: Cambridge University Press, 1984), p. 135; and in W. F. Church, *Richelieu and Reason of State* (Princeton, N.J.: Princeton University Press, 1972), p. 507.
10. Quoted in J. Wolf, *Louis XIV* (New York: W. W. Norton, 1968), p. 146.
11. John A. Lynn, "Recalculating French Army Growth," in *The Military Revolution Debate: Readings on the Military Transformation of Early Modern Europe*, ed. Clifford J. Rogers (Boulder, Colo.: Westview Press, 1995), p. 125.
12. J. H. Elliott, *Imperial Spain, 1469–1716* (New York: Mentor Books, 1963), pp. 306–308.
13. B. Bennassar, *The Spanish Character: Attitudes and Mentalities from the Sixteenth to the Nineteenth Century*, trans. B. Keen (Berkeley: University of California Press, 1979), p. 125.
14. For a revisionist interpretation, see J. Wormald, "James VI and I: Two Kings or One?" *History* 62 (June 1983): 187–209.
15. S. Schama, *The Embarrassment of Riches: An Interpretation of Dutch Culture in the Golden Age* (New York: Alfred A. Knopf, 1987), pp. 165–170; quotation is on p. 167.
16. C. J. Friedrich and C. Blitzer, *The Age of Power* (Ithaca, N.Y.: Cornell University Press, 1957), p. 112.

To assess your mastery of this chapter, go to **bedfordstmartins.com/mckaywestbrief**

The Court at Versailles

Although the Duc de Saint-Simon (1675–1755) was a soldier, courtier, and diplomat, his enduring reputation rests on The Memoirs (1788), *his eyewitness account of the personality and court of Louis XIV. A nobleman of extremely high status, Saint-Simon resented Louis's high-handed treatment of the ancient nobility and his promotion of newer nobles and the bourgeoisie.* The Memoirs, *excerpted here, remains a monument of French literature and an indispensable historical source, partly for its portrait of the court at Versailles.*

Very early in the reign of Louis XIV the Court was removed from Paris, never to return. The troubles of the minority had given him a dislike to that city; his enforced and surreptitious flight from it still rankled in his memory; he did not consider himself safe there, and thought cabals would be more easily detected if the Court was in the country, where the movements and temporary absences of any of its members would be more easily noticed. . . . No doubt that he was also influenced by the feeling that he would be regarded with greater awe and veneration when no longer exposed every day to the gaze of the multitude.

He availed himself of the frequent festivities at Versailles, and his excursions to other places, as a means of making the courtiers assiduous in their attendance and anxious to please him; for he nominated beforehand those who were to take part in them, and could thus gratify some and inflict a snub on others. He was conscious that the substantial favours he had to bestow were not nearly sufficient to produce a continual effect; he had therefore to invent imaginary ones, and no one was so clever in devising petty distinctions and preferences which aroused jealousy and emulation. . . .

Not only did he expect all persons of distinction to be in continual attendance at Court, but he was quick to notice the absence of those of inferior degree; at his *lever* (**LEV-ay**) [formal rising from bed in the morning], his *coucher* (**KOO-shay**) [preparations for going to bed], his meals, in the gardens of Versailles (the only place where the courtiers in general were allowed to follow him), he used to cast his eyes to right and left; nothing escaped him, he saw everybody. If any one habitually living at Court absented himself he insisted on knowing the reason; those who came there only for flying visits had also to give a satisfactory explanation; any one who seldom or never appeared there was certain to incur his displeasure. If asked to bestow a favour on

Louis XIV was extremely proud of the gardens at Versailles and personally led ambassadors and other highly ranked visitors on tours of the extensive palace grounds. (Erich Lessing/Art Resource, NY)

such persons he would reply haughtily: "I do not know him"; of such as rarely presented themselves he would say, "He is a man I never see"; and from these judgements there was no appeal.

He loved splendour, magnificence, and profusion in all things, and encouraged similar tastes in his Court; to spend money freely on equipages [horse carriages] and buildings, on feasting and at cards, was a sure way to gain his favour, perhaps to obtain the honour of a word from him. Motives of policy had something to do with this; by making expensive habits the fashion, and, for people in a certain position, a necessity, he compelled his courtiers to live beyond their income, and gradually reduced them to depend on his bounty for the means of subsistence. This was a plague which, once introduced, became a scourge to the whole country, for it did not take long to spread to Paris, and thence to the armies and the provinces; so that a man of any position is now estimated entirely according to his expenditure on his table and other luxuries. This folly, sustained by pride and ostenta-

tion, has already produced widespread confusion; it threatens to end in nothing short of ruin and a general overthrow.

Questions for Analysis

1. What was the role of etiquette and ceremony at the court of Versailles? How could Louis XIV use them in everyday life at court to influence and control nobles?

2. How important do you think Louis's individual character and personality were to his style of governing? What challenges might this present to his successors?

3. Consider the role of ceremony in some modern governments, such as the U.S. government. How does it compare to Louis XIV's use of ceremony as portrayed by Saint-Simon?

4. Do you think Saint-Simon is an objective and trustworthy recorder of life at court? Why?

Source: "The Court at Versailles" from *The Memoirs of the Duke de Saint Simon*, ed. F. Arkwright (New York: Brentano's, n.d.), Vol. V, pp. 271–274, 276–278.

CHAPTER 17

Absolutism in Central and Eastern Europe

to 1740

Chapter Preview

Warfare and Social Change in Central and Eastern Europe
What social and economic changes affected central and eastern Europe from 1400 to 1650?

The Rise of Austria and Prussia
How did the rulers of Austria and Prussia manage to build powerful absolute monarchies?

The Development of Russia and the Ottoman Empire
What were the distinctive features of Russian and Ottoman absolutism in this period?

INDIVIDUALS IN SOCIETY: Hürrem

IMAGES IN SOCIETY: Absolutist Palace Building

LISTENING TO THE PAST: A Foreign Traveler in Russia

Peter the Great's magnificent new crown, created for his joint coronation in 1682 with his half-brother Ivan. (State Museum of the Kremlin, Moscow)

The crises of the seventeenth century—religious division, economic depression, and war—were not limited to western Europe. Central and eastern Europe experienced even more catastrophic dislocation, with German lands serving as the battleground of the Thirty Years' War and borders constantly vulnerable to attack from the east. In Prussia and Habsburg Austria absolutist states emerged in the aftermath of this conflict.

Russia and the Ottoman Turks also developed absolutist governments. These empires seemed foreign and exotic to western Europeans, who saw them as the antithesis of their political, religious, and cultural values. To Western eyes, their own monarchs respected law—either divine or constitutional—while Eastern despots ruled with an iron fist. In this view, the Ottoman Muslim state was home to fanaticism and heresy, and even Russian Orthodoxy had rituals and traditions, if not core beliefs, that differed sharply from either Catholicism or Protestantism. Beneath the surface, however, these Eastern governments shared many similarities with Western ones.

The most successful Eastern empires lasted until 1918, far longer than monarchical rule endured in France, the model of absolutism under Louis XIV. Eastern monarchs had a powerful impact on architecture and the arts, encouraging new monumental construction to reflect their glory. Questions about the relationship between East and West remain potent today, as evidenced by the debate surrounding Turkey's bid for membership in the European Union.

Warfare and Social Change in Central and Eastern Europe

What social and economic changes affected central and eastern Europe from 1400 to 1650?

When absolute monarchy emerged in the seventeenth century, it built on social and economic foundations laid between roughly 1400 and 1650. In those years the elites of eastern Europe rolled back the gains made by the peasantry during the High Middle Ages and reimposed a harsh serfdom on the rural masses. The nobility also reduced the importance of the towns and the middle classes. This process differed from developments in western Europe, where peasants won greater freedom and the urban middle class continued its rise. The Thirty Years' War represented the culmination of these changes. Decades of war in central Europe led to depopulation and economic depression, which allowed lords to impose ever-harsher controls on the peasantry.

The Consolidation of Serfdom

The period from 1050 to 1300 was a time of general economic expansion in eastern Europe characterized by the growth of trade, towns, and population. The rulers of eastern Europe attracted settlers to the frontier beyond the Elbe River with economic and legal incentives and the offer of greater personal freedom. These benefits were also gradually extended to the local Slavic populations, even those of central Russia. Thus, by 1300 **serfdom** had all but disappeared in eastern Europe.

After the Black Death (1348), however, as Europe's population and economy declined grievously, lords sought to solve their economic problems by more heavily

serfdom A system used by nobles and rulers in which peasants were bound to the land they worked and to the lords they served.

Estonia in the 1660s
The Estonians were conquered by German military nobility in the Middle Ages and reduced to serfdom. The German-speaking nobles ruled the Estonian peasants with an iron hand, and Peter the Great reaffirmed their domination when Russia annexed Estonia (see Map 17.3 on page 445). (Mansell Collection/Time Life Pictures/Getty Images)

exploiting the peasantry. This reaction generally failed in the West, where by 1500 almost all peasants were free or had their serf obligations greatly reduced. East of the Elbe, however, the landlords won. They pushed for laws restricting or eliminating the peasants' right to move wherever they wished. They also took more of their peasants' land and imposed heavier labor obligations. Instead of being independent farmers paying freely negotiated rents, peasants became forced laborers on the lords' estates. By the early 1500s, lords in many territories could command their peasants to work without pay as many as six days a week. The peasants had no recourse through the courts to fight these injustices. The local lord was also the prosecutor, judge, and jailer.

Between 1500 and 1650 the social, legal, and economic conditions of peasants in eastern Europe continued to decline, and free peasants became serfs. Polish nobles gained complete control over their peasants in 1574, after which they could legally inflict the death penalty whenever they wished. In Prussia in 1653 peasants were assumed to be tied to their lords in hereditary subjugation—bound to their lords and the land from one generation to the next. In Russia a peasant's right to move from an estate was permanently abolished in 1603. In 1649 the tsar lifted the nine-year time limit on the recovery of runaways and eliminated all limits on lords' authority over their peasants.

Political factors were crucial to the re-emergence of serfdom in eastern Europe. In the late Middle Ages central and eastern Europe experienced innumerable wars and general political chaos, which allowed noble landlords to increase their power. There were, for example, many disputed royal successions, so that weak kings were forced to grant political favors to win the nobility's support. Thus while strong monarchs and effective central government were rising in Spain, France, and England, kings were generally losing power in the East and could not resist the demands of lords regarding peasants.

Moreover, most Eastern monarchs did not oppose the growth of serfdom. The typical king was only first among noble equals. He, too, wanted to squeeze his peasants. The Western concept of sovereignty, as embodied in a king who protected the interests of all his people, was not well developed in eastern Europe before 1650.

Not only the peasants suffered. Also with the approval of kings, landlords systematically undermined the medieval privileges of the towns and the power of the urban classes. Instead of selling products to local merchants, landlords sold directly to foreigners. For example, Dutch ships sailed up the rivers of Poland and eastern Germany to the loading docks of the great estates, completely bypassing the local towns. Moreover, "town air" no longer "made people free," for the Eastern towns had lost their medieval right of refuge and were now compelled to return runaways to their lords. The population of the towns and the importance of the urban middle classes declined greatly.

The Thirty Years' War

The Holy Roman Empire was a confederation of hundreds of principalities, independent cities, duchies, and other polities loosely united under an elected emperor. An uneasy truce had prevailed in the Holy Roman Empire since the Peace of Augsburg (AWGZ-burg) of 1555 (see page 350). According to the settlement, the faith of the prince determined the religion of his subjects. Later in the century, however, Catholics and Lutherans grew alarmed as the faiths of various areas shifted. Calvinists and Jesuits had converted some Lutheran princes; Lutherans had acquired Catholic bishoprics. Lutheran princes felt compelled to form the Protestant Union (1608), and Catholics retaliated with the Catholic League (1609). Each alliance was determined that the other should make no religious or territorial advance. Dynastic interests were also involved; the Spanish Habsburgs strongly supported the goals of their Austrian relatives—the unity of the empire and the preservation of Catholicism within it.

The immediate catalyst of violence was the closure of some Protestant churches by Ferdinand of Styria, the new Catholic king in Bohemia (boh-HEE-mee-uh) in 1617. On May 23, 1618, Protestants hurled two of Ferdinand's officials from a castle window in Prague. They fell seventy feet but survived: Catholics claimed that angels had caught them; Protestants said that the officials had fallen on a heap of soft horse manure. Called the "defenestration of Prague," this event marked the beginning of the Thirty Years' War (1618–1648).

The war is traditionally divided into four phases. The first, or Bohemian, phase (1618–1625) was characterized by civil war in Bohemia between the Catholic League, led by Ferdinand, and the Protestant Union, headed by Frederick, the elector of the Palatinate of the Rhine, one of the states of the Holy Roman Empire. The Protestant Union fought for religious liberty and independence from Habsburg rule. In 1620 Catholic forces defeated Frederick at the Battle of the White Mountain.

The second, or Danish, phase of the war (1625–1629)—so called because of the leadership of the Protestant king Christian IV of Denmark (r. 1588–1648)—witnessed additional Catholic victories. The Catholic imperial army led by Albert of Wallenstein swept through Silesia, north to the Baltic, and east into Pomerania, scoring smashing victories. Wallenstein, an unscrupulous opportunist who used his vast riches to build an army loyal only to himself, seemed more interested in carving out his own empire than in aiding the Catholic cause. He quarreled with the Catholic League, and soon the Catholic forces were divided. Religion was eclipsed as a basic issue of the war.

Habsburg power peaked in 1629. The emperor issued the Edict of Restitution, whereby all Catholic properties lost to Protestantism since 1552 were restored, and only Catholics and Lutherans were allowed to practice their faiths. When Wallenstein began ruthless enforcement, Protestants throughout Europe feared the collapse of the balance of power in north-central Europe.

CHRONOLOGY

ca. 1400–1650	Re-emergence of serfdom in eastern Europe
1462–1505	Reign of Ivan III in Russia
1533–1584	Reign of Ivan the Terrible in Russia
1618–1648	Thirty Years' War
1620	Habsburgs crush Protestantism in Bohemia
1620–1740	Growth of absolutism in Austria and Prussia
1640–1688	Reign of Frederick William in Prussia
1652	Nikon reforms Russian Orthodox Church
1670–1671	Cossack revolt led by Razin
ca. 1680–1750	Construction of palaces by absolutist rulers
1683–1718	Habsburgs defend Vienna; win war with Ottoman Turks
1702	Peter the Great founds St. Petersburg
1713–1740	Growth of Prussian military

The third, or Swedish, phase of the war (1630–1635) began with the arrival in Germany of the Swedish king Gustavus Adolphus (goo-STAV-us ah-DOLF-us) (r. 1594–1632). The ablest administrator of his day and a devout Lutheran, he intervened to support the empire's oppressed Protestants. The French chief minister, Cardinal Richelieu, subsidized the Swedes, hoping to weaken Habsburg power in Europe. Gustavus Adolphus won two important battles but was fatally wounded in combat. The Swedish victories ended the Habsburg ambition to unite the German states under imperial authority.

The last, or French, phase of the war (1635–1648) was prompted by Richelieu's concern that the Habsburgs would regain their strength after the death of Gustavus Adolphus. Richelieu declared war on Spain and sent military as well as financial assistance to the Swedes and the Protestant princes fighting in Germany. The war dragged on. The French, Dutch, and Swedes, supported by Scots, Finns, and German mercenaries, burned, looted, and destroyed German agriculture and commerce. Finally, in October 1648 peace was achieved.

Peace of Westphalia A series of treaties that concluded the Thirty Years' War, recognized the sovereign authority of over three hundred German princes, acknowledged the independence of the United Provinces, made Calvinism a permissible creed within Germany, and reduced the role of the Roman Catholic Church in European politics.

Consequences of the Thirty Years' War

The 1648 **Peace of Westphalia** (west-FEY-lee-uh) that ended the Thirty Years' War marked a turning point in European history. Conflicts fought over religious faith ended. The treaties recognized the sovereign, independent authority of more than three hundred German princes (see Map 17.1). Since the time of Holy Roman Emperor Frederick II (1194–1250), Germany had followed a pattern of state-building different from that of France and England: the emperor shared authority with the princes. After the Peace of Westphalia, the emperor's power continued to be severely limited, and the Holy Roman Empire remained a loosely knit federation.

The peace agreement acknowledged the independence of the United Provinces of the Netherlands. France acquired the province of Alsace along with the advantages of the weakened status of the empire. Sweden received a large cash indemnity and jurisdiction over German territories along the Baltic Sea, leaving it as a major threat to the future kingdom of Brandenburg-Prussia (BRAN-duhn-burg PRUHSH-uh). The papacy lost the right to participate in central European religious affairs and the Augsburg agreement of 1555 became permanent, adding Calvinism to Catholicism and Lutheranism as legally permissible creeds. The north German states remained Protestant; the south German states, Catholic.

The Thirty Years' War was probably the most destructive event for the central European economy and society prior to the twentieth century. Perhaps one-third of urban residents and two-fifths of the rural population died. Entire areas were depopulated by warfare, by the flight of refugees, and by disease. The trade of southern German cities such as Augsburg, already hard hit by the shift in transportation routes from the Mediterranean to the Atlantic, was virtually destroyed. All of Europe was experiencing severe inflation due to the influx of Spanish silver, but the destruction of land and foodstuffs made the price rise worse in central Europe than anywhere else. Agricultural areas suffered catastrophically. Many small farmers lacked the revenue to rework their holdings and had to become day laborers. In parts of central Europe, especially in areas east of the Elbe River, loss of land contributed to the consolidation of serfdom.[1]

Some people prospered, however. Nobles and landlords who controlled agricultural estates profited from rising food prices. They bought or seized the land of failed small farmers and then demanded more unpaid labor on those enlarged estates. Surpluses in wheat and timber were sold to foreign merchants, who exported them to the growing cities of the West.

Section Review

- The great decline in population and economy from the Black Death (1348), as well as many wars and political instability, led eastern European landlords to reimpose harsh serfdom on peasants and undermine the privileges of urban dwellers, a tactic that failed in western Europe, where by 1500 most peasants were free.

- Conflict between Lutheran and Catholic princes within the Holy Roman Empire broke the peace of Augsburg (1555), resulting in the outbreak of the Thirty Years' War (1618–1648).

- The Thirty Years' War erupted in Prague in 1618 and continued through four phases: Bohemian, Danish, Swedish, and French.

- Consequences of the Thirty Years' War included an end to conflicts over religious faith, legal inclusion of Calvinism, greater independence of princes in the Holy Roman Empire, severe inflation, the loss of small farms, and the destruction of a third of the population.

**Map labels (main map):**

NORWAY · SWEDEN · FINLAND · ESTONIA · LIVONIA · RUSSIA
SCOTLAND · Edinburgh · North Sea · See Inset · Copenhagen · DENMARK · Baltic Sea · Vilna
IRELAND · Dublin · ENGLAND · Danzig · PRUSSIA · POLAND-LITHUANIA
London · UNITED PROVINCES · Amsterdam · Magdeburg · Berlin · Warsaw
ATLANTIC OCEAN · Antwerp · Essen · Cologne · SAXONY · SILESIA · Dnieper R.
SPANISH NETHERLANDS · Rhine R. · Elbe R. · Vistula R.
Seine R. · Paris · LOWER PALATINATE · UPPER PALATINATE · Prague · BOHEMIA · MORAVIA
Metz · Nantes · Loire R. · FRANCE · BAVARIA · Augsburg · Vienna · AUSTRIA · STYRIA
FRANCHE-COMTÉ · Zurich · SWITZERLAND · Salzburg · TYROL · Trent · CARINTHIA · Buda · Pest · MOLDAVIA · JEDISAN
Geneva · SAVOY · PIEDMONT · MILAN · REPUBLIC OF VENICE · Venice · CARNIOLA · HUNGARY · TRANSYLVANIA · BESSARABIA
Rhône R. · GENOA · CROATIA · SLAVONIA · Belgrade · WALLACHIA · Black Sea
Ebro R. · SPAIN · BOSNIA · SERBIA · Danube R.
Tagus R. · TUSCANY · PAPAL STATES · HERZEGOVINA · MONTENEGRO · BULGARIA · OTTOMAN EMPIRE · Constantinople
Corsica (to Genoa) · Rome · Adriatic Sea
Balearic Is. · Sardinia · NAPLES · Naples
Palermo · Sicily · GREECE · Athens · Aegean Sea · Mediterranean Sea · Crete (to Rep. Of Venice)

**Inset labels:**

North Sea · SWEDEN · JUTLAND · Copenhagen · DENMARK · Baltic Sea · SCHLESWIG · WISMAR · POMERANIA · Lübeck · Hamburg · BREMEN · MECKLENBURG · VERDEN · Elbe R. · BRANDENBURG

Legend:

Austrian Habsburg lands
Spanish Habsburg lands
Other German states
Swedish lands by 1648
Ottoman Empire and tributary states
— Boundary of the Holy Roman Empire

0   150   300 Km.
0   150   300 Mi.

MAP 17.1   Europe After the Thirty Years' War

Which country emerged from the Thirty Years' War as the strongest European power? What dynastic house was that country's major rival in the early modern period?

The Rise of Austria and Prussia

How did the rulers of Austria and Prussia manage to build powerful absolute monarchies?

The monarchs of central and eastern Europe gradually gained political power in three key areas. First, they imposed permanent taxes without consent. Second, they maintained permanent standing armies to police the country and fight abroad. Third, they conducted relations with other states as they pleased. They were able to gain these powers by allowing the nobles greater control over serfs and by providing protection from outside invaders.

As with all general historical developments, there were important variations on the absolutist theme in eastern Europe. Royal absolutism in Prussia was stronger and more effective than in Austria. This would give Prussia a thin edge in the struggle for power in east-central Europe in the eighteenth century. Prussian-style absolutism had great long-term political significance, for it was a rising Prussia that unified the German people in the nineteenth century and imposed on them a militaristic stamp.

The Austrian Habsburgs

Like all of central Europe, the Habsburgs emerged from the Thirty Years' War impoverished and exhausted. Their efforts to destroy Protestantism in the German lands and to turn the weak Holy Roman Empire into a real state had failed. Although the Habsburgs remained the hereditary emperors, real power lay in the hands of a bewildering variety of separate political jurisdictions, including independent cities, small principalities, medium-sized states such as Bavaria and Saxony, and some of the territories of Prussia and the Habsburgs.

Defeat in central Europe encouraged the Habsburgs to turn away from a quest for imperial dominance and to focus inward and eastward in an attempt to unify their diverse holdings. If they could not impose Catholicism in the empire, at least they could do so in their own domains.

The Habsburg victory over Bohemia during the Thirty Years' War was an important step in this direction. The victorious king, Ferdinand II (r. 1619–1637), had drastically reduced the power of the **Bohemian Estates,** which was the largely Protestant representative assembly. He also confiscated the landholdings of many Protestant nobles and gave them to a few loyal Catholic nobles and to the foreign aristocratic mercenaries who led his armies. After 1650 a large portion of the Bohemian nobility was of recent origin and owed everything to the Habsburgs.

With the help of this new nobility, the Habsburgs established direct rule over Bohemia. The condition of the enserfed peasantry worsened substantially: three days per week of unpaid labor—the *robot*—became the norm, and a quarter of the serfs worked for their lords every day but Sundays and religious holidays. Protestantism was also stamped out. The reorganization of Bohemia was a giant step toward creating absolutist rule. As in France in the same years, the pursuit of religious unity was an essential element of absolutism.

Ferdinand III (r. 1637–1657) continued to build state power. He centralized the government in the hereditary German-speaking provinces, which formed the core Habsburg holdings. For the first time, a permanent standing army was ready to put down any internal opposition.

Bohemian Estates The largely Protestant representative body of the different estates in Bohemia. Significantly reduced in power by Ferdinand II.

Austrian Rule in Hungary

The Habsburg monarchy then turned east toward the plains of Hungary, which had been divided between the Ottomans and the Habsburgs in the early sixteenth century (see page 356). Between 1683 and 1699 the Habsburgs pushed the Ottomans from most of Hungary and Transylvania. The recovery of all of the former kingdom of Hungary was completed in 1718.

The Hungarian nobility, despite its reduced strength, effectively thwarted the full development of Habsburg absolutism. Throughout the seventeenth century Hungarian nobles—the most numerous in Europe—rose in revolt against attempts to impose absolute rule. They never triumphed decisively, but neither were they crushed the way the Czech nobility had been in 1620.

The Hungarians resisted because many of them remained Protestants, especially in areas formerly ruled by the Turks. In some of these regions, the Ottomans acted as military allies to the nobles, against the Habsburgs. Finally, the Hungarian nobility, and even part of the peasantry, became attached to a national ideal long before most of the other peoples of eastern Europe. Hungarian nobles were determined to maintain as much independence and local control as possible. In 1703, with the Habsburgs bogged down in the War of the Spanish Succession (see page 411), the Hungarians rose in one last patriotic rebellion under Prince Francis Rákóczy.

Rákóczy and his forces were eventually defeated, but the Habsburgs had to accept a compromise. Charles VI (r. 1711–1740) restored many of the traditional privileges of the aristocracy in return for Hungarian acceptance of hereditary Habsburg rule. Thus Hungary, unlike Austria and Bohemia, was never fully integrated into a centralized, absolute Habsburg state.

Despite checks on their ambitions in Hungary, the Habsburgs made significant achievements in state-building overall by forging consensus with the church and the nobility. A sense of common identity and loyalty to the monarchy grew among elites in Habsburg lands, even to a certain extent in Hungary. The best evidence for this consensus is the spectacular sums approved by the Estates for the growth of the army. German became the language of the common culture and zealous Catholicism also helped fuse a collective identity. Vienna became the political and cultural center of the empire. By 1700 it was a thriving city with a population of one hundred thousand, with its own version of Versailles, the royal palace of Schönbrunn. (SHUN-broon) (See the feature "Images in Society: Absolutist Palace Building" on pages 440–441.)

Prussia in the Seventeenth Century

In the fifteenth and sixteenth centuries, the Hohenzollern family had ruled parts of eastern Germany as the imperial electors of Brandenburg and the dukes of Prussia, but they had little real power. The **elector of Brandenburg** had the right to help choose the Holy Roman emperor, which bestowed prestige, but the elector had no military strength of his own. Nothing suggested that the Hohenzollern family and its territories would come to play as important a role in European affairs as they did.

The elector of Brandenburg was a helpless spectator in the Thirty Years' War, his territories alternately ravaged by Swedish and Habsburg armies. Yet foreign armies also dramatically weakened the political power of the Estates, which helped the elector Frederick William (r. 1640–1688) make significant progress toward royal absolutism. This constitutional struggle was the most crucial in Prussian history until that of the 1860s.

elector of Brandenburg One of the electors of the Holy Roman Empire, with the right to help choose the emperor, hereditarily held by the Hohenzollern family. Frederick William, "the Great Elector," was able to use and expand the office, ultimately resulting in the consolidation of the Prussian state under his successors.

Images in Society

Absolutist Palace Building

By 1700 palace building had become a veritable obsession for the rulers of central and eastern Europe. Their dramatic palaces symbolized the age of absolutist power, just as soaring Gothic cathedrals had expressed the idealized spirit of the High Middle Ages. With its classically harmonious, symmetrical, and geometric design, Versailles, shown in Image 1, served as the model for the wave of palace building that began in the last decade of the seventeenth century.

Located ten miles southwest of Paris, Versailles began as a modest hunting lodge built by Louis XIII in 1623. His son, Louis XIV, loved the site so much that he spent decades enlarging and decorating the original chateau. Between 1668 and 1670, his architect Louis Le Vau (**LOO-ee luh VOH**) enveloped the old building within a much larger second structure that still exists today. In 1682 the new palace became the official residence of the Sun King and his court, although construction continued until 1710, when the royal chapel was completed. At any one time, several thousand people lived in the bustling and crowded palace. The awesome splendor of the eighty-yard Hall of Mirrors, replete with floor to ceiling mirrors and ceiling murals illustrating the king's triumphs, contrasted with the strong odors from the courtiers who commonly relieved themselves in discreet corners. Royal palaces like Versailles were intended to overawe the people and proclaim their owners' authority and power.

In 1693 Charles XI of Sweden, having reduced the power of the aristocracy, ordered the construction of his Royal Palace, which dominates the center of Stockholm to this day. Another such palace was Schönbrunn, an enormous Viennese Versailles begun in 1695 by Emperor Leopold to celebrate Austrian military victories and Habsburg might. Image 2 shows architect Joseph Bernhard Fischer von Erlach's ambitious plan for

IMAGE 1 Pierre-Denis Martin: View of the Chateau de Versailles, 1722 (Châteaux de Versailles et de Trianon, Versailles/Réunion des Musées Nationaux/Art Resource, NY)

Schönbrunn palace. Erlach's plan emphasizes the palace's vast size and its role as a site for military demonstrations. Ultimately financial constraints resulted in a more modest building.

Petty German princes contributed mightily to the palace-building mania. Frederick the Great of Prussia noted that every descendant of a princely family "imagines himself to be something like Louis XIV. He builds his Versailles, has his mistresses, and maintains his army."[*] The elector-archbishop of Mainz, the ruling prince of that city, confessed apologetically that "building is a craze which costs much, but every fool likes his own hat."[†]

In central and eastern Europe, the favorite noble servants of royalty became extremely rich and powerful,

[*] Quoted in R. Ergang, *The Potsdam Fuhrer: Frederick William I, Father of Prussian Militarism* (New York: Octagon Books, 1972), p. 13.
[†] Quoted in J. Summerson, in *The Eighteenth Century: Europe in the Age of Enlightenment*, ed. A. Cobban (New York: McGraw-Hill, 1969), p. 80.

IMAGE 2 Project for the Palace at Schönbrunn (ca. 1700) (Austrian National Library, Vienna)

IMAGE 4 View of the Petit Parc at Versailles from the Canal (Bibliothèque nationale de France)

IMAGE 3 Prince Eugene's Summer Palace, Vienna (Erich Lessing/Art Resource, NY)

and they too built grandiose palaces in the capital cities. These palaces were in part an extension of the monarch, for they surpassed the buildings of less-favored nobles and showed all the high road to fame and fortune. Take, for example, the palaces of Prince Eugene of Savoy, a French nobleman who became Austria's most famous military hero. It was Eugene who led the Austrian army, smashed the Turks, fought Louis XIV to a standstill, and generally guided the triumph of absolutism in Austria. Rewarded with great wealth by his grateful king, Eugene called on the leading architects of the day, J. B. Fischer von Erlach and Johann Lukas von Hildebrandt, to consecrate his glory in stone and fresco. Fischer built Eugene's Winter (or Town) Palace in Vienna, and he and Hildebrandt collaborated on the prince's Summer Palace on the city's outskirts, shown in Image 3. The prince's summer residence featured two baroque gems, the Lower Belvedere and the lovely Upper Belvedere, completed in 1722 and shown here. The building's interior is equally stunning, with crouching giants serving as pillars and a magnificent great staircase.

Palace gardens were an extension of the architecture. The rational orderliness and symmetry of a garden showed that the ruler's force extended even to nature, which offered its subjugated pleasures to the delight of sovereign and courtiers. The terraces and waterworks of these gardens served as showcases for the latest techniques in military and civil engineering. Exotic plants and elaborate designs testified to the sovereign's global trading networks and elevated taste.

The gardens at Versailles, shown in Image 4, exemplify absolutist palace gardens. In the foreground of this image we see a mock naval campaign being enacted on the canal for the edification of courtiers. For diplomatic occasions, Louis XIV himself wrote lengthy guides for viewing the gardens of Versailles. Modern visitors can still follow his itineraries. The themes of the sculptures in the Versailles gardens also hailed Louis's power, with images of Apollo, the sun god, and Neptune, the sea god, making frequent appearances.

Compare the image of Prince Eugene's summer palace with the plans for Schönbrunn and the palace of Versailles. What did concrete objects and the manipulation of space accomplish for these rulers that mere words could not? What disadvantages might stem from using architecture in this way? Is the use of space and monumental construction still a political tool in today's world?

When he came to power in 1640, the twenty-year-old Frederick William, later known as the "Great Elector," was determined to unify his three provinces and enlarge them by diplomacy and war. These provinces were Brandenburg; Prussia, inherited in 1618; and scattered holdings along the Rhine, inherited in 1614 (see Map 17.2). Each was inhabited by German-speaking people, but each had its own Estates. Although the Estates had not met regularly during the chaotic Thirty Years' War, taxes could not be levied without their consent. The Estates of Brandenburg and Prussia were dominated by the nobility and the landowning classes, known as the **Junkers** (YOONG-kuhrs).

To pay for the permanent standing army he first established in 1660, Frederick William forced the Estates to accept the introduction of permanent taxation without consent. The Estates' power declined rapidly thereafter, for the Great Elector had both financial independence and superior force. The state's total revenue tripled during his reign, and the size of the army leaped by ten. In 1688 a population of one million was supporting a peacetime standing army of thirty thousand.

Two factors were central to the Great Elector's triumph. First, as in the formation of every absolutist state, war was a decisive factor. The ongoing struggle between Sweden and Poland for control of the Baltic after 1648 and the wars of Louis XIV in western Europe created an atmosphere of permanent crisis. The nomadic Tatars (TAY-terz) of the Crimea in southern Russia swept through Prussia in the winter of 1656–1657, killing and carrying off thousands as slaves. This invasion softened up the Estates and strengthened the urgency of the Great Elector's demands for more military funding.

Second, the nobility proved willing to accept Frederick William's new claims in exchange for reconfirmation of their own privileges, including authority over

Junkers The nobility of Brandenburg and Prussia. Reluctant allies of Frederick William in his consolidation of the Prussian state.

MAP 17.2   The Growth of Austria and Brandenburg-Prussia to 1748

Austria expanded to the southwest into Hungary and Transylvania at the expense of the Ottoman Empire. It was unable to hold the rich German province of Silesia, however, which was conquered by Brandenburg-Prussia.

Legend:
- Austrian territory at end of Thirty Years' War (1648)
- Austrian acquisitions by end of Turkish Wars (1699)
- Austrian acquisitions after decisive victory over Ottoman Empire (1718)
- Prussian territory at Great Elector's accession (1640)
- Prussian acquisitions by Great Elector's death (1688)
- Prussian acquisitions by end of War of the Austrian Succession (1748)
- Boundary of the Holy Roman Empire

the serfs. The Junkers chose not to join representatives of the towns in a common front against the elector. Instead, they accepted new taxes that fell primarily on towns. The elector used naked force to break the liberties of the towns; the main leader of urban opposition in the key city of Königsberg (KUHN-nigz-burg), for example, was arrested and imprisoned for life without trial.

Like Louis XIV, the Great Elector built his absolutist state in collaboration with traditional elites, reaffirming their privileges in return for loyal service and revenue. He also created a larger centralized government bureaucracy to oversee his realm and to collect the new taxes. Pre-existing representative institutions were bypassed. The Diet of Brandenburg did not meet again after 1652. In 1701 the elector's son, Frederick I (1701–1713), received the elevated title of king of Prussia (instead of elector) as a reward for aiding the Holy Roman emperor in the War of the Spanish Succession.

The Consolidation of Prussian Absolutism

Frederick William I, "the Soldiers' King" (r. 1713–1740), completed his grandfather's work. He created a strong centralized bureaucracy and eliminated the last traces of parliamentary estates and local self-government. He truly established Prussian absolutism and transformed Prussia into a military state. King Frederick William was intensely attached to military life. He always wore an army uniform, and he lived the highly disciplined life of the professional soldier. He began his work by five or six in the morning; at ten he almost always went to the parade ground to drill or inspect his troops. Years later he summed up his life's philosophy in his instructions to his son: "A formidable army and a war chest large enough to make this army mobile in times of need can create great respect for you in the world, so that you can speak a word like the other powers."[2]

The king's power grab brought him into considerable conflict with the Junkers. In his early years he even threatened to destroy them; yet, in the end, the Prussian nobility was not destroyed but enlisted—into the army. Responding to a combination of threats and opportunities, the Junkers became the officer caste. A new compromise was worked out whereby the proud nobility imperiously commanded the peasantry in the army as well as on the estates.

Through penny-pinching and hard work, Frederick William achieved results. Prussia, twelfth in Europe in population, had the fourth largest army by 1740. Moreover, soldier for soldier, the Prussian army was the best in Europe, astonishing foreign observers with its precision, skill, and discipline. For the next two hundred years Prussia and then Prussianized Germany would win many crucial military battles.

Frederick William and his ministers also built an exceptionally honest and conscientious bureaucracy to administer the country and foster economic

A Prussian Giant Grenadier
Frederick William I wanted tall, handsome soldiers. He dressed them in tight bright uniforms to distinguish them from the peasant population from which most soldiers came. He also ordered several portraits of his favorites from his court painter, J. C. Merk. Grenadiers (gren-AH-deers) wore the miter cap instead of an ordinary hat so that they could hurl their heavy grenades unimpeded by a broad brim. (The Royal Collection © 2008, Her Majesty Queen Elizabeth II)

- In the aftermath of the Thirty Years' War, monarchs of central and eastern Europe gained new power through increased taxation, the creation of permanent standing armies, and exercising a free hand in foreign policy.

- The Austrian Habsburgs gained control over Bohemia by reducing the power of the Estates and creating a new and loyal nobility, but were less successful in Hungary, where they were forced to compromise with a fiercely independent Protestant nobility.

- In Prussia, the elector of Brandenburg, Frederick William Hohenzollern, the "Great Elector," set out to unify his provinces under absolutist rule by restoring privileges to the Junker nobility and by using the threat of war to build the best army in Europe.

- His grandson, King Frederick William I, transformed Prussia into a military state, centralized government, eliminated parliament and local self-government, and incorporated the nobility within his army to enforce obedience.

- Palace building modeled on Versailles near Paris and Schönbrunn in Vienna spread through central and eastern Europe, as princes competed for power and aristocrats showcased the riches won through service to the monarchy.

Mongol Yoke The two-hundred-year rule of the Mongol khan over the former territories of Kievan Rus'; this period is considered a prelude to the rise of absolutist Russia.

development. And like the miser he was known to be, the king loved his "blue boys" so much that he hated to "spend" them. This most militaristic of kings was, paradoxically, almost always at peace.

Nevertheless, Prussians paid a heavy and lasting price for the obsessions of their royal drillmaster. Civil society became rigid and highly disciplined, and Prussia became the "Sparta of the North"; unquestioning obedience was the highest virtue. As a Prussian minister later summed up: "To keep quiet is the first civic duty."[3] Thus the policies of Frederick William I combined with harsh peasant bondage and Junker tyranny to lay the foundations for a highly militaristic country.

The Development of Russia and the Ottoman Empire

What were the distinctive features of Russian and Ottoman absolutism in this period?

A favorite parlor game of nineteenth-century intellectuals was debating whether Russia was a Western (European) or non-Western (Asian) society. This question was particularly fascinating because it was unanswerable. To this day, Russia differs from the West in some fundamental ways, though its history has paralleled that of the West in other aspects.

There was no question in the mind of Europeans, however, that the Ottomans were outsiders. Even absolutist rulers disdained Ottoman sultans as cruel and tyrannical despots. Despite stereotypes, the Ottomans were in many ways more tolerant than Westerners, providing protection and security to other religions while steadfastly maintaining their Muslim faith. The Ottoman state combined the Byzantine heritage of the territory they conquered with Persian and Arab traditions. Flexibility and openness to other ideas and practices were sources of strength for the empire.

The Mongol Yoke and the Rise of Moscow

In the thirteenth century the Kievan principality (see page 445) was conquered by the Mongols, a group of nomadic tribes from present-day Mongolia who had come together under Chinggis Khan (1162–1227). At its height, the Mongol empire stretched from Korea to eastern Europe, and the portion that encompassed Russia was known as the Golden Horde. The two-hundred-year period of rule under the Mongol khan (king), known as the **Mongol Yoke,** set the stage for the rise of absolutist Russia.

The Mongols forced the Slavic princes to submit to their rule and to give them tribute and slaves. Although the Mongols conquered, they were quite willing to use local princes as obedient servants and tax collectors. Thus, they did not abolish the title of "great prince," bestowing it instead on the prince who served them best and paid them most handsomely. Beginning with Alexander Nevsky in 1252, the princes of Moscow became particularly adept at serving the Mongols. They loyally put down popular uprisings and collected the khan's taxes. As reward, the princes of Moscow emerged as hereditary great princes. Eventually the Muscovite princes were able to destroy the other princes who were their rivals for power. Ivan III (r. 1462–1505) consolidated power around Moscow and won Novgorod (NOV-guh-rod), almost reaching the Baltic Sea (see Map 17.3).

By 1480 Ivan III felt strong enough to stop acknowledging the khan as his supreme ruler and cease tribute payments to the Mongols. To legitimize their new

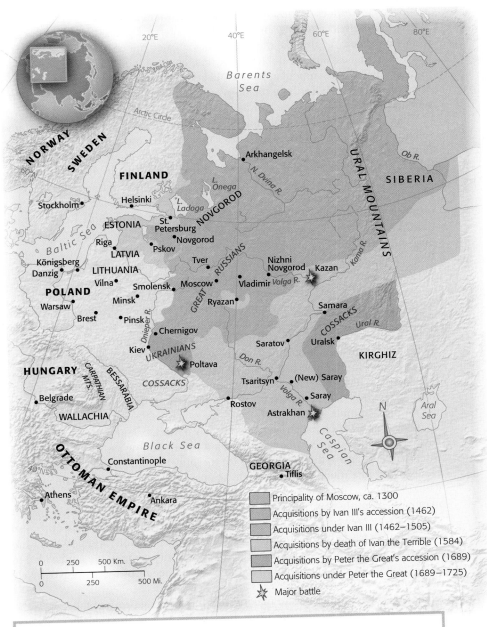

Principality of Moscow, ca. 1300
Acquisitions by Ivan III's accession (1462)
Acquisitions under Ivan III (1462–1505)
Acquisitions by death of Ivan the Terrible (1584)
Acquisitions by Peter the Great's accession (1689)
Acquisitions under Peter the Great (1689–1725)
✴ Major battle

MAPPING THE PAST

MAP 17.3   The Expansion of Russia to 1725

After the disintegration of the Kievan (KEE-ef-ahn) state and the Mongol conquest, the princes of Moscow and their descendants gradually extended their rule over an enormous territory. [1] Compare this map with Map 17.4, which shows Ottoman expansion from 1300. What explains the fantastic success of both the Russians and the Ottomans in expanding their territories? Why was the sixteenth century such an important period for expansion? [2] How do you explain the geographic direction that expansion followed in each case? [3] What happened after the periods shown on these maps? Did the territorial development of the two states diverge from each other or follow the same trajectory?

boyars The highest-ranking nobles in Russia.

authority, the princes of Moscow drew on two sources of authority. First, they declared themselves *autocrats*, meaning that, like the khans, they were the sole source of power. Yet also like the khans, they needed the cooperation of the local elites. The highest-ranking nobles, or **boyars,** enabled the tsars to rule with an extremely limited government apparatus. In addition to political authority, Moscow also took over Mongol tribute relations and borrowed institutions such as the tax system, postal routes, and the census.

The second source of legitimacy lay in Moscow's claim to the political and religious inheritance of the Byzantine Empire. After the fall of Constantinople (kon-stan-tun-OH-puhl) to the Turks in 1453, the princes of Moscow saw themselves as the heirs of both the caesars and Orthodox Christianity, the one true faith. The title **tsar,** first taken by Ivan IV in 1547, is a contraction of *caesar*. All the other kings of Europe were heretics; only the Russians were rightful and holy rulers. The idea was promoted by Orthodox churchmen, who spoke of "holy Russia" as the "Third Rome." Ivan's marriage to the daughter of the last Byzantine emperor further enhanced the aura of Moscow's imperial inheritance.

tsar A title first taken by Ivan IV, it is a contraction of the word *caesar*.

Tsar and People to 1689

Developments in Russia took a chaotic turn with the reign of Ivan IV (r. 1533–1584), the famous "Ivan the Terrible," who ascended to the throne at age three. His mother died, possibly poisoned, when he was eight, leaving Ivan to suffer insults and neglect from the boyars at court. At age sixteen he suddenly pushed aside his hated advisers, and in an awe-inspiring ceremony, complete with gold coins pouring down on his head, Ivan majestically crowned himself, taking the august title of tsar for the first time.

Ivan's reign was characterized by endless wars and violent purges. He was successful in defeating the remnants of Mongol power, adding vast new territories to the realm and laying the foundations for the huge, multiethnic Russian empire. He engaged in a much longer struggle against the large Polish-Lithuanian state, without success. After the sudden death of his beloved wife Anastasia [of the Romanov (ROH-muh-nawf) family], the increasingly demented Ivan jailed and executed any he suspected of opposing him. Many were intimates of the court from the leading boyar families, and their families, friends, servants, and peasants were also executed. Their large estates were broken up, with some of the land added to the tsar's domain and the rest given to the lower **service nobility,** a group of newly made nobles who served in the tsar's army.

service nobility A newly emerging class of nobles who held some of the tsar's land on the explicit condition that they serve in the tsar's army.

Ivan also took strides toward making all commoners servants of the tsar. As the service nobles demanded more from those peasants who survived the wars and persecutions, growing numbers fled toward wild, recently conquered territories to the east and south. There they joined free groups and outlaw armies known as **Cossacks** (KOS-akz) and maintained a precarious independence. The solution to the problem of peasant flight was to tie peasants ever more firmly to the land and to the noble landholders, who in turn served the tsar.

Cossacks Free groups and outlaw armies living on the steppes bordering Russia, whose numbers were increased by runaway peasants during the time of Ivan the Terrible.

Simultaneously, urban traders and artisans were also bound to their towns and jobs so that the tsar could tax them more heavily. Ivan assumed that the tsar owned Russia's trade and industry, just as he owned all the land. The urban classes had no security in their work or property, and even the wealthiest merchants were dependent agents of the tsar. These restrictions checked the growth of the Russian middle classes and stood in sharp contrast to developments in western Europe, where the middle classes were gaining security in their private property.

Saint Basil's Cathedral, Moscow

With its sloping roofs and colorful onion-shaped domes, Saint Basil's is a striking example of powerful Byzantine influences on Russian culture. According to tradition, an enchanted Ivan the Terrible blinded the cathedral's architects to ensure that they would never duplicate their fantastic achievement, which still dazzles the beholder in today's Red Square. (George Holton/Photo Researchers)

After the death of Ivan and his successor, Russia entered a chaotic period known as the "Time of Troubles" (1598–1618). While Ivan's relatives struggled for power, the Cossacks and peasants rebelled against nobles and officials, demanding fairer treatment. This social explosion from below brought the nobles, big and small, together. They crushed the Cossack rebellion at the gates of Moscow and elected Ivan's sixteen-year-old grandnephew, Michael Romanov, the new hereditary tsar (r. 1613–1645). Michael's election was represented as a restoration of tsarist autocracy. (See the feature "Listening to the Past: A Foreign Traveler in Russia" on pages 456–457.)

Although the new tsar successfully reconsolidated central authority, social and religious uprisings continued through the seventeenth century. One of the largest rebellions was led by the Cossack Stenka Razin, who attracted a great army of urban poor and peasants, killing landlords and government officials, and proclaiming freedom from oppression. Eventually this rebellion was defeated.

Despite the turbulence of the period, the Romanov tsars made several important achievements during the second half of the seventeenth century. After a long war, Russia gained a large mass of Ukraine from weak and decentralized Poland in 1667 (see Map 17.3) and completed the conquest of Siberia by the end of the century. Territorial expansion was accompanied by growth of the bureaucracy and the army. Foreign experts were employed to help build and reform the Russian army. The great profits from Siberia's natural resources, especially furs, funded the Romanov's bid for great power status.

The Reforms of Peter the Great

Heir to the first efforts at state-building, Peter the Great (r. 1682–1725) embarked on a tremendous campaign to accelerate and complete these processes. A giant for his time, at six feet seven inches, and possessing enormous energy and willpower, Peter was determined to build and improve the army. He was equally determined to continue the tsarist tradition of territorial expansion. After 1689 Peter ruled independently for thirty-six years, only one of which was peaceful.

Fascinated by weapons and foreign technology, the tsar led a group of two hundred fifty Russian officials and young nobles on an eighteen-month tour of western European capitals. Traveling unofficially to avoid lengthy diplomatic ceremonies, Peter worked with his hands at various crafts and met with foreign kings and experts. He was particularly impressed with the growing power of the Dutch and the English, and he considered how Russia could profit from their example.

Returning to Russia, Peter entered into a secret alliance with Denmark and Poland to wage a sudden war of aggression against Sweden, with the goal of securing access to the Baltic Sea and opportunities for westward expansion. Peter and his allies believed that their combined forces could win easy victories because Sweden was in the hands of a new and inexperienced king.

Eighteen-year-old Charles XII of Sweden (1697–1718) surprised Peter. He defeated Denmark quickly in 1700, then turned on Russia. In a blinding snowstorm, his well-trained professional army attacked and routed unsuspecting Russians besieging the Swedish fortress of Narva (NAHR-vuh) on the Baltic coast. Peter and the survivors fled in panic to Moscow. It was, for the Russians, a grim beginning to the long and brutal Great Northern War, which lasted from 1700 to 1721.

Suffering defeat and faced with a military crisis, Peter responded with measures designed to increase state power, strengthen his armies, and gain victory. He required every nobleman, great or small, to serve in the army or in the civil administration—for life. Since a more modern army and government required skilled technicians and experts, Peter created schools and universities to produce them. One of his most hated reforms was requiring a five-year education away from home for every young nobleman. Peter established an interlocking military-

Gustaf Cederstrom: The Swedish Victory at Narva (1701)
This poignant re-creation focuses on the contrast between the Swedish officers in handsome dress uniforms and the battered Russian soldiers laying down their standards in surrender. Charles XII of Sweden scored brilliant, rapid-fire victories over Denmark, Saxony, and Russia, but he failed to make peace with Peter while he was ahead and eventually lost Sweden's holdings on the Baltic coast. (The National Museum of Fine Arts, Stockholm)

civilian bureaucracy with fourteen ranks, and he decreed that all had to start at the bottom and work toward the top. Some people of non-noble origins rose to high positions in this embryonic meritocracy. Drawing on his experience abroad, Peter searched out talented foreigners and placed them in his service. These measures gradually combined to make the army and government more powerful and efficient.

Peter also greatly increased the service requirements of commoners. In the wake of the Narva disaster, he established a regular standing army of more than two hundred thousand peasant-soldiers commanded by officers from the nobility. In addition, special forces of Cossacks and foreigners numbered more than one hundred thousand. Taxes on peasants increased threefold during Peter's reign. Serfs were arbitrarily assigned to work in the growing number of factories and mines that supplied the military.

Peter's new war machine was able to crush the small army of Sweden in Ukraine at Poltava (pol-TAH-vah) in 1709, one of the most significant battles in Russian history. Russia's victory was conclusive in 1721, and Estonia and present-day Latvia (see Map 17.3) came under Russian rule for the first time. The cost was high—warfare consumed eighty to eighty-five percent of all revenues. But Russia became the dominant power in the Baltic and very much a European Great Power.

After his victory at Poltava, Peter channeled enormous resources into building a new Western-style capital on the Baltic to rival the great cities of Europe. Originally a desolate and swampy Swedish outpost, the magnificent city of St. Petersburg was designed to reflect modern urban planning, with wide, straight avenues; buildings set in a uniform line; and large parks.

Peter the Great dictated that all in society realize his vision. Just as the government drafted the peasants for the armies, so it drafted twenty-five thousand to forty thousand men each summer to labor in St. Petersburg without pay. Many peasant construction workers died from hunger, sickness, and accidents. Nobles were ordered to build costly stone houses and palaces in St. Petersburg and to live in them most of the year. Merchants and artisans were also commanded to settle and build in the new capital. These nobles and merchants were then required to pay for the city's infrastructure. The building of St. Petersburg was, in truth, an enormous direct tax levied on the wealthy, with the peasantry forced to do the manual labor.

There were other important consequences of Peter's reign. For Peter, modernization meant Westernization, and both Westerners and Western ideas flowed into Russia for the first time. He required nobles to shave their heavy beards and wear Western clothing, previously banned in Russia. He required them to attend parties where young men and women would mix together and freely choose their own spouses. He forced a warrior elite to accept administrative service as an honorable occupation. From these efforts a new class of Western-oriented Russians began to emerge.

At the same time, vast numbers of Russians hated Peter's massive changes. For nobles, one of Peter's most detested reforms was the imposition of unigeniture—inheritance of land by one son alone—cutting daughters and other sons from

Peter the Great in 1723

This compelling portrait by Grigory Musikiysky captures the strength and determination of the warrior tsar after more than three decades of personal rule. In his hand Peter holds the scepter, symbol of royal sovereignty, and across his breastplate is draped an ermine fur, a mark of honor. In the background are the battleships of Russia's new Baltic fleet and the famous St. Peter and St. Paul Fortress that Peter built in St. Petersburg. (Kremlin Museums, Moscow/The Bridgeman Art Library) family property. For peasants, the reign of the reforming tsar saw a significant increase in the bonds of serfdom. The gulf between the enserfed peasantry and the educated nobility increased, even though all were caught up in the tsar's demands.

Thus Peter built on the service obligations of old Muscovy (MUHS-kuh-vee). His monarchical absolutism was the culmination of the long development of a unique Russian civilization. Yet the creation of a more modern army and state introduced much that was new and Western to Russia. This development paved the way for Russia to move somewhat closer to the European mainstream in its thought and institutions during the Enlightenment, especially under Catherine the Great.

The Growth of the Ottoman Empire

Most Christian Europeans perceived the Ottomans as the antithesis of their own values and traditions and viewed the empire as driven by an insatiable lust for warfare and conquest. In their view the fall of Constantinople was a catastrophe and the taking of the Balkans a despotic imprisonment of those territories. From the perspective of the Ottomans, the world looked very different. The siege of Constantinople liberated a glorious city from its long decline under the Byzantines. Rather than being a despoiled captive, the Balkans became a haven for refugees fleeing the growing intolerance of Western Christian powers. The Ottoman Empire provided Jews, Muslims, and even some Christians safety from the Inquisition and religious war.

The Ottomans came out of Central Asia as conquering warriors, settled in Anatolia (present-day Turkey), and, at their peak in the mid-sixteenth century, they ruled one of the most powerful empires in the world. Their possessions stretched from western Persia across North Africa and into the heart of central Europe (see Map 17.4).

When the Ottomans captured Constantinople in 1453 they fulfilled a long-held Islamic dream. Under Suleiman the Magnificent (r. 1520–1566), they made great inroads into eastern Europe, capturing Bosnia, Croatia, Romania, Ukraine, and part of Hungary at the battle of Mohács in 1526. For the next hundred and fifty years, the Ottomans ruled the many different ethnic groups living in southeastern Europe and the eastern Mediterranean. In 1529 their European expansion was halted with a failed siege of the Habsburg capital, Vienna. The Ottoman loss at the battle of Lepanto (leh-PAN-toh) in 1571, against the Christian Holy League, confirmed the limits of their ambitions in Europe.

The Ottoman Empire was originally built on a unique model of state and society. There was an almost complete absence of private landed property. Agricultural land was the personal hereditary property of the **sultan** (SUHL-tun), and peasants paid taxes to use the land. There was therefore no security of landholding and no hereditary nobility.

The Ottomans also employed a distinctive form of government administration. The top ranks of the bureaucracy were staffed by the sultan's slave corps. Because Muslim law prohibited enslaving other Muslims, the sultan's agents purchased slaves along the borders of the empire. Within the realm, the sultan levied a "tax" of one thousand to three thousand male children on the conquered Christian populations in the Balkans every year. Young slaves were raised in Turkey as Muslims and were trained to fight and to administer. The most talented rose to the top of the bureaucracy, where they might acquire wealth and power; the less fortunate formed the brave and skillful core of the sultan's army, the **janissary** (JAN-uh-ser-ee) corps. These highly organized and efficient troops gave the Ottomans a formidable advantage in war with western Europeans. By 1683, service in the janissary

sultan The ruler of the Ottoman Empire; he owned all the agricultural land of the empire and was served by an army and bureaucracy composed of highly trained slaves.

janissary corps The core of the sultan's army, composed of conscripts from non-Muslim parts of the empire until 1683.

corps had become so prestigious that the sultan ceased recruitment by force and it became a volunteer force open to Christians and Muslims.

The Ottomans divided their subjects into religious communities, and each *millet*, or "nation," enjoyed autonomous self-government under its religious leaders. (The Ottoman Empire recognized Orthodox Christians, Jews, Armenian Christians, and Muslims as distinct millets.) The **millet** (MIL-it) **system** created a powerful bond between the Ottoman ruling class and the different religious leaders, who supported the sultan's rule in return for extensive authority over their own communities. Each millet collected taxes for the state, regulated group behavior, and maintained law courts, schools, synagogues, and hospitals for its people.

After 1453 Constantinople—renamed Istanbul (is-tahn-BOOL)—became the capital of the empire. The "old palace" was for the sultan's female family members, who lived in isolation under the care of eunuchs. The newly constructed Topkapi palace was where officials worked and young slaves trained for future administrative or military careers. To prevent wives from bringing foreign influence

millet system A system used by the Ottomans whereby subjects were divided into religious communities with each millet (nation) enjoying autonomous self-government under its religious leaders.

MAP 17.4 The Ottoman Empire at Its Height, 1566

The Ottomans, like their great rivals the Habsburgs, rose to rule a vast dynastic empire encompassing many different peoples and ethnic groups. The army and the bureaucracy served to unite the disparate territories into a single state under an absolutist ruler.

Major battle
Ottoman state, ca. 1300
Ottoman Empire under Suleiman, 1566
Tributary states of the sultan, 1566

The Sultan's Harem at Topkapi Palace, Istanbul

Sultan Suleiman I created separate quarters at the Topkapi Palace for his wife Hürrem and her ladies-in-waiting. His successors transferred all of their wives, concubines, and female family members to the harem (HAIR-uhm) at Topkapi, carefully situated out of sight of the staterooms and courtyards where public affairs took place. The harem was the object of intense curiosity and fascination in the West. (Vanni/Art Resource, NY)

into government—a constant concern in the West—sultans procreated only with their concubines and not with official wives. They also adopted a policy of allowing each concubine to produce only one male heir. At a young age, each son went to govern a province of the empire under his mother's supervision. These practices were intended to stabilize power and prevent a recurrence of the civil wars of the late fourteenth and early fifteenth centuries.

Sultan Suleiman undid these policies when he boldly married his concubine and had several children with her. He established a wing in the Topkapi palace for his own female family members and his brothers' families. Starting with Suleiman, imperial wives begin to take on more power. Marriages were arranged between sultans' daughters and high-ranking servants, creating powerful new members of the imperial household. Over time, the sultan's exclusive authority waned in favor of a more bureaucratic administration. These changes brought the Ottoman court closer to the European model of factionalism, intrigue, and informal female power. (See the feature "Individuals in Society: Hürrem.")

The Ottoman Empire experienced the same economic and social crises that affected the rest of Europe in this period. In the 1580s and 1590s rebellions broke out among many different groups in the vast empire: frustrated students, underpaid janissaries, and ambitious provincial governors. Revolts continued during the seventeenth century as the janissaries formed alliances with court factions that resulted in the overthrow or execution of several Ottoman sultans.

In the late seventeenth century the Ottomans succeeded in marshaling their forces for one last attack on the Habsburgs, and a huge Turkish army laid siege to Vienna in 1683. Not only did they fail to hold the city, but their retreat became a rout. As Russian and Venetian allies attacked on

Section Review

- The Mongols under Chinggis Khan added the Kievan principality in Russia to the Mongol Empire stretching from Korea to Eastern Europe, ruling the area as the Golden Horde for the next two hundred years through the Russian princes, who collected taxes and maintained order.

- By 1480 the prince of Moscow, Ivan III, defied the khan (Mongol ruler) and seized power to begin the dynasty of the tsars.

- The reign of Ivan IV "the Terrible" featured constant war, violent purges, peasant and outlaw army (Cossack) uprisings, and the addition of vast new territories.

- Following Ivan's death, a period of chaos known as the "Time of Troubles" (1598–1618) ensued, ending with the coronation of Ivan's grandnephew, Michael, the first Romanov tsar.

- Despite ongoing rebellions, the seventeenth-century Romanov tsars succeeded in consolidating royal authority, increasing the bureaucracy and army, and acquiring Siberia and parts of Ukraine.

- Peter the Great (r. 1682–1725) transformed Russian society and the Russian landscape by drafting citizens for military or civil service, enabling him to create a powerful war machine, enlarge the empire, and build the modern, Westernized capital city of St. Petersburg on Baltic coastal land conquered from Sweden.

- Despite Christian stereotypes, the Ottoman empire was tolerant of religious diversity and protected Jews and other religious refugees.

- The Ottomans captured Constantinople in 1453 and renamed it Istanbul, then conquered much of southeastern Europe until their expansion was halted with the failed siege of Vienna in 1529.

- Highly trained slaves staffed the elite of the sultan's administration and army; while the millet system allowed autonomous self-government to religious minority groups; all land in the empire belonged to the sultan.

- Starting with Sultan Suleiman, wives began to exercise more power and the sultan's exclusive authority gave way to more bureaucratic administration.

Individuals in Society

Hürrem

In Muslim culture *harem* means a sacred place or a sanctuary, which is forbidden to profane outsiders. The term was applied to the part of the household occupied by women and children and forbidden to men outside the family. The most famous member of the Ottoman sultan's harem was Hürrem, wife of Suleiman the Magnificent.

Hürrem (1505?–1558) came to the harem as a slave-concubine. Like many of the sultan's concubines, Hürrem was of foreign birth. Tradition holds that she was born Aleksandra Lisowska in what was then the kingdom of Poland and today is Ukraine. She was captured during a Tartar raid and enslaved. Between 1517 and 1520, when she was about fifteen years old, she entered the imperial harem. Venetian ambassadors' reports insist that she was not outstandingly beautiful but was possessed of wonderful grace, charm, and good humor. These qualities gained her the Turkish nickname Hürrem, or "joyful one." After her arrival in the harem, Hürrem quickly became the imperial favorite.

Suleiman's love for Hürrem led him to break all precedents for the role of a concubine, including the rule that concubines must cease having children once they gave birth to a male heir. By 1531 Hürrem had given birth to one daughter and five sons. In 1533 or 1534 Suleiman entered formal marriage with his consort—an unprecedented honor for a concubine. He reportedly gave his exclusive attention to his wife and also defied convention by allowing Hürrem to remain in the palace throughout her life instead of accompanying her son to a provincial governorship as other concubines had done.

Contemporaries were shocked by Hürrem's influence over the sultan and resentful of the apparent role she played in politics and diplomacy. The Venetian ambassador Bassano wrote that "the Janissaries and the entire court hate her and her children likewise, but because the Sultan loves her, no one dares to speak."* She was suspected of using witchcraft to control the sultan and accused of or-

dering the death of the sultan's first-born son (with another mother) in 1553. These stories were based on court gossip and rumor. The correspondence between Suleiman and Hürrem, unavailable until the nineteenth century, along with Suleiman's own diaries, confirms her status as the sultan's most trusted confidant and adviser. During his frequent absences, the pair exchanged passionate love letters. Hürrem included information about the political situation and warnings about any potential uprisings. She also intervened in affairs between the empire and her former home. She wrote to Polish king Sigismund Augustus and seems to have helped Poland attain its privileged diplomatic status.

Hürrem and her ladies in the harem. (Bibliothèque nationale de France)

She brought a particularly feminine touch to diplomatic relations, sending the Persian shah and the Polish king personally embroidered articles.

Hürrem used her enormous pension to contribute a mosque, two schools, a hospital, a fountain, and two public baths to Istanbul. In Jerusalem, Mecca, and Istanbul, she provided soup kitchens and hospices for pilgrims and the poor. She died in 1558. When her husband died in 1566, their son Selim II (r. 1566–1574) inherited the throne.

Drawing from reports of contemporary Western observers, historians depicted Hürrem as a manipulative and power-hungry social climber. They saw her career as the beginning of a "sultanate of women" in which strong imperial leadership gave way to court intrigue and dissipation. More recent historians have emphasized the intelligence and courage Hürrem demonstrated in navigating the ruthlessly competitive world of the harem.

Hürrem's journey from Ukrainian maiden to harem slave girl to sultan's wife captured enormous

* Cited in Galina Yermolenko, "Roxolana: The Greatest Empress of the East," in *The Muslim World* 95, 2 (2005).

public attention. She is the subject of numerous paintings, plays, and novels as well as an opera, a ballet, and a symphony by the composer Haydn. Interest in and suspicion of Hürrem continues. In 2003 a Turkish miniseries once more depicted her as a scheming intriguer.

Questions for Analysis

1. Compare Hürrem to other powerful early modern women such as Isabella of Castile, Elizabeth I of England, and Catherine de' Medici of France.

2. What can an exceptional woman like Hürrem reveal about the broader political and social world in which she lived?

Source: Leslie P. Pierce, *The Imperial Harem: Women and Sovereignty in the Ottoman Empire* (New York: Oxford University Press, 1993).

other fronts, the Habsburgs conquered almost all of Hungary and Transylvania by 1699 (see Map 17.4). The Habsburgs completed their victory in 1718, with the Treaty of Passarowitz. From this point on, a weakened Ottoman empire ceased to pose a threat to Western Europe.

Chapter Review

What social and economic changes affected central and eastern Europe from 1400 to 1650? (page 433)

From about 1400 to 1650 social and economic developments in eastern Europe diverged from those in western Europe. In the East, after enjoying relative freedom in the Middle Ages, peasants and townspeople lost freedom and fell under the economic, social, and legal authority of the nobles, who increased their power and prestige.

How did the rulers of Austria and Prussia manage to build powerful absolute monarchies? (page 438)

Within this framework of resurgent serfdom and entrenched nobility, Austrian and Prussian monarchs fashioned absolutist states in the seventeenth and early eighteenth centuries. These monarchs won absolutist control over standing armies, taxation, and representative bodies, but they did not question underlying social and economic relationships. Indeed, they enhanced the privileges of the nobles, who filled enlarged armies and growing state bureaucracies. In exchange for entrenched privileges over their peasants, nobles thus cooperated with the growth of state power.

Triumphant absolutism interacted spectacularly with the arts. Central and eastern European rulers built grandiose palaces, and even whole cities, like Saint Petersburg, to glorify their power and majesty.

What were the distinctive features of Russian and Ottoman absolutism in this period? (page 444)

In Russia the social and economic trends were similar, but the timing of political absolutism was different. Mongol conquest and rule were a crucial experience, and a harsh indigenous tsarist autocracy was firmly in place by the reign of Ivan the Terrible in the sixteenth century. More than a century later Peter the Great succeeded in modernizing Russia's traditional absolutism by reforming the army and the bureaucracy. Farther to the east, the Ottoman sultans developed a distinctive political and economic system in which all land theoretically belonged to the sultan, who was served by a slave corps of administrators and soldiers. The Ottoman Empire was relatively tolerant on religious matters and served as a haven for Jews and other marginalized religious groups.

Key Terms

serfdom (p. 433)
hereditary subjugation (p. 434)
Peace of Westphalia (p. 436)
Bohemian Estates (p. 438)
elector of Brandenburg (p. 439)
Junkers (p. 442)
Mongol Yoke (p. 444)
boyars (p. 446)
tsar (p. 446)
service nobility (p. 446)
Cossacks (p. 446)
sultan (p. 450)
millet system (p. 451)
janissary corps (p. 453)

Notes

1. H. Kamen, "The Economic and Social Consequences of the Thirty Years' War," *Past and Present* 39 (April 1968): 44–61.
2. H. Rosenberg, *Bureaucracy, Aristocracy, and Autocracy: The Prussian Experience, 1660–1815* (Boston: Beacon Press, 1966), p. 43.
3. Quoted in Rosenberg, *Bureaucracy, Aristocracy, and Autocracy*, p. 40.

To assess your mastery of this chapter, go to **bedfordstmartins.com/mckaywestbrief**

Listening to the Past

A Foreign Traveler in Russia

*Seventeenth-century Russia remained a remote and mysterious land for western and even central Europeans, who had few direct contacts with the tsar's dominion. Knowledge of Russia came mainly from occasional travelers who had visited Muscovy and sometimes wrote accounts of what they saw. The most famous of these accounts—*Travels in Muscovy*—was by the German Adam Olearius (ca. 1599–1671), who was sent to Moscow by the duke of Holstein on three diplomatic missions in the 1630s. Published in German in 1647 and soon translated into several languages (but not Russian), Olearius's unflattering study played a major role in shaping European ideas about Russia.*

The government of the Russians is what political theorists call a "dominating and despotic monarchy," where the sovereign, that is, the tsar or the grand prince who has obtained the crown by right of succession, rules the entire land alone, and all the people are his subjects, and where the nobles and princes no less than the common folk—townspeople and peasants—are his serfs and slaves, whom he rules and treats as a master treats his servants. . . .

If the Russians be considered in respect to their character, customs, and way of life, they are justly to be counted among the barbarians. . . . The vice of drunkenness is so common in this nation, among people of every station, clergy and laity, high and low, men and women, old and young, that when they are seen now and then lying about in the streets, wallowing in the mud, no attention is paid to it, as something habitual. If a cart driver comes upon such a drunken pig whom he happens to know, he shoves him onto his cart and drives him home, where he is paid his fare. No one ever refuses an opportunity to drink and to get drunk, at any time and in any place, and usually it is done with vodka. . . .

The Russians being naturally tough and born, as it were, for slavery, they must be kept under a harsh and strict yoke and must be driven to do their work with clubs and whips, which they suffer without impatience, because such is their station, and they are accustomed to it. Young and half-grown fellows sometimes come together on certain days and train themselves in fisticuffs, to accustom themselves to receiving blows, and, since habit is second nature, this makes blows given as punishment easier to bear. Each and all, they are slaves and serfs. . . .

Although the Russians, especially the common populace, living as slaves under a harsh yoke, can bear and endure a great deal out of love for their masters, yet if the pressure is beyond measure, then it can be said of them: "Patience, often wounded, finally turned into fury." A dangerous indignation

The brutality of serfdom is shown in this illustration from Olearius's *Travels in Muscovy.* (University of Illinois Library, Champaign)

results, turned not so much against their sovereign as against the lower authorities, especially if the people have been much oppressed by them and by their supporters and have not been protected by the higher authorities. And once they are aroused and enraged, it is not easy to appease them. Then, disregarding all dangers that may ensue, they resort to every kind of violence and behave like madmen. . . . They own little; most of them have no feather beds; they lie on cushions, straw, mats, or their clothes; they sleep on benches and, in winter, like the non-Germans [natives] in Livonia, upon the oven, which serves them for cooking and is flat on the top; here husband, wife, children, servants, and maids huddle together. In some houses in the countryside we saw chickens and pigs under the benches and the ovens.

Questions for Analysis

1. In what ways were all social groups in Russia similar, according to Olearius?

2. How did Olearius characterize the Russians in general? What supporting evidence did he offer for his judgment?

3. Does Olearius's account help explain Stenka Razin's rebellion? In what ways?

4. On the basis of these representative passages, why do you think Olearius's book was so popular and influential in central and western Europe?

Source: G. Vernadsky and R. T. Fisher, Jr., eds., *A Source Book for Russian History from Early Times to 1917*, 3 vols., vol. 1, pp. 249–251. Copyright © 1972. Reprinted by permission of the publisher, Yale University Press.

CHAPTER 18
Toward a New Worldview

1540–1789

Chapter Preview

The Scientific Revolution
What was revolutionary in the new attitudes toward the natural world?

The Enlightenment
How did the new worldview affect the way people thought about society and human relations?

The Enlightenment and Absolutism
What impact did this new way of thinking have on political developments and monarchical absolutism?

INDIVIDUALS IN SOCIETY: Moses Mendelssohn and the Jewish Enlightenment

LISTENING TO THE PAST: Voltaire on Religion

Voltaire, the renowned Enlightenment thinker, leans forward on the left to exchange ideas and witty conversation with Frederick the Great, king of Prussia. (Bildarchiv Preussischer Kulturbesitz/Art Resource, NY)

The intellectual developments of the seventeenth and eighteenth centuries created the modern worldview that the West continues to hold—and debate—to this day. In the seventeenth century fundamentally new ways of understanding the natural world emerged. In the nineteenth century scholars hailed these achievements as a "scientific revolution" that produced modern science as we know it. The new science created in the seventeenth century entailed the search for precise knowledge of the physical world based on the union of experimental observations with sophisticated mathematics.

In the eighteenth century philosophers extended the use of reason from the study of nature to the study of human society. They sought to bring the light of reason to bear on the darkness of prejudice, outmoded traditions, and ignorance. Self-proclaimed members of an "Enlightenment" movement, they wished to bring the same progress to human affairs as their predecessors had brought to the understanding of the natural world. While the scientific revolution ushered in modern science, the Enlightenment created concepts of human rights, equality, progress, universalism, and tolerance that still guide Western societies today.

While many view the scientific revolution and the Enlightenment as bedrocks of the achievement of Western civilization, others have seen a darker side. For these critics, the mastery over nature permitted by the scientific revolution now threatens to overwhelm the earth's fragile equilibrium, and the belief in the universal application of "reason" can lead to arrogance and intolerance, particularly intolerance of other people's spiritual values. Such vivid debate about the legacy of these intellectual and cultural developments testifies to their continuing importance in today's world.

The Scientific Revolution

What was revolutionary in the new attitudes toward the natural world?

The emergence of modern science was a development of tremendous long-term significance. A noted historian has said that the scientific revolution was "the real origin both of the modern world and the modern mentality."[1] With the scientific revolution Western society began to acquire its most distinctive traits.

Scientific Thought in 1500

Since developments in astronomy and physics were at the heart of the scientific revolution, one must begin with the traditional European conception of the universe. The practitioners of the scientific revolution did not consider their field *science* but rather **natural philosophy** and their intention was philosophical: to ask fundamental questions about the nature of the universe, its purpose, and how it functioned. In the early 1500s natural philosophy was still based primarily on the ideas of Aristotle, the great Greek philosopher of the fourth century B.C.E. Medieval theologians such as Thomas Aquinas brought Aristotelian philosophy into harmony with Christian doctrines. According to the revised Aristotelian view, a motionless earth was fixed at the center of the universe. Around it moved ten separate transparent crystal spheres. In the first eight spheres were embedded, in turn, the moon, the sun, the five known planets, and the fixed stars. Then followed two spheres added during the Middle Ages to account for slight changes in the positions of the stars over the centuries. Beyond the tenth sphere was Heaven, with the

natural philosophy An early modern term for the study of the nature of the universe, its purpose, and how it functioned; it encompassed what we would call today "science."

The Aristotelian Universe as Imagined in the Sixteenth Century

A round earth is at the center, surrounded by spheres of water, air, and fire. Beyond this small nucleus, the moon, the sun, and the five planets were imbedded in their own rotating crystal spheres, with the stars sharing the surface of one enormous sphere. Beyond, the heavens were composed of unchanging ether. (Image Select/Art Resource, NY)

Copernican hypothesis The idea that the sun, not the earth, was the center of the universe; this had tremendous scientific and religious implications.

throne of God and the souls of the saved. Angels kept the spheres moving in perfect circles. Thus human beings were at the center of the universe and were the critical link in a "great chain of being" that stretched from the throne of God to the lowliest insect on earth.

Aristotle's views, suitably revised by medieval philosophers, also dominated thinking about physics and motion on earth. Aristotle had distinguished sharply between the world of the celestial spheres and that of the earth. The celestial spheres consisted of a perfect, incorruptible "quintessence," or fifth essence. The earth was composed of four imperfect, changeable elements. The "light" elements (air and fire) naturally moved upward, while the "heavy" elements (water and earth) naturally moved downward. These natural directions of motion did not always prevail, however, for elements were often mixed together and could be affected by an outside force such as a human being. Aristotle and his followers also believed that a uniform force moved an object at a constant speed and that the object would stop as soon as that force was removed.

The Copernican Hypothesis

The first great departure from the medieval system came from Nicolaus Copernicus (koh-PUR-ni-kuhs) (1473–1543). As a young man Copernicus studied church law and astronomy in various European universities. He saw how professional astronomers still depended for their most accurate calculations on the second century B.C.E. work of Ptolemy. Copernicus felt that Ptolemy's cumbersome and occasionally inaccurate rules detracted from the majesty of a perfect Creator. He preferred an old Greek idea being discussed in Renaissance Italy: that the sun, rather than the earth, was at the center of the universe. Finishing his university studies and returning to a church position in East Prussia, Copernicus worked on his hypothesis from 1506 to 1530. Never questioning the Aristotelian belief in crystal spheres or the idea that circular motion was most perfect and divine, Copernicus theorized that the stars and planets, including the earth, revolved around a fixed sun. Yet fearing the ridicule of other astronomers, Copernicus did not publish his *On the Revolutions of the Heavenly Spheres* until 1543, the year of his death.

The **Copernican hypothesis** brought sharp attacks from religious leaders, especially Protestants, who objected to the idea that the earth moved but the sun did not. Martin Luther noted that the theory was counter to the Bible: "as the Holy Scripture tells us, so did Joshua bid the sun stand still and not the earth."[2] John Calvin also condemned Copernicus. Catholic reaction was milder at first. The Catholic Church had never held to literal interpretations of the Bible, and not until 1616 did it officially declare the Copernican hypothesis false.

This slow reaction also reflected the slow progress of Copernicus's theory for many years. Other events were almost as influential in creating doubts about traditional astronomical ideas. In 1572 a new star appeared and shone very brightly for almost two years. The new star, which was actually a distant exploding star, made an enormous impression on people. It seemed to contradict the idea that the heavenly spheres were unchanging and therefore perfect. In 1577 a new comet suddenly moved through the sky, cutting a straight path across the supposedly impenetrable crystal spheres. It was time, as a typical scientific writer put it, for "the radical renovation of astronomy."[3]

ca. 1540–1690	Scientific revolution
1543	Copernicus, *On the Revolutions of the Heavenly Spheres*
1564–1642	Life of Galileo
1571–1630	Life of Kepler
1662	Royal Society of London founded
1687	Newton, *Principia* and the law of universal gravitation
1690	Locke, *Essay Concerning Human Understanding*
ca. 1690–1780	Enlightenment
1694–1778	Life of Voltaire
1700–1789	Growth of book publishing
1720–1780	Rococo style in art and decoration
ca. 1740–1780	Salons led by elite women
1740–1786	Reign of Frederick the Great of Prussia
ca. 1750–1790	Enlightened absolutists
1751–1765	Diderot and d'Alembert, *Encyclopedia*
1762	Rousseau, *The Social Contract*
1762–1796	Reign of Catherine the Great of Russia
1780–1790	Reign of Joseph II of Austria

From Brahe to Galileo

One astronomer who agreed was Tycho Brahe (TEE-koh BRAH-hee) (1546–1601). Born into a prominent Danish noble family, Brahe was an imposing man who had lost a piece of his nose in a duel and replaced it with a special bridge of gold and silver alloy. He established himself as Europe's leading astronomer with his detailed observations of the new star of 1572. For twenty years he meticulously observed the stars and planets with the naked eye in the most sophisticated observatory of his day. His limited understanding of mathematics prevented him, however, from making much sense out of his mass of data. Part Ptolemaic, part Copernican, he believed that all the planets except the earth revolved around the sun and that the entire group of sun and planets revolved in turn around the earth-moon system.

It was left to Brahe's assistant, Johannes Kepler (YO-han-nis KEP-ler) (1571–1630), to rework Brahe's mountain of observations. A brilliant mathematician, Kepler would eventually move beyond his early belief that the universe was built on mystical mathematical relationships and a musical harmony of the heavenly bodies.

Kepler formulated three famous laws of planetary motion. First, building on Copernican theory, he demonstrated in 1609 that the orbits of the planets around the sun are elliptical rather than circular. Second, he demonstrated that the planets do not move at a uniform speed in their orbits. Third, in 1619 he showed that the time a planet takes to make its complete orbit is precisely related to its distance from the sun. Kepler's contribution was monumental. Whereas Copernicus had speculated, Kepler proved mathematically the precise relations of a sun-centered (solar) system. His work demolished the old system of Aristotle and Ptolemy, and in his third law he came close to formulating the idea of universal gravitation.

While Kepler was unraveling planetary motion, a young Florentine named Galileo Galilei (gal-uh-LAY-oh gal-uh-LAY-ee) (1564–1642) was challenging all the old ideas about motion. Like Kepler and so many early scientists, Galileo was a poor nobleman first marked for a religious career. Instead, his fascination with mathematics led to a professorship in which he examined motion and mechanics in a new way. Indeed, his great achievement was the elaboration and consolidation of the **experimental method.** That is, rather than speculate about what might or should happen, Galileo conducted controlled experiments to find out what actually *did* happen.

In some of these experiments Galileo measured the movement of a rolling ball across a surface that he constructed, repeating the action again and again to verify his results. In his famous acceleration experiment, he showed that a uniform force—in this case, gravity—produced a uniform acceleration. Through another experiment, he formulated the **law of inertia** (in-UR-shuh). Rest was not the

experimental method The approach, first developed by Galileo, that the proper way to explore the workings of the universe was through repeatable experiments rather than speculation.

law of inertia A law formulated by Galileo that stated that rest was not the natural state of an object. Rather, an object continues in motion forever unless stopped by some external force.

Galileo's Paintings of the Moon

When Galileo published the results of his telescopic observations of the moon, he added these paintings to illustrate the marvels he had seen. Galileo made two telescopes, which are shown here. The larger one magnifies fourteen times, the smaller one twenty times. (Biblioteca Nazionale Centrale, Florence/Art Resource, NY; Museum of Science, Florence/Art Resource, NY)

natural state of objects. Rather, an object continues in motion forever unless stopped by some external force. Aristotelian physics was in shambles.

In the tradition of Brahe, Galileo also applied the experimental method to astronomy. On hearing details about the invention of the telescope in Holland, Galileo made one for himself and trained it on the heavens. He wrote in 1610 in *Siderus Nuncius*:

> By the aid of a telescope anyone may behold [the Milky Way] in a manner which so distinctly appeals to the senses that all the disputes which have tormented philosophers through so many ages are exploded by the irrefutable evidence of our eyes, and we are freed from wordy disputes upon the subject. For the galaxy is nothing else but a mass of innumerable stars planted together in clusters.[4]

Reading these famous lines, one feels a crucial corner in Western civilization being turned. No longer should one rely on established authority. A new method of learning and investigating was being developed, one that proved capable of great extension. A historian investigating documents of the past, for example, is not so different from a Galileo studying stars and rolling balls.

Galileo was employed in Florence by the Medici grand dukes of Tuscany, and his work eventually aroused the ire of some theologians. The issue was presented in 1624 to Pope Urban VIII, who permitted Galileo to write about different possible systems of the world as long as he did not presume to judge which one actually existed. After the publication in Italian of his widely read *Dialogue on the Two Chief Systems of the World* in 1632, which openly lampooned the traditional views of Aristotle and Ptolemy and defended those of Copernicus, Galileo was tried for heresy by the papal Inquisition. Imprisoned and threatened with torture, the aging Galileo recanted, "renouncing and cursing" his Copernican errors.

Newton's Synthesis

The accomplishments of Kepler, Galileo, and other scientists had taken effect by about 1640. The old astronomy and physics were in ruins, and several fundamental breakthroughs had been made. But the new findings failed to explain what forces controlled the movement of the planets and objects on Earth. That challenge was taken up by the English scientist Isaac Newton (1642–1727).

Newton was born into the lower English gentry and he attended Cambridge University. A genius who spectacularly united the experimental and theoretical-mathematical sides of modern science, Newton was far from being the perfect rationalist eulogized by later centuries. Like many other practitioners of the new science, Newton was both intensely religious and fascinated by alchemy.

He arrived at some of his most basic ideas about physics in 1666 at age twenty-four but was unable to prove them mathematically. In 1684, after years of studying optics, Newton returned to physics for eighteen extraordinarily intensive months. The result was his towering accomplishment, a single explanatory system that could integrate the astronomy of Copernicus, as corrected by Kepler's laws, with the physics of Galileo and his predecessors. Newton did this by means of a set of mathematical laws that explain motion and mechanics. These laws of dynamics are complex, and it took scientists and engineers two hundred years to work out all their implications. Nevertheless, the key feature of the Newtonian synthesis was the **law of universal gravitation.** According to this law, every body in the universe attracts every other body in the universe in a precise mathematical relationship, whereby the force of attraction is proportional to the quantity of matter of the objects and inversely proportional to the square of the distance between them. The whole universe—from Kepler's elliptical orbits to Galileo's rolling balls—was unified in one majestic system. Newton's synthesis prevailed until the twentieth century.

law of universal gravitation Newton's law that every body in the universe attracts every other body in the universe in a precise mathematical relationship, whereby the force of attraction is proportional to the quantity of matter of the objects and inversely proportional to the square of the distance between them.

Causes of the Scientific Revolution

The scientific revolution drew on long-term developments in European culture. The first was the development of the medieval university. By the fourteenth and fifteenth centuries leading universities had evolved to include professorships of mathematics, astronomy, and physics (natural philosophy) within their faculties of philosophy. Although the prestige of the new fields was low, critical thinking was now applied to scientific problems by a permanent community of scholars. And an outlet existed for the talents of a Galileo or a Newton: all the great pathfinders either studied or taught at universities.

Second, the Renaissance also stimulated scientific progress. The recovery of ancient texts showed that classical mathematicians had their differences; Europeans were thus forced to try to resolve these ancient controversies by means of their own efforts. Renaissance patrons played a role in funding scientific investigations as well as artistic projects, as the Medicis of Florence did for Galileo.

The navigational problems of long sea voyages in the age of overseas expansion were a third factor in the scientific revolution. As early as 1484 the king of Portugal appointed a commission of mathematicians to perfect tables to help seamen find their latitude. Navigational problems were also critical in the development of many new scientific instruments, such as the telescope, barometer, thermometer, pendulum clock, microscope, and air pump. Better instruments, which permitted more accurate observations, often led to important new knowledge. Galileo with his telescope was by no means unique.

The fourth factor in the scientific revolution was the development of better ways of obtaining knowledge about the world. Two important thinkers, Francis

Bacon (1561–1626) and René Descartes (dey-KAHRT) (1596–1650) were influential in describing and advocating for improved scientific methods, based on experimentation and mathematical reasoning.

The English politician and writer Francis Bacon was the greatest early propagandist for the new scientific method. Bacon argued that the researcher who wants to learn more about leaves or rocks should not speculate about the subject but should rather collect a multitude of specimens and then compare and analyze them. General principles will then emerge. Bacon's contribution was to formalize the empirical method, which had already been used by Brahe and Galileo, into the general theory of inductive reasoning known as **empiricism.**

The French philosopher René Descartes was a true genius who made his first great discovery in mathematics. As a twenty-three-year-old soldier serving in the Thirty Years' War, he experienced a life-changing intellectual vision on a single night in 1619. Descartes saw that there was a perfect correspondence between geometry and algebra and that geometrical, spatial figures could be expressed as algebraic equations and vice versa. A major step forward in the history of mathematics, Descartes's discovery of analytic geometry provided scientists with an important new tool.

Descartes's greatest achievement was to develop his initial vision into a whole philosophy of knowledge and science. He decided it was necessary to doubt everything that could reasonably be doubted and then, as in geometry, to use deductive reasoning from self-evident principles to ascertain scientific laws. Descartes's reasoning ultimately reduced all substances to "matter" and "mind"—that is, to the physical and the spiritual. His view of the world as consisting of two fundamental entities is known as **Cartesian** (kahr-TEE-zhuhn) **dualism.** Descartes was a profoundly original and extremely influential thinker.

Bacon's inductive experimentalism and Descartes's deductive, mathematical reasoning are combined in the modern scientific method, which began to crystallize in the late seventeenth century. Neither man's extreme approach was sufficient by itself. Bacon's inability to appreciate the importance of mathematics and his obsession with practical results clearly showed the limitations of antitheoretical empiricism. Likewise, some of Descartes's positions—he believed, for example, that it was possible to deduce the whole science of medicine from first principles—demonstrated the inadequacy of rigid, dogmatic rationalism. Thus the modern scientific method has joined precise observations and experimentalism with the search for general laws that may be expressed in rigorously logical, mathematical language.

Science and Society

The rise of modern science had many consequences, some of which are still unfolding. First, it went hand in hand with the rise of a new and expanding social group—the international **scientific community.** Members of this community were linked together by common interests and shared values as well as by journals and the learned scientific societies founded in many countries in the later seventeenth and the eighteenth centuries. Their personal success depended on making new discoveries, and science became competitive. Second, as governments intervened to support and sometimes direct research, the new scientific community became closely tied to the state and its agendas. National academies of science were created under state sponsorship in London in 1662, Paris in 1666, Berlin in 1700, and later across Europe. At the same time, scientists developed a critical attitude toward established authority that would inspire thinkers to question traditions in other domains as well.

empiricism A theory of inductive reasoning that calls for acquiring evidence through observation and experimentation rather than reason and speculation.

Cartesian dualism Descartes's view that all of reality could ultimately be reduced to mind and matter.

scientific community The international social group that expanded with the rise of modern science; its members were linked together by common interests and shared values as well as by journals and the learned scientific societies founded in many countries in the later seventeenth and eighteenth centuries.

Metamorphoses of the Caterpillar and Moth

Maria Sibylla Merian (1647–1717), the stepdaughter of a Dutch painter, became a celebrated scientific illustrator in her own right. Her finely observed pictures of insects in the South American colony of Surinam introduced many new species, shown in their various stages of development. For Merian, science was intimately tied with art: she not only painted but also bred caterpillars and performed experiments on them. Her two-year stay in Surinam, accompanied by a teenaged daughter, was a daring feat for a seventeenth-century woman. (Bildarchiv Preussischer Kulturbesitz/Art Resource, NY)

Some things did not change in the scientific revolution. Scholars have recently analyzed representations of femininity and masculinity in the scientific revolution and have noted that nature was often depicted as a female, whose veil of secrecy needed to be stripped away and penetrated by male experts. (At the same time, the Americas were similarly depicted as a female terrain whose potentially fertile lands needed to be controlled and impregnated by male colonists.) New "rational" methods for approaching nature did not question traditional inequalities between the sexes—and may have worsened them in some ways. Women were largely shut out of the academies and then refused membership into scientific communities because they lacked academic credentials. (This continued for a long time. Marie Curie, the first person to win two Nobel prizes, was rejected by the French Academy of Science in 1911 because she was a woman.[5])

There were, however, a number of noteworthy exceptions. In Italy, universities and academies did offer posts to women, attracting some foreigners spurned by their own countries. Women were allowed to work as makers of wax anatomical models and as botanical and zoological illustrators. Women were also very much involved in informal scientific communities, attending salons, participating in scientific experiments, and writing learned treatises. Some female intellectuals were recognized as full-fledged members of the philosophical dialogue. In England, Margaret Cavendish, Anne Conway, and Mary Astell all contributed to debates about Descartes's mind-body dualism, among other issues. Descartes himself conducted an intellectual correspondence with the princess Elizabeth of Bohemia, of whom he stated: "I attach more weight to her judgement than to those messieurs the Doctors, who take for a rule of truth the opinions of Aristotle rather than the evidence of reason."[6]

The scientific revolution had few consequences for economic life and the living standards of the masses until the late eighteenth century. True, improvements in the techniques of navigation facilitated overseas trade and helped enrich states and merchant companies. But science had relatively few practical economic applications. Thus the scientific revolution of the seventeenth century was first and foremost an intellectual revolution. For more than a hundred years its greatest impact was on how people thought and believed.

Section Review

- Natural philosophy was based on Aristotle's ideas: the earth was the center of the universe, heaven was perfect, and the earth's four elements (air, fire, water, earth) were imperfect and changeable.

- The Copernican hypothesis stated that the sun, not the earth, was fixed and the planets and stars revolved around it—an idea the church rejected.

- Tycho Brahe, an astronomer, took detailed observations of the planets from which his assistant, Johannes Kepler, a mathematician, was able to determine and prove planetary motion, while Galileo Galilei developed the experimental method, using controlled experiments to verify results.

- Newton used a set of mathematical laws that explain motion and mechanics to synthesize his law of universal gravitation, which unified the universe into one magnificent system.

- The scientific revolution was a product of the medieval university, Renaissance funding, the need for navigational instruments, and the scientific method of experimentation and mathematical reasoning.

- The scientific revolution was an intellectual revolution, fostering international scientific communities and critical thinking in many fields beyond science.

The Enlightenment

How did the new worldview affect the way people thought about society and human relations?

Enlightenment The intellectual and cultural movement of the late seventeenth and eighteenth centuries that introduced a new worldview that has played a large role in shaping the modern mind. The three central concepts of the Enlightenment were the use of reason, the scientific method, and progress.

rationalism A secular, critical way of thinking in which nothing was to be accepted on faith, and everything was to be submitted to reason.

The scientific revolution was the single most important factor in the creation of the new worldview of the eighteenth-century **Enlightenment**. This worldview, which has played a large role in shaping the modern mind, grew out of a rich mix of diverse and often conflicting ideas. Despite the diversity, three central concepts stand at the core of Enlightenment thinking. The most important and original idea was that the methods of natural science could and should be used to examine and understand all aspects of life. This was what intellectuals meant by *reason*, a favorite word of Enlightenment thinkers. Nothing was to be accepted on faith. Everything was to be submitted to **rationalism**, a secular, critical way of thinking. A second important Enlightenment concept was that the scientific method was capable of discovering the laws of human society as well as those of nature. Thus was social science born. Its birth led to the third key idea, that of progress. Armed with the proper method of discovering the laws of human existence, Enlightenment thinkers believed, it was at least possible for human beings to create better societies and better people. Their belief was strengthened by some modest improvements in economic and social life during the eighteenth century.

The Emergence of the Enlightenment

Loosely united by certain key ideas, the European Enlightenment was a broad intellectual and cultural movement that gained strength gradually and did not reach its maturity until about 1750. Yet it was the generation that came of age between the publication of Newton's *Principia* (**prin-SIP-ee-uh, prin-KIP-ee-uh**) in 1687 and the death of Louis XIV in 1715 that tied the crucial knot between the scientific revolution and a new outlook on life. Talented writers of that generation popularized hard-to-understand scientific achievements for the educated elite.

A new generation came to believe that the human mind is capable of making great progress. Medieval and Reformation thinkers had been concerned primarily with sin and salvation. The humanists of the Renaissance had emphasized worldly matters, but their inspiration was the wisdom of the past. Enlightenment thinkers came to believe that, at least in science and mathematics, their era had gone far beyond antiquity. Progress, at least intellectual progress, was very possible.

The excitement of the scientific revolution also generated doubt and uncertainty, contributing to a widespread crisis in late seventeenth-century European thought. In the wake of the devastation wrought by the Thirty Years' War, some people asked whether ideological conformity in religious matters was really necessary. Others skeptically asked if religious truth could ever be known with absolute certainty and concluded that it could not. This was a new development because many seventeenth-century scientists, Catholic and Protestant, believed that their work exalted God and helped explain his creation to fellow believers.

The most famous of these skeptics was Pierre Bayle (1647–1706), a French Huguenot who despised Louis XIV and found refuge in the Netherlands. Bayle critically examined the religious beliefs and persecutions of the past in his *Historical and Critical Dictionary* (1697). Demonstrating that human beliefs had been extremely varied and very often mistaken, he concluded that nothing can ever be known beyond all doubt, a view known as **skepticism**. A very influential text, his

skepticism The belief that nothing can ever be known beyond all doubt and that humanity's best hope was open-minded toleration.

Popularizing Science

The frontispiece illustration of *Conversations on the Plurality of Worlds* by Bernard de Fontenelle (1657–1757) invites a nonscientific audience to share the pleasures of astronomy with an elegant lady and an entertaining teacher. The drawing shows the planets revolving around the sun.
(By permission of the Syndics of Cambridge University Library)

Dictionary was reprinted frequently in the Netherlands and in England and was found in more private libraries of eighteenth-century France than any other book.

The rapidly growing travel literature on non-European lands and cultures was another cause of uncertainty. In the wake of the great discoveries, Europeans were learning that the peoples of China, India, Africa, and the Americas all had their own very different beliefs and customs. Europeans shaved their faces and let their hair grow. Turks shaved their heads and let their beards grow. In Europe a man bowed before a woman to show respect. In Siam a man turned his back on a woman when he met her because it was disrespectful to look directly at her. Countless similar examples discussed in the travel accounts helped change the perspective of educated Europeans. They began to look at truth and morality in relative, rather than absolute, terms. If anything was possible, who could say what was right or wrong?

An additional cause and manifestation of European intellectual turmoil was John Locke's epochal *Essay Concerning Human Understanding* (1690). Locke's essay brilliantly set forth a new theory about how human beings learn and form their ideas, rejecting Descartes's view that all people are born with certain basic ideas and ways of thinking. Locke insisted that all ideas are derived from experience. The human mind at birth is like a blank tablet, or **tabula rasa** (TAB-yuh-luh RAH-suh), on which the environment writes the individual's understanding and beliefs. Human development is therefore determined by education and social institutions, for good or for evil. Locke's *Essay Concerning Human Understanding* passed through many editions and translations. Along with Newton's *Principia*, it was one of the dominant intellectual inspirations of the Enlightenment.

tabula rasa A blank tablet, incorporated into Locke's belief that all ideas are derived from experience, and that the human mind at birth is like a blank tablet on which the environment writes the individual's understanding and beliefs.

The Philosophes and the Public

By the time Louis XIV died in 1715, many of the ideas that would soon coalesce into the new worldview had been assembled. Yet Christian Europe was still strongly attached to its traditional beliefs, as witnessed by the powerful revival of religious orthodoxy in the first half of the eighteenth century (see pages 526–530). By the outbreak of the American Revolution in 1775, however, a large portion of western Europe's educated elite had embraced many of the new ideas. This acceptance was the work of the **philosophes** (FIL-uh-sawfz), a group of influential intellectuals who proudly proclaimed that they, at long last, were bringing the light of knowledge to their ignorant fellow creatures.

Philosophe is the French word for "philosopher," and it was in France that the Enlightenment reached its highest development. There were at least three reasons for this. First, French was the international language of the educated classes in the

philosophes Intellectuals in France who proclaimed that they were bringing the light of knowledge to their fellow creatures in the Age of Enlightenment.

eighteenth century, and France was still the wealthiest and most populous country in Europe. Second, although French intellectuals were not free to openly criticize either church or state, they were not as strongly restrained as intellectuals in eastern and east-central Europe. Philosophes like the baron de Montesquieu (MON-tuh-skyoo) (1689–1755) used satire and double meanings to spread their message to the public. Third, the French philosophes made it their goal to reach a larger audience of elites, many of whom were joined together in the eighteenth-century concept of the "republic of letters"—an imaginary, transnational realm of the well-educated.

The influence of writers like Montesquieu on the enlightened public can be seen in the results of his political writing. Disturbed by the growth in royal absolutism under Louis XIV and inspired by the example of the physical sciences, Montesquieu set out to apply the critical method to the problem of government. *The Spirit of Laws* (1748) was a complex comparative study of republics, monarchies, and despotisms—a great pioneering inquiry in the emerging social sciences.

separation of powers The idea, developed by the philosophe Montesquieu, that despotism could be avoided when political power was divided and shared by a variety of classes and legal estates holding unequal rights and privileges.

Showing that forms of government were shaped by history, geography, and customs, Montesquieu focused on the conditions that would promote liberty and prevent tyranny. He argued for a **separation of powers,** with political power divided and shared by a variety of classes and legal estates holding unequal rights and privileges. Admiring greatly the English balance of power among the king, the houses of Parliament, and the independent courts, Montesquieu believed that in France the thirteen high courts—the *parlements*—were frontline defenders of liberty against royal despotism. Apprehensive about the uneducated poor, Montesquieu was clearly no democrat, but his theory of separation of powers had a great impact on the constitutions of the young United States in 1789 and of France in 1791.

The most famous and in many ways most representative philosophe was François Marie Arouet, who was known by the pen name Voltaire (vohl-TAIR) (1694–1778). In his long career, this son of a comfortable middle-class family wrote more than seventy witty volumes, hobnobbed with kings and queens, and died a millionaire because of shrewd business speculations. His early career, however, was turbulent, and he was arrested on two occasions for insulting noblemen. Voltaire moved to England for three years in order to avoid a longer prison term in France, and there he came to share Montesquieu's enthusiasm for English institutions.

Returning to France and soon threatened again with prison in Paris, Voltaire had the great fortune of meeting Gabrielle-Emilie Le Tonnelier de Breteuil, marquise du Châtelet (SHA-tuh-lay) (1706–1749), an intellectually gifted woman from the high aristocracy with a passion for science. Inviting Voltaire to live in her country house at Cirey in Lorraine and becoming his long-time companion (under the eyes of her tolerant husband), Madame du Châtelet studied physics and mathematics and published scientific articles and translations.

Excluded from the Royal Academy of Sciences because of her gender, Madame du Châtelet depended on private tutors for instruction and became uncertain of her ability to make important scientific discoveries. She therefore concentrated on spreading the ideas of others, and her translation—with an accompanying commentary—of Newton's *Principia* into French for the first (and only) time was her greatest work. But she, who had patiently explained Newton's complex mathematical proofs to Europe's foremost philosophe, had no doubt that women's limited scientific contributions in the past were due to limited and unequal education. She once wrote that if she were a ruler "I would reform an abuse which cuts off, so to speak, half the human race. I would make women participate in all the rights of humankind, and above all in those of the intellect."[7]

While living at Cirey, Voltaire wrote various works praising England and popularizing English scientific progress. Newton, he wrote, was history's greatest man, for he had used his genius for the benefit of humanity. "It is," wrote Voltaire, "the man who sways our minds by the prevalence of reason and the native force of truth, not they who reduce mankind to a state of slavery by force and downright violence . . . that claims our reverence and admiration."[8] In the true style of the Enlightenment, Voltaire mixed the glorification of science and reason with an appeal for better individuals and institutions.

Yet like almost all of the philosophes, Voltaire was a reformer, not a revolutionary, in social and political matters. He pessimistically concluded that the best one could hope for in the way of government was a good monarch, since human beings "are very rarely worthy to govern themselves." Nor did he believe in social and economic equality in human affairs. The idea of making servants equal to their masters was "absurd and impossible." The only realizable equality, Voltaire thought, was that "by which the citizen only depends on the laws which protect the freedom of the feeble against the ambitions of the strong."[9]

Voltaire's philosophical and religious positions were much more radical. In the tradition of Bayle, his voluminous writings challenged, often indirectly, the Catholic Church and Christian theology at almost every point. Voltaire clearly believed in God, but his was a distant, deistic God, the great Clockmaker who built an orderly universe and then stepped aside and let it run. Above all, Voltaire and most of the philosophes hated all forms of religious intolerance, which they believed often led to fanaticism and savage, inhuman action. Simple piety and human kindness—as embodied in Christ's great commandments to "love God and your neighbor as yourself"—were religion enough, as may be seen in Voltaire's famous essay on religion. (See the feature "Listening to the Past: Voltaire on Religion" on pages 482–483.)

The ultimate strength of the French philosophes lay in their number, dedication, and organization. The philosophes felt keenly that they were engaged in a common undertaking that transcended individuals. Their greatest and most representative intellectual achievement was, quite fittingly, a group effort—the seventeen-volume *Encyclopedia: The Rational Dictionary of the Sciences, the Arts, and the Crafts*, edited by Denis Diderot (duh-nee DEE-duh-roe) (1713–1784) and Jean le Rond d'Alembert (al-em-BAHR) (1717–1783). From different circles and with different interests, the two men set out to find coauthors who would examine the rapidly expanding whole of human knowledge. Even more fundamentally, they set out to teach people how to think critically and objectively about all matters. As Diderot said, he wanted the *Encyclopedia* to "change the general way of thinking."[10]

Not every article was daring or original, but the overall effect was little short of revolutionary. Science and the industrial arts were exalted, religion and immortality questioned. Intolerance, legal injustice, and out-of-date social institutions were openly criticized. The encyclopedists were convinced that greater knowledge would result in greater human happiness, for knowledge was useful and made possible economic, social, and political progress. The *Encyclopedia* was widely read,

Madame du Châtelet

The marquise du Châtelet was fascinated by the new world system of Isaac Newton. She helped spread Newton's ideas in France by translating his *Principia* and by influencing Voltaire, her companion for fifteen years until her death. (Giraudon/Art Resource, NY)

especially in less-expensive reprint editions published in Switzerland, and it was extremely influential in France and throughout western Europe as well. It summed up the new worldview of the Enlightenment.

Urban Culture and the Public Sphere

Enlightenment ideas did not float on air. A series of new institutions and practices emerged in the late seventeenth and eighteenth centuries to facilitate their spread. First, the European production and consumption of books grew significantly in the eighteenth century. Moreover, the types of books people read changed dramatically. The proportion of religious and devotional books published in Paris declined after 1750; history and law held constant; the arts and sciences surged.

Reading more books on many more subjects, the educated public in France and throughout Europe increasingly approached reading in a new way. The result was what some scholars have called a **"reading revolution."** The old style of reading in Europe had been centered on a core of sacred texts that inspired reverence and taught earthly duty and obedience to God. Reading had been patriarchal and communal, with the father of the family slowly reading the text aloud and the audience savoring each word. Now reading involved a broader field of books that constantly changed. Reading became individual and silent, and texts could be

reading revolution The transition in Europe from a society where literacy consisted of patriarchal and communal reading of religious texts to a society where literacy was commonplace and reading material was broad and diverse.

Selling Books, Promoting Ideas

This appealing bookshop with its intriguing ads for the latest works offers to put customers "Under the Protection of Minerva," the Roman goddess of wisdom. Large packets of books sit ready for shipment to foreign countries. Book consumption surged in the eighteenth century.
(Musée des Beaux-Arts, Dijon/Art Resource, NY)

questioned. Subtle but profound, the reading revolution ushered in new ways of relating to the written word.

Conversation, discussion, and debate also played a critical role in the Enlightenment. Paris set the example, and other French and European cities followed. In Paris a number of talented, wealthy women presided over regular social gatherings in their elegant private drawing rooms, or **salons**. There they encouraged the exchange of witty, uncensored observations on literature, science, and philosophy. Talented hostesses, or *salonnières* (sal-lon-ee-AIRZ), mediated the public's free-wheeling examination of Enlightenment thought. As one philosophe described his Enlightenment hostess and her salon:

> *She could unite the different types, even the most antagonistic, sustaining the conversation by a well-aimed phrase, animating and guiding it at will. . . . Politics, religion, philosophy, news: nothing was excluded. Her circle met daily from five to nine. There one found men of all ranks in the State, the Church, and the Court, soldiers and foreigners, and the leading writers of the day.*[11]

As this passage suggests, the salons created a cultural realm free from religious dogma and political censorship. There a diverse but educated public could debate issues and form its own ideas. Through their invitation lists, salon hostesses brought together members of the intellectual, economic, and social elites. In such an atmosphere, the philosophes, the French nobility, and the prosperous middle classes intermingled and influenced one another. Thinking critically about almost any question became fashionable and flourished alongside hopes for human progress through greater knowledge and enlightened public opinion.

salons Regular social gatherings held by talented and rich Parisian women in their homes, where philosophes and their followers met to discuss literature, science, and philosophy.

Enlightenment Culture
An actor performs the first reading of a new play by Voltaire at the salon of Madame Geoffrin. Voltaire, then in exile, is represented by a bust statue. (Réunion des Musées Nationaux/Art Resource, NY)

rococo A popular style in Europe in the eighteenth century, known for its soft pastels, ornate interiors, sentimental portraits, and starry-eyed lovers protected by hovering cupids.

Elite women also exercised an unprecedented feminine influence on artistic taste. Soft pastels, ornate interiors, sentimental portraits, and starry-eyed lovers protected by hovering cupids were all hallmarks of the style they favored. This style, known as **rococo** (ruh-KOH-koh), was popular throughout Europe in the eighteenth century. It has been argued that feminine influence in the drawing room went hand in hand with the emergence of polite society and the general attempt to civilize a rough military nobility. Similarly, some philosophes championed greater rights and expanded education for women, claiming that the position and treatment of women were the best indicators of a society's level of civilization and decency.[12] To be sure, for these male philosophes greater rights for women did not mean equal rights, and the philosophes were not particularly disturbed by the fact that elite women remained legally subordinate to men in economic and political affairs. Elite women lacked many rights, but so did most men.

While membership at the salons was restricted to the well-born, the well-connected, and the exceptionally talented, a number of institutions emerged for the rest of society. Lending libraries served an important function for people who could not afford to buy their own books. The coffeehouses that first appeared in the late seventeenth century became meccas of philosophical discussion. In addition to these institutions, book clubs, Masonic lodges, and journals all played roles in the creation of a new **public sphere** that celebrated open debate informed by critical reason. The public sphere was an idealized space where members of society came together as individuals to discuss issues relevant to the society, economics, and politics of the day.

public sphere An idealized intellectual space that emerged in Europe during the Enlightenment, where members of society came together as individuals to discuss issues relevant to the society, economics, and politics of the day.

What of the common people? Did they participate in the Enlightenment? Enlightenment philosophes did not direct their message to peasants or urban laborers. They believed that the masses had no time or talent for philosophical speculation and that elevating them would be a long, slow, potentially dangerous process. Deluded by superstitions and driven by violent passions, they thought, the people were like little children in need of firm parental guidance. French philosophe d'Alembert characteristically made a sharp distinction between "the truly enlightened public" and "the blind and noisy multitude."[13]

There is some evidence, however, that the people were not immune to the words of the philosophes. At a time of rising literacy, book prices were dropping in cities and towns, and many philosophical ideas were popularized in cheap pamphlets. Moreover, even illiterate people had access to written material, through the practice of public reading. Although they were barred from salons and academies, ordinary people were not immune to the new ideas in circulation.

Late Enlightenment

After about 1770 a number of thinkers and writers began to attack the Enlightenment's faith in reason, progress, and moderation. The most famous of these was the Swiss Jean-Jacques Rousseau (1712–1778), the son of a poor watchmaker who made his way into the world of Paris salons through his brilliant intellect. Appealing but neurotic, Rousseau came to believe that his philosophe friends and the women of the Parisian salons were plotting against him. In the mid-1750s he broke with them, living thereafter as a lonely outsider with his uneducated common-law wife and going in his own highly original direction.

Like other Enlightenment thinkers, Rousseau was passionately committed to individual freedom. Unlike them, however, he attacked rationalism and civilization as destroying, rather than liberating, the individual. Warm, spontaneous feeling had to complement and correct cold intellect. Moreover, the basic goodness of the individual and the unspoiled child had to be protected from the cruel refinements of civilization. Rousseau's ideals greatly influenced the early romantic movement (see pages 517–518), which rebelled against the culture of the Enlightenment in the late eighteenth century.

Reconfirming Montesquieu's critique of women's influence in public affairs, Rousseau called for a rigid division of gender roles. According to Rousseau, women and men were radically different beings. Destined by nature to assume a passive role in sexual relations, women should also be passive in social life. Women's passion for fashion, attending salons, and pulling the strings of power was unnatural and had a corrupting effect on both politics and society. Rousseau thus rejected the sophisticated way of life of Parisian elite women. These views contributed to calls for privileged women to abandon their stylish corsets and to breast-feed their children.

Rousseau's contribution to political theory in *The Social Contract* (1762) was equally significant. His contribution was based on two fundamental concepts: the general will and popular sovereignty. According to Rousseau, the **general will** is sacred and absolute, reflecting the common interests of all the people, who have displaced the monarch as the holder of sovereign power. The general will is not necessarily the will of the majority, however. At times the general will may be the authentic, long-term needs of the people as correctly interpreted by a farseeing minority. (The concept has since been used by many dictators who have claimed that they, rather than some momentary majority of the voters, represent the general will.)

general will Rousseau's concept that the common interest of all the people is sacred and absolute, and is not necessarily reflected by the will of the majority but by the interpretation of a farseeing minority.

As the reading public developed, it joined forces with the philosophes to call for the autonomy of the printed word. Immanuel Kant (1724–1804), a professor in East Prussia and the greatest German philosopher of his day, posed the question of the age when he published a pamphlet in 1784 entitled *What Is Enlightenment?* Kant answered, "*Sapere Aude!* (**SAP-eh-ray OW-day**) [dare to know] Have courage to use your own understanding!—that is the motto of enlightenment." He argued that if serious thinkers were granted the freedom to exercise their reason publicly in print, enlightenment would almost surely follow. Kant was no revolutionary; he also insisted that in their private lives, individuals must obey all laws, no matter how unreasonable, and should be punished for "impertinent" criticism. Kant thus tried to reconcile absolute monarchical authority with a critical public sphere. This balancing act characterized experiments with "enlightened absolutism" in the eighteenth century.

Race and the Enlightenment

In recent years, historians have found in the scientific revolution and the Enlightenment a crucial turning point in European ideas about race. A primary catalyst for new ideas about race was the urge to classify nature, unleashed by the scientific revolution's insistence on careful empirical observation. In *The System of Nature* (1735) Swedish botanist Carl von Linné argued that nature was organized into a God-given hierarchy. As scientists developed more elaborate taxonomies of plant and animal species, they also began to classify humans into hierarchically ordered "races" and to investigate the origins of race. The Comte de Buffon (**komt duh buh-FAWN**) argued that humans originated with one species that then developed into distinct races due largely to climatic conditions. According to Immanuel Kant, there were four human races, each of which had derived from an original race of "white brunette" people.

Using the word *race* to designate biologically distinct groups of humans, akin to distinct animal species, was new. Previously, Europeans grouped other peoples

enlightened absolutism Term coined by historians to describe the rule of eighteenth-century monarchs who, without renouncing their own absolute authority, adopted Enlightenment ideals of rationalism, progress, and tolerance.

into "nations" based on their historical, political, and cultural affiliations, rather than on supposedly innate physical differences. Unsurprisingly, when European thinkers drew up a hierarchical classification of human species, their own "race" was placed at the top. Europeans had long believed they were culturally superior to "barbaric" peoples in Africa and, since 1492, the New World. Now emerging ideas about racial difference taught them they were biologically superior as well.

These ideas did not go unchallenged. James Beattie responded directly to claims of white superiority by pointing out that Europeans had started out as savage as nonwhites and that many non-European peoples in the Americas, Asia, and Africa had achieved high levels of civilization.

Scholars are only at the beginning of efforts to understand links between Enlightenment ideas about race and its notions of equality, progress, and reason. There are clear parallels, though, between the use of science to propagate racial hierarchies and its use to defend social inequalities between men and women. As Rousseau used women's "natural" passivity to argue for their passive role in society, so others used non-Europeans' "natural" inferiority to defend slavery and colonial domination. The new powers of science and reason were thus marshaled to imbue traditional stereotypes with the force of natural law.

The Enlightenment and Absolutism

What impact did this new way of thinking have on political developments and monarchical absolutism?

How did the Enlightenment influence political developments? To this important question there is no easy answer. Most Enlightenment thinkers outside of England and the Netherlands believed that political change could best come from above—from the ruler—rather than from below, especially in central and eastern Europe. It was necessary to educate and "enlighten" the monarch, who could then make good laws and promote human happiness.

Many government officials were attracted to and interested in philosophical ideas. They were among the best-educated members of society, and their daily involvement in complex affairs of state made them naturally interested in ideas for improving or reforming human society. Encouraged and instructed by these officials, some absolutist rulers of the later eighteenth century tried to govern in an "enlightened" manner. Yet the actual programs and accomplishments of these rulers varied greatly. It is necessary to examine the evolution of monarchical absolutism at close range before trying to judge the Enlightenment's effect and the meaning of what historians have often called the **enlightened absolutism** of the later eighteenth century.

Enlightenment teachings inspired European rulers in small as well as large states in the second half of the eighteenth century. Absolutist princes and monarchs in several west German and Italian states, as well as in Scandinavia, Spain, and Portugal, proclaimed themselves more enlightened. A few smaller states were actually the most successful in making reforms, perhaps because their rulers were not overwhelmed by the size and complexity of their realms. Denmark, for example, carried out extensive and progressive land reform in the 1780s that practically abolished serfdom and gave Danish peasants secure tenure on their farms. Yet by far the most influential of the new-style monarchs were in Prussia, Russia, and Austria, and they deserve primary attention.

Frederick the Great of Prussia

Frederick II (r. 1740–1786), commonly known as Frederick the Great, built masterfully on the work of his father, Frederick William I (see page 443). Although in his youth he embraced culture and literature rather than the crude life of the barracks, by the time he came to the throne Frederick was determined to use the splendid army that his father had left him.

Therefore, when Maria Theresa of Austria inherited the Habsburg dominions upon the death of her father Charles VI, Frederick pounced. He invaded her rich, mainly German province of Silesia (si-LEE-zhuh) in violation of the Pragmatic Sanction that had guaranteed her succession. In 1742, as other greedy powers were falling on her lands in the general European War of the Austrian Succession (1740–1748), Maria Theresa was forced to cede almost all of Silesia to Prussia (see Map 17.2 on page 442). In one stroke Prussia had doubled its population to six million people. Now Prussia unquestionably towered above all the other German states and stood as a European Great Power.

Though successful in 1742, Frederick had to spend much of his reign fighting against great odds to save Prussia from total destruction. When the ongoing competition between Britain and France for colonial empire brought another great conflict in 1756 (see page 497), Maria Theresa fashioned an aggressive alliance with the leaders of France and Russia. During the Seven Years' War (1756–1763), the aim of the alliance was to conquer Prussia and divide up its territory. Despite invasions from all sides, Frederick fought on with stoic courage. In the end he was miraculously saved: Peter III came to the Russian throne in 1762 and called off the attack against Frederick, whom he greatly admired.

The terrible struggle of the Seven Years' War tempered Frederick's interest in territorial expansion and brought him to consider how more humane policies for his subjects might also strengthen the state. Thus Frederick went beyond a superficial commitment to Enlightenment culture for himself and his circle. He tolerantly allowed his subjects to believe as they wished in religious and philosophical matters. He promoted the advancement of knowledge, improving his country's schools and permitting scholars to publish their findings. Moreover, Frederick tried to improve the lives of his subjects more directly. As he wrote his friend Voltaire, "I must enlighten my people, cultivate their manners and morals, and make them as happy as human beings can be, or as happy as the means at my disposal permit."

The legal system and the bureaucracy were Frederick's primary tools. Prussia's laws were simplified, torture of prisoners was abolished, and judges decided cases quickly and impartially. Prussian officials became famous for their hard work and honesty. After the Seven Years' War ended in 1763, Frederick's government energetically promoted the reconstruction of agriculture and industry in his war-torn country. Frederick himself set a good example. He worked hard and lived modestly, claiming that he was "only the first servant of the state." Thus Frederick justified monarchy in terms of practical results and said nothing of the divine right of kings.

Frederick's dedication to high-minded government went only so far, however. While he condemned serfdom in the abstract, he accepted it in practice and did not even free the serfs on his own estates. He accepted and extended the privileges of the nobility, who remained the backbone of the army and the entire Prussian state.

Nor did Frederick listen to thinkers like Moses Mendelssohn (MEN-dul-suhn) (1729–1786), who urged that Jews be given freedom and civil rights. (See the feature "Individuals in Society: Moses Mendelssohn and the Jewish Enlightenment.") The vast majority of Jews were confined to tiny, overcrowded ghettos, were

Individuals in Society

Moses Mendelssohn and the Jewish Enlightenment

In 1743 a small, humpbacked Jewish boy with a stammer left his poor parents in Dessau (**DES-ow**) in central Germany and walked eighty miles to Berlin, the capital of Frederick the Great's Prussia. According to one story, when the boy reached the Rosenthaler (**ROH-zuhn-taw-ler**) Gate, the

Lavater (*right*) attempts to convert Mendelssohn, in a painting by Moritz Oppenheim of an imaginary encounter. (Collection of the Judah L. Magnes Museum, Berkeley)

only one through which Jews could pass, he told the inquiring watchman that his name was Moses and that he had come to Berlin "to learn." The watchman laughed and waved him through. "Go Moses, the sea has opened before you."[*] Embracing the Enlightenment and seeking a revitalization of Jewish religious thought, Moses Mendelssohn did point his people in a new and uncharted direction.

In Berlin, the young Mendelssohn turned to a learned rabbi he had previously known in Dessau, studied Jewish law, and eked out a living copying Hebrew manuscripts in a beautiful hand. But he was soon fascinated by an intellectual world that had been closed to him in the Dessau ghetto. There, like most Jews throughout central Europe, he had spoken Yiddish—a mixture of German, Polish, and Hebrew. Now, working mainly on his own, he mastered German; learned Latin, Greek, French, and English; and studied mathematics and Enlightenment philosophy. Word of his exceptional abilities spread in Berlin's Jewish community (1,500 of the city's 100,000 inhabitants). He began tutoring the children of a wealthy Jewish silk merchant, and he soon became the merchant's clerk and later his partner. But his great passion remained the life of the mind and the spirit, which he avidly pursued in his off hours.

Gentle and unassuming in his personal life, Mendelssohn was a bold thinker. Reading eagerly in Western philosophy since antiquity, he was, as a pious Jew, soon convinced that Enlightenment teachings need not be opposed to Jewish thought and religion. Indeed, he concluded that reason could complement and strengthen religion, although each would retain its integrity as a separate sphere.[†] Developing his idea in his first great work, "On the Immortality of the Soul" (1767), Mendelssohn used the neutral setting of a philosophical dialogue between Socrates and his followers in ancient Greece to argue that the human soul lived forever. In refusing to bring religion and critical thinking into conflict, he was strongly influenced by contemporary German philosophers who argued similarly on behalf of Christianity. He reflected the way the German Enlightenment generally supported established religion, in contrast to the French Enlightenment, which attacked it. This was the most important difference in Enlightenment thinking between the two countries.

Mendelssohn's treatise on the human soul captivated the educated German public, which marveled that a Jew could have written a philosophical masterpiece. In the excitement, a Christian zealot named Lavater challenged Mendelssohn in a pamphlet to accept Christianity or to demonstrate how the Christian faith was not "reasonable." Replying politely but passionately, the Jewish philosopher affirmed that all his studies had only strengthened him in the faith of his fathers, although he certainly did not seek to convert anyone not born into Judaism. Rather, he urged toleration in religious matters. He spoke up courageously for his fellow Jews and decried the oppression they endured, and he continued to do so for the rest of his life.

Orthodox Jew and German philosophe, Moses Mendelssohn serenely combined two very different worlds. He built a bridge from the ghetto to the dominant culture over which many Jews would pass, including his novelist daughter Dorothea and his famous grandson, the composer Felix Mendelssohn.

Questions for Analysis

1. How did Mendelssohn seek to influence Jewish religious thought in his time?
2. How do Mendelssohn's ideas compare with those of the French Enlightenment?

[*] H. Kupferberg, *The Mendelssohns: Three Generations of Genius* (New York: Charles Scribner's Sons, 1972), p. 3.

[†] D. Sorkin, *Moses Mendelssohn and the Religious Enlightenment* (Berkeley: University of California Press, 1996), pp. 8 ff.

excluded by law from most business and professional activities, and could be ordered out of the kingdom at a moment's notice.

Catherine the Great of Russia

Catherine the Great of Russia (r. 1762–1796) was one of the most remarkable rulers of her age, and the French philosophes adored her. Catherine was a German princess from Anhalt-Zerbst (AHN-hahlt ZEHR-bst), a totally insignificant principality sandwiched between Prussia and Saxony. Her father commanded a regiment of the Prussian army, but her mother was related to the Romanovs of Russia, and that proved to be Catherine's chance.

At the age of fifteen she was married to the heir to the Russian throne. When her husband Peter III came to power in 1762, his decision to withdraw Russian troops from the coalition against Prussia alienated the army. At the end of six months Catherine and her conspirators deposed Peter III in a palace revolution, and the Orlov brothers murdered him. The German princess became empress of Russia.

Catherine had drunk deeply at the Enlightenment well. Never questioning the common assumption that absolute monarchy was the best form of government, she set out to rule in an enlightened manner. She had three main goals. First, she worked hard to continue Peter the Great's effort to bring the culture of western Europe to backward Russia. To do so, she imported Western architects,

Catherine the Great as Equestrian and Miniature of Count Grigory Grigoryevich Orlov
Catherine conspired with her lover Count Orlov to overthrow her husband Peter III and became empress of Russia. Strongly influenced by the Enlightenment, she cultivated the French philosophes and instituted moderate reforms, only to reverse them in the aftermath of Pugachev's rebellion. This equestrian portrait now hangs above her throne in the palace throne room. (left: Musée des Beaux-Arts, Chartres/The Bridgeman Art Library; right: State Hermitage Museum, St. Petersburg)

sculptors, musicians, and intellectuals. She bought masterpieces of Western art in wholesale lots and patronized the philosophes. An enthusiastic letter writer, she corresponded extensively with Voltaire and praised him as the "champion of the human race." When the French government banned the *Encyclopedia*, she offered to publish it in St. Petersburg, and she sent money to Diderot when he needed it. With these and countless similar actions, Catherine won good press in the West for herself and for her country. Moreover, this intellectual ruler, who wrote plays and loved good talk, set the tone for the entire Russian nobility. Peter the Great westernized Russian armies, but it was Catherine who Westernized the imagination of the Russian nobility.

Catherine's second goal was domestic reform, and she began her reign with sincere and ambitious projects. Better laws were a major concern. In 1767 she appointed a special legislative commission to prepare a new law code. No new unified code was ever produced, but Catherine did restrict the practice of torture and allowed limited religious toleration. She also tried to improve education and strengthen local government. The philosophes applauded these measures and hoped more would follow.

Such was not the case. In 1773 a common Cossack soldier named Emelian Pugachev (PEW-gah-chev) sparked a gigantic uprising of serfs, very much as Stenka Razin had done a century earlier (see page 447). Proclaiming himself the true tsar, Pugachev issued "decrees" abolishing serfdom, taxes, and army service. Thousands joined his cause, slaughtering landlords and officials over a vast area of southwestern Russia. Pugachev's untrained forces eventually proved no match for Catherine's noble-led regular army. Betrayed by his own company, Pugachev was captured and savagely executed.

Pugachev's rebellion put an end to any intentions Catherine might have had about reforming the system. The peasants were clearly dangerous, and her empire rested on the support of the nobility. After 1775 Catherine gave the nobles absolute control of their serfs. She extended serfdom into new areas, such as Ukraine. In 1785 she formalized the nobility's privileged position, freeing nobles forever from taxes and state service. Under Catherine the Russian nobility attained its most exalted position, and serfdom entered its most oppressive phase.

Catherine's third goal was territorial expansion, and in this respect she was extremely successful. Her armies subjugated the last descendants of the Mongols and the Crimean Tartars, and began the conquest of the Caucasus (KAW-kuh-suhs). Her greatest coup by far was the partition of Poland (see Map 18.1). When, between 1768 and 1772, Catherine's armies scored unprecedented victories against the Turks and thereby threatened to disturb the balance of power between Russia and Austria in eastern Europe, Frederick of Prussia obligingly came forward with a deal. He proposed that Turkey be let off easily and that Prussia, Austria, and Russia each compensate itself by taking a gigantic slice of the weakly ruled Polish territory. Catherine jumped at the chance. The first partition of Poland took place in 1772. Two more partitions, in 1793 and 1795, gave all three powers more Polish territory, and the ancient republic of Poland vanished from the map.

The Austrian Habsburgs

In Austria two talented rulers did manage to introduce major reforms, although traditional power politics was more important than Enlightenment teachings. One was the empress Maria Theresa (1740–1780), a remarkable but old-fashioned absolutist. The other was her son, Joseph II (r. 1780–1790), a fascinating individual.

MAPPING THE PAST

MAP 18.1 The Partition of Poland and Russia's Expansion, 1772–1795

By 1700 Poland had become a weak and decentralized republic with an elected king. All important decisions continued to require the unanimous agreement of all nobles elected to the Polish Diet, which meant that nothing could ever be done to strengthen the state. In 1772 war threatened between Russia and Austria over Russian gains from the Ottoman Empire. To satisfy desires for expansion without fighting, Prussia's Frederick the Great proposed that parts of Poland be divided among Austria, Prussia, and Russia. In 1793 and 1795 the three powers partitioned the remainder of the country. **[1]** Why was Poland vulnerable to partition in the latter half of the eighteenth century? What does it say about European politics at the time that a country could simply cease to exist on the map? Could that happen today? **[2]** Of the three powers that divided the kingdom of Poland, which benefited the most? How did the partition affect the geographical boundaries of each state, and what was the significance? **[3]** Which border with the former Poland remained unchanged? Why do you think this was the case?

For an earlier generation of historians, he was the "revolutionary emperor," a tragic hero whose lofty reforms were undone by the landowning nobility he dared to challenge. More recent scholarship has revised this romantic interpretation and has stressed how Joseph II continued the state-building work of his mother.

Emerging from the long War of the Austrian Succession in 1748 with the serious loss of Silesia, Maria Theresa and her closest ministers were determined to introduce reforms that would make the state stronger and more efficient. Three aspects of these reforms were most important. First, Maria Theresa introduced measures aimed at limiting the papacy's political influence in her realm. Second,

Section Review

- Frederick the Great of Prussia struggled militarily during the Seven Years' War but also promoted Enlightenment policies to improve the lives of his subjects.

- Moses Mendelssohn, an orthodox Jew and German philosophe who believed reason and religion could strengthen each other, promoted religious toleration and received the admiration of the educated German public.

- Catherine the Great of Russia enjoyed Enlightenment ideas and hosted Western intellectuals and artists while attempting domestic reform, but after a peasant-led revolt, instead increased the power of the nobility.

- Catherine focused on territorial expansion, defeating the Turks and accepting the division of Polish territory between Russia, Austria, and Prussia.

- Maria Theresa enacted Enlightenment policies to limit papal influence, strengthen bureaucracy, and improve conditions for the peasants.

- Her son Joseph II went further and abolished serfdom in favor of cash payments, but both the nobles and the peasants rejected his reforms and his brother and successor Leopold II re-established serfdom.

a whole series of administrative reforms strengthened the central bureaucracy, smoothed out some provincial differences, and revamped the tax system, taxing even the lands of nobles without special exemptions. Third, the government sought to improve the lot of the agricultural population, cautiously reducing the power of lords over their hereditary serfs and their partially free peasant tenants.

Coregent with his mother from 1765 onward and a strong supporter of change, Joseph II moved forward rapidly when he came to the throne in 1780. Most notably, Joseph abolished serfdom in 1781, and in 1789 he decreed that all peasant labor obligations be converted into cash payments. This measure was violently rejected not only by the nobility but also by the peasants it was intended to help, because they lacked the necessary cash. When a disillusioned Joseph died prematurely at forty-nine, the entire Habsburg empire was in turmoil. His brother Leopold II (r. 1790–1792) canceled Joseph's radical edicts in order to re-establish order. Peasants once again were required to do forced labor for their lords.

The eastern European absolutists of the later eighteenth century combined old-fashioned state-building with the culture and critical thinking of the Enlightenment. In doing so, they succeeded in expanding the role of the state in the life of society. They perfected bureaucratic machines that were to prove surprisingly adaptive and capable of enduring into the twentieth century. Their failure to implement policies we would recognize as humane and enlightened—such as abolishing serfdom—may reveal inherent limitations in Enlightenment thinking about equality and social justice, rather than in their execution of an Enlightenment program. The fact that leading philosophes supported rather than criticized Eastern rulers' policies suggests some of the blinders of the era.

Chapter Review

What was revolutionary in the new attitudes toward the natural world? (page 459)

Decisive breakthroughs in astronomy and physics in the seventeenth century demolished the imposing medieval synthesis of Aristotelian philosophy and Christian theology. These developments had only limited practical consequences at the time, but the impact of new scientific knowledge on intellectual life was enormous. The emergence of modern science was a distinctive characteristic of Western civilization and became a key element of Western identity. During the eighteenth century scientific thought fostered new ideas about racial differences and provided justifications for belief in Western superiority.

How did the new worldview affect the way people thought about society and human relations? (page 466)

Interpreting scientific findings and Newtonian laws in a manner that was both antitradition and antireligion, Enlightenment philosophes extolled the superiority of rational, critical thinking. This new method, they believed, promised not just increased knowledge but even the discovery of the fundamental laws of human society. Although

Key Terms

natural philosophy (p. 459)
Copernican hypothesis (p. 460)
experimental method (p. 461)
law of inertia (p. 461)
law of universal gravitation (p. 463)
empiricism (p. 464)
Cartesian dualism (p. 464)
scientific community (p. 464)
Enlightenment (p. 466)
rationalism (p. 466)
skepticism (p. 466)
tabula rasa (p. 467)

they reached different conclusions when they turned to social and political realities, they did stimulate absolute monarchs to apply reason to statecraft and the search for useful reforms. Above all, the philosophes succeeded in shaping an emerging public opinion and spreading their radically new worldview.

What impact did this new way of thinking have on political developments and monarchical absolutism? (page 474)

The ideas of the Enlightenment were an inspiration for monarchs, particularly absolutist rulers in central and eastern Europe who saw in them important tools for reforming and rationalizing their governments. Their primary goal was to strengthen their states and increase the efficiency of their bureaucracies and armies. Enlightened absolutists believed that these reforms would ultimately improve the lot of ordinary people, but this was not their chief concern. With few exceptions, they did not question the institution of serfdom. The fact that leading philosophes supported rather than criticized Eastern rulers' policies suggests some of the limitations of the era.

philosophes (p. 467)

separation of powers (p. 468)

reading revolution (p. 470)

salons (p. 471)

rococo (p. 472)

public sphere (p. 472)

general will (p. 473)

enlightened absolutism (p. 474)

Notes

1. H. Butterfield, *The Origins of Modern Science* (New York: Macmillan, 1951), p. viii.
2. Quoted in A. G. R. Smith, *Science and Society in the Sixteenth and Seventeenth Centuries* (New York: Harcourt Brace Jovanovich, 1972), p. 97.
3. Quoted in Butterfield, *The Origins of Modern Science*, p. 47.
4. Ibid., p. 120.
5. L. Schiebinger, *The Mind Has No Sex? Women in the Origins of Modern Science* (Cambridge, Mass.: Harvard University Press, 1989), p. 2.
6. Jacqueline Broad, *Women Philosophers of the Seventeenth Century* (Cambridge: Cambridge University Press, 2003), p. 17.
7. Schiebinger, *The Mind Has No Sex?* p. 64.
8. Quoted in L. M. Marsak, ed., *The Enlightenment* (New York: John Wiley & Sons, 1972), p. 56.
9. Quoted in G. L. Mosse et al., eds., *Europe in Review* (Chicago: Rand McNally, 1964), p. 156.
10. Quoted in P. Gay, "The Unity of the Enlightenment," *History* 3 (1960): 25.
11. Quoted in G. P. Gooch, *Catherine the Great and Other Studies* (Hamden, Conn.: Archon Books, 1966), p. 149.
12. See E. Fox-Genovese, "Women in the Enlightenment," in *Becoming Visible: Women in European History*, 2d ed., ed. R. Bridenthal, C. Koonz, and S. Stuard (Boston: Houghton Mifflin, 1987), esp. pp. 252–259, 263–265.
13. Jean Le Rond d'Alembert, *Eloges lus dans les séances publiques de l'Académie française* (Paris, 1779), p. ix, quoted in Mona Ozouf, "'Public Opinion' at the End of the Old Regime," *The Journal of Modern History* 60, Supplement: Rethinking French Politics in 1788 (September 1988), p. S9.

To assess your mastery of this chapter, go to **bedfordstmartins.com/mckaywestbrief**

Listening to the Past

Voltaire on Religion

Voltaire was the most renowned and probably the most influential of the French philosophes. His biting satirical novel Candide (1759) is still widely assigned in college courses, and his witty yet serious Philosophical Dictionary remains a source of pleasure and stimulation. The Dictionary consists of a series of essays on topics ranging from Adam to Zoroaster, from certainty to circumcision. The following passage is taken from the essay on religion. In it Voltaire describes being deep in meditation when a genie transported him to a desert filled with the bones of those who had been killed because of their religious practices or beliefs. The genie then led him to the "heroes of humanity, who tried to banish violence and plunder from the world."

An impish Voltaire, by the French sculptor Houdon. (Courtesy of Board of Trustees of the Victoria & Albert Museum)

[At last] I saw a man with a gentle, simple face, who seemed to me to be about thirty-five years old. From afar he looked with compassion upon those piles of whitened bones, through which I had been led to reach the sage's dwelling place. I was astonished to find his feet swollen and bleeding, his hands likewise, his side pierced, and his ribs laid bare by the cut of the lash. "Good God!" I said to him, "is it possible for a just man, a sage, to be in this state? I have just seen one who was treated in a very hateful way, but there is no comparison between his torture and yours. Wicked priests and wicked judges poisoned him; is it by priests and judges that you were so cruelly assassinated?"

With great courtesy he answered, "Yes."

"And who were these monsters?"

"They were hypocrites."

"Ah! that says everything; I understand by that one word that they would have condemned you to the cruelest punishment. Had you then proved to them, as Socrates did, that the Moon was not a goddess, and that Mercury was not a god?"

"No, it was not a question of planets. My countrymen did not even know what a planet was; they were all arrant ignoramuses. Their superstitions were quite different from those of the Greeks."

"Then you wanted to teach them a new religion?"

"Not at all; I told them simply: 'Love God with all your heart and your neighbor as yourself, for that is the whole of mankind's duty.' Judge yourself if this precept is not as old as the universe; judge yourself if I brought them a new religion." . . .

"But did you say nothing, do nothing that could serve them as a pretext?"

"To the wicked everything serves as pretext."

"Did you not say once that you were come not to bring peace, but a sword?"

"It was a scribe's error; I told them that I brought peace and not a sword. I never wrote anything; what I said can have been changed without evil intention."

"You did not then contribute in any way by your teaching, either badly reported or badly interpreted, to those frightful piles of bones which I saw on my way to consult with you?"

"I have only looked with horror upon those who have made themselves guilty of all these murders."

. . . [Finally] I asked him to tell me in what true religion consisted.

"Have I not already told you? Love God and your neighbor as yourself."

"Is it necessary for me to take sides either for the Greek Orthodox Church or the Roman Catholic?"

"When I was in the world I never made any difference between the Jew and the Samaritan."

"Well, if that is so, I take you for my only master." Then he made a sign with his head that filled me with peace. The vision disappeared, and I was left with a clear conscience.

Questions for Analysis

1. Who is the man that Voltaire meets in this passage? Why did the writer decide to leave this person unnamed?

2. What is Voltaire's message?

3. If a person today thought and wrote like Voltaire, would that person be called a defender or a destroyer of Christianity? Why?

Source: F. M. Arouet de Voltaire, *Oeuvres complètes*, vol. 8, trans. J. McKay (Paris: Firmin-Didot, 1875), pp. 188–190.

CHAPTER 19

The Expansion of Europe in the Eighteenth Century

Chapter Preview

Agriculture and the Land
What were the causes and effects of the agricultural revolution, and what nations led the way in these developments?

The Beginning of the Population Explosion
Why did European population rise dramatically in the eighteenth century?

Cottage Industry and Urban Guilds
What is cottage industry, and how did it contribute to Europe's economic and social transformation?

Building the Global Economy
How did colonial markets boost Europe's economic and social development, and what conflicts and adversity did world trade entail?

The East India Dock, London (detail), by Samuel Scott, a painting infused with the spirit of maritime expansion. (© Board of Trustees of the Victoria & Albert Museum)

The world of absolutism and aristocracy, a combination of raw power and elegant refinement, was a world apart from that of the common people. For most people in the eighteenth century, life remained a struggle with poverty and uncertainty, with the landlord and the tax collector. In 1700 peasants on the land and artisans in their shops lived little better than their ancestors had in the Middle Ages. Only in science and thought, and there only among intellectual elites and their followers, had Western society succeeded in going beyond the great achievements of the High Middle Ages, achievements that in turn owed much to Greece and Rome.

Everyday life was a struggle because European societies still could not produce very much by modern standards. Ordinary men and women might work like their beasts in the fields, but there was seldom enough good food, warm clothing, and decent housing. Life went on; history went on. The wars of religion ravaged Germany in the seventeenth century; Russia rose to become a Great Power; the state of Poland disappeared; monarchs and nobles continually jockeyed for power and wealth. In 1700 the idea of progress, of substantial and ongoing improvement in the lives of great numbers of people, was still the dream of a small elite in fashionable salons.

Yet the economic basis of European life was beginning to change. In the course of the eighteenth century the European economy emerged from the long crisis of the seventeenth century, responded to challenges, and began to expand once again. Population resumed its growth, while colonial empires developed and colonial elites prospered. Some areas were more fortunate than others. The rising Atlantic powers—Holland, France, and above all England—and their colonies led the way. The expansion of agriculture, industry, trade, and population marked the beginning of a surge comparable to that of the eleventh- and twelfth-century springtime of European civilization. But this time, broadly based expansion was not cut short. This time the response to new challenges led toward one of the most influential developments in human history, the Industrial Revolution, considered in Chapter 22.

Agriculture and the Land

What were the causes and effects of the agricultural revolution, and what nations led the way in these developments?

At the end of the seventeenth century the economy of Europe was agrarian. With the possible exception of Holland, at least 80 percent of the people of all western European countries drew their livelihoods from agriculture. In eastern Europe the percentage was considerably higher. Yet even in a rich agricultural region such as the Po Valley in northern Italy, every bushel of wheat sown yielded on average only five or six bushels of grain at harvest. By modern standards output was distressingly low.

In most regions of Europe in the sixteenth and seventeenth centuries, climatic conditions produced poor or disastrous harvests every eight or nine years. Unbalanced and inadequate food in famine years made people extremely susceptible to illnesses such as influenza and smallpox. In famine years the number of deaths soared far above normal. A third of a village's population might disappear in a year or two. But new developments in agricultural technology and methods gradually brought an end to the ravages of hunger in western Europe.

The Agricultural Revolution

One way for European peasants to improve their difficult position was to take land from those who owned it but did no labor. Yet the social and political conditions that sustained the ruling elites were ancient and deeply rooted, and powerful forces stood ready to crush protest. Only with the coming of the French Revolution were European peasants, mainly in France, able to improve their position by means of radical mass action.

Technological progress offered another possibility. If peasants (and their noble landlords) could eliminate the need to leave part of the land fallow, or unplanted, in order to restore fertility to the soil, they could greatly increase the land under cultivation. So remarkable were the possibilities and the results that historians have often spoken of the progressive elimination of the fallow, which occurred gradually throughout Europe from the mid-seventeenth century on, as an **agricultural revolution.** This revolution, which took longer than historians used to believe, was a great milestone in human development.

Because grain crops exhaust the soil and make fallowing necessary, the secret to eliminating the fallow lies in alternating grain with nitrogen-storing crops. The most important of these soil-reviving crops are peas and beans, root crops such as turnips and potatoes, and clovers and grasses. As the eighteenth century went on, the number of crops that were systematically rotated grew. New patterns of organization allowed some farmers to develop increasingly sophisticated patterns of **crop rotation** to suit different kinds of soils. For example, farmers in French Flanders near Lille in the late eighteenth century used a ten-year rotation, alternating a number of grain, root, and hay crops in a given field on a ten-year schedule. Continual experimentation led to more scientific farming.

Improvements in farming had multiple effects. The new crops made ideal feed for animals, and because peasants and larger farmers had more fodder, hay, and root crops for the winter months, they could build up their herds of cattle and sheep. More animals meant more meat and better diets. More animals also meant more manure for fertilizer and therefore more grain for bread and porridge.

Advocates of the new crop rotations, who included an emerging group of experimental scientists, some government officials, and a few big landowners, believed that new methods were scarcely possible within the traditional framework of open fields and common rights. A farmer who wanted to experiment with new methods would have to get all the landholders in a village to agree to the plan. Advocates of improvement argued that innovating agriculturalists needed to enclose and consolidate their scattered holdings into compact, fenced-in fields in order to farm more effectively. In doing so, the innovators also needed to enclose their individual shares of the natural pasture, the common. According to proponents of this movement, known as **enclosure,**

agricultural revolution The period in Europe from the mid-seventeenth century on, during which great agricultural progress was made and the fallow was gradually eliminated.

crop rotation The system by which farmers rotated the types of crops grown in each field so as to replenish the soil of its natural resources.

enclosure The movement to fence in fields in order to farm more effectively.

Enclosure in Streatley, Berkshire County, England

This map shows the results of enclosure in early-nineteenth-century Streatley, a village ten miles west of Reading on the River Thames. The area marked in yellow was the enclosed territory, appropriated mostly by a few large landowners and the city of Reading. The legend provides a detailed list of land ownership, including references to "old inclosures." (Courtesy, Berkshire Record Office, Ref # Streatley (1817), MRI 256) a revolution in village life and organization was the necessary price of technical progress.

That price seemed too high to many poor rural people who had small, inadequate holdings or very little land at all. Traditional rights were precious to these poor peasants. They used commonly held pastureland to graze livestock, and marsh or moor lands outside the village as a source for firewood, berries, and other foraged goods that could make the difference between survival and famine in harsh times. Thus when the small landholders and the village poor could effectively oppose the enclosure of the open fields and the common lands, they did so. Moreover, in many countries they found allies among the larger, predominately noble landowners who were also wary of enclosure because it required large investments and posed risks for them as well.

The old system of unenclosed fields and the new system of continuous rotation coexisted in Europe for a long time. Open fields could be found in much of France and Germany in the early years of the nineteenth century because peasants there had successfully opposed efforts to introduce the new techniques in the late eighteenth century. Until the end of the eighteenth century, the new system was extensively adopted only in the Low Countries and England.

ca. 1650–1790	Growth of Atlantic economy
ca. 1650–1850	Agricultural improvement and revolution
1651–1663	British Navigation Acts
1652–1674	Anglo-Dutch wars; rise of British mercantilism
ca. 1690–1790	Enlightenment
1700–1790	Height of Atlantic slave trade; expansion of rural industry in Europe
1701–1713	War of the Spanish Succession
1701–1763	Mercantilist wars of empire
1720–1722	Last of bubonic plague in Europe
1720–1789	Growth of European population
1740–1748	War of the Austrian Succession
1750–1790	Rise of economic liberalism
1756–1763	Seven Years' War
1759	Fall of Quebec
1760–1815	Height of parliamentary enclosure in England
1776	Smith, *Wealth of Nations*
1807	British slave trade abolished

The Leadership of the Low Countries and England

The new methods of the agricultural revolution originated in the Low Countries. One reason for early Dutch leadership in farming was that the area was one of the most densely populated in Europe. The Dutch were forced at an early date to seek maximum yields from their land and to increase the cultivated area through the steady draining of marshes and swamps. As the urban population of Amsterdam grew with its rise as an international trading hub, Dutch peasants found a huge market for their surplus crops. Each agricultural region specialized in what it did best. Thus the Low Countries became "the Mecca of foreign agricultural experts who came . . . to see Flemish agriculture with their own eyes, to write about it and to propagate its methods in their home lands."[1]

The English were the best students. In the first half of the seventeenth century Dutch experts made a great contribution to draining the extensive marshes, or fens, of wet and rainy England. Swampy wilderness was converted into thousands of acres of some of the most fertile land in England.

Jethro Tull (1674–1741), part crank and part genius, was an important English innovator. A true son of the early Enlightenment, Tull adopted a critical attitude toward accepted ideas about farming and tried to develop better methods through empirical research. He was especially enthusiastic about using horses, rather than slower-moving oxen, for plowing. He also advocated sowing seed with drilling equipment rather than scattering it by hand. Drilling distributed seed in an even manner and at the proper depth. Selective breeding of ordinary livestock was another marked improvement over the haphazard old pattern.

By the mid-eighteenth century English agriculture was in the process of a long but radical transformation. The eventual result was that by 1870 English farmers

proletarianization The transformation of large numbers of small peasant farmers into landless rural wage earners.

Section Review

- European economies were agrarian; low crop yields in years of poor climate resulted in famine, disease, and death.

- The agricultural revolution involved the gradual elimination of the practice of leaving land fallow and the development of crop rotation patterns that allowed crops to restore nutrients to the soil.

- Enclosure meant fencing in fields to farm more effectively, but most peasants opposed it and only the Low Countries and England used it extensively.

- Enclosure and the new methods of farming increased production but led to an estate agricultural system and proletarianization, changing peasant farmers into landless laborers.

were producing 300 percent more food than they had produced in 1700, although the number of people working the land had increased by only 14 percent. This great surge of agricultural production provided food for England's rapidly growing urban population. Growth in production was achieved in part by land enclosures. About half the farmland in England was enclosed through private initiatives prior to 1700; in the eighteenth century, a series of acts of Parliament enclosed most of the remaining common land.

The eighteenth-century enclosure movement marked the completion of two major historical developments in England—the rise of market-oriented estate agriculture and the emergence of a landless rural proletariat. By 1815 a tiny minority of wealthy English (and Scottish) landowners held most of the land and pursued profits aggressively, leasing their holdings to middle-sized farmers, who relied on landless laborers for their workforce. These landless laborers usually worked from dawn to dusk, six days a week, all year long. Moreover, landless laborers had lost that bit of independence and self-respect that common rights had provided and were completely dependent on cash wages. In no other European country had this **proletarianization** (proh-le-TAIR-ee-uh-nize-ay-shun)—this transformation of large numbers of small peasant farmers into landless rural wage earners—gone so far. And England's village poor found the cost of change heavy and unjust.

The Beginning of the Population Explosion

Why did European population rise dramatically in the eighteenth century?

Another factor that affected the existing order of life and forced economic changes in the eighteenth century was the beginning of the "population explosion." Explosive growth continued in Europe until the twentieth century, by which time it was affecting non-Western areas of the globe. What were the causes of this new population growth?

A common misperception holds that the population of Europe was always rising quickly. On the contrary, until 1700 the total population of Europe grew slowly much of the time, and it followed an irregular cyclical pattern (see Figure 19.1). The population dipped after 1350 as a result of the Black Death and, after recovering, population growth slowed and dipped again in the seventeenth century. Famine, epidemic disease, and war ravaged Europe during that century, as we have seen. There were, of course, some exceptions. Areas such as Russia and colonial New England, where there was a great deal of frontier to be settled, experienced population growth.

FIGURE 19.1   The Growth of Population in England, 1000–1800

England is a good example of both the uneven increase of European population before 1700 and the third great surge of growth, which began in the eighteenth century. (*Source:* "Long-Term Population Trends in England and Wales, 1000–1800," from E. A. Wrigley, *Population and History.* Copyright © 1969. Reprinted by permission of the author.)

In the eighteenth century the population of Europe began to grow markedly. This increase in numbers occurred in all areas of Europe, western and eastern, northern and southern, dynamic and stagnant. Growth was especially dramatic after about 1750 (see Figure 19.2).

What caused this population growth? In some areas women had more babies than before because new opportunities for employment in rural industry allowed them to marry at an earlier age. But the basic cause for Europe as a whole was a decline in mortality—fewer deaths.

The bubonic plague mysteriously disappeared. Following the Black Death in the fourteenth century, plagues had remained part of the European experience, striking again and again with savage force, particularly in towns. As late as 1720 a ship from Syria and the Levant brought the disease to Marseilles, killing up to one hundred thousand in the city and surrounding region. By 1722 the epidemic had passed, and that was the last time plague fell on western and central Europe. Exactly why plague disappeared is unknown. Stricter measures of quarantine in Mediterranean ports and along the Austrian border with Turkey helped by carefully isolating human carriers of plague. Chance and plain good luck were probably just as important.

Advances in medical knowledge did not contribute much to reducing the death rate in the eighteenth century. The most important advance in preventive medicine in this period was inoculation against smallpox, and this great improvement was long confined mainly to England, probably doing little to reduce deaths throughout Europe until the latter part of the century. However, improvements in the water supply and sewerage, which were frequently promoted by strong absolutist monarchies, resulted in somewhat better public health and helped reduce such diseases as typhoid and typhus in some urban areas of western Europe. Improvements in water supply and the drainage of swamps also reduced Europe's large insect population. Flies and mosquitoes played a major role in spreading diseases, especially those striking children and young adults. Thus early public health measures helped the decline in mortality that began with the disappearance of plague and continued into the early nineteenth century.

Human beings also became more successful in their efforts to safeguard the supply of food. The eighteenth century was a time of considerable canal and road building in western Europe. These advances in transportation, which were also among the more positive aspects of strong absolutist states, lessened the impact of local crop failure and famine. Emergency supplies could be brought in, and localized starvation became less frequent. Wars became more gentlemanly and less destructive than in the seventeenth century and spread fewer epidemics. New foods, particularly the potato from South America, were introduced. In short, population grew in the eighteenth century primarily because years of abnormal death rates were less catastrophic. Famines, epidemics, and wars continued to occur, but their severity moderated.

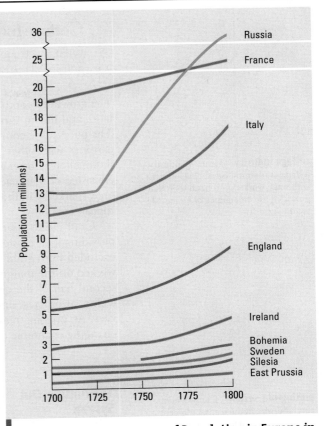

FIGURE 19.2   The Increase of Population in Europe in the Eighteenth Century
France's large population continued to support French political and intellectual leadership. Russia emerged as Europe's most populous state because natural increase was complemented by growth from territorial expansion.

Section Review

- The European population fell in the seventeenth century from famine, disease, and war, but in the eighteenth century it began to grow steadily, primarily due to a decline in mortality.

- The disappearance of epidemic disease and improvements in water supply and sewerage contributed to improved public health.

- Swamp drainage decreased the insect population and thus the diseases they caused; improved methods of food storage and transportation as well as less destructive warfare meant fewer deaths.

Cottage Industry and Urban Guilds

What is cottage industry, and how did it contribute to Europe's economic and social transformation?

The growth of population increased the number of rural workers with little or no land, and this in turn contributed to the development of industry in rural areas. The poor in the countryside increasingly needed to supplement their agricultural earnings with other types of work, and urban capitalists were eager to employ them, often at lower wages than urban workers were paid. **Cottage industry,** which consisted of manufacturing with hand tools in peasant cottages and work sheds, grew markedly in the eighteenth century and became a crucial feature of the European economy.

cottage industry Domestic industry; a stage of rural industrial development with wage workers and hand tools that preceded the emergence of large-scale factory industry.

Craft guilds (gildz) continued to dominate production in towns and cities, providing their masters with economic privileges as well as a social identity. Those excluded from guild membership—women, day laborers, Jews, and foreigners—worked on the margins of the urban economy. Critics attacked the guilds in the second half of the eighteenth century as outmoded institutions that obstructed technical progress and innovation. Until recently, most historians repeated that view. An ongoing reassessment of guilds now emphasizes their ability to adapt to changing economic circumstances.

The Putting-Out System

putting-out system The system of rural industry in the eighteenth century in which a merchant loaned raw materials to cottage workers who processed them and returned the finished products to the merchant.

Cottage industry was often organized through the **putting-out system.** The two main participants in the putting-out system were the merchant capitalist and the rural worker. The merchant loaned, or "put out," raw materials to cottage workers who processed the raw materials in their own homes and returned the finished products to the merchant. There were many variations on this basic relationship. Sometimes rural workers bought their own raw materials and worked as independent producers before they sold to the merchant. Sometimes whole families were involved in domestic industry; at other times the tasks were closely associated with one gender. Sometimes several workers toiled together to perform a complicated process in a workshop outside the home.

As industries grew in scale and complexity, production was often broken into many stages. For example, a merchant would provide raw wool to one group of workers for spinning into thread. He would then pass the thread to another group of workers to be bleached, to another for dying, and to another for weaving into cloth. The merchant paid outworkers by the piece and proceeded to sell the finished product to regional, national, or international markets.

The putting-out system grew because it had competitive advantages. Labor costs were cheaper in the countryside, where underemployed peasants were willing to work for less than their guild counterparts. Because they did not operate within guild guidelines, merchants and workers were able to experiment with procedures as they saw fit. While the goods that non-guild workers produced were not of exceptional quality, they were acceptable for everyday use. Textiles; all manner of knives, forks, and housewares; buttons and gloves; and clocks could be produced quite satisfactorily in the countryside.

Rural manufacturing did not spread across Europe at an even rate. It developed most successfully in England, particularly for the spinning and weaving of woolen cloth. By 1500 half of England's textiles were being produced in the countryside. By 1700 English industry was generally more rural than urban and heavily reliant on the putting-out system. Most continental countries, with the exception of Flanders and the Netherlands, developed rural industry more slowly. The latter part of the eighteenth century witnessed a remarkable expansion of rural industry in certain densely populated regions of continental Europe (see Map 19.1).

The Textile Industry

Until the nineteenth century, the industry that employed the most people in Europe was textiles. The making of linen, woolen, and eventually cotton cloth was the typical activity of cottage workers engaged in the putting-out system. A look inside the cottage of the English weaver illustrates a way of life as well as an economic system.

MAPPING THE PAST

MAP 19.1   Industry and Population in Eighteenth-Century Europe

The growth of cottage manufacturing in rural areas helped country people increase their income and contributed to population growth. The putting-out system began in England, and much of the work was in the textile industry. Cottage industry was also strong in the Low Countries—modern-day Belgium and Holland. **[1]** What types of textiles were produced in Europe? How would you account for the distribution of each type of cloth across Europe? **[2]** What was the relationship between population density and the growth of textile production? Was this a fixed or variable relationship? What geographic characteristics seem to have played a role in encouraging this industry? **[3]** Did metal production draw on different demographic and geographic conditions? Why do you think this was the case?

The Weaver's Repose

This painting by Decker Cornelis Gerritz (1594–1637) captures the pleasure of release from long hours of toil in cottage industry. The loom realistically dominates the cramped living space and the family's modest possessions. (Musées Royaux des Beaux-Arts, Brussels. Copyright A.C.I.)

The rural worker lived in a small cottage with tiny windows and little space. Indeed, the worker's cottage was often a single room that served as workshop, kitchen, and bedroom. There were only a few pieces of furniture, of which the weaver's loom was by far the largest and most important.

Handloom weaving was a family enterprise. All members of the family helped in the work, so that "every person from seven to eighty (who retained their sight and who could move their hands) could earn their bread," as one eighteenth-century English observer put it.[2] Operating the loom was considered a man's job, reserved for the male head of the family. Women and children worked at auxiliary tasks, such as winding threads on bobbins and mounting the threads on the frame.

There was always a serious imbalance in textile manufacture before mechanization: the work of four or five spinners was needed to keep one weaver steadily employed. Since the weaver's family usually could not produce enough thread, alternate sources of labor were needed. Merchants turned to the wives and daughters of agricultural workers, who took on spinning work in their spare time. Many widows and single women also became "spinsters," so many in fact that the word became a synonym for an unmarried woman. (In other parts of Europe, such as the Rhineland, spinning employed whole families and was not reserved for women.) As the industry expanded and merchants covered ever greater distances in search of workers, they sometimes turned to local shopkeepers to manage the spinners in their villages.

Conditions were particularly hard for female workers. While men could earn decent wages through long hours of arduous labor, women's wages were always terribly low. In the Yorkshire wool industry, a male wool comber earned a good wage of twelve shillings or more a week, while a spinner could hope for only three-and-a-half shillings.[3] A single or widowed spinner faced a desperate struggle against poverty. Any period of illness or unemployment could spell disaster for her and any dependent children.

Relations between workers and employers were often marked by sharp conflict. There were constant disputes over the weights of materials and the quality of finished work. Moreover, the pace of work depended on the agricultural calendar. In spring and late summer, planting and haymaking occupied all hands in the rural village, leading to shortages in the supply of thread. Merchants, whose livelihood depended on their ability to meet orders on time, bitterly resented their lack of control over rural labor. They accused workers—especially female spinners—of laziness, intemperance, and immorality. If workers failed to produce enough thread, they reasoned, it must be because their wages were too high and they had little incentive to work. Merchants thus insisted on maintaining the lowest possible wages to force the "idle" poor into productive labor. They also successfully lobbied for new police powers over workers. Imprisonment and public whipping became common punishments for pilfering small amounts of yarn or cloth. For poor workers, their right to hold onto the bits and pieces left over in the production process was akin to the traditional peasant right of gleaning in common lands.

Urban Guilds

The high point of the **guild system** in most of Europe occurred in the seventeenth and eighteenth centuries, rather than in the High Middle Ages as previously believed. Guilds grew in number in cities and towns across Europe during this period. In Louis XIV's France, for example, finance minister Jean-Baptiste Colbert revived the urban guilds and used them to encourage high-quality production and to collect taxes. The number of guilds in the city of Paris grew from 60 in 1672 to 129 in 1691.

Guild masters occupied the summit of the world of work. Each guild received a detailed set of privileges from the Crown, including exclusive rights to produce and sell certain goods, access to restricted markets in raw materials, and the rights to train apprentices, hire workers, and open shops. Any individual who violated these monopolies could be prosecuted. Guilds also served social and religious functions, providing a locus of sociability and group identity to the urban middle class.

To ensure that there was enough work to go around, guilds jealously restricted their membership to local men who were good Christians, had several years of work experience, paid stiff membership fees, and completed a masterpiece. They also favored family connections. A master's sons enjoyed automatic access to their father's guild, while outsiders were often barred from entering. In the 1720s, Parisian guild masters numbered only about thirty-five thousand in a population of five hundred thousand. Most men and women worked in non-guild trades, as domestic servants, as manual laborers, and as vendors of food and other small goods.

Critics of guilds in France derided them as outmoded and exclusionary institutions that obstructed technical innovation and progress. Indeed, French guilds were abolished by the Revolution of the late eighteenth century. (See the feature "Listening to the Past: The Debate over the Guilds" on pages 508–509.) Many historians have repeated that charge. More recent scholarship, however, has emphasized the flexibility and adaptability of the guild system and its vitality through the eighteenth century. Guild masters adopted new technologies and found creative ways to circumvent impractical rules. For many merchants and artisans, economic regulation did not hinder commerce but instead fostered the confidence necessary to stimulate it. In an economy where buyers' and sellers' access to information was so limited, regulation helped each side trust in the other's good faith.

During the eighteenth century some guilds grew more accessible to women. This was particularly the case in dressmaking; given the great increase in textile production, more hands were needed to fashion clothing for urban elites. In 1675 Colbert granted seamstresses a new all-female guild in Paris, and soon seamstresses joined tailors' guilds in parts of France, England, and the Netherlands. In the late seventeenth century new vocational training programs were established for poor girls in many European cities, mostly in needlework. There is also evidence that

guild system The organization of artisanal production into trade-based associations, or guilds, each of which received a monopoly over their trade and the right to train apprentices and hire workers; the system was abolished in France in 1791 but persisted into the nineteenth century in other parts of Europe.

The Linen Industry in Ireland Many steps went into making textiles. Here the women are beating away the woody part of the flax plant so that the man can comb out the soft part. The combed fibers will then be spun into thread and woven into cloth by this family enterprise. The increased labor of women and girls in the late seventeenth century helped produce an "industrious revolution." (Victoria and Albert Museum London/Eileen Tweedy/The Art Archive)

more women were hired as skilled workers by male guilds, often in defiance of official statutes.

While many artisans welcomed the economic liberalization that followed the French Revolution, some continued to espouse the ideals of the guilds. Because they had always been semi-clandestine, journeymen's associations frequently survived into the nineteenth century. They espoused the values of hand craftsmanship and limited competition, in contrast to the proletarianization and loss of skills endured in mechanized production. Nevertheless, by the middle of the nineteenth century economic deregulation was championed by most European governments and elites.

industrious revolution The shift that occurred as families in northwestern Europe worked harder and longer hours and focused on earning wages instead of producing goods for household consumption, especially among women and children; this reduced families' economic self-sufficiency but increased their ability to purchase consumer goods.

The Industrious Revolution

One scholar has used the term **industrious revolution** to describe the social and economic changes taking place in Europe in the late seventeenth and early eighteenth centuries.[4] This occurred as households in northwestern Europe reduced leisure time, stepped up the pace of work, and, most importantly, redirected the labor of women and children away from the production of goods for household consumption and toward wage work. By working harder and increasing the number of wageworkers, households could purchase more goods, even in a time of stagnant or falling real wages.

New sources and patterns of labor established important foundations for the Industrial Revolution of the late eighteenth and nineteenth centuries. They created households in which all members worked for wages rather than in a united family business and in which consumption relied on market-produced rather than homemade goods. It was not until the mid-nineteenth century, with rising industrial wages, that a new model emerged in which the male "breadwinner" was expected to earn enough to support the whole family and women and children were relegated back to the domestic sphere. With 77 percent of U.S. women between ages twenty-five and fifty-four in the workforce in the year 2000, today's world is experiencing a sec-

Section Review

- The increase of landless rural workers led to cottage industries where peasants manufactured products in their homes for urban capitalists.

- Urban merchants "put out" raw materials, which the cottage industry workers processed and returned to the merchants, who then sold the finished product.

- The textile industry employed the most people in Europe and was typically a family enterprise: the men wove while women and children spun the wool and did other tasks; wages were low and working conditions hard.

- Urban guild masters were at the top of the work world, enjoying exclusive rights to sell and produce some goods while the guilds served a social and religious function to their members.

- The "industrious revolution" describes a shift whereby families in northwestern Europe worked harder and longer hours and focused on earning wages instead of producing goods for household consumption, especially among women and children; this reduced their economic self-sufficiency but increased their ability to purchase consumer goods.

ond industrious revolution in a similar climate of stagnant wages and increased demand for consumer goods.

Building the Global Economy

How did colonial markets boost Europe's economic and social development, and what conflicts and adversity did world trade entail?

In addition to agricultural improvement, a decline in mortality, and growing cottage industry, the expansion of Europe in the eighteenth century was characterized by the growth of world trade. Spain and Portugal revitalized their empires and began drawing more wealth from renewed development. Yet once again the countries of northwestern Europe—the Netherlands, France, and above all Great Britain—benefited most. Great Britain, which was formed in 1707 by the union of England and Scotland into a single kingdom, gradually became the leading maritime power. Thus the British played the critical role in building a fairly unified Atlantic economy that provided remarkable opportunities for them and their colonists. They also conducted ruthless competition with France and the Netherlands for trade and territory in Asia.

Mercantilism and Colonial Wars

Britain's commercial leadership in the eighteenth century had its origins in the mercantilism of the seventeenth century (see page 409). Mercantilism aimed particularly at creating a favorable balance of foreign trade in order to increase a country's stock of gold. A country's gold holdings served as an all-important treasure chest that could be opened periodically to pay for war in a violent age.

Beginning with Oliver Cromwell in 1651, the English government enacted a series of laws designed to build English power and wealth under the mercantile system. Known as the **Navigation Acts,** these laws controlled the import of goods to Britain and British colonies. The most significant of these acts required the colonists to ship their products on British (or American) ships and to buy almost all European goods from Britain. It was believed that these economic regulations would help British merchants and workers as well as colonial plantation owners and farmers; and the emerging British Empire would develop a shipping industry with a large number of experienced seamen who could serve when necessary in the Royal Navy.

The Navigation Acts were a form of economic warfare. Their initial target was the Dutch, who were far ahead of the English in shipping and foreign trade in the mid-seventeenth century (see page 426). In conjunction with three Anglo-Dutch wars between 1652 and 1674, the Navigation Acts seriously damaged Dutch shipping and commerce. The British seized the thriving Dutch colony of New Amsterdam in 1664 and renamed it "New York." By the late seventeenth century the Netherlands was falling behind England in shipping, trade, and colonies.

Thereafter France stood clearly as England's most serious rival in the competition for overseas empire. Rich in natural resources, with a population three or four times that of England, and allied with Spain, continental Europe's leading military power was already building a powerful fleet and a worldwide system of rigidly monopolized colonial trade. Thus from 1701 to 1763 Britain and France were locked in a series of wars to decide, in part, which nation would become the leading maritime power and claim the profits of Europe's overseas expansion (see Map 19.2).

Navigation Acts A series of English laws that controlled the import of goods to Britain and British colonies.

Plantation zone

NORTH AMERICA
Azores
Madeira Is.
Canary Is.
Mexico City
Cuba
Jamaica
Puerto Rico
Hispaniola
Trinidad
Cape Verde Is.
Panama
Quito
PERU
Lima
SOUTH AMERICA
Potosi
BRAZIL
PACIFIC OCEAN
Santiago
Rio de Janeiro
Buenos Aires
ATLANTIC OCEAN
0   2,000 Km.
0   2,000 Mi.
Strait of Magellan
Cape Horn
N

NORTH AMERICA
Silver (to the Philippines)
Silks, spices porcelain
ARCTIC OCEAN
Hudson Bay
MEXICO
LOUISIANA
RUPERT'S LAND
Mississippi R.
NEW FRANCE
QUEBEC
Acapulco
Veracruz
THIRTEEN COLONIES
NOVA SCOTIA (ACADIA) (To Gr. Br., 1713)
NEWFOUNDLAND (To Gr. Br., 1713)
FLORIDA
Tobacco
Furs
GREAT BRITAIN
ASIA
EUROPE
Havana
Silver
Colonial products
NETHERLANDS
CUBA
JAMAICA
Sugar
FRANCE
Porto Bello
Hispaniola
SAINT-DOMINGUE (Fr.)
SANTO DOMINGO (Sp.)
Sugar
Manufactured goods
SPAIN
PORTUGAL
Silver
Guadeloupe (Fr.)
Martinique (Fr.)
Barbados (Gr. Br.)
Canary Is. (Spain)
Lima
NEW GRANADA
DUTCH GUIANA
FRENCH GUIANA
NORTH ATLANTIC OCEAN
AFRICA
PERU
Amazon R.
Sugar
Manufactured goods
Gold
Cape Verde Is. (Port.)
Cape Verde
Slave Coast
Gold Coast
Silver
SOUTH AMERICA
BRAZIL
Slaves
ANGOLA
Buenos Aires
SOUTH ATLANTIC OCEAN

Great Britain
France
Portugal
Spain
Netherlands
Trade from Europe
Trade from Africa
Trade from Americas
Trade from Asia

MAP 19.2   The Atlantic Economy in 1701

The growth of trade encouraged both economic development and military conflict in the Atlantic basin. Four continents were linked together by the exchange of goods and slaves.

The first round was the War of the Spanish Succession (see page 411), which started when Louis XIV of France accepted the Spanish crown willed to his grandson. Besides upsetting the continental balance of power, a union of France and Spain threatened to encircle and destroy the British colonies in North America (see Map 19.2). Defeated by a great coalition of states after twelve years of fighting, Louis XIV was forced in the Peace of Utrecht (YOO-trekt) (1713) to cede Newfoundland, Nova Scotia, and the Hudson Bay territory to Britain. Spain was compelled to give Britain control of its West African slave trade—the so-called *asiento* (a-SYEN-toh)—and to let Britain send one ship of merchandise into the Spanish colonies annually through Porto Bello on the Isthmus of Panama. France was still a mighty competitor, however. The War of the Austrian Succession (1740–1748) over Maria Theresa's Austrian empire (see page 475) brought France and England back into conflict. But the Seven Years' War (1756–1763) marked the decisive round in the Franco-British competition for colonial empire.

The fighting began in North America. The population of New France was centered in Quebec and along the St. Lawrence River, but French soldiers and Canadian fur traders had also built forts and trading posts along the Great Lakes, through the Ohio country, and down the Mississippi to New Orleans. Allied with many Native American tribes, the French built more forts in 1753 in what is now western Pennsylvania to protect their claims. The following year a Virginia force attacked a small group of French soldiers, and soon the war to conquer Canada was on.

French and Canadian forces under the experienced marquis de Montcalm fought well and scored major victories until 1758. Then, led by their new chief minister, William Pitt, the British diverted men and money from the war in Europe and used their superior sea power to destroy the French fleet and choke off French commerce around the world. In 1759 a combined British naval and land force defeated Montcalm's army in a dramatic battle that sealed the fate of France in North America.

British victory on all colonial fronts was ratified in the **Treaty of Paris** (1763), ending the Seven Years' War in Europe and the colonies. Canada and all French territory east of the Mississippi River passed to Britain, and France ceded Louisiana to Spain as compensation for Spain's loss of Florida to Britain. France also gave up most of its holdings in India, opening the way to British dominance on the subcontinent. By 1763 Britain had realized its goal of monopolizing a vast trading and colonial empire.

In the eighteenth century, stimulated by trade and empire building, London grew into the West's largest and richest city. (See the feature "Images in Society: London: The Remaking of a Great City" on pages 498–499.) Above all, the rapidly growing and increasingly wealthy agricultural populations of the mainland colonies of North America provided an expanding market for English manufactured goods. Foreign trade became the bread and butter of some industries; for example, by 1750 half the nails made in England were going to the colonies. Thus, the mercantilist system achieved remarkable success for England in the eighteenth century, and by the 1770s England stood on the threshold of the epoch-making industrial changes that are described in Chapter 22.

Despite their losses, the French still profited enormously from colonial trade. The colonies of Saint Domingue (san do-MANG) (modern-day Haiti) and Martinique and Guadeloupe (which remain French departments today) provided immense fortunes in sugar and coffee plantations and slave trading during the second half of the eighteenth century. By 1789 the population of Saint Domingue included five hundred thousand slaves whose labor had allowed the colony to

Treaty of Paris The treaty that ended the Seven Years' War in Europe and the colonies in 1763 and ratified British victory on all colonial fronts.

Images in Society

London: The Remaking of a Great City

The imperial capital and intercontinental trade center of London dominated Britain and astonished the visitor. Equal in population to Paris with four hundred thousand inhabitants in 1650, the super city of the West grew to nine hundred thousand in 1801, while second-place Paris had six hundred thousand. And as London grew, its citizens created a new urban landscape and style of living.

Image 1 shows the "true profile" of London and its built environment as viewed from the south before the Great Fire of 1666, which raged for four days and destroyed about 80 percent of the old, predominately wooden central city. With the River Thames flowing eastward toward the sea, one sees from left to right pre-fire St. Paul's Cathedral, London Bridge crowded with houses, ships at the wharves, and the medieval Tower of London. Clearly visible in the distance are the open fields of the large estates surrounding London, while beyond the view on the left are the royal palace and adjacent government buildings. Also missing is the famous London smog, the combination of fog and smoke from coal-burning fireplaces that already polluted the metropolis. How would you characterize pre-fire London?

Reconstruction proceeded quickly after the Great Fire so that people could regain shelter and employment. Brick construction was made mandatory to prevent fire, but only a few streets were straightened or widened. Thus social classes remained packed together in the rebuilt city. The rich merchant family in a first-class city residence (Image 2), built in the 1670s and still standing in 1939, shared a tiny courtyard and constantly rubbed shoulders with poor and middling people in everyday life.

As London rebuilt and kept growing, big noble landowners followed two earlier examples and sought to increase their incomes by setting up residential developments on their estates west of the city. A landowner would lay out a square with streets and building lots, which he or she would lease to speculative builders who put up fine houses for sale or rent. Soho Square, first laid out in the 1670s and shown in Image 3 as it appeared in 1731, was fairly typical. The spacious square with its gated park is

IMAGE 1 London Before the Great Fire (Hulton Archive/Getty Images)

IMAGE 2 Merchant Family's Residence (built 1670–1680)
(English Heritage/NMR)

IMAGE 3 Soho Square, 1731 (Private Collection/The Stapleton Collection/The Bridgeman Art Library)

IMAGE 4 Bloomsbury Square, 1787 (HarperCollins Publishers/The Art Archive)

surrounded by three-story row houses set on deep, narrow lots. Set in the country but close to the city, a square like Soho was a kind of elegant "village" with restrictive building codes that catered to aristocrats, officials, and successful professionals who were served by artisans and shopkeepers living in alleys and side streets. Do you see a difference between the houses on the square and on the street behind? How would you compare Soho Square with the hills in the distance and with the old London of Images 1 and 2? The classy, new area, known as the West End, contrasted sharply with the shoddy rentals and makeshift shacks of laborers and sailors in the mushrooming East End, which artists rarely painted. Thus residential segregation by income level increased substantially in eighteenth-century London.

As the suburban villages grew and gradually merged together, the West End increasingly attracted the well-to-do from all over England. Rural landowners and provincial notables came for the social season from October to May. Operating out of comfortable second homes purchased or rented in the West End, they played the national market

for mortgages, marriages, and recreation. Image 4, showing classy Bloomsbury Square in 1787 and the original country mansion of the enterprising noble developer, provides a glimpse into this well-born culture. How does Image 4 complement Image 3? What message is the artist conveying with the milkmaid and her cows? Some historians believe that London's West End was an important social innovation. Reconsidering these images, do you agree?

become the world's leading producer of coffee and sugar. It was the most profitable plantation colony in the New World and the one that consumed the greatest number of slaves.[5] The wealth generated from colonial trade fostered the confidence of the merchant classes in Paris, Bordeaux, and other large cities, and merchants soon joined other elite groups clamoring for more political responsibility.

The third major player in the Atlantic economy, Spain, saw its colonial fortunes improve during the eighteenth century. Not only did it gain Louisiana from France in 1763, but its influence expanded westward all the way to northern California through the efforts of Spanish missionaries and ranchers. Its mercantilist goals were boosted by a recovery in silver production, which had dropped significantly in the seventeenth century.

Silver mining also stimulated food production for the mining camps, and wealthy Spanish landowners developed a system of **debt peonage** (PEE-uh-nij) to keep indigenous workers on their estates. Under this system, which was similar to serfdom, a planter or rancher would keep workers in perpetual debt bondage by advancing them food, shelter, and a little money.

The profits from mining and agriculture gave the **Creoles** (KREE-ohlz)—people of Spanish blood born in America—the means to purchase more and more European luxuries and manufactured goods. A class of wealthy Creole merchants

debt peonage A system that allowed a planter or rancher to keep his workers or slaves in perpetual debt bondage by periodically advancing food, shelter, and a little money; it was a form of serfdom.

Creoles People of Spanish blood born in America.

mestizo Spanish term for a person of mixed racial origins, especially Native American and European.

Forming the Mexican People

It was not uncommon for Creole men in Latin America to take Indian wives, with the result that roughly 30 percent of the population was racially mixed by the end of the colonial period. This painting, by an unknown eighteenth-century artist, shows the union of a Spanish man and a Native American woman that has produced a racially mixed **mestizo** (mess-TEE-zoh) child on the left, and a group that features a mestizo woman and a Spaniard with their little daughter on the right. Paintings such as this reflect contemporary fascination with the spectrum of racial difference produced in the colonies. (Private Collection, Mexico) arose to handle this flourishing trade, which often relied on smuggled goods from Great Britain. The Creoles strove to become a genuine European aristocracy and looked upon the agents sent by Spain as meddlesome rivals.

The Atlantic Slave Trade

As Britain built its empire in North America, it secured an important outlet for surplus population, so that migration abroad limited poverty at home. The settlers also benefited, for they enjoyed privileged access to virtually free and unlimited land. And unlike the great majority of European peasants, American farmers kept most of what they produced. Indeed, on the eve of the American Revolution white men and women in the mainland British colonies had one of the highest living standards in the world.[6] Cheap land and the tremendous demand for scarce labor also fostered the growth of slavery in the British colonies. The Spanish and the Portuguese had first brought African slaves to the Americas in the sixteenth century. In the seventeenth century the Dutch aggressively followed their example and transported thousands of Africans first to Brazil and then to the Caribbean to work on highly profitable sugar plantations. The English established their own Caribbean sugar plantations, and, in the eighteenth century, tobacco planters in Virginia and Maryland embarked on plantation agriculture using slave labor.

Taken to the Americas in chains, Africans made a decisive contribution to the development of the Atlantic economy. Above all, the labor of enslaved Africans made possible large-scale production of valuable commodities for sale in Europe. Indeed, an important recent study concludes that in the years from 1761 to 1800 Africans and their descendants in Brazil, Spanish America, the Caribbean, and Britain's mainland slave colonies accounted for more than *four-fifths* of all the commodities produced in the Americas for sale in the Atlantic economy.[7] It was this flood of ever-cheaper sugar, coffee, tobacco, rice, and (in the nineteenth century) cotton that generated hard cash in the Americas—cash that paid for manufactured goods and services from Britain and Europe as well as for more slaves from Africa.

The forced migration of millions of Africans—cruel, unjust, and tragic—remained a key element in the Atlantic system and western European economic expansion throughout the eighteenth century. Indeed, the brutal **Atlantic slave trade** intensified dramatically after 1700 and especially after 1750. According to one authoritative estimate, European traders purchased and shipped over six million African slaves across the Atlantic between 1701 and 1800, fully 52 percent of the estimated total of almost 12 million Africans transported between 1450 and 1900.[8] In 1790, when the U.S. population was approaching 4 million, slaves accounted for almost 20 percent of the total.

Intensification of the slave trade resulted in fundamental changes in its organization. After 1700, as Britain became the undisputed leader in the slave trade, European governments and ship captains cut back on fighting among themselves and concentrated on commerce. They generally adopted the shore method of trading, which was less expensive than maintaining fortified trading posts. Thus European ships sent boats ashore or invited African dealers to bring traders and slaves out to their ships. This method allowed ships to move easily along the coast from market to market and to depart more quickly for the Americas.

Some African merchants and rulers who controlled exports profited from the greater demand for slaves, and some Africans secured foreign products that they found appealing because of price or quality. But generally such economic returns did not spread very far, and the negative consequences of the expanding slave trade

Atlantic slave trade The forced migration of Africans across the Atlantic for slave labor on plantations and in other industries; although many European countries participated, its peak was among the English in the eighteenth century and ultimately the trade involved almost twelve million Africans.

Slaves Harvesting Sugar Cane
In this 1828 print a long line of hard-working slaves systematically harvests the ripe cane on the island of Antigua, while on the right more slaves load cut cane into wagons for refining at the plantation's central crushing mill. The manager on horseback may be ordering the overseer to quicken the work pace, always brutal and unrelenting at harvest time. Slave labor made high-intensity capitalist production of sugar possible in the Americas. (John Carter Brown Library at Brown University)

predominated. Wars between Africans to obtain salable captives increased, and leaders purchased more arms and bought relatively fewer textiles and consumer goods. And while the population of Europe (and Asia) grew substantially in the eighteenth century, that of Africa stagnated or possibly declined.

Slaves were typically captives who had been taken in battles between African states, but as demand grew, slave dealers tried new approaches. Kidnappers seized and enslaved men and women like Olaudah Equiano (oh-LAU-duh ay-kwee-AHN-oh) and his sister, whose tragic separation, exile, and exploitation personified the full horror of the Atlantic slave trade. (See the feature "Individuals in Society: Olaudah Equiano.") Another approach was for African rulers to change the punishment for misdemeanors from fines to enslavement in order to generate more captives for sale.

Most Europeans did not personally witness the horrors of the slave trade between Africa and the Americas, and until 1700, and perhaps even 1750, they considered the African slave trade a legitimate business. But as details of the plight of slaves became known, a campaign to abolish slavery developed in Britain. Between 1788 and 1792, according to some recent scholarship, the abolition campaign grew into the first peaceful mass political movement based on the mobilization of public opinion in British history. British women played a critical role in this mass movement, denouncing the immorality of human bondage and stressing the cruel and sadistic treatment of female slaves and slave families. These attacks put the defenders of slavery on the defensive. In 1807 Parliament abolished the British

Individuals in Society

Olaudah Equiano

The slave trade was a mass migration involving millions of human beings. It was also the sum of individual lives spent partly or entirely in slavery. Although most of those lives remain hidden to us, Olaudah Equiano (1745–1797) is an important exception.

Equiano was born in Benin (modern Nigeria) of Ibo ethnicity. His father, one of the village elders (or chieftains), presided over a large household that included "many slaves," prisoners captured in local wars. All people, slave and free, shared in the cultivation of family lands. One day, when all the adults were in the fields, two strange men and a woman broke into the family compound, kidnapped the eleven-year-old boy and his sister, tied them up, and dragged them into the woods. Brother and sister were separated, and Olaudah was sold several times to various dealers before reaching the coast. As it took six months to walk there, his home must have been far inland.

The slave ship and the strange appearance of the white crew terrified the boy. Much worse was the long voyage from Benin to Barbados in the Caribbean, as Equiano later recounted. "The stench of the [ship's] hold . . . became absolutely pestilential . . . [and] brought on a sickness among the slaves, of which many died. . . . The shrieks of the women and the groans of the dying rendered the whole a scene of horror almost inconceivable." Placed on deck with the sick and dying, Equiano saw two and then three of his "enchained countrymen" escape somehow through the nettings and jump into the sea, "preferring death to such a life of misery."*

Equiano's new owner, an officer in the Royal Navy, took him to England and saw that the lad received some education. Engaged in bloody action in Europe for almost four years as a captain's boy in the Seven Years' War, Equiano hoped that his loyal service and Christian baptism would help secure his freedom. He also knew that slavery was generally illegal in England. But his master deceived him. Docking in London, he and his accomplices forced a protesting and heartbroken Equiano onto a ship bound for the Caribbean.

There he was sold to Robert King, a Quaker merchant from Philadelphia who dealt in sugar and rum.

Equiano developed his mathematical skills, worked hard to please as a clerk in King's warehouse, and became first mate on one of King's ships. Allowed to trade on the side for his own profit, Equiano amassed capital, repaid King his original purchase price, and received his deed of manumission at the age of twenty-one. King urged his talented former slave to stay on as a business partner, but Equiano hated the limitations and dangers of black freedom in the colonies—he was almost kidnapped back into slavery while loading a ship in Georgia—and could think only of England. Settling in London, Equiano studied, worked as a hairdresser, and went to sea periodically as a merchant seaman. He developed his ardent Christian faith and became a leading member of London's sizable black community.

Olaudah Equiano, in an engraving from his autobiography. (National Portrait Gallery, Smithsonian Institution/Art Resource, NY)

Equiano loathed the brutal slavery and the vicious exploitation that he saw in the West Indies and Britain's mainland colonies. A complex and sophisticated man, he also respected the integrity of Robert King and admired British navigational and industrial technologies. He encountered white oppressors and made white friends. He once described himself as "almost an Englishman." In the 1780s he joined with white and black activists in the antislavery campaign and wrote *The Interesting Narrative of the Life of Olaudah Equiano Written by Himself*, a well-documented autobiographical indictment of slavery. Above all, he urged Christians to live by the principles they professed and to treat Africans equally as free human beings and children of God. With the success of his widely read book, he carried his message to large audiences across Britain and Ireland and inspired the growing movement to abolish slavery.

Questions for Analysis

1. What aspects of Olaudah Equiano's life as a slave were typical? What aspects were atypical?
2. Describe Equiano's culture and personality. What aspects are most striking? Why?

---

* Olaudah Equiano, *The Interesting Narrative of the Life of Olaudah Equiano Written by Himself*, ed. with an introduction by Robert J. Allison (Boston: Bedford Books, 1995), pp. 56–57. Recent scholarship has re-examined Equiano's life and thrown some details of his identity into question.

slave trade, although slavery continued in British colonies and the Americas for years.

Trade and Empire in Asia

As the Atlantic economy took shape, Europeans continued to vie for dominance in the Asian trade. The Dutch, who had dominated as a supplier of Asian goods to Europeans in the seventeenth century, failed to diversify to meet changing consumption patterns. Spices continued to comprise much of its shipping, despite their declining importance in the European diet. Fierce competition from its main rival, the English East India Company (est. 1600), also severely undercut Dutch trade.

Britain initially struggled for a foothold in Asia. With the Dutch monopolizing the Indian Ocean, the British focused on India, where they were minor players throughout the seventeenth century. The English East India Company relied on trade concessions from the powerful Mughal emperor, who granted only piecemeal access to the subcontinent. Finally, in 1716 the Mughals conceded empire-

The British in India (ca. 1785)
This Indian miniature shows (*center*) the wife of a British officer attended by many Indian servants. A British merchant (*left*) awaits her attention. The picture reflects the luxurious lifestyle of the British elite in India; many returned home with colossal fortunes. (Scala/Art Resource, NY)

wide trading privileges. To further their economic interests, British company agents increasingly intervened in local affairs and made alliances or waged war against Indian princes. However, they faced competition from France, which also had company agents and troops stationed on the subcontinent. Forces from the two sides clashed in the 1740s.

With the Treaty of Paris that ended the Seven Years' War in 1763 (page 497), France lost its possessions in India. British ascendancy in India subsequently accelerated. In 1764 English East India Company forces defeated the Mughal emperor, leaving him on the throne as a ruler in title only. Robert Clive a company agent who had led its forces in battle, became the first British governor general of Bengal, in northeast India, with direct authority over the province. By the early 1800s the British had overcome vigorous Indian resistance to gain economic and political dominance of much of the subcontinent, and India was lauded as the "jewel" in the British Empire in the nineteenth century.

Adam Smith and Economic Liberalism

Although mercantilist policies strengthened European colonial empires in the eighteenth century, a strong reaction against mercantilism ultimately set in. Creole merchants chafed at regulations imposed from Madrid, while English merchants complained loudly about the trade monopoly enjoyed by the British East India Company. These independent merchants led the call for "free trade," borrowing from the ideas of Scottish Enlightenment philosopher Adam Smith (1723–1790), whose *Inquiry into the Nature and Causes of the Wealth of Nations* (1776) established the basis for modern economics.

Smith described eighteenth-century mercantilism as a combination of stifling government regulations and unfair privileges for state-approved monopolies and government favorites. Far preferable was free competition, which would best protect consumers from price gouging and give all citizens a fair and equal right to do what they did best. Fearful of political oppression, Smith argued that government should limit itself to "only three duties": it should provide a defense against foreign invasion, maintain civil order with courts and police protection, and sponsor certain indispensable public works and institutions that could never adequately profit private investors. He believed that the pursuit of self-interest in a competitive market would be sufficient to improve the living conditions of citizens.

In the nineteenth and twentieth centuries Smith was often seen as an advocate of unbridled capitalism, but his ideas were considerably more complex. In his own mind, Smith spoke for truth, not for special interests. Unlike many disgruntled merchant capitalists, he applauded the modest rise in real wages of British workers in the eighteenth century and went on to say that "No society can surely be flourishing and happy, of which the far greater part of the members are poor and miserable." He also deplored the deadening effects of the division of labor and called for government intervention to raise workers' living standards.

Smith's provocative work had a great international impact, going through eight editions in English and being translated into several languages within twenty years. It quickly emerged as the classic argument for **economic liberalism.**

economic liberalism Based on the writings of Adam Smith, a belief in free trade and competition. Smith argued that the invisible hand of free competition would benefit all individuals, rich and poor.

Section Review

- Britain imposed a form of economic warfare with the Navigation Acts, which required the transportation of British products on British ships.

- England went through a series of wars with the Dutch and then the French in the struggle for maritime supremacy and although Britain gained a trading monopoly and colonial empire, France and Spain continued to profit from their own colonial trade.

- The Atlantic slave trade grew enormously as colonial plantations used slaves to produce commodities for sale in Europe and although public outcry at its horrors led the British to end their involvement in the trade in 1807, slavery itself continued in the Americas and the British colonies.

- The Great Fire of 1666 destroyed much of London; reconstruction kept the social classes mixed in the old city but new suburbs created segregation by income level.

- The British East India Company vied with the French and the Dutch for trading dominance in Asia and emerged as dominant rulers within the Indian subcontinent.

- Adam Smith's writings gained international fame, promoting free trade in a competitive market, an arrangement he thought would protect consumers and benefit all citizens.

Chapter Review

What were the causes and effects of the agricultural revolution, and what nations led the way in these developments? (page 485)

While the European educated elite was developing a new view of the world in the eighteenth century, Europe as a whole was experiencing a gradual but far-reaching expansion. As agriculture began showing signs of modest improvement across the continent, first the Low Countries and then England launched changes that gradually revolutionized it. New crops and intensified crop rotation created new food sources for both people and livestock. Enclosure of common land allowed landowners to reap the fruits of agricultural innovation at the cost of excluding poor peasants from their traditional access to the land. The gap between wealthy landowner and landless poor stretched wider in this period.

Why did European population rise dramatically in the eighteenth century? (page 488)

For reasons historians do not yet understand, the recurring curse of bubonic plague disappeared. Less vulnerable to food shortages and free from the plague, the populations of all European countries grew significantly. During the eighteenth century the European population recovered from the stagnation and losses of the previous century to reach unprecedented new levels.

What is cottage industry, and how did it contribute to Europe's economic and social transformation? (page 490)

Population increases encouraged the growth of wage labor, cottage industry, and merchant capitalism. To escape the constraints of urban guilds, merchants transported production to the countryside. Peasant households set up industrial production within their cottages, allocating family members' labor during the slack seasons of agriculture or, in some cases, abandoning farming altogether for a new life of weaving or spinning. The spread of cottage industry was one sign of an "industrious revolution" that helped pave the path of the Industrial Revolution of the late eighteenth century. Women's labor was crucial to the spread of cottage industry and the renewed vitality of the urban trades.

How did colonial markets boost Europe's economic and social development, and what conflicts and adversity did world trade entail? (page 495)

The products of peasant industry were exported across Europe and even across the world. During the eighteenth century Europeans continued their overseas expansion, fighting for empire and profit and, in particular, consolidating their hold on the Americas. A revived Spain and its Latin American colonies participated fully in this expansion. As in agriculture and cottage industry, however, England and its empire proved most successful. The English concentrated much of the growing Atlantic trade in their hands, a development that challenged and enriched English industry and intensified interest in new methods of production and in an emerging economic liberalism. Thus, by the 1770s England was approaching an economic breakthrough as fully significant as the great political upheaval destined to develop shortly in neighboring France.

Key Terms

agricultural revolution (p. 486)
crop rotation (p. 486)
enclosure (p. 486)
proletarianization (p. 488)
cottage industry (p. 490)
putting-out system (p. 490)
guild system (p. 493)
industrious revolution (p. 494)
Navigation Acts (p. 495)
Treaty of Paris (p. 497)
debt peonage (p. 500)
Creoles (p. 500)
mestizo (p. 500)
Atlantic slave trade (p. 501)
economic liberalism (p. 505)

Notes

1. B. H. Slicher van Bath, *The Agrarian History of Western Europe*, A.D. 500–1850 (New York: St. Martin's Press, 1963), p. 240.
2. Quoted in I. Pinchbeck, *Women Workers and the Industrial Revolution, 1750–1850* (New York: F. S. Crofts, 1930), p. 113.
3. Richard J. Soderlund, " 'Intended as a Terror to the Idle and Profligate': Embezzlement and the Origins of Policing in the Yorkshire Worsted Industry, c. 1750–1777," *Journal of Social History* 31 (Spring 1998): 658.
4. Ibid. In addition, Jan de Vries, "The Industrious Revolution and the Industrious Revolution," *The Journal of Economic History* 54, 2 (June 1994): 249–270, discusses the second industrious revolution of the second half of the twentieth century.
5. Laurent Dubois and John D. Garrigus, *Slave Revolution in the Carribean, 1789–1904* (New York: Palgrave, 2006), p. 8.
6. G. Taylor, "America's Growth Before 1840," *Journal of Economic History* 24 (December 1970): 427–444.
7. J. Inikori, *Africans and the Industrial Revolution in England: A Study in International Trade and Economic Development* (Cambridge: Cambridge University Press, 2002), pp. 481–482.
8. P. E. Lovejoy, *Transformations in Slavery: A History of Slavery in Africa* (Cambridge: Cambridge University Press, 1983), p. 19.

To assess your mastery of this chapter, go to **bedfordstmartins.com/mckaywestbrief**

Listening to the Past

The Debate over the Guilds

Guilds, also known as trade corporations, claimed that their rules guaranteed fair wages, high-quality goods, and community values. However, both French philosophes and enlightened government officials increasingly disagreed. The following excerpt, from a 1776 law abolishing French guilds by the reform minister Jacques Turgot (tur-GOH), is an important example of the liberal critique in action. A vociferous response from the guilds led to the law's repeal only six months later. New guild regulations responded to some of the critiques, for example by allowing women to join all guilds. In 1791 French revolutionaries definitively abolished the guild system.

A German brush maker and guild member shows a customer his wares. (The Fotomas Index/The Bridgeman Art Library)

Edict Abolishing the Guilds in France

In nearly all the towns of our Kingdom the practice of different arts and crafts is concentrated in the hands of a small number of masters, united in a corporation, who alone have the exclusive right to manufacture and sell particular articles; so that those of our subjects who, through wish or necessity intend to practise in these fields, must have attained the mastership, to which they are admitted only after very long tests which are as difficult as they are useless, and after having satisfied rules or manifold exactions, which absorb part of the funds they need to set up in business or even to exist. . . .

God, in giving man needs, by making work necessary, has made the right to work a universal prerogative, and this is the first, the most sacred and the most indefeasible of all rights.

We regard it as one of the first duties of our law, and one of the acts most worthy of our charity, to free our subjects from all attacks against the inalienable right of mankind. Consequently, we wish to abolish these arbitrary institutions, which do not allow the poor man to earn his living; which reject a sex whose weakness has given it more needs and fewer resources, and which seem, in condemning it to an inevitable misery, to support seduction and debauchery; which destroy emulation and industry and nullify the talents of those whose circumstances have excluded them from membership of a corporation; which deprive the State and the arts of all the knowledge brought to them by foreigners; which retard the progress of these arts through the innumerable difficulties encountered by inventors with whom different corporations dispute the right to exploit their discoveries . . . which, by the huge expenses artisans are obliged to sustain to obtain the right to work, by their various exactions and frequent fines for alleged illegalities, by all kinds of expenditure, waste and interminable law suits, resulting from the respective claims of all these corporations on the extent of their exclusive privileges, burden industry with an oppressive tax, which bears heavily on the people, and is without benefit to the State; which finally, by the facility they provide for members of corporations to combine to force the poorest members to submit to the laws of the rich, become an instrument of privilege and encourage developments, the effect of which is to raise above their natural level the price of those goods which are most essential for the people.

Questions for Analysis

1. How did Turgot justify the abolition of French guilds? Do you think his reasons are valid? How might the guilds respond?

2. Do guilds—and modern-day unions—help or hurt workers? Defend your position.

Source: S. Pollard and C. Holmes, eds., *Documents of European Economic History,* Volume One: *The Process of Industrialization, 1750–1870,* 1968, pp. 53–56.

CHAPTER 20
The Changing Life of the People

Chapter Preview

Marriage and the Family
What changes occurred in marriage and the family in the course of the eighteenth century?

Children and Education
What was life like for children, and how did attitudes toward childhood evolve?

Food, Medicine, and New Consumption Habits
How did new patterns of consumption and changing medical care affect people's lives?

Religion and Popular Culture
What were the patterns of popular religion and culture, and how did they interact with the worldview of the educated public and the Enlightenment?

INDIVIDUALS IN SOCIETY: Madame du Coudray, the Nation's Midwife

LISTENING TO THE PAST: A Day in the Life of Paris

A quack doctor uses a snake and a dog to sell a miraculous cure-all in an Italian village market, in a painting (detail) by Michele Graneri (1736–1778). (Dagli Orti Private Collection/The Art Archive)

The discussion of agriculture and industry in the previous chapter showed the common people at work, straining to make ends meet within the larger context of population growth, gradual economic expansion, and ferocious political competition. The world of work was embedded in a rich complex of family organization, community practices, everyday experiences, and collective attitudes.

In recent years, historians have intensively studied all these aspects of popular life. The challenge has been formidable because regional variations abounded and the common people left few written records. Yet imaginative research has resulted in major findings and much greater knowledge. It is now possible to follow the common people into their homes, workshops, churches, and taverns and to ask, "What were the everyday experiences of ordinary people?"

Marriage and the Family

What changes occurred in marriage and the family in the course of the eighteenth century?

The basic unit of social organization is the family. Within the structure of the family human beings love, mate, and reproduce. It is primarily the family that teaches the child, imparting values and customs that condition an individual's behavior for a lifetime. The family is also an institution woven into the web of history. It evolves and changes, assuming different forms in different times and places.

Late Marriage and Nuclear Families

In the previous chapter, we noted the common misconception that populations of the past always grew quickly. Another popular error is that before the modern era people married at a young age and settled in large multigenerational households. In recent years historians have used previously neglected parish registers of births, deaths, and marriages to uncover details of European family life before the nineteenth century. It is now clear that the extended, three-generation family was a rarity in western and central Europe by 1700. Indeed, the extended family may never have been common in Europe, although it is hard to know about the early Middle Ages because very few records survive. When young European couples married, they normally established their own households and lived apart from their parents. If a three-generation household came into existence, it was usually because a widowed parent moved into the home of a married child.

Moreover, most people did not marry young in the seventeenth and eighteenth centuries. The average person who was neither rich nor aristocratic married surprisingly late, many years after reaching adulthood and beginning to work. In one well-studied, apparently typical English village in the seventeenth and eighteenth centuries, both men and women married for the first time at an average age of twenty-seven or older. A similar pattern existed in eighteenth-century France, where women married around age twenty-five and men around age twenty-seven. A substantial portion of men and women never married at all. The custom of late marriage combined with a nuclear-family household distinguished European society from other areas of the world.

Why was marriage delayed? The main reason was that couples normally did not marry until they could support themselves economically. Peasants often needed to wait until the father's death to inherit land and marry. In the towns, men and women worked to accumulate enough savings to start a small business and establish a household. In some areas couples needed the legal permission or tacit approval of the local lord or landowner in order to marry. Austria and Germany had legal restrictions on marriage, and well into the nineteenth century poor couples had particular difficulty securing the approval of local officials. This pattern helped society maintain some kind of balance between the number of people and the available economic resources.

Work Away from Home

Many young people worked within their families until they could start their own households. Boys plowed and wove; girls spun and tended the cows. Others left home to work elsewhere. In the towns a lad would begin apprenticeship around age fifteen and finish in his late teens or early twenties. During that time he would not be permitted to marry. In most trades he earned little and worked hard, but if he was lucky, he might eventually be admitted to a guild. Many poor families could not afford apprenticeship, and their sons drifted from one tough job to another: hired hand for a small farmer, wage laborer on a new road, carrier of water in a nearby town. They were always subject to economic fluctuations, and unemployment was a constant threat.

Many girls also left their families to work in adolescence. Some apprenticed to mistresses in traditionally female occupations, becoming seamstresses, linen drapers, or midwives. As the demand for skilled labor grew, even male guildsmen hired girls and women, despite guild restrictions.

Service in another family's household, though, was by far the most common job for girls, and even middle-class families often sent their daughters into service. The legions of young servant girls worked hard but had little independence. Sometimes the employer paid the girl's wages directly to her parents. Constantly under the eye of her mistress, the servant girl had many tasks—cleaning, shopping, cooking, caring for the baby. Court records are full of servant girls' complaints of physical mistreatment by their mistresses. There were many like the fifteen-year-old English girl in the early eighteenth century who told the judge that her mistress had not only called her "very opprobrious names, as Bitch, Whore and the like," but also "beat her without provocation and beyond measure."[1]

Male apprentices told similar tales of verbal and physical abuse at their masters' hands. Boys were far less vulnerable, though, to the sexual harassment and assault that threatened female servants. In theory, domestic service offered a young girl protection and security in a new family. But in practice

Boucher: The Pretty Cook

Increased migration to urban areas in the eighteenth century contributed to a loosening of traditional morals and soaring illegitimacy rates. Young women who worked as servants or shop girls could not be supervised as closely as those who lived at home. The themes of seduction, fallen virtue, and familial conflict were popular in eighteenth-century art, such as this painting by François Boucher (frahn-SWA boo-SHEY) (1703–1770), master of the rococo. (Réunion des Musées Nationaux/Art Resource, NY) she was often the easy prey of a lecherous master or his sons or friends. If the girl became pregnant, she could be quickly fired and thrown out in disgrace to make her own way, which often led to a life of prostitution and petty thievery. "What are we?" exclaimed a bitter Parisian prostitute. "Most of us are unfortunate women, without origins, without education, servants and maids for the most part."[2]

Prostitutes encountered increasingly harsh and repressive laws in the sixteenth and early seventeenth centuries, as officials across Europe began to close licensed brothels and declare prostitution illegal. Despite this repression, prostitution flourished in European cities and towns in the eighteenth century. Most prostitutes were working women who turned to the sex trade when confronted with unemployment or seasonal shortages of work. Farther up the social scale were courtesans whose wealthy protectors provided apartments, servants, beautiful clothing, and cash allowances. As she aged, such a woman could descend once more to streetwalking.

Premarital Sex and Community Controls

Did late marriage in preindustrial Europe go hand in hand with many illegitimate children? For most of western and central Europe until at least 1750, the answer is no. English parish registers seldom listed more than one illegitimate child out of every twenty children baptized. Some French parishes in the seventeenth century had extraordinarily low rates of illegitimacy, with less than 1 percent of the babies born out of wedlock. Illegitimate babies were apparently a rarity, at least as far as the official church records are concerned. This does not mean that premarital intercourse was unusual, however. A significant number of women were pregnant on their wedding day.

The combination of very low rates of illegitimate births with large numbers of pregnant brides reflects the powerful **community controls** of the traditional village, particularly the open-field village, with its pattern of cooperation and common action. No doubt many couples were already betrothed, or at least "going steady," before they entered into intimate relationships, and pregnancy simply set the marriage date once and for all. But if a couple wavered about marriage, they could expect to be pressured by irate parents, anxious village elders, indignant priests, and stern landlords. The prospect of an unwed (and therefore poor) mother was seen as a grave threat to the economic, social, and moral stability of the closely knit community.

Community controls extended to domestic disputes and marital scandals as well. The people in peasant communities gave such affairs loud and unfavorable publicity either at the time of the event or during the Carnival season (see page 530). The young men of the village would typically gang up on the person they wanted to punish and force him or her to sit astride a donkey facing backward and holding up the donkey's tail. They would parade the overly brutal spouse-beating husband (or wife), or the couple whose adultery had been discovered, all around the village, loudly proclaiming the offender's misdeeds with scorn and ridicule. The donkey ride and other colorful humiliations ranging from rotten vegetables splattered on the doorstep to obscene and insulting midnight serenades were common punishments throughout much of Europe. They epitomized the community's far-reaching effort to police personal behavior and maintain community standards.

community controls A pattern of cooperation and common action that was mobilized by perceived threats to the economic, social, and moral stability of the closely knit community.

New Patterns of Marriage and Illegitimacy

illegitimacy explosion The sharp increase in out-of-wedlock births that occurred in Europe between 1750 and 1850, caused by urbanization, unemployment, and the breakdown of community controls.

In the second half of the eighteenth century, the pattern of few births out of wedlock began to break down. The number of illegitimate births soared between about 1750 and 1850 as much of Europe experienced an **illegitimacy explosion.** In Frankfurt, Germany, for example, illegitimate births rose steadily from about 2 percent of all births in the early 1700s to a peak of about 25 percent around 1850. In Bordeaux, France, 36 percent of all babies were being born out of wedlock by 1840. Small towns and villages experienced less startling climbs, but between 1750 and 1850 increases from a range of 1 to 3 percent initially to 10 to 20 percent were commonplace. Fewer young people were abstaining from premarital intercourse, and, more important, fewer young men were marrying the women they got pregnant. Thus a profound sexual and cultural transformation took place.

Historians are still debating the meaning of this transformation, but one trend seems to explain the rise of illegitimate births in urban areas. The needs of a growing population sent many young villagers to towns and cities in search of employment. Most young women in urban areas found work only as servants or textile workers. Poorly paid and with little possibility of truly independent lives, they looked to marriage for security. But without the social controls of village life, their courtships could lead to illegitimate children rather than marriage. Because the lives of their partners were also insecure, many men hesitated to take on the financial burden of a wife and child. Thus the romantic aspirations of many young people were frustrated by low wages, inequality, and changing economic and social conditions. Old patterns of marriage and family were breaking down. Only in the late nineteenth century would more stable patterns reappear.

The pattern of late marriage also eroded in some areas in the second half of the eighteenth century. First, the growth of cottage industry created new opportunities for earning a living, opportunities not tied to the land. Cottage workers married at a younger age because they did not have to wait to inherit a farm. A scrap of

David Allan: The Penny Wedding (1795)

The spirited merrymaking of a peasant wedding was a popular theme of European artists. In rural Scotland "penny weddings" like this one were common: guests provided cash gifts; any money left after paying for the wedding went to the newlyweds to help them get started. Dancing, feasting, and drinking characterized these community parties, which led the Presbyterian church to oppose them and hasten their decline. (National Galleries of Scotland)

ground for a garden and a cottage for the loom and spinning wheel could be quite enough for a modest living. Couples married not only at an earlier age but also for different reasons. Nothing could be so businesslike as peasant marriages that were often dictated by the needs of the couples' families. After 1750, however, courtship became more extensive and freer as cottage industry grew. It was easier to yield to the attraction of the opposite sex and fall in love. Members of the older generation were often highly critical of the lack of responsibility they saw in the union of "people with only two spinning wheels and not even a bed." But such scolding did not stop cottage workers from marrying for love rather than for economic considerations as they blazed a path that factory workers would follow in the nineteenth century. Ironically, therefore, both the rise of illegitimate births and the new tendencies toward earlier marriage reflect a weakening of parental and communities' control over young people.

Children and Education

What was life like for children, and how did attitudes toward childhood evolve?

In the traditional framework of agrarian Europe, women married late but then began bearing children rapidly. If a woman married before she was thirty, and if both she and her husband lived to fifty, she would most likely give birth to six or more children. The newborn child entered a dangerous world. Newborns were vulnerable to infectious diseases of the chest and stomach, and many babies died of dehydration brought about by bad bouts of ordinary diarrhea. Of those who survived infancy, many more died in childhood. Even in rich families little could be done for an ailing child. Childbirth could also be dangerous. Women who bore six children faced a cumulative risk of dying in childbirth of 5 to 10 percent, a thousand times as great as the risk in Europe today.[3]

Schools and formal education played only a modest role in the lives of ordinary children, and many boys and many more girls never learned to read. Nevertheless, basic literacy was growing among the popular classes, whose reading habits have been intensively studied in recent years. Attempting to peer into the collective attitudes of the common people and compare them with those of the book-hungry cultivated public, historians have produced some fascinating insights.

Child Care and Nursing

In the countryside, women of the lower classes generally breast-fed their infants for two years or more. Breast-feeding decreases the likelihood of pregnancy for the average woman by delaying the resumption of ovulation. By nursing their babies, women limited their fertility and spaced their children from two to three years apart. If a newborn baby died, nursing stopped, and a new life could be created. Nursing also saved lives: the breast-fed infant received precious immunity-producing substances with its mother's milk and was more likely to survive than when it was given other food.

Women of the aristocracy and upper middle class seldom nursed their own children. The upper-class woman felt that breast-feeding was crude and undignified. Instead, she hired a live-in wet nurse to suckle her child (which usually meant sending the nurse's own infant away to be nursed). Urban mothers of more modest means also relied on wet nurses to free them for full-time work. Unable to afford

Arrival of the Wet Nurses
Wet-nursing was big business in eighteenth-century France, particularly in Paris and the north. Here, rural wet nurses bring their charges back to the city to be reunited with their families after around two years of care. These children were lucky survivors of a system that produced high mortality rates. (Réunion des Musées Nationaux/Art Resource, NY)

wet-nursing A widespread and flourishing business in the eighteenth century in which women would breast-feed other women's babies for money.

live-in wet nurses, they often turned to the cheaper services of women in the countryside. Rural **wet-nursing** was a widespread business in the eighteenth century, conducted within the framework of the putting-out system. The traffic was in babies rather than in yarn or cloth, and two or three years often passed before the wet-nurse worker in the countryside finished her task. The wet nurse generally had little contact with the family that hired her, and she was expected to privilege the newcomer at the expense of her own nursing child.

Reliance on wet nurses contributed to high levels of infant mortality. A study of parish registers in northern France during the late seventeenth and early eighteenth centuries reveals that 35 percent of babies died before their first birthdays, and another 20 percent before age ten.[4] In England, where more mothers nursed, only some 30 percent of children did not reach their tenth birthdays. French-women also gave birth to more children since nursing tends to slow down the return of fertility after childbirth.

In the second half of the eighteenth century critics mounted a harsh attack against wet-nursing. Upper-class women responded positively to the new mindset, but poor urban women who depended on jobs where nursing was not possible continued to rely on wet nurses. Not until the late-nineteenth-century introduction of sterilized cows' milk and artificial nipples did wet-nursing cease as a practice.

Foundlings and Infanticide

The young woman who could not provide for a child had few choices, especially if she had no prospect of marriage. Abortions were illegal, dangerous, and apparently rare. In desperation, some women, particularly in the countryside, hid unwanted pregnancies, delivered in secret, and smothered their newborn infants. If discovered, **infanticide** (in-fAN-tuh-side) was punishable by death.

Women in cities could leave their infants at foundling homes, which multiplied in the eighteenth century. In eighteenth-century England, for example, the government acted on a petition calling for a foundling hospital "to prevent the frequent murders of poor, miserable infants at birth" and "to suppress the inhuman custom of exposing newborn children to perish in the streets." As the number of homes increased, the number of foundlings being cared for surged. By the end of the century European foundling hospitals were admitting annually about one hundred thousand abandoned children, nearly all of them infants. While most of the children were the offspring of unwed mothers, others were the offspring of married couples, for whom an additional mouth to feed often meant tragedy.

Great numbers of babies entered foundling homes, but few left. Even in the best of these homes, 50 percent of the babies normally died within a year. In the worst, fully 90 percent did not survive.[5] They succumbed to long journeys over rough roads, intentional and unintentional neglect by their wet nurses, and customary childhood illnesses. So great were the losses that some contemporaries called the foundling hospitals "legalized infanticide."

> **infanticide** The willful destruction of a newborn infant.

Attitudes Toward Children

What were the typical circumstances of children's lives? The topic of parental attitudes toward children in the early modern period remains controversial. Some scholars have claimed that parents did not risk forming emotional attachments to young children because of high mortality rates. With a reasonable expectation that a child might die, some scholars believe, parents maintained an attitude of indifference, if not downright negligence.

The French essayist, Michel de Montaigne (mon-TAIN), exemplifies this attitude. He wrote: "I cannot abide that passion for caressing new-born children, which have neither mental activities nor recognisable bodily shape by which to make themselves loveable and I have never willingly suffered them to be fed in my presence."[6]

In contrast to this harsh picture, however, historians have drawn ample evidence from diaries, letters, and family portraits that many parents did cherish their children and suffered greatly when they died. The English poet Ben Jonson wrote movingly of the death of his seven-year-old son Benjamin:

> *On My First Son*
> *Farewell, thou child of my right hand, and joy;*
> *My sin was too much hope of thee, loved boy.*
> *Seven years thou wert lent to me, and I thee pay,*
> *Exacted by thy fate, on the just day.*

In a society characterized by violence and brutality, discipline of children was often severe. The novelist Daniel Defoe (duh-FOH) (1659–1731), who was always delighted when he saw young children working hard in cottage industry, coined the axiom "Spare the rod and spoil the child." He meant it. So did Susannah Wesley (1669–1742), mother of John Wesley, the founder of Methodism. According to her, the first task of a parent toward her children was "to conquer the will, and bring them to an obedient temper." She reported that her babies were "taught to fear the rod, and to cry softly; by which means they escaped the abundance of correction they might otherwise have had, and that most odious noise of the crying of children was rarely heard in the house."[7]

The Enlightenment produced an enthusiastic new discourse about childhood and child rearing. Starting around 1760, critics called for greater tenderness toward children and proposed imaginative new teaching methods. They objected to the practices of swaddling babies, using rigid whale-boned corsets to "straighten them out," and dressing children in miniature versions of adult clothing. Instead parents were urged to dress their children in simpler and more comfortable clothing to allow freedom of movement. For Enlightenment critics, the best hopes for creating a new society, untrammeled by the prejudices of the past, lay in a radical revision of child-rearing techniques according to "natural" laws.

One of the century's most influential works on child rearing was Jean-Jacques Rousseau's (zhahn-zhock roo-SOE) *Emile*, which fervently advocated breast-feeding and natural dress. Rousseau argued that boys' education should include plenty of fresh air and exercise and that they should be taught practical craft skills in addition to book learning. Reacting to what he perceived as the vanity and frivolity of upper-class Parisian women, Rousseau insisted girls' education focus on their future domestic responsibilities. For Rousseau, women's "nature" destined them solely for a life of marriage and child rearing. The ideas of Rousseau and other reformers were enthusiastically adopted by elite women, who did not adopt universal nursing but did at least begin to supervise their wet nurses more carefully.

For all his influence, Rousseau also reveals the occasional hypocrisy of Enlightenment thinkers. With regard to the child-rearing techniques he believed would create a better society, Rousseau had extremely high expectations; when it came to the five children he fathered with his common-law wife, however, he abandoned them all in foundling hospitals despite their mother's protests. None are known to have survived. For Rousseau, the idea of creating a natural man was more important than raising real children.

Schools and Popular Literature

The availability of formal education outside the home increased during the eighteenth century. Prussia led the way in the development of universal education, inspired by the Protestant idea that every believer should be able to read the Bible and by the new idea of a population capable of effectively serving the state. As early as 1717 Prussia made attendance at elementary schools compulsory, and more Protestant German states, such as Saxony and Württemberg (WUR-tuhm-burg), followed during the eighteenth century. In Scotland the focus on Bible study led to the creation of parish schools for all children, and in England "charity schools" were established for the poor. In Catholic France, some Christian schools were established to teach the catechism and prayers as well as reading and writing, and the Catholic Habsburg state went even further, promoting elementary education enthusiastically in the eighteenth century. Thus some elementary education was becoming a reality, and schools were of growing significance in the life of the child.

The result of these efforts was a remarkable growth in basic literacy between 1600 and 1800. Whereas in 1600 only one male in six was barely literate in France and Scotland, and one in four in England, by 1800 almost nine out of ten Scottish males, two out of three French males, and more than half of English males were literate. In all three countries, the bulk of the jump occurred in the eighteenth century. Women were also increasingly literate, although they lagged behind men.

Raoux: Young Woman Reading a Letter

Literacy rates for men and women rose substantially during the eighteenth century. The novel also emerged as a new literary genre in this period. With its focus on emotions, love, and family melodrama, the novel was seen as a particularly feminine genre, and it allowed women writers more access to publication. Writing and reading letters were also associated with women. Some contemporaries worried that women's growing access to reading and writing would excite their imagination and desires, leading to moral dissolution. (Réunion des Musées Nationaux/Art Resource, NY)

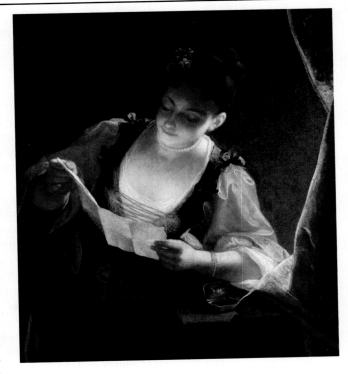

The growth in literacy promoted a growth in reading, and historians have carefully examined what the common people read in an attempt to discern what they were thinking. While the Bible remained the overwhelming favorite, especially in Protestant countries, short pamphlets known as chapbooks were the staple of popular literature. Printed on the cheapest paper available, many chapbooks dealt with religious subjects. They featured Bible stories, prayers, devotions, and the lives of saints and exemplary Christians. Promising happiness after death, devotional literature was also intensely practical. It gave the believer moral teachings and a confidence in God that helped in daily living.

Entertaining, often humorous stories formed a second element of popular literature. Fairy tales, medieval romances, true crime stories, and fantastic adventures were some of the delights that filled the peddler's pack as he approached a village. These tales presented a world of danger and magic, of supernatural powers, fairy godmothers, and evil trolls. The significance of these entertaining stories for the peasant reader is debated. Many scholars see them reflecting a desire for pure escapism and a temporary flight from harsh everyday reality. Others see the tales reflecting ancient folk wisdom and counseling prudence in a world full of danger and injustice, where wolves dress up like grandmothers and eat Little Red Riding Hoods.

Finally, some popular literature was highly practical, dealing with rural crafts, household repairs, useful plants, and similar matters. Much lore was stored in almanacs, where calendars listing secular, religious, and astrological events were mixed with agricultural schedules, arcane facts, and jokes. The almanac was universal, was not controversial, and was highly appreciated even by many in the comfortable classes. "Anyone who could would read an almanac."[8] In this way, elites still shared some elements of a common culture with the masses.

While the vast majority of ordinary people did not read the great works of the Enlightenment, that does not mean they were immune to its ideas. Urban working people were exposed to new ideas through public conversation and cheap publications that helped translate Enlightenment critiques into ordinary language. Servants who had overheard the discussions of their educated employers might disseminate new ideas on trips back to their villages.

Section Review

- Lower-class rural women generally breast-fed their infants, while urban and upper-class women most often hired a wet nurse, typically a rural woman, to suckle their infants.

- An unwanted pregnancy brought social and economic disaster, causing some women to turn to infanticide; in response, Europeans set up foundling hospitals that took in large numbers of infants, but few left, as infant death rates were high.

- The Enlightenment brought calls for a new tenderness and freedom for children; among the most influential was Rousseau's plea for boys to get exercise and practical life skills along with book learning and for girls to learn appropriate domestic skills.

- A growing number of schools contributed to increased literacy, and reading rates rose with the introduction of popular and devotional literature, novels, fairy tales, and books on practical subjects such as the almanac. The Bible and Bible stories remained favorite reading material.

Food, Medicine, and New Consumption Habits

How did new patterns of consumption and changing medical care affect people's lives?

One of the most important developments in European society in the eighteenth century was the emergence of a fledgling consumer culture. Much of the expansion took place in the upper and upper-middle classes, but a boom in cheap reproductions of luxury items also permitted people of modest means to purchase more objects. From food to ribbons and from coal stoves to umbrellas, the material world of city dwellers grew richer and more diverse. These developments created new expectations for comfort and hygiene in daily life. Medical practitioners greatly increased in number, although their techniques did not differ much from those of previous generations.

The possibility of picking and choosing among a new variety of consumer goods and provisioners encouraged the development of new notions of individuality and self-expression. A shop girl could stand out from her peers by her choice of a striped jacket, a colored parasol, or simply a new ribbon for her hair. New attitudes about privacy and intimate life also emerged. Whereas families previously shared common living spaces, in the eighteenth century they erected new partitions within their homes to create private nooks. Alongside an upturn in economic production, this "consumer revolution," as it has been called, dramatically changed European life in the eighteenth century. As in other developments, England led the way.

Diets and Nutrition

At the beginning of the eighteenth century, ordinary men and women depended on grain as fully as they had in the past. Brown bread and gruel remained the mainstays of people's diets, and while they did eat vegetables, their choices were typically limited to peas, beans, cabbage, carrots, and wild greens. Patterns of food consumption changed markedly as the century progressed. There was a general growth of market gardening, and a greater variety of vegetables appeared in towns and cities. This was particularly the case in the Low Countries and England, which pioneered new methods of farming.

The Columbian exchange of foods was also responsible for dietary changes. Originating in the Americas—along with corn, squash, tomatoes, and many other useful plants—the humble potato provided an excellent new food source for Europeans. Containing a good supply of carbohydrates, calories, and vitamins A and C, the potato offset the lack of vitamins from green vegetables in the poor person's diet, and it provided a much higher caloric yield than grain for a given piece of land. After initial resistance, the potato became an important dietary supplement in much of Europe by the end of the century. In the course of the eighteenth century the large towns and cities of maritime Europe also began to receive semitropical fruits, such as oranges and lemons, from Portugal and the West Indies, but they remained expensive.

The most remarkable dietary change in the eighteenth century was in the consumption of sugar and tea. No other commodities grew so quickly in consumption. Previously expensive and rare luxury items, they became dietary staples for people of all social classes. This was possible because of the steady drop in prices created by the expansion of colonial production and slave labor. Other colonial

Royal Interest in the Potato
Frederick the Great of Prussia, shown here supervising cultivation of the potato, used his influence and position to promote the new food on his estates and throughout Prussia. Peasants could grow potatoes with the simplest hand tools, but it was backbreaking labor, as this painting by R. Warthmüller suggests. *(Private Collection, Hamburg/akg-images)*

goods also became important items of daily consumption in this period, including coffee, tobacco, and chocolate.

Part of the motivation for consuming these products was a desire to emulate the habits of "respectable" people. The accelerating pace of work in the eighteenth century also seems to have created new needs for stimulants among working people. (See the feature "Listening to the Past: A Day in the Life of Paris" on pages 533–534.) Whereas the gentry took tea as a leisurely and genteel ritual, the lower classes usually drank tea at work. With the widespread adoption of these products (which turned out to be mildly to extremely addictive), working people in Europe became increasingly dependent on faraway colonial economies. Their understanding of daily necessities and how to procure those necessities shifted definitively, linking them into a globalized capitalism far beyond their ability to shape or control.

Toward a Consumer Society

Along with foodstuffs, all manner of other goods increased in variety and number in the eighteenth century. This proliferation led to a growth in consumption and new attitudes toward consumer goods so wide-ranging that some historians have referred to an eighteenth-century "**consumer revolution.**" The long-term result of this revolution was the birth of a new type of society, in which people had greater access to finished goods and derived their self-identity as much from their consuming practices as from their working lives and place in the production process. The full emergence of a consumer society did not take place until much later, but its roots lie in the developments of the eighteenth century.

consumer revolution The growth in consumption and new attitudes toward consumer goods as a result of an increase in quantity and variety of foodstuffs and other goods in the eighteenth century.

Increased demand for consumer goods was not merely an innate response to increased supply. Eighteenth-century merchants cleverly pioneered new techniques to incite demand: they initiated marketing campaigns, opened fancy boutiques with large windows, and advertised the patronage of royal princes and princesses. By diversifying their product lines and greatly accelerating the turnover of styles, they seized the reins of fashion from the courtiers who had earlier controlled it. Instead of setting new styles, duchesses and marquises now bowed to the dictates of fashion merchants. Fashion also extended beyond court circles to touch many more items and social groups.

Clothing was one of the chief indicators of nascent consumerism. The wiles of entrepreneurs made fashionable clothing seem more desirable, while legions of women entering the textile and needle trades made it ever cheaper. As a result, eighteenth-century western Europe witnessed a dramatic rise in the consumption of clothing, particularly in large cities. One historian has documented an enormous growth in the size and value of Parisians' wardrobes from 1700 to 1789, as well as a new level of diversity in garments and accessories, colors, and fabrics. Colonial economies played an important role, supplying new materials, such as cotton and vegetable dyes, at low cost. Cheaper copies of elite styles made it possible for working people to aspire to follow fashion for the first time.[9]

Women were typically more interested in acquiring a fashionable wardrobe than were their husbands, brothers, and fathers. This was true across the social spectrum; in ribbons, shoes, gloves, and lace, French working women reaped in the consumer revolution what they had sewn in the industrious revolution (see pages 494–495). There were also new gender distinctions in dress. Previously, noblemen vied with women in the magnificence and ostentation of their dress; by the end of the eighteenth century men had begun to don early versions of the plain dark suit that remains standard male formalwear in the West. This was one

The Fashion Merchant's Shop
Shopping in fancy boutiques became a favorite leisure pastime of the rich in the eighteenth century. Whereas shops had previously been dark, cramped spaces, now they were filled with light from large plate-glass windows, staffed by finely dressed attendants, and equipped with chairs and large mirrors for a comfortable shopping experience. Fashion merchants (or milliners) sold hats, shawls, parasols, and an infinite variety of accessories and decorations. (Courtesy, University of Illinois Library)

more aspect of the increasingly rigid distinction drawn between appropriate male and female behavior.

The consumer revolution extended into the home as well. In 1700 a meal might be served in a common dish, with each person dipping his or her spoon into the pot. By the end of the eighteenth century even humble households contained a much greater variety of cutlery and dishes, making it possible for each person to eat from his or her own plate. More books and prints, which also proliferated at lower prices, decorated the walls. Improvements in glass-making provided more transparent glass, which allowed daylight to penetrate into gloomy rooms. Cold and smoky hearths were increasingly replaced by more efficient and cleaner coal stoves, which also eliminated the backache of cooking over an open fire. People began to assign specific functions to rooms, moving away from the practice of using the same room for sleeping, receiving guests, and working. Inner walls or screens were added to create these specific areas along with greater privacy. Rooms became warmer, better lit, more comfortable, and more personalized.

The scope of the new consumer economy should not be exaggerated. These developments were concentrated in large cities in northwestern Europe and in North America. Even in these centers the elite benefited the most from new modes of life. This was not yet the society of mass consumption that emerged toward the end of the nineteenth century with the full expansion of the Industrial Revolution. The eighteenth century did, however, lay the foundations for one of the most distinctive features of modern Western life: societies based on the consumption of goods and services obtained through the market in which individuals form their identities and self-worth through the goods they consume.

Medical Practitioners

With these advances in daily life, how did the care of sickness, pain, and disease evolve? Medical science continued to struggle in vain against these scourges. Yet the Enlightenment's focus on research and experimentation, along with a remarkable rise in the number of medical practitioners, laid the foundation for significant breakthroughs in the middle and late nineteenth century.

Care of the sick in the eighteenth century was the domain of several competing groups: faith healers, apothecaries (or pharmacists), physicians, surgeons, and midwives. Both men and women were prominent in the healing arts, as had been the case since the Middle Ages. But by 1700 the range of medical activities open to women was severely restricted because women were generally denied admission to medical colleges and lacked the diplomas necessary to practice. In the course of the eighteenth century, the position of women as midwives and healers further eroded.

Faith healers remained active. They and their patients believed that demons and evil spirits caused disease by lodging in the body and that the proper treatment was to exorcise, or drive out, the offending devil. This demonic view of disease was strongest in the countryside, where popular belief placed great faith in the healing power of religious relics, prayer, and the laying on of hands.

In the larger towns and cities, apothecaries sold a vast number of herbs, drugs, and patent medicines for every conceivable "temperament and distemper." Their prescriptions were incredibly complex—a hundred or more drugs might be included in a single prescription—and often very expensive. Like all varieties of medical practitioners, apothecaries advertised their wares, their high-class customers, and their miraculous cures in newspapers and commercial circulars. Medicine, like food and fashionable clothing, thus joined the era's new commercial culture.

Physicians, who were invariably men, were apprenticed in their teens to practicing physicians for several years of on-the-job training. This training was then rounded out with hospital work or some university courses. Because such prolonged training was expensive, physicians came mainly from prosperous families, and they usually concentrated on urban patients from similar social backgrounds. They had little contact with urban workers and less with peasants. While physicians in the eighteenth century were increasingly willing to experiment with new methods, they continued to practice the medieval cures of blood-letting and purging of the bowels.

Surgeons, in contrast to physicians, made considerable medical and social progress in the eighteenth century. Long considered to be ordinary male artisans comparable to butchers and barbers, surgeons began studying anatomy seriously and improved their art. They learned to perform amputations when faced with severely wounded limbs, but they labored in the face of incredible difficulties. Almost all operations were performed without painkillers, for the anesthesias of the day were hard to control and were believed too dangerous for general use. Many patients died from the agony and shock of such operations. Surgery was also performed in utterly unsanitary conditions, for there was no knowledge of bacteriology and the nature of infection. The simplest wound treated by a surgeon could fester and lead to death.

Midwives continued to deliver the overwhelming majority of babies throughout the eighteenth century. Trained initially by another woman practitioner—and regulated by a guild in many cities—the midwife primarily assisted in labor and delivering babies but also handled other medical issues specific to women and infants. In France one enterprising Parisian midwife secured royal financing for her campaign to teach better birthing techniques to village midwives, which reinforced the position of women practitioners. (See the feature "Individuals in Society: Madame du Coudray, the Nation's Midwife.") However, their profession came under attack by surgeon-physicians, who used their monopoly over the new instrument of the forceps to seek lucrative new business. While midwives generally lost no more babies than did male doctors, the doctors persuaded growing numbers of wealthy women of the superiority of their services.

Experimentation and the intensified search for solutions to human problems led to some real advances in medicine after 1750. The eighteenth century's greatest medical triumph was the conquest of smallpox. With the progressive decline of bubonic plague, smallpox became the most terrible of the infectious diseases, and it is estimated that 60 million Europeans died of it in the eighteenth century. Fully 80 percent of the population was stricken at some point in life.

The first step in the conquest of this killer in Europe came in the early eighteenth century. Lady Mary Wortley Montagu (MON-tuh-gyoo) brought the practice of **smallpox inoculation** to England from the Muslim lands of western Asia where she had lived as the wife of the British ambassador. But inoculation with the pus of a smallpox victim was risky because about one person in fifty died from it. In addition, people who had been inoculated were infectious and often spread the disease.

While the practice of inoculation with the smallpox virus was refined over the century, the crucial breakthrough was made by Edward Jenner (1749–1823), a talented country doctor. His starting point was the countryside belief that dairy maids who had contracted cowpox did not get smallpox. Cowpox produces sores that resemble those of smallpox, but the disease is mild and is not contagious. For eighteen years Jenner practiced a kind of Baconian science, carefully collecting data. Finally, in 1796 he performed his first vaccination on a young boy using

smallpox inoculation The practice of vaccinating people with cowpox so that they would not come down with smallpox.

Individuals in Society

Madame du Coudray, the Nation's Midwife

In 1751 a highly esteemed Parisian midwife left the capital for a market town in central France. Having accepted an invitation to instruct local women in the skills of childbirth, Madame Angelique Marguerite Le Boursier du Coudray (kood-RAY) soon demonstrated a marvelous ability to teach students and win their respect. The thirty-six-year-old midwife found her mission: she would become the nation's midwife.

For eight years Madame du Coudray taught young women from the impoverished villages of Auvergne (oh-VAIRN). In doing so, she entered into the world of unschooled midwives who typically were solid matrons with several children who relied on traditional birthing practices and folk superstitions. Trained in Paris through a rigorous three-year apprenticeship and imbued with an Enlightenment faith in the power of knowledge, du Coudray had little sympathy for these village midwives. Many peasant mothers told her about their difficult deliveries and their many uterine "infirmities," which they attributed to "the ignorance of the women to whom they had recourse, or to that of some inexperienced village [male] surgeons."* Du Coudray agreed. Botched deliveries by incompetents resulted in horrible deformities and unnecessary deaths.

Determined to raise standards, Madame du Coudray saw that her unlettered pupils learned through the senses, not through books. Thus she made, possibly for the first time in history, a life-sized obstetrical model—a "machine"—out of fabric and stuffing for use in her classes. "I had . . . the students maneuver in front of me on a machine . . . which represented the pelvis of a woman, the womb, its opening, its ligaments, the conduit called the vagina, the bladder, and *rectum intestine*. I added an [artificial] child of natural size, whose joints were flexible enough to be able to be put in different positions." Now du Coudray could demonstrate the problems of childbirth, and each student could practice on the model in the "lab session."

As her reputation grew, Madame du Coudray sought to reach a national audience. In 1757 she published the first of several editions of her *Manual on the Art of Childbirth*. Handsomely and effectively illustrated (see the image below), the *Manual* incorporated her hands-on teaching method and served as a text and reference for students and graduates. In 1759 the government authorized Madame du Coudray to carry her instruction "throughout the realm" and promised financial support. Her reception was not always warm, for she was a self-assured and demanding woman who could anger old midwives, male surgeons, and skeptical officials. But aided by servants, a niece, and her husband, this inspired and indefatigable woman took her course from town to town until her retirement in 1784. Typically her students were young peasant women on tiny stipends who came into town from surrounding villages for two to three months of instruction. Classes met

Plate from Madame du Coudray's manual, illustrating "another incorrect method of delivery." (Rare Books Division, Countway [Francis A.] Library of Medicine)

mornings and afternoons six days a week, with ample time to practice on the mannequin (MAN-uh-kin). After a recuperative break, Madame du Coudray and her entourage moved on.

Teaching thousands of fledgling midwives, Madame du Coudray may well have contributed to the decline in infant mortality and to the increase in population occurring in France in the eighteenth century—an increase she and her royal supporters fervently desired. Certainly she spread better knowledge about childbirth from the educated elite to the common people.

Questions for Analysis

1. How do you account for Madame du Coudray's remarkable success?
2. Does Madame du Coudray's career reflect tensions between educated elites and the common people? If so, how?

* Quotes are from Nina Gelbart, *The King's Midwife: A History and Mystery of Madame du Coudray* (Berkeley: University of California Press, 1998), pp. 60–61. This definitive biography is excellent.

526 Chapter 20 The Changing Life of the People

- Potatoes and new vegetables from the colonies added to the diet as did sugar and tea; their falling prices helped them become staples for all social classes.

- Increased availability of finished goods and new techniques for marketing them helped produce a consumer revolution in some parts of Europe, especially among women, thus marking the first step toward a society in which people derive self-identity from the possessions they consume.

- Eighteenth-century medical practitioners included countryside faith healers, apothecaries selling a wide range of advertised treatments, physicians and surgeons who worked primarily with the wealthy and were almost all men, and midwives who assisted women in birthing and faced new competition from male doctors.

- Madame du Coudray was a French midwife who brought her training and knowledge of childbirth to the masses by holding classes and offering hands-on training.

- The biggest breakthrough in medicine was the smallpox inoculation, which William Jenner perfected using cowpox to vaccinate people.

matter taken from a milkmaid with cowpox. After performing more successful vaccinations, Jenner published his findings in 1798. The new method of treatment spread rapidly, and smallpox soon declined to the point of disappearance in Europe and then throughout the world.

Religion and Popular Culture

What were the patterns of popular religion and culture, and how did they interact with the worldview of the educated public and the Enlightenment?

Though the critical spirit of the Enlightenment made great inroads in the eighteenth century, the majority of ordinary men and women, especially those in rural areas, remained committed Christians. Religious faith promised salvation and eternal life, and it gave comfort and courage in the face of sorrow and death. Religion also remained strong because it was usually embedded in local traditions, everyday social experience, and popular culture.

Yet the popular religion of the European village was everywhere enmeshed in a larger world of church hierarchies and state power. These powerful outside forces sought to regulate religious life at the local level. Their efforts created tensions that helped set the scene for a vigorous religious revival in Germany and England. Similar tensions arose in Catholic countries, where powerful elites criticized and attacked popular religious practices that their increasingly rationalistic minds deemed foolish and superstitious.

The Institutional Church

As in the Middle Ages, the local parish church remained the focal point of religious devotion and community cohesion. Congregations gossiped and swapped stories after services, and neighbors came together in church for baptisms, marriages, funerals, and special events. Priests and parsons kept the community records of births, deaths, and marriages, distributed charity, looked after orphans, and provided primary education to the common people. Thus the parish church was woven into the very fabric of community life.

While the parish church remained central to the community, it was also subject to greater control from the state. In Protestant areas, princes and monarchs headed the official church, and they regulated their "territorial churches" strictly, selecting personnel and imposing detailed rules. By the eighteenth century, the radical ideas of the Reformation had resulted in another version of church bureaucracy. Catholic monarchs in this period also took greater control of religious matters in their kingdoms, weakening papal authority. Spain, a deeply Catholic country with devout rulers, took firm control of ecclesiastical appointments. Papal proclamations could not even be read in Spanish churches without prior approval from the government. Spain also asserted state control over the Spanish Inquisition, which pursued heresy as an independent agency under Rome's direction and went far toward creating a "national" Catholic Church, as France had done earlier.

A more striking indication of state power and papal weakness was the fate of the Society of Jesus, or Jesuits. The well-educated Jesuits were extraordinary teachers, missionaries, and agents of the papacy. In many Catholic countries, they exercised tremendous political influence, holding high government positions and educating the nobility in their colleges. Yet by playing politics so effectively, the

Jesuits eventually elicited a broad coalition of enemies. Bitter controversies led Louis XV to order the Jesuits out of France in 1763 and to confiscate their property. France and Spain then pressured Rome to dissolve the Jesuits completely. In 1773 a reluctant pope caved in, although the order was revived after the French Revolution.

Some Catholic rulers also believed that the clergy in monasteries and convents should make a more practical contribution to social and religious life. Austria, a leader in controlling the church (see page 479) and promoting primary education, showed how far the process could go. Maria Theresa began by sharply restricting entry into "unproductive" orders. In his Edict on Idle Institutions, her successor Joseph II abolished contemplative orders, henceforth permitting only orders that were engaged in teaching, nursing, or other practical work. The state also expropriated the dissolved monasteries and used their wealth for charitable purposes and higher salaries for ordinary priests. These measures recalled the radical transformation of the Protestant Reformation.

Protestant Revival

By the late seventeenth century the vast reforms of the Reformation were complete and routinized in most Protestant churches. Indeed, many official Protestant churches had settled into a smug complacency. In the Reformation heartland, one concerned German minister wrote that the Lutheran church "had become paralyzed in forms of dead doctrinal conformity" and badly needed a return to its original inspiration.[10] His voice was one of many that prepared and then guided a powerful Protestant revival that succeeded because it answered the intense but increasingly unsatisfied needs of common people.

The Protestant revival began in Germany. It was known as **Pietism** (PIE-uh-tiz-um), and three aspects helped explain its powerful appeal. First, Pietism called for a warm, emotional religion that everyone could experience. Enthusiasm—in prayer, in worship, in preaching, in life itself—was the key concept. "Just as a drunkard becomes full of wine, so must the congregation become filled with spirit," declared one exuberant writer. Another said simply, "The heart must burn."[11]

Second, Pietism reasserted the earlier radical stress on the priesthood of all believers, thereby reducing the gulf between official clergy and Lutheran laity. Bible reading and study were enthusiastically extended to all classes, and this provided a powerful spur for popular education as well as individual religious development (see page 518). Finally, Pietists believed in the practical power of Christian rebirth in everyday affairs. Reborn Christians were expected to lead good, moral lives and to come from all social classes.

Pietism had a major impact on John Wesley (1703–1791), who served as the catalyst for popular religious revival in England. As a teaching fellow at Oxford University, Wesley organized a Holy Club for similarly minded students, who were soon known contemptuously as **Methodists** because they were so methodical in their devotion. Yet like the young Luther, Wesley remained intensely troubled about his own salvation even after his ordination as an Anglican priest in 1728.

Wesley's anxieties related to grave problems of the faith in England. The government shamelessly used the Church of England to provide favorites with high-paying jobs. Building of churches practically stopped while the population grew, and in many parishes there was a shortage of pews. Churches were customarily locked on weekdays. Services and sermons had settled into an uninspiring routine. Moreover, Enlightenment skepticism was making inroads among the educated classes, and deism was becoming popular. Some bishops and church leaders

Pietism The name for the Protestant revival that began in Germany; it stressed enthusiasm, the priesthood of all believers, and the practical power of Christian rebirth in everyday affairs.

Methodists The name given to a Protestant religious group started by John Wesley, so named because of their methodical devotion.

Hogarth's Satirical View of the Church
William Hogarth (1697–1764) was one of the foremost satirical artists of his day. This image mocks a London Methodist meeting, where the congregation swoons in enthusiasm over the preacher's sermon. The woman in the foreground giving birth to rabbits refers to a hoax perpetrated in 1726 by a servant named Mary Tofts; the credulousness of those who believed Tofts is likened to that of the Methodist congregation. (HIP/Art Resource, NY)

seemed to believe that doctrines such as the Virgin Birth were little more than elegant superstitions.

Spiritual counseling from a sympathetic Pietist minister from Germany prepared Wesley for a mystical, emotional "conversion" in 1738. He described this critical turning point in his *Journal*:

> *In the evening I went to a [Christian] society in Aldersgate Street where one was reading Luther's preface to the Epistle to the Romans. About a quarter before nine, while he was describing the change which God works in the heart through faith in Christ, I felt my heart strangely warmed. I felt I did trust in Christ, Christ alone for salvation; and an assurance was given me that he had taken away my sins, even mine, and saved me from the law of sin and death.*[12]

Wesley took the good news of salvation to the people, traveling some 225,000 miles by horseback and preaching more than forty thousand sermons in fifty years. Crowds assembled in open fields to hear him speak. Of critical importance was Wesley's rejection of Calvinist predestination—the doctrine of salvation granted to only a select few. Instead, he preached that *all* men and women who earnestly sought salvation might be saved. It was a message of hope and joy, of free will and universal salvation.

Wesley's ministry won converts, formed Methodist cells, and eventually resulted in a new denomination. And as Wesley had been inspired by the Pietist revival in Germany, so evangelicals in the Church of England and the old dissenting groups now followed Wesley's example, giving impetus to an even broader awakening among the lower classes. In Protestant countries, religion remained a vital force in the lives of the people.

Catholic Piety

Jansenism A form of Catholic revival that originated with the Flemish theologian, Cornelius Jansen, emphasizing the heavy weight of original sin and accepting the doctrine of predestination, rejected as heresy by the official church.

Catholicism had its own version of the Pietist revivals that shook Protestant Europe. **Jansenism** (JAN-suh-niz-uhm) has been described by one historian as the "illegitimate off-spring of the Protestant Reformation and the Catholic Counter-Reformation."[13] It originated with the Flemish theologian Cornelius Jansen (1585–1638), who called for a return to the austere early Christianity of Saint Augustine. In contrast to the worldly Jesuits, Jansen emphasized the heavy weight of original sin and accepted the doctrine of predestination.

Although outlawed by papal and royal edicts as Calvinist heresy, Jansenism attracted Catholic followers eager for religious renewal, particularly in France.

Many members of elite French society, especially judicial nobles and some parish priests, became known for their Jansenist piety and spiritual devotion. Such stern religious values encouraged the judiciary's increasing opposition to the monarchy in the second half of the eighteenth century. Among the poor, a different strain of Jansenism took hold. Prayer meetings brought men and women together in ecstatic worship, and some participants fell into convulsions and spoke in tongues.

Jansenism was an urban phenomenon. In the countryside, many peasants in Catholic countries held religious beliefs that were marginal to the Christian faith altogether, often of obscure or even pagan origin. On the Feast of Saint Anthony, for example, priests were expected to bless salt and bread for farm animals to protect them from disease. One saint's relics could help cure a child of fear, and there were healing springs for many ailments. The ordinary person combined strong Christian faith with a wealth of time-honored superstitions.

Inspired initially by the fervor of the Catholic Counter-Reformation and then to some extent by the critical rationalism of the Enlightenment, parish priests and Catholic hierarchies sought increasingly to "purify" popular religious practice. French priests particularly denounced the "various remnants of paganism" found in popular bonfire ceremonies during Lent, in which young men, "yelling and screaming like madmen," tried to jump over the bonfires in order to help the crops

Procession of Nuns at Port-Royal des Champs

The convent of Port-Royal, located twenty miles southwest of Paris, was a center of Jansenist activity throughout the seventeenth century. Angered by the nuns' defiance, Louis XIV ordered them forcibly relocated in 1709. To generate support, the artist Magdelaine Horthemels painted a series of images depicting the pious and placid religious life at the convent. The convent was nonetheless destroyed by Louis's forces in 1710. This image is one of many copies of Horthemels' work made by Jansenists in the eighteenth century. (Réunion des Musées Nationaux/ Art Resource, NY) grow and protect themselves from illness. One priest saw rational Christians regressing into pagan animals—"the triumph of Hell and the shame of Christianity."[14]

In contrast with Protestant reformers, many Catholic priests and hierarchies preferred a compromise between theological purity and the people's piety. Thus, the severity of the attack on popular Catholicism varied widely by country and region. Where authorities pursued purification vigorously, as in Austria under Joseph II, pious peasants saw only an incomprehensible attack on the true faith and drew back in anger.

Carnival The pre-Lent festival of reveling and excess in Catholic and Mediterranean Europe.

Leisure and Recreation

The combination of religious celebration and popular recreation was most strikingly displayed at **Carnival,** a time of reveling in Catholic and Mediterranean Europe. Carnival preceded Lent—the forty days of fasting and penitence before Easter—and for a few exceptional days in February or March, a wild release of drinking, masquerading, and dancing reigned. Moreover, a combination of plays, processions, and rowdy spectacles turned the established order upside down. Peasants dressed up as nobles and men as women, and rich masters waited on their servants at the table. This annual holiday gave people a much-appreciated chance to release their pent-up frustrations and aggressions before life returned to the usual pattern of hierarchy and hard work.

Despite the spread of literacy, the culture of the common people was largely oral rather than written. In the cold, dark winter months, families gathered around the fireplace to talk, sing, tell stories, do craftwork, and keep warm. In some parts of Europe, women would gather together in groups in someone's cottage to chat, sew, spin, and laugh. Sometimes a few young men would be invited so that the daughters (and mothers) could size up potential suitors in a supervised atmosphere. A favorite recreation of men was drinking and talking with buddies in public places, and it was a sorry village that had no tavern.

Towns and cities offered a wide range of amusements. Many of these had to be paid for because the eighteenth century saw a sharp increase in the commercialization of leisure-time activities. Urban fairs featured prepared foods, acrobats, freak shows, open-air performances, optical illusions, and the like. Such entertainments attracted a variety of social classes. So did the growing number of commercial, profit-oriented spectator sports. These ranged from traveling circuses and horse races to boxing matches and bullfights. Modern sports heroes, such as brain-bashing heavyweight champions and haughty matadors, made their appearance on the historical scene.

blood sports Spectator sports involving torture and forced combat of animals, such as bullbaiting and cockfighting.

Blood sports, such as bullbaiting and cockfighting, remained popular with the masses. In bullbaiting, the bull, usually staked on a chain in the courtyard of an inn, was attacked by ferocious dogs for the amusement of the innkeeper's clients. Eventually the maimed and tortured animal was slaughtered by a butcher and sold as meat. In cockfighting two roosters, carefully trained by their owners and armed with razor-sharp steel spurs, slashed and clawed each other in a small ring until the victor won—and the loser died. An added attraction of cockfighting was that the screaming spectators could bet on the lightning-fast combat and its uncertain outcome.

In trying to place the vibrant popular culture of the common people in broad perspective, historians have stressed the growing criticism levied against it by the educated elites in the second half of the eighteenth century. These elites, who had previously shared the popular enthusiasm for religious festivals, Carnival, drinking in taverns, blood sports, and the like, now tended to see these activities as superstition, sin, disorder, and vulgarity.[15] The resulting attack on popular culture, which

Section Review

- The local parish was still the center of community life but increasingly the state exerted more control and, in Catholic areas, weakened papal authority.

- Protestant revival was known as Pietism and became popular because it included emotion and enthusiasm, enforced the priesthood of all believers, and promoted morality for all social classes.

- John Wesley, frustrated with uninspiring services and routines, attracted followers, later called Methodists, with his message of universal salvation, hope, and joy.

- In Catholic countries, especially France, Jansenism gained a hold in the cities and focused on a return to piety and on a belief in original sin and predestination, while in the countryside a combination of Christian and pagan beliefs was common.

- For recreation people got together to tell stories, drink in taverns, watch sporting events, attend an urban fair, or celebrate, dance, and let loose during Carnival—all pastimes increasingly frowned upon as sinful by educated elites.

had its more distant origins in the Protestant clergy's efforts to eliminate frivolity and superstition, was intensified as an educated public embraced the critical worldview of the Enlightenment.

Chapter Review

| What changes occurred in marriage and the family in the course of the eighteenth century? (page 511)

In the current generation, imaginative research has greatly increased our understanding of ordinary life and social patterns of the past. In the eighteenth century the life of the people remained primarily rural and oriented toward the local community. Tradition, routine, and well-established codes of behavior framed much of the everyday experience. Thus, just as the three-field agricultural cycle and its pattern of communal rights had determined traditional patterns of grain production, so did community values in the countryside strongly encourage a late marriage age and a low rate of illegitimate births. Yet powerful forces also worked for change. Many changes came from outside and above, from the aggressive capitalists, educated elites, and government officials. Closely knit villages began to lose control over families and marital practices, as can be seen in the earlier marriages of cottage workers and in the beginning of the explosion in illegitimate births.

| What was life like for children, and how did attitudes toward childhood evolve? (page 515)

Infancy and childhood were highly vulnerable stages of life. In some parts of Europe fewer than half of all children reached the age of ten. Infant mortality was high in areas like France, in which wet-nursing was commonly practiced. Treatment of children could be harsh in an early modern society that was characterized by much higher levels of violence and brutality than Western societies today. The second half of the eighteenth century witnessed a new concern with methods of child raising inspired by Enlightenment efforts to reform human society. Schools for non-elite children spread across Europe, leading to a growth in literacy rates.

| How did new patterns of consumption and changing medical care affect people's lives? (page 520)

The urban populace benefited from the surge in agricultural and industrial production. People found a greater variety of food products at the market, including new stimulants produced in the colonies that soon became staples of elite and popular consumption. Within homes, standards of comfort and hygiene increased, and the emerging consumer society offered new possibilities for self-expression and individuality. Medical techniques continued to follow traditional patterns, but the number of practitioners grew, and great strides were made against smallpox.

| What were the patterns of popular religion and culture, and how did they interact with the worldview of the educated public and the Enlightenment? (page 526)

Patterns of recreation and leisure, from churchgoing and religious festivals to sewing and drinking in groups within an oral culture, reflected and reinforced community ties

Key Terms

community controls (p. 513)

illegitimacy explosion (p. 514)

wet-nursing (p. 516)

infanticide (p. 517)

consumer revolution (p. 521)

smallpox inoculation (p. 524)

Pietism (p. 527)

Methodists (p. 527)

Jansenism (p. 528)

Carnival (p. 530)

blood sports (p. 530)

and values. Many long-standing beliefs and practices remained strong forces and sustained continuity in popular life. A wave of religious revival counteracted the secular tendencies of the Enlightenment, ensuring that religion continued to have a strong hold over the popular classes. The next great wave of change would be inaugurated by revolution in politics.

Notes

1. Quoted in J. M. Beattie, "The Criminality of Women in Eighteenth-Century England," *Journal of Social History* 8 (Summer 1975): 86.
2. Quoted in R. Cobb, *The Police and the People: French Popular Protest, 1789–1820* (Oxford: Clarendon Press, 1970), p. 238.
3. Pier Paolo Viazzo, "Mortality, Fertility, and Family," in *Family Life in Early Modern Times, 1500–1789*, ed. David I. Kertzer and Marzio Barbagli (New Haven: Yale University Press, 2001), p. 180.
4. Robert Woods, "Did Montaigne Love His Children? Demography and the Hypothesis of Parental Indifference," *Journal of Interdisciplinary History* 33, 3 (2003): 426.
5. Alysa Levene, "The Estimation of Mortality at the London Foundling Hospital, 1741–99," *Population Studies* 59, 1 (2005): 87–97.
6. Cited in Woods, "Did Montaigne Love His Children?," p. 421.
7. Ibid., pp. 13, 16.
8. E. Kennedy, *A Cultural History of the French Revolution* (New Haven: Yale University Press, 1989), p. 47.
9. Daniel Roche, *The Culture of Clothing: Dress and Fashion in the Ancien Regime.* Translated by Jean Birrell (Cambridge: Cambridge University Press, 1996).
10. Quoted in K. Pinson, *Pietism as a Factor in the Rise of German Nationalism* (New York: Columbia University Press, 1934), p. 13.
11. Ibid., pp. 43–44.
12. Quoted in S. Andrews, *Methodism and Society* (London: Longmans, Green, 1970), p. 327.
13. Dale Van Kley, "The Rejuvenation and Rejection of Jansenism in History and Historiography," *French Historical Studies* 29 (Fall 2006): 649–684.
14. Quoted in T. Tackett, *Priest and Parish in Eighteenth-Century France* (Princeton, N.J.: Princeton University Press, 1977), p. 214.
15. Woloch, *Eighteenth-Century Europe*, pp. 220–221; see also pp. 214–220 for this section.

To assess your mastery of this chapter, go to **bedfordstmartins.com/mckaywestbrief**

Listening to the Past

A Day in the Life of Paris

Louis-Sébastien Mercier (1740–1814) was the best chronicler of everyday life in eighteenth-century Paris. His masterpiece was the Tableau de Paris (1781–1788), a multi-volume work composed of 1,049 chapters that covered subjects ranging from convents to cafés, bankruptcy to booksellers, the latest fashions to royal laws. He aimed to convey the infinite diversity of people, places, and things he saw around him, and in so doing he left future generations a precious record of the changing dynamics of Parisian society in the second half of the eighteenth century.

Mercier was born in 1740 to a weapons-maker father and a mother similarly descended from the respectable artisan classes. Neither rich nor poor, the family enjoyed a comfortable lifestyle without luxury. This middling position ideally suited Mercier for observing the extremes of wealth and poverty around him. Although these volumes contain many wonderful glimpses of daily life, they should not be taken for an objective account. Mercier brought his own moral and political sensibilities, influenced by Jean-Jacques Rousseau, to the task.

A page from Mercier's original manuscript.
(Bibliothèque nationale de France)

At one in the morning six thousand peasants arrive, bringing the town's provision of vegetables and fruits and flowers, and make straight for the Halles;* their beasts have come eighteen leagues perhaps, and are weary. As for the market itself, it never sleeps. Morpheus never shakes his poppy-seed there. Perpetual noise, perpetual motion, the curtain never rings down on the enormous stage; first come the fishmongers, and after these the egg-dealers, and after these the retail buyers; for the Halles keep all the other markets of Paris going; they are the warehouses whence these draw their supplies. The food of the whole city is shifted and sorted in high-piled baskets; you may see eggs, pyramids of eggs, moved here and there, up steps and down, in and out of the throngs, miraculous; not one is ever broken. . . .

This impenetrable din contrasts oddly with the sleeping streets, for at that hour none but thieves and poets are awake.

Twice a week, at six, those distributors of the staff of life, the bakers of Gonesse,† bring in an enormous quantity of loaves to the town, and may take none back through the barriers. And at this same hour workmen take up their tools, and trudge off to their day's labour. Coffee with milk is, unbelievably, the favoured drink among these stalwarts nowadays.

At street-corners, where the pale light from a street lamp falls, the coffee women stand, carrying their tin urns on their backs; they sell their coffee in earthenware cups, two sous a cup, one penny, and not too well sugared at that; but our workmen find it very much to their taste. . . .

So coffee-drinking has become a habit, and one so deep-rooted that the working classes will start the day on nothing else. It is not costly, and has more flavour to it, and more nourishment too, than anything else they can afford to drink; so they consume immense quantities, and say that if a man can only have coffee for breakfast it will keep him going till nightfall. They take only two meals in the

* The city's central wholesale food market.

† A suburb of Paris, famous for the excellent bread baked there.

twenty-four hours; that at midday and the evening snack of supper, what they call the *persillade*. . . .

If the sybarites of Paris, those who like to lie abed till noon, had their way, there would be no smiths in the city, no horses shod, and no pots and pans mended; all such noise would be banished without the walls. . . .

Their complaint is well founded; but if their remedy were followed, and carried to extremes, there would be no hats made in Paris, because of the stink of the felt; no leather tanned, no varnish nor perfume made for the same reason, although they themselves make use of these commodities. . . . Privilege would allow no shop-windows, but only porticoes to shelter carriages; would strew straw in the streets from midnight till midday, when Privilege does the world the honor of waking . . . for only Privilege may be privileged to fill the streets with the clatter of wheels and hoofs and to keep others from sleeping.

Questions for Analysis

1. What different social groups does Mercier describe in Paris? On what basis does he categorize people?

2. What is Mercier's attitude toward the poor and the rich? Does he approve or disapprove of Parisian society as he describes it?

Source: From *Panorama of Paris: Selections from "Le Tableau de Paris,"* Louis Sebastien Mercier, based on the translation by Helen Simpson, edited and with a new preface and translations by Jeremy D. Popkin. Copyright © 1999 The Pennsylvania State University. Reprinted by permission of Penn State Press.

In this painting by the female artist Nanine Vallain, the figure of Liberty bears a copy of the Declaration of the Rights of Man in one hand and a pike to defend them in the other. The painting hung in the Jacobin Club until its fall from power. (Musée de la Revolution Française, Vizille/The Bridgeman Art Library)

CHAPTER 21

The Revolution in Politics

1775–1815

Chapter Preview

Background to Revolution
What social, political, and economic factors formed the background to the French Revolution?

Revolution in Metropole and Colony (1789–1791)
What were the immediate events that sparked the Revolution, and how did they result in the formation of a constitutional monarchy in France? How did the ideals and events of the early Revolution raise new aspirations in the colonies?

World War and Republican France (1791–1799)
How and why did the Revolution take a radical turn at home and in the colonies?

The Napoleonic Era (1799–1815)
Why did Napoleon Bonaparte assume control of France, and what factors led to his downfall? How did the new republic of Haiti gain independence from France?

INDIVIDUALS IN SOCIETY: Toussaint L'Ouverture

LISTENING TO THE PAST: Revolution and Women's Rights

The last years of the eighteenth century were a time of great upheaval. A series of revolutions and revolutionary wars challenged the old order of monarchs and aristocrats. The ideas of freedom and equality, ideas that continue to shape the world, flourished and spread. The revolutionary era began in North America in 1775. Then in 1789 France, the most influential country in Europe, became the leading revolutionary nation. It established first a constitutional monarchy, then a radical republic, and finally a new empire under Napoleon. Inspired by both the ideals of the Revolution and internal colonial conditions, the slaves of Saint-Domingue rose up in 1791. Their rebellion led to the creation of the new independent nation of Haiti in 1805.

The armies of France violently exported revolution beyond the nation's borders in an effort to establish new governments throughout much of Europe. The world of modern domestic and international politics was born.

Background to Revolution

What social, political, and economic factors formed the background to the French Revolution?

estates The three legal categories, or orders, of France's inhabitants: the clergy, the nobility, and everyone else.

The origins of the French Revolution have been one of the most debated topics in history. In order to understand the path to revolution, numerous interrelated factors must be taken into account. These include deep social changes in France, a long-term political crisis that eroded monarchical legitimacy, the impact of new political ideas derived from the Enlightenment, the emergence of a "public sphere" in which such opinions were formed and shared, and, perhaps most importantly, a financial crisis created by France's participation in expensive overseas wars.

A FAUT ESPERER Q'EU JEU LA FINIRA BEN TOT.

l'auteur en Campagne Ap. 1789.

Legal Orders and Social Change

As in the Middle Ages, France's 25 million inhabitants were still legally divided into three orders, or **estates**—the clergy, the nobility, and everyone else. As the nation's first estate, the clergy numbered about one hundred thousand and had important privileges, including exemption from regular taxes and the ability to tax landowners. The second estate consisted of some four hundred thousand nobles who owned about 25 percent of the land in France outright. The nobility also enjoyed special privileges associated with their exalted social position, including lighter taxes, exclusive hunting and fishing rights, monopolies on bread baking and wine pressing equipment, and the right to wear swords. The third estate was a conglomeration of very different social groups—prosperous merchants, lawyers, and officials along with

The Three Estates

In this political cartoon from 1789 a peasant of the third estate struggles under the crushing burden of a happy clergyman and a plumed nobleman. The caption—"Let's hope this game ends soon"—sets forth a program of reform that any peasant could understand. (Réunion des Musées Nationaux/Art Resource, NY) poorer peasants, urban artisans, and unskilled day laborers—united only by their shared legal status as distinct from the nobility and clergy.

In discussing the origins of the French Revolution, historians long focused on growing tensions between the nobility and the comfortable members of the third estate, the *bourgeoisie* (boor-zwah-ZEE) or upper middle class. In this formulation, the French bourgeoisie eventually rose up to lead the entire third estate in a great social revolution that destroyed feudal privileges and established a capitalist order based on individualism and a market economy.

In recent years, a flood of new research has challenged these accepted views. Above all, revisionist historians have questioned the existence of growing social conflict between a progressive capitalistic bourgeoisie and a reactionary feudal nobility in eighteenth-century France. Instead, they see both bourgeoisie and nobility as highly fragmented, riddled with internal rivalries. The sword nobility, for example, who descended from the oldest noble families, was separated by differences in wealth, education, and worldview from the newer and less prestigious robe nobility, who acquired noble titles through service in the royal administration and judiciary. Differences within the bourgeoisie—between wealthy financiers and local lawyers, for example—were no less profound. Rather than standing as unified blocs against each other, nobility and bourgeoisie formed two parallel social ladders increasingly linked together at the top by wealth, marriage, and Enlightenment culture.

Revisionist historians note that the nobility and the bourgeoisie were not really at odds in the economic sphere. Investment in land and government service were the preferred activities of both groups, and the ideal of the merchant capitalist was to gain enough wealth to retire from trade, purchase an estate, and live nobly as a large landowner. Indeed, wealthy members of the third estate could even move into the second estate by serving the government and purchasing noble positions. At the same time, wealthy nobles often acted as aggressive capitalists, investing especially in mining, metallurgy, and foreign trade. In addition, until the revolution actually began, key sections of the nobility were liberal and generally joined the bourgeoisie in opposition to the government.

Revisionists have clearly shaken the belief that the bourgeoisie and the nobility were inevitably locked in growing conflict before the Revolution. Yet they also make clear that the Old Regime had ceased to correspond with social reality by the 1780s. Legally, society was still based on rigid orders inherited from the Middle Ages. In reality, France had already moved far toward being a society based on wealth and education in which an emerging elite that included both aristocratic and bourgeois notables was frustrated by a bureaucratic monarchy that continued to claim the right to absolute power.

The Crisis of Political Legitimacy

Overlaying these social changes was a century-long political and fiscal struggle between the monarchy and its opponents that was primarily enacted in the law courts. When Louis XIV died, his successor Louis XV (r. 1715–1774) was only five years

CHRONOLOGY

1775–1783	American Revolution
1786–1789	Financial crisis in France
1789	Feudalism abolished in France; ratification of U.S. Constitution; storming of the Bastille
1789–1799	French Revolution
1790	Burke, *Reflections on the Revolution in France*
1791	Slave insurrection in Saint-Domingue
1792	Wollstonecraft, *A Vindication of the Rights of Woman*
1793	Execution of Louis XVI
1793–1794	Economic controls to help poor in France; Robespierre's Reign of Terror
1794	Robespierre deposed and executed
1794–1799	Thermidorian reaction
1799–1815	Napoleonic era
1804	Haitian republic declares independence
1812	Napoleon invades Russia
1814–1815	Napoleon defeated and exiled

old. The high courts of France—the *parlements*—regained the ancient right to evaluate royal decrees publicly in writing before they were registered and given the force of law. The parlements used this power to prevent the king from imposing taxes after the War of the Austrian Succession, and then the Seven Years' War plunged France into a fiscal crisis. During the latter crisis, the Parlement of Paris asserted that it was acting as the representative of the entire nation when it checked the king's power to levy taxes.

After years of attempting to compromise with the parlements, Louis XV roused himself for a determined defense of his absolutist inheritance. His appointee as chancellor, René de Maupeou (maw-POO), abolished the existing parlements, exiled the vociferous members of the Parlement of Paris to the provinces, and began to tax the privileged groups. Public opinion as a whole sided with the old parlements, however, and there was widespread criticism of "royal despotism." The king also came under attack for sexual scandals and lost the sacred aura of God's anointed on earth.

desacralization The stripping away of the sacred aura of the king as God's anointed on earth.

Despite this progressive **desacralization** (dee-SAY-kruh-lie-ZAY-shun) of the monarchy, its power was still great enough to ride over the opposition, and Louis XV would probably have prevailed if he had lived to a ripe old age, but he died in 1774. The new king, Louis XVI (r. 1774–1792), was a shy twenty-year-old with good intentions. Taking the throne, he is reported to have said, "What I should like most is to be loved."[1] The eager-to-please monarch yielded in the face of vehement opposition from France's educated elite. He dismissed chancellor Maupeou and repudiated the strong-willed minister's work. Louis also waffled on the economy, dismissing controller general Turgot when his attempts to liberalize the economy drew fire. A weakened but unreformed monarchy now faced a judicial opposition that claimed to speak for the entire French nation. Increasingly locked in stalemate, the country was drifting toward renewed financial crisis and political upheaval.

The Impact of the American Revolution

Coinciding with the first years of Louis XVI's reign, the American Revolution had an enormous impact on France both in practical and ideological terms. French expenses to support the colonists bankrupted the Crown, while the ideals of liberty and equality provided heady inspiration for political reform.

Like the French Revolution some years later, the American Revolution had its immediate origins in struggles over increased taxes. The high cost of the Seven Years' War—fought with little financial contribution from the colonies—doubled the British national debt. When the government tried to recoup some of the losses in increased taxes on the colonies in 1765, the colonists reacted with anger.

The key questions were political rather than economic. To what extent could the home government assert its power while limiting the authority of colonial legislatures and their elected representatives? Accordingly, who should represent the colonies, and who had the right to make laws for Americans? The British government replied that Americans were represented in Parliament, albeit indirectly (like most British people themselves), and that the absolute supremacy of Parliament throughout the empire could not be questioned. Many Americans felt otherwise.

A series of disputes between the American colonies and the British government ultimately led to open rebellion. The uncompromising attitude of the British government and its use of German mercenaries dissolved loyalties to the home country and rivalries among the separate colonies. On July 4, 1776, an assembly of colonists adopted the Declaration of Independence. Written by Thomas Jefferson, it boldly listed the tyrannical acts committed by George III (r. 1760–1820) and confidently proclaimed the sovereignty of the American states. It also universalized the traditional rights of English people, stating that "all men are created equal. . . . They are endowed by their Creator with certain unalienable rights. . . . Among these are life, liberty, and the pursuit of happiness."

On the international scene, the French wanted revenge for the humiliating defeats of the Seven Years' War. They sympathized with the rebels and supplied guns and gunpowder from the beginning. By 1777 French volunteers were arriving in Virginia, and a dashing young nobleman, the marquis de Lafayette (1757–1834), quickly became one of Washington's most trusted generals. In 1778 the French government offered a formal alliance to the American ambassador in Paris, Benjamin Franklin, and in 1779 and 1780 the Spanish and Dutch declared war on Britain. Catherine the Great of Russia helped organize the League of Armed Neutrality in order to protect neutral shipping rights, which Britain refused to recognize.

Thus by 1780 Great Britain was engaged in an imperial war against most of Europe as well as against the thirteen colonies. In these circumstances, and in the face of severe reverses, a new British government offered peace on extremely generous terms. By the Treaty of Paris of 1783, Britain recognized the independence of the thirteen colonies and ceded all its territory between the Allegheny Mountains and the Mississippi River to the Americans. Out of the bitter rivalries of the Old World, the Americans snatched dominion over a vast territory.

Europeans who dreamed of a new era were fascinated by the political lessons of the American Revolution. The Americans had begun with a revolutionary defense against tyrannical oppression, and they had been victorious. They had then shown how rational beings could assemble together to exercise sovereignty and write a new social contract. All this gave greater reality to the concepts of individual liberty and representative government and reinforced one of the primary ideas of the Enlightenment: that a better world was possible.

No country felt the consequences of the American Revolution more directly than France. Hundreds of French officers served in America and were inspired by the experience, the marquis de Lafayette chief among them. French intellectuals and publicists engaged in passionate analysis of the new federal Constitution (1789) as well as the constitutions of the various states of the new United States. Perhaps more importantly, the expenses of supporting the revolutionary forces provided the last nail in the coffin for the French treasury.

Financial Crisis

The French Revolution thus had its immediate origins in the king's financial difficulties. Thwarted by the Parlement of Paris in its efforts to raise revenues by reforming the tax system, the government was forced to finance all of its enormous expenditures during the American war with borrowed money. As a result, the national debt and the annual budget deficit soared.

By the 1780s, fully 50 percent of France's annual budget went for interest payments on the debt. Another 25 percent went to maintain the military, while 6 percent was absorbed by the king and his court at Versailles. Less than 20 percent of the entire national budget was available for the productive functions of the state, such as transportation and general administration. This was an impossible financial situation.

Louis XVI's minister of finance revived old proposals to impose a general tax on all landed property as well as to form provincial assemblies to help administer

Assembly of Notables A group of important noblemen and high-ranking clergy called by Louis XVI to impose a general tax, but who ended up opposing it.

Section Review

- French society had three social orders or estates: the clergy, nobility, and everyone else, including the bourgeoisie or upper middle class that was increasingly frustrated with the monarchy's right to absolute power.

- The monarchy and the high courts, the parlements, were at odds over financial and political power; Louis XV's attempt to rein in the parlements failed as Louis XVI restored them to power.

- The French supported the American Revolution with money, volunteers, and arms; the rebels in turn inspired the French by their ability to oppose the British and create their own sovereign nation.

- The royal government, indebted from the American war, attempted to raise taxes, but parlement thwarted it, so finally Louis XVI called for a session of the Estates General.

Estates General A legislative body in pre-revolutionary France made up of representatives of each of the three classes, or estates; it was called into session in 1789 for the first time since 1614.

the tax, and he convinced the king to call an **Assembly of Notables** to gain support for the idea. The notables, who were mainly important noblemen and high-ranking clergy, opposed the new tax. In exchange for their support, they demanded that control over all government spending be given to the provincial assemblies. When the government refused, the notables responded that such sweeping tax changes required the approval of the Estates General, the representative body of all three estates, which had not met since 1614.

Facing imminent bankruptcy, the king tried to reassert his authority. He dismissed the notables and established new taxes by decree. In stirring language, the judges of the Parlement of Paris promptly declared the royal initiative null and void. When the king tried to exile the judges, a tremendous wave of protest swept the country. Frightened investors also refused to advance more loans to the state. Finally, in July 1788, Louis XVI bowed to public opinion and called for a spring session of the Estates General.

Revolution in Metropole and Colony (1789–1791)

What were the immediate events that sparked the Revolution, and how did they result in the formation of a constitutional monarchy in France? How did the ideals and events of the early Revolution raise new aspirations in the colonies?

Although inspired by the ideals of the American Revolution, the French Revolution did not mirror the American example. It was more radical and more complex, more influential and more controversial, more loved and more hated. For Europeans and most of the rest of the world, it was the great revolution of the eighteenth century, *the* revolution that opened the modern era in politics. In turn, the slave insurrection in Saint-Domingue—which ultimately resulted in the second independent republic of the Americas—inspired liberation movements across the world.

The Formation of the National Assembly

Once Louis had agreed to hold the **Estates General,** following precedent, he set elections for the three orders. Elected officials from the noble order were primarily conservatives from the provinces, but fully one-third of the nobility's representatives were liberals committed to major changes. The third estate elected lawyers and government officials to represent them, with few delegates representing business or the working poor.

As at previous meetings of the Estates General, local assemblies were to prepare a list of grievances for their representatives to bring to the next electoral level. The petitions for change coming from the three estates showed a surprising degree of consensus. There was general agreement that royal absolutism should give way to a constitutional monarchy in which laws and taxes would require the consent of the Estates General in regular meetings. All agreed that individual liberties would have to be guaranteed by law and that economic regulations should be loosened. The striking similarities in the grievance petitions of the clergy, nobility, and third estate reflected a shared commitment to a basic reform platform among the educated elite.

Yet an increasingly bitter quarrel undermined this consensus during the intense electoral campaign: *how* would the Estates General vote, and precisely *who* would lead in the political reorganization that was generally desired? The Estates

General of 1614 had sat as three separate houses. Each house held one vote, despite the fact that the third estate represented the majority population of France. Given the close ties between them, the nobility and clergy would control all decisions. As soon as the estates were called, the aristocratic Parlement of Paris ruled that the Estates General should once again sit separately. In response to protests from some reform-minded critics, the government agreed that the third estate should have as many delegates as the clergy and the nobility combined but then rendered this act meaningless by upholding voting by separate order.

In May 1789 the twelve hundred delegates of the three estates paraded in medieval pageantry through the streets of Versailles to an opening session resplendent with feudal magnificence. The estates were almost immediately deadlocked. Delegates of the third estate refused to transact any business until the king ordered the clergy and nobility to sit with them in a single body. Finally, after a six-week war of nerves, a few parish priests began to go over to the third estate, which on June 17 voted to call itself the **National Assembly**. On June 20 the delegates of the third estate, excluded from their hall because of "repairs," moved to a large indoor tennis court. There they swore the famous Oath of the Tennis Court, pledging not to disband until they had written a new constitution.

The king's response was ambivalent. On June 23 he made a conciliatory speech urging reforms to a joint session, and four days later he ordered the three estates to meet together. At the same time, the vacillating and indecisive monarch apparently followed the advice of relatives and court nobles who urged him to dissolve the Estates General by force. Belatedly asserting his "divine right" to rule, the king called an army of eighteen thousand troops toward Versailles, and on July 11 he dismissed his finance minister and his other more liberal ministers.

National Assembly The first French revolutionary legislature; a constituent assembly made up of primarily of representatives of the third estate and a few nobles and clergy who joined them, in session from 1789 to 1791.

The Revolt of the Poor and the Oppressed

While delegates of the third estate pressed for political rights, economic hardship gripped the common people. A poor grain harvest in 1788 caused the price of bread to soar, unleashing a classic economic depression of the preindustrial age. With food so expensive and with so much uncertainty, the demand for manufactured goods collapsed. Thousands of artisans and small traders were thrown out of work. By the end of 1789 almost half of the French people would be in need of relief. One person in eight was a pauper living in extreme want. In Paris perhaps 150,000 of the city's 600,000 people were without work in July 1789.

Against this background of poverty and ongoing political crisis, the people of Paris entered decisively onto the revolutionary stage. They believed in a general, though ill-defined, way that the economic distress had human causes. They believed that they should have steady work and enough bread at fair prices to survive. Specifically, they feared that the dismissal of the king's moderate finance minister would put them at the mercy of aristocratic landowners and grain speculators. Rumors that the king's troops would sack the city began to fill the air. Angry crowds formed, and passionate voices urged action. On July 13 the people began to seize arms for the defense of the city as the king's armies moved toward Paris, and on July 14 several hundred people marched to the Bastille (bass-TEE) to search for weapons and gunpowder.

The Bastille, once a medieval fortress, was a royal prison guarded by eighty retired soldiers and thirty Swiss mercenaries. The governor of the fortress-prison refused to hand over the powder, panicked, and ordered his men to resist, killing ninety-eight people attempting to enter. Cannon were brought to batter the main gate, and fighting continued until the prison surrendered. The governor of the prison was later hacked to death, and his head was stuck on a pike and paraded through the streets. The next day a committee of citizens appointed the marquis de Lafayette commander of the city's armed forces. Paris was lost to the king, who was forced to recall the finance minister and disperse his troops. The popular uprising had broken the power monopoly of the royal army and thereby saved the National Assembly.

As the delegates resumed their inconclusive debates at Versailles, the countryside sent them a radical and unmistakable message. Throughout France peasants began to rise in insurrection against their lords, ransacking manor houses and burning feudal documents that recorded their obligations. In some areas peasants reinstated traditional village practices, undoing recent enclosures and reoccupying old common lands. They seized forests, and taxes went unpaid. Fear of vagabonds and outlaws—called the **Great Fear** by contemporaries—seized the countryside and fanned the flames of rebellion. The long-suffering peasants were doing their best to free themselves from manorial rights and exploitation. In the end, they were successful. On the night of August 4, 1789, the delegates at Versailles agreed to abolish all the old noble privileges—peasant serfdom where it still existed, exclusive hunting rights, fees for justice, village monopolies, and a host of other dues. Thus the French peasantry, which already owned about 30 percent of all the land, achieved an unprecedented victory in the early days of revolutionary upheaval. Henceforth, French peasants would seek mainly to protect and consolidate their triumph. As the Great Fear subsided in the countryside, they became a force for order and stability.

Great Fear In the summer of 1789, the fear of vagabonds and outlaws that seized the French countryside and fanned the flames of revolution.

A Limited Monarchy

The National Assembly moved forward. On August 27, 1789, it issued the Declaration of the Rights of Man and of the Citizen, which stated, "Men are born and remain free and equal in rights." The declaration also maintained that mankind's natural rights are "liberty, property, security, and resistance to oppression" and that "every man is presumed innocent until he is proven guilty." As for law, "it is an expression of the general will; all citizens have the right to concur personally or through their representatives in its formation. . . . Free expression of thoughts and opinions is one of the most precious rights of mankind: every citizen may therefore speak, write, and publish freely." In short, this clarion call of the liberal revolutionary ideal guaranteed equality before the law, representative government for a sovereign people, and individual freedom. This revolutionary credo, only two pages long, was disseminated throughout France and Europe and around the world.

Moving beyond general principles to draft a constitution proved difficult. The questions of how much power the king should retain and whether he could permanently veto legislation led to another deadlock. Once again the decisive answer came from the poor—in this instance, the poor women of Paris.

Women customarily bought the food and managed the poor family's slender resources. The economic crisis worsened after the fall of the Bastille, as aristocrats fled the country and the luxury market collapsed. Foreign markets also shrunk in the aftermath of the crisis, and unemployment grew. In addition, household managers could no longer look to the church for grants of food and money.

On October 5 some seven thousand desperate women marched the twelve miles from Paris to Versailles to demand action. This great crowd invaded the Assembly, "armed with scythes, sticks and pikes." One tough old woman defiantly shouted into the debate, "Who's that talking down there? Make the chatterbox

The Women of Paris March to Versailles

On October 5, 1789, a large group of Parisian market women marched to Versailles to protest the price of bread. For the people of Paris, the king was the baker of last resort, responsible for feeding his people during times of scarcity. The crowd forced the royal family to return with them and to live in Paris, rather than remain isolated from their subjects at court. (Erich Lessing/Art Resource, NY)

shut up. That's not the point: the point is that we want bread."[2] Hers was the genuine voice of the people, essential to any understanding of the French Revolution.

The women invaded the royal apartments, slaughtered some of the royal bodyguards, and furiously searched for the queen, Marie Antoinette (ann-twah-NET), who was widely despised for her frivolous and supposedly immoral behavior. "We are going to cut off her head, tear out her heart, fry her liver, and that won't be the end of it," they shouted, surging through the palace in a frenzy. It seems likely that only the intervention of Lafayette and the National Guard saved the royal family. But the only way to calm the disorder was for the king to live in Paris, as the crowd demanded.

The National Assembly followed the king to Paris, and the next two years, until September 1791, saw the consolidation of the liberal revolution. Under middle-class leadership, the National Assembly abolished the French nobility as a legal order and pushed forward with the creation of a **constitutional monarchy,** which Louis XVI reluctantly agreed to accept in July 1790. In the final constitution, the king remained the head of state, but all lawmaking power was placed in the hands of the National Assembly, elected by the economic upper half of French males. New laws broadened women's rights to seek divorce, to inherit property, and to obtain financial support for illegitimate children from fathers, but women were not allowed to hold political office or even vote. The men of the National Assembly believed that civic virtue would be restored if women focused on child rearing and domestic duties.

The National Assembly replaced the complicated patchwork of historic provinces with eighty-three departments of approximately equal size. The jumble of weights and measures that varied from province to province was reformed, leading

constitutional monarchy A form of government in which the king retains his position as head of state, while the authority to tax and make new laws resides in an elected body.

to the introduction of the metric system in 1793. Monopolies, guilds, and workers' associations were prohibited, and barriers to trade within France were abolished in the name of economic liberty. Thus the National Assembly applied the critical spirit of the Enlightenment in a thorough reform of France's laws and institutions.

The Assembly also imposed a radical reorganization on the country's religious life. It granted religious freedom to the small minority of French Jews and Protestants. Of greater impact, it then nationalized the Catholic Church's property and abolished monasteries as useless relics of a distant past. The government used all former church property as collateral to guarantee a new paper currency, the *assignats* (**AS-ig-nat**), and then sold the property in an attempt to put the state's finances on a solid footing. Although the church's land was sold in large blocks, peasants eventually purchased much when it was subdivided. These purchases strengthened their attachment to the new revolutionary order in the countryside.

Imbued with the rationalism and skepticism of the eighteenth-century philosophes, many delegates distrusted popular piety and "superstitious religion." Thus they established a national church, with priests chosen by voters. The National Assembly then forced the Catholic clergy to take a loyalty oath to the new government. The pope formally condemned this attempt to subjugate the church, and only half the priests of France swore the oath. Many sincere Christians, especially those in the countryside, were upset by these changes in the religious order. The attempt to remake the Catholic Church, like the Assembly's abolition of guilds and workers' associations, sharpened the conflict between the educated classes and the common people that had been emerging in the eighteenth century.

Revolutionary Aspirations in Saint-Domingue

The French Revolution radically transformed not only the territorial nation of France but its overseas colonies as well. On the eve of the Revolution, Saint-Domingue—the most profitable of all Caribbean colonies—was even more rife with social tensions than France itself. The island was composed of a variety of social groups who resented and mistrusted one another. The European population included French colonial officials, wealthy plantation owners and merchants, and poor immigrants. Greatly outnumbering the white population were the colony's five hundred thousand slaves, along with a sizable population of free people of African and mixed African European descent. This last group referred to themselves as "free coloreds" or **free people of color.**

free people of color Sizable population of free people of African and mixed African-European descent living in the French isles of the Caribbean.

The political and intellectual turmoil of the 1780s, with its growing rhetoric of liberty, equality, and fraternity, raised new challenges and possibilities for each of these groups. For slaves, news of abolitionist movements in France, and the royal government's own attempts to rein in the worst abuses of slavery, led to hopes that the mother country might grant them freedom. Free people of color found in such rhetoric the principles on which to base a defense of their legal and political rights. They looked to political reforms in Paris as a means of gaining political enfranchisement and regaining legal rights that had been rescinded by colonial administrators. The white elite looked to revolutionary ideals of representative government for the chance to gain control of their own affairs, as had the American colonists before them. The meeting of the Estates General and the Declaration of the Rights of Man and of the Citizen raised these conflicting colonial aspirations to new levels.

The National Assembly, however, frustrated the hopes of all these groups. It ruled that each colony would draft its own constitution, with free rein over decisions on slavery and the enfranchisement of free people of color. After dealing this blow to the aspirations of slaves and free coloreds, the committee also reaffirmed French monopolies over colonial trade, thereby angering planters as well.

Following a failed revolt in Saint-Domingue led by Vincent Ogé (oh-ZHAY), a free man of color, the National Assembly attempted a compromise. It granted political rights to free people of color born to two free parents who possessed sufficient property. When news of this legislation arrived in Saint-Domingue, the white elite was furious and the colonial governor refused to enact it. Violence now erupted between groups of whites and free coloreds in parts of the colony. The liberal revolution had failed to satisfy the contradictory ambitions in the colonies.

World War and Republican France (1791–1799)

How and why did the Revolution take a radical turn at home and in the colonies?

When Louis XVI accepted the final version of the National Assembly's constitution in September 1791, a young and still obscure provincial lawyer and delegate named Maximilien Robespierre (ROBES-pee-air) (1758–1794) concluded, "The Revolution is over." Robespierre was both right and wrong. He was right in the sense that the most constructive and lasting reforms were in place. Nothing substantial in the way of liberty and fundamental reform would be gained in the next generation. He was wrong in the sense that a much more radical stage lay ahead. New heroes and new ideologies were to emerge in revolutionary wars and international conflict in which Robespierre himself would play a central role.

Foreign Reactions and the Beginning of War

The outbreak and progress of revolution in France produced great excitement and a sharp division of opinion in Europe and the United States. Liberals and radicals saw a mighty triumph of liberty over despotism. In Great Britain especially, they hoped that the French example would lead to a fundamental reordering of Parliament, which was in the hands of the aristocracy and a few wealthy merchants. After the French Revolution began, conservative leaders such as Edmund Burke (1729–1797) were deeply troubled by the aroused spirit of reform. In 1790 Burke published *Reflections on the Revolution in France*, one of the great defenses of European conservatism. He defended inherited privileges in general and those of the English monarchy and aristocracy. He glorified the unrepresentative Parliament and predicted that thoroughgoing reform like that occurring in France would lead only to chaos and tyranny. Burke's work sparked much debate.

One passionate rebuttal came from a young writer in London, Mary Wollstonecraft (WOOL-stuhn-kraft) (1759–1797). Incensed by Burke's book, Wollstonecraft immediately wrote a blistering, widely read attack, *A Vindication of the Rights of Man* (1790). Then she made a daring intellectual leap, developing for the first time the logical implications of natural-law philosophy in her masterpiece, *A Vindication of the Rights of Woman* (1792). To fulfill the still-unrealized potential of the French Revolution and to eliminate the sexual inequality she had felt so keenly, she demanded that

> the Rights of Women be respected . . . [and] JUSTICE for one-half of the human race. . . . It is time to effect a revolution in female manners, time to restore to them

their lost dignity, and make them, as part of the human species, labor, by reform-
ing themselves, to reform the world.

Setting high standards for women — "I wish to persuade women to endeavor to acquire strength, both of mind and body"[3] — Wollstonecraft broke with those who had a low opinion of women's intellectual potential. She advocated rigorous co-education, which would make women better wives and mothers, good citizens, and economically independent. Women could manage businesses and enter politics if only men would give them the chance. Wollstonecraft's analysis testified to the power of the Revolution to excite and inspire outside of France. Paralleling ideas put forth independently in France by Olympe de Gouges (oh-LIMP duh GOOJ) (1748–1793), a self-taught writer and woman of the people (see the feature "Listening to the Past: Revolution and Women's Rights" on pages 563–564), Wollstonecraft's work marked the birth of the modern women's movement for equal rights, and it was ultimately very influential.

The kings and nobles of continental Europe, who had at first welcomed the revolution in France as weakening a competing monarchy, realized that their power was also threatened. In June 1791, Louis XVI and Marie Antoinette were arrested and returned to Paris after trying unsuccessfully to slip out of France. The shock of this arrest led the monarchs of Austria and Prussia to issue the Declaration of Pillnitz in August 1791. This carefully worded statement declared their willingness to intervene in France in certain circumstances and was expected to have a sobering effect on revolutionary France without causing war.

But the crowned heads of Europe misjudged the revolutionary spirit in France. The representative body that convened in October 1791 had completely new delegates and a different character. The great majority of the legislators were still prosperous, well-educated middle-class men, but they were younger and less cautious than their predecessors. Many of the deputies belonged to a political club called the **Jacobin** (JAK-uh-bin) **club,** after the name of the former monastery in which they held their meetings. Such clubs had proliferated in Parisian neighborhoods since the beginning of the Revolution, drawing men and women to debate the burning political questions of the day.

Jacobin club A political club in Revolutionary France whose members were radical republicans.

The new representatives to the Assembly whipped themselves into a patriotic fury against the Declaration of Pillnitz. If the kings of Europe were attempting to incite a war against France, then "we will incite a war of people against kings. . . . Ten million Frenchmen, kindled by the fire of liberty, armed with the sword, with reason, with eloquence would be able to change the face of the world and make the tyrants tremble on their thrones."[4] In April 1792 France declared war on Francis II, the Habsburg monarch.

France's crusade against tyranny went poorly at first. Prussian forces joined Austria against the French, who broke and fled at their first military encounter with this First Coalition. The road to Paris lay open, and it is possible that only conflict between the Eastern monarchs over the division of Poland saved France from defeat.

The Assembly declared the country in danger, and volunteers rallied to the capital. In this supercharged wartime atmosphere, rumors of treason by the king and queen spread in Paris. On August 10, 1792, a revolutionary crowd attacked the royal palace at the Tuileries (TWEE-luh-reez), while the king and his family fled for their lives to the nearby Legislative Assembly. Rather than offering refuge, the Assembly suspended the king from all his functions, imprisoned him, and called for a new National Convention to be elected by universal male suffrage. Monarchy in France was on its deathbed, mortally wounded by war and popular upheaval.

The Second Revolution

The fall of the monarchy marked a rapid radicalization of the Revolution, a phase that historians often call the **second revolution.** Louis's imprisonment was followed by the September Massacres. Wild stories that imprisoned counter-revolutionary aristocrats and priests were plotting with the allied invaders seized the city. As a result, angry crowds invaded the prisons of Paris and slaughtered half the men and women they found. In late September 1792 the new, popularly elected National Convention proclaimed France a republic.

The republic sought to create a new popular culture, fashioning compelling symbols that broke with the past and glorified the new order. Its new revolutionary calendar eliminated saints' days and renamed the days and the months after the seasons of the year, while also adding secular holidays designed to instill a love of nation. These secular celebrations were less successful in villages, where Catholicism was stronger.

All the members of the National Convention were republicans, and at the beginning almost all belonged to the Jacobin club of Paris. But the Jacobins themselves were increasingly divided into two bitterly competitive groups—the **Girondists (juh-RON-dists),** named after a department in southwestern France that was home to several of their leaders, and **the Mountain,** led by Robespierre and another young lawyer, Georges Jacques Danton. The Mountain was so called because its members sat on the uppermost benches on the left side of the assembly hall. A majority of the indecisive Convention members, seated in the "Plain" below, floated back and forth between the rival factions.

This division emerged clearly after the National Convention overwhelmingly convicted Louis XVI of treason. The Girondists accepted his guilt but did not wish to put the king to death. By a narrow majority, the Mountain carried the day, and Louis was executed on January 21, 1793, on the newly invented guillotine. Both the Girondists and the Mountain were determined to continue the "war against tyranny." The Prussians had been stopped at the Battle of Valmy on September 20, 1792, one day before the republic was proclaimed. French armies then invaded Savoy and captured Nice, moved into the German Rhineland, and by November 1792 were occupying the entire Austrian Netherlands (modern Belgium). Everywhere they went French armies of occupation chased the princes, abolished feudalism, and "liberated" the people.

But the French armies also lived off the land, requisitioning food and supplies and plundering local treasures. The liberators looked increasingly like foreign invaders. International tensions mounted. In February 1793 the National Convention, at war with Austria and Prussia, declared war on Britain, Holland, and Spain as well. Republican France was now at war with almost all of Europe, a great war that would last almost without interruption until 1815.

Groups within France added to the turmoil. Peasants in western France revolted against being drafted into the army, and devout Catholics, royalists, and foreign agents encouraged their rebellion. In Paris the National Convention was locked in a life-and-death political struggle between the Mountain and the more moderate Girondists. With the middle-class delegates so bitterly divided, the laboring poor of Paris emerged as the decisive political factor. The laboring poor and the petty traders were often known as the **sans-culottes (sanz-koo-LOT),** "without breeches," because their men wore trousers instead of the knee breeches of the aristocracy and the solid middle class. They demanded radical political action to guarantee them their daily bread. The Mountain joined with sans-culottes activists in the city government to engineer a popular uprising that forced the Convention to arrest thirty-one Girondist deputies for treason on June 2. All power passed to the Mountain.

second revolution From 1792 to 1795, the second phase of the French Revolution during which the fall of the French monarchy introduced a rapid radicalization of politics.

Girondists A group contesting control of the National Convention in France, named after a department in southwestern France.

the Mountain The radical faction of the National Convention led by Robespierre and Danton, so called because its members sat in the uppermost benches of the assembly hall.

sans-culottes The name for the laboring poor of Paris, so called because the men wore trousers instead of the knee breeches of the aristocracy and middle class; it came to refer to the militant radicals of the city.

Des Tetes !_du Sang !_ la Mort !_ à la Lanterne !_ à la Guillotine.
point de Reine ! Je suis la Deesse de la Liberté !_ l'egalité !_ que
Londres soit brulé !_ que Paris soit Libre !_ Vive la Guillotine !_

Mfs Mary Stokes delt.

A PARIS BELLE.

Pub. Sept 26th 1794. by H. Humphrey No. 18 Old Bond Street

Contrasting Visions of the Sans-Culottes

The woman on the left, with her playful cat and calm simplicity, suggests how the French sans-culottes saw themselves as democrats and virtuous citizens. The ferocious sans-culotte harpy on the right, a creation of wartime England's vivid counter-revolutionary imagination, screams for more blood, more death: "I am the Goddess of Liberty! Long live the guillotine!" (Bibliothèque nationale de France)

The Convention also formed the Committee of Public Safety to deal with the threats from within and outside France. The committee, which Robespierre came to lead, was given dictatorial power to deal with the national emergency. Moderates in leading provincial cities, such as Lyons and Marseilles, revolted and demanded a decentralized government. The peasant revolt also spread, and the republic's armies were driven back on all fronts. By July 1793 only the areas around Paris and on the eastern frontier were firmly held by the central government. Defeat seemed imminent.

Total War and the Terror

A year later, in July 1794, the Austrian Netherlands and the Rhineland were once again in the hands of conquering French armies, and the First Coalition was falling apart. This remarkable change of fortune was due to the revolutionary government's success in harnessing, for perhaps the first time in history, the explosive forces of a planned economy, revolutionary terror, and modern nationalism in a total war effort.

Robespierre and the Committee of Public Safety first collaborated with the fiercely patriotic sans-culottes to establish a **planned economy** with egalitarian social overtones. Rather than let supply and demand determine prices, the government set maximum allowable prices for key products. Though the state was too weak to enforce all its price regulations, it did fix the price of bread in Paris at levels the poor could afford. Rationing was introduced, and bakers were permitted

planned economy In response to inflation and high unemployment, Robespierre and the government set maximum prices for products, rather than relying on supply and demand.

The French Revolution

May 5, 1789	Estates General convene at Versailles.
June 17, 1789	Third estate declares itself the National Assembly.
June 20, 1789	Oath of the Tennis Court is sworn.
July 14, 1789	Storming of the Bastille occurs.
July–August 1789	Great Fear ravages the countryside.
August 4, 1789	National Assembly abolishes feudal privileges.
August 27, 1789	National Assembly issues Declaration of the Rights of Man.
October 5, 1789	Women march on Versailles and force royal family to return to Paris.
November 1789	National Assembly confiscates church lands.
July 1790	Civil Constitution of the Clergy establishes a national church.
	Louis XVI reluctantly agrees to accept a constitutional monarchy.
June 1791	Royal family is arrested while attempting to flee France.
August 1791	Austria and Prussia issue the Declaration of Pillnitz.
	Slave insurrections break out in Saint-Domingue.
April 1792	France declares war on Austria.
August 1792	Parisian mob attacks the palace and takes Louis XVI prisoner.
September 1792	September Massacres occur.
	National Convention declares France a republic and abolishes monarchy.
January 1793	Louis XVI is executed.
February 1793	France declares war on Britain, Holland, and Spain.
	Revolts take place in some provincial cities.
	Slavery abolished in French colonies.
March 1793	Bitter struggle occurs in the National Convention between Girondists and the Mountain.
April–June 1793	Robespierre and the Mountain organize the Committee of Public Safety and arrest Girondist leaders.
September 1793	Price controls are instituted to aid the sans-culottes and mobilize the war effort.
	British troops invade Saint-Domingue.
1793–1794	Reign of Terror darkens Paris and the provinces.
February 1794	National Convention abolishes slavery in all French territories.
Spring 1794	French armies are victorious on all fronts.
July 1794	Robespierre is executed.
	Thermidorian reaction begins.
1795–1799	Directory rules.
1795	Economic controls are abolished, and suppression of the sans-culottes begins.
	Toussaint L'Ouverture named brigadier general.
1797	Napoleon defeats Austrian armies in Italy and returns triumphant to Paris.
1798	Austria, Great Britain, and Russia form the Second Coalition against France.
1799	Napoleon overthrows the Directory and seizes power.

to make only the "bread of equality"—a brown bread made of a mixture of all available flours. White bread and pastries were outlawed as luxuries. The poor of Paris may not have eaten well, but at least they ate.

They also worked, mainly to produce arms and munitions for the war effort. The government told craftsmen what to produce, nationalized many small workshops, and requisitioned raw materials and grain. The second revolution and the ascendancy of the sans-culottes had produced an embryonic emergency socialism, which thoroughly frightened Europe's propertied classes and had great influence on the subsequent development of socialist ideology.

Second, while radical economic measures supplied the poor with bread and the armies with weapons, the **Reign of Terror** (1793–1794) used revolutionary terror to solidify the home front. Special revolutionary courts responsible only to Robespierre's Committee of Public Safety tried rebels and "enemies of the nation" for political crimes. Some forty thousand French men and women were executed or died in prison. Another three hundred thousand suspects were arrested.

The third and perhaps most decisive element in the French republic's victory over the First Coalition was its ability to draw on the explosive power of patriotic dedication to a national state and a national mission. An essential part of modern **nationalism**, this commitment was something new in history. With a common language and a common tradition newly reinforced by the ideas of popular sovereignty and democracy, large numbers of French people were stirred by a common loyalty. They developed an intense emotional commitment to the defense of the nation and saw the war as a life-and-death struggle between good and evil.

The fervor of nationalism, combined with the all-out mobilization of resources, made the French army unstoppable. After August 1793 all unmarried young men were subject to the draft, resulting in the largest fighting force in the history of European warfare. Recent research concludes that the French armed forces outnumbered their enemies almost four to one.[5] French generals used mass assaults at bayonet point to overwhelm the enemy. "No maneuvering, nothing elaborate," declared the fearless General Hoche. "Just cold steel, passion and patriotism."[6] By spring 1794 French armies were victorious on all fronts. The republic was saved.

Reign of Terror The period from 1793 to 1794, during which Robespierre used revolutionary terror to solidify the home front of France, resulting in the death of some 40,000 French men and women.

nationalism Patriotic dedication to a national state and mission; it was a decisive element in the French republic's victory.

Revolution in Saint-Domingue

The second stage of revolution in Saint-Domingue also resulted from decisive action from below. In August 1791 groups of slaves organized a revolt that spread across much of the northern plain. By the end of August the uprising was "10,000 strong, divided into 3 armies, of whom 700 or 800 are on horseback, and tolerably well-armed."[7] During the next month slaves attacked and destroyed hundreds of sugar and coffee plantations.

On April 4, 1792, as war loomed with the European states, the National Assembly issued a new decree enfranchising all free blacks and free people of color. The Assembly hoped this measure would win the loyalty of free blacks and their aid in defeating the slave rebellion.

Less than two years later, on February 4, 1794, slavery was abolished in the entire French Caribbean, and in 1795 the former slaves won full political rights. The National Convention was forced to make these concessions when Saint-Domingue came under siege from Spanish and British troops hoping to capture the profitable colony. With the former slaves and free colored forces on their side, the French gradually regained control of the island in 1796.

The key leader in the French victory was General Toussaint L'Ouverture (too-SAN loo-ver-CHORE) (1743–1803). (See the feature "Individuals in Society: Toussaint L'Ouverture.") L'Ouverture was then named commander of the western province of Saint-Domingue. The increasingly conservative nature of the French government, however, threatened to undo the gains made by former slaves and free people of color. As exiled planters gained a stronger voice in French policy-making, L'Ouverture and other local leaders grew ever more wary of what the future might hold.

The Thermidorian Reaction and the Directory (1794–1799)

With the French army victorious, Robespierre and the Committee of Public Safety relaxed the emergency economic controls, but they extended the political Reign of Terror. In March 1794, to the horror of many sans-culottes, Robespierre wiped out many of his critics. Two weeks later, Robespierre sent many of his long-standing collaborators, including the famous orator Danton, up the steps to the guillotine. A strange assortment of radicals and moderates in the Convention, knowing that they might be next, organized a conspiracy. They howled down Robespierre when he tried to speak to the National Convention on 9 Thermidor (July 27, 1794). The next day it was Robespierre's turn to be shaved by the revolutionary razor.

As Robespierre's closest supporters followed their leader to the guillotine, France unexpectedly experienced a thorough reaction to the despotism of the Reign of Terror. In a general way, this **Thermidorian** (thur-mi-DAWR-ee-uhn) **reaction** recalled the early days of the Revolution. The middle-class lawyers and professionals who had led the liberal revolution of 1789 reasserted their authority, drawing support from their own class, the provincial cities, and the better-off peasants. The National Convention abolished many economic controls, let prices rise sharply, and severely restricted the local political organizations in which the sans-culottes had their strength.

> **Thermidorian reaction** The period after the execution of Robespierre in 1794; it was a reaction to the violence of the Reign of Terror.

The collapse of economic controls, coupled with runaway inflation, hit the working poor very hard. After the Convention used the army to suppress the sans culottes' protests, the urban poor lost their revolutionary fervor. Excluded and disillusioned, they would have little interest in and influence on politics until 1830. The poor of the countryside turned toward religion as a relief from earthly cares. Rural women, especially, brought back the Catholic Church and the open worship of God as the government began to soften its antireligious revolutionary stance.

As for the middle-class members of the National Convention, in 1795 they wrote yet another constitution that they believed would guarantee their economic position and political supremacy. As in previous elections, the mass of the population voted only for electors, whose number was cut back to men of substantial means. Electors then elected

The Execution of Robespierre
The guillotine was painted red and was completely wooden except for the heavy iron blade. Large crowds witnessed the executions in a majestic public square in central Paris, then known as the Place de la Revolution and now called the Place de la Concorde (Harmony Square).
(Snark/Art Resource, NY)

- The revolution in France brought mixed reactions elsewhere, from Edmund Burke's book defending conservatism to Mary Wollstonecraft's passionate plea to eliminate sexual inequality.

- The monarchs of Austria and Prussia responded to the arrest of the royal family with the Declaration of Pillnitz, inciting such anger that the National Assembly, led by members of the Jacobin political club, declared war on the Habsburg monarch and then suspended the king from all his functions.

- The National Convention declared France a republic, executed the king in 1793, and sought to create a new republican, secular culture.

- The National Convention faced division between the moderate Girondists and the radical Mountain as French armies battled Prussian and Austrian forces, ending up at war against most of Europe.

- Robespierre and the Committee of Public Safety established a planned economy, fixed the price of bread, provided work to aid the war effort, initiated the Reign of Terror, and worked to promote a strong sense of nationalism, all of which helped to save the republic, though at the cost of many lives.

- In the Caribbean island of Saint-Domingue (today's Haiti), slaves revolted and, under the pressure of war, the French government first enfranchised free people of color, then abolished slavery and extended political rights to former slaves.

- Under the leadership of Toussaint L'Ouverture, a former slave, French forces in Saint-Domingue defeated Spanish and British invaders.

- The Thermidorian Reaction led to the execution of Robespierre, a new National Convention, the end of economic controls, a new constitution, the establishment of the Directory, and a coup d'état by Napoleon.

the members of a reorganized legislative assembly as well as key officials throughout France. The new assembly also chose a five-man executive—the Directory.

The Directory continued to support French military expansion abroad. War was no longer so much a crusade as a means to meet ever-present, ever-unsolved economic problems. Large, victorious French armies reduced unemployment at home and were able to live off the territories they conquered and plundered.

The unprincipled action of the Directory reinforced widespread disgust with war and starvation. This general dissatisfaction revealed itself clearly in the national elections of 1797, which returned a large number of conservative and even monarchist deputies who favored peace at almost any price. The members of the Directory, fearing for their skins, used the army to nullify the elections and began to govern dictatorially. Two years later Napoleon Bonaparte (nuh-POH-lee-uhn BOH-nuh-pahrt) ended the Directory in a coup d'état (koo day-TA) and substituted a strong dictatorship for a weak one. The effort to establish stable representative government had failed.

The Napoleonic Era (1799–1815)

Why did Napoleon Bonaparte assume control of France, and what factors led to his downfall? How did the new republic of Haiti gain independence from France?

For almost fifteen years, from 1799 to 1814, France was in the hands of a keen-minded military dictator of exceptional ability. One of history's most fascinating leaders, Napoleon Bonaparte (1769–1821) realized the need to put an end to civil strife in France in order to create unity and consolidate his rule. And he did. But Napoleon saw himself as a man of destiny, and the glory of war and the dream of universal empire proved irresistible. For years he spiraled from victory to victory, but in the end he was destroyed by a mighty coalition united in fear of his restless ambition.

Napoleon's Rule of France

In 1799 when he seized power, young General Napoleon Bonaparte was a national hero. Born in Corsica into an impoverished noble family in 1769, Napoleon left home and became a lieutenant in the French artillery in 1785. After a brief and unsuccessful adventure fighting for Corsican independence in 1789, he returned to France as a French patriot and a dedicated revolutionary. Rising rapidly in the new army, Napoleon was placed in command of French forces in Italy and won brilliant victories there in 1796 and 1797. His next campaign, in Egypt, was a failure, but Napoleon returned to France before the fiasco was generally known, and his reputation remained intact.

Napoleon soon learned that some prominent members of the legislature were plotting against the Directory. The dissatisfaction of these plotters stemmed not so much from the fact that the Directory was a dictatorship as from the fact that it was a weak dictatorship. Ten years of upheaval and uncertainty had convinced these disillusioned revolutionaries that a strong military ruler was needed to restore order. Thus the conspirators and Napoleon organized a takeover. On November 9, 1799, they ousted the Directors, and the following day soldiers disbanded the legislature at bayonet point. Napoleon was named first consul of the republic, and a new constitution consolidating his position was overwhelmingly approved in a

The Napoleonic Era

November 1799	Napoleon overthrows the Directory.
December 1799	French voters overwhelmingly approve Napoleon's new constitution.
1800	Napoleon founds the Bank of France.
1801	France defeats Austria and acquires Italian and German territories in the Treaty of Lunéville.
	Napoleon signs the Concordat with the pope.
1802	France signs the Treaty of Amiens with Britain.
	French forces arrive in Saint-Domingue.
April 1803	Toussaint L'Ouverture dies in France.
January 1804	Jean Jacques Dessalines declares Haitian independence.
March 1804	Napoleonic Code comes into force.
December 1804	Napoleon crowns himself emperor.
May 1805	First Haitian constitution promulgated.
October 1805	Britain defeats the French and Spanish fleet at the Battle of Trafalgar.
December 1805	Napoleon defeats Austria and Russia at the Battle of Austerlitz.
1807	Napoleon redraws the map of Europe in the treaties of Tilsit.
1810	The Grand Empire is at its height.
June 1812	Napoleon invades Russia with 600,000 men.
Fall–Winter 1812	Napoleon makes a disastrous retreat from Russia.
March 1814	Russia, Prussia, Austria, and Britain sign the Treaty of Chaumont, pledging alliance to defeat Napoleon.
April 1814	Napoleon abdicates and is exiled to Elba.
February–June 1815	Napoleon escapes from Elba and rules France until he is defeated at the Battle of Waterloo.

plebiscite in December 1799. Republican appearances were maintained, but Napoleon was already the real ruler of France.

The essence of Napoleon's domestic policy was to use his great and highly personal powers to maintain order and end civil strife. He did so by working out unwritten agreements with powerful groups in France whereby the groups received favors in return for loyal service. Napoleon's bargain with the solid middle class was codified in the famous Civil Code of 1804, which reasserted two of the fundamental principles of the liberal and essentially moderate revolution of 1789: equality of all male citizens before the law and absolute security of wealth and private property. Napoleon and the leading bankers of Paris established the privately owned Bank of France, which loyally served the interests of both the state and the financial oligarchy. Peasants were also appeased when Napoleon defended the gains in land and status they had claimed during the revolution.

At the same time Napoleon perfected a thoroughly centralized state. As recent scholarship shows, Napoleon consolidated his rule by recruiting disillusioned revolutionaries for the network of ministers, prefects, and centrally appointed mayors that depended on him and came to serve him well. Only former revolutionaries who leaned too far to the left or to the right were pushed to the sidelines.[8] Nor were members of the old nobility slighted. In 1800 and again in 1802 Napoleon granted amnesty to one hundred thousand émigrés on the condition that they return to France and take a loyalty oath. Members of this returning elite soon ably occupied many high posts in the expanding centralized state. Napoleon also created a new imperial nobility in order to reward his most talented generals and officials.

Napoleon applied his diplomatic skills to healing the Catholic Church in France so that it could serve as a bulwark of order and social peace. After arduous negotiations, Napoleon and Pope Pius VII (1800–1823) signed the Concordat (kon-KAWR-dat) of 1801. The pope gained the precious right for French Catholics to practice their religion freely, but Napoleon gained political power: his government now nominated bishops, paid the clergy, and exerted great influence over the church in France.

The domestic reforms of Napoleon's early years were his greatest achievement. Much of his legal and administrative reorganization has survived in France to this day. More generally, Napoleon's domestic initiatives gave the great majority of French people a welcome sense of stability and national unity.

Order and unity had a price: Napoleon's authoritarian rule. Women, who had often participated in revolutionary politics, lost many of the gains they had made in the 1790s. Under the law of the new Napoleonic Code, women were dependents of either their fathers or their husbands, and they could not make contracts or even have bank accounts in their own names. Indeed, Napoleon and his advisers aimed at re-establishing a family monarchy, where the power of the husband and father was as absolute over the wife and the children as that of Napoleon was over his subjects.

Free speech and freedom of the press were continually violated. By 1811 only four newspapers were left, and they were little more than organs of government propaganda. The occasional elections were a farce. Later laws prescribed harsh penalties for political offenses, and people were watched carefully under an efficient spy system. People suspected of subversive activities were arbitrarily detained, placed under house arrest, or consigned to insane asylums. After 1810 political suspects were held in state prisons, as they had been during the Terror. There were about twenty-five hundred such political prisoners in 1814.

Napoleon's Expansion in Europe

Napoleon was above all a military man, and a great one. After coming to power in 1799 he sent peace feelers to Austria and Great Britain, the two remaining members of the Second Coalition that had been formed against France in 1798. When these overtures were rejected, French armies led by Napoleon decisively defeated the Austrians. In the Treaty of Lunéville (1801), Austria accepted the loss of almost all its Italian possessions, and German territory on the west bank of the Rhine was incorporated into France. The British agreed to the Treaty of Amiens in 1802, allowing France to remain in control of Holland, the Austrian Netherlands, the west bank of the Rhine, and most of the Italian peninsula. The Treaty of Amiens was clearly a diplomatic triumph for Napoleon, and peace with honor and profit increased his popularity at home.

In 1802 Napoleon was secure but driven to expand his power. Aggressively redrawing the map of Germany so as to weaken Austria and encourage the secondary states of southwestern Germany to side with France, Napoleon tried to restrict

The Coronation of Napoleon, 1804 (detail)
In this grandiose painting by Jacques-Louis David, Napoleon prepares to crown his wife, Josephine, in an elaborate ceremony in Notre Dame Cathedral. Napoleon, the ultimate upstart, also crowned himself. Pope Pius VII, seated glumly behind the emperor, is reduced to being a spectator. (Louvre/Réunion des Musées Nationaux/Art Resource, NY)

British trade with all of Europe. He then plotted to attack Great Britain, but his Mediterranean fleet was virtually annihilated by Lord Nelson at the Battle of Trafalgar on October 21, 1805. Invasion of England was henceforth impossible. Renewed fighting had its advantages, however, for the first consul used the wartime atmosphere to have himself proclaimed emperor in late 1804.

Austria, Russia, and Sweden joined with Britain to form the Third Coalition against France shortly before the Battle of Trafalgar. Actions such as Napoleon's assumption of the Italian crown had convinced both Alexander I of Russia and Francis II of Austria that Napoleon was a threat to their interests and to the European balance of power. Yet the Austrians and the Russians were no match for Napoleon, who scored a brilliant victory over them at the Battle of Austerlitz (AW-ster-lits) in December 1805. Alexander I decided to pull back, and Austria accepted large territorial losses in return for peace as the Third Coalition collapsed.

Napoleon then proceeded to reorganize the German states to his liking. In 1806 he abolished many of the tiny German states as well as the ancient Holy Roman Empire and established by decree the German Confederation of the Rhine, a union of fifteen German states minus Austria, Prussia, and Saxony. Naming himself "protector" of the confederation, Napoleon firmly controlled western Germany.

Napoleon's intervention in German affairs alarmed the Prussians, who mobilized their armies after more than a decade of peace with France. Napoleon attacked and won two more brilliant victories in October 1806 at Jena (YEY-nah) and Auerstädt (OW-er-stat), where the Prussians were outnumbered two to one.

The war with Prussia, now joined by Russia, continued into the following spring. After Napoleon's larger armies won another victory, Alexander I of Russia was ready to negotiate the peace. In the subsequent treaties of Tilsit, Prussia lost half of its population, while Russia accepted Napoleon's reorganization of western and central Europe and promised to enforce Napoleon's economic blockade against British goods.

The War of Haitian Independence

With Toussaint L'Ouverture acting increasingly as an independent ruler of the western province of Saint-Domingue, another general, André Rigaud, set up his own government in the southern peninsula, which had long been more isolated from France than the rest of the colony. Civil war broke out between the two sides in 1799, when L'Ouverture's forces, led by his lieutenant Jean Jacques Dessalines (dey-sa-LEEN), invaded the south. Victory over Rigaud gave Toussaint control of the entire colony. (See the feature "Individuals in Society: Toussaint L'Ouverture.")

L'Ouverture's victory was soon challenged, however, by Napoleon's arrival in power. Napoleon intended to reinvigorate the Caribbean plantation economy as a basis for expanding French power. He ordered his brother-in-law General Charles-Victor-Emmanuel Leclerc to crush the new regime.

In 1802 Leclerc landed in Saint-Domingue. Although Toussaint L'Ouverture cooperated with the French and turned his army over to them, he was arrested and deported to France, along with his family, where he died in 1803. Jean Jacques Dessalines united the resistance under his command and led it to a crushing victory over the French forces. Of the fifty-eight thousand French soldiers, fifty thousand were lost in combat and to disease. On January 1, 1804, Dessalines formally declared the independence of Saint-Domingue and the creation of the new sovereign nation of Haiti, the name used by the pre-Columbian inhabitants of the island. (France's other Caribbean colonies were not granted independence. Slavery was re-established and remained in force until 1848.)

Haiti, the second independent state in the Americas and the first in Latin America, was thus born from the first successful large-scale slave revolt in history. Fearing the spread of slave rebellion to the United States, President Thomas Jefferson refused to recognize Haiti. Both the American and the French Revolutions thus exposed their limits by acting to protect economic interests at the expense of revolutionary ideals of freedom and equality. Yet, Haitian independence had fundamental repercussions for world history. As one recent historian of the Haitian revolution commented:

> The slave insurrection of Saint-Domingue led to the expansion of citizenship beyond racial barriers despite the massive political and economic investment in the slave system at the time. If we live in a world in which democracy is meant to exclude no one, it is in no small part because of the actions of those slaves in Saint-Domingue who insisted that human rights were theirs too.[9]

The Grand Empire and Its End

Napoleon resigned himself to the loss of Saint-Domingue, but he still maintained imperial ambitions in Europe. Increasingly, he saw himself as the emperor of Europe and not just of France. The so-called **Grand Empire** he built had three parts. The core, or first part, was an ever-expanding France, which by 1810 included Belgium, Holland, parts of northern Italy, and much German territory on the east bank of the Rhine. Beyond French borders Napoleon established the

Grand Empire Napoleon's name for the European empire over which he intended to rule. This Grand Empire would consist of France, a number of lesser dependent states ruled by his relations, and several major allied states (Austria, Prussia, and Russia).

Individuals in Society

Toussaint L'Ouverture

Little is known of the early life of the brilliant military and political leader Toussaint L'Ouverture. He was born in 1743 on a plantation outside Le Cap owned by the Count de Bréda (bree-DAH). According to tradition, Toussaint was the eldest son of a captured African prince from modern-day Benin. Toussaint Bréda, as he was then called, occupied a privileged position among slaves. Instead of performing backbreaking labor in the fields, he served his master as a coachman and livestock keeper. During the 1770s, after being freed, he leased his own small coffee plantation, worked by slaves. A devout Catholic who led a frugal and ascetic life, L'Ouverture impressed others with his enormous physical energy, intellectual acumen, and air of mystery.

Toussaint L'Ouverture entered history in 1791 when he joined the slave uprisings that swept Saint-Domingue. (At some point he took on the cryptic *nom de guerre* "l'ouverture" meaning "the opening.") Toussaint rose to prominence among rebel slaves allied with Spain and by early 1794 controlled his own army. In 1794 he defected to the French side and led his troops to a series of victories against the Spanish. In 1795 France's National Convention promoted L'Ouverture to brigadier general.

Over the next three years L'Ouverture successively eliminated rivals for authority on the island. First he freed himself of the French commissioners sent to govern the colony. With a firm grip on power in the northern province, Toussaint defeated General André Rigaud in 1800 to gain control in the south. His army then marched on the capital of Spanish Santo Domingo on the eastern half of the island, meeting little resistance. The entire island of Hispaniola was now under his command.

With control of Saint-Domingue in his hands, L'Ouverture was confronted with the challenge of building a postemancipation society, the first of its kind. The task was made even more difficult by the chaos wreaked by war, the destruction of plantations, and bitter social and racial tensions. For L'Ouverture the most pressing concern was to re-establish the plantation economy.

Without revenue to pay his army, the gains of the rebellion could be lost. He therefore encouraged white planters to return and reclaim their property. He also adopted harsh policies toward former slaves, forcing them back to their plantations and restricting their ability to acquire land. When they resisted, he sent troops across the island to enforce submission.

In 1801 L'Ouverture convened a colonial assembly to draft a new constitution that reaffirmed his draconian labor policies. The constitution named L'Ouverture governor for life, leaving Saint-Domingue as a colony in name alone. When news of the constitution arrived in France, an angry Napoleon dispatched General Leclerc (luh-CLAIR) to re-establish French control. In June 1802 Leclerc's forces arrested L'Ouverture and took him to France. He was jailed at Fort de Joux (for duh ZHOO) in the Jura Mountains near the Swiss border, where he died of pneumonia on April 7, 1803. It was left to his lieutenant, Jean Jacques Dessalines, to win independence for the new Haitian nation.

Equestrian portrait of Toussaint L'Ouverture. (Réunion des Musées Nationaux/Art Resource, NY)

Questions for Analysis

1. Toussaint L'Ouverture was both slave and slave owner. How did each experience shape his life and actions?

2. Despite their differences, what did Toussaint L'Ouverture and Napoleon Bonaparte have in common? Why did they share a common fate?

second part: a number of dependent satellite kingdoms, on the thrones of which he placed (and replaced) the members of his large family. The third part comprised the independent but allied states of Austria, Prussia, and Russia. After 1806 both satellites and allies were expected to support Napoleon's continental system and to cease trade with Britain.

The impact of the Grand Empire on the peoples of Europe was considerable. In the areas incorporated into France and in the satellites (see Map 21.1), feudal dues and serfdom had been abolished. Some of the peasants and middle class benefited from these reforms. Yet Napoleon had to put the prosperity and special interests of France first in order to safeguard his power base. Levying heavy taxes in money and men for his armies, he came to be regarded more as a conquering tyrant than as an enlightened liberator. Thus French rule encouraged the growth of reactive nationalism, for individuals in different lands developed patriotic feelings for their own lands in opposition to Napoleon's imperialism.

The first great revolt occurred in Spain. In 1808 a coalition of Catholics, monarchists, and patriots rebelled against Napoleon's attempts to make Spain a French satellite with a Bonaparte as its king. French armies occupied Madrid, but the foes of Napoleon fled to the hills and waged uncompromising guerrilla warfare. Spain was a clear warning: resistance to French imperialism was growing.

Yet Napoleon pushed on, determined to hold his complex and far-flung empire together. In 1810, when the Grand Empire was at its height, Britain still remained at war with France, helping the guerrillas in Spain and Portugal. The continental system, organized to exclude British goods from the continent and force that "nation of shopkeepers" to its knees, was a failure. Instead, it was France that suffered from Britain's counter-blockade, which created hard times for French artisans and the middle class. Perhaps looking for a scapegoat, Napoleon turned on Alexander I of Russia, who in 1811 openly repudiated Napoleon's war of prohibitions against British goods.

Napoleon's invasion of Russia began in June 1812 with a force that eventually numbered 600,000, probably the largest force yet assembled in a single army. Only one-third of this Great Army was French, however; nationals of all the satellites and allies were drafted into the operation. Originally planning to winter in the Russian city of Smolensk (smoh-LENSK) if Alexander did not sue for peace, Napoleon reached Smolensk and recklessly pressed on toward Moscow. The great Battle of Borodino that followed was a draw, and the Russians retreated in good order. Alexander ordered the evacuation of Moscow, which then burned in part, and he refused to negotiate. Finally, after five weeks in the abandoned city, Napoleon ordered a retreat. That retreat was one of the greatest military disasters in history. The Russian army, the Russian winter, and starvation cut Napoleon's army to pieces.

MAPPING THE PAST

MAP 21.1   Napoleonic Europe in 1810

Only Great Britain remained at war with Napoleon at the height of the Grand Empire. Many British goods were smuggled through Helgoland, a tiny but strategic British possession off the German coast. Compare this map with Map 16.1, which shows the division of Europe in 1715. **[1]** How had the balance of power shifted in Europe from 1715 to 1810? What changed, and what remained the same? **[2]** Why did Napoleon succeed in achieving vast territorial gains where Louis XIV did not? **[3]** In comparing Map 16.1 with this map, what was the impact of Napoleon's wars on Germany and the Italian peninsula? What significance do you think this had for these regions in the nineteenth century?

ATLANTIC OCEAN

North Sea

Baltic Sea

Black Sea

Mediterranean Sea

GREAT BRITAIN

London

KINGDOM OF NORWAY AND DENMARK

KINGDOM OF SWEDEN

Stockholm

Copenhagen

St. Petersburg

RUSSIAN EMPIRE

Moscow

Borodino 1812

Smolensk

Kiev

Lübeck

Hamburg

Bremen

Berlin

WESTPHALIA

Auerstädt 1806

Jena 1806

SAXONY

PRUSSIA

SWEDISH POMERANIA

Danzig

Königsberg

Tilsit

Friedland 1807

Neman R.

GRAND DUCHY OF WARSAW

CONFEDERATION OF THE RHINE

Rhine R.

Elbe R.

WÜRTTEMBERG

BADEN

BAVARIA

Zurich

SWITZERLAND

Vienna

Austerlitz 1805

Wagram 1809

Pressburg

Buda

Pest

AUSTRIAN EMPIRE

Danube R.

ILLYRIAN PROVINCES

OTTOMAN EMPIRE

Constantinople

Athens

Ionian Is. (Gr. Br.)

KINGDOM OF ITALY

Milan

Marengo 1800

Genoa

Corsica

Elba

Sardinia

Rome

Naples

KINGDOM OF NAPLES

Palermo

KINGDOM OF SICILY

Malta (Gr. Br.)

Brussels

Waterloo 1815

Paris

Lunéville

Amiens

FRANCE

Marseilles

SPAIN

Madrid

GIBRALTAR (Gr. Br.)

Trafalgar 1805

PORTUGAL

Lisbon

French empire
Dependent states
Allied with Napoleon
At war with Napoleon
Major battle

400 Mi.
400 Km.
200
0

50° N
60° N
40° N
10° W
0
10° E
20° E
30° E

Section Review

- Napoleon brought about civil order by offering favors for loyal service, letting the poor keep land, appointing disillusioned revolutionaries and amnestied nobles to government posts, and exercising the power to nominate clergy to posts in exchange for granting religious freedom for Catholics.

- Civil liberties and freedoms for women suffered under Napoleon's authoritarian rule.

- Napoleon defeated the Austrians, proclaimed himself emperor, defeated Prussia and Russia at Austerlitz and then abolished the Holy Roman Empire by creating the German Confederation of the Rhine, and gained Russia's support in a blockade against the British, who had thwarted him at Trafalgar.

- Civil war in Saint-Domingue ended with victory for Toussaint L'Ouverture, who allowed white planters to return, forced former slaves to return to their plantations, and named himself governor for life, but Napoleonic forces captured him and deported him to France.

- The resistance led by Dessalines crushed the French and Saint-Domingue became the sovereign nation of Haiti.

- Napoleon's Grand Empire faced a Spanish revolt supported by the British, a failed French coalition invasion of Russia, and a Europe united against France.

- Napoleon abdicated and was exiled to the island of Elba, but he escaped and after the Hundred Days the allies defeated him at Waterloo; the French restored the Bourbon dynasty under Louis XVIII.

When the frozen remnants staggered into Poland and Prussia in December, 370,000 men had died and another 200,000 had been taken prisoner.[10]

Leaving his troops to their fate, Napoleon raced to Paris to raise yet another army. Austria and Prussia deserted Napoleon and joined Russia and Great Britain in the Treaty of Chaumont in March 1814, by which the four powers pledged allegiance to defeat the French emperor. All across Europe patriots called for a "war of liberation" against Napoleon's oppression. Less than a month later, on April 4, 1814, a defeated Napoleon abdicated his throne. After this unconditional abdication, the victorious allies granted Napoleon the island of Elba off the coast of Italy as his own tiny state. Napoleon was even allowed to keep his imperial title, and France was required to pay him a yearly income of 2 million francs.

The allies also agreed to the restoration of the Bourbon dynasty under Louis XVIII (r. 1814–1824) and promised to treat France with leniency in a peace settlement. The new monarch tried to consolidate support among the people by issuing the Constitutional Charter, which accepted many of France's revolutionary changes and guaranteed civil liberties.

Yet Louis XVIII—old, ugly, and crippled by gout—totally lacked the glory and magic of Napoleon. Hearing of political unrest in France and diplomatic tensions in Vienna, Napoleon staged a daring escape from Elba in February 1815. Landing in France, he issued appeals for support and marched on Paris with a small band of followers. French officers and soldiers who had fought so long for their emperor responded to the call. Louis XVIII fled, and once more Napoleon took command. But Napoleon's gamble was a desperate long shot, for the allies were united against him. At the end of a frantic period known as the Hundred Days, they crushed his forces at Waterloo on June 18, 1815, and imprisoned him on the rocky island of St. Helena, far off the western coast of Africa.

Louis XVIII returned again and recommenced his reign. The allies now dealt more harshly with the apparently incorrigible French. As for Napoleon, he took revenge by writing his memoirs, skillfully nurturing the myth that he had been Europe's revolutionary liberator, a romantic hero whose lofty work had been undone by oppressive reactionaries. An era had ended.

Chapter Review

What social, political, and economic factors formed the background to the French Revolution? (page 536)

The French Revolution was forged by multiple and complex factors. Whereas an earlier generation of historians was convinced that the origins of the Revolution lay in class struggle between the entrenched nobility and the rising bourgeoisie, it is now clear that many other factors were involved. Certainly, French society had undergone significant transformations during the eighteenth century, which dissolved many economic and social differences among elites without removing the legal distinction between them. These changes were accompanied by political struggles between the monarchy and its officers, particularly in the high law courts. Emerging public opinion focused on the shortcomings of monarchical rule, and a rising torrent of political theory, cheap pamphlets, gossip, and innuendo offered scathing and even pornographic

Key Terms

estates (p. 536)

desacralization (p. 538)

Assembly of Notables (p. 540)

Estates General (p. 540)

National Assembly (p. 541)

Great Fear (p. 542)

constitutional monarchy (p. 543)

depictions of the king and his court. With their sacred royal aura severely tarnished, Louis XV and his successor Louis XVI found themselves unable to respond to the financial crises generated by French involvement in the Seven Years' War and the American Revolution. Louis XVI's half-hearted efforts to redress the situation were quickly overwhelmed by elite and popular demands for fundamental reform.

What were the immediate events that sparked the Revolution, and how did they result in the formation of a constitutional monarchy in France? How did the ideals and events of the early Revolution raise new aspirations in the colonies? (page 540)

Forced to call a meeting of the Estates General for the first time in almost two centuries, Louis XVI fell back on the traditional formula of one vote for each of the three orders of society. Debate over the composition of the assembly called forth a bold new paradigm: that the Third Estate in itself constituted the French nation. By 1791 the National Assembly had eliminated Old Regime privileges and had established a constitutional monarchy. Talk in France of liberty, equality, and fraternity raised new and contradictory aspirations in the colony of Saint-Domingue. White planters lobbied for increased colonial autonomy; free people of color sought the return of legal equality; slaves of African birth or descent took direct action on revolutionary ideals by rising in rebellion against their masters.

How and why did the Revolution take a radical turn at home and in the colonies? (page 545)

With the execution of the royal couple and the declaration of terror as the order of the day, the French Revolution took an increasingly radical turn from the end of 1792. Popular fears of counter-revolutionary conspiracy combined with the outbreak of war against a mighty alliance of European monarchs convinced many that the Revolution was vulnerable and must be defended against its multiple enemies. In a spiraling cycle of accusations and executions, the Jacobins eliminated their political opponents and then factions within their own party. The Directory government that took power after the fall of Robespierre restored political equilibrium at the cost of the radical platform of social equality he had pursued.

Why did Napoleon Bonaparte assume control of France, and what factors led to his downfall? How did the new republic of Haiti gain independence from France? (page 552)

Wearied by the weaknesses of the Directory, a group of conspirators gave Napoleon Bonaparte control of France. His brilliant reputation as a military leader and his charisma and determination made him seem ideal to lead France to victory over its enemies. As is so often the case in history, Napoleon's relentless ambitions ultimately led to his downfall. His story is paralleled by that of Toussaint L'Ouverture, another soldier who emerged to the political limelight from the chaos of revolution only to endure exile and defeat. Unlike Napoleon, L'Ouverture's cause ultimately prevailed. After his exile, war between the French forces and the armies he had led and inspired led to French defeat and independence for Saint-Domingue.

As complex as its origins are the legacies of the French Revolution. These included liberalism, assertive nationalism, radical democratic republicanism, embryonic socialism, self-conscious conservatism, abolitionism, decolonization, and movements for racial and sexual equality. The Revolution also left a rich and turbulent history of electoral competition, legislative assemblies, and even mass politics. Thus the French Revolution and conflicting interpretations of its significance presented a whole range of political options and alternative visions of the future. For this reason, it was truly the revolution in modern European politics.

Notes

1. Quoted in G. Wright, *France in Modern Times*, 4th ed. (New York: W. W. Norton, 1987), p. 34.
2. G. Pernoud and S. Flaisser, eds., *The French Revolution* (Greenwich, Conn.: Fawcett, 1960), p. 61.
3. Quotations from Wollstonecraft are drawn from E. W. Sunstein, *A Different Face: The Life of Mary Wollstonecraft* (New York: Harper & Row, 1975), pp. 208, 211; and H. R. James, *Mary Wollstonecraft: A Sketch* (London: Oxford University Press, 1932), pp. 60, 62, 69.
4. Quoted in L. Gershoy, *The Era of the French Revolution, 1789–1799* (New York: Van Nostrand, 1957), p. 150.
5. T. Blanning, *The French Revolutionary Wars, 1787–1802* (London: Arnold, 1996), pp. 116–128.
6. Quoted ibid., p. 123.
7. Quoted in Laurent Dubois, *Avengers of the New World: The Story of the Haitian Revolution* (Cambridge: Harvard University Press, 2004), p. 97.
8. I. Woloch, *Napoleon and His Collaborators: The Making of a Dictatorship* (New York: W. W. Norton, 2001), pp. 36–65.
9. Ibid., p. 3.
10. D. Sutherland, *France, 1789–1815: Revolution and Counterrevolution* (New York: Oxford University Press, 1986), p. 420.

To assess your mastery of this chapter, go to **bedfordstmartins.com/mckaywestbrief**

Listening to the Past

Revolution and Women's Rights

The 1789 Declaration of the Rights of Man was a revolutionary call for legal equality, representative government, and individual freedom that excluded women from its manifesto. Among those who saw the contradiction in granting supposedly universal rights to only half the population was Marie Gouze (1748–1793), known to history as Olympe de Gouges. The daughter of a provincial butcher and peddler, she pursued a literary career in Paris after the death of her husband. De Gouges's great work was her Declaration of the Rights of Woman (1791). Excerpted here, it called on males to end their oppression of women and to give women equal rights. A radical on women's issues, de Gouges sympathized with the monarchy and criticized Robespierre in print. Convicted of sedition, she was guillotined in November 1793.

Olympe de Gouges in 1784; aquatint by Madame Aubry (1748–1793). (Musée de la Ville de Paris, Musée Carnavalet, Paris, France/The Bridgeman Art Library)

. . . Man, are you capable of being just? . . . Tell me, what gives you sovereign empire to oppress my sex? Your strength? Your talents? Observe the Creator in his wisdom . . . and give me, if you dare, an example of this tyrannical empire. Go back to animals, consult the elements, study plants . . . and distinguish, if you can, the sexes in the administration of nature. Everywhere you will find them mingled; everywhere they cooperate in harmonious togetherness in this immortal masterpiece.

Man alone has raised his exceptional circumstances to a principle. . . . [H]e wants to command as a despot a sex which is in full possession of its intellectual faculties; he pretends to enjoy the Revolution and to claim his rights to equality in order to say nothing more about it. . . . Mothers, daughters, sisters and representatives of the nation demand to be constituted into a national assembly. Believing that ignorance, omission, or scorn for the rights of woman are the only causes of public misfortunes and of the corruption of governments, [the women] have resolved to set forth in a solemn declaration the natural, inalienable, and sacred rights of woman. . . .

I. Woman is born free and lives equal to man in her rights. Social distinctions can be based only on the common utility.

II. The purpose of any political association is the conservation of the natural and imprescriptible rights of woman and man; these rights are liberty, property, security, and especially resistance to oppression.

III. The principle of all sovereignty rests essentially with the nation, which is nothing but the union of woman and man. . . .

IV. Liberty and justice consist of restoring all that belongs to others; thus, the only limits on the exercise of the natural rights of woman are perpetual male tyranny; these limits are to be reformed by the laws of nature and reason.

V. Laws of nature and reason proscribe all acts harmful to society. . . .

VI. The law must be the expression of the general will; all female and male citizens must contribute either personally or through their representatives to its formation; it must be the same for all: male and female citizens, being equal in the eyes of the law, must be equally admitted to all honors, positions, and public employment according to their capacity and without other distinctions besides those of their virtues and talents. . . .

IX. Once any woman is declared guilty, complete rigor is [to be] exercised by the law.

X. No one is to be disquieted for his very basic opinions; woman has the right to mount the scaffold; she must equally have the right to mount the rostrum, provided that her demonstrations do not disturb the legally established public order.

XI. The free communication of thoughts and opinions is one of the most precious rights of woman, since that liberty assures the recognition of children by their fathers. Any female citizen thus may say freely, I am the mother of a child which belongs to you, without being forced by a barbarous prejudice to hide the truth. . . .

XIII. For the support of the public force and the expenses of administration, the contributions of woman and man are equal; she shares all the duties . . . and all the painful tasks; therefore, she must have the same share in the distribution of positions, employment, offices, honors, and jobs. . . .

XVI. No society has a constitution without the guarantee of rights and the separation of powers; the constitution is null if the majority of individuals comprising the nation have not cooperated in drafting it.

XVII. Property belongs to both sexes whether united or separate; for each it is an inviolable and sacred right. . . .

Questions for Analysis

1. On what basis did de Gouges argue for gender equality? Did she believe in natural law?

2. What consequences did "scorn for the rights of woman" have for France, according to de Gouges?

3. Did de Gouges stress political rights at the expense of social and economic rights? If so, why?

Source: Olympe de Gouges, "Declaration of the Rights of Woman," from *Women in Revolutionary Paris, 1789–1795: Selected Documents Translated with Notes and Commentary.* Translated with notes and commentary by Darline Gay Levy, Harriet Branson Applewhite, and Mary Durham Johnson. Copyright © 1979 Board of Trustees. Used with permission of the editors and the University of Illinois Press.

LONDON TO FOLKSTONE IN 3 HOURS.

LONDON & DOVER RAILWAY

LONDON AND FOLKSTONE TIME TABLE.

A colorful timetable poster lists the trains from London to Folkstone, the English Channel's gateway port to the European continent, and proudly proclaims the speed of the journey. (Private Collection/The Bridgeman Art Library)

CHAPTER 22

The Revolution in Energy and Industry

ca. 1780–1860

Chapter Preview

The Industrial Revolution in Britain
What were the origins of the Industrial Revolution in Britain, and how did it develop between 1780 and 1850?

Industrialization in Continental Europe
How after 1815 did continental countries respond to the challenge of industrialization?

Relations Between Capital and Labor
How did the Industrial Revolution affect social classes, the standard of living, and patterns of work? What measures were taken to improve the conditions of workers?

INDIVIDUALS IN SOCIETY: The Strutt Family

LISTENING TO THE PAST: Testimony Concerning Young Mine Workers

W hile the revolution in France was opening a new political era, another revolution was beginning to transform economic and social life. This was the Industrial Revolution, which began in Great Britain around the 1780s and started to influence continental Europe after 1815. Although the Industrial Revolution was less dramatic than the French Revolution, it brought about numerous radical changes. Quite possibly only the development of agriculture during Neolithic times had a comparable impact and significance.

The Industrial Revolution profoundly modified much of human experience. It changed patterns of work, transformed the social class structure, and eventually even altered the international balance of political power. The Industrial Revolution also helped ordinary people gain a higher standard of living as the widespread poverty of the preindustrial world was gradually reduced.

Unfortunately, the improvement in the European standard of living was quite limited until about 1850 for at least two reasons. First, even in Britain, only a few key industries experienced a technological revolution, holding down the increase in total production. Second, Europe's population continued to grow rapidly, leaving most individuals poorer and making the wrenching transformation all the more difficult.

The Industrial Revolution in Britain

What were the origins of the Industrial Revolution in Britain, and how did it develop between 1780 and 1850?

The Industrial Revolution began in Great Britain, that historic union of England, Scotland, and Wales. It was something new in history, and it was quite unplanned. With no models to copy and no idea of what to expect, Britain had to pioneer not only in industrial technology but also in social relations and urban living. Between 1793 and 1815, these formidable tasks were complicated by almost constant war with France. As the trailblazer in economic development—while France was undergoing political change—Britain must command special attention.

Eighteenth-Century Origins

Although many aspects of the British Industrial Revolution are still matters for scholarly debate, it is generally agreed that the industrial changes that did occur grew out of a long process of development. First, the British economy was expanding both domestically and abroad. The North American colonial empire that Britain aggressively built, augmented by a strong position in Latin America and in the African slave trade, provided a growing market for British manufactured goods. Within Britain, goods flowed easily between markets along miles of navigable water. Beginning in the 1770s, a canal-building boom greatly enhanced this natural transportation advantage. Rivers and canals also provided easy movement of England's and Wales's enormous deposits of iron and coal, raw materials that would be critical to Europe's early industrial age.

Second, improved agricultural methods played a central role in bringing about the Industrial Revolution in Britain. The result, especially before 1760, was a period of bountiful crops and low food prices that freed up the family budget for other purchases.

Third, Britain had other assets that helped give rise to industrial leadership. Unlike eighteenth-century France, Britain had an effective central bank and well-developed credit markets. The monarchy and the aristocratic oligarchy, which had jointly ruled the country since 1688, provided stable and predictable government. At the same time, the government let the domestic economy operate with few controls, encouraging personal initiative, technical change, and a free market. Finally, Britain had long had a large class of hired agricultural laborers who were relatively mobile—compared to village-bound peasants in France and western Germany, for example—and along with cottage workers they formed a potential industrial labor force for capitalist entrepreneurs.

All these factors combined to initiate the **Industrial Revolution,** a term first coined by awed contemporaries in the 1830s to describe the burst of major inventions and technical changes they had witnessed in certain industries. This technical revolution went hand in hand with an impressive quickening in the annual rate of industrial growth in Britain. The decisive quickening of growth probably came in the 1780s, after the American War of Independence and just before the French Revolution.

The Industrial Revolution was, however, a longer process than the political revolutions that began around the same time. It was not complete in Britain until 1850 at the earliest, and it had no real impact on continental countries until after 1815.

ca. 1765	Hargreaves invents spinning jenny
1769	Watt creates modern steam engine
1775–1783	American Revolution
1780s–1850	Industrial Revolution
1780–1851	Population boom in England
1789–1799	French Revolution
1798	Malthus, *Essay on the Principle of Population*
1799	Combination Acts passed
1810	Strike of Manchester cotton spinners
1824	Combination Acts repealed
1830	Stephenson's *Rocket;* first important railroad
1830s	Industrial banks in Belgium
1833	Factory Act
1842	Mines Act
1844	Engels, *The Condition of the Working Class in England*
1851	Great Exhibition held at Crystal Palace

Industrial Revolution A term first coined by awed contemporaries in the 1830s to describe the burst of major inventions and technical changes they had witnessed in certain industries.

The First Factories

The first decisive breakthrough of the Industrial Revolution was the creation of large factories for the British cotton textile industry in the 1770s and 1780s. Technological innovations in the manufacture of cotton cloth led to a new system of production and social relationships. Since no other industry experienced such a rapid or complete transformation before 1830, these trailblazing developments deserve special consideration.

Although the putting-out system of merchant capitalism (see page 490) was expanding all across Europe in the eighteenth century, this pattern of rural industry was most fully developed in Britain. There, as demand for product grew, the system's limitations began to outweigh its advantages for the first time. This was especially true in the British textile industry after about 1760.

A constant shortage of thread in the textile industry prompted many a tinkering worker to come up with a better spinning wheel; James Hargreaves succeeded with his cotton-spinning jenny about 1765. At almost the same moment, Richard Arkwright invented (or possibly pirated) another kind of spinning machine, the water frame. These breakthroughs produced an explosion in the infant cotton textile industry in the 1780s, and by 1790 the new machines were producing ten times as much cotton yarn as had been made in 1770.

Hargreaves's **spinning jenny** was simple, inexpensive, and could be hand-operated by a single person. Arkwright's **water frame,** however, quickly acquired a capacity of several hundred spindles and demanded much more power—waterpower. The water frame thus required large specialized mills, factories that

spinning jenny A spinning machine created by James Hargreaves in 1765 that used six to twenty-four spindles mounted on a sliding carriage to spin a fine thread.

water frame A spinning machine created by Richard Arkwright that had a capacity of several hundred spindles and used water power; it therefore required a larger and more specialized mill but the thread it spun was thicker; generally the thread was then spun on a spinning jenny to achieve the desired thickness.

Woman Working a Hargreaves Spinning Jenny
The loose cotton strands on the slanted bobbins passed up to the sliding carriage and then on to the spindles in back for fine spinning. The worker, almost always a woman, regulated the sliding carriage with one hand, and with the other she turned the crank on the wheel to supply power. By 1783 one woman could spin by hand a hundred threads at a time on an improved model. (Mary Evans Picture Library)

employed as many as one thousand workers from the very beginning. The water frame could spin only coarse, strong thread, which was then put out for respinning on hand-powered cottage jennies. Around 1790 an alternative technique invented by Samuel Crompton also began to require more power than the human arm could supply. After that time, all cotton spinning was gradually concentrated in factories.

The first consequences of these revolutionary developments were generally beneficial to Westerners. Millions of poor people, who had earlier worn nothing underneath their coarse, filthy outer garments, could afford the comfort and cleanliness of cotton slips and underpants as well as cotton dresses and shirts.

Families using cotton in cottage industry were freed from their constant search for thread, which could now be spun in the cottage on the jenny or obtained from a nearby factory. The wages of weavers rose markedly until about 1792. They were known to walk proudly through the streets with 5-pound notes stuck in their hatbands, and they dressed like the middle class. As a result, large numbers of agricultural laborers became hand-loom weavers, while mechanics and capitalists sought to invent a power loom to save on labor costs. This Edmund Cartwright achieved in 1785. But the power looms of the factories worked poorly at first, and hand-loom weavers continued to receive good wages until at least 1800.

Most people preferred to work in their cottages rather than in early factories, so factory owners often turned to children who had been abandoned by their parents and put in the care of local parishes. Apprenticed as young as five or six years of age, boy and girl workers were forced by law to labor for their "masters" for as many as fourteen years. Housed, fed, and locked up nightly in factory dormitories, the young workers received little or no pay. Hours were appalling—commonly thirteen or fourteen hours a day, six days a week. Harsh physical punishment maintained discipline. To be sure, poor children typically worked long hours outside the home for brutal masters, but this was exploitation on a truly unprecedented scale. This exploitation ultimately sparked an increase in humanitarian attitudes toward child laborers in the early nineteenth century.

The Steam Engine Breakthrough

In order to grow, the cotton textile industry needed a more expandable source of power than rivers and streams. The iron industry was also stagnating because of its dependence on processed wood (charcoal), which was in ever shorter supply as forests were depleted. The shortage of energy had become particularly severe in Britain by the eighteenth century. As this early energy crisis grew worse, Britain looked toward its abundant and widely scattered reserves of coal as an alternative to its vanishing wood. Coal was first used in Britain in the late Middle Ages as a source of heat. By 1640 most homes in London were heated with it, and it also provided heat for making beer, glass, soap, and other products. The breakthrough came when industrialists began to use coal to produce mechanical energy and to power machinery.

As more coal was produced, mines were dug deeper and deeper and were constantly filling with water. Mechanical pumps, usually powered by animals walking in circles at the surface, had to be installed. At one mine, fully five hundred horses were used in pumping. Such power was expensive and bothersome. In an attempt to overcome these disadvantages, Thomas Savery in 1698 and Thomas Newcomen in 1705 invented the first primitive **steam engines.** Both engines were extremely inefficient. Both burned coal to produce steam, which was then used to operate a pump. However, by the early 1770s, many of the Savery engines and hundreds of the Newcomen engines were operating successfully, though inefficiently, in English and Scottish mines.

In 1763, a gifted young Scot named James Watt (1736–1819) was called on to repair a Newcomen engine. Watt saw that the Newcomen engine's waste of energy could be reduced by adding a separate condenser. This splendid invention, patented in 1769, greatly increased the efficiency of the steam engine.

To invent something in a laboratory is one thing; to make it a practical success is quite another. Watt needed skilled workers, precision parts, and capital, and the relatively advanced nature of the British economy proved essential. A partnership with a wealthy English toymaker provided risk capital and a manufacturing plant. In the craft tradition of locksmiths, tinsmiths, and millwrights, Watt found skilled mechanics who could install, regulate, and repair his sophisticated engines. From ingenious manufacturers such as the cannonmaker John Wilkinson, Watt was gradually able to purchase precision parts. In more than twenty years of constant effort, Watt made many further improvements. By the late 1780s, the steam engine had become a practical and commercial success in Britain.

The steam engine of Watt and his followers was the Industrial Revolution's most fundamental advance in technology. For the first time in history, humanity had, at least for a few generations, almost unlimited power at its disposal. For the first time, inventors and engineers could devise and implement all kinds of power

steam engines A breakthrough invention by Thomas Savery in 1698 and Thomas Newcomen in 1705 that burned coal to produce steam, which was then used to operate a pump; although inefficient they were used successfully in English and Scottish mines.

The Saltash Bridge

Railroad construction presented innumerable challenges, such as the building of bridges to span rivers and gorges. Civil engineers responded with impressive feats, and their profession bounded ahead. This painting portrays the inauguration of I. K. Brunel's Saltash Bridge, where the railroad crosses the Tamar River into Cornwall in southwest England. The high spans allow large ships to pass underneath. (Elton Collection, Ironbridge Gorge Museum Trust)

equipment to aid people in their work. For the first time, abundance was at least a possibility for ordinary men and women.

The steam engine was quickly put to use in several industries in Britain. It drained mines and made possible the production of ever more coal to feed steam engines elsewhere. The steam-power plant began to replace waterpower in the cotton-spinning mills during the 1780s, contributing greatly to that industry's phenomenal rise. Steam took the place of waterpower in flour mills, in the malt mills used in breweries, in the flint mills supplying the china industry, and in the sugar mills of the West Indies colonies. It was put to use in the British iron industry, which grew from producing 17,000 tons in 1740 to 3 million tons in 1844. Once scarce and expensive, iron became the cheap, basic, indispensable building block of the economy.

The Coming of the Railroads

As industry grew, so did the need to transport large quantities of goods over long distances. Overland shipment of freight, relying solely on horsepower, was still quite limited and frightfully expensive; shippers used rivers and canals for heavy freight whenever possible. It was logical, therefore, that inventors would try to use steam power for transportation.

As early as 1800, an American ran a "steamer on wheels" through city streets. Other experiments followed. In the 1820s, English engineers created steam cars capable of carrying fourteen passengers at ten miles an hour—as fast as the mail coach. But the noisy, heavy steam automobiles frightened passing horses and damaged themselves as well as the roads with their vibrations. For the rest of the century, horses continued to reign on highways and city streets.

The coal industry had long been using plank roads and rails to move coal wagons within mines and at the surface. Rails reduced friction and allowed a horse or a human being to pull a heavier load. Thus once a rail capable of supporting a heavy locomotive was developed in 1816, all sorts of experiments with steam engines on rails went forward. In 1830 George Stephenson's **Rocket** sped down the track of the just-completed Liverpool and Manchester Railway at sixteen miles per hour. This was the world's first important railroad, fittingly steaming in the heart of industrial England. The line from Liverpool to Manchester was a financial as well as a technical success, and many private companies were organized to build more rail lines. Within twenty years, they had completed the main trunk lines of Great Britain. Other countries were quick to follow.

Rocket The name given to George Stephenson's effective locomotive that was first tested in 1830 on the Liverpool and Manchester Railway at 16 miles per hour.

The economic consequences of the railroad were tremendous. As the barrier of high transportation costs was lowered, markets became larger and even nationwide. Larger markets encouraged larger factories with more sophisticated machinery in a growing number of industries. Such factories could make goods more cheaply and gradually subjected most cottage workers and many urban artisans to severe competitive pressures.

In all countries, the construction of railroads required a large number of laborers. Many landless farm laborers and poor peasants, long accustomed to leaving their villages for temporary employment, went to build railroads. By the time the work was finished, urban life seemed more appealing. By the time they sent for their wives and sweethearts to join them, they had become urban workers.

The railroad, with trains reaching speeds of fifty miles per hour by 1850, gave the entire society a new sense of power and speed. Painters such as Joseph M. W. Turner (1775–1851), succeeded in expressing this sense of power and awe. So did the massive new train stations, the cathedrals of the industrial age. Leading railway engineers such as Isambard Kingdom Brunel (IZ-uhm-bahrd broo-NEL) and Thomas Brassey, whose tunnels pierced mountains and whose bridges spanned valleys, became public idols—the astronauts of their day. Everyday speech absorbed the images of railroading. After you got up a "full head of steam," you "highballed" along. And if you didn't "go off the track," you might "toot your own whistle." The railroad fired the imagination.

Industry and Population

In 1851 London was the site of a famous industrial fair. This Great Exhibition was held in the newly built **Crystal Palace**, an architectural masterpiece made entirely of glass and iron, both of which were now cheap and abundant. For the millions who visited, one fact stood out: the little island of Britain was the "workshop of the world." It alone produced two-thirds of the world's coal and more than one-half of its iron and cotton cloth. More generally, it has been carefully estimated that in 1860 Britain produced a truly remarkable 20 percent of the entire world's output of industrial goods, whereas it had produced only about 2 percent of the world total in 1750.[1] Experiencing revolutionary industrial change, Britain became the first industrial nation (see Map 22.1).

Crystal Palace The location of the Great Exposition in 1851 in London, an architectural masterpiece made entirely of glass and iron, both of which were now cheap and abundant.

MAP 22.1 The Industrial Revolution in England, ca. 1850

Industry concentrated in the rapidly growing cities of the north and the Midlands, where rich coal and iron deposits were in close proximity.

Towns with over 20,000 people are shown

50 / 400 Thousand / 2.4 Million

Cities with over 100,000 people are labeled

Exposed coalfields

Industrial areas

Centers of woolen cloth production, 18th century

Principal railroads

Section Review

- The causes of the Industrial Revolution included an expanding British economy, improved agricultural methods, effective banking and credit markets, stable government, a relatively free market, and a mobile labor force.

- The invention of the spinning jenny and then the water frame revolutionized the cotton textile industry, increasing wages for weavers, but requiring large factories where owners apprenticed young children who worked long hours under harsh conditions.

- The invention of—and subsequent improvements to—the steam engine was the catalyst to the industrial revolution, replacing water power in the production of coal, flour, malt, sugar, flint, and, most importantly, iron.

- The steam engine was a financial and technical success, lowering transportation costs, enlarging consumer markets and factories, lowering prices, increasing employment, and expanding urbanization.

- At the same time that Britain's industry was booming, the population was growing rapidly as well, providing more workers for the labor force.

At the same time that Britain's gross national product (GNP) was skyrocketing, its population was exploding as well. Although the question is still debated, many economic historians now believe that rapid population growth in Great Britain was not harmful because it facilitated industrial expansion. More people meant a more mobile labor force, with a wealth of young workers in need of employment and ready to go where the jobs were.

Contemporaries were much less optimistic. In his famous and influential *Essay on the Principle of Population* (1798), Thomas Malthus (1766–1834) argued that population would always tend to grow faster than the food supply. In Malthus's opinion, the only hope of warding off such "positive checks" to population growth as war, famine, and disease was "prudential restraint." That is, young men and women had to limit the growth of population by the old tried-and-true means of marrying late in life. While Malthus and his followers were proved wrong in the long term, until the 1820s, or even the 1840s, contemporary observers might reasonably have concluded that the economy and the total population were racing neck and neck, with the outcome very much in doubt.

Industrialization in Continental Europe

How after 1815 did continental countries respond to the challenge of industrialization?

The new technologies developed in the British Industrial Revolution were adopted by business in continental Europe to a considerable but variable degree and at different rates of change. Continental Europe faced a number of challenges in attempting to develop new industries, but all European states (as well as the United States, Canada, and Japan) managed to raise per capita industrial levels in the nineteenth century.

The Challenge of Industrialization

In 1750 all the countries of Europe were fairly close together on a per capita level of industrialization—that is, according to how much industrial product was produced, on average, for each person in a year. But Britain had opened up a noticeable lead over all continental countries by 1800, and that gap progressively widened as the British Industrial Revolution accelerated to 1830 and reached full maturity by 1860. The British level of per capita industrialization was twice the French level in 1830, for example, and more than three times the French level in 1860. All other large countries (except the United States) had fallen even farther behind Britain than France had at both dates.

Posing the greatest obstacle to European expansion was the political and social turmoil caused by the French Revolution and its aftermath. On the continent, the upheavals that began with the French Revolution disrupted trade, created runaway inflation, and fostered social anxiety. War severed normal communications between Britain and the continent, severely handicapping continental efforts to use new British machinery and technology. Moreover, the years from 1789 to 1815 were, even for those of the privileged French economic classes, who received special favors from Napoleon after 1800, a time of "national catastrophe"—in the graphic words of a famous French scholar.[2] Thus France and the rest of Europe were further behind Britain in 1815 than in 1789.

This widening gap made it more difficult, if not impossible, for other countries to follow the British pattern in energy and industry after peace was restored in 1815. Above all, in the newly mechanized industries, British goods were being produced very economically, and these goods had come to dominate world markets completely while the continental states were absorbed in war between 1792 and 1815. In addition, British technology had become so advanced and complicated that very few engineers or skilled technicians outside England understood it. Moreover, the technology of steam power had grown much more expensive. It involved large investments in the iron and coal industries and, after 1830, required the existence of railroads, which were very costly. Continental business people had great difficulty finding the large sums of money the new methods demanded, and there was a shortage of laborers accustomed to working in factories. All these disadvantages slowed the spread of modern industry (see Map 22.2).

After 1815, however, when continental countries began to face up to the British challenge, they had at least three important advantages over non-Western countries. First, most continental countries had a rich tradition of putting-out enterprise, merchant capitalists, and skilled urban artisans. Second, continental capitalists were able to "borrow" knowledgeable engineers and skilled factory

MAPPING THE PAST

Map 22.2   Continental Industrialization, ca. 1850

Although continental countries were beginning to make progress by 1850, they still lagged far behind Britain. For example, continental railroad building was still in an early stage, whereas the British rail system was essentially complete (review Map 22.1, page 572). Coal played a critical role in nineteenth-century industrialization both as a power source for steam engines and as a raw material for making iron and steel. **[1]** Locate the major exposed (that is, known) coal deposits in 1850. Which countries and areas appear rich in coal resources, and which appear poor? Is there a difference between northern and southern Europe? **[2]** What is the relationship between known coal deposits and emerging industrial areas?

workers from England, even though English laws tried to prevent the export of talent and equipment. English entrepreneurs also set up their own factories in Europe, some producing the machinery needed for other industries. Third, continental countries were independent of foreign control and could act in their own self-interest to foster industry.

tariff protection A government's way of supporting and aiding their own economy by laying high taxes on the cheaper, imported goods of another country, as when France responded to cheaper British goods flooding their country by imposing high tariffs on British imports.

Government Support and Corporate Banking

Continental governments played an important role in helping business people develop new industries. These governments fashioned economic policies to serve their own interests; **tariff protection** was one such policy.

For example, after Napoleon's wars ended in 1815, France was suddenly flooded with cheaper and better British goods. The French government responded by laying high tariffs on many British imports in order to protect the French economy. The governments of German states formed a customs union or Zollverein (TSOLL-feh-rine), allowing goods to move between the German member states without tariffs, while erecting a single uniform tariff against other nations. Without such protections, the German writer Friedrich List (1789–1846) argued, Britain could "make the rest of the world, like the Hindus, its serfs in all industrial and commercial relations."

After 1815 continental governments bore the cost of building roads and canals to improve transportation. They also bore to a significant extent the cost of building railroads. Belgium led the way in the 1830s and 1840s. In an effort to tie the newly independent nation together, the Belgian government decided to construct a state-owned system that helped make the country an early industrial leader. Several of the smaller German states also built state systems.

The Prussian government provided another kind of invaluable support for the construction of a national rail system. It guaranteed that the state treasury would pay the interest and principal on railroad bonds if the closely regulated private companies in Prussia were unable to do so. Thus railroad investors in Prussia ran little risk, and capital was quickly raised.

In France the state shouldered all the expense of acquiring and laying roadbed, including bridges and tunnels. Finished roadbed was leased to a carefully supervised private company, which usually benefited from a state guarantee of its

A German Ironworks, 1845
This big business enterprise, the Borsig ironworks in Berlin, mastered the new British method of smelting iron ore with coke. Germany, and especially the state of Prussia, was well endowed with both iron and coal, and the rapid exploitation of these resources after 1840 transformed a poor agricultural country into an industrial powerhouse. (akg-images)

debts. In short, governments helped pay for railroads, the all-important leading sector in continental industrialization.

Finally, banks, like governments, also played a larger and more creative role on the continent than in Britain. Previously, banks in Europe had generally avoided industrial investment as being too risky because the partners in these private banks risked losing their entire personal fortunes if an investment failed. In the 1830s, two important Belgian banks pioneered in a new direction. They received permission from the growth-oriented government to establish themselves as corporations enjoying limited liability. That is, a stockholder could lose only his or her original investment in the bank's common stock and could not be assessed for any additional losses. Publicizing the risk-reducing advantage of limited liability, these Belgian banks were able to attract many shareholders, large and small. They mobilized impressive resources for investment in big companies, became industrial banks, and successfully promoted industrial development.

Similar corporate banks became important in France and Germany in the 1850s and 1860s. Usually working in collaboration with governments, they established and developed many railroads and many companies working in heavy industry, which were increasingly organized as limited liability corporations.

The combined efforts of skilled workers, entrepreneurs, governments, and industrial banks meshed successfully between 1850 and the financial crash of 1873. This was a period of unprecedented economic growth on the continent. In Belgium, Germany, and France, key indicators of modern industrial development—such as railway mileage, iron and coal production, and steam-engine capacity—increased at average annual rates of 5 to 10 percent. As a result, rail networks were completed in western and much of central Europe, and the leading continental countries mastered the industrial technologies that had first been developed in Great Britain. In the early 1870s, Britain was still Europe's most industrial nation, but a select handful of countries were closing the gap that had been opened up by the Industrial Revolution.

Europe's continent-wide increases stood in stark contrast to the large and tragic decreases that occurred at the same time in many non-Western countries, most notably in China and India. European countries industrialized to a greater or lesser extent even as most of the non-Western world de-industrialized. Thus differential rates of wealth- and power-creating industrial development, which heightened disparities within Europe, also greatly magnified existing inequalities between Europe and the rest of the world. We shall return to this momentous change in world economic relationships in Chapter 26.

Relations Between Capital and Labor

How did the Industrial Revolution affect social classes, the standard of living, and patterns of work? What measures were taken to improve the conditions of workers?

Industrial development brought new social relations and intensified long-standing problems between capital and labor in both urban workshops and cottage industry. A new group of factory owners and industrial capitalists arose. These men and women and their families strengthened the wealth and size of the middle class, which had previously been made up mainly of merchants and professional people. The nineteenth century became the golden age of the middle class. Modern industry also created a much larger group, the factory workers. For the first time, large

Section Review

- The countries of Europe faced a great challenge to keep up with Britain's industry and were hindered by disruptions caused by war and by the lack of skilled engineers, railroads, funding, and laborers accustomed to factory work.

- Continental governments paved the way for industry in their own countries by imposing tariffs on foreign goods and by encouraging and financing railroad-building.

- Banks mobilized funding for investments by offering limited liability, causing a rapid rise in economic growth across Europe, the completion of rail networks, and the adaptation of new industrial technologies.

numbers of men, women, and children came together under one roof to work with complicated machinery for a single owner or a few partners in large companies.

The growth of new occupational groups in industry stimulated new thinking about social relations. Often combined with reflections on the French Revolution, this thinking led to the development of a new overarching interpretation—a new paradigm—regarding social relationships (see Chapter 23). Briefly, this paradigm argued, with considerable success, that individuals were members of economically determined classes, which had conflicting interests. Accordingly, the comfortable, well-educated "public" of the eighteenth century came increasingly to see itself as the backbone of the middle class (or the middle classes), and the "people" gradually transformed themselves into the modern working class (or working classes). And if the new class interpretation was more of a deceptive simplification than a fundamental truth for some critics, it appealed to many because it seemed to explain what was happening. Therefore, conflicting classes existed, in part, because many individuals came to believe they existed and they developed an appropriate sense of class feeling—what Marxists call **class-consciousness.**

class-consciousness A sense of class differentiation that existed, in part, because many individuals came to believe that conflicting classes existed.

The New Class of Factory Owners

Early industrialists operated in a highly competitive economic system, and success and large profits were by no means certain. Manufacturers waged a constant battle to cut their production costs while also investing profits back into the business for new and better machinery. "Dragged on by the frenzy of this terrible life," according to one of the dismayed critics, the struggling manufacturer had "no time for niceties. He must conquer or die, make a fortune or drown himself."[3]

Most early industrialists drew upon their families and friends for labor and capital, but they came from a variety of backgrounds. Many were from well-established merchant families, which provided a rich network of contacts and support. Others were of modest means, especially in the early days. Artisans and skilled workers of exceptional ability had unparalleled opportunities. Members of ethnic and religious groups who had been discriminated against in the traditional occupations controlled by the landed aristocracy jumped at the new chances and often helped each other. Scots, Quakers, and other Protestant dissenters were tremendously important in Britain; Protestants and Jews dominated banking in Catholic France. Many of the industrialists were newly rich, and, not surprisingly, they were very proud and self-satisfied.

As factories and firms grew larger, opportunities declined, at least in well-developed industries. It became considerably harder for a gifted but poor young mechanic to start a small enterprise and end up as a wealthy manufacturer. Formal education (for males) became more important as a means of success and advancement, and at the advanced level it was very expensive. In Britain by 1830 and in France and Germany by 1860, leading industrialists were more likely to have inherited their well-established enterprises, and they were financially much more secure than their struggling fathers and mothers had been. They also had a greater sense of class-consciousness, fully aware that ongoing industrial development had widened the gap between themselves and their workers.

The wives and daughters of successful businessmen also found fewer opportunities for active participation in Europe's increasingly complex business world. Rather than contributing as vital partners in a family-owned enterprise, as so many middle-class women such as Elizabeth Strutt had done (see the feature "Individuals in Society: The Strutt Family"), these women were increasingly valued for their ladylike gentility. By 1850 some influential women writers and most businessmen

Individuals in Society

The Strutt Family

For centuries economic life in Europe revolved around hundreds of thousands of small family enterprises. These family enterprises worked farms, crafted products, and traded goods. They built and operated the firms and factories of the early industrial era, with the notable exceptions of the capital-hungry railroads and a few big banks. Indeed, until late in the nineteenth century, close-knit family groups continued to control most successful businesses, including those organized as corporations.

One successful and fairly well-documented family enterprise began with the marriage of Jedediah Strutt (1726–1797) and Elizabeth Woollat (1729–1774) in Derbyshire in northern England in 1755. The son of a farmer, Jedediah fell in love with Elizabeth when he lodged with her parents. Both young people grew up in the close-knit dissenting Protestant community, which did not accept the doctrines of the state-sponsored Church of England, and the well-educated Elizabeth worked in a local school for dissenters and then for a dissenter minister in London.

Aided by Elizabeth, who was "obviously a very capable woman" and who supplied some of the drive her husband had previously lacked, Jedediah embarked on a new career.* He invented a machine to make handsome, neat-fitting ribbed silk stockings, which had previously been made by hand. He secured a patent, despite strong opposition from competitors, and went into production. Elizabeth helped constantly in the enterprise, which was nothing less than an informal partnership between husband and wife.†

In 1757, for example, when Jedediah was fighting to uphold his patent in the local court, Elizabeth left her son of nine months and journeyed to London to seek a badly needed loan from her former employer. She also canvassed her London relatives and dissenter friends for orders for stockings and looked for sales agents and sources of capital. Elizabeth's letters reveal a detailed knowledge of ribbed stockings and the prices and quality of different kinds of thread. The family biographers conclude that her husband "owed much of his success to her energy and counsel." Elizabeth was always "active in the business—a partner in herself."‡ Despite the invaluable business contribution of wives like Elizabeth, the legal rights and consequences of partnership were denied to married women in Britain and Europe in the eighteenth and nineteenth centuries.

The Strutt enterprise grew and gradually prospered, but it always retained its family character. The firm built a large silk mill and then went into cotton spinning in partnership with Richard Arkwright, the inventor of the water frame (see page 567). The brothers of both Jedediah and Elizabeth worked for the firm, and their eldest daughter worked long hours in the warehouse. Bearing three sons, Elizabeth fulfilled yet another vital task because the typical family firm looked to its own members for managers and continued success. All three sons entered the business and became cotton textile magnates. Elizabeth never saw these triumphs. The loyal and talented wife in the family partnership died suddenly at age forty-five while in London with Jedediah on a business trip.

Jedediah Strutt (ca. 1790), by Joseph Wright of Derby. (Derby Museum & Art Gallery/The Bridgeman Art Library)

Questions for Analysis

1. How and why did the Strutts succeed?
2. What does Elizabeth's life tell us about the role of British women in the early Industrial Revolution?

---

* R. Fitton and A. Wadsworth, *The Strutts and the Arkwrights, 1758–1830: A Study of the Early Factory System* (Manchester, England: Manchester University Press, 1958), p. 23.
† See the excellent discussion by C. Hall, "Strains in the 'Firm of Wife, Children and Friends'? Middle-Class Women and Employment in Early Nineteenth-Century England," in P. Hudson and W. Lee, eds., *Women's Work and the Family Economy in Historical Perspective* (Manchester, England: Manchester University Press, 1990), pp. 106–132.
‡ Fitton and Wadsworth, *The Strutts*, pp. 110–111.

assumed that middle-class wives and daughters should steer clear of undignified work in offices and factories. Rather, a middle-class lady should protect and enhance her femininity. She should concentrate on her proper role as wife and mother, preferably in an elegant residential area far removed from ruthless commerce and the volatile working class.

The New Factory Workers

The social consequences of the Industrial Revolution have long been hotly debated. The condition of British workers during the transformation has always generated the most controversy among historians because Britain was the first country to industrialize and because the social consequences seemed harshest there. Before 1850 other countries had not proceeded very far with industrialization, and almost everyone agrees that the economic conditions of European workers improved after 1850. Thus the experience of British workers to about 1850 deserves special attention. (Industrial growth also promoted rapid urbanization, with its own awesome problems, as will be shown in Chapter 24.)

From the beginning, the Industrial Revolution in Britain had its critics. Among the first were the romantic poets. William Blake (1757–1827) called the early factories "satanic mills" and protested against the hard life of the London poor. William Wordsworth (1770–1850) lamented the destruction of the rural way of life and the pollution of the land and water. Some handicraft workers—notably the **Luddites** (LUD-eytes), who attacked whole factories in northern England in 1812 and after—smashed the new machines, which they believed were putting them out of work. Doctors and reformers wrote eloquently of problems in the factories and new towns.

Was the new poverty of industrial workers worse than the old poverty of cottage workers and agricultural laborers? Friedrich Engels (ENG-guhlz) (1820–1895), the future revolutionary and colleague of Karl Marx, charged that it was. After studying conditions in northern England, this young middle-class German issued a blistering indictment of the middle classes in *The Condition of the Working Class in England.* "At the bar of world opinion," he wrote, "I charge the English middle classes with mass murder, wholesale robbery, and all the other crimes in the calendar." Engels's extremely influential charge of middle-class exploitation and increasing worker poverty was embellished by Marx and later socialists.

Meanwhile, other observers believed that conditions were improving for the working people. Andrew Ure (yoo-RAY) wrote in 1835 in his study of the cotton industry that conditions in most factories were not harsh and were even quite good. Edwin Chadwick, a conscientious government official well acquainted with the problems of the working population, concluded that the "whole mass of the laboring community" was increasingly able "to buy more of the necessities and minor luxuries of life."[4] Nevertheless, if all the contemporary assessments had been counted up, those who thought conditions were getting worse for working people would probably have been the majority.

In an attempt to go beyond the contradictory judgments of contemporaries, some historians have looked at different kinds of sources. The most recent studies also confirm the view that the early years of the Industrial Revolution were hard ones for British workers. There was little or no increase in the purchasing power of the average British worker from about 1780 to about 1820. The years from 1792 to 1815, a period of almost constant warfare with France, were particularly difficult. Food prices rose faster than wages, and the living conditions of the laboring poor declined. Only after 1820, and especially after 1840, did real wages rise substantially,

Luddites Handicraft workers who attacked whole factories in northern England in 1812 and after, smashing the new machines that they believed were putting them out of work.

so that the average worker earned and consumed roughly 50 percent more in real terms in 1850 than in 1770.[5] In short, there was considerable economic improvement for workers throughout Great Britain by 1850, but that improvement was hard won and slow in coming.

This important conclusion must be qualified, however. The hours in the average workweek increased, as some economic historians now believe it had been increasing in parts of northern Europe since the seventeenth century. Thus, to a large extent, workers earned more simply because they worked more. Indeed, significant recent research shows that in England nonagricultural workers labored about 250 days per year in 1760 as opposed to 300 days per year in 1830, while the normal workday remained an exhausting eleven hours throughout the entire period.[6]

Another way to consider the workers' standard of living is to look at the goods that they purchased. Again the evidence is somewhat contradictory. Speaking generally, workers ate somewhat more food of higher nutritional quality as the Industrial Revolution progressed, except during wartime. Diets became more varied; people ate more potatoes, dairy products, fruits, and vegetables. Clothing improved, but housing for working people probably deteriorated somewhat. In short, per capita use of specific goods supports the position that the standard of living of the working classes rose, at least moderately, after the long wars with France.

Conditions of Work

What about working conditions? Did workers eventually earn more only at the cost of working longer and harder? Were workers exploited harshly by the new factory owners?

The first factories were cotton mills, which began functioning along rivers and streams in the 1770s. Cottage workers, accustomed to the putting-out system, were reluctant to work in the new factories even when they received relatively good wages because factory work was unappealing. In the factory, workers had to keep up with the machine and follow its tempo. They had to show up every day and work long, monotonous hours. Factory workers had to adjust their daily lives to the shrill call of the factory whistle.

Cottage workers were not used to that kind of schedule. All members of the family worked hard and long, but in spurts, setting their own pace. They could interrupt their work when they wanted to. Women and children could break up their long hours of spinning with other tasks. On Saturday afternoon the head of the family delivered the week's work to the merchant manufacturer and got paid. Saturday night was a time of relaxation and drinking, especially for the men. Recovering from his hangover on Tuesday, the weaver bent to his task on Wednesday and then worked frantically to meet his deadline on Saturday. Like some students today, he might "pull an all-nighter" on Thursday or Friday in order to get his work finished.

Also, early factories resembled English poorhouses, where totally destitute people went to live at public expense. Some poorhouses were industrial prisons, where the inmates had to work in order to receive their food and lodging. The similarity between large brick factories and large stone poorhouses increased the cottage workers' aversion to factories.

By 1790 the factory system was gaining greater acceptance. Many more factories were being built, mainly in urban areas, where they could use steam power rather than waterpower and attract a workforce more easily than in the countryside. The need for workers was great, especially when the practice of using abandoned and orphaned children was outlawed by Parliament in 1802. Indeed, people came from near and far to work in the cities, both as factory workers and as laborers, builders, and domestic servants. Yet as they took these new jobs, working people did not simply give in to a system of labor that had formerly repelled them. Rather, they helped modify the system by carrying over old, familiar working traditions.

For one thing, they often came to the mills and the mines as family units. This was how they had worked on farms and in the putting-out system. The mill or mine owner bargained with the head of the family and paid him or her for the work of the whole family. In the cotton mills, children worked for their mothers or fathers, collecting scraps and "piecing" broken threads together. In the mines, children sorted coal and worked the ventilation equipment. Their mothers hauled coal in the tunnels below the surface, while their fathers hewed with pick and shovel at the face of the seam.

The preservation of the family as an economic unit in the factories from the 1790s on made the new surroundings more tolerable, and parents felt that their children were still under their control when they worked side by side. Adult workers were not particularly interested in limiting the minimum working age or hours of their children as long as family members worked together. Only when technical changes threatened to place control and discipline in the hands of impersonal managers and overseers did adult workers protest against inhuman conditions in the name of their children.

Some enlightened employers and social reformers in Parliament worked to change this practice, arguing that more humane standards were necessary. For example, Robert Owen (1771–1858), a very successful manufacturer in Scotland, testified in 1816 before an investigating committee on the basis of his experience. He stated that "very strong facts" demonstrated that employing children under ten years of age as factory workers was "injurious to the children, and not beneficial to the proprietors."[7] Workers also provided graphic testimony at such hearings as the reformers pressed Parliament to pass corrective laws. They scored some important successes.

Their most significant early accomplishment was the **Factory Act of 1833.** It limited the factory workday for children between nine and thirteen to eight hours and that of adolescents between fourteen and eighteen to twelve hours, although the act made no effort to regulate the hours of work for children at home or in small businesses. Children under nine were to be enrolled in the elementary schools that factory owners were required to establish. The employment of children declined rapidly. Thus the Factory Act broke the pattern of whole families working together in the factory because efficiency required standardized shifts for all workers.

Ties of blood and kinship were important in other ways in Great Britain in the formative years between about 1790 and 1840. Many manufacturers and builders hired subcontractors, who in turn hired the work crews. The subcontractor might be as harsh as the greediest capitalist, but the relationship between subcontractor and work crew was close and personal because many of his hires were friends and relatives. This kind of personal relationship had traditionally existed in cottage industry and in urban crafts, and it was more acceptable to many workers than impersonal factory discipline.

Ties of kinship were particularly important for newcomers, who often traveled great distances to find work. Many urban workers in Great Britain were from Ireland. Forced out of rural Ireland by population growth and deteriorating economic conditions from 1817 on, Irish in search of jobs could not be choosy; they took what they could get. As early as 1824, most of the workers in the Glasgow cotton

Factory Act of 1833 This act limited the factory workday for children between nine and thirteen to eight hours and that of adolescents between fourteen and eighteen to twelve hours.

mills were Irish; in 1851 one-sixth of the population of Liverpool was Irish. Like many other immigrant groups held together by ethnic and religious ties, the Irish worked together, formed their own neighborhoods, and not only survived but also thrived.

Changes in the Division of Labor by Gender

The era of the Industrial Revolution witnessed major changes in the gender division of labor. In preindustrial Europe most people generally worked in family units. By tradition, certain jobs were defined by gender—women and girls for milking and spinning, men and boys for plowing and weaving—but many tasks might go to either sex. Family employment carried over into early factories and subcontracting, but it collapsed as child labor was restricted and new attitudes emerged. A different sexual division of labor gradually arose to take its place. The man emerged as the family's primary wage earner, while the woman found only limited job opportunities. Generally denied good jobs at good wages in the growing urban economy, women were expected to concentrate on unpaid housework, child care, and craftwork at home.

separate spheres A rigid gender division of labor with the wife as mother and homemaker and the husband as wage earner.

This new pattern of **separate spheres** had several aspects. First, all studies agree that married women from the working classes were much less likely to work full-time for wages outside the house after the first child arrived, although they often

Workers at a Large Cotton Mill

This 1833 engraving shows adult women operating power looms under the supervision of a male foreman, and it accurately reflects both the decline of family employment and the emergence of a gender-based division of labor in many English factories. The jungle of belts and shafts connecting the noisy looms to the giant steam engine on the ground floor created a constant din. (Time Life Pictures/Getty Images) earned small amounts doing putting-out handicrafts at home and taking in boarders. Second, when married women did work for wages outside the house, they usually came from the poorest families, where the husbands were poorly paid, sick, unemployed, or missing. Third, these poor married (or widowed) women were joined by legions of young unmarried women, who worked full-time but only in certain jobs. Fourth, all women were generally confined to low-paying, dead-end jobs. Virtually no occupation open to women paid a wage sufficient for a person to live independently. Men predominated in the better-paying, more promising employments. Evolving gradually, but largely in place by 1850, the new sexual division of labor in Britain constituted a major development in the history of women and of the family.

If the reorganization of paid work along gender lines is widely recognized, there is no agreement on its causes. One school of scholars sees little connection with industrialization and finds the answer in the deeply ingrained sexist attitudes of a "patriarchal tradition," which predated the economic transformation. These scholars stress the role of male-dominated craft unions in denying working women access to good jobs and relegating them to unpaid housework. Other scholars, stressing that the gender roles of women and men can vary enormously with time and culture, look more to a combination of economic and biological factors in order to explain the emergence of a sex-segregated division of labor.

Three ideas stand out in this more recent interpretation. First, relentless factory discipline conflicted with child care in a way that labor on the farm or in the cottage had not. A woman operating earsplitting spinning machinery could mind a child of seven or eight working beside her (until such work was outlawed), but she could no longer pace herself through pregnancy or breast-feed her baby on the job. One mother of four, in describing her past experience of working in the mines, provided a real insight into why many women accepted the emerging gender division of labor:

> While working in the pit I was worth to my [miner] husband seven shillings a week, out of which we had to pay 2½ shillings to a woman for looking after the younger children. I used to take them to her house at 4 o'clock in the morning, out of their own beds, to put them into hers. Then there was one shilling a week for washing; besides, there was mending to pay for, and other things. The house was not guided. The other children broke things; they did not go to school when they were sent; they would be playing about, and get ill-used by other children, and their clothes torn. Then when I came home in the evening, everything was to do after the day's labor, and I was so tired I had no heart for it; no fire lit, nothing cooked, no water fetched, the house dirty, and nothing comfortable for my husband. It is all far better now, and I wouldn't go down again.[8]

Second, running a household in conditions of primitive urban poverty was an extremely demanding job in its own right. There were no supermarkets or public transportation. Everything had to be done on foot, with children in tow. Yet another brutal job outside the house—a "second shift"—had limited appeal for the average married woman. Thus women might well have accepted the emerging division of labor as the best available strategy for family survival in the industrializing society.[9]

Third, why were the women who did work for wages outside the home confined to certain "women's jobs"? No doubt the desire of males to monopolize the best opportunities and hold women down provides part of the answer. Yet as some feminist scholars have argued, sex-segregated employment was also a collective response to the new industrial system, where young people mingled without parental supervision. Continuing to mix after work, they were "more likely to form liaisons, initiate courtships, and respond to advances."[10] Such intimacy also led to more unplanned pregnancies and fueled the illegitimacy explosion that had begun in the late eighteenth century and that gathered force until at least 1850 (see pages 514–515). Thus segregation of jobs by gender was partly an effort by older people to help control the sexuality of working-class youths. The **Mines Act of 1842,** for example, prohibited underground work for all women as well as for boys under ten.

Mines Act of 1842 This act prohibited underground work for all women as well as for boys under ten.

The Early Labor Movement in Britain

Many kinds of employment changed slowly during and after the Industrial Revolution in Great Britain. In 1850 more British people still worked on farms than in any other occupation. The second-largest occupation was domestic service, with more than one million household servants, 90 percent of whom were women. Thus many old, familiar jobs outside industry lived on and provided alternatives for individual workers. This helped ease the transition to industrial civilization.

Within industry itself, the pattern of artisans working with hand tools in small shops remained unchanged in many trades, even as some others were revolutionized by technological change. For example, as in the case of cotton and coal, the British iron industry was completely dominated by large-scale capitalist firms by 1850. Many large ironworks had more than one thousand people on their payrolls. Yet the firms that fashioned iron into small metal goods, such as tools, tableware, and toys, employed on average fewer than ten wage workers, who used time-honored handicraft skills. Only gradually after 1850 did some owners find ways to reorganize some handicraft industries with new machines and new patterns of work. The survival of small workshops gave many workers an alternative to factory employment.

Combination Acts Passed in 1799, these acts outlawed unions and strikes. They were repealed by Parliament in 1824.

THE WORKSHOP

Working-class solidarity and class-consciousness developed in small workshops as well as in large factories. In the northern factory districts, where thousands of "hired hands" looked across at a tiny minority of managers and owners, anti-capitalist sentiments were frequent by the 1820s. Commenting in 1825 on a strike in the woolen center of Bradford and the support it had gathered from other regions, one paper claimed with pride that "it is all the workers of England against a few masters of Bradford."[11] Modern technology had created a few versus a many.

As in France during the French Revolution, the British government attacked monopolies, guilds, and workers combinations in the name of economic freedom, adding to the ill will between classes. In 1799 Parliament passed the **Combination Acts,** which outlawed unions and strikes. In 1813 and 1814, Parliament repealed an old law regulating the wages of artisans and the conditions of apprenticeship. As a result of

Celebrating Skilled Labor

This handsome engraving embellished the membership certificate of the British carpenters union, one of the leading "new model unions" that represented skilled workers effectively after 1850. The upper panel shows carpenters building the scaffolding for a great arch; the lower panel captures the spirit of a busy workshop. (E & E Image Library/Art Resource, NY) these and other measures, certain skilled artisan workers, such as bootmakers and high-quality tailors, found aggressive capitalists ignoring traditional work rules and flooding their trades with unorganized women workers and children to beat down wages.

The liberal capitalist attack on artisan guilds and work rules was bitterly resented by many craftworkers, who subsequently played an important part in gradually building a modern labor movement to improve working conditions and to serve worker needs. The Combination Acts were widely disregarded by workers. Printers, papermakers, carpenters, tailors, and other such craftsmen continued to take collective action, and societies of skilled factory workers also organized unions. They were not afraid to strike; there was, for example, a general strike of adult cotton spinners in Manchester in 1810. In the face of widespread union activity, Parliament repealed the Combination Acts in 1824, and unions were tolerated, though not fully accepted, after 1825.

The next stage in the development of the British trade-union movement was the attempt to create a single large national union. This effort was led not so much by working people as by social reformers such as Robert Owen, a self-made cotton manufacturer. In 1834 Owen organized one of the largest and most visionary of the early national unions, the **Grand National Consolidated Trades Union.** When this and other grandiose schemes collapsed, the British labor movement moved once again after 1851 in the direction of craft unions. The most famous of these "new model unions" was the Amalgamated Society of Engineers, which represented skilled machinists. These unions won real benefits for members and became an accepted part of the industrial scene.

British workers also engaged in direct political activity in defense of their own interests. After the collapse of Owen's national trade union, many working people went into the Chartist movement, which sought political democracy. The key Chartist demand—that all men be given the right to vote—became the great hope of millions. Workers were also active in campaigns to limit the workday in factories to ten hours and to permit duty-free importation of wheat into Great Britain to secure cheap bread. Thus working people developed a sense of their own identity and played an active role in shaping the new industrial system. They were neither helpless victims nor passive beneficiaries.

Grand National Consolidated Trades Union Organized by Robert Owen in 1834, this was one of the largest and most visionary early national unions.

Section Review

- Early industrialists worked hard to establish their factories, but the next generation inherited already prosperous businesses so they had a new class-consciousness, prizing their wealth and role in society.
- Conditions for factory workers improved over time but were harsh, with long hours and low wages; although clothing and diets improved, housing conditions did not.
- Critics of the harsh new conditions included William Blake and Friedrich Engels, while apologists such as Andrew Ure depicted conditions in optimistic terms.
- Factories often employed whole families until the Factory Act of 1833 limited the number of hours children and adolescents could work and required children under age nine to attend school.
- The division of labor between men and women emerged, with men the primary wage earners while married women were confined to the home and unmarried women to low-paying jobs.
- Farmers, domestic service, and small artisans coexisted with industry and formed the working class, organizing unions and taking collective action against capitalists to improve working conditions, wages, and democratic political rights, such as in the Chartist movement.

Chapter Review

What were the origins of the Industrial Revolution in Britain, and how did it develop between 1780 and 1850? (page 566)

Western society's industrial breakthrough grew out of a long process of economic and social change in which the rise of capitalism, overseas expansion, and the growth of rural industry stood out as critical preparatory developments. Eventually taking the lead in all of these developments, and also profiting from stable government, abundant natural resources, and a flexible labor force, Britain experienced between the 1780s and the 1850s an epoch-making transformation, one that is still aptly termed the Industrial Revolution.

Key Terms
Industrial Revolution (p. 567)
spinning jenny (p. 567)
water frame (p. 567)
steam engines (p. 569)

(continued)

How after 1815 did continental countries respond to the challenge of industrialization? (page 573)

Building on technical breakthroughs, power-driven equipment, and large-scale enterprise, the Industrial Revolution in England greatly increased output in certain radically altered industries, stimulated the large handicraft and commercial sectors, and speeded up overall economic growth. By 1850 the level of British per capita industrial production was surpassing continental levels by a growing margin, and Britain savored a near monopoly in world markets for mass-produced goods.

Continental countries inevitably took rather different paths to the urban industrial society. They relied more on handicraft production in both towns and villages. Only in the 1840s did railroad construction begin to create the strong demand for iron, coal, and railway equipment that speeded up the process of industrialization in the 1850s and 1860s.

How did the Industrial Revolution affect social classes, the standard of living, and patterns of work? What measures were taken to improve the conditions of workers? (page 576)

The rise of modern industry had a profound impact on people and their lives. In the early stages, Britain again led the way, experiencing in a striking manner the long-term social changes accompanying the economic transformation. Factory discipline and Britain's stern capitalist economy weighed heavily on working people, who, however, actively fashioned their destinies and refused to be passive victims. Improvements in the standard of living came slowly, but they were substantial by 1850. The era of industrialization fostered new attitudes toward child labor, encouraged protective factory legislation, and called forth a new sense of class feeling and an assertive labor movement. It also promoted a more rigid division of roles and responsibilities within the family that was detrimental to women, another gradual but profound change of revolutionary proportions.

Notes

1. P. Bairoch, "International Industrialization Levels from 1750 to 1980," *Journal of European Economic History* 11 (Spring 1982): 269–333.
2. M. Lévy-Leboyer, *Les banques européennes et l'industrialisation dans la première moitié du XIXe siècle* (Paris: Presses Universitaires de France, 1964), p. 29.
3. J. Michelet, *The People*, trans. with an introduction by J. P. McKay (Urbana: University of Illinois Press, 1973; original publication, 1846), p. 64.
4. Quoted in W. A. Hayek, ed., *Capitalism and the Historians* (Chicago: University of Chicago Press, 1954), p. 126.
5. N. Crafts, *British Economic Growth During the Industrial Revolution* (Oxford University Press, 1985), p. 95.
6. H-J. Voth, *Time and Work in England, 1750–1830* (Oxford: Oxford University Press, 2000), pp. 268–270; also pp. 118–133.
7. Quoted in E. R. Pike, *"Hard Times": Human Documents of the Industrial Revolution* (New York: Praeger, 1966), p. 109.
8. Ibid., *"Hard Times,"* p. 208.
9. See especially J. Brenner and M. Rama, "Rethinking Women's Oppression," *New Left Review* 144 (March–April 1984): 33–71, and sources cited there.
10. J. Humphries, ". . . 'The Most Free from Objection' . . . : The Sexual Division of Labor and Women's Work in Nineteenth-Century England," *Journal of Economic History* 47 (December 1987): 948.
11. Quoted in D. Geary, ed., *Labour and Socialist Movements in Europe Before 1914* (Oxford: Berg, 1989), p. 29.

To assess your mastery of this chapter, go to **bedfordstmartins.com/mckaywestbrief**

Listening to the Past

Testimony Concerning Young Mine Workers

The use of child labor in British industrialization quickly attracted the attention of humanitarians and social reformers. This interest led to investigations by parliamentary commissions, which resulted in laws limiting the hours and the ages of children working in large factories. Designed to build a case for remedial legislation, parliamentary inquiries gave large numbers of workers a rare chance to speak directly to contemporaries and to historians.

The moving passages that follow are taken from testimony gathered in 1841 and 1842 by the Ashley Mines Commission. Interviewing employers and many male and female workers, the commissioners focused on the physical condition of the youth and on the sexual behavior of workers far underground. The subsequent Mines Act of 1842 sought to reduce immoral behavior and sexual bullying by prohibiting underground work for all women (and for boys younger than ten).

Mr. Payne, coal master:

That children are employed generally at nine years old in the coal pits and sometimes at eight. In fact, the smaller the vein of coal is in height, the younger and smaller are the children required; the work occupies from six to seven hours per day in the pits; they are not ill-used or worked beyond their strength; a good deal of depravity exists but they are certainly not worse in morals than in other branches of the Sheffield trade, but upon the whole superior; the morals of this district are materially improving; Mr. Bruce, the clergyman, has been zealous and active in endeavoring to ameliorate their moral and religious education. . . .

Patience Kershaw, hurrier, aged 17:

My father has been dead about a year; my mother is living and has ten children, five lads and five lasses; the oldest is about thirty, the youngest is four; three lasses go to mill; all the lads are colliers, two getters and three hurriers [workers who move coal wagons underground]; one lives at home and does nothing; mother does nought but look after home.

All my sisters have been hurriers, but three went to the mill. Alice went because her legs swelled from hurrying in cold water when she was hot. I never went to day-school; I go to Sunday-school, but I cannot read or write; I go to pit at five o'clock in the morning and come out at five in the evening; I get my breakfast of porridge and milk first; I take my dinner with me, a cake, and eat it as I go; I do not stop or rest any time for the purpose; I get nothing else until I get home, and then have potatoes and meat, not every day meat. I hurry in the clothes I have now got on, trousers and ragged jacket; the bald place upon my head is made by thrusting the

This illustration of a girl dragging a coal wagon was one of several that shocked public opinion and contributed to the Mines Act of 1842. (The British Library)

corves [coal wagons]; my legs have never swelled, but sisters' did when they went to mill; I hurry the corves a mile and more under ground and back; they weigh 300; I hurry 11 a day; I wear a belt and chain at the workings to get the corves out; the put-ters [miners] that I work for are *naked* except their caps; they pull off all their clothes; I see them at work when I go up; sometimes they beat me, if I am not quick enough, with their hands; they strike me upon my back; the boys take liberties with me, sometimes, they pull me about; I am the only girl in the pit; there are about 20 boys and 15 men; all the men are naked; I would rather work in mill than in coal-pit.

Questions for Analysis

1. To what extent is the testimony of Patience Kershaw in harmony with that of Payne?

2. Describe Kershaw's work. What do you think of her work? Why?

3. The witnesses were responding to questions from middle-class commissioners. What did the commissioners seem interested in? Why?

Source: From *Voices of the Industrial Revolution*, edited by J. Bowditch and C. Ramsland. Copyright © 1961. Re-printed by permission of University of Michigan Press.

Revolutionaries in Transylvania. Ana Ipatescu, of the first group of revolutionaries in Transylvania against Russia, 1848. (National Historical Museum, Bucharest/The Art Archive)

CHAPTER 23

Ideologies and Upheavals

1815–1850

Chapter Preview

The Peace Settlement
How did the victorious allies fashion a general peace settlement, and how did Metternich uphold a conservative European order?

Radical Ideas and Early Socialism
What were the basic tenets of liberalism, nationalism, and socialism, and what groups were most attracted to these ideologies?

The Romantic Movement
What were the characteristics of the romantic movement, and who were some of the great romantic artists?

Reforms and Revolutions
How after 1815 did liberal, national, and socialist forces challenge conservatism in Greece, Great Britain, and France?

The Revolutions of 1848
Why in 1848 did revolution triumph briefly throughout most of Europe, and why did it fail almost completely?

INDIVIDUALS IN SOCIETY: Jules Michelet

LISTENING TO THE PAST: Speaking for the Czech Nation

589

The momentous economic and political transformation of modern times began in the late eighteenth century with the Industrial Revolution in England and then the French Revolution. Until about 1815, these economic and political revolutions were separate, involving different countries and activities and proceeding at very different paces. After peace returned in 1815, the situation changed. Economic and political changes tended to fuse, reinforcing each other and bringing about what historian Eric Hobsbawn has incisively called the **dual revolution.** For instance, the growth of the industrial middle class encouraged the drive for representative government, and the demands of the French sans-culottes in 1793 and 1794 inspired many socialist thinkers. Gathering strength, the dual revolution rushed on to alter completely first Europe and then the rest of the world. Much of world history in the past two centuries can be seen as the progressive unfolding of the dual revolution.

The dual revolution posed a tremendous intellectual challenge. The meanings of the economic, political, and social changes that were occurring, as well as the ways they would be shaped by human action, were anything but clear. These changes fascinated observers and stimulated the growth of new ideas and powerful ideologies. The most important of these ideological forces were revitalized conservatism and three ideologies of change—liberalism, nationalism, and socialism. All played critical roles in the political and social battles of the era and the great popular upheaval that eventually swept across Europe in the revolutions of 1848.

dual revolution A term that historian Eric Hobsbawn used for the economic and political changes that tended to fuse after 1815, reinforcing each other.

The Peace Settlement

How did the victorious allies fashion a general peace settlement, and how did Metternich uphold a conservative European order?

The eventual triumph of revolutionary economic and political forces was by no means certain as the Napoleonic era ended. Quite the contrary. The conservative, aristocratic monarchies of Russia, Prussia, Austria, and Great Britain—the Quadruple Alliance—had finally defeated France and reaffirmed their determination to hold France in line. But many other international questions were outstanding, and the allies agreed to meet at the **Congress of Vienna** to fashion a general peace settlement.

Most people felt a profound longing for peace. The great challenge for political leaders in 1814 was to construct a settlement that would last and not sow the seeds of another war. Their efforts were largely successful and contributed to a century unmarred by destructive, generalized war (see Map 23.1).

Congress of Vienna A meeting of Russia, Prussia, Austria, and Great Britain to fashion a peace settlement after defeating France.

The European Balance of Power

The allied powers were concerned first and foremost with the defeated enemy, France. Agreeing to the restoration of the Bourbon dynasty (see page 560), the allies were quite lenient toward France after Napoleon's abdication. The first Peace of Paris gave to France the boundaries it possessed in 1792, which were larger than those of 1789, and France did not have to pay any war reparations. Thus the victorious powers did not foment a spirit of injustice and revenge in the defeated country.

When the four allies of the Quadruple Alliance (plus a representative of the restored monarchy in France) met together at the Congress of Vienna, they also agreed to raise a number of formidable barriers against renewed French aggression. Above all, Prussia received considerably more territory on France's eastern border so as to stand as the "sentinel on the Rhine" against France. In these ways, the Quadruple Alliance combined leniency toward France with strong defensive measures.

In their moderation toward France, the allies were motivated by self-interest and traditional ideas about the balance of power. To Klemens von Metternich (MET-uhr-nik) and Robert Castlereagh (KAS-uhl-rey), the foreign ministers of Austria and Great Britain, respectively, as well as their French counterpart, Charles Talleyrand, the balance of power meant an international equilibrium that would discourage aggression by any combination of states or, worse, the domination of Europe by any single state.

The Great Powers—Austria, Britain, Prussia, Russia, and France—used the balance of power to settle their own dangerous disputes at the Congress of Vienna. There was general agreement among the victors that each of them should receive compensation in the form of territory for their successful struggle against the French. Great Britain had already won colonies and strategic outposts during the long wars. Metternich's Austria gave up territories in Belgium and

Adjusting the Balance
The Englishman on the left uses his money to counterbalance the people that the Prussian and the fat Metternich are gaining in Saxony and Italy. Alexander I sits happily on his prize, Poland. This cartoon captures the essence of how most people thought about balance-of-power diplomacy at the Congress of Vienna. (Bibliothèque nationale de France)

Kingdom of Prussia
Austrian Empire
Boundary of German Confederation

MAPPING THE PAST

MAP 23.1 Europe in 1815

Europe's leaders re-established a balance of political power after the defeat of Napoleon. Prussia gained territory on the Rhine and in Saxony, consolidating its position as a Great Power. Austria gained the Italian provinces of Lombardy and Venetia as well as Galicia and land along the Adriatic Sea. In 1815 Europe contained many different states, but international politics was dominated by the five Great Powers (or six, if one includes the Ottoman Empire). Trace the political boundaries of each Great Power, and compare their geographical strengths and weaknesses. **[1]** In which directions might the different Great Powers seek to expand further and gain more people and territory? **[2]** At what points might these states then come into conflict with one another?

southern Germany but expanded greatly elsewhere, taking the rich provinces of Venetia and Lombardy in northern Italy as well as former Polish possessions and new lands on the eastern coast of the Adriatic. More contentious was the push for greater territory by Russia and Prussia. When France, Austria, and Great Britain allied against these central European powers, Russia accepted a small Polish kingdom, and Prussia took only part of Saxony (see Map 23.1). This compromise was very much within the framework of balance-of-power ideology.

Following Napoleon's escape from Elba and his final defeat at Waterloo, a second Peace of Paris was convened. Again the Quadruple Alliance was relatively moderate toward France, and the previously agreed-upon balance of power was left intact. The members of the Quadruple Alliance and France also agreed to meet periodically to discuss their common interests and to consider appropriate measures for the maintenance of peace in Europe. This agreement marked the beginning of the European "congress system," which lasted long into the nineteenth century and settled many international crises through international conferences and balance-of-power diplomacy.

Intervention and Repression

There was also a domestic political side to the reestablishment of peace. Within their own countries, the leaders of the victorious states were much less flexible. In 1815 under Metternich's leadership, Austria, Prussia, and Russia were determined to uphold a conservative European order. Thus they embarked on a crusade against the ideas and politics of the dual revolution. This crusade lasted until 1848. The first step was the **Holy Alliance,** formed by Austria, Prussia, and Russia in September 1815. First proposed by Russia's Alexander I, the alliance soon became a symbol of the repression of liberal and revolutionary movements all over Europe.

In 1820 revolutionaries succeeded in forcing the monarchs of Spain and the southern Italian kingdom of the Two Sicilies to grant liberal constitutions. Metternich was horrified: revolution was rising once again. Calling a conference at Troppau in Austria under the provisions of the Quadruple Alliance, he and Alexander I proclaimed the principle of active intervention to maintain all autocratic regimes whenever they were threatened. Austrian forces then marched into Naples in 1821 and restored Ferdinand I to the throne of the Two Sicilies, while French armies likewise restored the Spanish regime.

In the following years, Metternich continued to battle against liberal political change. Sometimes he could do little, as in the case of the new Latin American republics that broke away from Spain. Nor could he undo the dynastic changes of 1830 and 1831 in France and Belgium. Nonetheless, until 1848 Metternich's system proved quite effective in central Europe, where his power was the greatest.

Metternich's policies dominated not only Austria and the Italian peninsula but also the entire German Confederation, which the peace settlement of Vienna had called into being. The confederation was composed of thirty-eight independent German states, including Prussia and Austria (see Map 23.1). These states met in complicated assemblies dominated by Austria, with Prussia a willing junior partner in the execution of repressive measures.

Through this German Confederation, Metternich had the infamous **Carlsbad Decrees** issued in 1819. These decrees required the thirty-eight German member states to root out subversive ideas in their universities and newspapers. The decrees also established a permanent committee with spies and informers to investigate and punish any liberal or radical organizations.

In his efforts to hold back liberalism, Metternich was supported by the Russian Empire and, to a lesser extent, by the Ottoman Empire. Bitter enemies and often at war with each other, these far-flung empires also shared several basic characteristics. Both the Russian and Ottoman empires were absolutist states with powerful armies and long traditions of expansion and conquest. Both were multinational empires made up of many peoples, languages, and religions, but in each case most of the ruling elite came from the dominant ethnic group — the Orthodox Christian

Holy Alliance An alliance formed by Austria, Russia, and Prussia in September of 1815 that became a symbol of the repression of liberal and revolutionary movements all over Europe.

Carlsbad Decrees Issued in 1819, these decrees required the thirty-eight German member states to root out subversive ideas in their universities and newspapers.

Russians centered in central and northern Russia, and the Muslim Ottoman Turks of Anatolia (much of modern Turkey). After 1815, both multinational, absolutist states worked to preserve their respective traditional, conservative orders. Only in the middle of the nineteenth century did each in turn experience a profound crisis and embark on a program of fundamental reform and modernization, as we shall see in Chapter 25.

Radical Ideas and Early Socialism

What were the basic tenets of liberalism, nationalism, and socialism, and what groups were most attracted to these ideologies?

In the years following the peace settlement of 1815 intellectuals and social observers sought to understand the revolutionary changes that had occurred and were still taking place. These efforts led to ideas that still motivate people throughout the world.

Almost all of these basic ideas were radical. In one way or another, they rejected conservatism, with its stress on tradition, a hereditary monarchy, a strong and privileged landowning aristocracy, and an official church. Instead, they developed and refined alternative visions—alternative ideologies—and tried to convince society to act on them. With time, they were very successful.

liberalism The principal ideas of this movement were equality and liberty; liberals demanded representative government and equality before the law as well as individual freedoms such as freedom of the press, freedom of speech, freedom of assembly, and freedom from arbitrary arrest.

Liberalism

The principal ideas of **liberalism**—liberty and equality—were by no means defeated in 1815. First realized successfully in the American Revolution and then achieved in part in the French Revolution, this political and social philosophy continued to pose a radical challenge to revived conservatism. Liberalism demanded representative government as opposed to autocratic monarchy, equality before the law as opposed to legally separate classes. The idea of liberty also meant specific individual freedoms: freedom of the press, freedom of speech, freedom of assembly, and freedom from arbitrary arrest. In Europe only France with Louis XVIII's Constitutional Charter and Great Britain with its Parliament and historic rights of English men and women had realized much of the liberal program in 1815. Even in those countries, liberalism had not fully succeeded.

Liberalism was also aligned with the doctrine of **laissez faire** (lay-say FAIR), which called for unrestricted private enterprise and no government interference in the economy. (This form of liberalism is often called "classical liberalism" in the United States in order to distinguish it sharply from modern American liberalism, which usually favors more government programs to meet social needs and to regulate the economy.)

laissez faire A doctrine of economic liberalism that believes in unrestricted private enterprise and no government interference in the economy.

As we have seen (Chapter 19), Adam Smith posited the idea of a free economy in opposition to mercantilism, in which the government placed major restrictions on trade. Smith argued that freely competitive private enterprise would give all citizens a fair and equal opportunity to do what they did best and would result in greater income for everyone, not just the rich.

In early-nineteenth-century Britain, economic liberalism was embraced most enthusiastically by business groups and thus became a doctrine associated with business interests. Businessmen used the doctrine to defend their right to do as they wished in their factories. Labor unions were outlawed because they supposedly restricted free competition and the individual's "right to work."

Liberal political ideals in the early nineteenth century also became more closely associated with narrow class interests. Liberals favored representative government, but they generally wanted property qualifications attached to the right to vote. In practice, this meant limiting the vote to well-to-do aristocratic landowners, substantial businessmen, and successful members of the professions. Workers and peasants, as well as the lower middle class of shopkeepers, clerks, and artisans, did not own the necessary property and thus could not vote.

As liberalism became increasingly identified with the middle class after 1815, some intellectuals and foes of conservatism felt that liberalism did not go nearly far enough. Inspired by memories of the French Revolution and the example of the young American republic, they called for universal voting rights, at least for males, and for democracy. These democratic republicans were more radical than the liberals, and they were more willing than most liberals to endorse violent upheaval to achieve goals. All of this meant that liberals and radical, democratic republicans could join forces against conservatives only up to a point.

nationalism The idea that each people had its own genius and its own *cultural* unity, which was self-evident, manifesting itself especially in a common language, history, and territory.

Nationalism

With immediate origins in the French Revolution and the Napoleonic wars, **nationalism** was based on the idea that each people had its own genius and its own *cultural* unity. For nationalists this cultural unity was basically self-evident, manifesting itself especially in a common language, history, and territory. In fact, in the early nineteenth century such cultural unity was more a dream than a reality. Within each ethnic grouping only an elite spoke a standardized written language. Local dialects abounded, and peasants from nearby villages often failed to understand each other. As for historical memory, it divided the inhabitants of the different German or Italian states as much as it unified them. Moreover, a variety of ethnic groups shared the territory of most states.

Despite these basic realities, sooner or later European nationalists usually sought to turn the cultural unity that they perceived into a *political* reality. They sought to make the territory of each people coincide with well-defined boundaries in an independent nation-state. This political goal was what made nationalism so explosive in central and eastern Europe after 1815, when there were either too few states (Austria, Russia, and the Ottoman Empire) or too many (the Italian peninsula and the German Confederation) and when different peoples overlapped and intermingled.

Of fundamental importance in the rise of nationalism was the push to use a standardized national language in order to facilitate communication in an increasingly complex industrial and urban society. As the entire population was educated in the national language, at least a superficial cultural unity took root. Citizens might also be brought together with emotionally charged symbols and ceremonies, such as independence holidays and patriotic parades. On such fleeting occasions the imagined nation of spiritual equals might celebrate its most hallowed traditions, which were often recent

Building German Nationalism

As popular upheaval in France spread to central Europe in March 1848, Germans from the solid middle classes came together in Frankfurt to draft a constitution for a new united Germany. This woodcut commemorates the solemn procession of delegates entering Saint Paul's Cathedral in Frankfurt, where the delegates would have their deliberations. Festivals, celebrations, and parades helped create a feeling of belonging to a large unseen community, a nation binding millions of strangers together. (akg-images) inventions.[1] Liberals and nationalists agreed that the benefits of self-government would be possible only if the people were united by common traditions that transcended local interests and even class differences.

Early nationalists usually believed that every nation, like every citizen, had the right to exist in freedom and to develop its character and spirit. They were confident that a symphony of nations would promote the harmony and ultimate unity of all peoples. The great Italian patriot Guiseppe Mazzini (1805–1872) believed that "in laboring according to the true principles of our country we are laboring for Humanity." Thus the liberty of the individual and the love of a free nation overlapped greatly in the early nineteenth century.

Yet early nationalists also stressed the differences among peoples and they developed a strong sense of "we" and "they." To this "we-they" outlook, it was all too easy for nationalists to add two highly volatile ingredients: a sense of national mission and a sense of national superiority. Even the French historian Jules Michelet (zhul meesh-uh-LEY), so alive to the national aspirations of other peoples, could not help speaking in 1846 of the "superiority of France"; the principles espoused in the French Revolution had made France the "salvation of mankind." (See the feature "Individuals in Society: Jules Michelet" on page 608.)

Russian and German nationalists had a very different opinion of France. In the narratives they constructed, the French often seemed oppressive, as the Russians did to the Poles and as the Germans did to the Czechs. (See the feature "Listening to the Past: Speaking for the Czech Nation" on pages 615–616.) Thus "they" often emerged as the enemy.

socialism A backlash against the emergence of individualism and the fragmentation of society, and a move toward cooperation and a sense of community; the key ideas were economic planning, greater economic equality, and state regulation of property.

French Utopian Socialism

Socialism, the new radical doctrine after 1815, began in France, despite the fact that France lagged far behind Great Britain in developing modern industry. Early French socialist thinkers were acutely aware that the political revolution in France, the rise of laissez faire, and the emergence of modern industry in Britain were transforming society. They were disturbed because they saw these developments as fomenting selfish individualism and splitting the community into isolated fragments. There was, they believed, an urgent need for a further reorganization of society to establish cooperation and a new sense of community.

Early French socialists believed in economic planning. Inspired by the emergency measures of 1793 and 1794 in France, they argued that the government should rationally organize the economy and not depend on destructive competition to do the job. Early socialists also shared an intense desire to help the poor, and they preached that the rich and the poor should be more nearly equal economically. Finally, socialists believed that private property should be strictly regulated by the government or that it should be abolished and replaced by state or community ownership. Planning, greater economic equality, and state regulation of property—these were the key ideas of early French socialism and of all socialism since.

One of the most influential early socialist thinkers was a nobleman, Count Henri de Saint-Simon (on-REE duh san-see-MAWN) (1760–1825). Saint-Simon optimistically proclaimed the tremendous possibilities of industrial development: "The age of gold is before us!" The key to progress was a social organization that required the parasites—the court, the aristocracy, lawyers, and churchmen—to surrender power to the doers—the leading scientists, engineers, and industrialists. The doers would guide the economy forward by undertaking vast public works projects and establishing investment banks. Saint-Simon also stressed that every social institution ought to have as its main goal improved conditions for the poor.

The journalist Louis Blanc (1811–1882) urged workers to agitate for universal voting rights and to take control of the state peacefully. Blanc believed that the state should set up government-backed workshops and factories to guarantee full employment. The right to work had to become as sacred as any other right.

Of great importance, the message of French utopian socialists interacted with the experiences of French urban workers. Workers cherished the memory of the radical phase of the French Revolution, and they became violently opposed to laissez-faire laws that denied workers the right to organize. Developing a sense of class in the process, workers favored collective action and government intervention in economic life. Thus the aspirations of workers and utopian theorists reinforced each other, and a genuine socialist movement emerged in Paris in the 1830s and 1840s. To Karl Marx was left the task of establishing firm foundations for modern socialism.

The Birth of Marxian Socialism

In 1848 Karl Marx (1818–1883) and Friedrich Engels (1820–1895) published *The Communist Manifesto,* which became the bible of socialism. The son of a Jewish lawyer who had converted to Christianity, the atheistic young Marx had studied philosophy at the University of Berlin before turning to journalism and economics. By the time Marx was twenty-five, he was developing his own socialist ideas.

Early French socialists often appealed to the middle class and the state to help the poor. Marx ridiculed such appeals as naive. He argued that the interests of the middle class and those of the industrial working class were inevitably opposed to each other. Indeed, according to the *Manifesto,* the "history of all previously existing society is the history of class struggles." In Marx's view, one class had always exploited the other, and with the advent of modern industry, society was split more clearly than ever before: between the middle class—the **bourgeoisie** (boor-zwah-ZEE) and the modern working class—the **proletariat** (proh-li-TAIR-ee-uht).

| **bourgeoisie** The middle class.

| **proletariat** The modern working class.

Just as the bourgeoisie had triumphed over the feudal aristocracy, Marx predicted that the proletariat would conquer the bourgeoisie in a violent revolution. While a tiny minority owned the means of production and grew richer, the ever-poorer proletariat was constantly growing in size and in class-consciousness. In this process, the proletariat was aided, according to Marx, by a portion of the bourgeoisie who had gone over to the proletariat and who (like Marx and Engels) "had raised themselves to the level of comprehending theoretically the historical moment." The critical moment, Marx thought, was very near. "Let the ruling classes tremble at a Communist revolution. The proletarians have nothing to lose but their chains. They have a world to win.

Karl Marx
Active in the revolution of 1848, Marx fled from Germany in 1849 and settled in London. There he wrote *Capital,* the weighty exposition of his socialist theories, and worked to organize the working class. Marx earned a modest living as a journalist, supplemented by financial support from his coauthor, Friedrich Engels. (The Granger Collection, New York)

WORKING MEN OF ALL COUNTRIES, UNITE!" So ends *The Communist Manifesto*.

Marx's debt to England was great. He was the last of the classical economists. Following David Ricardo, who had taught that labor was the source of all value, Marx went on to argue that profits were really wages stolen from the workers. Moreover, Marx incorporated Engels's charges of terrible oppression of the new class of factory workers in England; thus Marx's doctrines seemed to be based on hard facts.

Marx's theory of historical evolution was built on the philosophy of the German Georg Hegel (HEY-guhl) (1770–1831). Hegel believed that each age is characterized by a dominant set of ideas; this produces opposing ideas and eventually a new synthesis. Marx retained Hegel's view of history as a dialectic process of change but made economic relationships between classes the driving force. Marx's next idea, that it was now the bourgeoisie's turn to give way to the socialism of revolutionary workers, appeared to many the irrefutable capstone of a brilliant interpretation of humanity's long development. Thus Marx synthesized a number of early-nineteenth-century ideas to create a powerful ideology that would have a major impact on world history.

The Romantic Movement

What were the characteristics of the romantic movement, and who were some of the great romantic artists?

The early nineteenth century was a time of change in literature and other arts as well as in politics. The romantic movement was in part a revolt against the emphasis on rationality, order, and restraint that characterized the Enlightenment and the controlled style of classicism.

Forerunners of the romantic movement appeared from about 1750 on. Of these, Rousseau (see page 472)—the passionate advocate of feeling, freedom, and natural goodness—was the most influential. Romanticism then crystallized fully in the 1790s, primarily in England and Germany. The French Revolution kindled the belief that radical reconstruction was also possible in cultural and artistic life (even though many early English and German romantics became disillusioned with events in France and turned from liberalism to conservatism in politics). Romanticism gained strength until the 1840s.

romanticism A movement that a revolt against classicism and the Enlightenment, characterized by a belief in emotional exuberance, unrestrained imagination, and spontaneity in both art and personal life.

Sturm und Drang The name adopted by German early Romantics of the 1770s and 1780s who lived lives of tremendous emotional intensity; it means "Storm and Stress."

Romanticism's Tenets

Romanticism was characterized by a belief in emotional exuberance, unrestrained imagination, and spontaneity in both art and personal life. In Germany early romantics of the 1770s and 1780s called themselves the **Sturm und Drang** ("Storm and Stress"), and many romantic artists of the early nineteenth century lived lives of tremendous emotional intensity. Suicide, duels to the death, madness, and strange illnesses were not uncommon among leading romantics. Romantic artists typically led bohemian lives, wearing their hair long and uncombed in preference to powdered wigs and rejecting the materialism of refined society. Great individualists, the romantics believed the full development of one's unique human potential to be the supreme purpose in life.

Nowhere was the break with classicism more apparent than in romanticism's general conception of nature. Classicism in art was not particularly interested in nature. In the words of the eighteenth-century English author Samuel Johnson, "A blade of grass is always a blade of grass; men and women are my subjects of inquiry." The romantics, in contrast, were enchanted by nature. For some it was awesome and tempestuous, while others saw nature as a source of spiritual inspiration. As the great English landscape artist John Constable declared, "Nature is Spirit visible."

Most romantics saw the growth of modern industry as an ugly, brutal attack on their beloved nature and on the human personality. They sought escape—in the unspoiled Lake District of northern England, in exotic North Africa, in an idealized Middle Ages.

Diverse, exciting, and important, the study of history became a romantic passion. History was the key to a universe that was now perceived to be organic and dynamic, not mechanical and static as the Enlightenment thinkers had believed. Historical studies also promoted the growth of national aspirations, encouraging entire peoples to seek in the past their special destinies.

Literature

Romanticism found its distinctive voice in poetry, as the Enlightenment had in prose. Its first great poets were British: Wordsworth and Coleridge were all active by 1800, to be followed shortly by Byron, Shelley, and Keats.

A towering leader of English romanticism, William Wordsworth (1770–1850) was deeply influenced by Rousseau and the spirit of the early French Revolution. Wordsworth settled in the rural Lake District of England with his sister, Dorothy, and poet Samuel Taylor Coleridge (1772–1834). In 1798 Wordsworth and Coleridge published their *Lyrical Ballads*, which abandoned flowery classical conventions for the language of ordinary speech and endowed simple subjects with the loftiest majesty. One of the best examples of Wordsworth's romantic credo and genius is "Daffodils." After describing the joyful experience of wandering into a field of flowers, the poet reflects on the power of that single experience in the last stanza of the poem:

> For oft, when on my couch I lie
> In vacant or in pensive mood,
> They flash upon that inward eye
> Which is the bliss of solitude;
> And then my heart with pleasure fills,
> And dances with the daffodils.

Here indeed are simplicity and love of nature in commonplace forms that could be appreciated by everyone. Wordsworth's conception of poetry as the "spontaneous overflow of powerful feeling recollected in tranquility" is well illustrated in this stanza.

Classicism remained strong in France under Napoleon and inhibited the growth of romanticism there. In 1813 Germaine de Staël (duh STAHL) (1766–1817), a Franco-Swiss writer living in exile, urged the French to throw away their worn-out classical models. Her study *On Germany* (1810) extolled the spontaneity and enthusiasm of German writers and thinkers, and it had a powerful impact on the post-1815 generation in France. Between 1820 and 1850, the romantic impulse broke through in the poetry and prose of Lamartine, de Vigny, Dumas, Hugo, and Sand.

The powerful novels of Victor Hugo (1802–1885) exemplified the romantic fascination with fantastic characters, exotic historical settings, and human emotions.

The hero of Hugo's famous *Hunchback of Notre Dame* (1831) is the great cathedral's deformed bell-ringer, a "human gargoyle" overlooking the teeming life of fifteenth-century Paris. Renouncing his early conservatism, Hugo equated freedom in literature with liberty in politics and society.

Amandine Aurore Lucie Dupin (1804–1876), generally known by her pen name, George Sand, defied the narrow conventions of her time in an unending search for sexual and personal freedom. After eight years of unhappy marriage she abandoned her husband and took her two children to Paris to pursue a career as a writer. There Sand soon achieved fame, notoriety, and wealth, eventually writing over eighty novels on a variety of romantic and social themes.

In central and eastern Europe, literary romanticism and early nationalism often reinforced each other. Some romantic writers became fascinated with peasant life and transcribed the folk songs, tales, and proverbs that the cosmopolitan Enlightenment had disdained. The brothers Jacob and Wilhelm Grimm were particularly successful at rescuing German fairy tales from oblivion. In the Slavic lands, romantics played a decisive role in converting spoken peasant languages into modern written languages. The greatest of all Russian poets, Aleksander Pushkin (1799–1837), rejected eighteenth-century attempts to force Russian poetry into a classical straitjacket and used his lyric genius to mold the modern literary language.

Art and Music

France's master of the romantic style in painting was Eugène Delacroix (OO-gene duh-la-KWAH) (1798–1863), probably the illegitimate son of French foreign minister Talleyrand. Delacroix's dramatic, colorful depictions of the violent struggle for freedom stirred the emotions. He was also fascinated with remote and exotic subjects, whether lion hunts in Morocco or dreams of languishing, sensuous women in a sultan's harem.

In England the most notable romantic painters were Joseph M. W. Turner (1775–1851) and John Constable (1776–1837). Both were fascinated by nature, but their interpretations of it contrasted sharply, aptly symbolizing the tremendous emotional range of the romantic movement. Turner depicted nature's power and terror; wild storms and sinking ships were favorite subjects. Constable painted the idyllic and soothing countryside of unspoiled rural England.

In music, the romantic movement endured well into the late nineteenth century. Abandoning well-defined structures, the great romantic composers used a wide range of forms to create a thousand musical landscapes and evoke a host of powerful emotions. Romantic composers also transformed the small classical orchestra, tripling its size by adding wind instruments, percussion, and more brass and strings. The crashing chords evoking the surge of the masses in Chopin's "Revolutionary Etude" and the bottomless despair of the funeral march in Beethoven's Third Symphony plumbed the depths of human feeling.

This range and intensity gave music and musicians much greater prestige than in the past. Music no longer simply complemented a church service or helped a nobleman digest his dinner. Music became a sublime end in itself, most perfectly realizing the endless yearning of the soul. The unbelievable one-in-a-million performer—the great virtuoso who could transport the listener to ecstasy and hysteria—became a cultural hero. People swooned for Franz Liszt (frahnts list) (1811–1886), the greatest pianist of his age, as they scream for rock stars today.

The first great romantic composer is also the most famous today. Ludwig van Beethoven (BEY-toe-vuhn) (1770–1827) used contrasting themes and tones to

Section Review

- Romanticism's tenets included a belief in emotional expression and imagination, living life to the fullest by developing one's potential, and being captivated by nature and the study of history.

- Poetry was the language of the romantics, who used ordinary speech, simple subjects, and novels with fantastic characters, historical settings, and heightened human emotions.

- Romantic art depicted the full range of expression in nature, from power and terror to the calm and serene; in music, too, the romantic goal was to evoke a range of emotions by using contrasting themes and tones.

produce dramatic conflict and inspiring resolutions. As one contemporary admirer wrote, "Beethoven's music sets in motion the lever of fear, of awe, of horror, of suffering, and awakens just that infinite longing which is the essence of Romanticism."

Reforms and Revolutions

How after 1815 did liberal, national, and socialist forces challenge conservatism in Greece, Great Britain, and France?

While the romantic movement was developing, liberal, national, and socialist forces battered against the conservatism of 1815. In some countries, change occurred gradually and peacefully. Elsewhere, pressures built and eventually caused an explosion in 1848. Three countries—Greece, Great Britain, and France—experienced variations on this basic theme between 1815 and 1848.

National Liberation in Greece

National, liberal revolution, frustrated in Italy and Spain by conservative statesmen, succeeded first in Greece after 1815. Since the fifteenth century, the Greeks had been living under the domination of the Ottoman Turks. In spite of centuries of foreign rule, the Greeks had survived as a people, united by their language and the Greek Orthodox religion. Inspired by the general growth of nationalism and independence movements in the early nineteenth century, a rising Greek national movement took root. Under Alexander Ypsilanti (ip-suh-LAN-tee), a Greek patriot and a general in the Russian army, revolution broke out in 1821.

The Great Powers, particularly Metternich, were opposed to all revolution, even revolution against the Islamic Turks. They refused to back Ypsilanti and supported the Ottoman Empire. Yet for many Europeans, the Greek cause became a holy one. Educated Americans and Europeans were in love with the culture of classical Greece; Russians were stirred by the piety of their Orthodox brethren. Writers and artists, moved by the romantic impulse, responded enthusiastically to the Greek national struggle. The famous English romantic poet Lord Byron even joined the Greeks and died fighting "that Greece may yet be free."

The Greeks, though often quarreling among themselves, battled on against the Turks and hoped for the eventual support of European governments. In 1827 Great Britain, France, and Russia responded to popular demands at home and directed Turkey to accept an armistice. When the Turks refused, the navies of these three powers trapped the Turkish fleet at Navarino and destroyed it. Russia then declared another of its periodic wars of expansion against the Turks. This led to the establishment of a Russian protectorate over much of present-day Romania, which had also been under Turkish rule. Great Britain, France, and Russia finally declared Greece independent in 1830 and installed a German prince as king of the new country in 1832. In the end, the Greeks had won: a small nation had gained its independence in a heroic war of liberation against a foreign empire.

Liberal Reform in Great Britain

Eighteenth-century British society had been both flexible and remarkably stable. It was dominated by the landowning aristocracy, but that class was neither closed nor rigidly defined. Successful business and professional people could buy land and become gentlefolk, while the common people had more than the usual opportunities of the preindustrial world. Nonetheless, the British Parliament was thoroughly undemocratic.

By the 1780s there was growing interest in some kind of political reform, but the French Revolution made the British aristocracy fearful and extremely hostile to any attempts to change the status quo. Conflicts between the ruling class and laborers were sparked in 1815 with revision of the **Corn Laws.** Britain had been unable to import cheap grain from eastern Europe during the war years, leading to high prices and large profits for the landed aristocracy. With the war over, grain could be imported again, allowing the price of wheat and bread to go down and benefiting almost everyone except the aristocracy. The aristocracy, however, rammed far-reaching changes in the Corn Laws through Parliament. The new regulation prohibited the importation of foreign grain unless the price at home rose to improbable levels. Seldom has a class legislated more selfishly for its own narrow economic advantage or done more to promote a class-based view of political action.

The change in the Corn Laws, coming as it did at a time of widespread unemployment and postwar economic distress, triggered protests and demonstrations. In

Corn Laws British laws, revised in 1815, that prohibited the importation of foreign grain unless the price at home rose to improbable levels.

1817 the Tory government, which was completely controlled by the landed aristocracy, responded by temporarily suspending the traditional rights of peaceable assembly and habeas corpus. Two years later, Parliament passed the infamous Six Acts, which, among other things, placed controls on a heavily taxed press and practically eliminated all mass meetings. These acts followed an enormous but orderly protest, at Saint Peter's Fields in Manchester, that had been savagely broken up by armed cavalry. Nicknamed the **Battle of Peterloo,** in scornful reference to the British victory at Waterloo, this incident demonstrated the government's determination to repress dissenters.

Battle of Peterloo A protest that took place at Saint Peter's Fields in Manchester in reaction to the revision of the Corn Laws; it was broken up by armed cavalry.

As their wealth grew, the new manufacturing and commercial groups insisted on a place in the framework of political power and social prestige, and they called for many kinds of liberal reform. In the 1820s, a less frightened Tory government responded with reforms that offered better urban administration, greater economic liberalism, civil equality for Catholics, and limited imports of foreign grain. These actions encouraged the middle classes to press on for reform of Parliament so they could have a larger say in government.

The Whig Party, though led like the Tories by great aristocrats, had by tradition been more responsive to commercial and manufacturing interests. After a series of setbacks, their Reform Bill of 1832 was propelled into law by a mighty surge of popular support. The Reform Bill of 1832 moved politics in a democratic direction. It increased the power in Parliament of the House of Commons at the expense of the House of Lords. The new industrial areas of the country also gained representation in the Commons, and many old "rotten boroughs"—electoral districts that had very few voters and that the landed aristocracy had bought and sold—were eliminated. As a result of the **Reform Bill of 1832,** the number of voters increased by about 50 percent, giving about 12 percent of adult men in Britain and Ireland the right to vote. Comfortable middle-class groups in the urban population, as well as some larger-scale farmers, received the vote. Thus the pressures building in Great Britain were temporarily released. A major reform had been achieved peacefully. Continued fundamental reform within the system appeared difficult but not impossible.

Reform Bill of 1832 A major British political reform that increased the number of male voters by about 50 percent and gave political representation to new industrial areas.

The movement to grant voting rights to all men gained momentum. Hundreds of thousands of people signed gigantic petitions calling on Parliament to grant universal male suffrage, first and most seriously in 1839, again in 1842, and yet again in 1848. Parliament rejected all three petitions. In the short run, the working poor failed with their demands, but they learned a valuable lesson in mass politics.

While calling for universal male suffrage, many working-class people joined with middle-class manufacturers in the Anti–Corn Law League, founded in Manchester in 1839. The League argued that lower food prices and more jobs in industry depended on repeal of the Corn Laws. Finally, in 1846, Parliament allowed for free imports of grain when the failure of the Irish potato crop threatened famine. Thereafter the liberal doctrine of free trade became almost sacred dogma in Great Britain.

The following year, the Tories passed a bill designed to help the working classes, but in a different way. The Ten Hours Act of 1847 limited the workday for women and young people in factories to ten hours. Tory aristocrats continued to champion legislation regulating factory conditions. They were competing vigorously with the middle class for the support of the working class. This healthy competition between a still-vigorous aristocracy and a strong middle class was a crucial factor in Great Britain's peaceful evolution. The working classes could make temporary alliances with either competitor to better their own conditions.

The Prelude to 1848

March 1814	Russia, Prussia, Austria, and Britain form the Quadruple Alliance to defeat France.
April 1814	Napoleon abdicates.
May–June 1814	Bourbon monarchy is restored; Louis XVIII issues the Constitutional Charter providing for civil liberties and representative government.
	First Peace of Paris: allies combine leniency with a defensive posture toward France.
October 1814–June 1815	Congress of Vienna peace settlement establishes balance-of-power principle and creates the German Confederation.
February 1815	Napoleon escapes from Elba and marches on Paris.
June 1815	Napoleon defeated at the Battle of Waterloo.
September 1815	Austria, Prussia, and Russia form the Holy Alliance to repress liberal and revolutionary movements.
November 1815	Second Peace of Paris and renewal of Quadruple Alliance punish France and establish the European "congress system."
1819	In Carlsbad Decrees, Metternich imposes harsh measures throughout the German Confederation.
1820	Revolution occurs in Spain and the kingdom of the Two Sicilies.
	At the Congress of Troppau, Metternich and Alexander I of Russia proclaim the principle of intervention to maintain autocratic regimes.
1821	Austria crushes a liberal revolution in Naples and restores the Sicilian autocracy.
	Greeks revolt against the Ottoman Turks.
1823	French armies restore the Spanish regime.
1824	Reactionary Charles X succeeds Louis XVIII in France.
1830	Charles X repudiates the Constitutional Charter; insurrection and collapse of the government follow. Louis Philippe succeeds to the throne and maintains a narrowly liberal regime until 1848.
	Greece wins independence from the Ottoman Empire.
1832	Reform Bill expands British electorate and encourages the middle class.
1839	Louis Blanc publishes *Organization of Work*.
1840	Pierre Joseph Proudhon publishes *What Is Property?*
1846	Jules Michelet publishes *The People*.
1848	Karl Marx and Friedrich Engels publish *The Communist Manifesto*.

Ireland and the Great Famine

The people of Ireland did not benefit from the political competition in Britain. The great mass of the population (outside of the northern counties of Ulster, which were partly Presbyterian) were Irish Catholics, who rented their land from a tiny minority of Church of England Protestants. These landlords were content to use their power to grab as much as possible.

The result was that the condition of the Irish peasantry around 1800 was abominable. The typical peasant lived in a wretched cottage and could afford neither shoes nor stockings. Hundreds of shocking accounts describe hopeless poverty. Yet in spite of terrible conditions, population growth sped onward. The 3 million of 1725 reached 4 million in 1780 and doubled to 8 million by 1840.

The population grew so quickly for three reasons: extensive cultivation of the potato, early marriage, and exploitation of peasants by landlords. Once peasants began to cultivate potatoes in the late sixteenth century, a larger population could be supported. A single acre of land spaded and planted with potatoes could feed an Irish family of six for a year, whereas two to four acres of grain and pasture were needed to feed the same number. Needing only a big potato patch to survive, Irish men and women married early. Because landlords leased land for short periods only, peasants had no incentive to make permanent improvements or hold off on marriage until they were settled. Rural poverty was inescapable and better shared with a spouse, while dutiful children were an old person's best hope of escaping destitution.

As population and potato dependency grew, conditions became more precarious. From 1820 onward deficiencies and diseases in the potato crop became more common. In 1845 and 1846, and again in 1848 and 1851, the potato crop failed in Ireland.

The result was unmitigated disaster—the **Great Famine.** Blight attacked the young plants, the leaves withered, and the tubers rotted. Widespread starvation and mass fever epidemics followed. Yet the British government, committed to rigid laissez-faire ideology, was slow to act. When it did, its relief efforts were tragically inadequate. Moreover, the government continued to collect taxes, and landlords demanded their rents. Tenants who could not pay were evicted and their homes destroyed. Famine or no, Ireland remained the conquered jewel of foreign landowners.

The Great Famine shattered the pattern of Irish population growth. Fully 1 million emigrants fled the famine between 1845 and 1851, and at least 1.5 million died or went unborn because of the disaster. Alone among the countries of

Great Famine The result of four years of crop failure in Ireland, a country that had grown dependent on potatoes as a dietary staple.

Daniel McDonald: The Discovery of the Potato Blight

Although the leaves of diseased plants usually shriveled and died, they could also look deceptively healthy. This Irish family has dug up its potato harvest and just discovered to its horror that the blight has rotted the crop. Like thousands of Irish families, this family now faces the starvation and the mass epidemics of the Great Famine. (Delargy Centre for Irish Folklore, University College, Dublin)

Europe, Ireland experienced a declining population in the nineteenth century, from about 8 million in 1845 to 4.4 million in 1911. Ireland became a land of continuous out-migration, late marriage, and widespread celibacy.

The Great Famine also intensified anti-British feeling and promoted Irish nationalism, for the bitter memory of starvation, exile, and British inaction was burned deeply into the popular consciousness. Patriots could call on powerful collective emotions in their campaigns for land reform, home rule, and, eventually, Irish independence.

The Revolution of 1830 in France

France won a liberal constitution under Louis XVIII. His Constitutional Charter of 1814 protected the economic and social gains made by sections of the middle class and the peasantry in the French Revolution, permitted great intellectual and artistic freedom, and allowed for the creation of a parliament with upper and lower houses. Immediately after Napoleon's abortive Hundred Days, the moderate king refused the counsel of reactionary aristocrats such as his brother Charles, who wished to sweep away all the revolutionary changes and return to a bygone age of royal absolutism and aristocratic pretension. Instead, Louis appointed as his ministers moderate royalists, who sought and obtained the support of a majority of the representatives elected to the lower Chamber of Deputies.

Louis XVIII's charter was anything but democratic. Only about 100,000 of the wealthiest males out of a total population of 30 million had the right to vote for the deputies who, with the king and his ministers, made the laws of the nation. Nonetheless, the "notable people" who did vote came from very different backgrounds. There were wealthy businessmen, war profiteers, successful professionals, ex-revolutionaries, large landowners from the old aristocracy and the middle class, Bourbons, and Bonapartists.

The old aristocracy, with its pre-1789 mentality, was a minority within the voting population. It was this situation that Louis's successor, Charles X (r. 1824–1830), could not abide. Crowned in a lavish, utterly medieval, five-hour ceremony in the cathedral of Reims (reemz) in 1824, Charles was a true reactionary. He wanted to re-establish the old order in France. Increasingly blocked by the opposition of the deputies, Charles's government turned in 1830 to military adventure in an effort to rally French nationalism and gain popular support. A long-standing economic and diplomatic dispute with Muslim Algeria, a vassal state of the Ottoman Empire, provided the opportunity.

In June 1830, a French force of 37,000 crossed the Mediterranean, landed to the west of Algiers, and took the capital city in three short weeks. Victory seemed complete, but in 1831 Muslims from the interior revolted and waged a fearsome war until 1847, when French armies finally subdued the country. Bringing French, Spanish, and Italian settlers to Algeria and leading to the expropriation of large tracts of Muslim land, the conquest of Algeria marked the rebirth of French colonial expansion.

Emboldened by the good news from Algeria, Charles repudiated the Constitutional Charter and issued decrees stripping much of the wealthy middle class of its voting rights. He also censored the press. The immediate reaction, encouraged by journalists and lawyers, was an insurrection in the capital by printers, other artisans, and small traders. In "three glorious days," the government collapsed. Paris boiled with revolutionary excitement, and Charles fled. Then the upper middle class, which had fomented the revolt, skillfully seated Charles's cousin, Louis Philippe, duke of Orléans, on the vacant throne.

Louis Philippe (r. 1830–1848) accepted the Constitutional Charter of 1814; adopted the red, white, and blue flag of the French Revolution; and admitted that he was merely the "king of the French people." Yet the situation in France remained fundamentally unchanged. The vote was extended from 100,000 to just 170,000 citizens. The upper middle class wanted only to protect their interests and the narrowly liberal institutions of 1815. Republicans, democrats, social reformers, and the poor of Paris were bitterly disappointed. They had made a revolution, but it seemed for naught. The social and political divisions that so troubled Jules Michelet in the 1840s were clear for all to see. (See the feature "Individuals in Society: Jules Michelet.")

The Revolutions of 1848

Why in 1848 did revolution triumph briefly throughout most of Europe, and why did it fail almost completely?

In 1848 revolutionary political and social ideologies combined with a severe economic crisis to produce a vast upheaval across Europe. Only reforming Great Britain and immobile Russia escaped untouched. Governments toppled; monarchs and ministers bowed or fled. National independence, liberal-democratic constitutions, and social reform: the lofty aspirations of a generation seemed at hand. Yet in the end, the revolutions failed.

A Democratic Republic in France

The late 1840s in Europe were hard economically and tense politically. The potato famine in Ireland in 1845 and 1846 had many echoes on the continent. Bad harvests jacked up food prices and caused misery and unemployment in the cities. "Prerevolutionary" outbreaks occurred all across Europe: an abortive Polish revolution in the northern part of Austria in 1846, a civil war between radicals and conservatives in Switzerland in 1847, and an armed uprising in Naples, Italy, in January 1848. Revolution was almost universally expected, but it took revolution in Paris—once again—to turn expectations into realities.

Louis Philippe's "bourgeois monarchy" had been characterized by stubborn inaction and complacency. There was a glaring lack of social legislation, and politics was dominated by corruption and selfish special interests. With only the rich voting for deputies, many of the deputies were docile government bureaucrats.

The government's stubborn refusal to consider electoral reform heightened a sense of class injustice among middle-class shopkeepers, skilled artisans, and unskilled working people, and it eventually touched off a popular revolt in Paris. Barricades went up on the night of February 22, 1848, and by February 24 Louis Philippe had abdicated in favor of his grandson. But the common people in arms would tolerate no more monarchy. This refusal led to the proclamation of a provisional republic, headed by a ten-man executive committee and certified by cries of approval from the revolutionary crowd.

The revolutionaries immediately set about drafting a constitution for France's Second Republic. Moreover, they wanted a truly popular and democratic republic so that the common people—the peasants, the artisans, and the unskilled workers—could participate in reforming society. In practice, building such a republic meant giving the right to vote to every adult male, and this was quickly done. Revolutionary

Jules Michelet

Famous proponent of democratic nationalism and generally recognized as France's pre-eminent romantic historian, Jules Michelet (1798–1874) was born and educated in Paris, the only child in a loving family of poor printers. Largely self-taught in the family print shop in his early years, the awkward apprentice-turned-student entered the prestigious Charlemagne College in 1813 and had to repeat his first year. Then he sped forward, winning prizes, earning a professorship, and building a brilliant academic career. Yet Michelet remained true to his roots in the common people, and he drew from history a vision of a generous France that would embrace all its children and heal their social divisions.

Jules Michelet, in a portrait by Joseph Court. (Photo12.com)

The young Michelet was strongly influenced by the still largely ignored Italian philosopher Giovanni Battista Vico (1668–1744), who viewed history as the development of societies and human institutions, as opposed to the biographies of great men or the work of divine providence.

After being appointed the historical director of the National Archives after the revolution of 1830, Michelet was able to combine teaching and writing with intense research in still largely unexplored documentary collections and he presented what he believed to be the first genuine history of his country and its people. Many historians, though not Michelet himself, believe that his history of France in the Middle Ages—published between 1833 and 1844 and becoming the first six volumes in his multivolume *History of France* (1833–1867)—is his most solid, useful, and lasting accomplishment. These volumes single out his vast knowledge of the sources, his uncanny evocation of times and places, and his empathic and balanced understanding of different views and individuals. His treatment of the national revival under Joan of Arc in the fifteenth century is a famous example of his early work.

Finishing his study of the Middle Ages and shaken by his wife's death, Michelet became eager to write the history of the French Revolution as the ultimate achievement, the time the French people reached maturity and began the long-delayed liberation of mankind. Yet, confronted by growing social divisions and seeing "France sinking hour by hour," he tried first to write a book that would save France. Published in 1846, *The People* drew on personal experience, history, and contemporary debates, painting a vivid picture of French society and the social dislocation that afflicted all classes. Rejecting socialism as an unrealistic fantasy, Michelet pleaded instead for national unity: "One people! one country! one France! Never, never, I beg you, must we become two nations! Without unity, we perish!"* He also called for universal secular education as a way to create a unified and stable citizenry. Michelet's book was widely read and discussed.

Sickened by the failure of the revolution of 1848 and refusing to swear allegiance to Louis Napoleon, Michelet lost his government positions and turned to full-time writing. He completed his seven-volume history of the French Revolution, filled in the history of the early modern period of France with another eleven volumes, and wrote popular impressions of nature and anticlerical polemics. Michelet's later history is often criticized for being overly emotional and biased against the monarchy, the nobility, and the clergy while idealizing popular forces and revolutionary upheaval. A great individualist, Michelet was a gifted writer with a grand, heartfelt historical narrative of compassionate nationhood for a noble people.

Questions for Analysis

1. How would you describe Michelet's conception of history, and how did it evolve over time?
2. Does the study of history help solve contemporary problems? Debate this question, and defend your position.

* Jules Michelet, *The People*, trans. with an introduction by John P. McKay (Urbana: University of Illinois Press, 1973), p. 21.

compassion and sympathy for freedom were expressed in the freeing of all slaves in French colonies, the abolition of the death penalty, and the establishment of a ten-hour workday for Paris.

Yet there were profound differences within the revolutionary coalition in Paris. On the one hand, there were the moderate, liberal republicans of the middle class. They viewed universal male suffrage as the ultimate concession to be made to popular forces, and they strongly opposed any further radical social measures. On the other hand, there were radical republicans and hard-pressed artisans. Influenced by a generation of utopian socialists, and appalled by the poverty and misery of the urban poor, the radical republicans were committed to some kind of socialism. So were many artisans, who hated the unrestrained competition of cutthroat capitalism and who advocated a combination of strong craft unions and worker-owned businesses.

Worsening depression and rising unemployment brought these conflicting goals to the fore in 1848. Louis Blanc, who along with a worker named Albert represented the republican socialists in the provisional government, pressed for recognition of a socialist right to work. Blanc asserted that permanent government-sponsored cooperative workshops should be established for workers. Such workshops would be an alternative to capitalist employment and a decisive step toward a new, noncompetitive social order.

The moderate republicans wanted no such thing. They were willing to provide only temporary relief. The resulting compromise set up national workshops—soon to become little more than a vast program of pick-and-shovel public works—and established a special commission under Blanc to "study the question." This satisfied no one. The national workshops were, however, better than nothing. An army of desperate poor from the French provinces and even from foreign countries streamed into Paris to sign up. As the economic crisis worsened, the number enrolled in the workshops soared from 10,000 in March to 120,000 by June, and another 80,000 were trying unsuccessfully to join.

While the workshops in Paris grew, the French masses went to the election polls in late April. Voting in most cases for the first time, the people of France elected to the new Constituent Assembly about five hundred moderate republicans, three hundred monarchists, and one hundred radicals who professed various brands of socialism. One of the moderate republicans was the author of *Democracy in America*, Alexis de Tocqueville (TOHK-vil) (1805–1859), who had predicted the overthrow of Louis Philippe's government.

Tocqueville observed that the socialist movement in Paris was an anathema to France's peasants as well as to the upper and middle classes. The French peasants owned land, and according to Tocqueville, "private property had become with all those who owned it a sort of bond of fraternity."[2] Returning from Normandy to take his seat in the new Constituent Assembly, Tocqueville saw that a majority of the members were firmly committed to the republic and strongly opposed to the socialists and their artisan allies, and he shared their sentiments.

This clash of ideologies—of liberal capitalism and socialism—became a clash of classes and arms after the elections. The new government's executive committee dropped Blanc and thereafter included no representative of the Parisian working class. Fearing that their socialist hopes were about to be dashed, artisans and unskilled workers invaded the Constituent Assembly on May 15 and tried to proclaim a new revolutionary state. But the government was ready and used the middle-class National Guard to squelch this uprising. As the workshops continued to fill and grow more radical, the fearful but powerful propertied classes in the Assembly took the offensive. On June 22, the government dissolved the national workshops in Paris, giving the workers the choice of joining the army or going to workshops in the provinces.

The result was a spontaneous and violent uprising. Frustrated in attempts to create a socialist society, masses of desperate people were now losing even their life-sustaining relief. As a voice from the crowd cried out when the famous astronomer François Arago counseled patience, "Ah, Monsieur Arago, you have never been hungry!"[3] Barricades sprang up in the narrow streets of Paris, and a terrible class war began. Working people fought with the courage of utter desperation, but the government had the army and the support of peasant France. After three terrible "June Days" and the death or injury of more than ten thousand people, the republican army under General Louis Cavaignac triumphed.

The revolution in France thus ended in spectacular failure. The February coalition of the middle and working classes had in four short months become locked in mortal combat. In place of a generous democratic republic, the Constituent Assembly completed a constitution featuring a strong executive. This allowed Louis Napoleon, nephew of Napoleon Bonaparte, to win a landslide victory in the election of December 1848. The appeal of his great name as well as the desire of the propertied classes for order at any cost had produced a semi-authoritarian regime.

The Austrian Empire in 1848

Throughout central Europe, the first news of the upheaval in France evoked feverish excitement and eventually revolution. Liberals demanded written constitutions, representative government, and greater civil liberties from authoritarian regimes. When governments hesitated, popular revolts followed. Urban workers and students served as the shock troops, but they were allied with middle-class liberals and peasants. In the face of this united front, monarchs collapsed and granted almost everything. The popular revolutionary coalition, having secured great and easy victories, then broke down as it had in France. The traditional forces—the monarchy, the aristocracy, the regular army—recovered their nerve, reasserted their authority, and took back many, though not all, of the concessions. Reaction was everywhere victorious.

The revolution in the Austrian Empire began in Hungary in 1848, where nationalistic Hungarians demanded national autonomy, full civil liberties, and universal suffrage. When the monarchy in Vienna hesitated, Viennese students and workers took to the streets, and peasant disorders broke out in parts of the empire. The Habsburg emperor Ferdinand I (r. 1835–1848) capitulated and promised reforms and a liberal constitution. Metternich, who had foreseen the disruptive potential of nationalism, fled in disguise toward London. The old absolutist order seemed to be collapsing with unbelievable rapidity.

The coalition of revolutionaries was not stable, however. When the monarchy abolished serfdom as part of its promised reforms, the newly free peasants then lost interest in the political and social questions agitating the cities. Meanwhile, the coalition of urban revolutionaries broke down along class lines over the issue of socialist workshops and universal voting rights for men.

The revolutionary coalition was also weakened, and ultimately destroyed, by conflicting national aspirations. In March the Hungarian revolutionary leaders pushed through an extremely liberal, almost democratic, constitution. But the Hungarian revolutionaries also sought to transform the mosaic of provinces and peoples that was the kingdom of Hungary into a unified, centralized, Hungarian nation. To the minority groups that formed half of the population—the Croats,

Serbs, and Romanians—such unification was completely unacceptable. Each felt entitled to political autonomy and cultural independence. In a somewhat similar way, Czech nationalists based in Bohemia and the city of Prague came into conflict with German nationalists. (See the feature "Listening to the Past: Speaking for the Czech Nation" on pages 615–616.) Thus conflicting national aspirations within the Austrian Empire enabled the monarchy to play off one ethnic group against the other.

Finally, the conservative aristocratic forces regained their nerve under the rallying call of the archduchess Sophia, a Bavarian princess married to the emperor's brother. Deeply ashamed of the emperor's collapse before a "mess of students," she insisted that Ferdinand, who had no heir, abdicate in favor of her son, Francis Joseph.[4] Powerful nobles organized around Sophia in a secret conspiracy to reverse and crush the revolution.

Their first breakthrough came when the army bombarded Prague and savagely crushed a working-class revolt there on June 17. Other Austrian officials and nobles began to lead the minority nationalities of Hungary against the revolutionary government. At the end of October, the well-equipped, predominately peasant troops of the regular Austrian army attacked the student and working-class radicals in Vienna and retook the city at the cost of more than four thousand casualties. Thus the determination of the Austrian aristocracy and the loyalty of its army were the final ingredients in the triumph of reaction and the defeat of revolution.

When Francis Joseph (r. 1848–1916) was crowned emperor of Austria immediately after his eighteenth birthday in December 1848, only Hungary had yet to be brought under control. But another determined conservative, Nicholas I of Russia (r. 1825–1855), obligingly lent his iron hand. On June 6, 1849, 130,000 Russian troops poured into Hungary and subdued the country after bitter fighting. For a number of years, the Habsburgs ruled Hungary as a conquered territory.

Prussia and the Frankfurt Assembly

After Austria, Prussia was the largest and most influential German kingdom. Prior to 1848, the goal of middle-class Prussian liberals had been to transform absolutist Prussia into a liberal constitutional monarchy, which would lead the thirty-eight states of the German Confederation into a liberal, unified nation. The agitation following the fall of Louis Philippe in France encouraged Prussian liberals to press their demands. When the artisans and factory workers in Berlin exploded in March and joined temporarily with the middle-class liberals in the struggle against the monarchy, Frederick William IV (r. 1840–1861) promised to grant Prussia a liberal constitution and to merge Prussia into a new national German state that was to be created. But urban workers wanted much more and the Prussian aristocracy wanted much less than the moderate constitutional liberalism the king conceded. The workers issued a series of democratic and vaguely socialist demands that troubled their middle-class allies, and the conservative clique gathered around the king to urge counter-revolution.

As an elected Prussian Constituent Assembly met in Berlin to write a constitution for the Prussian state, a self-appointed committee of liberals from various German states began organizing for the creation of a unified German state. Meeting in Frankfurt in May, a National Assembly composed of lawyers, professors, doctors, officials, and businessmen convened to write the German federal constitution. However, their attention shifted from drafting a constitution to deciding how to respond to Denmark's claims on the provinces of Schleswig (SCHLES-wig) and Holstein, which where inhabited primarily by Germans.

Street Fighting in Frankfurt, 1848
Workers and students could tear up the cobblestones, barricade a street, and make it into a fortress. But urban revolutionaries were untrained and poorly armed. They were no match for professional soldiers led by tough officers who were sent against them after frightened rulers had recovered their nerve. (The Granger Collection, New York)

Section Review

- Jules Michelet, a romantic historian and prolific writer on the history of France, called for French unity instead of socialism and had a vision of France that would provide universal education and heal social divisions.

- King Louis Philippe ruled with the help of the wealthy and corrupt; his failure to provide social programs led to revolt and an end to monarchy in 1848, and the establishment of the Second Republic.

- The moderate republicans and the republican socialists disagreed about reforms, not going far enough for the working class, who unsuccessfully revolted in the "June Days"; the reaction replaced the generous democratic republic with Bonaparte's nephew Louis Napoleon, who consolidated power once again in the hands of the propertied elite under a semi-authoritarian regime.

- Revolution in France inspired popular revolts in the Austrian Empire in 1848 and led to reforms, but conflicting national aspirations and poor organization brought defeat to the revolutionaries by the Austrian aristocracy and its loyal army.

- At the Frankfurt Assembly, Prussian liberals demanded a constitutional monarchy but urban workers wanted more radical reforms; Prussian king Frederick William refused the constitutional crown they offered and with the help of Austria and Russia reasserted his conservative and autocratic royal authority, forcing a return to the German Confederation.

Thus delayed, the National Assembly did not complete its draft of a liberal constitution until March 1849, at which time it elected King Frederick William of Prussia emperor of the new German national state (minus Austria and Schleswig-Holstein). By early 1849, however, reaction had been successful almost everywhere. Frederick William had reasserted his royal authority, disbanded the Prussian Constituent Assembly, and granted his subjects a limited, essentially conservative constitution. Reasserting that he ruled by divine right, Frederick William contemptuously refused to accept the "crown from the gutter." Bogged down by their preoccupation with nationalist issues, the reluctant revolutionaries in Frankfurt had waited too long and acted too timidly.

When Frederick William, who really wanted to be emperor but only on his own authoritarian terms, tried to get the small monarchs of Germany to elect him emperor, Austria balked. Supported by Russia, Austria forced Prussia to renounce all of its schemes of unification in late 1850. The German Confederation was reestablished. Attempts to unite the Germans—first in a liberal national state and then in a conservative Prussian empire—had failed completely.

Chapter Review

How did the victorious allies fashion a general peace settlement, and how did Metternich uphold a conservative European order? (page 590)

In 1814 the victorious allied powers sought to restore peace and stability in Europe. Dealing moderately with France and wisely settling their own differences, the allies laid the foundations for beneficial international cooperation throughout much of the nineteenth century. Led by Metternich, the conservative powers also used intervention and repression as they sought to prevent the spread of subversive ideas and radical changes in domestic politics.

What were the basic tenets of liberalism, nationalism, and socialism, and what groups were most attracted to these ideologies? (page 594)

European thought has seldom been more powerfully creative than after 1815, and ideologies of liberalism, nationalism, and socialism all developed to challenge the existing order in this period of early industrialization and rapid population growth. The basic tenets in one way or another rejected conservatism, with its stress on tradition, hereditary monarchy and aristocracy, and an official church.

What were the characteristics of the romantic movement, and who were some of the great romantic artists? (page 598)

The romantic movement, breaking decisively with the dictates of classicism, reinforced the spirit of change and revolutionary anticipation. The romantic movement was characterized by a belief in self-expression, imagination, and spontaneity, in art as well as in personal life. Some of the artists and thinkers who embodied the romantic movement include Rousseau, Wordsworth, George Sand, Delacroix, and Chopin.

How after 1815 did liberal, national, and socialist forces challenge conservatism in Greece, Great Britain, and France? (page 601)

Inspired by modern nationalism, Greek patriots rebelled against their Turkish rulers and won national independence. In Great Britain the liberal challenge to the conservative order led to fundamental reforms, as more men gained the right to vote, high tariffs on grain were abolished, and the factory workday was reduced. Elsewhere in Europe the old order held firm, and political, economic, and social pressures kept building.

Why in 1848 did revolution triumph briefly throughout most of Europe, and why did it fail almost completely? (page 607)

In 1848 the increasing pressures exploded dramatically as they culminated in liberal and nationalistic revolutions. Monarchies panicked and crumbled as revolutionaries triumphed, first in France and then all across the continent. Yet very few revolutionary

Key Terms

dual revolution (p. 590)
Congress of Vienna (p. 590)
Holy Alliance (p. 593)
Carlsbad Decrees (p. 593)
liberalism (p. 594)
laissez faire (p. 594)
nationalism (p. 595)
socialism (p. 596)
bourgeoisie (p. 597)
proletariat (p. 597)
romanticism (p. 598)
Sturm und Drang (p. 598)
Corn Laws (p. 602)
Battle of Peterloo (p. 603)
Reform Bill of 1832 (p. 603)
Great Famine (p. 605)

goals were realized. The moderate, nationalistic middle classes were unable to consolidate their initial victories. Instead, they drew back when artisans, factory workers, and radical socialists rose up to present their own much more revolutionary demands. This retreat facilitated the efforts of dedicated aristocrats in central Europe to reassert their power. And it made possible the crushing of Parisian workers by a coalition of solid bourgeoisie and landowning peasantry in France. Thus the lofty ideals of a generation drowned in a sea of blood and disillusion. Soon tough-minded realists would take command to confront the challenges of the day.

Notes

1. This paragraph draws on the influential views of B. Anderson, *Imagined Communities: Reflections on the Origins and Spread of Nationalism*, rev. ed. (London/New York: Verso, 1991), and E. J. Hobsbawm and T. Ranger, eds., *The Invention of Tradition* (Cambridge: Cambridge University Press, 1983).
2. A. de Tocqueville, *Recollections* (New York: Columbia University Press, 1949), p. 94.
3. M. Agulhon, *1848* (Paris: Éditions du Seuil, 1973), pp. 68–69.
4. W. L. Langer, *Political and Social Upheaval, 1832–1852* (New York: Harper & Row, 1969), p. 361.

To assess your mastery of this chapter, go to **bedfordstmartins.com/mckaywestbrief**

Listening to the Past

Speaking for the Czech Nation

The creation of national consciousness and nationalism often began with a cultural revival that focused on a people's language and history. In Austria, the influential historian Frantisek Palacky (1798–1876) created a portrait of the Czechs as progressive and democratic before the Counter-Reformation and the long process of Germanization under Habsburg rule.

In the revolution of 1848, the German National Assembly in Frankfurt asked Palacky to represent the Austrian province of Czech Bohemia in its efforts to form a unified Germany. In the famous letter that follows Palacky rejected this invitation, asserting the reality of a Czech nation and warning of both Russian and German expansionism, he proposed a "union of equals" in a radically transformed Austria. A version of Palacky's proposal was passed by Austria's constituent assembly in 1849, but the resurgent absolutist government vetoed it.

Frantisek Palacky, in a frontispiece portrait accompanying his most important work on Czech history. (Visual Connection Archive)

I am a Czech of Slav descent and with all the little I own and possess I have devoted myself wholly and forever to the service of my nation. That nation is small, it is true, but from time immemorial it has been an independen0t nation with its own character; its rulers have participated since old times in the federation of German princes, but the nation never regarded itself nor was it regarded by others throughout all the centuries, as part of the German nation. The whole union of the Czech lands first with the Holy German Empire and then with the German Confederation was always a purely dynastic one of which the Czech nation, the Czech Estates, hardly wished to know and which they hardly noticed. . . . If anyone asks that the Czech nation should now unite with the German nation, beyond this heretofore existing federation between princes, this is then a new demand which has no historical legal basis. . . . The second reason which prevents me from participating in your deliberations is the fact that . . . you . . . are . . . aiming to undermine Austria forever as an independent empire and to make its existence impossible—an empire whose preservation, integrity and consoli-

dation is, and must be, a great and important matter not only for my own nation but for the whole of Europe, indeed for mankind and civilization itself. [Palacky goes on to argue that a strong Austrian empire is needed as a barrier to Russian expansion.]

But why have we seen this state, which by nature and history is destined to be the bulwark and guardian of Europe against Asiatic elements of every kind—why have we seen it in a critical moment helpless and almost unadvised in the face of the advancing storm? It is because in an unhappy blindness which has lasted for very long, Austria has not recognized the real legal and moral foundation of its existence and has denied it: the fundamental rule that all the nationalities united under its scepter should enjoy complete equality of rights and respect. The right of nations is truly a natural right; no nation on earth has the right to demand that its neighbour should sacrifice itself for its benefit, no nation obliged to deny or sacrifice itself for the good of its neighbour. Nature knows neither ruling nor subservient nations. If the union which unites several different nations is to be firm and lasting, no nation must have cause to fear that by that union it will lose any of the goods which it holds most dear; on the contrary each must have the certain hope that it will find in the central authority defense and protection against possible violations of equality by neighbours; then every nation will do its best to strengthen that central authority so that it can successfully provide the aforesaid defense.

Questions for Analysis

1. Why did Palacky refuse to participate in the German National Assembly?

2. What Enlightenment ideas does Palacky draw upon in his letter?

3. Why might an absolutist government reject Palacky's argument?

Source: Slightly adapted from Hans Kohn, *Pan-Slavism: Its Ideology and History*, pp. 65–69. Copyright © 1953 by the University of Notre Dame Press. Reprinted with permission.

CHAPTER 24

Life in the Emerging Urban Society in the Nineteenth Century

John Perry, *A Bill-poster's Fantasy* (1855), explores the endless diversity of big-city entertainment. (Dunhill Museum & Archive, 48 Jermyn Street, St. James's, London)

Chapter Preview

Taming the City
What was life like in the cities, and how did urban life change in the nineteenth century?

Rich and Poor and Those in Between
What did the emergence of urban industrial society mean for rich and poor and those in between?

The Changing Family
How did families change as they coped with the challenges and the opportunities of the developing urban civilization?

Science and Thought
What major changes in science and thought reflected and influenced the new urban society?

INDIVIDUALS IN SOCIETY: Franziska Tiburtius

IMAGES IN SOCIETY: Class and Gender Boundaries in Women's Fashion, 1850–1914

LISTENING TO THE PAST: Middle-Class Youth and Sexuality

617

The era of intellectual and political upheaval that culminated in the revolutions of 1848 was also an era of rapid urbanization. After 1848 Western political development veered off in a novel and uncharted direction, but the growth of towns and cities rushed forward with undiminished force. Thus Western society was urban and industrial in 1900 as surely as it had been rural and agrarian in 1800. The urbanization of society was both a result of the Industrial Revolution and a reflection of its enormous long-term impact.

Taming the City

What was life like in the cities, and how did urban life change in the nineteenth century?

The growth of industry posed enormous challenges for all members of Western society, from young factory workers confronting relentless discipline to aristocratic elites maneuvering to retain political power. As we saw in Chapter 22, the early consequences of economic transformation were mixed and far-reaching and by no means wholly negative. By 1850 at the latest, working conditions were improving and real wages were rising for the mass of the population, and they continued to do so until 1914. Thus given the poverty and uncertainty of preindustrial life, some historians maintain that the history of industrialization in the nineteenth century is probably better written in terms of increasing opportunities than in terms of greater hardships.

Critics of this relatively optimistic view of industrialization claim that it neglects the quality of life in urban areas. They stress that the new industrial towns and cities were awful places where people, especially poor people, suffered from bad housing, lack of sanitation, and a sense of hopelessness. They ask if these drawbacks did not more than cancel out higher wages and greater opportunity. An examination of the development of cities in the nineteenth century provides some answers to this complex question.

Industry and the Growth of Cities

Since the Middle Ages, European cities had been centers of government, culture, and large-scale commerce. They had also been congested, dirty, and unhealthy. People were packed together almost as tightly as possible within the city limits. Infectious disease spread with deadly speed in overcrowded cities, and in the larger towns, yearly deaths outnumbered births. Urban populations were able to maintain their numbers only because newcomers were continually arriving from rural areas.

Clearly, deplorable urban conditions did not originate with the Industrial Revolution. What the Industrial Revolution did was to amplify those conditions. The steam engine freed industrialists from dependence on water power and allowed them to build factories in any location. Cities were desirable sites because they offered better access to shipping facilities, materials and markets, and a large pool of workers. Therefore, as industry grew, there was also a rapid expansion of already overcrowded and unhealthy cities.

The challenge of the urban environment was felt first and most acutely in Great Britain. The number of people living in cities of 20,000 or more in England and Wales jumped from 1.5 million in 1801 to 6.3 million in 1851 and reached 15.6 million in 1891. Such cities accounted for 17 percent of the total English

ca. 1850–1870	Modernization of Paris
1850–1914	Condition of working classes improves
1854	Pasteur studies fermentation and develops pasteurization
1854–1870	Development of germ theory
1857	Flaubert, *Madame Bovary*
1859	Darwin, *On the Origin of Species*
1869	Mendeleev creates periodic table
1880–1881	Dostoevski, *The Brothers Karamazov*
1880–1913	Birthrate steadily declines in Europe
1890s	Electric streetcars introduced in Europe

population in 1801, 35 percent as early as 1851, and fully 54 percent in 1891. Other countries duplicated the English pattern as they industrialized (see Map 24.1). An American observer was hardly exaggerating when he wrote in 1899 that "the most remarkable social phenomenon of the present century is the concentration of population in cities."[1]

As the population climbed, each town or city utilized every scrap of land to the fullest extent. Parks and open areas were almost nonexistent. Narrow houses were built wall to wall in long rows. These row houses had neither front nor back yards, and only a narrow alley in back separated one row from the next. Or buildings were built around tiny courtyards completely enclosed on all four sides. "Six, eight, and even ten occupying one room is anything but uncommon," wrote one observer in 1842.

These highly concentrated urban populations lived in extremely unsanitary and unhealthy conditions. Open drains and sewers flowed alongside or down the middle of unpaved streets. Toilet facilities were primitive in the extreme. In parts of Manchester, as many as two hundred people shared a single outhouse. Sewage often overflowed and seeped into cellar dwellings. Moreover, some courtyards in poorer neighborhoods became dunghills, collecting excrement that was sometimes sold as fertilizer.

Who or what was responsible for these awful conditions? The crucial factors were the tremendous pressure of more people and the *total* absence of public transportation. People simply had to jam themselves together if they were to be able to walk to shops and factories. Another factor was that governments, on the continent as well as in Great Britain, were slow to provide sanitary facilities and establish adequate building codes. This slow pace was probably attributable more to uncertainty about what precisely should be done than to rigid middle-class opposition to government action. Moreover, because of the sad legacy of rural housing conditions in preindustrial society, ordinary people generally took dirt and filth for granted. One English miner told an investigator, "I do not think it usual for the lasses [in the coal mines] to wash their bodies; my sisters never wash themselves." As for the men, "their legs and bodies are as black as your hat."[2]

Public Health and the Bacterial Revolution

Although cleanliness was not next to godliness in most people's eyes, it was becoming so for some reformers. The most famous of these was Edwin Chadwick, a commissioner charged with the administration of relief to paupers. Chadwick was a follower of radical philosopher Jeremy Bentham (1748–1832), whose approach to social problems, called **utilitarianism,** aimed for a solution that provided the "greatest good for the greatest number." Chadwick believed that unsanitary conditions led to illness and that the sickness or death of a wage earner pushed the family deeper into poverty. His goal was to ward off disease and thus poverty by cleaning up the urban environment.

Chadwick documented the "sanitary conditions of the laboring populations" in an 1842 report and argued that the excrement of communal outhouses could be dependably carried off by water through sewers at less than one-twentieth the cost of removing it by hand. The cheap iron pipes and tile drains of the industrial age would provide running water and sewerage for all sections of town, not just the wealthy ones. In 1848, with the cause strengthened by the cholera epidemic of

utilitarianism The idea of Jeremy Bentham that social policies should promote the "greatest good for the greatest number."

1800

1900

MAPPING THE PAST

MAP 24.1   European Cities of 100,000 or More, 1800 and 1900

There were more large cities in Great Britain in 1900 than in all of Europe in 1800. A careful comparison of these historical snapshots reveals key aspects of nineteenth-century urbanization. **[1]** In 1800, what common characteristics were shared by many large European cities? (For example, how many big cities were capitals and/or leading ports?) **[2]** Compare the spatial distribution of cities in 1800 with the distribution in 1900. Where and why in 1900 are many large cities concentrated in two clusters?

1846, Chadwick's report became the basis of Great Britain's first public health law, which created a national health board and gave cities broad authority to build modern sanitary systems.

The public health movement won dedicated supporters in the United States, France, and Germany from the 1840s on. Governments accepted at least limited responsibility for the health of all citizens, and their programs broke decisively with the age-old fatalism of urban populations in the face of shockingly high mortality. By the 1860s and 1870s, European cities were making real progress toward adequate water supplies and sewerage systems, city dwellers were beginning to reap the rewards of better health, and death rates began to decline (see Figure 24.1).

Still, effective control of communicable disease required an understanding of the connection between germs and disease. This was to evolve through the work of Louis Pasteur (**pa-STUR**) (1822–1895), a French chemist who began studying fermentation in 1854 at the request of brewers. Using his microscope to study the fermentation process, Pasteur found that it depended on the growth of living organisms and that the activity of these organisms could be suppressed by heating the beverage—by pasteurization. The breathtaking implication was that specific diseases were caused by specific living organisms—germs—and that those organisms could be controlled.

By 1870 the work of Pasteur and others had demonstrated the general connection between germs and disease. Next the German country doctor Robert Koch (**kawkh**) and his coworkers developed pure cultures of harmful bacteria and described their life cycles, paving the way for researchers—mainly Germans—to identify the organisms responsible for disease after disease. These discoveries led to the development of a number of effective vaccines. Medical procedures became much more effective as well when the English surgeon Joseph Lister (1827–1912) reasoned that a chemical disinfectant applied to a wound dressing would destroy airborne germs.

The evolution of **germ theory** coupled with the ever more sophisticated public health movement saved millions of lives, particularly after about 1880. Diphthe-

germ theory The idea that disease was spread through filth and not caused by it.

FIGURE 24.1   The Decline of Death Rates in England and Wales, Germany, France, and Sweden, 1840–1913

A rising standard of living, improvements in public health, and better medical knowledge all contributed to the dramatic decline of death rates in the nineteenth century.

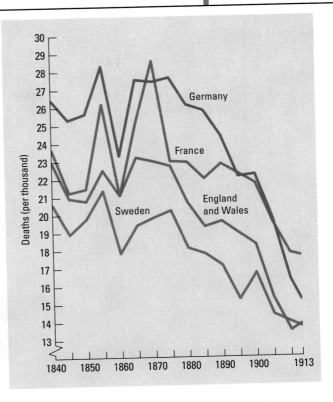

ria, typhoid, typhus, cholera, and yellow fever claimed fewer victims, and mortality rates began to decline dramatically (see Figure 24.1). By 1910 a great silent revolution had occurred: the death rates for people of all ages in urban areas were generally no higher than those for people in rural areas, and sometimes they were lower.

Urban Planning and Public Transportation   More effective urban planning was one of the keys to improving the quality of urban life. France took the lead during the rule of Napoleon III (r. 1848–1870), who sought to stand above class conflict and promote the welfare of all his subjects through government action. He believed that rebuilding much of Paris would provide employment, improve living conditions, and testify to the power and glory of his empire. Under his appointee, the baron Georges Haussmann (HOUSE-muhn) (1809–1884), Paris was transformed.

Haussmann and his fellow planners proceeded on many interrelated fronts. With a bold energy that often shocked their contemporaries, they razed old buildings in order to cut broad, straight, tree-lined boulevards through the center of the city as well as in new quarters on the outskirts. These boulevards, designed in part to prevent the easy construction and defense of barricades by revolutionary crowds, permitted traffic to flow freely and afforded impressive vistas. Their creation also demolished some of the worst slums.

New streets stimulated the construction of better housing, especially for the middle classes. Small neighborhood parks and open spaces were created throughout the city, and two very large parks suitable for all kinds of holiday activities were developed—one on the wealthy west side and one on the poor east side. The city also improved its sewers, and a system of aqueducts more than doubled the city's supply of good fresh water.

The Parisian model of urban planning spread throughout Europe, particularly after 1870. In city after city, public authorities mounted a coordinated attack on many of the interrelated problems of the urban environment. They razed structures to build new boulevards, office buildings, town halls, theaters, opera houses, and museums, while also placing pipes for sewage and water underground. Zoning expropriation laws, which allowed a majority of the owners of land in a given quarter of the city to impose major street or sanitation improvements on a reluctant minority, were an important mechanism of the new urbanism.

The development of mass public transportation also contributed to better living conditions. In the 1870s, horse-drawn streetcars carried riders along the growing number of major thoroughfares. Then in the 1890s, the real revolution occurred: European countries adopted the electric streetcar.

The Urban Landscape: Madrid in 1900
This wistful painting of a Spanish square on a rainy day, by Enrique Martinez Cubells y Ruiz (1874–1917), includes a revealing commentary on public transportation. Coachmen wait atop their expensive hackney cabs for a wealthy clientele, while modern electric streetcars that carry the masses converge on the square from all directions. (Museo Municipal, Madrid/The Bridgeman Art Library)

Section Review

- Industrialization meant increasing opportunities but also greater hardships including population density, lack of public transportation, and little government oversight, resulting in unsanitary, overcrowded conditions.

- The development of germ theory and the implementation of public health laws improved sanitation in the cities and mortality rates fell dramatically.

- Beginning in France, modern urban planning included organized streets and parks, better housing, sewers and fresh water supplies, and horse-drawn and then electric streetcars.

Electric streetcars were cheaper, faster, more dependable, and more comfortable than their horse-drawn counterparts. Service improved dramatically. Millions of Europeans—workers, shoppers, schoolchildren—hopped on board during the workweek. And on weekends and holidays, streetcars carried millions on happy outings to parks and countryside, racetracks and music halls. Good mass transit helped greatly in the struggle for decent housing. While horse-drawn streetcars had allowed the middle classes to move to better housing, electric streetcars made better housing accessible to those of modest means. The still-crowded city was able to expand and become less congested.

Rich and Poor and Those in Between

What did the emergence of urban industrial society mean for rich and poor and those in between?

General improvements in health and in the urban environment had beneficial consequences for all kinds of people. Yet differences in living conditions among social classes remained gigantic.

Social Structure

How much did the almost-completed journey to an urban, industrialized world change the social framework of rich and poor and those in between? The first great change was a substantial and undeniable increase in the standard of living for the average person. The real wages of British workers, for example, which had already risen by 1850, almost doubled between 1850 and 1906. Similar increases occurred in continental countries as industrial development quickened after 1850. Ordinary people took a major step forward in the centuries-old battle against poverty, reinforcing efforts to improve many aspects of human existence.

There is another side to the income coin, however. Greater economic rewards for the average person did *not* eliminate hardship and poverty, nor did they make the wealth and income of the rich and the poor significantly more equal. In almost every advanced country around 1900, the richest 5 percent of all households in the population received 33 percent of all national income. The richest 20 percent of households received anywhere from 50 to 60 percent of all national income. Moreover, income taxes on the wealthy were light or nonexistent. Thus the gap between rich and poor remained enormous at the beginning of the twentieth century. It was probably almost as great as it had been in the age of agriculture and aristocracy before the Industrial Revolution.

The great gap between rich and poor endured, in part, because industrial and urban development made society more diverse and less unified. There developed an almost unlimited range of jobs, skills, and earnings; one group or subclass shaded off into another in a complex, confusing hierarchy. Thus the very rich and the dreadfully poor were separated from each other by a range of subclasses, each filled with individuals struggling to rise or at least to hold their own in the social order. In this atmosphere of competition and hierarchy, neither the middle classes nor the working classes acted as a unified force, counter to Marx's predictions. This social and occupational hierarchy developed enormous variations, but the age-old pattern of great economic inequality remained firmly intact.

The Middle Classes

By the beginning of the twentieth century, the diversity and range within the urban middle classes were striking. At the top stood the most successful business families from banking, industry, and large-scale commerce. As people in this upper middle class gained in income and progressively lost all traces of radicalism after the trauma of 1848, they were almost irresistibly drawn toward the aristocratic lifestyle. They purchased country places or built beach houses for weekend and summer use. They employed a staff of servants and hired private coaches and carriages to signal their rising social status.

The topmost reaches of the upper middle class tended to shade off into the old aristocracy to form a new upper class of at most 5 percent of the population. Much of the aristocracy welcomed this development. Having experienced a sharp decline in its relative income in the course of industrialization, the landed aristocracy was often delighted to trade titles, country homes, and snobbish elegance for good hard cash. Some of the best bargains were made through marriages to American heiresses. Correspondingly, wealthy aristocrats tended increasingly to exploit their agricultural and mineral resources as if they were business people. Below the wealthy upper middle class were much larger, much less wealthy, and increasingly diversified middle-class groups. Here one found the moderately successful industrialists and merchants as well as professionals in law and medicine. This was the middle middle class, solid and quite comfortable but lacking great wealth. Below it were independent shopkeepers, small traders, and tiny manufacturers—the lower middle class. Both of these traditional elements of the middle class expanded modestly in size with economic development.

As industry and technology developed, new occupations entered the middle-class sphere. Engineering, for example, emerged from the world of skilled labor as a full-fledged profession of great importance, considerable prestige, and many branches. Architects, chemists, accountants, and surveyors, to name only a few, first achieved professional standing in this period. Management of large public and private institutions also emerged as a kind of profession as governments provided more services and as very large corporations such as railroads came into being.

Industrialization also expanded and diversified the lower middle class. The number of independent, property-owning shopkeepers and small business people grew, and so did the number of white-collar employees—a mixed group of traveling salesmen, bookkeepers, store managers, and clerks who staffed the offices and branch stores of large corporations. White-collar employees were propertyless and often earned no more than the better-paid skilled or semiskilled workers did. Yet white-collar workers were fiercely committed to the middle class and to the ideal of moving up in society. In the Balkans, for example, clerks let their fingernails grow very long to distinguish themselves from people who worked with their hands. The tie, the suit, and soft, clean hands were no-less-subtle marks of class distinction than wages.

Relatively well educated but without complex technical skills, many white-collar groups aimed at achieving professional standing and solid middle-class status. Elementary school teachers largely succeeded in this effort. From being miserably paid part-time workers in the early nineteenth century, teachers rode the wave of mass education to respectable middle-class status and income. Nurses also rose from the lower ranks of unskilled labor to precarious middle-class standing. Dentistry was taken out of the hands of working-class barbers and placed in the hands of highly trained (and middle-class) professionals.

Middle-Class Culture

In spite of their diversity, the middle classes were loosely united by a certain style of life and culture. Food was the largest item in the household budget, and a well-off family might spend 10 percent of its substantial earnings on meat and fully 25 percent of its income on food and drink. The dinner party was this class's favored social occasion. A wealthy family might host eight to twelve almost every week, whereas more modest households would settle for once a month.

The middle-class wife could cope with this endless procession of meals, courses, and dishes because she had both servants and money at her disposal. Indeed, the employment of at least one full-time maid was the best single sign that a family had crossed the cultural divide separating the working classes from what some contemporary observers called the "servant-keeping classes." The greater a family's income, the greater the number of servants it employed. Food and servants together absorbed about 50 percent of income at all levels of the middle class.

Well fed and well served, the middle classes were also well housed by 1900. Many quite prosperous families chose to rent apartments, complete with tiny rooms for servants under the eaves of the top floor. By 1900 the middle classes were also quite clothes-conscious. The factory, the sewing machine, and the department store had all helped reduce the cost and expand the variety of clothing. Middle-class women were particularly attentive to the fickle dictates of fashion.

"A Corner of the Table"
With photographic precision, the French academic artist Paul-Émile Chabas (1869–1937) idealizes the elegance and intimacy of a sumptuous dinner party. Throughout Europe, such dinners were served in eight or nine separate courses, beginning with appetizers and ending with coffee and liqueurs. (Archives Charmet/The Bridgeman Art Library)

(See the feature "Images in Society: Class and Gender Boundaries in Women's Fashion, 1850–1914" on pages 626–627.)

Education was another growing expense, as middle-class parents tried to provide their children with ever more crucial advanced education. The keystones of culture and leisure were books, music, and travel. The long realistic novel, the heroics of composers Wagner and Verdi, the diligent striving of the dutiful daughter at the piano, and the packaged tour to a foreign country were all sources of middle-class pleasure.

Finally, the middle classes were loosely united by a strict code of morality. This code laid great stress on hard work, self-discipline, and personal achievement. Drunkenness and gambling were denounced as vices; sexual purity and fidelity were celebrated as virtues. Men and women who fell into crime or poverty were generally assumed to be responsible for their own downfall.

The Working Classes

About four out of five people belonged to the working classes at the turn of the century. Many members of the working classes—that is, people whose livelihoods depended on physical labor and who did not employ domestic servants—were still small landowning peasants and hired farm hands. This was especially true in eastern Europe. In western and central Europe, however, the typical worker had left the land. In Great Britain, fewer than 8 percent of the people worked in agriculture, and in rapidly industrializing Germany only 25 percent were employed in agriculture and forestry. Even in less industrialized France, fewer than 50 percent of the people depended on the land in 1900.

The urban working classes were even less unified and homogeneous than the middle classes. Not only were there divides based on skill level (see Figure 24.2),

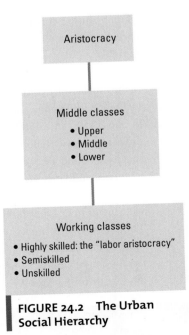

FIGURE 24.2   The Urban Social Hierarchy

Aristocracy

Middle classes
- Upper
- Middle
- Lower

Working classes
- Highly skilled: the "labor aristocracy"
- Semiskilled
- Unskilled

Images in Society

Class and Gender Boundaries in Women's Fashion, 1850–1914

Women's fashion was big business in the nineteenth century. Long the dominant industrial pursuit in human history, the production of textiles took off with the Industrial Revolution. In the later nineteenth century fashionable clothing, especially for middle-class women, became the first modern consumer industry as careful buyers snapped up the constantly changing ready-to-wear goods sold by large department stores.

In the nineteenth century, before society fragmented into many different groups expressing themselves in many dress styles, clothing patterns focused mainly on perceived differences in class and gender. The four illustrations presented here allow one to analyze the social information communicated through women's clothing. As you study these illustrations, note the principal characteristics and then try to draw out the larger implications. What does the impractical, restrictive clothing in these images reveal about society's view of women during this period? What is the significance of the emergence of alternative styles of well-groomed dress?

Most changes in women's fashion originated in Paris in the nineteenth century. Image 1 shows the attire worn by French aristocratic and wealthy middle-class women in the 1850s and 1860s. Note that these expensive dresses, flawlessly tailored by an army of skilled seamstresses, abound in elaborate embroidery, rich velvety materials, and fancy accessories. The circular spread of these floor-sweeping gowns is due to the crinoline, a slip with metal hoops that holds the skirt out on all sides. These women also are wearing the corset, the century's most characteristic women's undergarment, which was laced up tightly in back and pressed unmercifully from the breasts to the hips. What does this image tell you about the life of these women (their work, leisure activities, and so on)?

The intriguing 1875 painting by Atkinson Grimshaw, *Summer* (Image 2), shows a middle-class interior and the evolution of women's summer fashion two decades later. The corset still binds, but crinoline hoops have given way to the bustle, a cotton fan with steel reinforcement that pushes the dress out in back and exaggerates gender differences. The elaborate costume of the wealthy elite, available in cheaper ready-to-wear versions sold through department stores and mail-order catalogues throughout Europe, had become the standard for middle-class women. Emulating the elite in

IMAGE 1 Crinoline Dresses, Paris, 1859 (ILN/Mary Evans Picture Library)

IMAGE 2 Summer Dress with Bustle, England, 1875
(Roy Miles, Esq./The Bridgeman Art Library)

IMAGE 3 Alternative
Fashion, England, 1893
(© Manchester City Art Galleries)

style, conventional middle-class women shopped care-fully, scouting for sales, and drew a boundary separating themselves from working-class women in their simple cotton clothes. What implications, if any, do you see this having on class distinctions?

The young middle-class Englishwoman in an 1893 photo (Image 3) has chosen a woman's tailored suit, the only major English innovation in nineteenth-century women's fashion. This "alternative dress" combines the tie, suit jacket, vest, and straw hat—all initially items of male attire—with typical feminine elements, such as the skirt and gloves. This practical, socially accepted al-ternative dress appealed to the growing number of women in paid employment in the 1890s. The historian Diana Crane has argued that this departure from the dominant style can be seen as a symbolic, nonverbal as-sertion of independence and equality with men.* Do you agree with this? If so, what was the significance of the pre-1914 turn from stifling corset to the more flex-ible brassiere and the mainstream embrace of loose-fitting garments, such as the 1910 dress in Image 4? Did the greater freedom of movement in clothing reflect the emerging emancipation of Western women? Or was the

coquettish femininity of these loose, flowing dresses only a repackaging of the dominant culture's sharply defined gender boundaries?

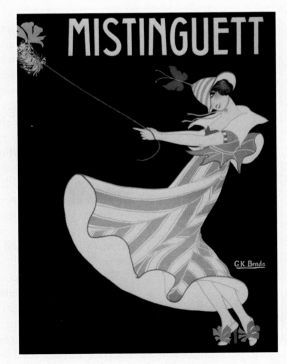

IMAGE 4 Loose-fitting Dress, France, 1910 (© Corbis)

*Diana Crane, *Fashion and Its Social Agendas: Class, Gender, and Identity in Clothing* (Chicago: University of Chicago Press, 2000), pp. 99–114.

but there were also great differences in lifestyles and cultural values. These differences contributed to a keen sense of social status and hierarchy within the working classes.

Highly skilled workers, who made up about 15 percent of the working classes, became a real **labor aristocracy.** These workers earned only about two-thirds of the income of the bottom ranks of the servant-keeping classes, but that was fully twice as much as the earnings of unskilled workers. The most "aristocratic" of the highly skilled workers were construction bosses and factory foremen, men who had risen from the ranks and were fiercely proud of their achievement. The labor aristocracy also included members of the traditional highly skilled handicraft trades that had not been mechanized or placed in factories, such as cabinetmakers, jewelers, and printers.

This group as a whole was under constant pressure. Over time, many skilled artisans such as woodcarvers and watchmakers were replaced by lower-paid semiskilled factory workers. At the same time, new kinds of skilled workers such as shipbuilders and railway locomotive engineers entered the labor aristocracy. Thus the labor elite remained in a state of flux as individuals and whole crafts moved in and out of it.

To maintain their precarious standing, the upper working class adopted straitlaced, almost puritanical values. Like the middle classes, the labor aristocracy was strongly committed to the family and to economic improvement. Families in the upper working class saved money regularly, worried about their children's education, and valued good housing. Despite these similarities, skilled workers viewed themselves not as aspirants to the middle class but as the pacesetters and natural leaders of all the working classes. Well aware of the degradation not so far below them, they practiced self-discipline and stern morality.

The upper working class in general frowned on heavy drinking and sexual permissiveness. An organized temperance movement was strong in the countries of northern Europe. As one German labor aristocrat somberly warned, "The path to the brothel leads through the tavern" and from there quite possibly to drastic decline or total ruin for person and family.[3] Men and women of the labor aristocracy were also quick to find fault with those below them who failed to meet their standards.

Below the labor aristocracy stood semiskilled and unskilled urban workers. The enormous complexity of this sector of the world of labor is not easily summarized. Workers in the established crafts—carpenters, bricklayers, pipe fitters—stood near the top of the semiskilled hierarchy. A large number of the semiskilled were factory workers who earned highly variable but relatively good wages and whose relative importance in the labor force was increasing.

Below the semiskilled workers was a larger group of unskilled workers that included day laborers such as longshoremen, wagon-driving teamsters, teenagers, and every kind of "helper." Many of these people had real skills and performed valuable services, but they were unorganized and divided, united only by the common fate of meager earnings. The same lack of unity characterized street vendors and market people—self-employed workers who competed savagely with each other and with the established shopkeepers of the lower middle class.

Domestic servants comprised a large and steadily growing segment of the unskilled group in the nineteenth century. The great majority were women; indeed, one out of every three girls in Britain between the ages of fifteen and twenty was a domestic servant. Throughout Europe and America, a great many female domestics in the cities were recent migrants from rural areas. As in earlier times, domestic service was still hard work at low pay with limited personal independence and the danger of sexual exploitation. Nonetheless, domestic service had real attrac-

labor aristocracy The highly skilled workers who made up about 15 percent of the working classes at the turn of the twentieth century.

A School for Servants

Although domestic service was poorly paid, there was always plenty of competition for the available jobs. Schools sprang up to teach young women the manners and the household skills that employers in the "servant-keeping classes" demanded. (Corporation of London: London Metropolitan Archives)

tions for "rough country girls": higher wages than agricultural work, more varied marriage prospects, and access to a broader range of entertainment.

Many young domestics from the countryside made a successful transition to working-class wife and mother, yet they often needed to supplement the family income by working in the **sweated industries.** Like the putting-out and cottage industries of earlier times, these industries paid by the piece for work done off-site, in the home. While some women hand-decorated objects, most made clothing, especially after the advent of the sewing machine. An army of poor women accounted for the bulk of the inexpensive "ready-made" clothes displayed on department store racks and in tiny shops.

sweated industries Poorly paid handicraft production, often by married women paid by the piece and working at home.

Working-Class Leisure and Religion While the middle classes gathered over dinner in their homes, the working classes mingled in taverns, cafés, and pubs. Working-class political activities, both moderate and radical, were also concentrated in drinking establishments. Moreover, social drinking in public places by married couples and sweethearts became an

- The standard of living increased for the average person during the nineteenth century, but poverty still existed and income disparity remained enormous; taxes on the rich were low and the working classes were not unified.

- The middle classes had an upper middle class of business owners, a diverse middle middle class, and a lower middle class of white-collar workers and shopkeepers.

- The middle classes had some common cultural interests, including socializing at dinner parties, employing servants, wearing fashionable clothing, educating their children, and abiding by a strict moral code.

- The working class had an upper working class, or labor aristocracy, skilled workers with high moral standards who viewed themselves as leaders of the working classes; below them were the semi-skilled and unskilled workers, both highly diverse groups that were not organized.

- Social and political gatherings of the working classes took place in taverns and pubs and for the first time included women; sports and music were other favored pastimes, while church attendance declined.

accepted and widespread practice for the first time. This greater participation by women undoubtedly helped civilize the world of drink and hard liquor.

The two other leisure-time passions of the working classes were sports and music halls. A great decline in "blood sports," such as bullbaiting and cockfighting, had occurred throughout Europe by the late nineteenth century. Their place was filled by modern spectator sports, of which racing and soccer were the most popular. Men and women also frequented music halls and vaudeville theaters, the working-class counterparts of middle-class opera and classical theater. Drunkenness, sexual intercourse and pregnancy before marriage, marital difficulties, and problems with mothers-in-law were favorite themes of broad jokes and bittersweet songs.

The working poor continued to find solace and meaning in religion. Yet historians also recognize that by the last two or three decades of the nineteenth century, a considerable decline in both church attendance and church donations was occurring in most European countries. And it seems clear that this decline was greater for the urban working classes than for their rural counterparts or for the middle classes.

Why did working-class church attendance decline? Part of the reason was that the vibrant, materialistic urban environment undermined popular religious impulses, which were poorly served in the cities. Equally important, however, was the fact that throughout the nineteenth century both Catholic and Protestant churches were normally seen as conservative institutions defending social order and custom. Therefore, as the European working classes became more politically conscious, they tended to see the established (or quasi-established) "territorial church" as defending what they wished to change and as allied with their political opponents. Especially the men of the urban working classes developed vaguely antichurch attitudes, even though they remained neutral or positive toward religion. They tended to regard regular church attendance as "not our kind of thing"—not part of urban working-class culture. The pattern was different in those places where the church or synagogue had never been linked to the state and served as a focus for ethnic cohesion. Irish Catholic churches in Protestant Britain and Jewish synagogues in Russia were outstanding examples.

The Changing Family

How did families change as they coped with the challenges and the opportunities of the developing urban civilization?

Urban life wrought many fundamental changes in the family. Although much is still unknown, it seems clear that in the second half of the nineteenth century the family had stabilized considerably after the disruption of the late eighteenth and early nineteenth centuries. The home became more important for both men and women. The role of women and attitudes toward children underwent substantial change, and adolescence emerged as a distinct stage of life. These are but a few of the transformations that affected all social classes in varying degrees.

Premarital Sex and Marriage

By 1850 the ideal of romantic love had triumphed among the working classes. Couples were ever more likely to come from different, even distant, towns and to be more nearly the same age, further indicating that romantic sentiment was replacing tradition and financial considerations.

For the middle classes, however, economic considerations continued to play a major role in marriage arrangements. In France dowries and elaborate legal marriage contracts were common practice among the middle classes in the later nineteenth century, and marriage was for many families one of life's most crucial financial transactions. As in the past, this preoccupation with money led many men to marry late, after they had been established economically, and to choose women considerably younger than themselves. A young woman of the middle class found her romantic life carefully supervised by her well-meaning mother, who schemed for a proper marriage and guarded her daughter's virginity like the family's credit. After marriage, middle-class morality sternly demanded fidelity. Middle-class boys were watched, too, but not as vigilantly. By the time they reached late adolescence, they had usually attained considerable sexual experience with maids or prostitutes. (See the feature "Listening to the Past: Middle-Class Youth and Sexuality" on pages 643–644.)

In Paris alone, 155,000 women were registered as prostitutes between 1871 and 1903, and 750,000 others were suspected of prostitution in the same years. Men of all classes visited prostitutes, but the middle and upper classes supplied much of the motivating cash. Thus, though many middle-class men abided by the publicly professed code of stern puritanical morality, others indulged their appetites for prostitutes and sexual promiscuity. For many poor young women, prostitution, like domestic service, was a stage of life and not a permanent employment. They went on to marry (or live with) men of their own class and establish homes and families.

A woman's virginity before marriage was not as important to the working classes, and in urban Europe around 1900, as many as one woman in three was going to the altar an expectant mother. Unmarried young people in western, northern, and central Europe were probably engaging in just as much sexual activity as their parents and grandparents who had created the illegitimacy explosion of 1750 to 1850 (see page 514). However, the rising rate of illegitimacy was reversed in the second half of the nineteenth century: more babies were born to married mothers. What accounts for this reversal? Pregnancy led increasingly to marriage and the establishment of a two-parent household. Skipping out was less acceptable, and marriage was less of an economic challenge. Thus the urban working-class couple became more stable, and that stability strengthened the family as an institution.

Kinship Ties

Within working-class homes, ties to relatives after marriage—kinship ties—were in general much stronger than many social observers have recognized. Most newlyweds tried to live near their parents, though not in the same house. Indeed, for many married couples in later-nineteenth-century cities, ties to mothers and fathers, uncles and aunts, were more important than ties to unrelated acquaintances.

Although governments were generally providing more welfare services by 1900, many people turned to their families for help in coping with sickness, unemployment, old age, and death. Relatives were also valuable at less tragic moments. If a couple was very poor, an aged relation often moved in to cook and mind the children so that the wife could earn badly needed income outside the home. Sunday dinners were often shared, as were outgrown clothing and useful information. Often the members of a large family group all lived in the same neighborhood.

Gender Roles and Family Life

Industrialization and the growth of modern cities brought great changes to the lives of European women. These changes were particularly consequential for married women, and in the nineteenth century most women did marry.

The rigid gender roles that had developed with industrialization were firmly entrenched after 1850. Men and women occupied separate spheres: the wife as mother and homemaker, the husband as wage earner. Well-paying jobs were off-limits to women, and married women were subordinated to their husbands by law.

With all women facing discrimination in education and employment and with middle-class women suffering especially from a lack of legal rights, there is little wonder that some women rebelled and began the long-continuing fight for equality of the sexes and the rights of women. Their struggle proceeded on two main fronts. First, following in the steps of women such as Mary Wollstonecraft (see page 545), organizations founded by middle-class feminists campaigned for equal legal rights for women as well as access to higher education and professional employment. These middle-class feminists argued that unmarried women and middle-class widows with inadequate incomes simply had to have more opportunities to support themselves. Middle-class feminists also recognized that paid (as opposed to unpaid) work could relieve the monotony that some women found in their sheltered middle-class existence and put greater meaning into their lives.

In the later nineteenth century, these organizations scored some significant victories, such as the 1882 law giving English married women full property rights. More women found professional and white-collar employment, especially after about 1880. But progress was slow and hard won. For example, in Germany before 1900, women were not admitted as fully registered students at a single university, and it was virtually impossible for a woman to receive certification and practice as a lawyer or doctor. (See the feature "Individuals in Society: Franziska Tiburtius.") In the years before 1914, middle-class feminists increasingly focused their attention on political action and fought for the right to vote for women.

Women inspired by utopian and especially Marxian socialism blazed a second path. Often scorning the programs of middle-class feminists, socialist women leaders argued that the liberation of working-class women would come only with the liberation of the entire working class through revolution. In the meantime, they championed the cause of working women and won some practical improvements, especially in Germany, where the socialist movement was most effectively organized. In a general way, these different approaches to women's issues reflected the diversity of classes in urban society.

While the ideology and practice of rigidly separate spheres made women powerless outside the home, within it their power grew stronger. Among the English working classes, it was the wife who generally determined how the family's money was spent. In many families, the husband gave all his earnings to his wife to manage, whatever the law might read. She returned to him only a small allowance for carfare, beer, tobacco, and union dues. All the major domestic decisions, from the children's schooling and religious instruction to the selection of new furniture or a new apartment, were hers. Despite this power, however, a good deal of her effort was directed toward pampering her husband as he expected. In countless humble households, she saw that he had meat while she ate bread, that he relaxed by the fire while she did the dishes.

The woman's guidance of the household went hand in hand with the increased emotional importance of home and family. The home she ran was idealized as a warm shelter in a hard and impersonal urban world. For a child of the English slums in the early 1900s,

home, however poor, was the focus of all love and interests, a sure fortress against a hostile world. Songs about its beauties were ever on people's lips. "Home, sweet home," first heard in the 1870s, had become "almost a second national anthem."

Franziska Tiburtius

Why did a small number of women in the late nineteenth century brave great odds and embark on professional careers? And how did a few of those manage to reach their objectives? The career and personal reflections of Franziska Tiburtius (tie-bur-TEE-us), a pioneer in German medicine, suggest that talent, determination, and economic necessity were critical ingredients.*

Like many women of her time who would study and pursue professional careers, Franziska Tiburtius (1843–1927) was born into a property-owning family of modest means. The youngest of nine children on a small estate in northeastern Germany, the sensitive child wilted with a harsh governess but flowered with a caring teacher and became an excellent student.

Graduating at sixteen and needing to support herself, Tiburtius had few opportunities. A young woman from a "proper" background could work as a governess or a teacher without losing her respectability and spoiling her matrimonial prospects, but that was about it. She tried both avenues. Working for six years as a governess in a noble family and no doubt learning that poverty was often one's fate in this genteel profession, she then turned to teaching. Called home from her studies in Britain in 1871 to care for her brother, who had contracted typhus as a field doctor in the Franco-Prussian War, she found her calling. She decided to become a medical doctor.

Supported by her family, Tiburtius's decision was truly audacious. In all of Europe, only the University of Zurich in republican Switzerland accepted female students. Moreover, if it became known that she had studied medicine and failed, she would never get a job as a teacher. No parent would entrust a daughter to an "emancipated" radical who had carved up dead bodies!

Although the male students at the university sometimes harassed the women with crude pranks, Tiburtius thrived. The revolution of the microscope and the discovery of microorganisms was rocking Zurich, and she was fascinated by her studies. She became close friends with a fellow female medical student from Germany, Emilie Lehmus, with whom she would form a lifelong partnership in medicine. She did her internship with families of cottage workers around Zurich and loved her work.

Graduating at age thirty-three in 1876, Tiburtius went to stay with her brother, a doctor in Berlin. Though well qualified to practice, she ran into pervasive discrimination. She was not even permitted to take the state medical exams and could practice only as an unregulated (and unprofessional) "natural healer." But after persistent fighting with the bureaucrats, she was able to display her diploma and practice as "Franziska Tiburtius, M.D. University of Zurich." She and Lehmus were in business.

Soon the two women realized their dream and opened a clinic, subsidized by a wealthy industrialist, for female factory workers. The clinic filled a great need and was soon treating many patients. A room with beds for extremely sick women was later expanded into a second clinic.

Franziska Tiburtius, pioneering woman physician in Berlin. (Ullstein Bilderdienst/The Granger Collection, New York)

Tiburtius and Lehmus became famous. For fifteen years, they were the only women doctors in all Berlin. An inspiration for a new generation of women, they added the wealthy to their thriving practice. But Tiburtius's clinics always concentrated on the poor, providing them with subsidized and up-to-date treatment. Talented, determined, and working with her partner, Tiburtius experienced the joys of personal achievement and useful service, joys that women and men share in equal measure.

Questions for Analysis

1. How does Franziska Tiburtius's life reflect both the challenges and the changing roles of middle-class women in the later nineteenth century?

2. In what ways was Tiburtius's career related to improvements in health in urban society and to the expansion of the professions?

*This portrait draws on Conradine Lück, *Frauen: Neun Lebensschicksale* (Reutlingen: Ensslin & Laiblin, n.d.), pp. 153–185.

Few walls in lower-working-class houses lacked "mottoes"—colored strips of paper, about nine inches wide and eighteen inches in length, attesting to domestic joys: EAST, WEST, HOME'S BEST; BLESS OUR HOME; GOD IS MASTER OF THIS HOUSE; HOME IS THE NEST WHERE ALL IS BEST.[4]

By 1900 home and family were what life was all about for millions of people of all classes.

Married couples also developed stronger emotional ties to each other. Affection and eroticism became more central to the couple after marriage. Gustave Droz (**drose**), whose bestseller *Mr., Mrs., and Baby* went through 121 editions between 1866 and 1884, saw love within marriage as the key to human happiness. Many French marriage manuals of the late 1800s stressed that women had legitimate sexual needs, such as the "right to orgasm." Perhaps the French were a bit more enlightened in these matters than other nationalities. But the rise of public socializing by couples in cafés and music halls as well as franker affection within the family suggests a more erotic, pleasurable intimate life for women throughout Western society. This, too, helped make the woman's role as mother and homemaker acceptable and even satisfying.

Child Rearing

Within the family, attitudes toward children and child rearing also shifted. As more babies survived, parents allowed themselves to form emotional attachments earlier in their children's lives. Mothers increasingly breast-fed their infants, for example, rather than paying wet nurses to do so. Breast feeding involved sacrifice—a

SUNDAY MORNING
WORKMANS HOME
LEATHER LANE

A Working-Class Home, 1875
Emotional ties within ordinary families grew stronger in the nineteenth century. Parents gave their children more love and better care.
(ILN/Mary Evans Picture Library)

temporary loss of freedom, if nothing else. Yet in an age when there was no good alternative to mother's milk, it saved lives. This surge of parental feeling also gave rise to a wave of specialized books on child rearing and infant hygiene, such as Droz's phenomenally successful book. Droz urged fathers to get into the act and pitied those "who do not know how to roll around on the carpet, play at being a horse and a great wolf, and undress their baby."[5]

The loving care lavished on infants was matched by greater concern for older children and adolescents. They, too, were wrapped in the strong emotional ties of a more intimate and protective family. For one thing, European couples began to limit their number of children in order to care adequately for those they had. It was evident by the end of the nineteenth century that the birthrate was declining across Europe, as Figure 24.3 shows, and it continued to do so until after World War II. The Englishwoman who married in the 1860s, for example, had an average of about six children; her daughter marrying in the 1890s had only four; and her granddaughter marrying in the 1920s had only two or possibly three.

The most important reason for this revolutionary reduction in family size, in which the comfortable and well-educated classes took the lead, was parents' desire to improve their economic and social position and that of their children. Children were no longer contributors to the family income; indeed, parents saved to provide their children with such advantages as music lessons and summer vacations and long, expensive university educations and suitable dowries. A young German skilled worker with only one child spoke for many in his class when he said, "We want to get ahead, and our daughter should have things better than my wife and sisters did."[6] Thus the growing tendency of couples in the late nineteenth century to use a variety of contraceptive methods—rhythm method, withdrawal method, and mechanical devices—certainly reflected increased concern for children.

Indeed, many parents, especially in the middle classes, probably became *too* concerned about their children, unwittingly subjecting them to an emotional pressure cooker of almost unbearable intensity. The result was that many children and especially adolescents came to feel trapped and in need of greater independence.

The rigid division of gender roles within the family contributed to feelings of tension and anxiety. It was widely believed that mother and child loved each other easily but that relations between father and child were necessarily difficult and often tragic. The father was a stranger; his world of business was far removed from the maternal world of spontaneous affection. Moreover, the father was demanding, often expecting the child to succeed where he himself had failed and making his love conditional on achievement. Little wonder that the imaginative literature of the late nineteenth century came to deal with the emotional and destructive elements of

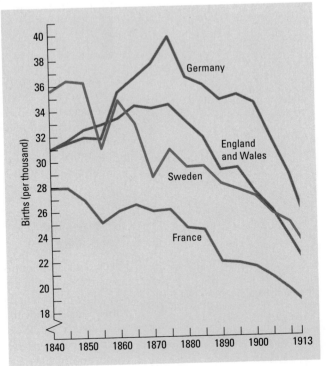

FIGURE 24.3   The Decline of Birthrates in England and Wales, Germany, France, and Sweden, 1840–1913
Women had fewer babies for a variety of reasons, including the fact that their children were increasingly less likely to die before reaching adulthood. Compare with Figure 24.1.

- Members of the working classes now often married for love but in the middle classes marriage was still an economic arrangement, with young women carefully supervised while young men frequented prostitutes.

- Kinship ties remained important for members of a working-class family, who often lived near each other and provided needed help and care.

- Rigid gender roles led to the development of organizations that pursued women's rights.

- Within the home a woman typically had more power, managing the household's income and making domestic decisions, but her primary responsibility was still to care for her husband and family.

- Love and emotional bonding to children occurred earlier, as infant survival rates grew, and couples, for economic reasons, generally had fewer children.

- Freud blamed tension and anxiety in young adulthood on early childhood experiences, while popular literature questioned parent-child relationships; for working-class youths, escape was possible as they could find work and leave home, but for middle-class youths there was no easy escape.

father-son relationships. In the Russian Feodor Dostoevski's (dos-tuh-YEF-skee) great novel *The Brothers Karamazov* (1880–1881), for example, four sons work knowingly or unknowingly to destroy their father. Later at the murder trial, one of the brothers claims to speak for all mankind and screams out, "Who doesn't wish his father dead?"

Sigmund Freud (froid) (1856–1939), the Viennese founder of psychoanalysis, formulated the most striking analysis of the explosive dynamics of the family, particularly the middle-class family in the late nineteenth century. A physician by training, Freud began his career treating mentally ill patients. He noted that the hysteria of his patients appeared to originate in bitter early-childhood experiences wherein the child had been obliged to repress strong feelings. When these painful experiences were recalled and reproduced under hypnosis or through the patient's free association of ideas, the patient could be brought to understand his or her unhappiness and eventually deal with it.

The working classes probably had more avenues of escape from such tensions than did the middle classes. Unlike their middle-class counterparts, who remained economically dependent on their families until a long education was finished or a proper marriage secured, working-class boys and girls went to work when they reached adolescence. Earning wages on their own, they could bargain with their parents for greater independence within the household by the time they were sixteen or seventeen. If they were unsuccessful, they could and did leave home to live cheaply as paying lodgers in other working-class homes. Thus the young person from the working classes broke away from the family more easily when emotional ties became oppressive. In the twentieth century, middle-class youths would follow this lead.

Science and Thought

What major changes in science and thought reflected and influenced the new urban society?

Major changes in Western science and thought accompanied the emergence of urban society. Two aspects of these complex intellectual developments stand out as especially significant. First, scientific knowledge expanded rapidly, influencing the Western worldview even more profoundly than before and spurring the creation of new products and whole industries. Second, between about the 1840s and the 1890s, European literature underwent a shift from soaring romanticism to tough-minded realism.

The Triumph of Science

The pace of scientific discoveries accelerated from the 1830s onward, stimulated by breakthroughs in industrial technology. While ordinary citizens continued to lack detailed scientific knowledge, they became convinced of the importance of science to human advancement.

The new branch of physics known as **thermodynamics** was one example of a theoretical field with roots in industry and obvious practical applications. Building on Isaac Newton's laws of mechanics and on studies of steam engines, thermodynamics investigated the relationship between heat and mechanical energy. By midcentury, physicists had formulated the fundamental laws of thermodynamics,

thermodynamics A branch of physics built on Newton's laws of mechanics that investigated the relationship between heat and mechanical energy.

which were then applied to mechanical engineering, chemical processes, and many other fields. The law of conservation of energy held that different forms of energy—such as heat, electricity, and magnetism—could be converted but neither created nor destroyed. Nineteenth-century thermodynamics demonstrated that the physical world was governed by firm, unchanging laws, leaving little room for either divine intervention or human will.

Chemistry and electricity were two other fields characterized by extremely rapid scientific progress. And in both fields, "science was put in the service of industry," as the influential economist Alfred Marshall (1842–1924) argued at the time.

Chemists devised ways of measuring the atomic weight of different elements, and in 1869 the Russian chemist Dmitri Mendeleev (men-duh-LEY-uhf) (1834–1907) codified the rules of chemistry in the periodic law and the periodic table. Chemistry was subdivided into many specialized branches, such as **organic chemistry**—the study of the compounds of carbon. Applying theoretical insights gleaned from this new field, researchers in large German chemical companies discovered ways of transforming the dirty, useless coal tar that accumulated in coke ovens into beautiful, expensive synthetic dyes for the world of fashion. The basic discoveries of Michael Faraday (FAR-uh-dee) (1791–1867) in electromagnetism in the 1830s and 1840s resulted in the first dynamo (generator) and opened the way for the subsequent development of the telegraph, electric motor, electric light, and electric streetcar.

organic chemistry The study of the compounds of carbon.

The successful application of scientific research in the fast-growing electrical and organic chemical industries promoted solid economic growth between 1880 and 1913 and provided a model for other industries. Systematic "R & D"—research and development—was born in the late nineteenth century.

The methods of science acquired unrivaled prestige after 1850. For many, the union of careful experiment and abstract theory was the only reliable route to truth and objective reality. The "unscientific" intuitions of poets and the revelations of saints seemed hopelessly inferior.

Social Science and Evolution

From the 1830s onward, many thinkers tried to apply the objective methods of science to the study of society. In some ways, these efforts simply perpetuated the critical thinking of the philosophes. Yet there were important differences. The new "social scientists" had access to the massive sets of numerical data that governments had begun to collect on everything from children to crime, from population to prostitution. In response, social scientists developed new statistical methods to analyze these facts "scientifically" and supposedly to test their theories. And the systems of the leading nineteenth-century social scientists were more unified, all-encompassing, and dogmatic than those of the philosophes. Marx was a prime example (see pages 597–598).

Another extremely influential system builder was French philosopher Auguste Comte (komt) (1798–1857), author of the six-volume *System of Positive Philosophy* (1830–1842). Comte postulated that all intellectual activity progresses through predictable stages:

> The great fundamental law . . . is this:—that each of our leading conceptions— each branch of our knowledge—passes successively through three different theoretical conditions: the Theological, or fictitious; the Metaphysical, or abstract; and the Scientific, or positive. . . . The first is the necessary point of departure of human understanding, and the third is the fixed and definitive state. The second is merely a transition.[7]

DARWIN! — par GILL

Satirizing Darwin's Ideas

The heated controversies over Darwin's theory of evolution also spawned innumerable jokes and cartoons. This cartoon depicts a bearded Charles Darwin and the atheistic materialist Emile Littré performing as monkeys in a circus. *(Musée de la Ville de Paris, Musée Carnavalet/Archives Charmet/The Bridgeman Art Library)*

By way of example, Comte noted that the prevailing explanation of cosmic patterns had shifted, as knowledge of astronomy developed, from the will of God (the theological) to the will of an orderly nature (the metaphysical) to the rule of unchanging laws (the scientific). Later, this same intellectual progression took place in increasingly complex fields—physics, chemistry, and, finally, the study of society. Comte believed that by applying the scientific method, also called the **positivist method,** his new discipline of sociology would soon discover the eternal laws of human relations.

Comte's stages of knowledge exemplify the nineteenth-century fascination with the idea of **evolution** and dynamic development. Thinkers in many fields, such as the romantic historians and "scientific" Marxists, shared and applied this basic concept. In geology, Charles Lyell (LAHY-uhl) (1797–1875) effectively discredited the long-standing view that the earth's surface had been formed by short-lived cataclysms, such as biblical floods and earthquakes. Instead, Lyell posited that the earth's surface changed and continues to change over an immensely long time. The evolutionary view of biological development, first proposed by the

positivist method Auguste Comte's discipline of sociology, which postulated that each branch of our knowledge passes successively through three different theoretical conditions; the theological, or fictitious; the metaphysical, or abstract; and the scientific, or positive.

evolution The idea, applied by thinkers in many fields, that stresses gradual change and continuous adjustment.

Greek Anaximander in the sixth century B.C.E., re-emerged in a more modern form in the work of Jean Baptiste Lamarck (luh-MAHRK) (1744–1829). Lamarck asserted that all forms of life had arisen through a long process of continuous adjustment to the environment.

Lamarck's work was flawed—he believed that the characteristics parents acquired in the course of their lives could be inherited by their children—and was not accepted, but it helped prepare the way for Charles Darwin (1809–1882), the most influential of all nineteenth-century evolutionary thinkers. Convinced by fossil evidence that he had collected and also persuaded by his friend Lyell that the earth and life on it were immensely ancient, Darwin came to doubt the general belief in a special divine creation of each species of animal. Instead, he concluded, all life had gradually evolved from a common ancestral origin in an unending "struggle for survival."

Darwin's great originality lay in suggesting precisely *how* biological evolution might have occurred. His theory is summarized in the title of his work *On the Origin of Species by the Means of Natural Selection* (1859). Decisively influenced by Thomas Malthus's (MAL-thuhs) gloomy theory that populations naturally grow faster than their food supplies (see page 572), Darwin argued that chance differences among the members of a given species help some survive while others die. Thus the variations that prove useful in the struggle for survival are selected naturally and gradually spread to the entire species through reproduction.

Darwin was hailed throughout Europe as the great scientist par excellence, the "Newton of biology," who had revealed once again the powers of objective science. Darwin's findings also reinforced the teachings of secularists such as Comte and Marx, who scornfully dismissed religious belief in favor of agnostic or atheistic materialism. In the great cities especially, religion was on the defensive. Finally, many writers applied the theory of biological evolution to human affairs. Herbert Spencer (1820–1903) saw the idea of the "survival of the fittest" at work in economic progress: the poor were the ill-fated weak; the prosperous were the chosen strong. Understandably, Spencer and other **Social Darwinists** were especially popular with the upper middle class.

Social Darwinists A group of thinkers popular with the upper middle class who saw the human race as driven forward to ever-greater specialization and progress by the unending economic struggle that would determine the survival of the fittest.

realism A literary movement that stressed the depiction of life exactly as it was.

Realism in Literature

In literature, the key themes of **realism** and naturalism emerged in the 1840s and continued to dominate Western culture and style until the 1890s. The major realist writers focused their extraordinary powers of observation on contemporary everyday life. Emphatically rejecting the romantic search for the exotic and the sublime, they energetically pursued the typical and the commonplace. Beginning with a dissection of the middle classes, from which most of them sprang, many realists eventually focused on the urban working classes, which had been neglected in imaginative literature before this time. The realists put a microscope to many unexplored and taboo subjects—sex, strikes, violence, alcoholism—and were charged by middle-class critics with sensationalism and undermining public morality.

Unlike the romantics, who had gloried in individual freedom and an unlimited universe, realists were strict determinists. Human beings, like atoms, were components of the physical world, and all human actions were caused by unalterable natural laws. Heredity and environment determined human behavior; good and evil were merely social conventions.

The realist movement began in France and was home to three of its greatest practitioners—Balzac, Flaubert, and Zola. Honoré de Balzac (BAWL-zak) (1799–1850) spent thirty years writing a vastly ambitious panorama of postrevolutionary

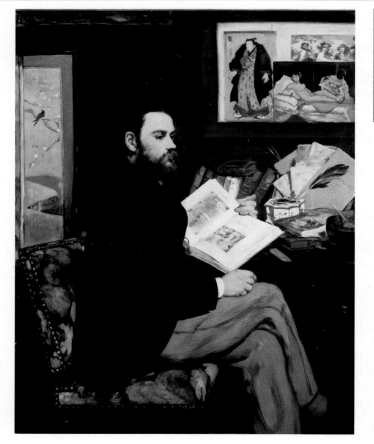

Manet: Emile Zola

The young novelist's sensitivity and strength of character permeate this famous portrait by the great French painter Edouard Manet. Focusing on nuances and subtle variations, Manet was at first denounced by the critics, and after Zola lost a newspaper job defending Manet they became close friends. Manet was strongly influenced by Japanese prints, seen in the background. (Erich Lessing/Art Resource, NY)

French life. Known collectively as *The Human Comedy*, this series of nearly one hundred books vividly portrays more than two thousand characters from virtually all sectors of French society. Balzac pictures urban society as grasping, amoral, and brutal, characterized by a Darwinian struggle for wealth and power.

Madame Bovary (1857), the masterpiece of Gustave Flaubert (floh-BAIR) (1821–1880), is far narrower in scope than Balzac's work but unparalleled in its depth and accuracy of psychological insight. The story of a frustrated middle-class housewife who has an adulterous love affair and is betrayed by her lover, *Madame Bovary* portrays the provincial middle class as petty, smug, and hypocritical.

Emile Zola (1840–1902) was most famous for his seamy, animalistic view of working-class life. Like many later realists, Zola sympathized with socialism—a sympathy evident in his overpowering novel *Germinal* (1885).

Realism quickly spread beyond France. In England, Mary Ann Evans (1819–1880), who wrote under the pen name George Eliot, brilliantly achieved a deeply felt, less sensational kind of realism. Her great novel *Middlemarch: A Study of Provincial Life* (1871–1872) examines masterfully the ways in which people are shaped by their social medium as well as their own inner strivings, conflicts, and moral choices. Thomas Hardy (1840–1928) was more in the Zola tradition. His novels, such as *Tess of the D'Urbervilles* (1891) and *The Return of the Native* (1878), depict men and women crushed by society, their own impulses, and bad luck.

The greatest Russian realist, Count Leo Tolstoy (1828–1910), combined realism in description and character development with an atypical moralizing, which came to dominate his later work. Tolstoy's greatest work is *War and Peace* (1864–1869), a monumental novel set against the historical background of Napoleon's invasion of Russia in 1812. Tolstoy went to great pains to develop his fatalistic theory of history, which regards free will as an illusion and the achievements of even the greatest leaders as only the channeling of historical necessity. Yet Tolstoy's central message is one that most of the people discussed in this chapter would have readily accepted: human love, trust, and everyday family ties are life's enduring values.

Section Review

- Scientific breakthroughs began to occur rapidly and their application to industry in the fields of physics, electrical engineering, and organic chemistry encouraged research and development to supplant the unscientific ideas of poets, philosophers, and religion.

- Social scientists studied society using scientific methods such as August Comte's positivist method.

- Charles Darwin built on Lyell's and Lamarck's ideas of evolution to propose that life on earth was immensely ancient and evolved in a slow process without the need for miraculous divine intervention.

- Herbert Spencer and other Social Darwinists applied evolution to human relations, arguing that "survival of the fittest" meant that society should accept the wealthy as the "most fit" and need not help the unsuccessful poor.

- Realism in literature branched away from the romantics and pursued middle and urban working class subjects, believing that heredity and environment were responsible for human behavior.

Chapter Review

What was life like in the cities, and how did urban life change in the nineteenth century? (page 618)

The revolution in industry had a decisive influence on the urban environment. The populations of towns and cities grew rapidly because it was economically advantageous to locate factories and offices in urban areas. This rapid growth worsened long-standing overcrowding and unhealthy living conditions and posed a frightening challenge for society. Eventually government leaders, city planners, reformers, scientists, and ordinary citizens responded. They took effective action in public health and provided themselves with other badly needed urban services. Gradually they tamed the ferocious savagery of the traditional city.

What did the emergence of urban industrial society mean for rich and poor and those in between? (page 622)

As the quality of urban life improved, the class structure became more complex and diversified than before. Urban society featured many distinct social groups, which existed in a state of constant flux and competition. The gap between rich and poor remained enormous and really quite traditional in mature urban society, although there were countless gradations between the extremes. Large numbers of poor women in particular continued to labor as workers in sweated industries, as domestic servants, and as prostitutes in order to satisfy the demands of their masters in the servant-keeping classes.

How did families change as they coped with the challenges and the opportunities of the developing urban civilization? (page 630)

Major changes in family life accompanied the more complex and diversified class system. Especially among the working classes, family life became more stable, more loving, and less mercenary. These improvements had a price, however. Gender roles for men and women became sharply defined and rigidly separate. Women especially tended to be locked into a subordinate and stereotypical role. Nonetheless, on balance, the quality of family life improved for all family members. Better, more stable family relations reinforced the benefits for the masses of higher real wages, increased social security, political participation, and education. Urban society in the late nineteenth century represented a long step forward for humanity, but it remained very unequal.

What major changes in science and thought reflected and influenced the new urban society? (page 636)

Inequality was a favorite theme of realist novelists such as Balzac and Zola. More generally, literary realism reflected Western society's growing faith in science, material progress, and evolutionary thinking. The emergence of urban, industrial civilization accelerated the secularization of the Western worldview.

Key Terms

utilitarianism (p. 619)
germ theory (p. 620)
labor aristocracy (p. 628)
sweated industries (p. 629)
thermodynamics (p. 636)
organic chemistry (p. 637)
positivist method (p. 638)
evolution (p. 638)
Social Darwinists (p. 639)
realism (p. 639)

Notes

1. A. Weber, *The Growth of Cities in the Nineteenth Century* (New York: Columbia University Press, 1899), p. 1.
2. Quoted in E. Chadwick, *Report on the Sanitary Condition of the Labouring Population of Great Britain*, ed. M. W. Flinn (Edinburgh: University of Edinburgh Press, 1965; original publication, 1842), pp. 315–316.

3. Quoted in R. P. Neuman, "The Sexual Question and Social Democracy in Imperial Germany," *Journal of Social History* 7 (Winter 1974): 276.
4. Quoted in R. Roberts, *The Classic Slum: Salford Life in the First Quarter of the Century* (Manchester, England: University of Manchester Press, 1971), p. 35.
5. Quoted in T. Zeldin, *France, 1848–1945*, vol. 1 (Oxford: Clarendon Press, 1973), p. 328.
6. Quoted in Neuman, "The Sexual Question," p. 281.
7. A. Comte, *The Positive Philosophy of Auguste Comte*, trans. H. Martineau, vol. 1 (London: J. Chapman, 1853), pp. 1–2.

To assess your mastery of this chapter, go to **bedfordstmartins.com/mckaywestbrief**

Listening to the Past

Middle-Class Youth and Sexuality

Growing up in Vienna in a prosperous Jewish family, Stephan Zweig (zwahyg) (1881–1942) became an influential voice calling for humanitarian values and international culture in early twentieth-century Europe. The following passage from his autobiography, The World of Yesterday *(1943), offers a glimpse into late nineteenth-century attitudes toward the sexuality of young adults and Zweig's assessment of the social consequences of these attitudes.*

An elegant ball for upper-class youth, with debutantes, junior officers, and vigilant chaperons watching in the background (State Russian Museum, St. Petersburg, Russia/The Bridgeman Art Library)

During the eight years of our higher schooling [beyond grade school], something had occurred which was of great importance to each one of us: we ten-year-olds had grown into virile young men of sixteen, seventeen, and eighteen, and Nature began to assert its rights. . . . It did not take us long to discover that those authorities in whom we had previously confided—school, family, and public morals—manifested an astonishing insincerity in this matter of sex. But what is more, they also demanded secrecy and reserve from us in this connection. . . .

This "social morality," which on the one hand privately presupposed the existence of sexuality and its natural course, but on the other would not recognize it openly at any price, was doubly deceitful. While it winked one eye at a young man and even encouraged him with the other "to sow his wild oats," as the kindly language of the home put it, in the case of a woman it studiously shut both eyes and acted as if it were blind. That a man could experience desires, and was permitted to experience them, was silently admitted by custom. But to admit frankly that a woman could be subject to similar desires, or that creation for its eternal purposes also required a female polarity, would have transgressed the conception of the "sanctity of womanhood." In the pre-Freudian era, therefore, the axiom was agreed upon that a female person could have no physical desires as long as they had not been awakened by man, and that, obviously, was officially permitted only in marriage. . . .

What [sexual] possibilities actually existed for a young man of the middle-class world? . . . Only a very few particularly rich young men could afford the luxury of keeping a mistress, that is, taking an apartment and paying her expenses. And only a very few fortunate young men achieved the literary ideal of love of the times—the only one which it was permitted to describe in novels—an affair with a married woman. The others helped themselves for the most part with shopgirls and waitresses, and this offered little inner satisfaction. . . . But, generally speaking, prostitution was still the foundation of the erotic life outside of marriage; in a certain sense it constituted a dark underground vault over which rose the gorgeous structure of middle-class society with its faultless, radiant façade.

We should not permit ourselves to be misled by sentimental novels or stories of that epoch. It was a bad time for youth. The young girls were hermetically locked up under the control of the family, hindered in their free bodily as well as intellectual development. The young men were forced to secrecy and reticence by a morality which fundamentally no one believed or obeyed. Unhampered, honest relationships—in other words, all that could have made youth happy and joyous according to the laws of Nature—were permitted only to the very few.

Questions for Analysis

1. According to Zweig, how did the sex lives of young middle-class women and young middle-class men differ? What accounted for these differences?

2. Was there nonetheless a basic underlying unity in the way society treated both the young men and the young women of the comfortable middle class? If so, what was that unity?

3. Zweig ends this passage with a value judgment: "It was a bad time for youth." Do you agree or disagree? Why?

Source: "Middle-Class Youth and Sexuality," from *The World of Yesterday* by Stephan Zweig, translated by Helmut Ripperger, copyright © 1943 by the Viking Press, Inc. Used by permission of Viking Penguin, a division of Penguin Group (USA) Inc., and Williams Verlag AG.

CHAPTER 25

The Age of Nationalism

1850–1914

France's Napoleon III and Empress Eugénie greet Britain's Queen Victoria and Prince Albert in a dazzling ceremony in Paris in 1855.

(The Royal Collection, © 2008 Her Majesty Queen Elizabeth II)

Chapter Preview

Napoleon III in France
How in France did Napoleon III seek to reconcile popular and conservative forces in an authoritarian nation-state?

Nation Building in Italy and Germany
How did the process of unification in Italy and Germany create conservative nation-states?

Nation Building in the United States
In what ways did the United States experience the full drama of nation building?

The Modernization of Russia and the Ottoman Empire
What steps did Russia and the Ottoman Turks take toward modernization, and how successful were they?

The Responsive National State (1871–1914)
Why after 1871 did ordinary citizens feel a growing loyalty to their governments?

Marxism and the Socialist Movement
Why did the socialist movement grow, and how revolutionary was it?

INDIVIDUALS IN SOCIETY: Theodor Herzl

LISTENING TO THE PAST: The Making of a Socialist

645

The revolutions of 1848 closed one era and opened another. Urban industrial society began to take a strong hold on the continent and in the young United States, as it already had in Great Britain. Internationally, the repressive peace and diplomatic stability of Metternich's time were replaced by a period of war and rapid change. In thought and culture, exuberant romanticism gave way to hardheaded realism. In the Atlantic economy, the hard years of the 1840s were followed by good times and prosperity throughout most of the 1850s and 1860s. Perhaps most important of all, Western society progressively developed, for better or worse, a new and effective organizing principle capable of coping with the many-sided challenge of the dual revolution and the emerging urban civilization. That principle was nationalism—dedication to an identification with the nation-state.

The triumph of nationalism is an enormously significant historical development that was by no means completely predictable. After all, nationalism had been a powerful force since at least 1789, but it had repeatedly failed to realize its goals, most spectacularly so in 1848. Yet by 1914 nationalism had become in one way or another an almost universal faith in Europe and in the United States, a faith that had evolved to appeal not only to predominately middle-class liberals but also to the broad masses of society. To understand this fateful evolution is the task of this chapter.

Napoleon III in France

How in France did Napoleon III seek to reconcile popular and conservative forces in an authoritarian nation-state?

The ideas of nationhood and popular sovereignty posed a fearful revolutionary threat to conservatives like Metternich. Yet from the vantage point of the twenty-first century, it is clear that nationalism wears many masks: it may be narrowly liberal or democratic and radical, as it was for Mazzini and Michelet, but it can also flourish in dictatorial states, which may be conservative, fascist, or communist. Napoleon I's France had already combined national feeling with authoritarian rule. Significantly, it was Napoleon's nephew, Louis Napoleon, who revived and extended this merger. In doing so, he provided a model for political leaders elsewhere.

The Second Republic and Louis Napoleon

Although Louis Napoleon Bonaparte had played no part in French politics before 1848, he was elected president by a resounding majority. There were several reasons for his success. First, he had the great name of his uncle, whom romantics had transformed through legend from a dictator into a hero. Second, middle-class and peasant property owners wanted a tough ruler to curb the socialist agitation of workers. Third, in late 1848 Louis Napoleon had a positive "program" for France, which had been elaborated in widely circulated pamphlets before the election. He argued that the state and its leader had a sacred duty to provide jobs and stimulate the economy. Large numbers of French peasants and workers believed his claim that he would champion the interests of all classes.

Elected to a four-year term, President Louis Napoleon had to share power with a conservative National Assembly. But in 1851, after the Assembly failed to change the constitution so he could run for a second term, Louis Napoleon seized power in a coup d'état. Restoring universal male suffrage, Louis Napoleon called on the French people, as his uncle had done, to legalize his actions. They did: 92 percent voted to make him president for ten years. A year later, by the greatest electoral margin yet, the authoritarian Louis Napoleon was made emperor of the French nation.

1852–1871	Reign of Napoleon III in France
1859–1870	Unification of Italy
1860–1900	Industrialization of Russia
1861	Freeing of Russian serfs
1861–1865	U.S. Civil War
1866	Austro-Prussian War
1870–1871	Franco-Prussian War
1870–1878	Kulturkampf, Bismarck's attack on Catholic Church
1880s	Educational reforms affect Catholic schools in France
1883	First social security laws to help workers in Germany
1905	Bloody Sunday in Russia
1908	Young Turks in Power

Napoleon III's Second Empire

Louis Napoleon—now proclaimed Emperor Napoleon III—experienced both success and failure between 1852 and 1870. His greatest success was with the economy, particularly in the 1850s. His government encouraged the new investment banks and massive railroad construction that were at the heart of the Industrial Revolution on the continent. The government also fostered general economic expansion through an ambitious program of public works, which included the rebuilding of Paris to improve the urban environment (see page 621). Profits soared while unemployment declined.

Louis Napoleon aimed to garner the support of workers as well as business owners. In the 1850s he regulated pawnshops, supported credit unions, and provided better housing for the working classes. In the 1860s, he granted workers the right to form unions and the right to strike—important economic rights denied by earlier governments.

At first, political power remained in the hands of the emperor. At the same time, Napoleon III restricted but did not abolish the Assembly. Members were elected by universal male suffrage every six years, and Louis Napoleon and his government took the parliamentary elections very seriously. By persuading voters that the election of government candidates was the key to roads, tax rebates, and a thousand other benefits, Napoleon III's supporters won big victories in 1857 and 1863. Yet in the 1860s, Napoleon III encountered opposition when he attempted to reorganize Europe on the principle of nationality and gain influence and territory for France and himself in the process. Problems in Italy and the rising power of Prussia led to increasing criticism at home. With increasing effectiveness, the middle-class liberals who had always wanted a less authoritarian regime continued to denounce his rule.

Napoleon was always sensitive to the public mood. Public opinion, he once said, always wins the last victory. Thus in the 1860s, he progressively liberalized his empire. He gave the Assembly greater powers and the opposition candidates greater freedom, which they used to good advantage. In 1869 the opposition, consisting of republicans, monarchists, and liberals, polled almost 45 percent of the vote.

The next year, a sick and weary Louis Napoleon again granted France a new constitution, which combined a basically parliamentary regime with a hereditary emperor as chief of state. In a final great plebiscite on the eve of the disastrous war with Prussia, 7.5 million Frenchmen voted in favor of the new constitution, and only 1.5 million opposed it. Napoleon III's attempt to reconcile a strong national state with universal male suffrage was still evolving and was doing so in a democratic direction.

Section Review

- Louis Napoleon Bonaparte had several things in his favor: his name, the middle and peasant classes wanted a tough ruler, and he had a positive program for the economy.

- After his election he shared power with the National Assembly but when they would not allow him to run again, he seized power, successfully faced re-election and then took the title of emperor Napoleon III, ending the Second Republic.

- Napoleon III liberalized the Second Empire, improving the French economy through his public works program, and allowing universal male suffrage, but by the late 1860s, facing an imminent war with Prussia, his power waned in favor of the Assembly and a new constitution.

Nation Building in Italy and Germany

How did the process of unification in Italy and Germany create conservative nation-states?

Louis Napoleon's triumph in 1848 and his authoritarian rule in the 1850s provided the old ruling classes of Europe with a new model in politics. To what extent might the expanding urban middle classes and even portions of the growing working classes rally to a strong and essentially conservative national state? This was one of the great political questions in the 1850s and 1860s. In central Europe, a resounding answer came with the national unification of Italy and Germany.

Cavour and Garibaldi in Italy

Italy, which had been a collection of competing city-states during the Middle Ages and Renaissance, was reorganized at the Congress of Vienna in 1815. The rich northern provinces of Lombardy and Venetia were taken by Metternich's Austria. Sardinia and Piedmont were under the rule of an Italian monarch, and Tuscany, with its famous capital Florence, shared north-central Italy with several smaller states. Central Italy and Rome were ruled by the papacy; Naples and Sicily were ruled, as they had been for almost a hundred years, by a branch of the Bourbons. Metternich was not wrong in dismissing Italy as "a geographical expression."

Between 1815 and 1848, the goal of an Italian nation captured the imaginations of many Italians. For many, the kingdom of Sardinia-Piedmont was ideally suited to achieve the goal of national unification. Its constitution provided for a fair degree of civil liberties and real parliamentary government, with deputies elected by a limited franchise based on income. Its leaders had the diplomatic and military skills needed to unify the peninsula.

Sardinia was ruled by King Victor Emmanuel, who had appointed Count Camillo Benso di Cavour (kah-VOOR) to prime minister in 1850. A brilliant statesman, Cavour came from a noble family, but he had also made a substantial fortune in business before entering politics. Cavour's national goals were limited and realistic. Until 1859 he sought unity only for the states of northern and perhaps central Italy in a greatly expanded kingdom of Sardinia.

In the 1850s, Cavour worked to consolidate Sardinia as a liberal constitutional state capable of leading northern Italy. His program of highways and railroads, of civil liberties and opposition to clerical privilege, increased support for Sardinia throughout northern Italy. Yet Cavour realized that Victor Emmanuel could not drive Austria out of Lombardy and Venetia and unify northern Italy without the help of a powerful ally. Accordingly, he worked for a secret diplomatic alliance with Napoleon III against Austria.

Finally, in July 1858 Cavour succeeded and goaded Austria into attacking Sardinia in 1859. Napoleon III came to Sardinia's defense. Then, after the victory of the combined Franco-Sardinian forces, Napoleon III did a sudden about-face. Deciding it was not in his interest to have too strong a state on his southern border and criticized by French Catholics for supporting the pope's declared enemy, Napoleon III abandoned Cavour and made a compromise peace with the Austrians.

Yet Cavour's plans were salvaged by the skillful maneuvers of his allies in the moderate nationalist movement. While the war against Austria had raged in the north, nationalists in central Italy had fanned popular revolts and driven out their easily toppled princes. With the nationalists holding firm, Cavour gained Napoleon III's support by ceding Savoy and Nice to France. The people of central Italy then voted overwhelmingly to join a greatly enlarged kingdom of Sardinia-Piedmont. Cavour had achieved his original goal of a northern Italian state (see Map 25.1).

Meanwhile, in southern Italy, nationalists united under the superpatriot Giuseppe Garibaldi (juh-SEP-ee gar-uh-BAWL-dee) (1807–1882). The son of a poor sailor, Garibaldi personified the romantic, revolutionary nationalism and republicanism of Mazzini and 1848. Partly to use him and partly to get rid of him, Cavour secretly supported Garibaldi's bold plan to "liberate" the kingdom of the Two Sicilies. Landing on the shores of Sicily in May 1860, Garibaldi's guerrilla band of a thousand **Red Shirts** captured the imagination of the Sicilian peasantry. With their support, the guerrilla leader took Palermo. Then he and his men crossed to the mainland, marched triumphantly toward Naples, and prepared to attack Rome and the pope. But the wily Cavour quickly sent his forces to intercept Garibaldi.

Cavour realized that an attack on Rome would bring about war with France, and he also feared Garibaldi's radicalism and popular appeal. Thus he immediately organized a plebiscite in the conquered territories. Despite the urging of some radical supporters, the patriotic Garibaldi did not oppose Cavour, and the people

Red Shirts The guerrilla army of Giuseppe Garibaldi, who invaded Sicily in 1860 in an attempt to liberate it and won the hearts of the Sicilian peasantry.

MAP 25.1 The Unification of Italy, 1859–1870
The leadership of Sardinia-Piedmont, nationalist fervor, and Garibaldi's attack on the kingdom of Two Sicilies were decisive factors in the unification of Italy.

of the south voted to join Sardinia. When Garibaldi and Victor Emmanuel rode through Naples to cheering crowds, they symbolically sealed the union of north and south, of monarch and nation-state.

Cavour had succeeded. He had controlled Garibaldi and had turned popular nationalism in a conservative direction. The new kingdom of Italy, which expanded to include Venice in 1866 and Rome in 1870, was a parliamentary monarchy under Victor Emmanuel, neither radical nor democratic. Despite political unity, only a small minority of Italian males had the right to vote. The propertied classes and the common people were divided. A great and growing social and cultural gap separated the progressive, industrializing north from the stagnant, agrarian south. The new Italy was united on paper, but profound divisions remained.

Bismarck and the Austro-Prussian War (1866)

In the aftermath of 1848, the German states were locked in a political stalemate. After Austria and Russia blocked Frederick William's attempt to unify Germany "from above," tension grew between Austria and Prussia.

At the same time, powerful economic forces were contributing to the Austro-Prussian rivalry. By the end of 1853, Austria was the only German state that had not joined the German customs union, or **Zollverein**. Middle-class and business groups in the Zollverein were enriching themselves and finding solid economic reasons to bolster their idealistic support of national unification. Prussia's leading role within the Zollverein gave it a valuable advantage in its struggle against Austria's supremacy in German political affairs.

Prussia's king William I (r. 1861–1888), who had replaced the unstable Frederick William IV, was convinced of the need for a larger army, which meant a bigger defense budget and higher taxes. His plans were opposed by parliament, however, which was in the hands of the liberal middle class. The wealthy middle class wanted society to be less, not more, militaristic. Above all, middle-class representatives wanted to establish once and for all that the parliament, not the king, had the ultimate political power and that the army was responsible to Prussia's elected representatives. King William then called on Count Otto von Bismarck to head a new ministry and defy the parliament. This was a momentous choice.

The most important figure in German history between Luther and Hitler, Otto von Bismarck (1815–1898) was a master of politics and a devoted servant of his Prussian sovereign. "One must always have two irons in the fire," he once said. He kept his options open, pursuing one policy and then another as he moved with skill and cunning toward his goal.

When the aristocratic Bismarck took office as chief minister in 1862, he made a strong but unfavorable impression. Declaring that the government would rule without parliamentary consent, Bismarck lashed out at the middle-class opposition: "The great questions of the day will not be decided by speeches and resolutions— that was the blunder of 1848 and 1849—but by blood and iron." Bismarck had the Prussian bureaucracy go right on collecting taxes, even though the parliament refused to approve the budget. Bismarck reorganized the army. And for four years, from 1862 to 1866, the voters of Prussia continued to express their opposition by sending large liberal majorities to the parliament.

Opposition at home spurred the search for success abroad. An opportunity presented itself in 1864, when the Danish king tried again, as in 1848, to bring the provinces into a more centralized Danish state against the will of the German Confederation. Prussia joined Austria in a short and successful war against Den-

Zollverein A German customs union founded in 1834 to stimulate trade and increase the revenues of member states.

mark. However, Bismarck was convinced that Austria should be expelled from German affairs so that Prussia could be in control. He knew that a war with Austria would have to be a localized one that would not provoke a mighty alliance against Prussia. By skillfully neutralizing Russia and France, he was in a position to engage in a war of his own making.

The Austro-Prussian War of 1866 lasted only seven weeks. Utilizing railroads to mass troops and the new breechloading needle gun to achieve maximum firepower, the reorganized Prussian army overran northern Germany and defeated Austria decisively at the Battle of Sadowa (SAD-daw-vah) in Bohemia. Anticipating Prussia's future needs, Bismarck offered Austria realistic, even generous, peace terms. Austria paid no reparations and lost no territory to Prussia, although Venetia was ceded to Italy. But the German Confederation was dissolved, and Austria agreed to withdraw from German affairs. The states north of the Main River were grouped in the new North German Confederation, led by an expanded Prussia. The mainly Catholic states of the south remained independent while forming alliances with Prussia. Bismarck's fundamental goal of Prussian expansion was being realized (see Map 25.2).

The Taming of the Parliament

In the aftermath of victory, Bismarck fashioned a federal constitution for the new North German Confederation. Each state retained its own local government, but the king of Prussia became president of the confederation, and the chancellor—Bismarck—was responsible only to the president. King and chancellor controlled the army and foreign affairs. There was also a legislature with members of the lower house elected by universal male suffrage. With this radical innovation, Bismarck opened the door to popular participation and the possibility of going over the head of the middle class directly to the people, much as Napoleon III had done in France. All the while, however, ultimate power rested in the hands of Prussia and its king and army.

Marshaling all his diplomatic skill, Bismarck reached out to parliament and asked them to pass a special indemnity bill to approve after the fact all the government's spending between 1862 and 1866. Most of the liberals jumped at the chance to cooperate. With German unity in sight, the German middle class accepted the conservative, authoritarian government that Bismarck represented. In the years before 1914, the values of the aristocratic Prussian army officer increasingly replaced those of the middle-class liberal in public esteem and set the social standard.[1]

The Franco-Prussian War (1870–1871)

The final act in the drama of German unification followed quickly. Bismarck realized that a patriotic war with France would drive the south German states into his arms. The French obligingly played their part. The apparent issue—whether a distant relative of Prussia's William I (and France's Napoleon III) might become king of Spain—was only a diplomatic pretext. By 1870 the French leaders of the Second Empire, goaded by Bismarck and alarmed by their powerful new neighbor on the Rhine, had decided on a war to teach Prussia a lesson.

As soon as war against France began in 1870, Bismarck had the wholehearted support of the south German states. With other governments standing still—Bismarck's generosity to Austria in 1866 was paying big dividends—German forces under Prussian leadership decisively defeated the main French army at Sedan on

Prussia before 1866

Conquered by Prussia in Austro-Prussian War, 1866

Austrian territories excluded from North German Confederation, 1867

Joined with Prussia to form North German Confederation, 1867

South German states joining with Prussia to form German Empire, 1871

Won by Prussia in Franco-Prussian War, 1871

★ Major battle
— German Confederation boundary, 1815–1866
— Bismarck's German Empire, 1871

MAPPING THE PAST

Map 25.2 The Unification of Germany, 1866–1871

This map shows how Prussia expanded and a new German empire was created through two wars, the Austro-Prussian War of 1866 and the Franco-Prussian War of 1870–1871. It deserves careful study because it highlights how central Europe was remade and the power of Prussia-Germany was greatly increased. **[1]** What were the results of the Austro-Prussian War? Specifically, how did Prussia treat its neighbors in the north, such as Hanover and Saxony? **[2]** What losses did Austria experience in 1866? **[3]** What were the results of the Franco-Prussian War for France and for the predominately Catholic states of southern Germany, such as Bavaria and Württemberg?

September 1, 1870. Louis Napoleon himself was captured and humiliated. Three days later, French patriots in Paris proclaimed yet another French republic and vowed to continue fighting. But after five months, in January 1871, a starving Paris surrendered, and France went on to accept Bismarck's harsh peace terms. By this time, the south German states had agreed to join a new German empire.

Proclaiming the German Empire, January 1871

This commemorative painting by Anton von Werner testifies to the nationalistic intoxication in Germany after the victory over France. William I of Prussia stands on a platform surrounded by princes and generals in the famous Hall of Mirrors in the palace of Versailles, while officers from all the units around a besieged Paris cheer and salute him with uplifted swords as emperor of a unified Germany. Bismarck, like a heroic white knight, stands between king and army. (akg-images)

The victorious William I was proclaimed emperor of Germany in the Hall of Mirrors in the palace of Versailles. Europe had a nineteenth-century German "sun king." As in the 1866 constitution, the king of Prussia and his ministers had ultimate power in the new German Empire, and the lower house of the legislature was elected by universal male suffrage.

The Franco-Prussian War released an enormous surge of patriotic feeling in Germany while poisoning relations with France. Prussia had become, with fortification by the other German states, the most powerful state in Europe in less than a decade. Most Germans were enormously proud, blissfully imagining themselves the fittest and best of the European species. Semi-authoritarian nationalism and a "new conservatism," which was based on an alliance of the propertied classes and sought the active support of the working classes, had triumphed in Germany.

Nation Building in the United States

In what ways did the United States experience the full drama of nation building?

Closely linked to European developments in the nineteenth century, the United States experienced the full drama of bloody nation building. The "United" States was divided by slavery from its birth, as economic development in the young republic carried free and slaveholding states in very different directions. Northerners extended family farms westward and began building English-model factories in the Northeast. By 1850 an industrializing, urbanizing North was also building a system of canals and railroads and attracting most of the European immigrants. In the South, cotton plantations dominated the economy, producing 5 million bales a year and satisfying an apparently insatiable demand from textile mills in Europe and New England.

The rise of the cotton empire revitalized slave-based agriculture, spurred exports, and played a key role in igniting rapid U.S. economic growth. The large profits flowing from cotton also led influential Southerners to defend slavery. Even though three-quarters of all Southern white families were small farmers and owned no slaves in 1850, Southern whites developed a strong cultural identity and came to see themselves as a closely knit "we" distinct from the Northern "they." Northern whites viewed their free-labor system as being morally superior. Thus regional antagonisms intensified.

These antagonisms came to a climax after 1848 when a defeated Mexico ceded to the United States a vast area stretching from west Texas to the Pacific Ocean. Debate over the extension of slavery in this new territory caused attitudes to harden on both sides. In Abraham Lincoln's famous words, the United States was a "house divided."

Lincoln's election as president in 1860 gave Southern "fire-eaters" the chance they had been waiting for. Eventually eleven states left the Union, determined to win their own independence, and formed the Confederate States of America. When Southern troops fired on a Union fort in South Carolina's Charleston harbor, war began.

The long Civil War (1861–1865) was the bloodiest conflict in American history, but in the end the South was decisively defeated and the Union preserved. While Northern causalities were high, many people there prospered during the war years and certain dominant characteristics of American life and national culture took shape. Powerful business corporations emerged, steadfastly supported by the Republican party during and after the war. The **Homestead Act** of 1862, which gave western land to settlers, and the Thirteenth Amendment of 1865, which ended slavery, reinforced the concept of free labor taking its chances in a market economy. Finally, the triumph of the Union seemed to confirm that the nation's "manifest destiny" was indeed to straddle a continent as a great world power. Thus a new American nationalism grew out of civil war.

The Modernization of Russia and the Ottoman Empire

What steps did Russia and the Ottoman Turks take toward modernization, and how successful were they?

The Russian and the Ottoman empires also experienced profound political crises in the mid-nineteenth century. These crises were unlike those occurring in Italy and Germany, for neither Russia nor the Ottoman Empire aspired to build a single powerful state out of a jumble of principalities. Both empires were already vast multinational states, built on long traditions of military conquest and absolutist rule by elites from the dominant ethnic groups—the Russians and the Ottoman Turks. In the early nineteenth century these governing elites in both states were strongly opposed to representative government and national self-determination, and they continued to concentrate on absolutist rule and competition with other great powers.

For both states relentless power politics led to serious trouble. It became clear to the leaders of both empires that they had to embrace the process of **modernization,**

Homestead Act A result of the American Civil War that gave western land to settlers, reinforcing the concept of free labor in a market economy.

Section Review

- Differences between the urbanized North and the agricultural slave-owning plantations in the South led to the American Civil War.
- The factories and free market society of the North were victorious over Southern rebels in the Civil War, fostering a new American nationalism.
- The Homestead Act providing western land to settlers and the abolishment of slavery reinforced the concept of "manifest destiny," that the Union was destined to occupy the continent and become a great nation.

modernization The changes that enable a country to compete effectively with the leading countries at a given time.

defined narrowly and usefully as the changes that enable a country to compete effectively with the leading countries at a given time. This limited conception of modernization fits Russia after the Crimean War particularly well, and it helps explain developments in the Ottoman Empire.

The "Great Reforms"

In the 1850s, almost 90 percent of the Russian population lived on the land and industry was little developed. Agricultural techniques were backward, and serfdom was still the basic social institution. Bound to the lord on a hereditary basis, the peasant serf was little more than a slave.

Serfdom had become the great moral and political issue for the government by the 1840s. Then the Crimean War of 1853 to 1856, arising out of a dispute with France over who should protect certain Christian shrines in the Ottoman Empire, brought crisis. Because the fighting was concentrated in the Crimean peninsula on the Black Sea, Russia's transportation network of rivers and wagons failed to supply the distant Russian armies adequately. France and Great Britain, aided by Sardinia and the Ottoman Empire, inflicted a humiliating defeat on Russia.

This military defeat demonstrated that Russia had fallen behind the rapidly industrializing nations of western Europe. At the very least, Russia needed railroads, better armaments, and reorganization of the army if it was to maintain its international position. Moreover, the disastrous war had caused hardship and raised the specter of massive peasant rebellion. Reform of serfdom was imperative. Military disaster thus forced Alexander II (r. 1855–1881) and his ministers along the path of rapid social change and general modernization.

The first and greatest of the reforms was the freeing of the serfs in 1861. Human bondage was abolished forever, and the emancipated peasants received, on average, about half of the land. Yet they had to pay fairly high prices for their land, and because the land was owned collectively, each peasant village was jointly responsible for the payments of all the families in the village. Collective ownership and responsibility made it very difficult for individual peasants to improve agricultural methods or leave their villages. Thus the effects of the reform were limited.

Most of the later reforms were also halfway measures. In 1864 Alexander II established a new institution of local government, the **zemstvo** (ZEMST-voh). Russian liberals hoped that this reform would lead to an elected national parliament, but they were soon disappointed. The local zemstvo remained subordinate to the traditional bureaucracy and the local nobility. More successful was reform of the legal system, which established independent courts and equality before the law. Education and policies toward Russian Jews were also liberalized somewhat, and censorship was relaxed but not removed.

Until the twentieth century, Russia's greatest strides toward modernization were economic rather than political. Industry and transport, both so vital to the military, were transformed when the government subsidized private railway companies. The railroads enabled agricultural Russia to export grain and thus earn money for further industrialization. Industrial suburbs grew up around Moscow and St. Petersburg, and a class of modern factory workers began to take shape.

Industrial development strengthened Russia's military forces and gave rise to territorial expansion to the south and east. Imperial expansion greatly excited many ardent Russian nationalists and superpatriots, who became some of the government's most enthusiastic supporters. Industrial development also contributed mightily to the spread of Marxian thought and the transformation of the Russian revolutionary movement after 1890.

zemstvo A new institution of local government in reformed Russia, whose members were elected by a three-class system of towns, peasant villages, and noble landowners.

In 1881 Alexander II was assassinated by a small group of terrorists. The era of reform came to an abrupt end, for the new tsar (zahr), Alexander III (r. 1881–1894), was a determined reactionary. Nevertheless, economic modernization sped forward under Sergei Witte (sur-GEY VIT-uh), the tough, competent minister of finance from 1892 to 1903. Inspired by the writings of Friedrich List (see pages 575–576), Witte believed that the harsh reality of industrial backwardness was threatening Russia's power and greatness.

Therefore, under Witte's leadership the government built state-owned railroads rapidly, doubling the network to thirty-five thousand miles by the end of the century. Witte established high protective tariffs to build Russian industry, and he put the country on the gold standard of the "civilized world" in order to strengthen Russian finances.

Witte's greatest innovation was to use the West to catch up with the West. His efforts to entice Westerners to locate their factories in Russia were especially successful in southern Russia. There, in eastern Ukraine, foreign capitalists and their engineers built an enormous and very modern steel and coal industry.[2] In 1900 peasants still constituted the great majority of the population, but Russia was catching up with the industrialized West.

The Revolution of 1905

Catching up partly meant vigorous territorial expansion, for this was the age of Western imperialism. By 1903 Russia had established a sphere of influence in Chinese Manchuria and was eyeing northern Korea. When the diplomatic protests of equally imperialistic Japan were ignored, the Japanese launched a surprise attack in February 1904. After Japan scored repeated victories, Russia was forced in September 1905 to accept a humiliating defeat.

As is often the case, military disaster abroad brought political upheaval at home. The business and professional classes had long wanted a liberal, representative government. Urban factory workers had all the grievances of early industrialization and were organized in a radical and still illegal labor movement. Peasants had gained little from the era of reforms and were suffering from poverty and overpopulation. At the same time, nationalist sentiment was emerging among the empire's minorities, and subject nationalities such as the Poles and Ukrainians were calling for self-rule. With the army pinned down in Manchuria, all these currents of discontent converged in the **revolution of 1905.**

On a Sunday in January 1905, a massive crowd of workers and their families converged peacefully on the Winter Palace in St. Petersburg to present a petition to Tsar Nicholas II (1894–1917). Suddenly troops opened fire, killing and wounding hundreds. The **Bloody Sunday** massacre turned ordinary workers against the tsar and produced a wave of general indignation.

Outlawed political parties came out into the open, and by the summer of 1905 strikes, peasant uprisings, revolts among minority nationalities, and troop mutinies were sweeping the country. The revolutionary surge culminated in October 1905 in a great paralyzing general strike, which forced the government to capitulate. The tsar issued the **October Manifesto,** which granted full civil rights and promised a popularly elected **Duma** (DOO-muh) (parliament) with real legislative power. The manifesto split the opposition. Frightened middle-class leaders helped the government repress the uprising and survive as a constitutional monarchy.

On the eve of the opening of the first Duma in May 1906, the government issued the new constitution, the Fundamental Laws. The tsar retained great powers. The Duma, elected indirectly by universal male suffrage, and a largely appointive

revolution of 1905 A popular upheaval that overturned absolute tsarist rule and made Russia into a conservative constitutional monarchy.

Bloody Sunday A massacre of peaceful protesters at the Winter Palace in St. Petersberg in 1905 that turned ordinary workers against the tsar and produced a wave of general indignation.

October Manifesto The result of a great general strike in October 1905, it granted full civil rights and promised a popularly elected Duma (parliament) with real legislative power.

Duma The Russian parliament that opened in 1906, elected indirectly by universal male suffrage but controlled after 1907 by the tsar and the conservative classes.

upper house, could debate and pass laws, but the tsar had an absolute veto. As in Bismarck's Germany, the emperor appointed his ministers, who did not need to command a majority in the Duma.

The disappointed, predominately middle-class liberals, the largest group in the newly elected Duma, saw the Fundamental Laws as a step backwards. Efforts to cooperate with the tsar's ministers soon broke down. After months of deadlock, the tsar dismissed the Duma and rewrote the electoral law so as to increase greatly the weight of the propertied classes. When elections were held, the tsar could count on a loyal majority in the Duma. His chief minister then pushed through important agrarian reforms designed to break down collective village ownership of land and encourage the more enterprising peasants—his "wager on the strong." In 1914, Russia was partially modernized, a conservative constitutional monarchy with a peasant-based but industrializing economy.

Decline and Reform in the Ottoman Empire

The Ottoman Empire had reached its high point of development under Suleiman the Magnificent in the sixteenth century. By the eighteenth century it fell rapidly behind western Europe in science, industrial skill, and military technology. Also during the eighteenth century, Russia's powerful westernized army was able to occupy Ottoman provinces on the Danube River.

Pasha Halim Receiving Archduke Maximilian of Austria

As this painting suggests, Ottoman leaders became well versed in European languages and culture. They also mastered the game of power politics, playing one European state off against another and securing the Ottoman Empire's survival. The black servants on the right may be slaves from the Sudan. (Miramare Palace Trieste/Dagli Orti/The Art Archive)

Caught up in the Napoleonic wars and losing more territory to Russia, the Ottomans were forced in 1816 to grant Serbia local autonomy. In 1830, the Greeks won their national independence, while French armies began their long and bloody conquest of Algeria (see page 606). The Ottoman Empire was losing territory and power.

Another threat to the empire came from within, with the rise of Muhammad Ali, the Ottoman governor in Egypt. In 1831, and again in 1839, his French-trained forces occupied the Ottoman provinces of Syria and then Iraq and appeared ready to depose Sultan Mahmud II (r. 1808–1839). The Ottoman sultan survived, but only because the European powers forced Muhammad Ali to withdraw. The European powers, minus France, preferred a weak and dependent Ottoman state to a strong and revitalized Muslim entity under a dynamic leader such as Muhammad Ali.

Tanzimat A set of reforms that were designed to remake the Ottoman Empire on a western European model.

Young Turks Fervent patriots who seized power in the revolution of 1908 in the Ottoman Empire.

Realizing their precarious position, liberal Ottoman statesmen launched in 1839 an era of radical reforms, which lasted with fits and starts until 1876 and culminated in a constitution and a short-lived parliament. Known as the **Tanzimat** (TAHNZ-ee-MAT) (literally, regulations or orders), these reforms were designed to remake the empire on a western European model. New decrees called for the equality of Muslims, Christians, and Jews before the law and a modernized administration and military. New commercial laws allowed free importation of foreign goods and permitted foreign merchants to operate freely throughout the empire. Of great importance for later developments, growing numbers among the elite and the upwardly mobile embraced Western education and accepted secular values to some extent.

Intended to bring revolutionary modernization, the Tanzimat permitted partial recovery but fell short of its goals for several reasons. First, the liberal reforms failed to halt the growth of nationalism among Christian subjects in the Balkans (see Chapter 27), which resulted in crises and defeats that undermined all reform efforts. Second, the Ottoman initiatives did not curtail the appetite of Western imperialism, which secured a stranglehold on the Ottoman economy. Finally, equality before the law for all citizens and religious communities actually increased religious disputes, which were in turn exacerbated by the relentless interference of the European powers. This development embittered relations between the religious communities, distracted the government from its reform mission, and split Muslims into secularists and religious conservatives. These Islamic conservatives became the most dependable support of Sultan Abdülhamid (ahb-dool-hah-MEED) (r. 1876–1909), who abandoned the model of European liberalism in his long and repressive reign.

The combination of declining international power and conservative tyranny eventually led to a powerful resurgence of the modernizing impulse among idealistic Turkish exiles in Europe and young army officers in Istanbul. These fervent patriots, the so-called **Young Turks,** seized power in the revolution of 1908, and they forced the sultan to implement reforms. Failing to stop the rising tide of anti-Ottoman nationalism in the Balkans, the Young Turks helped to prepare the way for the birth of modern secular Turkey after the defeat and collapse of the Ottoman Empire in World War I (see page 705).

Section Review

- The Russians began to catch up with the West by modernizing, abolishing serfdom, building railroads, and attracting industry from the West, which built huge coal and steel factories.

- The rise in industrialization contributed to the spread of Marxist thought, leading to the Russian revolutionary movement.

- The Revolution of 1905 arose from defeat abroad by the Japanese and upheaval at home; when the army fired on a peaceful demonstration, revolts and strikes began and the tsar issued the October Manifesto, granting civil rights and an elected Duma (parliament).

- The Duma and the new constitution were a disappointment to the middle-class liberals because the tsar rewrote laws to secure his power and that of the propertied classes, ending collective village ownership of land and preserving the conservative constitutional monarchy with a peasant-based but industrialized economy.

- The Ottoman Empire embarked on a partially successful series of reforms, the Tanzimat, in an attempt to gain territory and power, but increasing disputes over religion and Western imperialism allowed the Young Turks to seize power in the revolution of 1908.

The Responsive National State (1871–1914)

Why after 1871 did ordinary citizens feel a growing loyalty to their governments?

For central and western Europe, the unification of Italy and Germany by "blood and iron" marked the end of a dramatic period of nation building. After 1871 the heartland of Europe was organized into strong national states. Only on the borders of Europe—in Ireland and Russia, in Austria-Hungary and the Ottoman Empire— did subject peoples still strive for political unity and independence.

General Trends

Despite some major differences between countries, European domestic politics after 1871 had in common the emergence of mass politics and growing mass loyalty toward the national state.

For good reason, ordinary people felt increasing loyalty to their governments. By 1914 most men had gained the right to vote and felt that they counted; they could influence the government to some extent. They were becoming "part of the system." Women also made some gains in their suffrage movement. By 1913

"Votes for Women!"

The long-simmering campaign for women's suffrage in England came to a rapid boil after 1903, as militants took to the streets, disrupted political meetings, and tried to storm Parliament. Manhandled by the police and often jailed, some activists responded by damaging public property and going on hunger strikes in prison. This 1908 illustration shows demonstrators giving a hero's welcome to Mary Leigh, the first suffragette imprisoned for property damage after she threw rocks through the windows of the prime minister's house. (The Art Archive) women could vote in twelve of the western United States. In 1914 Norway gave the vote to most women. Elsewhere, the efforts of more militant feminists prepared the way for the triumph of the women's suffrage movement immediately after World War I.

As the right to vote spread, politicians and parties in national parliaments represented the people more responsively. Governments also passed laws to alleviate general problems, thereby acquiring greater legitimacy and appearing more worthy of support.

There was a manipulative aspect to building support for strong nation-states after 1871. Conservative and moderate leaders found that workers who voted socialist would rally around the flag in a diplomatic crisis or cheer when distant territory was seized in Africa or Asia (see Chapter 26). Therefore, after 1871 governing elites frequently used militaristic policies to help manage domestic conflicts, but at the expense of increasing international tensions. Some leaders fanned anti-Semitism in order to unite Christians around their party.

The German Empire

Politics in Germany after 1871 developed within the new framework of a federal union of Prussia and twenty-four smaller states. This federal government was run by a chancellor—until 1890, Bismarck—and a popularly elected lower house, called the **Reichstag** (RIKES-tog). Although Bismarck refused to be bound by a parliamentary majority, he tried nonetheless to maintain one. This situation gave the political parties opportunities. For most of his chancellorship Bismarck relied mainly on the National Liberals, who supported legislation useful for further economic and legal unification of the country.

Bismarck's moves against the Catholic Church, however, gradually lost the National Liberals their parliamentary majority. Known as the **Kulturkampf** (kool-TOOR-kahmpf), or "struggle for civilization," Bismarck's anti-Catholic legislation was a response to Pope Pius IX's declaration of papal infallibility in 1870, which seemed to make the pope and not the government the ultimate source of authority for Catholics. Catholics throughout the country turned to the Catholic Center party, which blocked passage of national laws hostile to the church. Bismarck was forced to abandon his attack and instead court the support of the Catholic Center party, whose supporters included many small farmers in western and southern Germany. By enacting high tariffs on cheap grain from the outside the country, he won over both the Catholic Center and the Protestant Junkers, who had large landholdings in the east. With the tariffs, then, Bismark won Catholic and conservative support.

Bismarck had been looking for a way to increase taxes, and the solution he chose was higher tariffs. Many other governments acted similarly. The 1880s and 1890s saw a widespread return to protectionism. France, in particular, established very high tariffs to protect agriculture and industry, peasants and manufacturers, from foreign competition. Thus the German government and other governments responded effectively to a major economic problem and won greater loyalty. The general rise of protectionism in this period was also an outstanding example of the dangers of self-centered nationalism: new tariffs led to international name-calling and nasty trade wars.

Like other European leaders, Bismarck feared the revolutionary language of socialism. In 1878, after two attempts on the life of William I by radicals (though not socialists), Bismarck used a carefully orchestrated national outcry to ram through the Reichstag a law that outlawed the Social Democratic party and restricted so-

Reichstag The popularly elected lower house of government of the new German Empire after 1871.

Kulturkampf A struggle for civilization, Bismarck's attack on the Catholic church resulting from Pius IX's declaration of papal infallibility in 1870.

cialist meetings. However, German socialists displayed a discipline and organization worthy of the Prussian army itself. Bismarck decided to try another tack.

Bismarck's new approach was to create social programs that would win him the support of working-class people. In 1883 and 1884 the government established national sickness and accident insurance; in 1889 it established old-age pensions and retirement benefits. This national social security system, paid for through compulsory contributions by wage earners and employers as well as grants from the state, was the first of its kind anywhere. Bismarck's social security system did not wean workers from voting socialist, but it did give them a small stake in the system and protect them from some of the uncertainties of the complex urban industrial world. This enormously significant development was a product of political competition and government efforts to win popular support.

Increasingly, the great issues in German domestic politics were socialism and the Marxian Social Democratic party. In 1890 the new emperor, the young, idealistic, and unstable William II (r. 1888–1918), opposed Bismarck's attempt to renew the law outlawing the Social Democratic party. Eager to rule in his own right and to earn the support of the workers, William II forced Bismarck to resign.

Yet William II was no more successful than Bismarck in getting workers to renounce socialism. Indeed, Social Democrats won more and more seats in the Reichstag, until it became the largest single party in the Reichstag in 1912. This victory shocked aristocrats and their wealthy conservative middle-class allies, heightening the fears of an impending socialist upheaval. Yet the "revolutionary" socialists were actually becoming less radical in Germany. In the years before World War I, the German Social Democratic party broadened its base by adopting a more patriotic tone, allowing for greater military spending and imperialist expansion. German socialists concentrated instead on gradual social and political reform.

Republican France

France's progress toward a unified national state suffered in the immediate aftermath of the Franco-Prussian War (see pages 651–653). Parisians, who had bravely defended their city against Prussian forces, exploded in patriotic frustration when the National Assembly of France agreed to surrender Alsace (al-SAS) and Lorraine to Prussia. They proclaimed the Paris Commune in March 1871, with the goal of governing Paris without interference from the conservative French countryside. The National Assembly, led by the aging politician Adolphe Thiers (tyer), would hear none of it. The Assembly ordered the French army into Paris and brutally crushed the Commune. Twenty thousand people died in the fighting. As in June 1848, it was Paris against the provinces, French against French.

Out of this tragedy, France slowly formed a new national unity, achieving considerable stability before 1914. How is one to account for this? Luck played a part. Although the monarchists had gained the majority in the National Assembly, they could not find an acceptable king. Meanwhile, the middle class and people from the provinces were persuaded by Thiers's actions that the Third Republic might be moderate and socially conservative. France therefore retained the republic, though reluctantly. As President Thiers cautiously said, this was "the government which divides us least."

Another stabilizing factor was the skill and determination of the moderate republican leaders in the early years. The most famous of these was Léon Gambetta (gam-BET-uh), the son of an Italian grocer, a warm, easygoing, unsuccessful lawyer who had turned professional politician. By 1879 the great majority of members of both the upper and the lower houses of the National Assembly were republicans, and the Third Republic had firm foundations after almost a decade.

The moderate republicans sought to endure politically by appealing to the next generation. They worked to expand the state system of public schools, so that conservative Catholic schoolteachers were no longer the primary shapers of young minds. New laws made elementary education for girls and boys both free and compulsory. Public education served to reinforce nationalism and the value of republican government.

Although the educational reforms of the 1880s disturbed French Catholics, many of them rallied to the republic in the 1890s. The limited acceptance of the modern world by the more liberal Pope Leo XIII (1878–1903) eased tensions. The **Dreyfus affair,** however, would lead to the separation of church and state in France.

Dreyfus affair A divisive case in which Alfred Dreyfus, a Jewish captain in the French army was falsely accused and convicted of treason. The Catholic Church sided with the anti-Semites against Dreyfus; after Dreyfus was declared innocent, the French government severed all ties between the state and church.

Alfred Dreyfus, a Jewish captain in the French army, was falsely accused and convicted of treason. In 1898 and 1899, the case split France apart. On one side was the army, which had manufactured evidence against Dreyfus, joined by anti-Semites and most of the Catholic establishment. On the other side stood the civil libertarians and most of the more radical republicans.

This battle, which eventually led to Dreyfus's being declared innocent, revived republican feeling against the church. Between 1901 and 1905, the French government severed all ties to the Catholic Church. The salaries of priests and bishops were no longer paid by the government, and all churches were given to local committees of lay Catholics. Catholic schools were put on their own financially and soon lost a third of their students. In France only the growing socialist movement, with its very different and thoroughly secular ideology, stood in opposition to patriotic, republican nationalism.

Great Britain and Ireland

Britain in the late nineteenth century has often been seen as a shining example of peaceful and successful political evolution, where an effective two-party parliament skillfully guided the country from classical liberalism to full-fledged democracy with hardly a misstep. This view of Great Britain is not so much wrong as it is incomplete. The House of Commons did gradually widen the right to vote, so that by 1884 almost every adult male could participate in elections. The House of Lords, however, remained a bastion of aristocratic conservatism, ruling against labor unions and vetoing several measures passed by the Commons in the first decade of the twentieth century. The turning point came when the Lords vetoed the so-called **People's Budget,** which was designed to increase spending on social welfare services. The king threatened to create enough new peers to pass the bill, and aristocratic conservatism was forced to yield to popular democracy once and for all.

People's Budget A bill proposed after the Liberal party came to power in England in 1906, it was designed to increase spending on social welfare issues, but was vetoed in the House of Lords.

Between 1906 and 1914, extensive social welfare measures, slow to come to Great Britain, were passed in a spectacular rush. During those years, the Liberal party, inspired by the fiery Welshman David Lloyd George (1863–1945), substantially raised taxes on the rich as part of the People's Budget. This income helped the government pay for national health insurance, unemployment benefits, old-age pensions, and a host of other social measures. The state was integrating the urban masses socially as well as politically.

This record of accomplishment was only part of the story, however. On the eve of World War I, the unanswered question of Ireland brought Great Britain to the brink of civil war. The terrible Irish famine had fueled an Irish revolutionary move-

"No Home Rule"

Posters like this one helped to foment pro-British, anti-Catholic sentiment in the northern Irish counties of Ulster before the First World War. The rifle raised defiantly and the accompanying rhyme are a thinly veiled threat of armed rebellion and civil war. (Photograph reproduced courtesy of the Trustees of National Museums Northern Ireland)

ment. Thereafter, the English slowly granted concessions, such as the abolition of the privileges of the Anglican Church and rights for Irish peasants. Yet the question of self-rule for Ireland was divisive. Bills giving Ireland self-government failed to pass in 1886 and 1893. In 1913, however, Irish nationalists in the British Parliament were able to obtain a new home-rule bill for Ireland.

Within Ireland, the home-rule bill unleashed hostilities between north and south. The Protestants of Ulster in Northern Ireland refused to submerge themselves into Catholic Ireland and vowed to resist home rule in northern counties. By December 1913 they had raised 100,000 armed volunteers, and they were supported by much of English public opinion. Thus in 1914 the Liberals in the House of Lords introduced a compromise home-rule bill that did not apply to the northern counties. This bill, which openly betrayed promises made to Irish nationalists, was rejected, and in September the original home-rule bill was passed but simultaneously suspended for the duration of the hostilities. The momentous Irish question was then overtaken by an earth-shattering world war in August 1914.

Irish developments illustrated once again the power of national movements in the nineteenth century. Moreover, they were proof that governments could not elicit greater loyalty unless they could capture and control that elemental current of national feeling. Though Great Britain had much going for it—power, Parliament, prosperity—none of these availed in the face of the conflicting nationalisms created by Catholics and Protestants in Northern Ireland. Similarly, progressive Sweden was powerless to stop the growth of the Norwegian national movement, which culminated in Norway's breaking away from Sweden and becoming a fully independent nation in 1905. In this light, one can also see how hopeless was the case of the Ottoman Empire in Europe in the later nineteenth century. It was only a matter of time before the Serbs, Bulgarians, and Romanians would break away, and they did.

The Austro-Hungarian Empire

The dilemma of conflicting nationalisms also tore at the Austro-Hungarian Empire in the early twentieth century. In the wake of defeat in the Austro-Prussian War of 1866, a weakened Austria was forced to strike a compromise with its subjects in Hungary who had wanted independence. Through the so-called dual monarchy, the empire was divided, and the nationalistic Magyars gained virtual independence for Hungary. The two states were joined only by a shared monarch and common ministries for finance, defense, and foreign affairs.

The dual monarchy did not diffuse nationalist tensions, however. In Austria, many Germans saw their traditional dominance threatened by Czechs, Poles, and other Slavs. A particularly emotional issue in the Austrian parliament was the language used in government and elementary education at the local level. From 1900 to 1914 the parliament was so divided that ministries generally could not obtain a majority and ruled instead by decree. Even attempts to find common ground on economic issues were unsuccessful. In Hungary the Magyar nobility restricted voting to the wealthiest one-fourth of adult males, making the parliament the creature of the elite. Laws promoting the use of the Magyar (Hungarian) language in schools and government were rammed through and bitterly resented, especially by the Croatians and Romanians. While Hungarian extremists campaigned loudly for total separation from Austria, Croatian and Romanian radicals agitated for independence from Hungary. Unlike most major countries, which harnessed nationalism to strengthen the state after 1871, the Austro-Hungarian Empire was progressively weakened and destroyed by it.

Jewish Emancipation and Modern Anti-Semitism

Revolutionary changes in politics brought equally revolutionary changes in Jewish life in western and central Europe. The decisive turning point came in 1848, when Jews formed part of the revolutionary vanguard in Vienna and Berlin and the Frankfurt Assembly endorsed full rights for German Jews. In 1871 the constitution of the new German Empire consolidated the process of Jewish emancipation in central Europe. It abolished all restrictions on Jewish marriage, choice of occupation, place of residence, and property ownership. Exclusion from government employment and discrimination in social relations remained. However, according to one leading historian, by 1871 "it was widely accepted in Central Europe that the gradual disappearance of anti-Jewish prejudice was inevitable."[3]

The process of emancipation presented Jews with challenges and opportunities. Traditional Jewish occupations, such as court financial agent, village moneylender, and peddler, were undermined by free-market reforms, but careers in business, the professions, and the arts were opening to Jewish talent. By 1871 a majority of Jewish people in western and central Europe had improved their economic situation and entered the middle classes. Most Jewish people also identified strongly with their respective nation-states and with good reason saw themselves as patriotic citizens.

Vicious anti-Semitism reappeared after the stock market crash of 1873, beginning in central Europe. While Europe had a long history of anti-Semitism, this time it had modern elements. Resentment was aimed against Jewish achievement and Jewish "financial control," while fanatics claimed that the Jewish race (rather than the Jewish religion) posed a biological threat to the German people. Anti-Semitic beliefs were particularly popular among conservatives, extremist nationalists, and people who felt threatened by Jewish competition, such as small shopkeepers, officeworkers, and professionals.

Anti-Semites also created modern political parties to attack and degrade Jews. In Austrian Vienna in the early 1890s, Karl Lueger (LEW-ay-ger) and his "Christian socialists" won striking electoral victories, spurring Theodor Herzl to turn from German nationalism and advocate political **Zionism** and the creation of a Jewish state. (See the feature "Individuals in Society: Theodor Herzl.") Lueger, the popular mayor of Vienna from 1897 to 1910, combined fierce anti-Semitic rhetoric with municipal ownership of basic services, and he appealed especially to

Zionism A movement toward Jewish political nationhood, started by Theodor Herzl.

Individuals in Society

Theodor Herzl

In September 1897, only days after his vision and energy had called into being the First Zionist Congress in Basel, Switzerland, Theodor Herzl (1860–1904) assessed the results in his diary: "If I were to sum up the Congress in a word—which I shall take care not to publish—it would be this: At Basel I founded the Jewish state. If I said this out loud today I would be greeted by universal laughter. In five years perhaps, and certainly in fifty years, everyone will perceive it."* Herzl's buoyant optimism, which so often carried him forward, was prophetic. Leading the Zionist movement until his death at age forty-four in 1904, Herzl guided the first historic steps toward modern Jewish political nationhood and the creation of Israel in 1948.

Theodor Herzl was born in Budapest, Hungary, into an upper-middle-class, German-speaking Jewish family. When Herzl was eighteen, his family moved to Vienna, where he studied law. As a university student, he soaked up the liberal beliefs of most well-to-do Viennese Jews, who also championed the assimilation of German culture. Wrestling with his nonreligious Jewishness and his strong pro-German feeling, Herzl embraced German nationalism and joined a German dueling fraternity. There he discovered that full acceptance required openly anti-Semitic attitudes and a repudiation of all things Jewish. This Herzl could not tolerate, and he resigned. After receiving his law degree, he embarked on a literary career. In 1889 Herzl married into a wealthy Viennese Jewish family, but he and his socialite wife were mismatched and never happy together.

Herzl achieved considerable success as both a journalist and a playwright. His witty comedies focused on the bourgeoisie, including Jewish millionaires trying to live like aristocrats. Accepting many German stereotypes, Herzl sometimes depicted eastern Jews as uneducated and grasping. But as a dedicated, highly educated liberal, he mainly believed that the Jewish shortcomings he

perceived were the results of age-old persecution and would disappear through education and assimilation. Herzl also took a growing pride in Jewish steadfastness in the face of victimization and suffering. He savored memories of his early Jewish education and going with his father to the synagogue.

The emergence of modern anti-Semitism shocked Herzl, as it did many acculturated Jewish Germans. Moving to Paris in 1891 as the correspondent for Vienna's leading liberal newspaper, Herzl studied politics and pondered recent historical developments. He then came to a bold conclusion, published in 1896 as *The Jewish State: An Attempt at a Modern Solution to the Jewish Question*. According to Herzl, Jewish assimilation had failed, and attempts to combat anti-Semitism would never succeed. Only by building an independent Jewish state could the Jewish people achieve dignity and renewal. As recent scholarship shows, Herzl developed his political nationalism, or Zionism, before the anti-Jewish agitation accompanying the Dreyfus affair, which only strengthened his faith in his analysis.

Theodor Herzl (Library of Congress)

Generally rebuffed by skeptical Jewish elites in western and central Europe, Herzl turned for support to youthful idealists and the poor Jewish masses. He became an inspiring man of action, rallying the delegates to the annual Zionist congresses, directing the growth of the worldwide Zionist organization, and working himself to death. Herzl also understood that national consciousness required powerful emotions and symbols, such as a Jewish flag. Flags build nations, he said, because people "live and die for a flag."

Putting the Zionist vision before non-Jews and world public opinion, Herzl believed in international diplomacy and political agreements. He traveled constantly to negotiate with European rulers

*Quotes are from Theodor Herzl, *The Diaries of Theodor Herzl*, trans. and ed. with an introduction by Marvin Lowenthal (New York: Grosset & Dunlap, 1962), pp. 224, 22, xxi.

and top officials, seeking their support in securing territory for a Jewish state, usually in the Ottoman Empire. Aptly described by an admiring contemporary as "the first Jewish statesman since the destruction of Jerusalem," Herzl proved most successful in Britain. He paved the way for the 1917 Balfour Declaration, which solemnly pledged British support for a "Jewish homeland" in Palestine.

Questions for Analysis

1. Describe Theodor Herzl's background and early beliefs. Do you see a link between Herzl's early German nationalism and his later Zionism?

2. How did Herzl work as a leader to turn his Zionist vision into a reality?

the German-speaking lower middle class—and an unsuccessful young artist named Adolf Hitler.

Before 1914 anti-Semitism was most oppressive in eastern Europe, where Jews also suffered from terrible poverty. In the Russian empire, where there was no Jewish emancipation and 4 million of Europe's 7 million Jewish people lived in 1880, officials used anti-Semitism to channel popular discontent away from the government and onto the Jewish minority. Russian Jews were denounced as foreign exploiters who corrupted national traditions, and in 1881 through 1882 a wave of violent pogroms commenced in southern Russia. The police and the army stood aside for days while peasants looted and destroyed Jewish property. Official harassment continued in the following decades, and large numbers of Russian Jews emigrated to western Europe and the United States. About 2.75 million Jews left eastern Europe between 1881 and 1914.

Marxism and the Socialist Movement

Why did the socialist movement grow, and how revolutionary was it?

Nationalism served, for better or worse, as a new unifying principle. But what about socialism? Socialist parties, which were generally Marxian parties dedicated to an international proletarian revolution, grew rapidly in these years. Did this mean that national states had failed to gain the support of workers? Certainly, many prosperous and conservative citizens were greatly troubled by the socialist movement. And numerous historians have portrayed the years before 1914 as a time of increasing conflict between revolutionary socialism, on the one hand, and a nationalist alliance of the conservative aristocracy and the prosperous middle class, on the other.

The Socialist International

The growth of socialist parties after 1871 was phenomenal. (See the feature "Listening to the Past: The Making of a Socialist" on pages 671–672.) Neither Bismarck's antisocialist laws nor his extensive social security system checked the growth of the German Social Democratic party, which espoused the Marxian ideology. By 1912 it had millions of followers—mostly working-class people—and was the largest party in the Reichstag. Socialist parties also grew in other countries, though nowhere else with such success. In 1883 Russian exiles in Switzerland founded the Russian Social Democratic party, and various socialist parties were unified in 1905 in the French Section of the Workers International. Belgium and Austria-Hungary also had strong socialist parties.

As the name of the French party suggests, Marxian socialist parties were eventually linked together in an international organization. Marx believed that "the working men have no country," and he had urged proletarians of all nations to unite. Marx himself played an important role in founding the First International of socialists—the International Working Men's Association. Then Marx enthusiastically embraced the passionate, vaguely radical patriotism of the Paris Commune and its terrible conflict with the French National Assembly as a giant step toward socialist revolution. This impetuous action frightened many of his early supporters, especially the more moderate British labor leaders. The First International collapsed.

Yet international proletarian solidarity remained an important objective for Marxists. In 1889, as the individual parties in different countries grew stronger,

Section Review

- Ordinary people were becoming more nationalistic as they had more representation in governments; women, too, were slowly winning the right to vote, and governing elites took advantage of nationalistic sentiments using militaristic policies to manage domestic social conflicts.

- Chancellor Bismarck won popular support by imposing high tariffs on foreign grain and in an effort to take support away from the socialists, enacted the first social security system, but Emperor William II forced Bismarck to resign while the German Social Democratic party broadened its base by focusing on gradual social and political reform.

- France's mostly republican National Assembly led by Adolphe Thiers struggled to unite France and brought stabilization by expanding the state system of public schools and separating completely from the Catholic church after the Dreyfus Affair.

- Britain's House of Commons yielded to public pressure and enacted extensive social welfare measures benefiting the urban masses socially and politically, but Irish calls for home rule continued to be a problem along with Catholic-Protestant conflict in Northern Ireland.

- Conflicting nationalisms created friction as Hungarians wanted total separation from Austria while Croatians and Romanians agitated for independence from Hungary.

- German Jews won full political rights in 1848 and again in 1871, although they were still excluded from government employment and suffered from the growth of anti-Semitism in Austria, eastern Europe, and Russia.

"Greetings from the May Day Festival"
Workers participated enthusiastically in the annual one-day strike on May 1 to honor internationalist socialist solidarity, as this postcard from a happy woman visitor to her cousin suggests. Speeches, picnics, and parades were the order of the day, and workers celebrated their respectability and independent culture. Picture postcards developed with railroads and mass travel. (akg-images)

socialist leaders came together to form the Second International, which lasted until 1914. The International was only a federation of national socialist parties, but it had a great psychological impact. Every three years, delegates from the different parties met to interpret Marxian doctrines and plan coordinated action. May 1 (May Day) was declared an annual international one-day strike, a day of marches and demonstrations. A permanent executive for the International was established. Many feared and many others rejoiced in the growing power of socialism and the Second International.

Unions and Revisionism

Was socialism really radical in these years? On the whole, it was not. Indeed, as socialist parties grew, they looked more and more toward gradual change and steady improvement for the working class and less and less toward revolution. The mainstream of European socialism increasingly combined radical rhetoric with sober action.

Workers themselves were progressively less inclined to follow radical programs. There were several reasons for this. As workers gained the right to vote and to participate politically in the nation-state, they focused their attention more on elections than on revolutions. And as workers won real, tangible benefits, this furthered the process. Workers were also not immune to patriotic education and indoctrination during military service, and many responded positively to drum-beating parades and aggressive foreign policy as they loyally voted for socialists. Nor were workers a unified social group.

Perhaps most important of all, workers' standard of living rose gradually but substantially after 1850. Workers experienced gradual wage increases in most continental countries after 1850, though much less strikingly in late-developing Russia. The quality of life in urban areas improved dramatically as well. Therefore, workers tended more and more to become militantly moderate: they demanded gains, but they were less likely to take to the barricades in pursuit of them.

The growth of labor unions reinforced this trend toward moderation. In Germany, for example, unions had been denied rights and were viewed with suspicion as socialist fronts during their early years. But as German industrialization stormed ahead, almost all legal harassment of unions was eliminated, and union membership skyrocketed. Increasingly, unions in Germany focused on bread-and-butter issues—wages, hours, working conditions—rather than on the dissemination of pure socialist doctrine. Genuine collective bargaining, long opposed by socialist intellectuals as a "sellout," was officially recognized as desirable by the German Trade Union Congress in 1899. When employers proved unwilling to bargain, a series of strikes forced them to change their minds. Germany was the most industrialized, socialized, and unionized continental country by 1914.

The German trade unions and their leaders were in fact, if not in name, thoroughgoing revisionists. **Revisionism** was an effort by various socialists to update Marxian doctrines to reflect the realities of the time. Thus the socialist Edward Bernstein (BURN-stine) (1850–1932) argued in 1899 in his *Evolutionary Socialism* that socialists should combine with other progressive forces to win gradual evolutionary gains for workers through legislation, unions, and further economic development. These views were denounced as heresy by the German Social Democratic party and later by the entire Second International. Yet the revisionist, gradualist approach continued to gain the tacit acceptance of many German socialists, particularly in the trade unions.

Socialist parties before 1914 had clear-cut national characteristics. Russians and socialists in the Austro-Hungarian Empire tended to be the most radical. The German party talked revolution but practiced reformism, greatly influenced by its enormous trade-union movement. The French party talked revolution and tried to practice it, unrestrained by a trade-union movement that was both very weak and very radical. In England the socialist but non-Marxian Labour party, reflecting the well-established union movement, was formally committed to gradual reform. In Spain and Italy, Marxian socialism was very weak. There anarchism, seeking to smash the state rather than the bourgeoisie, dominated radical thought and action.

In short, socialist policies and doctrines varied from country to country. Socialism itself was to a large extent "nationalized" behind the imposing façade of international unity. This helps explain why when war came in 1914, almost all socialist leaders supported their governments.

revisionism An effort by various socialists to update Marxian doctrines to reflect the realities of the time.

Section Review

- The Socialist International was an organized group of socialist parties from many countries; after the First International collapsed, a Second formed in 1889, meeting every three years until 1914 to discuss Marxian doctrines and make plans, declaring each May 1 as an international one-day strike with marches and demonstrations.

- For the working class, socialism became more a means for gradual change than for revolution as they reaped the benefits of voting, union bargaining, and an increased standard of living.

- Edward Bernstein's revisionism was an attempt to make socialism less revolutionary and more gradual by combining it with legislation, unions, and economic development, but the German Social Democratic party and the Second International denounced it.

Chapter Review

How in France did Napoleon III seek to reconcile popular and conservative forces in an authoritarian nation-state? (page 646)

After 1850, Western society became nationalistic as well as urban and industrial. Conservative monarchical governments, recovering from the revolutionary trauma of 1848, learned to remodel early so as to build stronger states with greater popular support. Napoleon III in France led the way, combining authoritarian rule with economic prosperity and positive measures for the poor.

Key Terms
Red Shirts (p. 649)
Zollverein (p. 650)

(continued)

How did the process of unification in Italy and Germany create conservative nation-states? (page 648)

In Italy, Cavour joined traditional diplomacy with national revolt in the north and Garibaldi's revolutionary patriotism in the south, expanding the liberal monarchy of Sardinia-Piedmont into a conservative nation-state. Bismarck also combined traditional statecraft with national feeling to expand the power of Prussia and its king in a new German empire.

In what ways did the United States experience the full drama of nation building? (page 653)

In the mid-century years, the United States also experienced a crisis of nation building. The United States overcame sectionalism in a war that prevented an independent South and seemed to confirm America's destiny as a great world power.

What steps did Russia and the Ottoman Turks take toward modernization, and how successful were they? (page 654)

In autocratic Russia, defeat in the Crimean War led to the emancipation of the serfs, economic modernization with railroad building and industrialization, and limited political reform. The Ottoman Empire also sought to modernize to protect the state, but it was considerably less successful.

Why after 1871 did ordinary citizens feel a growing loyalty to their governments? (page 659)

Nation-states gradually enlisted widespread popular support, providing men and women with a greater sense of belonging, and giving them specific political, social, and economic improvements.

Why did the socialist movement grow, and how revolutionary was it? (page 667)

Even the growing socialist movement became increasingly national in orientation, gathering strength as a champion of working-class interests in domestic politics. Yet even though nationalism served to unite peoples, it also drove them apart—obvious not only in the United States before the Civil War and in Austria-Hungary and Ireland, but also throughout Europe. There the universal national faith, which usually reduced social tensions within states, promoted a bitter, almost Darwinian, competition between states and thus threatened the progress and unity it had helped to build, as we shall see in Chapters 26 and 27.

Notes

1. H. Schulze, *States, Nations and Nationalism: From the Middle Ages to the Present* (Oxford: Blackwell, 1994), pp. 222–223, 246–247.
2. J. McKay, *Pioneers for Profit: Foreign Entrepreneurship and Russian Industrialization, 1885–1913* (Chicago: University of Chicago Press, 1970), pp. 112–157.
3. R. Seltzer, *Jewish People, Jewish Thought: The Jewish Experience in History* (New York: Macmillan, 1980), p. 533.

To assess your mastery of this chapter, go to **bedfordstmartins.com/mckaywestbrief**

Listening to the Past

The Making of a Socialist

Nationalism and socialism appeared to be competing ideologies, but both fostered political awareness. A working person who became interested in politics and developed nationalist beliefs might well convert to socialism at a later date.

This was the case for Adelheid Popp (1869–1939), the editor of a major socialist newspaper for German workingwomen. Born into a desperately poor working-class family in Vienna, she was forced by her parents to quit school at age ten to begin full-time work. She struggled with low-paying piecework for years before she landed a solid factory job, as she recounts in the following selection from her widely read autobiography. She told her life story so that all working women might share her truth: "Socialism could change and strengthen others, as it did me."

1890 engraving of a meeting of workers in Berlin (Bildarchiv Preussischer Kulturbesitz/Art Resource, NY)

[At age fifteen] I was recommended to a great factory which stood in the best repute. . . . In none of the neighbouring factories were the wages so high; we were envied everywhere. . . . And even here, in this paradise, all were badly nourished. Those who stayed at the factory for the dinner hour would buy themselves for a few pennies a sausage or the leavings of a cheese shop. . . . In spite of all the diligence and economy, every one was poor, and trembled at the thought of losing her work. . . .

I did not only read novels and tales; I had begun . . . to read the classics and other good books. I also began to take an interest in public events. . . . I was not democratically inclined. I was full of enthusiasm then for emperors, and kings and highly placed personages played no small part in my fancies. . . . I bought myself a strict Catholic paper, that criticised very adversely the workers' movement, which was attracting notice. Its aim was to educate in a patriotic and religious direction. . . . I took the warmest interest in the events that occurred in the royal families, and I took the death of the Crown Prince of Austria so much to heart that I wept a whole day. . . .

Later on my mother and I lived with one of my brothers who had married. Friends came to him, among them some intelligent workmen. One of these workmen was particularly intelligent, and . . . could talk on many subjects. He was the first Social Democrat I knew. He brought me many books, and explained to me the difference between Anarchism and Socialism. I heard from him, also for the first time, what a republic was, and in spite of my former enthusiasm for royal dynasties, I also declared myself in favour of a republican form of government. I saw everything so near and so clearly, that I actually counted the weeks which must still elapse before the revolution of state and society would take place.

From this workman I received the first Social Democratic party organ. . . . I first learned from it to understand and judge of my own lot. I learned to see that all I had suffered was the result not of a divine ordinance, but of an unjust organization of society. . . .

In the factory I became another woman. . . . I told my [female] comrades all that I had read of the workers' movement. Formerly I had often told stories when they had begged me for them. But instead of narrating . . . the fate of some queen, I now held forth on oppression and exploitation. I told of accumulated wealth in the hands of a few, and introduced as a contrast the shoemakers who had no shoes and the tailors who had no clothes. On breaks I read aloud the articles in the Social Democratic paper and explained what Socialism was as far as I understood it. . . . [While I was reading] it often happened that one of the clerks passing by shook his head and said to another clerk: "The girl speaks like a man."

Questions for Analysis

1. How did Popp describe and interpret work in the factory?

2. To what extent did her socialist interpretation of factory life fit the facts she described?

3. What were Popp's political interests before she became a socialist?

4. Was this account likely to lead other working-women to socialism? Why or why not?

Source: Slightly adapted from A. Popp, *The Autobiography of a Working Woman,* trans. E. C. Harvey (Chicago: F. G. Browne, 1913), pp. 29, 34–35, 39, 66–69, 71, 74, 82–90.

CHAPTER 26

The West and the World

1815–1914

Africans in Madagascar transport a French diplomat in 1894, shortly before France annexed the island. (Snark/Art Resource, NY)

Chapter Preview

While industrialization and nationalism were transforming urban life and Western society, Western society itself was reshaping the world. At the peak of its power, the West entered the third and most dynamic phase of expansion that had begun with the Crusades and continued with the great discoveries and the rise of seaborne colonial empires. An ever-growing stream of products, people, and ideas flowed out of Europe in the nineteenth century. Hardly any corner of the globe was left untouched. The most spectacular manifestations of Western expansion came in the late nineteenth century when the leading European nations established or enlarged their far-flung political empires. The political annexation of territory in the 1880s—the "new imperialism," as it is often called by historians—was the capstone of a profound underlying economic and technological process.

Industrialization and the World Economy

What were some of the global consequences of European industrialization between 1815 and 1914?

The Industrial Revolution created, first in Great Britain and then in continental Europe and North America, a tremendously dynamic economic system. In the course of the nineteenth century, Europeans extended that system across the face of the earth through both peaceful and militaristic means. In general, they fashioned the global economic system so that the largest share of gains flowed to the West and its propertied classes.

The Rise of Global Inequality

Third World A term widely used by international organizations and by scholars to group the nonindustrialized nations Africa, Asia, and Latin America into a single unit.

The Industrial Revolution marked a momentous turning point in human history. It allowed those regions of the world that industrialized to increase their wealth and power enormously in comparison to those that did not. As a result, a gap between the industrializing regions (mainly Europe and North America) and the nonindustrializing or **Third World** regions (mainly Africa, Asia, and Latin America) opened up and grew steadily throughout the nineteenth century. Moreover, this pattern of uneven global development became institutionalized, or built into the structure of the world economy. Thus we evolved a "lopsided world," a world of rich lands and poor.

The enormous income disparities between developed and Third World countries (see Figure 26.1) are poignant indicators of equal disparities in food and clothing, health and education, life expectancy and general material well-being. The reason for these disparities has

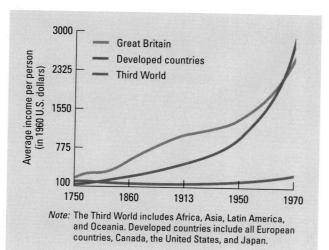

Note: The Third World includes Africa, Asia, Latin America, and Oceania. Developed countries include all European countries, Canada, the United States, and Japan.

FIGURE 26.1   The Growth of Average Income per Person in the Third World, Developed Countries, and Great Britain, 1750–1970

Growth is given in 1960 U.S. dollars and prices. (*Source:* P. Bairoch and M. Lévy-Leboyer, eds., *Disparities in Economic Development Since the Industrial Revolution.* Copyright © 1981. Reproduced with permission of Palgrave Macmillan.)

generated a great deal of debate. One school of interpretation stresses that the West used science, technology, capitalist organization, and even its critical worldview to create its wealth and greater physical well-being. Another school argues that the West used its political and economic power to steal much of its riches, continuing in the nineteenth (and twentieth) century the rapacious colonialism born of the era of expansion. These issues are complex, and there are few simple answers. It is helpful to consider them in the context of the dynamics of world trade in the nineteenth century.

The World Market

Trade between nations has always stimulated economic development. In the nineteenth century, an enormous increase in international commerce was directed by Europe. Great Britain took the lead in cultivating export markets for its booming industrial output. British manufacturers looked first to Europe and then around the world.

Take the case of cotton textiles. By 1820 Britain was exporting 50 percent of its production. Europe bought 50 percent of these cotton textile exports, while India bought only 6 percent. Then as European nations and the United States erected protective tariff barriers and promoted domestic industry, British cotton textile manufacturers aggressively sought and found other foreign markets in non-Western areas. By 1850 India was buying 25 percent and Europe only 16 percent of a much larger total. As a British colony, India could not raise tariffs to protect its ancient cotton textile industry, and thousands of Indian weavers lost their livelihoods.

International trade also grew as transportation systems improved. Wherever railroads were built, they drastically reduced transportation costs, opened new economic opportunities, and called forth new skills and attitudes. Much of the railroad construction undertaken in Latin America, Asia, and Africa connected seaports with inland cities and regions, as opposed to linking and developing cities and regions within a given country. Thus these railroads supported Western economic interests, facilitating the inflow and sale of Western manufactured goods and the export of local raw materials.

The power of steam revolutionized transportation by sea as well as by land. Steam power began to supplant sails on the oceans of the world in the late 1860s. Passenger and freight rates tumbled as ship design became more sophisticated, and the intercontinental shipment of low-priced raw materials became feasible. The opening of the Suez and Panama Canals shortened transport time considerably, and port facilities were also modernized to make loading and unloading cheaper, faster, and more dependable.

New communications systems directed the flow of goods across global networks. Transoceanic telegraph cables inaugurated rapid communications among the financial centers of the world. While a British tramp freighter steamed from Calcutta to New York, a broker in London was arranging by telegram for it to carry an American cargo to Australia. The same communications network conveyed world commodity prices instantaneously.

The revolution in transportation and communications encouraged European entrepreneurs to open up vast new territories around the world and develop agricultural products and raw materials there for sale in Europe. Improved transportation also enabled European ventures in Asia, Africa, and Latin America to ship not only the traditional tropical products—spices, tea, sugar, coffee—but also new raw materials for industry, such as jute, rubber, cotton, and coconut oil.

As their economies grew, Europeans began to make massive foreign investments beginning about 1840. By the outbreak of World War I in 1914, wealthy Europeans had invested more than $40 billion abroad. Great Britain, France, and Germany were the principal investing countries. Most of the capital exported did not go to European colonies or protectorates in Asia and Africa. Europeans found the most profitable opportunities for investment in construction of the railroads, ports, and utilities that were necessary for white settlers to develop the lands in such places as Australia and the Americas. Much of this investment was peaceful and mutually beneficial for lenders and borrowers. The victims were Native American Indians and Australian aborigines, who were decimated by the diseases, liquor, and weapons of an aggressively expanding Western society.

The Opening of China and Japan

While Europeans looked primarily to North America, Australia, and much of Latin America to absorb huge quantities of goods, investments, and migrants, they also hoped to penetrate the markets of Asia. In China and Japan they demonstrated their willingness to use force to remove trade barriers.

Traditional Chinese civilization was self-sufficient. For centuries China had sent more goods and inventions to Europe than it had received, and this was still the case in the early nineteenth century. Trade with Europe was carefully regulated by the Chinese imperial government—the Qing (ching), or Manchu (man-CHOO), Dynasty—which required all foreign merchants to live in the southern city of Canton and to buy from and sell to only the local merchant monopoly. Goods considered harmful to Chinese interests, such as opium, were forbidden.

For years the little community of foreign merchants in Canton accepted the Chinese system. By the 1820s, however, British merchants began flexing their muscles. They had found in opium a product the Chinese desired, and they wanted to stop smuggling and sell it openly. They pressured the British government to help them establish an independent British colony in China with "safe and unrestricted liberty" in trade. British merchants in Canton also enlisted the support of British manufacturers with visions of vast Chinese markets.

At the same time, the Qing government decided that the **opium trade** had to be stamped out. It was ruining the people and hurting the economy, as silver for opium was flowing to British merchants. The government began to prosecute Chinese drug dealers vigorously and in 1839 it ordered the foreign merchants to obey China's laws. The British merchants refused and were expelled, whereupon war soon broke out.

The British were able to call troops from India and used their superior sea power to occupy several coastal cities. China submitted to the Treaty of Nanking in 1842 and was forced to cede the island of Hong Kong to Britain forever, pay an indemnity of $100 million, and open up four large cities to foreign trade with low tariffs.

Thereafter the opium trade flourished, and Hong Kong developed rapidly as an Anglo-Chinese enclave. The British, joined by the French, attacked China again between 1856 and 1860, culminating in the occupation of Beijing. Another round of harsh treaties gave European merchants and missionaries greater privileges and protection and forced the Chinese to accept trade and investment on unfavorable terms for several more cities. Thus did Europeans use military aggression to open China to foreign trade and foreign ideas.

opium trade Opium was grown legally in British-occupied India and smuggled into China by means of fast ships and bribed officials; it became a destructive and ensnaring vice of the Chinese.

Britain and China at War, 1841
Britain capitalized on its overwhelming naval superiority, and this British aquatint celebrates a dramatic moment in a crucial battle near Guangzhou. Having received a direct hit from a steam-powered British ironclad, a Chinese sailing ship explodes into a wall of flame. The Chinese lost eleven ships and five hundred men in the two-hour engagement; the British suffered only minor damage. (National Maritime Museum, London)

China's neighbor Japan had decided by 1640 to seal off the country from all European influences in order to preserve traditional Japanese culture and society. When American and British whaling ships began to appear off Japanese coasts almost two hundred years later, the policy of exclusion was still in effect. An order of 1825 commanded Japanese officials to "drive away foreign vessels without second thought."[1]

Japan's refusal to share its ports complicated the provisioning of whaling ships and trading vessels in the eastern Pacific. It also thwarted the hope of trade and profit. Americans came to see it as their duty to force the Japanese to behave as a "civilized" nation.

After several unsuccessful American attempts to establish commercial relations with Japan, Commodore Matthew Perry steamed into Edo (**ED-doe**) (now Tokyo) Bay in 1853 and demanded diplomatic negotiations with the emperor. Japan entered a grave crisis. Some Japanese warriors urged resistance, but senior officials realized how defenseless their cities were against naval bombardment. Shocked and humiliated, they reluctantly signed a treaty with the United States that opened two ports and permitted trade. Over the next five years, more treaties spelled out the rights and privileges of the Western nations and their merchants in Japan. Japan was "opened."

Western Penetration of Egypt

Unlike China and Japan, nineteenth-century Egypt was attracted to European models of modernization and open to European business ventures. But it too was forced to make concessions to European powers, eventually falling under British rule.

Egypt emerged as an autonomous country in the nineteenth century under the leadership of the extraordinary Albanian-born Turkish general, Muhammad Ali (1769–1849). First appointed governor of Egypt by the Turkish sultan, Muhammad Ali set out to build his own state on the strength of a large, powerful army organized along European lines. He drafted for the first time the peasants of Egypt, and he hired French and Italian army officers to train these raw recruits and their Turkish officers. The government was also reformed, new lands were cultivated, and communications were improved. By the time of his death in 1849, Muhammad Ali had established a strong and virtually independent Egyptian state, to be ruled by his family on a hereditary basis within the Turkish empire.

Muhammad Ali's policies of modernization attracted large numbers of Europeans to the banks of the Nile. The port city of Alexandria had more than fifty thousand Europeans by 1864. Europeans served not only as army officers but also as engineers, doctors, government officials, and police officers. Others turned to trade, finance, and shipping.

Muhammad Ali's grandson Ismail (is-mah-EEL) (r. 1863–1879) continued to Westernize Egypt during his rule as the country's **khedive** (kuh-DEEV), or prince. The large irrigation networks he promoted caused cotton production and exports to Europe to boom, and with his support the Suez Canal was completed by a French company in 1869. Cairo acquired modern boulevards and Western hotels.

As French-educated Ismail proudly declared, "My country is no longer in Africa, we now form part of Europe."[2]

Yet Ismail's projects were enormously expensive, and by 1876 Egypt owed foreign bondholders a colossal debt that it could not pay. The governments of France and Great Britain intervened to protect the European bondholders, forcing Ismail to appoint French and British commissioners to oversee Egyptian finances.

Foreign financial control evoked a violent nationalistic reaction among Egyptian religious leaders, young intellectuals, and army officers. The British pushed Ismail out and brought in his weak son, Tewfig (r. 1879–1892), sparking anti-European riots in Alexandria. The British fleet then bombarded the city, which led to a country-wide revolt. But a British expeditionary force put down the rebellion and occupied all of Egypt.

The British said their occupation was temporary, but British armies remained in Egypt until 1956. They maintained the façade of the khedive's government as an autonomous province of the Ottoman Empire, but the khedive was a mere puppet. British rule did result in tax reforms and somewhat better conditions for peasants, while foreign bondholders received their interest and Egyptian nationalists nursed their injured pride.

British rule in Egypt provided a new model for European expansion in Africa and Asia. Such expansion was based on military force, political domination, and a self-justifying ideology of beneficial reform. This model was to predominate until 1914. Thus did Europe's Industrial Revolution lead to tremendous political as well as economic expansion throughout the world after 1880.

| **khedive** A prince in Egypt.

Section Review

- An expanding gap between industrialized countries and "Third World" non-industrializing countries developed with enormous economic disparities between them.

- Improvements in communication, such as the telegraph and transportation, including railroads and steamships, facilitated the establishment of a Western-driven global trade network, often at the expense of indigenous peoples.

- China had strict regulations for trade and when British merchants desired more favorable conditions for their opium trade, the Chinese government resisted, so Britain invaded, claiming Hong Kong and several other cities, forcing the Chinese to lift restrictions on foreign trade.

- Japan was closed to foreign trade until the Americans demanded diplomatic relations under threat of force and the Japanese reluctantly agreed to open some of their ports.

- Muhammad Ali and Ismail modernized Egypt and opened the door to foreign investors and immigrants but the expense of his projects, including the Suez Canal, put Egypt in debt and foreign commissioners took over financial control; when the Egyptians revolted the British used force to occupy Egypt until 1956.

The Great Migration

How was massive migration an integral part of Western expansion?

A poignant human drama was interwoven with economic expansion: millions of people pulled up stakes and left their ancestral lands in the course of history's greatest migration. To millions of ordinary people, for whom the opening of China and the interest on the Egyptian debt had not the slightest significance, this great movement was the central experience in the saga of Western expansion. It was, in part, because of this **great migration** that the West's impact on the world in the nineteenth century was so powerful and many-sided.

great migration A great movement of people that was the central experience in the saga of Western expansion; one reason why the West's impact on the world in the nineteenth century was so powerful and many-sided.

European Migrants

Population growth was a driving force behind European migration. The trend of falling death rates continued until the early twentieth century, mainly because of the rising standard of living but also because of improvements in medicine. Millions of country folk, seeing little available land and few opportunities, went abroad as well as to nearby cities in search of work and economic opportunity.

The United States absorbed the largest number of European migrants, but less than half of all migrants went there (see Figure 26.2). Moreover, migrants accounted for a larger proportion of the total population in Argentina, Brazil, and Canada than in the United States. The common American assumption that European migration meant migration to the United States is quite inaccurate.

Determined to maintain or improve their status, migrants were a great asset to the countries that received them. The vast majority came in the prime of life and were ready to work hard in the new land, at least for a time. Many Europeans moved but remained within Europe, settling temporarily or permanently in another European country. Jews from eastern Europe and peasants from Ireland migrated to Great Britain; Russians and Poles sought work in Germany; and Latin peoples from Spain, Portugal, and Italy entered France. Many Europeans were

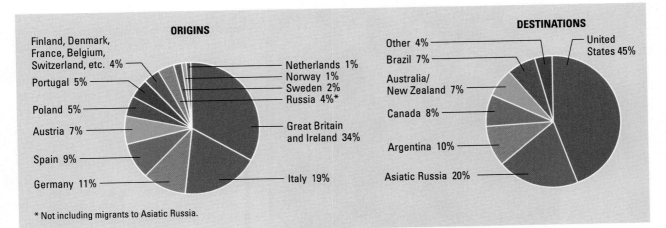

FIGURE 26.2   Origins and Destinations of European Emigrants, 1851–1960

Source: From *Impact of Western Man,* by W. Woodruff. Copyright © 1982. Reprinted by permission of University Press of America.

truly migrants as opposed to immigrants—that is, they returned home after some time abroad. One in two migrants to Argentina and probably one in three to the United States eventually returned to their native land. Once again, the possibility of buying land in the old country was of central importance.

Ties of family and friendship played a crucial role in the movement of peoples. Many people from a given province or village settled together in rural enclaves or tightly knit urban neighborhoods thousands of miles away. Very often a strong individual—a businessman, a religious leader—would blaze the way and others would follow, forming a "migration chain."

Many landless young European men and women were spurred to leave by a spirit of revolt and independence. In Sweden and in Norway, in Jewish Russia and in Italy, these young people felt frustrated by the small privileged classes, which often controlled both church and government and resisted demands for change and greater opportunity. Many a young Norwegian seconded the passionate cry of Norway's national poet, Martinius Bjørnson (**BYURN-suhn**): "Forth will I! Forth! I will be crushed and consumed if I stay."[3] Thus for many, migration was a radical way to "get out from under." Migration slowed down when the people won basic political and social reforms, such as the right to vote and social security.

Asian Migrants

Not all migration was from Europe. A substantial number of Chinese, Japanese, Indians, and Filipinos—to name only four key groups—responded to rural hardship with temporary or permanent migration. At least 3 million Asians (as opposed to more than 60 million Europeans) moved abroad before 1920. Most went as indentured laborers to work under incredibly difficult conditions on the plantations or in the gold mines of Latin America, southern Asia, Africa, California, Hawaii, and Australia. White estate owners very often used Asians to replace or supplement blacks after the suppression of the slave trade.

Such migration from Asia would undoubtedly have grown to much greater proportions if planters and mine owners in search of cheap labor had been able to hire as many Asian workers as they wished. But they could not. By the 1880s, Americans and Australians were building **great white walls**—discriminatory laws designed to keep Asians out.

great white walls Laws designed by Americans and Australians to keep Asians out.

Vaccinating Migrants Bound for Hawaii, 1904

First Chinese, then Japanese, and finally Koreans and Filipinos went in large numbers across the Pacific to labor in Hawaii on American-owned sugar plantations in the late nineteenth century. The native Hawaiians had been decimated by disease, preparing the way for the annexation of Hawaii by the United States in 1898. (Corbis)

A crucial factor in the migrations before 1914 was, therefore, the general policy of "whites only" in the open lands of possible permanent settlement. This, too, was part of Western dominance in the increasingly lopsided world. Largely successful in monopolizing the best overseas opportunities, Europeans and people of European ancestry reaped the main benefits from the great migration. By 1913 people in Australia, Canada, and the United States all had higher average incomes than people in Great Britain, still Europe's wealthiest nation.

Western Imperialism (1880–1914)

How and why after 1875 did European nations rush to build political empires in Africa and Asia?

The expansion of Western society reached its apex between about 1880 and 1914. In those years, the leading European nations not only continued to send massive streams of migrants, money, and manufactured goods around the world, but also rushed to create or enlarge vast *political* empires abroad. This political empire building contrasted sharply with the economic penetration of non-Western territories between 1816 and 1880, which had left a China or a Japan "opened" but politically independent. By contrast, the empires of the late nineteenth century recalled the old European colonial empires of the seventeenth and eighteenth centuries and led contemporaries to speak of the **new imperialism.**

Characterized by a frantic rush to plant the flag over as many people and as much territory as possible, the new imperialism had momentous consequences. It resulted in new tensions among competing European states, and it led to wars and rumors of war with non-European powers. The new imperialism was aimed primarily at Africa and Asia and subjugated millions under European rule.

The Scramble for Africa

The most spectacular manifestation of the new imperialism was the scramble for Africa. As late as 1880, European nations controlled only 10 percent of the African continent (see inset, Map 26.1). Between 1880 and 1900, the situation changed drastically. Britain, France, Germany, and Italy raced one another for African possessions (see Map 26.1). By 1900 nearly the whole continent had been carved up and placed under European rule: only Ethiopia in northeast Africa, which repulsed Italian invaders, and Liberia on the West African coast, which had been settled by freed slaves from the United States, remained independent. In the years before 1914, the European powers tightened their control and established colonial governments to rule their gigantic empires.

The situation in South Africa had a different final outcome. The British had taken possession of the Dutch settlements at Cape Town during the wars with Napoleon I. The descendents of Dutch settlers, known as Boers (bores) or **Afrikaners (af-rih-KAHN-uhrs)**, moved north and settled the regions later known as the Orange Free State and the Transvaal (**trans-VAHL**), proclaiming their political independence. Then in the early 1890s, Cecil Rhodes led the British farther north, establishing protectorates over Bechuanaland (**bech-oo-AH-nuh-land**) (now Botswana) and Rhodesia (**roh-DEE-zhuh**) (now Zimbabwe and Zambia).

Trying unsuccessfully to undermine the stubborn Afrikaners in the Transvaal, where English-speaking capitalists like Rhodes were developing fabulously rich gold mines, the British conquered their white rivals in the bloody South African

Section Review

- Population growth and the search for better economic and social opportunities drove European migration, which slowed when these conditions improved in the home country.

- Migrants were an asset to the receiving countries as they worked hard and often arrived with family and friends forming a "migration chain," all settling in the same neighborhoods or in specific areas.

- Asian migrants went to work most often as indentured laborers in awful conditions after the suppression of the slave trade, but laws allowing only whites to settle permanently limited their numbers.

new imperialism The drive to create vast political empires abroad, recalling the old European colonial empires of the seventeenth and eighteenth centuries and contrasting with the economic penetration of non-Western territories between 1816 and 1880.

Afrikaners Descendants of the Dutch in the Cape Colony.

MAP 26.1 The Partition of Africa

British
French
German
Italian

Portuguese
Belgian
Spanish
Independent African states

COLONIAL PRESENCE IN AFRICA, 1878

MAPPING THE PAST

MAP 26.1 The Partition of Africa

The European powers carved up Africa after 1880 and built vast political empires. European states also seized territory in Asia in the nineteenth century, although some Asian states and peoples managed to maintain their political independence, as may be seen on Map 26.2, page 686. The late nineteenth century was the peak of European imperialism. Compare the patterns of European imperialism in Africa and Asia, using this map and Map 26.2. **[1]** What European countries were leading imperialist states in both Africa and Asia, and what lands did they hold? **[2]** What countries in Africa and Asia maintained their political independence? **[3]** From an imperialist perspective, what in 1914 did the United States and Japan, two very different countries, have in common in Africa and Asia?

War (1899–1902). In 1910 their territories were united in a new Union of South Africa, established—unlike any other territory in Africa—as a largely "self-governing" colony. This enabled the defeated Afrikaners to use their numerical superiority over the British settlers to gradually take political power, as even the most educated nonwhites lost the right to vote outside the Cape Colony. (See the feature "Individuals in Society: Cecil Rhodes.")

In the complexity of the European seizure of Africa, certain events and individuals stand out. Of enormous importance was the British occupation of Egypt in 1882, which established the new model of formal political control. There was also the role of Leopold II of Belgium (r. 1865–1909), an energetic, strong-willed monarch with a lust for empire. "Steam and electricity have annihilated distance, and all the non-appropriated lands on the surface of the globe can become the field of our operations and of our success,"[4] he had exclaimed in 1861. Leopold ignited a gold rush mentality after sending the part-time explorer Henry M. Stanley to plant his flag in the Congo. The French rushed to stake their claim in the region, and the race for territory was on.

The leaders of Europe met at the **Berlin conference** in 1884 and 1885 to agree on some basic rules for this new and dangerous game of imperialist competition in sub-Saharan Africa. The conference established the principle that European claims to African territory had to rest on "effective occupation" in order to be recognized by other states. The conference recognized Leopold's personal rule over a neutral Congo free state and agreed to work to stop slavery and the slave trade in Africa.

Bismarck, who saw little value in colonies, had a change of stance when Germans clamored for a stake in Africa. In 1884 and 1885, Germany established protectorates over a number of small African kingdoms and tribes in Togo, Cameroons, southwest Africa, and, later, East Africa. In acquiring colonies, Bismarck worked with France's Jules Ferry against the British. With Bismarck's tacit approval, the French pressed southward from Algeria, eastward from their old forts on the Senegal coast, and northward from their protectorate on the Congo River.

Meanwhile, the British began enlarging their West African enclaves and impatiently pushing northward from the Cape Colony and westward from Zanzibar. Their attempt to move southward from Egypt was blocked by Muslim forces in the Sudan in 1885. A decade later, another British force, under General Horatio H. Kitchener (KICH-uh-ner), moved cautiously and more successfully up the Nile River, building

Berlin conference A meeting of European leaders held in 1884 and 1885 in order to lay down some basic rules for imperialist competition in sub-Saharan Africa; they established the principle that European claims to African territory had to rest on effective occupation in order to be recognized by other states.

H. M. Leopold, King of the Congo, in his national dress.

European Imperialism at its Worst

This 1908 English cartoon, "Leopold, King of the Congo, in his native dress," focuses on the barbaric practice of cutting off the hands and feet of Africans who refused to gather as much rubber as Leopold's company demanded. In 1908 an international human rights campaign forced the Belgian king to cede his personal fief to the Belgian state. (The Granger Collection, New York)

Individuals in Society

Cecil Rhodes

Cecil Rhodes (1853–1902) epitomized the dynamism and the ruthlessness of the new imperialism. He built a corporate monopoly, claimed vast tracts in Africa, and established the famous Rhodes scholarships to develop colonial (and American) leaders who would love and strengthen the British Empire. But to Africans, he left a bitter legacy.

Rhodes came from a large middle-class family and at seventeen went to southern Africa to seek his fortune. He soon turned to diamonds, newly discovered at Kimberley,

Cecil Rhodes, after crushing the last African revolt in Rhodesia in 1896. (Brown Brothers)

picked good partners, and was wealthy by 1876. But Rhodes, often called a dreamer, wanted more. He entered Oxford University, while returning periodically to Africa, and his musings crystallized in a belief in progress through racial competition and territorial expansion. "I contend," he wrote, "that we [English] are the finest race in the world and the more of the world we inhabit the better it is for the human race."*

Rhodes's belief in British expansion never wavered. In 1880 he formed the De Beers Mining Company, and by 1888 his firm monopolized southern Africa's diamond production and earned fabulous profits. Rhodes also entered the Cape Colony's legislature and became the all-powerful prime minister from 1890 to 1896. His main objective was to dominate the Afrikaner republics and to impose British rule on as much land as possible beyond their northern borders. Working through a state-approved private company financed in part by De Beers, Rhodes's agents forced and cajoled African kings to accept British "protection," then put down rebellions with Maxim machine guns. Britain thus obtained a great swath of empire on the cheap.

But Rhodes, like many high achievers obsessed with power and personal aggrandizement, went too far. He backed, and then in 1896 failed to call back, a failed invasion of the Transvaal, which was designed to topple the Dutch-speaking republic. Repudiated by top British leaders who had encouraged his plan, Rhodes had to resign as prime minister. In declining health, he continued to agitate against the Afrikaner republics. He died at age forty-nine as the South African War (1899–1902) ended.

In accounting for Rhodes's remarkable but flawed achievements, both sympathetic and critical biographers stress his imposing size, enormous energy, and powerful personality. His ideas were commonplace, but he believed in them passionately, and he could persuade and inspire others to follow his lead. Rhodes the idealist was nonetheless a born negotiator, a crafty dealmaker who believed that everyone could be had for a price. According to his best biographer, Rhodes's homosexuality—discreet, partially repressed, and undeniable—was also "a major component of his magnetism and his success."† Never comfortable with women, he loved male companionship. He drew together a "band of brothers," both gay and straight, to share in the pursuit of power.

Rhodes cared nothing for the rights of blacks. Ever a combination of visionary and opportunist, he looked forward to an eventual reconciliation of Afrikaners and British in a united white front. Therefore, as prime minister of the Cape Colony, he broke with the colony's liberal tradition and supported Afrikaner demands to reduce drastically the number of black voters and limit black freedoms. This helped lay the foundation for the Union of South Africa's brutal policy of racial segregation known as *apartheid* after 1948.

Questions for Analysis

1. How did Rhodes relate to Afrikaners and to black Africans? How do you account for the differences and the similarities?

2. In what ways does Rhodes's career throw additional light on the debate over the causes of the new imperialism?

*Robert Rotberg, *The Founder: Cecil Rhodes and the Pursuit of Power* (New York: Oxford University Press, 1988), p. 150.

†Ibid., p. 408.

a railroad to supply arms and reinforcements as it went. Finally, in 1898 these British troops met their foe at Omdurman (om-door-MAHN) (see Map 26.1), where Muslim tribesmen armed with spears charged time and time again, only to be cut down by the recently invented machine gun. In the end, eleven thousand brave Muslim tribesmen lay dead, while only twenty-eight Britons had been killed.

Continuing up the Nile after the Battle of Omdurman, Kitchener's armies found that a small French force had beaten them to the village of Fashoda (fuh-SHOH-duh). The result was a serious diplomatic crisis and even the threat of war. Eventually, wracked by the Dreyfus affair (see page 662) and unwilling to fight, France backed down and withdrew its forces, allowing the British to take over.

The British conquest of Sudan exemplifies the general process of empire building in Africa. The fate of the Muslim force at Omdurman was eventually inflicted on all native peoples who resisted European rule: they were blown away by vastly superior armaments. But however much the European powers squabbled for territory and privilege around the world, they always had the sense to stop short of actually fighting each other. Imperial ambitions were not worth a great European war.

Imperialism in Asia

Although the sudden division of Africa was more spectacular, Europeans also extended their political control in Asia. In 1815 the Dutch ruled little more than the island of Java in the East Indies. Thereafter they gradually brought almost all of the three-thousand-mile archipelago under their political authority, although they had to grant some territory to Britain and Germany. In the critical decade of the 1880s, the French under the leadership of Jules Ferry took Indochina. The Russians expanded to the south in the Caucasus and to the east in Central Asia and China's outlying provinces. India, Japan, and China also experienced a profound imperialist impact (see Map 26.2).

The United States's great conquest was the Philippines, taken from Spain in 1898 after the Spanish-American War. When it quickly became clear that the United States had no intention of granting independence, Philippine patriots rose in revolt and were suppressed only after long, bitter fighting. Some Americans protested the taking of the Philippines, but to no avail. Thus another great Western power joined the imperialist ranks in Asia.

Causes of the New Imperialism

Many factors contributed to the late-nineteenth-century rush for territory and empire, among them economics, nationalism, ideology, military technology, and the ambitions of individuals. While these reasons do not constitute a defense of imperialism, they are helpful in understanding what drove it.

Economic motives were a factor in the new imperialism, especially in the British Empire. By the late 1870s, Great Britain was losing its early lead in industrialization and facing increasingly tough competition from France, Germany, and the United States. When continental powers began to grab territory in the 1880s, the British followed suit immediately. They feared that France and Germany would seal off their empires with high tariffs and restrictions and that potential markets would be lost forever. In actuality, however, the overall economic gains of the new imperialism proved quite limited before 1914. The new colonies were simply too poor to buy much, and they offered few immediately profitable investments.

Colonies also seemed important for political and diplomatic reasons. For instance, the British occupation of Egypt was motivated in part by the desire to

MAP 26.2 Asia in 1914

India remained under British rule, while China precariously preserved its political independence. The Dutch empire in modern-day Indonesia was old, but French control of Indochina was a product of the new imperialism.

Territories held by Western powers

- Great Britain
- France
- Netherlands
- United States
- Russian Empire
- Japan and its territories
- Independent Asian states
- Ottoman Empire
- Major railroads

PACIFIC OCEAN

JAPANESE EMPIRE

Sea of Okhotsk

Sakhalin

Karafuto (1905)

Sea of Japan

Khabarovsk (1858)

Vladivostok (1860)

KOREA (1905, 1910)

Lüshun (Port Arthur) (Japan 1905)

Weihai (Gr. Br. 1898)

Jiaozhou (Ger. 1898)

Shanghai (Gr. Br. 1842)

East China Sea

Ryuku Is. (Jap.)

Formosa (1895)

Philippine Is. (U.S. 1898)

Manila

SIBERIA

AMUR DISTRICT (1858)

MANCHURIA

Harbin

JEHOL

Shenyang (Mukden)

Beijing

Tianjin

Nanjing

Wuhan

Fuzhou

Xiamen

Guangzhou (Gr. Br. 1842)

Macao (Port. 1557)

Hong Kong (Gr. Br. 1842)

Zhanjiang (France 1898)

Hainan

Haiphong

South China Sea

BRITISH NORTH BORNEO (1888)

SARAWAK (1888)

Borneo

DUTCH EAST INDIES

Celebes

New Guinea

Timor (Portugal 1859)

(Neth.)

Chita

Irkutsk

Lake Baikal

OUTER MONGOLIA (Russian Influence, 1912)

INNER MONGOLIA

Huang He R.

CHINA

Chongqing

Kunming

Hanoi

FRENCH INDOCHINA (1859, 1907)

Saigon

SIAM

Bangkok

MALAY STATES (1874, 1909)

Singapore (Gr. Br. 1819)

Sumatra

Java (1619)

Batavia

RUSSIAN EMPIRE

SINKIANG

TIBET

HIMALAYA MTS.

BHUTAN

NEPAL

Ganges R.

Yangzi R.

BURMA (1852, 1885)

Rangoon

Bay of Bengal

Andaman Is. (Gr. Br.)

Calcutta

St. Petersburg

Helsinki

Riga

Moscow

Kiev

Warsaw

Brest-Litovsk

Omsk

Trans-Siberian Railway

Samara

Orenburg

Kazalinsk

Aral Sea

Tashkent (1864)

Andizhan (1871)

Samarkand (1868)

Bukhara

Merv (1884)

Krasnovodsk

Ashkhabad (1881)

Kushka

AFGHANISTAN

KASHMIR (1846)

PUNJAB

Indus R.

Delhi

INDIA

BRITISH SPHERE (1907)

BALUCHISTAN (1883)

Karachi

Diu (Port.)

Bombay

Goa (Port.)

Madras

Pondicherry (Fr.)

Karikal (Fr.)

Yanaon (Fr.)

Ceylon

Caspian Sea

Baku

Batum (1878)

Kars (1878)

Tehran

RUSSIAN SPHERE (1907)

PERSIA

Baghdad

Persian Gulf

OMAN (1891)

Black Sea

Constantinople

Angora

Damascus

Beirut

OTTOMAN EMPIRE

Mediterranean Sea

Red Sea

KUWAIT (1899)

ARABIA

Medina

HADRAMAUT (1888)

WEST ADEN (1903)

Nile R.

AFRICA

Danube R.

Dnieper R.

Volga R.

INDIAN OCEAN

Arabian Sea

20°N

40°N

Equator 0°

Tropic of Cancer

80°E

100°E

110°E

40°E

N

0   500   1,000 Km.

0   500   1,000 Mi.

Lake Balkash

safeguard the Suez Canal. Far-flung possessions guaranteed ever-growing navies the safe havens and the dependable coaling stations they needed in times of crisis or war.

Imperialism also served European rulers who were dealing with social tensions and political conflicts at home. The tabloid press whipped up feelings of patriotism over foreign triumphs, while leaders stressed that colonies benefited workers as well as capitalists by providing cheap raw materials for industry. In short, conservative leaders used imperialism to justify the status quo and their hold on power.

European leaders were themselves pressured to acquire colonies by special-interest groups. Shipping companies wanted lucrative subsidies. White settlers demanded more land and greater protection. Missionaries and humanitarians wanted to spread religion and stop the slave trade. Military men and colonial officials, whose role has often been overlooked, foresaw rapid advancement and high-paid positions in growing empires. The actions of such groups pushed the course of empire forward.

Many Westerners were convinced that colonies were essential to achieving greatness. "There has never been a great power without great colonies," wrote one French publicist in 1877. "Every virile people has established colonial power," echoed the famous nationalist historian of Germany, Heinrich von Treitschke (HAHYN-rikh fuhn TRAHYCH-kuh). "All great nations in the fullness of their strength have desired to set their mark upon barbarian lands and those who fail to participate in this great rivalry will play a pitiable role in time to come."[5]

As Treitschke's statement suggests, Social Darwinism and racist doctrines also fostered imperialist expansion. As one prominent English economist argued, the "strongest nation has always been conquering the weaker . . . and the strongest tend to be best." In the words of another, "The path of progress is strewn with the wreck . . . of inferior races." Thus imperialism was justified as the inevitable triumph of the superior European race.

Convinced of their moral and intellectual superiority, Europeans also came to believe that they should "civilize" nonwhite peoples. According to this view, nonwhites would eventually receive the benefits of modern economies, cities, advanced medicine, and higher standards of living. In time, they might be ready for self-government and Western democracy. Thus the French spoke of their sacred "civilizing mission." In 1899 Rudyard Kipling (1865–1936), who wrote masterfully of Anglo-Indian life and was perhaps the most influential British writer of the 1890s, exhorted Europeans (and Americans in the United States) to unselfish service in distant lands:

> *Take up the White Man's Burden—*
> *Send forth the best ye breed—*
> *Go bind your sons to exile*
> *To serve your captives' need,*
> *To wait in heavy harness,*
> *On fluttered folk and wild—*
> *Your new-caught, sullen peoples*
> *Half-devil and half-child.*[6]

Many Americans also accepted the ideology of the **white man's burden.** It was an important factor in the decision to rule, rather than liberate, the Philippines after the Spanish-American War. Like their European counterparts, these Americans sincerely believed that their civilization had reached unprecedented heights and that they had unique benefits to bestow on all "less advanced" peoples. Another argument was that imperial government protected natives from tribal warfare as well as cruder forms of exploitation by white settlers and business people.

white man's burden The idea that Europeans could and should civilize more primitive, nonwhite peoples and that nonwhites would eventually receive the benefits of modern economics, cities, advanced medicine, and higher standards of living.

Peace and stability under European control also facilitated the spread of Christianity. In Africa, Catholic and Protestant missionaries competed with Islam south of the Sahara, seeking converts and building schools to spread the Gospel. Many Africans' first real contact with whites was in mission schools. Some peoples, such as the Ibo in Nigeria, became highly Christianized.

Such occasional successes in black Africa contrasted with the general failure of missionary efforts in India, China, and the Islamic world. There Christians often preached in vain to peoples with ancient, complex religious beliefs. Yet the number of Christian believers around the world did increase substantially in the nineteenth century, and missionary groups kept trying. Unfortunately, "many missionaries had drunk at the well of European racism," and this probably prevented them from doing better.[7]

Critics of Imperialism

Not all Westerners were convinced of the value of imperialism. The radical English economist J. A. Hobson (1858–1940), in his *Imperialism*, contended that the rush to acquire colonies was due to the need of the rich to find outlets for their surplus capital. Yet, Hobson argued, imperial possessions did not pay off economically for the country as a whole. Moreover, Hobson argued that the quest for empire diverted popular attention away from domestic reform and the need to reduce the great gap between rich and poor. Most people, however, did not believe Hobson's economic argument and believed instead that imperialism profited the homeland.

Hobson and many other critics struck home, however, with their moral condemnation of whites imperiously ruling nonwhites. They rebelled against crude Social Darwinian thought: "Blessed are the strong, for they shall prey on the weak."[8] Kipling and his kind were lampooned as racist bullies whose rule rested on brutality, racial contempt, and the Maxim machine gun. In the novel *Heart of Darkness*, Joseph Conrad (1857–1924) castigated the "pure selfishness" of Europeans in "civilizing" Africa and dramatized how both whites and nonwhites are destroyed in the process. Henry Labouchère, a member of Parliament and prominent spokesman for this position, mocked Kipling's famous poem:

Pile on the Brown Man's burden!
And if ye rouse his hate,
Meet his old-fashioned reasons
With Maxims up to date,
With shells and Dum-Dum bullets
A hundred times plain
The Brown Man's loss must never
Imply the White Man's gain.[9]

Critics charged Europeans with applying a degrading double standard and failing to live up to their own noble ideals. At home Europeans had won or were winning representative government, individual liberties, and a certain equality of opportunity. In their empires, Europeans imposed military dictatorships on Africans and Asians; forced them to work involuntarily, almost like slaves; and discriminated against them shamelessly. Europeans who denounced the imperialist tide provided colonial peoples with a Western ideology of liberation.

Section Review

- The struggle between Dutch settlers (Afrikaners) and the British for control of South Africa led to a bloody South African war, resulting in a self-governing colony with the more numerous Afrikaners gaining political dominance, disenfranchising nonwhites.
- European leaders met at the Berlin conference (1884–1885) to set rules for the imperialistic competition for African territory, agreeing on "effective occupation" as the basis for European control of Africa.
- Asia also fell to imperialist Westerners, the Dutch occupying Indonesia, the French taking Indochina, the Russians expanding into the Caucasus, Central Asia, and China, and the United States taking over the Philippines.
- Causes of the new imperialism were: economic, as imperialistic countries feared they would lose markets; political, as leaders promoted nationalism to cover social and political tensions at home; and ideological, with social Darwinism and racist doctrines fueling the "superior" European need to "civilize" nonwhite peoples and for Christian missionaries to convert them.
- Dissenters toward European imperialism, such as J. A. Hobson, denounced its diverting attention away from domestic reform and condemned its false morality, charging that civil liberties won at home were not practiced in colonies.

Responding to Western Imperialism

What was the general pattern of non-Western responses to Western expansion, and how did India, Japan, and China meet the imperialist challenge?

To peoples in Africa and Asia, Western expansion represented a profoundly disruptive assault. Everywhere it threatened traditional ruling classes, traditional economies, and traditional ways of life. Christian missionaries and European secular ideologies challenged established beliefs and values. Non-Western peoples experienced a crisis of identity, one made all the more painful by the power and arrogance of the white intruders.

The Pattern of Response

Generally, the initial response of African and Asian rulers to aggressive Western expansion was to try to drive the unwelcome foreigners away. When that proved impossible, conquered peoples responded in a variety of ways. At one end of the spectrum were "traditionalists," who concentrated on preserving their cultural traditions at all costs. "Westernizers" or "modernizers" stood at the other, and many shades of opinion rested in between. Both before and after European domination, the struggle among these groups was often intense. With time, however, the modernizers usually prevailed.

When the power of both the traditionalists and the modernizers was thoroughly shattered by superior force, the great majority of Asians and Africans accepted imperial rule. Political participation in non-Western lands was historically limited to small elites, and the masses were used to doing what their rulers told them. Nevertheless, support for European rule was shallow and weak. Thus the conforming masses followed with greater or lesser enthusiasm a few determined personalities who came to oppose the Europeans. Such leaders always arose, both when Europeans ruled directly and when they manipulated native governments.

Those individuals who would lead the fight against imperialism found in the Western world the ideologies and justification for their protest. They discovered liberalism, with its credo of civil liberty and political self-determination. Above all, they found themselves attracted to modern nationalism, which asserted that every people had the right to control its own destiny. After 1917 anti-imperialist revolt would find another weapon in Lenin's version of Marxian socialism. Thus the anti-imperialist search for dignity drew strength from Western thought and culture, as is apparent in the development of three major Asian countries—India, Japan, and China.

Empire in India

India was the jewel of the British Empire, and no colonial area experienced a more profound British impact. Unlike Japan and China, which maintained a real or precarious independence, and unlike African territories, which were annexed by Europeans only at the end of the nineteenth century, India was ruled more or less absolutely by Britain for a very long time.

Arriving in India on the heels of the Portuguese in the seventeenth century, the British East India Company had conquered the last independent native state by 1848. In the **Great Rebellion** of 1857 and 1858, people throughout northern

Great Rebellion The 1857 and 1858 insurrection by Muslim and Hindu mercenaries in the British army that spread throughout northern and central India before finally being crushed, primarily by loyal native troops from southern India. Britain thereafter ruled India directly.

and central India tried to drive the British out, but the rebellion was crushed, primarily by native troops from southern India. Thereafter the British Parliament in London ruled India directly, with white administrators in India carrying out their orders. Many British shared the sentiments of Lord Kitchener in justifying British hegemony:

> It is this consciousness of the inherent superiority of the European which has won for us India. However well educated and clever a native may be, and however brave he may prove himself, I believe that no rank we can bestow on him would cause him to be considered an equal of the British officer.[10]

British women played an important part in the imperial enterprise, especially after the opening of the Suez Canal in 1869 made it much easier for civil servants and businessmen to bring their wives and children with them to India. These British families tended to live in their own separate communities, where they occu-

Imperial Complexities in India
Britain permitted many native princes to continue their rule, if they accepted British domination. This photo shows a road-building project designed to facilitate famine relief in a southern native state. Officials of the local Muslim prince and their British "advisers" watch over workers drawn from the Hindu majority. (Nizam's Good Works Project—Famine Relief: Road Building, Aurangabad 1895–1902, from Judith Mara Gutman, *Through Indian Eyes.* Courtesy, Private Collection)

pied large houses with well-shaded porches, handsome lawns, and a multitude of servants. It was the wife's responsibility to direct their households and servants with the same self-confident authoritarianism that characterized British political rule in India. (See the feature "Listening to the Past: A British Woman in India" on pages 696–697.)

With British men and women sharing a sense of mission as well as strong feelings of racial and cultural superiority, the British established a modern system of progressive secondary education in which all instruction was in English. Thus through education and government service, the British offered some Indians opportunities for both economic and social advancement. High-caste Hindus, particularly quick to respond, emerged as skillful intermediaries between the British rulers and the Indian people, and soon they formed a new elite profoundly influenced by Western thought and culture.

This new bureaucratic elite played a crucial role in modern economic development, which was a second result of British rule. Irrigation projects for agriculture, the world's third-largest railroad network for good communications, and large tea and jute plantations geared to the world economy were all developed. Unfortunately, the lot of the Indian masses improved little, for the increase in production was eaten up by population increase.

Finally, with a well-educated, English-speaking Indian bureaucracy and modern communications, the British created a unified, powerful state. They placed under the same general system of law and administration the vanquished kingdoms of the entire subcontinent—groups that had fought each other for centuries and had been repeatedly conquered by Muslim and Mongol invaders.

In spite of these achievements, the decisive reaction to European rule was the rise of nationalism among the Indian elite. No matter how anglicized and necessary a member of the educated classes became, he or she could never become the white ruler's equal. The top jobs, the best clubs, the modern hotels, and even certain railroad compartments were sealed off to brown-skinned Indians. The peasant masses might accept such inequality as the latest version of age-old oppression, but the well-educated, English-speaking elite eventually could not. For the elite, racial discrimination meant bitter injustice. It flagrantly contradicted those cherished Western concepts of human rights and equality. Moreover, it was based on dictatorship, no matter how benign.

By 1885, when educated Indians came together to found the predominately Hindu Indian National Congress, demands were increasing for the equality and self-government that Britain had already granted white-settler colonies, such as Canada and Australia. By 1907, emboldened in part by Japan's success (see the next section), the radicals in the Indian National Congress were calling for complete independence. Even the moderates were demanding home rule for India through an elected parliament. Although there were sharp divisions between Hindus and Muslims, Indians were finding an answer to the foreign challenge. The common heritage of British rule and Western ideals, along with the reform and revitalization of the Hindu religion, had created a genuine movement for national independence.

The Example of Japan

When Commodore Matthew Perry arrived in Japan in 1853 with his crude but effective gunboat diplomacy, Japan was a complex feudal society. At the top stood a figurehead emperor, but real power was in the hands of a hereditary military governor, the **shogun** (SHOH-guhn). With the help of a warrior nobility known as

shogun The hereditary governor in feudal Japan.

samurai Japanese warrior nobility who were often poor, restless, and intensely proud.

samurai (SAH-muh-rye), the shogun governed an unindustrialized country of peasants and city dwellers.

When foreign diplomats and merchants began to settle in Yokohama (yoh-kuh-HAH-muh), radical samurai reacted with a wave of antiforeign terrorism and antigovernment assassinations between 1858 and 1863. The imperialist response was swift. An allied fleet of American, British, Dutch, and French warships demolished key forts, further weakening the power and prestige of the shogun's government. Then in 1867, a coalition led by patriotic samurai seized control of the government and restored the political power of the emperor. This was the Meiji (MAY-jee) Restoration, a great turning point in Japanese development.

The immediate, all-important goal of the new government was to meet the foreign threat. The battle cry of the Meiji reformers was "Enrich the state and strengthen the armed forces." Yet how were these tasks to be done? In a remarkable about-face, the leaders of Meiji Japan dropped their antiforeign attacks and initiated a series of measures to reform Japan along modern lines. In the broadest sense, the Meiji leaders tried to harness the power inherent in Europe's dual revolution in order to protect their country and catch up with the West.

In 1871 the new leaders abolished the old feudal structure and declared social equality. They decreed freedom of movement in a country where traveling abroad had been a most serious crime. They created a free, competitive, government-stimulated economy. Japan began to build railroads and modern factories. Thus the new generation adopted many principles of a free, liberal society, and, as in Europe, such freedom resulted in a tremendously creative release of human energy.

Yet the overriding concern of Japan's political leadership was always a powerful state, and to achieve this, more than liberalism was borrowed from the West. A powerful modern navy was created, and the army was completely reorganized along European lines, so that an army of draftees and a professional officer corps replaced the aristocratic samurai warriors. Japan also adapted skillfully the West's science and modern technology, particularly in industry, medicine, and education. Many Japanese were encouraged to study abroad, and the government paid large salaries to attract foreign experts. These experts were always carefully controlled, however, and replaced by trained Japanese as soon as possible.

By 1890, the new state was firmly established. Following the model of the German Empire, Japan established an authoritarian constitution and rejected democracy. The power of the emperor and his ministers was vast; that of the legislature, limited.

Japan successfully copied the imperialism of Western society. Expansion not only proved that Japan was

The Rapid Modernization of the Japanese Army
This woodcut from about 1870 shows Japanese soldiers outfitted in Western uniforms and marching in Western formation. Japanese reformers, impressed by Prussian discipline and success on the battlefield, looked to Germany for their military models. (Ryogoku Tsuneo Tamba Collection/Laurie Platt Winfrey)

strong; it also cemented the nation together in a great mission. Having "opened" Korea with the gunboat diplomacy of imperialism in 1876, Japan decisively defeated China in a war over Korea in 1894 and 1895 and took Formosa (modern-day Taiwan). In the next years, Japan competed aggressively with the leading European powers for influence and territory in China, particularly Manchuria (man-CHOOR-ee-uh). There Japanese and Russian imperialism met and collided. In 1904 Japan attacked Russia without warning, and after a bloody war, Japan emerged with a valuable foothold in China. By 1910, with the annexation of Korea, Japan had become a major imperialist power.

Toward Revolution in China

In 1860 the two-hundred-year-old Qing Dynasty in China appeared on the verge of collapse. Efforts to repel foreigners had failed, and rebellion and chaos wracked the country. Yet the government made a surprising comeback that lasted more than thirty years. Loyal scholar-statesmen and generals quelled disturbances such as the great Tai Ping (tie-PING) rebellion, while the empress dowager Tzu Hsi (TSOO SHEE) revitalized the bureaucracy with some help from European advisers. Foreign aggression also lessened during this period, for the Europeans had obtained their primary goal of commercial and diplomatic relations.

The Qing Dynasty moved again toward collapse in the wake of the Sino-Japanese War of 1894 to 1895, which had revealed China's helplessness in the face of aggression. European powers seized the opportunity to grab concessions and protectorates in China. At the high point of this rush in 1898, it appeared that the European powers might actually divide China among themselves, as they had recently divided Africa. Probably only the jealousy each nation felt toward its imperialist competitors saved China from partition, although the U.S. Open Door policy, which opposed formal annexation of Chinese territory, may have helped tip the balance. In any event, the tempo of foreign encroachment greatly accelerated after 1894.

So, too, did the intensity and radicalism of the Chinese reaction. Like the leaders of the Meiji Restoration, some modernizers saw salvation in Western institutions. In 1898 the government launched a desperate **hundred days of reform** in an attempt to meet the foreign challenge. More radical reformers, such as the revolutionary Sun Yat-sen (soon yot-SEN) (1866–1925), who came from the peasantry and was educated in Hawaii by Christian missionaries, sought to overthrow the dynasty altogether and establish a republic.

On the other side, some traditionalists turned back toward ancient practices, political conservatism, and fanatical hatred of the "foreign devils." "Protect the country, destroy the foreigner" was their simple motto. In the agony of defeat and unwanted reforms, secret societies such as the Boxers rebelled. In northeastern China, more than two hundred foreign missionaries and several thousand Chinese Christians were killed. Once again the imperialist response was swift and harsh. Peking was occupied and plundered by foreign armies. A heavy indemnity was imposed.

The years after the Boxer Rebellion (1900–1903) were ever more troubled. Anarchy and foreign influence spread as the power and prestige of the Qing Dynasty declined still further. Antiforeign, antigovernment revolutionary groups agitated and plotted. Finally in 1912, a spontaneous uprising toppled the Qing Dynasty. After thousands of years of emperors and empires, a loose coalition of revolutionaries proclaimed a Western-style republic and called for an elected parliament. The transformation of China under the impact of expanding Western society entered a new phase, and the end was not in sight.

hundred days of reform A series of Western-style reforms launched in 1898 by the Chinese government in an attempt to meet the foreign challenge.

Section Review

- Natives initially met Western expansion militarily to get rid of the white invaders, but when that failed, a variety of responses ensued, from struggles to maintain "traditionalist" culture to "modernists" who assimilated Western culture within their own.

- Support for European rule was generally weak, allowing native anti-imperialist leaders to use Western ideas of nationalism to inspire the masses to revolt.

- In British-ruled India, native Indians, no matter how educated, were only second class, leading to the formation of the Indian National Congress that began to call for complete independence or at least home rule through an elected parliament.

- Japan met the imperialist threat with counterforce, restoring the emperor and completely reorganizing their nation along the Western lines of a competitive, free, liberal society; they revamped the army and navy while retaining an authoritarian constitution and competing with the West for territory and influence in China.

- The Qing Dynasty struggled to maintain control of China in a climate of rebellion, chaos, and threats on all sides from foreign imperialists, but after the failed Boxer rebellion, another uprising in 1912 finally ended the empire, calling for a republic and an elected Western-style parliament.

Chapter Review

What were some of the global consequences of European industrialization between 1815 and 1914? (page 674)

In the nineteenth century, the industrializing West entered the third and most dynamic phase of its centuries-old expansion into non-Western lands. In so doing, Western nations promoted a prodigious growth of world trade, forced reluctant countries such as China and Japan into the globalizing economy, and profitably subordinated many lands to their own economic interests.

How was massive migration an integral part of Western expansion? (page 679)

In response to population pressures at home and economic opportunities abroad, Western nations also sent forth millions of emigrants to the sparsely populated areas of European settlement in North and South America, Australia, and Asiatic Russia. Migration from Asia was much more limited, mainly because European settlers raised high barriers against Asian immigrants.

How and why after 1875 did European nations rush to build political empires in Africa and Asia? (page 681)

After 1875, Western countries grabbed vast political empires in Africa and rushed to establish political influence in Asia. The reasons for this culminating surge were many, but the economic thrust of robust industrial capitalism, an ever-growing lead in technology, and the competitive pressures of European nationalism were particularly important.

What was the general pattern of non-Western responses to Western expansion, and how did India, Japan, and China meet the imperialist challenge? (page 689)

Western expansion had far-reaching consequences. The world became in many ways a single unit, as European expansion diffused the ideas and techniques of a highly developed civilization. Yet the West relied on force to conquer and rule, and it treated non-Western peoples as racial inferiors. Thus non-Western elites, often armed with Western doctrines, responded gradually but effectively to the Western challenge. In India, a well-educated English-speaking elite rejected racial discrimination, and in 1885 it launched the Indian National Congress, which was calling for complete independence by 1907. In Japan, the Meiji reformers reorganized the society, promoted modernization, and embraced imperialism. In China, less successful at reform, a popular uprising deposed the emperor in 1912 and established a republic. By 1914 non-Western elites in all three countries were engaged in a national, anti-imperialist struggle for dignity, genuine independence, and modernization.

Key Terms

Third World (p. 674)

opium trade (p. 676)

khedive (p. 678)

great migration (p. 679)

great white walls (p. 680)

new imperialism (p. 681)

Afrikaners (p. 681)

Berlin conference (p. 683)

white man's burden (p. 687)

Great Rebellion (p. 689)

shogun (p. 691)

samurai (p. 692)

hundred days of reform (p. 693)

Notes

1. Quoted in J. W. Hall, *Japan, from Prehistory to Modern Times* (New York: Delacorte Press, 1970), p. 250.
2. Quoted in Earl of Cromer, *Modern Egypt* (London, 1911), p. 48.
3. Quoted in T. Blegen, *Norwegian Migration to America*, vol. 2 (Northfield, Minn.: Norwegian-American Historical Association, 1940), p. 468.
4. Quoted in W. L. Langer, *European Alliances and Alignments, 1871–1890* (New York: Vintage Books, 1931), p. 290.

5. Quoted in G. H. Nadel and P. Curtis, eds., *Imperialism and Colonialism* (New York: Macmillan, 1964), p. 94.
6. Rudyard Kipling, *The Five Nations* (London, 1903).
7. E. H. Berman, "African Responses to Christian Mission Education," *African Studies Review* 17 (1974): 530.
8. Quoted in W. L. Langer, *The Diplomacy of Imperialism*, 2d ed. (New York: Alfred A. Knopf, 1951), p. 88.
9. "The Brown Man's Burden," by Henry Labouchère, 1899. Quoted in Ellis, *The Social History of the Machine Gun* (New York: Pantheon Books, 1975), pp. 99–100.
10. Quoted in K. M. Panikkar, *Asia and Western Dominance: A Survey of the Vasco da Gama Epoch of Asian History* (London: George Allen & Unwin, 1959), p. 116.

To assess your mastery of this chapter, go to **bedfordstmartins.com/mckaywestbrief**

Listening to the Past

A British Woman in India

Guides for housekeeping became popular in Europe in the nineteenth century as middle-class women funneled great energy into their homes. A British woman in India probably consulted The Complete Indian Housekeeper and Cook by Flora Annie Steel and Grace Gardiner, a bestseller published in 1888 and frequently updated.

The following passage focuses on how the British mistress should manage her Indian servants, and along with practical suggestions it lays bare some basic attitudes and assumptions of Europeans in colonial settings.

An English lady attended by her Indian servants.
(Stapleton Collection, UK/The Bridgeman Art Library)

Easy, however, as the actual housekeeping is in India, the personal attention of the mistress is quite as much needed here as at home. The Indian servant, it is true, learns more readily, and is guiltless of the sniffiness with which Mary Jane [the servant in England] receives suggestions, but a few days of absence or neglect on the part of the mistress, results in the servants falling into their old habits with the inherited conservatism of dirt. This is, of course, disheartening, but it has to be faced as a necessary condition of life, until a few generations of training shall have started the Indian servant on a new inheritance of habit. It must never be forgotten that at present those mistresses who aim at anything beyond keeping a good table are in the minority, and that pioneering is always arduous work.

The first duty of a mistress is, of course, to be able to give intelligible orders to her servants; therefore it is necessary she should learn to speak Hindustani. . . .

The next duty is obviously to insist on her orders being carried out. And here we come to the burning question: "How is this to be done?" Certainly, there is at present very little to which we can appeal in the average Indian servant, but then, until it is implanted by training, there is very little sense of duty in a child; yet in some well-regulated nurseries obedience is a foregone conclusion. The secret lies in making rules, and *keeping to them*. The Indian servant is a child in everything save age, and should

be treated as a child; that is to say, kindly, but with the greatest firmness. The laws of the household should be those of the Medes and Persians, and first faults should never go unpunished. By overlooking a first offence, we lose the only opportunity we have of preventing it becoming a habit.

But it will be asked, How are we to punish our servants when we have no hold either on their minds or bodies? . . .

In their own experience the authors have found a system of rewards and punishments perfectly easy of attainment. One of them has for years adopted the plan of engaging her servants at so much a month—the lowest rate at which such servant is obtainable—and so much extra as *buksheesh* (buk-SHEESH) [a bonus], conditional on good service. For instance, a *khitmutgâr* (KID-muht-gahr) [male table servant] is engaged permanently on Rs. 9 a month, but the additional rupee which makes the wage up to that usually demanded by good servants is a fluctuating assessment! . . . That plan has never been objected to, and . . . the household quite en-

696

ters into the spirit of the idea, infinitely preferring it to volcanic eruptions of fault-finding. . . .

We do not wish to advocate an unholy haughtiness; but an Indian household can no more be governed peacefully, without dignity and prestige, than an Indian Empire. For instance, if the mistress wishes to teach the cook a new dish, let her give the order for everything, down to charcoal, to be ready at a given time, and the cook in attendance; and let her do nothing herself that the servants can do, if only for this reason, that the only way of teaching is to *see* things done, not to let others see *you* do them.

Questions for Analysis

1. What challenges does the British housekeeper face in India? How, according to Steel and Gardiner, should she meet them?

2. In what ways do the authors' comments and housekeeping policies reflect the attitudes of European imperialism?

Source: F. A. Steel and G. Gardiner, *The Complete Indian Housekeeper and Cook* (London: William Heinemann, 1902), chap. 1. Reprinted in L. DiCaprio and M. Wiesner, eds., *Lives and Voices: Sources in European Women's History* (Boston: Houghton Mifflin, 2001), pp. 323–328.

CHAPTER 27

The Great Break: War and Revolution

1914–1919

Chapter Preview

The First World War
What caused the Great War, and why did it have such revolutionary consequences?

The Home Front
What was the impact of total war on civilian populations?

The Russian Revolution
Why did World War I bring socialist revolution in Russia?

The Peace Settlement
How did the Allies fashion a peace settlement, and why was it unsuccessful?

INDIVIDUALS IN SOCIETY: Vera Brittain

LISTENING TO THE PAST: Arab Political Aspirations in 1919

French soldiers in the trenches man a machine gun, the weapon that killed so many, in this chilling work by Christopher Nevinson. (© Tate, London/Art Resource, NY)

I n the summer of 1914, the nations of Europe went willingly to war. They believed they had no other choice. Moreover, both peoples and governments confidently expected a short war leading to a decisive victory. Such a war, they believed, would "clear the air," and European society would be able to go on as before.

These expectations were almost totally mistaken. The First World War was long, indecisive, and tremendously destructive. To the shell-shocked generation of survivors, it was known simply as the Great War: the war of unprecedented scope and intensity. From today's perspective, it is clear that the First World War marked a great break in the course of modern Western history. World War I was a revolutionary conflict of gigantic proportions.

The First World War

What caused the Great War, and why did it have such revolutionary consequences?

The First World War was extremely long and destructive because it involved all the Great Powers and because it quickly degenerated into a senseless military stalemate. Like evenly matched boxers in a championship bout, the two sides tried to wear each other down. But there was no referee to call a draw, only the blind hammering of a life-or-death struggle.

The Bismarckian System of Alliances

In ten short years, from 1862 to 1871, Prussia-Germany had risen to become the most powerful nation in Europe, opening a new era in international relations. Yet, as Bismarck never tired of repeating after his victory over France in 1871, Germany was a "satisfied" power. Within Europe, Germany had no territorial ambitions and wanted only peace.

But how was peace to be preserved? Bismarck's first concern was to keep an embittered France from gaining military allies. His second concern was the threat to peace posed from the east, from Austria-Hungary and from Russia. Those two enormous multinational empires had many conflicting interests, particularly in southeastern Europe where the strength of the Ottoman Empire was ebbing fast. There was a real threat that Germany might be dragged into a great war between the two rival empires. Bismarck's solution was a system of alliances to restrain both Russia and Austria-Hungary, to prevent conflict between them, and to isolate France.

A first step was the creation in 1873 of the conservative **Three Emperors' League,** which linked the monarchs of Prussia-Germany, Austria-Hungary, and Russia in an alliance against radical movements. In 1877 and 1878, when Russia's victories in a war with the Ottoman Empire threatened the balance of Austrian and Russian interests in the Balkans and the balance of British and Russian interests in the entire Middle East, Bismarck played the role of sincere peacemaker. But his balancing efforts at the Congress of Berlin in 1878 infuriated Russian nationalists, and this led Bismarck to conclude a defensive military alliance with Austria against Russia in 1879. This alliance lasted until 1918 and the end of World War I. Motivated by tensions with France, Italy joined Germany and Austria in 1882, thereby forming what became known as the Triple Alliance.

Three Emperors' League A conservative alliance that linked the monarchs of Austria-Hungary, Germany, and Russia against radical movements.

Bismarck also maintained good relations with Britain, while encouraging France in Africa but keeping France isolated in Europe. While he was not able to maintain an alliance with Russia, he was able to substitute an agreement by which both states promised neutrality if the other was attacked. In sum, Bismarck's accomplishments in foreign policy after 1871 were great. For almost a generation, he maintained German leadership in international affairs, and he worked successfully for peace by managing conflicts and by restraining Austria-Hungary and Russia with defensive alliances.

The Rival Blocs

In 1890 the young, impetuous Emperor William II dismissed Bismarck, in part because of the chancellor's friendly policy toward Russia since the 1870s. William then adamantly refused to renew the neutrality agreement with Russia, prompting France to seize the chance to gain a powerful new ally. The alliance of France and Russia was to remain in effect as long as the Triple Alliance of Austria, Germany, and Italy existed. As a result, continental Europe was dangerously divided into two rival blocs.

Great Britain's foreign policy became increasingly crucial. Long content with "splendid isolation" and no permanent alliances, Britain after 1891 was the only uncommitted Great Power. Could Britain afford to remain isolated, or would it feel compelled to take sides? Many Germans and some Britons felt that a "natural alliance" of shared ancestry united the Germanic and Anglo-Saxon peoples. However, the generally good relations that had prevailed between Prussia and Great Britain ever since the mid-eighteenth century gave way to commercial and naval rivalries.

Above all, Germany's decision in 1900 to expand greatly its battle fleet posed a challenge to Britain's long-standing naval supremacy. This decision coincided with the hard-fought South African War (1899–1902) between the British and the tiny Dutch republics of southern Africa, a war of British imperialism that was widely denounced in the European press. Thus British leaders prudently set about shoring up their exposed position with alliances and agreements.

Britain improved its often-strained relations with the United States and in 1902 concluded a formal alliance with Japan. Britain then responded favorably to the advances of France's skillful foreign minister, Théophile Delcassé (tey-aw-FEEL del-ka-SEY), who wanted better relations with Britain and was willing to accept British rule in Egypt in return for British support of French plans to dominate Morocco. The resulting Anglo-French Entente of 1904 settled all outstanding colonial disputes between Britain and France.

Germany's leaders foolishly decided to test the strength of the entente by insisting in 1905 on an international conference on the whole Moroccan question. But Germany's crude bullying forced France and Britain closer together, and the conference left Germany empty-handed and isolated (except for Austria-Hungary).

The result of the Moroccan crisis was something of a diplomatic revolution. Britain, France, Russia, and even the United States began to see Germany as a potential threat, a would-be intimidator that might seek to dominate all Europe. At the same time, German leaders began to see sinister plots to "encircle" Germany and block its development as a world power.

Germany's decision to add a large, enormously expensive fleet of big-gun battleships to its already expanding navy also heightened tensions after 1907. Again the British saw it as a challenge to their power, and they resented having to invest in a competing fleet. Unscrupulous journalists and special-interest groups in both countries also fanned hostilities with talk of economic warfare between the trade giants. In 1909 the mass-circulation London *Daily Mail* hysterically informed its readers that "Germany is deliberately preparing to destroy the British Empire."[1] By then Britain was psychologically, if not officially, in the Franco-Russian camp.

The Outbreak of War

In the early years of the twentieth century, nationalism was destroying the Ottoman Empire in Europe and threatening to break up the Austro-Hungarian Empire. War in the Balkans seemed inevitable.

In 1875 widespread nationalist rebellion resulted in the partial division of Ottoman Turkish possessions in Europe. Serbia and Romania won independence, and a part of Bulgaria won local autonomy, but Austria-Hungary obtained the right to "occupy and administer" Bosnia and Herzegovina (her-tsuh-goh-VEE-nuh), and the Ottoman Empire retained important Balkan holdings (see Map 27.1).

By 1903, however, nationalism in southeastern Europe was on the rise once again. Serbia led the way, hoping to expand its territories at the expense of Austria-Hungary and the Ottoman Empire. The Serbs looked to

CHRONOLOGY

1912	First Balkan War
1914	Assassination of Archduke Francis Ferdinand
1914–1918	World War I
1915	Italy and Bulgaria enter World War I
1916	German males between seventeen and sixty required to work only for war effort; Rasputin murdered
1916–1918	Growth of antiwar movement throughout Europe
1917	Russian Revolution
1918–1920	Great Civil War in Russia
1919	Treaty of Versailles

German Warships Under Full Steam

As these impressive ships engaged in battle exercises in 1907 suggest, Germany did succeed in building a large modern navy. But Britain was equally determined to maintain its naval superiority, and the spiraling arms race helped poison relations between the two countries. (Bibliothèque des Arts Décoratifs/Archives Charmet/The Bridgeman Art Library)

MAP 27.1   The Balkans After the Congress of Berlin, 1878

The Ottoman Empire suffered large territorial losses but remained a power in the Balkans.

MAP 27.2   The Balkans in 1914

Ethnic boundaries did not follow political boundaries, and Serbian national aspirations threatened Austria-Hungary.

Slavic Russia for support of their national aspirations. To block Serbian expansion and to take advantage of Russia's weakness after the revolution of 1905, Austria in 1908 formally annexed Bosnia and Herzegovina, with their large Serbian, Croatian, and Muslim populations. The kingdom of Serbia erupted in rage but could do nothing without Russian support.

Then, in 1912, in the First Balkan War, Serbia joined Greece and Bulgaria to attack the Ottoman Empire and then quarreled with Bulgaria over the spoils of victory—a dispute that led in 1913 to the Second Balkan War. Austria intervened in 1913 and forced Serbia to give up Albania. After centuries, nationalism had finally destroyed the Ottoman Empire in Europe (see Map 27.2). This sudden but long-awaited event elated the Balkan nationalists and dismayed the leaders of multinational Austria-Hungary. The former hoped and the latter feared that Austria might be broken apart next.

Within this tense context, Archduke Francis Ferdinand, heir to the Austrian and Hungarian thrones, and his wife, Sophie, were assassinated by Serbian revolutionaries living in Bosnia on June 28, 1914, during a state visit to the Bosnian capital of Sarajevo (sar-uh-YEY-voh). After some hesitation, the leaders of Austria-Hungary concluded that Serbia was implicated and had to be severely punished once and for all. On July 23 Austria-Hungary presented Serbia with an unconditional ultimatum. The Serbian government had forty-eight hours in which to agree to demands that would amount to ceding control of the Serbian state. When Serbia replied moderately but evasively, Austria began to mobilize and then declared war on Serbia on July 28. Thus a desperate multinational Austria-Hungary deliberately chose war in a last-ditch attempt to stem the rising tide of hostile nationalism within its borders. The Third Balkan War had begun.

Of prime importance in Austria-Hungary's fateful decision was Germany's unconditional support. Germany's leaders realized that a resurgent Russia (and therefore France) would probably enter the war in support of Serbia, but they hoped that Great Britain would remain neutral.

In fact, the diplomatic situation was already out of control. Military plans and timetables began to dictate policy. Russia, a vast country, would require much longer to mobilize its armies than Germany and Austria-Hungary. All the complicated mobilization plans of the Russian general staff had assumed a war with both Austria and Germany: Russia could not mobilize against Austria-Hungary alone. Therefore, on July 29 Tsar Nicholas II ordered full mobilization and in effect declared general war.

The German general staff had also assumed a two-front war, and following its plans meant striking France as well as Russia. France was to be knocked out first with a lightning attack through neutral Belgium before turning on Russia. So on August 3 German armies attacked Belgium, whose neutrality had been solemnly guaranteed in 1839 by all the great states including Prussia. In the face of this act of aggression, Great Britain joined the **Triple Entente** (on-TONT) with France and Russia and declared war on Germany the following day. The First World War had begun.

"Never Forget!"

This 1915 French poster with its passionate headline dramatizes Germany's brutal invasion of Belgium in 1914. Neutral Belgium is personified as a traumatized mother, assaulted and ravished by savage outlaws. The "rape of Belgium" featured prominently—and effectively—in anti-German propaganda. (Mary Evans Picture Library)

Triple Entente The alliance of Great Britain, France, and Russia in the First World War.

Stalemate and Slaughter

When the Germans invaded Belgium in August 1914, everyone believed that their side would secure a swift victory: "The boys will be home by Christmas." But German forces had been slowed by Belgian and British troops near the Franco-Belgian border, and by the end of August they were still making their way to Paris.

On September 6 the French attacked a gap in the German line at the Battle of the Marne. For three days, France threw everything into the attack. At one point, the French government desperately requisitioned all the taxis of Paris to rush reserves to the troops at the front. Finally, the Germans fell back. Paris and France had been saved (see Map 27.3 on page 706).

Soon, with the armies stalled, both sides began to dig trenches to protect themselves from machine-gun fire. By November 1914, an unbroken line of trenches extended from the Belgian ports through northern France, past the fortress of Verdun, and on to the Swiss frontier. Stalemate and slaughter followed. The defenders on both sides dug in behind rows of trenches, mines, and barbed wire. For days and even weeks, ceaseless shelling by heavy artillery supposedly "softened up" the enemy in a given area (and also signaled the coming attack). Then young draftees

The Tragic Absurdity of Trench Warfare
Soldiers charge across a scarred battlefield and overrun an enemy trench. The dead defender on the right will fire no more. But this is only another futile charge that will yield much blood and little land. A whole generation is being decimated by the slaughter. (By courtesy of the Trustees of the Imperial War Museum)

trench warfare A type of fighting behind rows of trenches, mines, and barbed wire; the cost in lives was staggering and the gains in territory minimal.

and their junior officers went "over the top" of the trenches in frontal attacks on the enemy's line.

The cost in lives of this **trench warfare** was staggering, the gains in territory minuscule. The massive French and British offensives during 1915 never gained more than 3 miles of blood-soaked earth from the enemy. In the Battle of the Somme in the summer of 1916, the British and French gained an insignificant 125 square miles at the cost of 600,000 dead or wounded, while the Germans lost 500,000 men. In that same year the unsuccessful German campaign against Verdun cost 700,000 lives on both sides. British poet Siegfried Sassoon (1886–1967) wrote of the Somme offensive, "I am staring at a sunlit picture of Hell."

The year 1917 was equally terrible. The hero of Erich Remarque's (ri-MAHRK) great novel *All Quiet on the Western Front* (1929) describes one attack:

> We see men living with their skulls blown open; we see soldiers run with their two feet cut off. . . . Still the little piece of convulsed earth in which we lie is held. We have yielded no more than a few hundred yards of it as a prize to the enemy. But on every yard there lies a dead man.

Such was war on the western front.

Trench warfare shattered an entire generation of young men. Millions who could have provided political creativity and leadership after the war were forever missing. Moreover, those who lived through the slaughter were maimed, shell-shocked, embittered, and profoundly disillusioned. The young soldiers went to war believing in the world of their leaders and elders—the pre-1914 world of order, progress, and patriotism. Then, in Remarque's words, the "first bombardment showed us our mistake, and under it the world as they had taught it to us broke in pieces."

The Widening War

On the eastern front, soldiers were spared trench warfare but the costs were equally high. The "Russian steamroller" immediately moved into eastern Germany but was badly damaged at the Battles of Tannenberg and the Masurian (mah-ZOOR-ee-an) Lakes in August and September 1914. Thereafter, Russia never threatened Germany again. On the Austrian front, armies seesawed back and forth, suffering enormous losses. Austro-Hungarian armies were repulsed twice by Serbia in bitter fighting. The Russians advanced on Austria's northwestern border in 1914, but Austro-Hungarian and German armies forced the Russians to retreat deep into their own territory in the eastern campaign of 1915. A staggering 2.5 million Russians were killed, wounded, or taken prisoner that year.

The war widened as previously neutral countries joined the fighting (see Map 27.3). Italy, once allied with Austria and Germany, joined the Triple Entente of Great Britain, France, and Russia in return for promises of Austrian territory. In October 1914 the Ottoman Empire joined with Austria and Germany, by then known as the Central Powers. The following September Bulgaria decided to follow the Ottoman Empire's lead in order to settle old scores with Serbia. The Balkans, with the exception of Greece, came to be occupied by the Central Powers. The entry of the Ottoman Turks carried the war into the Middle East. Heavy fighting between the Ottomans and the Russians saw battle lines seesawing back and forth and enveloping the Armenians, who lived on both sides of the border and had experienced brutal repression by the Turks in 1909. When in 1915 some Armenians welcomed Russian armies as liberators, the Ottoman government ordered a genocidal mass deportation of its Armenian citizens from their homeland. A million Armenians died from murder, starvation, and disease during World War I. In 1915 British forces tried to take the Dardanelles (dahr-den-ELZ) and Constantinople from the Ottomans but were badly defeated.

The British were more successful at inciting the Arabs to revolt against the Ottoman Turks. They bargained with the foremost Arab leader, Hussein ibn-Ali (hoo-SEYN IB-uhn ah-LEE) (1856–1931), who managed in 1915 to win vague British commitments for an independent Arab kingdom. Thus in 1916 Hussein revolted against the Turks, proclaiming himself king of the Arabs. He joined forces with the British under T. E. Lawrence, who in 1917 led Arab tribesmen and Indian soldiers in a highly successful guerrilla war against the Turks on the Arabian peninsula.

Similar victories were eventually scored in the Ottoman province of Iraq. Britain occupied the southern Iraqi city of Basra in 1914 and captured Baghdad (BAG-dad) in 1917. In September 1918 British armies and their Arab allies rolled into Syria. This offensive culminated in the triumphal entry of Hussein's son Faisal (FIE-suhl) into Damascus. Throughout Syria and Iraq there was wild Arab rejoicing. Many patriots expected a large, unified Arab nation-state to rise from the dust of the Ottoman collapse.

MAP 27.3   The First World War in Europe

Trench warfare on the western front was concentrated in Belgium and northern France, while the war in the east encompassed an enormous territory.

The Armenian Atrocities

When in 1915 some Armenians welcomed Russian armies as liberators after years of persecution, the Ottoman government ordered a genocidal mass deportation of its Armenian citizens from their homeland in the empire's eastern provinces. This photo, taken in Kharpert in 1915 by a German businessman from his hotel window, shows Turkish guards marching Armenian men off to a prison, where they will be tortured to death. A million Armenians died from murder, starvation, and disease during World War I. (Courtesy of the Armenian Library and Museum of America [ALMA], Watertown, MA)

As world war engulfed and revolutionized the Middle East, it also spread to some parts of East Asia and Africa. Instead of revolting as the Germans hoped, the colonial subjects of the British and French generally supported their foreign masters, providing crucial supplies and fighting in Europe and the Ottoman Empire. They also helped local British and French commanders seize Germany's colonies around the globe.

The Japanese, allied in Asia with the British since 1902, similarly used the war to grab German outposts in the Pacific Ocean and on the Chinese mainland, infuriating Chinese patriots and heightening long-standing tensions between China and Japan. More than a million Africans and Asians served in the various armies of the warring powers; more than double that number served as porters to carry equipment. The French, facing a shortage of young men, made especially heavy use of colonial troops.

In April 1917 the United States declared war on Germany, another crucial development in the expanding conflict. American intervention grew out of the war at sea, sympathy for the Triple Entente, and the increasing desperation of total war. At the beginning of the war, Britain and France had established a total naval blockade to strangle the Central Powers. No neutral ship was permitted to sail to

Lusitania The British passenger liner sunk by a German submarine that claimed 1,000 lives.

Section Review

- German chancellor Bismarck maintained peace in Europe by managing a balance-of-power system with the other European powers, forming first the Three Emperors' League with Austria-Hungary and Russia, and then the Triple Alliance with Italy and Austria.

- German emperor William II dismissed Bismarck, refused to renew neutrality with Russia, and, after arguing with France and Britain over Morocco, isolated himself and Austria-Hungary while Britain, formerly neutral, found itself siding with France and Russia.

- Nationalist problems in eastern Europe caused the decline of the Ottoman Empire and Serbian revolutionaries assassinated the heir to the Austrian throne, causing Austria to declare war on Serbia; confusion over military mobilization plans led Russia to declare general war, Germany overran Belgium to attack France, and Great Britain joined France and Russia to form the Triple Entente.

- The German offensive to take Paris ended as a stalemate with the Germans facing the French and British in horrific trench warfare that led to huge losses on both sides for little ground gained, resulting in disillusioned, maimed, and bitter soldiers.

- The war widened to include Italy with the Triple Entente and the Ottomans with the Central Powers, which opened fighting in the Middle East; the colonies generally supported their masters, Japan allied with the British, and finally the United States joined the Triple Entente in response to German submarine warfare.

total war In each country during the First World War, a government of national unity that began to plan and control economic and social life in order to make the greatest possible military effort.

Germany with any cargo. In early 1915 Germany retaliated with a counter-blockade using the murderously effective submarine, a new weapon that violated traditional niceties of fair warning under international law. In May 1915 a German submarine sank the British passenger liner *Lusitania,* claiming more than 1,000 lives, among them 139 Americans. President Woodrow Wilson protested vigorously. Germany was forced to relax its submarine warfare for almost two years; the alternative was almost certain war with the United States.

Early in 1917, the German military command—confident that improved submarines could starve Britain into submission before the United States could come to its rescue—resumed unrestricted submarine warfare. Like the invasion of Belgium, this was a reckless gamble. "German submarine warfare against commerce," President Wilson had told a sympathetic Congress and people, "is a warfare against mankind." Thus the last uncommitted great nation, as fresh and enthusiastic as Europe had been in 1914, entered the world war in April 1917, almost three years after it began. Eventually the United States was to tip the balance in favor of the Triple Entente and its allies.

The Home Front

What was the impact of total war on civilian populations?

Before looking at the last year of the Great War, let us turn our attention to the people on the home front. They were tremendously involved in the titanic struggle. War's impact on them was no less massive than on the men crouched in the trenches.

Mobilizing for Total War

In August 1914, most people greeted the outbreak of hostilities enthusiastically. In every country, the masses believed that their nation was in the right and defending itself from aggression. With the exception of a few extreme left-wingers, even socialists supported the war. Everywhere the support of the masses and working class contributed to national unity and an energetic war effort.

By mid-October generals and politicians had begun to realize that more than patriotism would be needed to win the war, whose end was not in sight. In each country, a government of national unity began to plan and control economic and social life in order to wage **total war.** Free-market capitalism was abandoned, at least "for the duration." Instead, government planning boards established priorities and decided what was to be produced and consumed.

Rationing, price and wage controls, and even restrictions on workers' freedom of movement were imposed by government. Only through such regimentation could a country make the greatest possible military effort. Thus, though there were national variations, the great nations all moved toward planned economies commanded by the established political leadership. However awful the war was, the ability of governments to manage and control highly complicated economies strengthened the cause of socialism. With the First World War, state socialism became for the first time a realistic economic blueprint rather than a utopian program.

The social impact of total war was no less profound than the economic impact, though again there were important national variations. The millions of men at the front and the insatiable needs of the military created a tremendous demand for

Waging Total War

A British war plant strains to meet the insatiable demand for trench-smashing heavy artillery shells. Quite typically, many of these defense workers are women. (By courtesy of the Trustees of the Imperial War Museum, neg. #Q30011)

workers. Jobs were available for everyone. This situation—seldom, if ever, seen before 1914—brought about momentous changes.

One such change was greater power and prestige for labor unions. Having proved their loyalty in August 1914, labor unions cooperated with war governments on work rules, wages, and production schedules in return for real participation in important decisions. This entry of labor leaders and unions into policymaking councils paralleled the entry of socialist leaders into the war governments.

The role of women changed dramatically. In every country, large numbers of women left home and domestic service to work in industry, transportation, and offices. Moreover, women became highly visible—not only as munitions workers but as bank tellers, mail carriers, even police officers. Women also served as nurses and doctors at the front. (See the feature "Individuals in Society: Vera Brittain.") In general, the war greatly expanded the range of women's activities and changed attitudes toward women. As a direct result of women's many-sided war effort, Britain, Germany, and Austria granted women the right to vote immediately after the war. Women also showed a growing spirit of independence during the war, as they started to bob their hair, shorten their skirts, and smoke in public.

War promoted greater social equality, blurring class distinctions and lessening the gap between rich and poor. This blurring was most apparent in Great Britain, where wartime hardship was never extreme. In fact, the bottom third of the population generally lived *better* than they ever had, for the poorest gained most from the severe shortage of labor. In continental countries, greater equality was reflected in full employment, rationing according to physical needs, and a sharing of hardships. There, too, society became more uniform and more egalitarian, in spite of some war profiteering.

Individuals in Society

Vera Brittain

Although the Great War upended millions of lives, it struck Europe's young people with the greatest force. For Vera Brittain (1893–1970), as for so many in her generation, the war became life's defining experience, which she captured forever in her famous autobiography, *Testament of Youth* (1933).

Brittain grew up in a wealthy business family in northern England, bristling at small-town conventions and discrimination against women. Very close to her brother Edward, two years her junior, Brittain read voraciously and dreamed of being a successful writer. Finishing boarding school and beating down her father's objections, she prepared for Oxford's rigorous entry exams and won a scholarship to its women's college. Brittain also fell in love with Roland Leighton (**LEYT-un**), an equally brilliant student from a literary family and her brother's best friend. All three, along with two more close friends, Victor Richardson and Geoffrey Thurlow, confidently prepared to enter Oxford in late 1914.

Vera Brittain, marked forever by her wartime experiences. (Vera Brittain Archive, William Ready Division of Archives and Research Collections, McMaster University Library)

When war suddenly approached in July 1914, Brittain shared with millions of Europeans a thrilling surge of patriotic support for her government, a pro-war enthusiasm she later played down in her published writings. She wrote in her diary that her "great fear" was that England would declare its neutrality and commit the "grossest treachery" toward France.* She seconded Roland's decision to enlist, agreeing with her sweetheart's glamorous view of war as "very ennobling and very beautiful." Later, exchanging anxious letters in 1915 with Roland in France, Vera began to see the conflict in personal, human terms. She wondered if any victory or defeat could be worth Roland's life.

Struggling to quell her doubts, Brittain redoubled her commitment to England's cause and volunteered as an army nurse. For the next three years she served with distinction in military hospitals in London, Malta, and northern France, repeatedly torn between the vision of noble sacrifice and the reality of human tragedy. She lost her sexual inhibitions caring for mangled male bodies, and she longed to consummate her love with Roland. Awaiting his return on leave on Christmas Day in 1915, she was greeted instead with a telegram: Roland had been killed two days before.

Roland's death was the first of the devastating blows that eventually overwhelmed Brittain's idealistic patriotism. In 1917, first Geoffrey and then Victor died from gruesome wounds. In early 1918, as the last great German offensive covered the floors of her war-zone hospital with maimed and dying German prisoners, the bone-weary Vera felt a common humanity and saw only more victims. A few weeks later brother Edward—her last hope—died in action. When the war ended, she was, she said, a "complete automaton," with "my deepest emotions paralyzed if not dead."

Returning to Oxford and finishing her studies, Brittain gradually recovered. She formed a deep, restorative friendship with another talented woman writer, Winifred Holtby, published novels and articles, and became a leader in the feminist campaign for gender equality. She also married and had children. But her wartime memories were always there. Finally, Brittain succeeded in coming to grips with them in *Testament of Youth*, her powerful antiwar autobiography. The unflinching narrative spoke to the experiences of an entire generation and became a runaway bestseller. Above all, perhaps, Brittain captured the ambivalent, contradictory character of the war, when millions of young people found excitement, courage, and common purpose but succeeded only in destroying their lives with their superhuman efforts and futile sacrifices. Becoming ever more committed to pacifism, Brittain opposed England's entry into World War II.

Questions for Analysis

1. What were Brittain's initial feelings toward the war? How did they change as the conflict continued? Why did they change?

2. Why did Brittain volunteer as a nurse, as many women did? Judging from her account, how might wartime nursing have influenced women of her generation?

3. In portraying the ambivalent, contradictory character of World War I for Europe's youth, was Brittain describing the character of all modern warfare?

*Quoted in the excellent study by P. Berry and M. Bostridge, *Vera Brittain: A Life* (London: Virago Press, 2001), p. 59; additional quotes are from pp. 80 and 136. This work is highly recommended.

Growing Political Tensions

During the first two years of war, most soldiers and civilians supported their governments. Belief in a just cause, patriotic nationalism, the planned economy, and a sharing of burdens united peoples behind their various national leaders.

Each government employed rigorous censorship to control public opinion, and each used both crude and subtle propaganda to maintain popular support. German propaganda hysterically pictured black soldiers from France's African empire raping German women, while German atrocities in Belgium and elsewhere were ceaselessly recounted and exaggerated by the French and British. Patriotic posters and slogans, slanted news, and biased editorials inflamed national hatreds and helped sustain superhuman efforts. However, by the spring of 1916, people were beginning to crack under the strain of total war. Strikes and protest marches over inadequate food began to flare up on every home front.

Soldiers' morale also began to decline. Italian troops mutinied. Numerous French units refused to fight after the disastrous French offensive of May 1917. Only tough military justice for leaders and a tacit agreement with the troops that there would be no more grand offensives enabled the new general in chief, Henri Philippe Pétain (pey-TAN), to restore order. A rising tide of war-weariness and defeatism also swept France's civilian population before Georges Clemenceau (zhorzh cluh-mon-SO) emerged as a ruthless and effective wartime leader in November 1917. Clemenceau (1841–1929) established a virtual dictatorship, pouncing on strikers and jailing without trial journalists and politicians who dared to suggest a compromise peace with Germany.

The strains were worse for the Central Powers. In October 1916, the chief minister of Austria was assassinated by a young socialist crying, "Down with Absolutism! We want peace!"[2] The following month, when feeble old Emperor Francis Joseph died, a symbol of unity disappeared. In spite of absolute censorship, political dissatisfaction and conflicts among nationalities grew. In April 1917, Austria's chief minister summed up the situation in the gloomiest possible terms. The country and army were exhausted. Another winter of war would bring revolution and disintegration. Both Czech and Yugoslav leaders demanded autonomous democratic states for their peoples. The British blockade kept tightening; people were starving.

The strain of total war was also evident in Germany. In the winter of 1916 to 1917, Germany's military position appeared increasingly desperate. The social conflict of prewar Germany re-emerged, and revolutionary agitation and strikes by war-weary workers occurred in early 1917. Thus militaristic Germany, like its ally Austria-Hungary (and its enemy France), was beginning to crack in 1917. Yet it was Russia that collapsed first and saved the Central Powers—for a time.

Section Review

- Almost all governments fostered national unity by implementing "total war" using temporary socialist measures, rationing, and price and wage controls.

- Wartime conditions improved worker conditions, strengthened women's roles in the labor market, and promoted greater social equality, strengthening the cause of socialism.

- Popular support for the war remained strong during the first years through propaganda, media censorship, and patriotism, but as the war dragged on, inadequate food inflamed public sentiment, and strikes and protests began.

- The war fronts on all sides began to decline as well, with soldiers exhausted and morale low; people were starving and social conflict became evident in Italy, France, Germany, Austria-Hungary, and in Russia, which collapsed first.

The Russian Revolution

Why did World War I bring socialist revolution in Russia?

The Russian Revolution of 1917 was one of modern history's most momentous events. Directly related to the growing tensions of World War I, it had a significance far beyond the wartime agonies of a single European nation. The Russian Revolution opened a new era. For some, it was Marx's socialist vision come true; for others, it was the triumph of dictatorship. To all, it presented a radically new prototype of state and society.

The Fall of Imperial Russia

Like its allies and its enemies, Russia embraced war with patriotic enthusiasm in 1914. Crowds rallied around Tsar Nicholas II (r. 1894–1917) as he took an oath never to make peace as long as the enemy stood on Russian soil. Conservatives anticipated expansion in the Balkans, while liberals and most socialists believed alliance with Britain and France would bring democratic reforms. For a moment, Russia was united.

The Russian war machine was underprepared, however, and mobilized less effectively for total war than the other warring nations. Its supplies of shells and ammunition were quickly depleted, and substantial numbers of soldiers were expected to find the rifles they needed on the battlefield among the dead. There were 2 million Russian casualties in 1915 alone.

The great problem was leadership. A kindly, slightly stupid man, Nicholas failed to form a close partnership with his citizens in order to fight the war more effectively. He came to rely instead on the old bureaucratic apparatus, distrusting the moderate Duma (the parliament), rejecting popular involvement, and resisting calls to share power.

As a result, the Duma, the educated middle classes, and the masses became increasingly critical of the tsar's leadership. In September 1915 parties ranging from conservative to moderate socialist formed the Progressive bloc, which called for a completely new government responsible to the Duma instead of the tsar. In answer, Nicholas temporarily adjourned the Duma and announced that he was traveling to the front in order to lead and rally Russia's armies.

His departure was a fatal turning point. With the tsar in the field with the troops, control of the government fell to the empress, Tsarina Alexandra. Nicholas's wife was a strong-willed woman with a hatred of parliaments. Having constantly urged her husband to rule absolutely, Alexandra tried to do so herself in his absence. She seated and unseated the top ministers. Her most trusted adviser was "our Friend Grigori," an uneducated Siberian preacher who was appropriately nicknamed "Rasputin" (ra-SPYOO-tin)—the "Degenerate." Rasputin's extraordinary influence rested on his seeming ability to stop the bleeding of Alexis, Alexandra's fifth child and heir to the throne, who suffered from the rare blood disease hemophilia.

In a desperate attempt to right the situation and end unfounded rumors that Rasputin was the empress's lover, three members of the high aristocracy murdered Rasputin in December 1916. The empress went into semipermanent shock. Food shortages in the cities worsened; morale declined. On March 8, women calling for bread in Petrograd (formerly St. Petersburg) started riots, which spontaneously spread to the factories and then elsewhere throughout the city. From the front, the tsar ordered troops to restore order, but discipline broke down, and the soldiers joined the revolutionary crowd. The Duma responded by declaring a provisional government on March 12, 1917. Three days later, Nicholas abdicated.

The Provisional Government

The March revolution was the result of an unplanned uprising of hungry, angry people in the capital, but it was joyfully accepted throughout the country. Patriots rejoiced at the prospect of a more determined and effective war effort, while workers happily anticipated better wages and more food. All classes and political parties called for liberty and democracy. They were not disappointed. After generations of arbitrary authoritarianism, the provisional government quickly established equality before the law; freedom of religion, speech, and assembly; the right of unions to organize and strike; and the rest of the classic liberal program.

The reorganized government formed in May 1917 made the patriotic socialist Alexander Kerensky (kuh-REN-skee) its prime minister in July. For Kerensky and other moderate socialists, the continuation of war was still the all-important national duty. Human suffering and war-weariness grew, sapping the limited strength of the provisional government.

From its first day, the provisional government had to share power with a formidable rival—the **Petrograd Soviet** (or council) of Workers' and Soldiers' Deputies. Modeled on the revolutionary soviets of 1905, the Petrograd Soviet was a huge, fluctuating mass meeting of two thousand to three thousand workers, soldiers, and socialist intellectuals. Seeing itself as a true grassroots revolutionary democracy, this counter- or half-government suspiciously watched the provisional government and issued its own radical orders, further weakening the provisional government. Its **Army Order No. 1** stripped officers of their authority and placed power in the hands of elected committees of common soldiers. Designed primarily to protect the revolution from some counter-revolutionary Bonaparte on horseback, the order instead led to a total collapse of army discipline.

Meanwhile, masses of peasant soldiers began "voting with their feet," to use Lenin's graphic phrase. That is, they began returning to their villages to help their families get a share of the land, which peasants were simply seizing as they settled old scores in a great agrarian upheaval. All across the country, liberty was turning into anarchy in the summer of 1917. It was an unparalleled opportunity for the most radical and most talented of Russia's many socialist leaders, Vladimir Ilyich Lenin (VLAD-uh-meer IL-yich LEN-in) (1870–1924).

Petrograd Soviet A huge, fluctuating mass meeting of 2,000 to 3,000 workers, soldiers, and socialist intellectuals, modeled on the revolutionary soviets of 1905.

Army Order No. 1 A radical order of the Petrograd Soviet that stripped officers of their authority and placed power in the hands of elected committees of common soldiers.

Lenin and the Bolshevik Revolution

From his youth, Lenin's whole life had been dedicated to the cause of revolution. Born into the middle class, Lenin became an implacable enemy of imperial Russia when his older brother was executed for plotting to kill the tsar in 1887. Exiled to Siberia for three years for his own revolutionary activity, Lenin continued the intense study of Marxian doctrines that he had begun as a law student. After his release, he joined fellow socialists in western Europe and developed his own revolutionary interpretations of the body of Marxian thought.

Three interrelated ideas were central for Lenin. First, he stressed that capitalism could be destroyed only by violent revolution and denounced all revisionist theories of a peaceful evolution to socialism. Lenin's second, more original, idea was that a socialist revolution was possible even in non-industrial countries like Russia if an underclass was exploited. Lenin also believed that at a given moment revolution was determined more by human leadership than by vast historical laws. Thus was born his third basic idea: the necessity of a highly disciplined workers' party, strictly controlled by a dedicated elite of intellectuals and full-time revolutionaries like Lenin himself. An opposing camp of Russian Marxists wanted a more democratic party with mass membership. Lenin's camp was called the **Bolsheviks** (BOHL-shuh-viks), or "majority group." While his majority did not hold, he kept the fine-sounding name and developed the party he wanted: tough, disciplined, revolutionary.

Unlike most other socialists, Lenin did not rally round the national flag in 1914. Observing events from neutral Switzerland, he saw the war as a product of imperialistic rivalries and as a marvelous opportunity for class war and socialist upheaval. Hoping that Lenin would undermine the Russian war effort, the German government provided him with safe passage across Germany and back into Russia after the March revolution.

Bolsheviks Meaning "majority group," the name for Lenin's camp of the Russian party of Marxian socialism.

Arriving triumphantly in Petrograd on April 3, Lenin attacked at once. He had no intentions to cooperate with the "bourgeois" provisional government, instead declaring a radical program: "All power to the soviets"; "All land to the peasants"; "Stop the war now." But an attempt by the Bolsheviks to seize power in July collapsed, and Lenin fled and went into hiding. He was charged with being a German agent, and indeed he and the Bolsheviks were getting money from Germany.[3] But no matter. Intrigue between Kerensky and his commander in chief, General Lavr Kornilov, resulted in Kornilov's leading a feeble attack against the provisional government in September. In the face of this rightist "counter-revolutionary" threat, the Bolsheviks were rearmed and redeemed. Kornilov's forces disintegrated, but Kerensky lost all credit with the army, the only force that might have saved him and democratic government in Russia.

Trotsky and the Seizure of Power

By October the Bolsheviks had gained a fragile majority in the Petrograd Soviet by appealing very effectively to its workers and soldiers. It was now Lenin's supporter Leon Trotsky (TROT-skee) (1879–1940), a spellbinding revolutionary orator and independent radical Marxist, who brilliantly executed the Bolshevik seizure of power.

Trotsky convinced the Petrograd Soviet that it was at risk and needed to make him the leader of a special military-revolutionary committee. Then, on the night of November 6, militants from Trotsky's committee joined with trusty Bolshevik soldiers to seize government buildings and pounce on members of the provisional government. Then they went on to the congress of soviets. There a Bolshevik majority declared that all power had passed to the soviets and named Lenin head of the new government.

The Bolsheviks came to power for three key reasons. First, by late 1917 democracy had given way to anarchy: power was there for those who would take it. Second, in Lenin and Trotsky the Bolsheviks had an utterly determined and truly superior leadership, which both the tsarist government and the provisional government lacked. Third, in 1917 the Bolsheviks succeeded in appealing to many soldiers and urban workers, people who were exhausted by war and eager for socialism. With time, many workers would become bitterly disappointed, but for the moment they had good reason to believe that they had won what they wanted.

Dictatorship and Civil War

History is full of short-lived coups and unsuccessful revolutions. The truly monumental accomplishment of Lenin, Trotsky, and the rest of the Bolsheviks was not taking power but keeping it. In the next four years, the Bolsheviks went on to conquer the chaos they had helped create, and they began to build their kind of dictatorial socialist society. The conspirators became conquerors. How was this done?

Lenin had the genius to profit from developments over which he and the Bolsheviks had no control. Thus Lenin's first law, which supposedly gave land to the peasants, actually merely approved what peasants were already doing. Urban workers' great demand in November was direct control of individual factories by local workers' committees. This, too, Lenin ratified with a decree in November.

Lenin also acknowledged that Russia had lost the war with Germany and that the only realistic goal was peace. He was able to convince the majority of the Central Committee to accept Germany's demand that the Soviet government give up all its western territories. Poles, Finns, Lithuanians, and other non-Russians inhabited these areas—lands that had been conquered by the tsars over three centuries. With the Treaty of Brest-Litovsk (brest lih-TOFSK) in March 1918, Lenin had escaped the certain disaster of continued war and could pursue his goal of absolute political power for the Bolsheviks—now renamed Communists—within Russia.

In November 1917, the Bolsheviks had promised that a freely elected **Constituent Assembly** would draw up a new constitution. But free elections produced a stunning setback for the Bolsheviks, and Bolshevik soldiers acting under Lenin's orders permanently disbanded the Assembly after its first day. Thus even before the peace with Germany, Lenin was forming a one-party government.

The destruction of the democratically elected Constituent Assembly helped feed the flames of civil war. The officers of the old army took the lead in organizing the so-called White opposition to the Bolsheviks in southern Russia, Ukraine, Siberia, and west of Petrograd. The Whites came from many social groups and were united only by their hatred of the Bolsheviks—the Reds.

By the summer of 1918, fully eighteen self-proclaimed regional governments—several of which represented minority nationalities—were competing with Lenin's Bolsheviks in Moscow. By the end of the year, White armies were on the attack. In October 1919, it appeared they might triumph, as they closed in on Lenin's government from three sides. Yet they did not. By the spring of 1920, the White armies had been almost completely defeated, and the Bolshevik Red Army had retaken Belorussia and Ukraine. The following year, the Communists also reconquered the independent nationalist governments of the Caucasus. The civil war was over; Lenin had won.

Lenin Rallies Worker and Soldier Delegates
At a midnight meeting of the Petrograd Soviet, the Bolsheviks rise up and seize power on November 6, 1917. This painting from the 1940s idealizes Lenin, but his great talents as a revolutionary leader are undeniable. In this re-creation Stalin, who actually played only a small role in the uprising, is standing behind Lenin, already his trusty right-hand man. (Sovfoto)

Lenin and the Bolsheviks won for several reasons. Strategically, they controlled the center, while the Whites were always on the fringes and disunited. Moreover, the poorly defined political program of the Whites was vaguely conservative, and it did not unite all the foes of the Bolsheviks under a progressive, democratic banner. Most important, the divided Whites were no match for Trotsky's Red Army. Manned through a draft and severely disciplined by former tsarist officers, the Red Army was a superior fighting force. Through **war communism,** resources were marshaled from civilians to keep the army supplied. Civil opposition to the Bolsheviks was silenced by the **Cheka** (CHE-kah), a new incarnation of the tsarist secret police.

Together, the Russian Revolution and the Bolshevik triumph were one of the reasons the First World War was such a great turning point in modern history. A radically new government, based on socialism and one-party dictatorship, came to power in a great European state, maintained power, and eagerly encouraged worldwide revolution. Although halfhearted constitutional monarchy in Russia was undoubtedly headed for some kind of political crisis before 1914, it is hard to

Constituent Assembly A freely elected assembly promised by the Bolsheviks, but permanently disbanded within one day under Lenin's orders after the Bolsheviks won less than one-fourth of the elected delegates.

war communism The application of the total war concept to a civil conflict, the Bolsheviks seized grain from peasants, introduced rationing, nationalized all banks and industry, and required everyone to work.

Cheka The re-established tsarist secret police, which hunted down and executed thousands of real or suspected foes, sowing fear and silencing opposition.

imagine the triumph of the most radical proponents of change and reform except in a situation of total collapse. That was precisely what happened to Russia in the First World War.

The Peace Settlement

How did the Allies fashion a peace settlement, and why was it unsuccessful?

In the spring of 1918, the combined forces of the United States, Great Britain, and France decisively defeated Germany. The guns of world war finally fell silent. Then as civil war spread in Russia and as chaos engulfed much of eastern Europe, the victorious Western Allies came together in Paris to establish a lasting peace.

Expectations were high; optimism was almost unlimited. Nevertheless, the hopes of peoples and politicians were soon disappointed, for the peace settlement of 1919 turned out to be a failure. Rather than creating conditions for peace, it sowed the seeds of another war. Surely this was the ultimate tragedy of the Great War, a war that directly and indirectly cost $332 billion and left 10 million dead and another 20 million wounded.

The End of the War

Victory over revolutionary Russia boosted sagging German morale, and in the spring of 1918 the Germans launched their last major attack against France under the command of General Erich Ludendorff (**LOOD-n-dawrf**). For a time, German armies pushed forward, coming within thirty-five miles of Paris. But Ludendorff's exhausted, overextended forces never broke through. They were decisively stopped in July at the second Battle of the Marne, where 140,000 fresh American soldiers saw action. Adding 2 million men in arms to the war effort by August, the late but massive American intervention decisively tipped the scales in favor of Allied victory.

By September British, French, and American armies were advancing steadily on all fronts, and a panicky General Ludendorff realized that Germany had lost the war. Yet he insolently insisted that moderate politicians shoulder the shame of defeat, and on October 4 the emperor formed a new, more liberal German government to sue for peace.

As negotiations over an armistice dragged on, an angry and frustrated German people finally rose up. On November 3, sailors in Kiel (**keel**) mutinied, and throughout northern Germany soldiers and workers began to establish revolutionary councils on the Russian soviet model. The same day, Austria-Hungary surrendered to the Allies and began breaking apart. Revolution broke out in Germany, and masses of workers demonstrated for peace in Berlin. With army discipline collapsing, the emperor abdicated and fled to Holland. Moderate socialist leaders in Berlin proclaimed a German republic on November 9 and simultaneously agreed to tough Allied terms of surrender. The armistice went into effect on November 11, 1918. The war was over.

Revolution in Germany

Military defeat brought political revolution to Germany and Austria-Hungary, as it had to Russia. In Austria-Hungary the revolution was primarily nationalistic and republican in character. Having started the war to preserve an antinationalistic dynastic state, the Habsburg empire had perished in the attempt. In its place, independent Austrian, Hungarian, and Czechoslovakian republics were proclaimed, while a greatly expanded Serbian monarchy united the South Slavs and took the name Yugoslavia.

In Germany, the empire was replaced by the Weimar Republic, which was composed largely of Social Democrats and the Catholic party. The German Revolution of November 1918 resembled the Russian Revolution of March 1917. In both cases, a genuine popular uprising welled up from below, toppled an authoritarian monarchy, and brought the establishment of a liberal provisional republic. In both countries, liberals and moderate socialists took control of the central government, while workers' and soldiers' councils formed a counter-government. In Germany, however, the moderate socialists and their liberal allies won, and the Lenin-like radical revolutionaries in the councils lost.

The Treaty of Versailles

The peace conference opened in Paris in January 1919 with seventy delegates representing twenty-seven victorious nations. There were great expectations. A young British diplomat later wrote that the victors "were journeying to Paris . . . to found a new order in Europe. We were preparing not Peace only, but Eternal Peace."[4] This general optimism and idealism had been greatly strengthened by President Wilson's January 1918 peace proposal, the Fourteen Points, which stressed national self-determination and the rights of small countries.

The real powers at the conference were the United States, Great Britain, and France. Germany was not allowed to participate; Russia was locked in civil war; and Italy's role was limited. Almost immediately the three great Allies began to quarrel. President Wilson passionately believed that only a permanent international organization could protect member states from aggression and avert future wars, and he insisted that the creation of a **League of Nations** come first on the agenda. Wilson had his way, although Lloyd George of Great Britain and especially Clemenceau of France were unenthusiastic. They were primarily concerned with punishing Germany.

Playing on British nationalism, David Lloyd George had already won a smashing electoral victory as prime minister in December on the popular platform of making Germany pay for the war. As Kipling summed up the general British feeling at the end of the war, the Germans were "a people with the heart of beasts."[5]

France's Georges Clemenceau, "the Tiger" who had broken wartime defeatism and led his country to victory, wholeheartedly agreed. Like most French people, Clemenceau wanted old-fashioned revenge as well as lasting security for France. This, he believed, required the creation of a buffer state between France and Germany, the permanent demilitarization of Germany, and vast German reparations. Clemenceau's demands seemed vindictive to Wilson and Lloyd George, violating morality and the principle of national self-determination. By April the countries attending the conference were deadlocked on the German question, and Wilson packed his bags to go home.

In the end, Clemenceau agreed to a compromise. He gave up the French demand for a Rhineland buffer state in return for Wilson and Lloyd George's promise that their countries would come to France's aid in the event of a German attack. Thus Clemenceau appeared to win his goal of French security, as Wilson had won his of a permanent international organization. The Allies moved quickly to finish the settlement, believing that any adjustments would later be possible within the dual framework of a strong Western alliance and the League of Nations (see Map 27.4).

League of Nations A permanent international organization established during the peace conference in Paris in January 1919, designed to protect member states from aggression and avert future wars.

MAPPING THE PAST

MAP 27.4 Shattered Empires and Territorial Changes After World War I

The Great War brought tremendous changes in eastern Europe. New nations and new boundaries were established, generally on the principle of national self-determination. A dangerous power vacuum was created by the new, usually small states established between Germany and Soviet Russia. **[1]** Identify the boundaries of Germany, Austria-Hungary, and Russia in 1914, and note carefully the changes caused by the war. **[2]** What territory did Germany lose, and why did France, Poland, and even Denmark receive it? Why was Austria sometimes called a head without a body in the 1920s? **[3]** What new independent states (excluding disputed Bessarabia) were formed from the old Russian Empire, and what nationalities lived in these states?

Map legend:
- Boundaries of German, Russian, and Austro-Hungarian Empires in 1914
- Areas lost by Austro-Hungarian Empire
- Areas lost by Russian Empire
- Areas lost by German Empire
- Areas lost by Bulgaria
- Demilitarized Zones
- Boundaries of 1926

The **Treaty of Versailles** between the Allies and Germany was the key to the settlement, and the terms were not unreasonable as a first step toward re-establishing international order. Had Germany won, it seems certain that France and Belgium would have been treated with greater severity, as Russia had been at Brest-Litovsk. Germany's colonies were given to France, Britain, and Japan as League of Nations mandates. Germany's territorial losses within Europe were minor, thanks to Wilson. Alsace-Lorraine (**AL-sas-law-REYN**) was returned to France. Parts of Germany inhabited primarily by Poles were ceded to the new Polish state, in keeping with the principle of national self-determination. Germany had to limit its army to 100,000 men and agree to build no military fortifications in the Rhineland.

More harshly, the Allies declared that Germany (with Austria) was responsible for the war and had therefore to pay reparations equal to all civilian damages caused by the war. This unfortunate and much-criticized clause expressed inescapable popular demands for German blood, but the actual figure was not set, and there was the clear possibility that reparations might be set at a reasonable level in the future when tempers had cooled.

When presented with the treaty, the German government protested vigorously. But there was no alternative, especially considering that Germany was still starving because the Allies had not yet lifted their naval blockade. On June 28, 1919, German representatives of the ruling moderate Social Democrats and the Catholic party signed the treaty in the Sun King's Hall of Mirrors at Versailles, where Bismarck's empire had been joyously proclaimed almost fifty years before.

Separate peace treaties were concluded with the other defeated European powers—Austria, Hungary, and Bulgaria. For the most part, these treaties merely ratified the existing situation in east-central Europe following the breakup of the Austro-Hungarian Empire. Like Austria, Hungary was a particularly big loser, as its "captive" nationalities (and some interspersed Hungarians) were ceded to Romania, Czechoslovakia, Poland, and Yugoslavia.

Treaty of Versailles The treaty by which Germany's army was limited to 100,000 men and Germany was declared responsible for the war and had therefore to pay reparations equal to all civilian damages caused by the war.

The Peace Settlement in the Middle East

Although Allied leaders at Versailles focused mainly on European questions, they also imposed a political settlement on what had been the Ottoman Empire. This settlement brought radical changes to the Middle East, and it became very controversial. Basically, the Ottoman Empire was broken up, Britain and France expanded their power and influence in the Middle East, and Arab nationalists felt cheated and betrayed.

The British government had encouraged the wartime Arab revolt against the Ottoman Turks (see page 705) and had even made vague promises of an independent Arab kingdom. However, when the fighting stopped, the British and the French chose instead to honor secret wartime agreements to divide and rule the Ottoman lands. Arab nationalists were also angered by the **Balfour Declaration** of November 1917, named after the British foreign secretary. It announced that Britain favored a "National Home for the Jewish People" in Palestine, but without prejudicing the civil and religious rights of the non-Jewish communities already living in Palestine. The "National Home for the Jewish People" implied to the Arabs—and to the Zionist Jews as well—the establishment of some kind of Jewish state that would be incompatible with rule by the majority Arab population.

The Arab leader Hussein ibn-Ali sent his son Faisal (1885–1933) to the Versailles Peace Conference with the goal of securing Arab independence. Although President Wilson wanted to give the Arab case serious consideration, the British and the French were determined to rule Syria, Iraq, Transjordan, and Palestine as

Balfour Declaration A 1917 British statement that declared British support of a "National Home for the Jewish People" in Palestine.

Prince Faisal at the Versailles Peace Conference, 1919

Standing in front, Faisal is supported by his allies and black slave. Nur-as-Said, an officer in the Ottoman army who joined the Arab revolt, is second from the left, and the British officer T. E. Lawrence—popularly known as Lawrence of Arabia—is fourth from the left in back. Faisal failed to win political independence for the Arabs, as the British backed away from the vague promises they had made during the war. (Courtesy of the Trustees of the Imperial War Museum, neg. #Q55581)

League of Nations mandates, and they confirmed only the independence of Hussein's kingdom of Hejaz along the western coast of contemporary Saudi Arabia. In response Arab nationalists met in Damascus to call for political independence. (See the feature "Listening to the Past: Arab Political Aspirations in 1919" on pages 724–725.) Brushing aside Arab opposition, the British mandate in Palestine formally incorporated the Balfour Declaration and its commitment to a Jewish national home. When Faisal returned to Syria, his followers repudiated the agreement he had reluctantly accepted. In March 1920 they met as the Syrian National Congress and proclaimed Syria independent, with Faisal as king. A similar congress declared Iraq an independent kingdom.

Western reaction to events in Syria and Iraq was swift and decisive. A French army stationed in Lebanon attacked Syria, taking Damascus in July 1920. Faisal fled, and the French took over. Meanwhile, the British put down an uprising in Iraq with bloody fighting and established effective control there. Western imperialism, in the form of League of Nations mandates, appeared to have replaced Ottoman rule in the Arab Middle East. The Allies laid claim to the Turkish heartland as well. Great Britain and France occupied parts of modern-day Turkey, and Italy and Greece also claimed shares. There was a sizable Greek minority in western Turkey, and Greek nationalists wanted to build a modern Greek empire modeled on long-dead Christian Byzantium. In 1919 Greek armies carried by British ships landed on the Turkish coast at Smyrna (SMUR-nuh) and advanced unopposed into the interior. Turkey seemed finished.

But Turkey revived under the leadership of Mustafa Kemal (MOOS-tah-fah kuh-MAHL) (1881–1938), later known as Atatürk (AT-uh-turk) ("father of the Turks"). Kemal was a military man who had directed the successful defense of the Dardanelles against British attack. Watching the Allies' aggression and the sultan's cowardice after the armistice, in early 1919 he moved to central Turkey and gradually unified the Turkish resistance. After a year of defeat in battle, they won a great victory in central Turkey, and the Greeks and their British allies sued for peace. The Treaty of Lausanne (loh-ZAN) (1923) recognized the territorial integrity of a truly independent Turkey. Turkey lost only its former Arab provinces.

Mustafa Kemal, a nationalist without religious faith, believed that Turkey should modernize and secularize along Western lines. He established a republic, had himself elected president, and created a one-party system—partly inspired by the Bolshevik example—in order to transform his country. Profoundly influenced by the example of western Europe, Mustafa Kemal set out to limit the place of religion and religious leaders in daily affairs. He decreed a revolutionary separation of church and state, promulgated law codes inspired by European models, and established a secular public school system. Women received rights that they never had before. By the time of his death in 1938, Mustafa Kemal had implemented successfully much of his revolutionary program. He had moved Turkey much closer to Europe, foretelling current efforts by Turkey to join the European Union as a full-fledged member.

American Rejection of the Versailles Treaty

The rapidly concluded Versailles Treaty of early 1919 was not perfect, but within the context of war-shattered Europe it was an acceptable beginning. The principle of national self-determination, which had played such a large role in starting the war, served as an organizing framework. Germany had been punished but not dismembered. A new world organization complemented a traditional defensive alliance of satisfied powers. The serious remaining problems could be worked out in the future. Moreover, Allied leaders had seen speed as essential for another reason: they detested Lenin and feared that his Bolshevik Revolution might spread. They realized that their best answer to Lenin's unending calls for worldwide upheaval was peace and tranquillity for war-weary peoples.

There were, however, two great, interrelated obstacles to such peace: Germany and the United States. Plagued by communist uprisings, reactionary plots, and popular disillusionment with losing the war, Germany's moderate socialists and their liberal and Catholic supporters faced an enormous challenge. Like French republicans after 1871, they needed time (and luck) if they were to establish firmly a peaceful and democratic republic. Progress in this direction required understanding but firm treatment of Germany by the victorious Western Allies, particularly by the United States.

However, the United States Senate and, to a lesser extent, the American people, rejected Wilson's handiwork. Republican senators led by Henry Cabot Lodge refused to ratify the Treaty of Versailles without changes in the articles creating the League of Nations. Lodge and others believed that this requirement gave away Congress's constitutional right to declare war. Moreover, the Senate refused to ratify Wilson's treaties forming a defensive alliance with France and Great Britain. Wilson, in failing health, refused to compromise.

The Wilson-Lodge fiasco and the newfound gospel of isolationism represented a tragic and cowardly renunciation of America's responsibility. Using America's action as an excuse, Great Britain, too, refused to

Section Review

- The entry of the United States into the war finally gave the Allies the edge and although Germany tried to hold on, the exhausted and angry Germans revolted and the emperor abdicated and fled; moderate socialists declared a German republic and agreed to an armistice.

- Post-war Austria-Hungary became independent Austria, Hungary, Czechoslovakia, and the monarchy of Yugoslavia; in Germany, an internal revolution led to a provisional republic led by the moderate Social Democrats.

- The United States, Britain, and France were at odds over how to create a lasting peace; U.S. president Wilson got a permanent League of Nations—an international organization to protect its members from aggression—while Britain and France pressed for German demilitarization and reparations.

- The Arabs in the Ottoman Empire were angered when the Allies denied their independence, forcibly occupying Syria and Iraq and attempting to control Turkey, but Atatürk was able to establish a republic and modernize Turkey.

- The United States Senate did not ratify the treaty of Versailles because Republican senators feared it gave away congress's right to declare war and they did not want to form a defensive alliance with Britain and France; Britain, too, refused to enter the alliance, leaving France alone and hopes for lasting peace unstable.

ratify its defensive alliance with France. Bitterly betrayed by its allies, France stood alone. Very shortly France was to take actions against Germany that would feed the fires of German resentment and seriously undermine democratic forces in the new republic. The great hopes of early 1919 had turned to ashes by the end of the year. The Western alliance had collapsed, and a grandiose plan for permanent peace had given way to a fragile truce. For this and for what came later, the United States must share a large part of the guilt.

Chapter Review

What caused the Great War, and why did it have such revolutionary consequences? (page 699)

World War I had truly revolutionary consequences because, first and foremost, it was a war of committed peoples. In France, Britain, and Germany in particular, governments drew on genuine popular support. This support reflected in part the diplomatic origins of the war, which citizens saw as growing out of an unwanted crisis in the Balkans and an inflexible alliance system of opposing blocs. More importantly, popular support reflected the way western European society had been unified under the nationalist banner in the later nineteenth century, despite the fears that the growing socialist movement aroused in conservatives.

What was the impact of total war on civilian populations? (page 708)

The relentlessness of total war helps explain why so many died, why so many were crippled physically and psychologically, and why Western civilization would in so many ways never be the same again. More concretely, the war swept away monarchs and multinational empires. National self-determination apparently triumphed across Europe, not only in Austria-Hungary but also in many of Russia's western borderlands. Except in Ireland and parts of Soviet Russia and the Arab Middle East, the revolutionary dream of national unity, born of the French Revolution, had finally come true.

Why did World War I bring socialist revolution in Russia? (page 711)

Two other revolutions were products of the war. In Russia the Bolsheviks established a radical regime, smashed existing capitalist institutions, and stayed in power with a new kind of authoritarian rule. Whether the new Russian regime was truly Marxian or socialist was questionable, but it indisputably posed a powerful, ongoing revolutionary challenge to Europe and its colonial empires.

More subtle but quite universal in its impact was an administrative revolution. This revolution, born of the need to mobilize entire societies and economies for total war, greatly increased the power of government. Freewheeling market capitalism and a well-integrated world economy were among the many casualties of the administrative revolution, and greater social equality was everywhere one of its results. Thus even in European countries where a communist takeover never came close to occurring, society still experienced a great revolution.

Key Terms

Three Emperors' League (p. 699)
Triple Entente (p. 703)
trench warfare (p. 704)
Lusitania (p. 708)
total war (p. 708)
Petrograd Soviet (p. 713)
Army Order No. 1 (p. 713)
Bolsheviks (p. 713)
Constituent Assembly (p. 715)
war communism (p. 715)
Cheka (p. 715)
League of Nations (p. 717)
Treaty of Versailles (p. 719)
Balfour Declaration (p. 719)

How did the Allies fashion a peace settlement, and why was it unsuccessful? (page 716)

Finally, the "war to end war" did not bring peace—only a fragile truce. In the West, the Allies failed to maintain their wartime solidarity. Germany remained unrepentant and would soon have more grievances to nurse. Moreover, the victory of national self-determination in eastern Europe created small, weak states and thus a power vacuum between a still-powerful Germany and a potentially mighty communist Russia. A vast area lay open to military aggression from two sides.

Notes

1. Quoted in J. Remak, *The Origins of World War I* (New York: Holt, Rinehart & Winston, 1967), p. 84.
2. Quoted in R. O. Paxton, *Europe in the Twentieth Century* (New York: Harcourt Brace Jovanovich, 1975), p. 109.
3. A. B. Ulam, *The Bolsheviks* (New York: Collier Books, 1968), p. 349.
4. H. Nicolson, *Peacemaking 1919* (New York: Grosset & Dunlap Universal Library, 1965), pp. 8, 31–32.
5. Quoted ibid., p. 24.

To assess your mastery of this chapter, go to **bedfordstmartins.com/mckaywestbrief**

Listening to the Past

Arab Political Aspirations in 1919

Great Britain and France had agreed to divide up the Arab lands, and the British also had made conflicting promises to Arab and Jewish nationalists. However, President Wilson insisted at Versailles that the right of self-determination should be applied to the conquered Ottoman territories, and he sent an American commission of inquiry to Syria, even though the British and French refused to participate. The commission canvassed political views throughout greater Syria, and its long report with many documents reflected public opinion in the region in 1919.

To present their view to the Americans, Arab nationalists from present-day Syria, Lebanon, Israel, and Jordan came together in Damascus as the General Syrian Congress, and they passed the following resolution on July 2, 1919.

We the undersigned members of the General Syrian Congress, meeting in Damascus on Wednesday, July 2nd, 1919, . . . provided with credentials and authorizations by the inhabitants of our various districts, Moslems, Christians, and Jews, have agreed upon the following statement of the desires of the people of the country who have elected us to present them to the American Section of the International Commission; the fifth article was passed by a very large majority; all the other articles were accepted unanimously.

1. We ask absolutely complete political independence for Syria within these boundaries. [Describes the area including the present-day states of Syria, Lebanon, Israel, and Jordan.]

2. We ask that the Government of this Syrian country should be a democratic civil constitutional Monarchy on broad decentralization principles, safeguarding the rights of minorities, and that the King be the Emir Faisal, who carried on a glorious struggle in the cause of our liberation and merited our full confidence and entire reliance. . . .

6. We do not acknowledge any right claimed by the French Government in any part whatever of our Syrian country and refuse that she should assist us or have a hand in our country under any circumstances and in any place.

7. We oppose the pretensions of the Zionists to create a Jewish commonwealth in the southern part of Syria, known as Palestine, and oppose Zionist migration to any part of our country; for we do not acknowledge their title but consider them a grave peril to our people from the national, economical, and political points of view. Our Jewish compatriots shall enjoy our common rights and assume the common responsibilities.

8. We ask that there should be no separation of the southern part of Syria, known as Palestine,

Palestinian Arabs protest against large-scale Jewish migration into Palestine.
(Roger-Viollet/Getty Images)

724

nor of the littoral western zone, which includes Lebanon, from the Syrian country. We desire that the unity of the country should be guaranteed against partition under whatever circumstances.

9. We ask complete independence for emancipated Mesopotamia [today's Iraq] and that there should be no economical barriers between the two countries. . . .

The noble principles enunciated by President Wilson strengthen our confidence that our desires emanating from the depths of our hearts, shall be the decisive factor in determining our future; and that President Wilson and the free American people will be our supporters for the realization of our hopes, thereby proving their sincerity and noble sympathy with the aspiration of the weaker nations in general and our Arab people in particular.

We also have the fullest confidence that the Peace Conference will realize that we would not have risen against the Turks, with whom we had participated in all civil, political, and representative privileges, but for their violation of our national rights, and so will grant us our desires in full in order that our political rights may not be less after the war than they were before, since we have shed so much blood in the cause of our liberty and independence.

We request to be allowed to send a delegation to represent us at the Peace Conference to defend our rights and secure the realization of our aspirations.

Questions for Analysis

1. What kind of state did the delegates want?

2. Did the delegates view their "Jewish compatriots" and the Zionists in different ways? Why?

3. How did the delegates appeal to American sympathies?

Source: "Resolution of the General Syrian Congress at Damascus, 2 July 1919," from the King-Crane Commission Report, in *Foreign Relations of the United States: Paris Peace Conference*, 1919, 12: 780–781.

CHAPTER 28
The Age of Anxiety

ca. 1900–1940

Chapter Preview

This detail of George Grosz's *Draussen und Drinnen* (Outside and Inside) captures the uncertainty and anxiety of the 1920s. (akg-images/Art@Estate of George Grosz/Licensed by VAGA, New York, NY)

726

With the end of the terrible trauma of total war, most people hoped that once again life would make sense in the familiar prewar terms of peace, prosperity, and progress. These hopes were in vain. The Great Break—the First World War and the Russian Revolution—had mangled too many things beyond repair. Life would no longer fit neatly into the old molds.

Instead, great numbers of men and women felt themselves increasingly adrift in a strange, uncertain, and uncontrollable world. They saw themselves living in an age of anxiety, an age of continual crisis (this age lasted until at least the early 1950s). In almost every area of human experience, people went searching for ways to put meaning back into life.

Modernism and the Crisis of Western Thought

In what ways did new and disturbing ideas in philosophy, physics, psychology, and the arts reflect the general crisis in Western thought?

Before 1914 most people still believed in the Enlightenment ideals of progress, reason, and the rights of the individual. Yet a small band of serious thinkers and creative writers had been attacking these well-worn optimistic ideas since the 1880s. These critics rejected the general faith in progress and the power of the rational human mind. An expanding chorus of thinkers echoed and enlarged their views after the experience of history's most destructive war—a war that suggested to many that human beings were a pack of violent, irrational animals quite capable of tearing the individual and his or her rights to shreds. Disorientation and pessimism were particularly acute in the 1930s, when the rapid rise of harsh dictatorships and the Great Depression transformed old certainties into bitter illusions, as we shall see in Chapter 29.

In the midst of economic, political, and social disruptions, the French poet and critic Paul Valéry (va-ley-REE) (1871–1945) saw the "cruelly injured mind," besieged by doubts and suffering from anxieties. This was the general intellectual crisis of the twentieth century, which touched almost every field of thought. The implications of new ideas and discoveries in philosophy, physics, psychology, and the arts played a central role in this crisis, disturbing "thinking people" everywhere.

Modern Philosophy

The work of the nineteenth-century German philosopher Friedrich Nietzsche (NEE-chee) (1844–1900) laid the foundation for the twentieth-century rejection of Enlightenment ideals. His first great work in 1872 argued that ever since classical Athens, the West had overemphasized rationality and stifled the passion and animal instinct that drive human activity and true creativity. Nietzsche went on to question all values. He claimed that Christianity embodied a "slave morality" that glorified weakness, envy, and mediocrity. In Nietzsche's most famous line, a wise fool proclaims that "God is dead," dead because he has been murdered by lackadaisical modern Christians who no longer really believe in him. Nietzsche viewed the pillars of conventional morality—reason, democracy, progress, respectability—as outworn social and psychological constructs whose influence was suffocating self-realization and excellence.

Nietzsche painted a dark world, foreshadowing perhaps his loss of sanity in 1889. The West was in decline; false values had triumphed. The only hope for the individual was to accept the meaninglessness of human existence and then make that very meaninglessness a source of self-defined personal integrity and hence liberation. Little read during his active years, Nietzsche attracted growing attention in the early twentieth century, especially from German radicals who found inspiration in Nietzsche's ferocious assault on the conventions of pre-1914 imperial Germany. Subsequent generations have each discovered new Nietzsches, and his influence remains enormous to this day.

This growing dissatisfaction with established ideas before 1914 was apparent in other important thinkers. In the 1890s, French philosophy professor Henri Bergson (1859–1941) convinced many young people through his writing that immediate experience and intuition were as important as rational and scientific thinking for understanding reality. Indeed, according to Bergson, a religious experience or a mystical poem could be more meaningful than a scientific law or a mathematical equation.

The First World War accelerated the revolt against established certainties in philosophy, but that revolt went in two very different directions. In English-speaking countries, the main development was the acceptance of logical empiricism (or logical positivism) in university circles. In continental countries, the primary development in philosophy was existentialism.

logical empiricism A revolt against established certainties in philosophy that rejected most of the concerns of traditional philosophy, from the existence of God to the meaning of happiness, as nonsense and hot air.

Logical empiricism was truly revolutionary. This outlook began primarily with the Austrian philosopher Ludwig Wittgenstein (VIT-guhn-shtine) (1889–1951), who later immigrated to England, where he trained numerous disciples. Wittgenstein argued that the traditional concerns of philosophy—God, freedom, morality, and so on—are quite literally senseless, a great waste of time, for statements about them can be neither tested by scientific experiments nor demonstrated by the logic of mathematics. Statements about such matters reflect only the personal preferences of a given individual. As Wittgenstein put it in the famous last sentence of his work, "Of what one cannot speak, of that one must keep silent." People could no longer look to philosophy for answers to the great questions of life.

Another direction in philosophy, **existentialism**, argued that philosophy was necessary to understand the truth of the human condition. Most existential thinkers in the twentieth century did not believe a supreme being had established humanity's fundamental nature and given life meaning. In the words of the famous French existentialist, Jean-Paul Sartre (zhahn-pawl sahrt) (1905–1980), "existence precedes essence." The existentialist thinker sees the world without a caring God or an underlying order. In the face of a world without God, only the actions of individuals can give life meaning. Individuals must become "engaged" and choose their own actions courageously and consistently and in full awareness of their inescapable responsibility for their own behavior. In the end, existentialists argued, human beings can overcome life's absurdity.

existentialism A highly diverse and even contradictory system of thought that was loosely united in a courageous search for moral values in a world of terror and uncertainty.

Not all twentieth-century philosophers rejected the possibility of God, however. Sometimes described as Christian existentialists because they shared the loneliness and despair of atheistic existentialists, they stressed the human being's sinful nature, the need for faith, and the mystery of God's forgiveness. The revival of fundamental Christian belief after World War I was fed by the rediscovery of the work of nineteenth-century Danish religious philosopher Søren Kierkegaard (KEER-ki-gahrd) (1813–1855), whose ideas became extremely influential. Having rejected formalistic religion, Kierkegaard had eventually resolved his personal anguish over his imperfect nature by making a total religious commitment to a remote and majestic God.

Similar ideas were brilliantly developed by Swiss Protestant theologian Karl Barth (1886–1968), whose many influential writings after 1920 sought to re-create the religious intensity of the Reformation. Barth urged people to accept God's word and the supernatural revelation of Jesus Christ with awe, trust, and obedience. Lowly mortals should not expect to "reason out" God and his ways. Among Catholics, the leading existential thinker was Gabriel Marcel (mahr-SEL) (1887–1973), who found in the Catholic Church an answer to what he called the postwar "broken world." Catholicism and religious belief provided the hope, humanity, honesty, and piety for which he hungered.

After 1914 religion became much more relevant and meaningful to intellectuals than it had been before the war. In addition to Barth and Marcel, many other illustrious individuals turned to religion between about 1920 and 1950. Poets T. S. Eliot and W. H. Auden, novelists Evelyn Waugh (waw) and Aldous Huxley, historian Arnold Toynbee (TOIN-bee), Oxford professor C. S. Lewis, psychoanalyst Karl Stern, physicist Max Planck (plahngk), and philosopher Cyril Joad were all either converted to religion or attracted to it for the first time. Religion, often of a despairing, existential variety, was one meaningful answer to terror and anxiety. In the words of a famous Roman Catholic convert, English novelist Graham Greene, "One began to believe in heaven because one believed in hell."[1]

The New Physics

Ever since the scientific revolution of the seventeenth century, progressive minds believed that science, unlike religion and philosophical speculation, was based on hard facts and controlled experiments. Science seemed to have achieved an unerring and almost complete picture of reality. Unchanging natural laws seemed to determine physical processes and permit useful solutions to more and more problems. All this was comforting, especially to people who were no longer committed to traditional religious beliefs. And all this was challenged by the new physics.

The work of Polish-born physicist Marie Curie (KYOOR-ee) (1867–1934) and German physicist Max Planck (1858–1947) called into question the old view of atoms as the stable, basic building blocks of nature, with a different kind of unbreakable atom for each of the ninety-two chemical elements. In 1905 the German-Jewish genius Albert Einstein (AHYN-stine) (1879–1955) went further than Curie and Planck in undermining Newtonian physics. His famous theory of special relativity postulated that time and space are relative to the viewpoint of the observer and that only the speed of light is constant for all frames of reference in the universe. The closed framework of Newtonian physics was quite limited compared to that of Einsteinian physics, which unified an apparently infinite universe with the incredibly small, fast-moving subatomic world. Moreover, Einstein's theory stated clearly that matter and energy are interchangeable and that even a particle of matter contains enormous levels of potential energy.

The 1920s opened the "heroic age of physics," in the apt words of one of its leading pioneers, Ernest Rutherford (1871–1937). Breakthrough followed breakthrough. In 1919 Rutherford showed that the atom could be split. By 1944 seven

Unlocking the Power of the Atom
Many of the fanciful visions of science fiction came true in the twentieth century, although not exactly as first imagined. This 1927 cartoon satirizes a professor who has split the atom and unwittingly destroyed his building and neighborhood in the process. In the Second World War the professors harnessed the atom in bombs and decimated faraway cities and foreign civilians. (Mary Evans Picture Library)

neutron The most important of the subatomic particles because its capacity to pass through other atoms allowed for intense experimental bombardment of matter, leading to chain reactions of unbelievable force.

subatomic particles had been identified, of which the most important was the **neutron** (NOO-tron). The neutron's capacity to pass through other atoms allowed for even more intense experimental bombardment of matter, leading to chain reactions of unbelievable force. This was the road to the atomic bomb.

Although few nonscientists understood this revolution in physics, the implications of the new theories and discoveries, as presented by newspapers and popular writers, were disturbing to millions of men and women in the 1920s and 1930s. The new universe was strange and troubling. It lacked any absolute objective reality. Everything was "relative," that is, dependent on the observer's frame of reference. Moreover, the universe was uncertain and undetermined, without stable building blocks. In 1927 German physicist Werner Heisenberg (VER-nuhr HI-zuhn-burg) (1901–1976) formulated the "principle of uncertainty," which postulates that because it is impossible to know the position and speed of an individual electron, it is therefore impossible to predict its behavior. Instead of Newton's dependable, rational laws, there seemed to be only tendencies and probabilities in an extraordinarily complex and uncertain universe.

id, ego, and superego Freudian terms to describe human behavior, which Freud saw as basically irrational.

Freudian Psychology

While physics presented an unpredictable universe, the findings and speculations of leading psychologist Sigmund Freud (see page 636) suggested that human behavior was basically irrational.

According to Freud, the key to understanding the mind is the primitive, irrational unconscious, which he called the **id**. The unconscious is driven by sexual, aggressive, and pleasure-seeking desires and is locked in a constant battle with the other parts of the mind: the rationalizing conscious, the **ego**, which mediates what a person *can* do; and ingrained moral values (the **superego**), which specify what a person *should* do. Human behavior is a product of a fragile compromise between instinctual drives and the controls of rational thinking and moral values. Since the instinctual drives are extremely powerful, the ever-present danger for individuals and whole societies is that unacknowledged drives will overwhelm the control mechanisms in a violent, distorted way. Yet Freud also agreed with Nietzsche that the mechanisms of rational thinking and traditional moral values can be too strong. They can repress sexual desires too effectively, crippling individuals and entire peoples with guilt and neurotic fears.

Freudian psychology and clinical psychiatry had become an international movement by 1910, but only after 1918 did they receive popular attention, especially in the Protestant countries of northern Europe and in the United States. Many opponents and even some enthusiasts interpreted Freud as saying that the first requirement for mental health is an uninhibited sex life. Thus after the First World War, the popular interpretation of Freud reflected and encouraged growing sexual experimentation, particularly among middle-class women. For more serious students, the psychology of Freud and his followers drastically undermined the old, easy optimism about the rational and progressive nature of the human mind.

The Modern Novel

Freud's ideas about the complexity and irrationality of the human mind found expression in the **stream-of-consciousness technique** of modern novelists. In *Jacob's Room* (1922), Virginia Woolf (1882–1941) created a novel made up of a series of internal monologues, in which a character's ideas and emotions from different periods of time bubble up as randomly as from a patient on a psychoanalyst's couch. William Faulkner (1897–1962), perhaps America's greatest twentieth-century novelist, used the same technique in *The Sound and the Fury* (1929), much of whose intense drama is confusedly seen through the eyes of an idiot. The most famous stream-of-consciousness novel—and surely the most disturbing novel of its generation—is *Ulysses* (1922), in which Irish novelist James Joyce (1882–1941) weaves an extended ironic parallel between his ordinary hero's aimless wanderings through the streets and pubs of Dublin and the heroic adventures of Homer's Ulysses on his way home from Troy. Abandoning conventional grammar and blending foreign words, puns, bits of knowledge, and scraps of memory together in bewildering confusion, the language of *Ulysses* mirrors the riddle of everyday life.

As creative writers turned their attention from society to the individual and from realism to psychological relativity, they rejected the idea of progress. Some even described "anti-utopias," nightmare visions of things to come. Franz Kafka's (1883–1924) novels and stories, such as *The Trial* (1925) and

stream-of-consciousness technique
A literary technique, used by Virginia Woolf, James Joyce, and others, that used interior monologue to explore the human psyche.

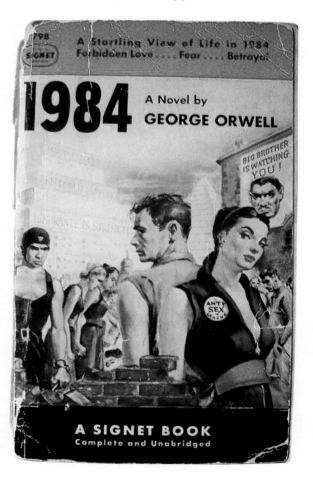

1984

This intriguing cover for an early edition of Orwell's brilliant novel hints at the tragic love affair between Winston and Julia. Considered a crime in Orwell's totalitarian dictatorship of the future, the love affair leads to the couple's arrest, torture, and betrayal. No one can escape the scrutiny of Big Brother and the Thought Police. (Signet Books/New American Library, 1949, cover illustration, James Avati. Private Collection)

The Castle (1926), portray helpless individuals crushed by inexplicably hostile forces. The German-Jewish Kafka died young, at forty-one, and so did not see the world of his nightmares materialize in the Nazi state.

Englishman George Orwell (1903–1950), however, had seen both that reality and its Stalinist counterpart by 1949, when he wrote perhaps the ultimate in anti-utopian literature: *1984*. Orwell set the action in the future, in 1984. Big Brother—the dictator—and his totalitarian state use a new kind of language, sophisticated technology, and psychological terror to strip a weak individual of his last shred of human dignity. The supremely self-confident chief of the Thought Police tells the tortured, broken, and framed Winston Smith, "If you want a picture of the future, imagine a boot stamping on a human face—forever."[2] A phenomenal bestseller, *1984* spoke to millions of people in the closing years of the age of anxiety.

Modernism in Art and Design

Like the scientists and writers who were partaking of the same culture, visual artists rejected old forms and old values. Modernism in art and music meant constant experimentation and a search for new kinds of expression. And though many people find the numerous and varied modern visions of the arts strange, disturbing, and even ugly, the first half of the twentieth century, so dismal in many respects, will probably stand as one of Western civilization's great artistic eras.

Modernism in the arts was loosely unified by a revolution in architecture. This revolution intended nothing less than a transformation of the physical framework of urban society according to a new principle: **functionalism.** Buildings, like industrial products, should be useful and "functional"—that is, they should serve, as well as possible, the purpose for which they were made. Moreover, they had to throw away useless ornamentation and find beauty and aesthetic pleasure in the clean lines of practical constructions and efficient machinery. Franco-Swiss genius Le Corbusier (luh cor-booz-YEH) (1887–1965) insisted that "a house is a machine for living in."[3] Featuring low lines, open interiors, and mass-produced building materials, the work of American architect Frank Lloyd Wright (1869–1959) embodied the modernist aesthetic.

In post-war Germany, Walter Gropius (GROH-pee-uhs) (1883–1969) established a new kind of interdisciplinary art school, called the **Bauhaus** (BOU-hous). The Bauhaus brought together many leading modern architects, designers, and theatrical innovators to work as a team, combining the study of fine art, such as painting and sculpture, with the study of applied art in the crafts of printing, weaving, and furniture making. Throughout the 1920s, the Bauhaus, with its stress on functionalism and good design for everyday life, attracted enthusiastic students from all over the world. It had a great and continuing impact.

In painting, the early twentieth century saw a move away from representing reality to an interest in the arrangement of color, line, and form as an end in itself. (See the feature "Images in Society: Pablo Picasso and Modern Art" on pages 734–735.) Another concern was to express a complicated psychological view of reality as well as an overwhelming emotional intensity. "The observer," said Russian-born Wassily Kandinsky (VAS-uh-lee kan-DIN-skee) (1866–1944), "must learn to look at [my] pictures . . . as form and color combinations . . . as a representation of mood and not as a representation of *objects*."[4] On the eve of the First World War, extreme expressionism and abstract painting were developing rapidly not only in Paris but also in Russia and Germany. Modern art had become international.

In the 1920s and 1930s, the artistic movements of the prewar years were extended and consolidated. The most notable new developments were dadaism

functionalism The principle that buildings, like industrial products, should serve as well as possible the purpose for which they were made.

Bauhaus A German interdisciplinary school of fine and applied arts that brought together many leading modern architects, designers, and theatrical innovators.

Walter Gropius: The Fagus Shoe Factory, 1911
The factory's sleek exterior is inspired by the revolutionary principles of functionalism. The striking glass façade creates a feeling of lightness and eliminates the traditional separation between interior and exterior. The glass façade also provides workers with healthy, natural light—a practical, "functional" concern. (Vanni/Art Resource, NY)

(DAH-dah-izm) and surrealism. **Dadaism** attacked all accepted standards of art and behavior, delighting in outrageous conduct. Its name is deliberately nonsensical. A famous example of dadaism is a reproduction of Leonardo da Vinci's *Mona Lisa* in which the famous woman with the mysterious smile sports a mustache and is ridiculed with an obscene inscription. After 1924 many dadaists were attracted to surrealism, which became very influential in art in the late 1920s and 1930s. Surrealists painted a fantastic world of wild dreams and complex symbols, where watches melted and giant metronomes beat time in precisely drawn but impossible alien landscapes. Refusing to depict ordinary visual reality, surrealist painters made powerful statements about the age of anxiety.

Dadaism An artistic movement of the 1920s and 1930s that attacked all accepted standards of art and behavior and delighted in outrageous conduct.

Modern Music

Developments in modern music were strikingly parallel to those in painting. Composers, too, were attracted by the emotional intensity of expressionism. The ballet *The Rite of Spring* by Igor Stravinsky (struh-VIN-skee) (1882–1971) practically caused a riot when it was first performed in Paris, in 1913, by Sergei Diaghilev's (dee-AH-guh-lef) famous Russian dance company. The combination of pulsating, dissonant rhythms from the orchestra pit and an earthy representation of lovemaking by the dancers on the stage seemed a shocking, almost pornographic enactment of a primitive fertility rite.

Images in Society

Pablo Picasso and Modern Art

Pablo Picasso (pi-KAH-soh) (1881–1973) was probably the most significant artist of the early twentieth century. For more than seventy years, he personified the individuality, freedom, and revolutionary creativity of the modern artist.

Born at Málaga in southern Spain, Picasso quickly demonstrated a precocious talent. At nineteen he headed for Paris, Europe's art capital. Suffering from poverty and falling into depression, he painted the weak and the poor in somber blue and purple tones. These pessimistic paintings of Picasso's "Blue Period" (1901–1904) are masterpieces in the tradition of Spanish realism.

Yet the young Picasso soon sought a new visual reality. In 1907 his arduous struggle to create a new style resulted in *Les Demoiselles d'Avignon* (dem-wuh-ZEL duh-a-vee-NYAWN) (Image 1), a painting originating in memories of a brothel scene in Barcelona. This work was considered a revolutionary upheaval in art. Since the Renaissance, artists had been expected to follow established rules, seeing objects in an orderly perspective from a single viewpoint and creating "beauty" and unified human forms. Do the faces of the central figures in this work conform to these rules? Regard the figures on either side, who were painted later. Notice how the light fails to combine with the shadow to create bodies

with continuous, three-dimensional contours. The figures appear broken into large, flat planes with heads that are twisted, fractured dislocations. Do you see the magical violence of a pictorial breakthrough or a grotesque, ugly departure?

Picasso extended his revolutionary experiments, and after 1910 he was joined by others. A critic called the new school cubism because these artists used many geometric forms in intersecting planes. Objects, viewed from many shifting viewpoints, often emerged as purely abstract designs.

Three Musicians (Image 2), painted in 1921, represents mature cubism. Many people believe that it marks the culmination of Picasso's cubist style. What similarities and differences do you see between this picture and Image 1? Notice the limited number of viewpoints, with the white clown,

IMAGE 1 Les Demoiselles d'Avignon (1907).

the harlequin, the monk, their instruments, and the table in front cut up into rectangular shapes and reassembled in recognizable form on a shallow series of planes. What is the effect of the bright primary colors and the harmonious, decorative order? Picasso had been making the sets for Sergei Diaghilev's famous Russian dance company in Paris, and these three jagged figures from traditional Italian comedy seem to convey the atmosphere of the theater and the dissonant, syncopated rhythm of modern music. Picasso always drew back from pure abstraction because he began with real objects and used models.

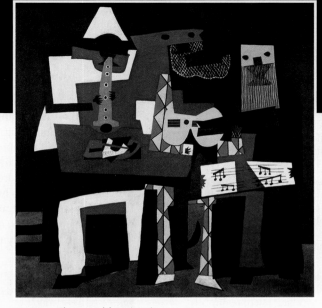

IMAGE 2 Three Musicians (1921). (Digital image © The Museum of Modern Art/ Licensed by Scala/Art Resource, NY/© 2004 Estate of Pablo Picasso/Artists Rights Society [ARS], New York)

Picasso's passionate involvement in his times infuses his immense painting *Guernica* (Image 3), often considered his greatest work. Painted for the Spanish pavilion at the Paris International Exhibition in 1937, this mural, with its mournful white, black, and blue colors, was inspired by the Spanish civil war and the deadly terror bombing of Guernica by fascist planes in a single night. In this complex work, a shrieking woman falls from a burning house on the far right. On the left, a woman holds a dead child, while toward the center are fragments of a warrior and a screaming horse pierced by a spear. Do cubist techniques heighten the effect? Picasso also draws on the surrealist aspect of the modernist revolution in this painting.

IMAGE 3 Guernica (1937). (Bridgeman-Giraudon/Art Resource, NY/© 2004 Estate of Pablo Picasso/Artists Rights Society [ARS], New York)

- After the terrible trauma of the First World War, philosophers turned to ideas of logical empiricism, which argued that concerns with God, freedom, or morality were a waste of time because you cannot test or prove them; existentialists argued that only one's actions have meaning; Christianity and Catholicism also attempted to give life meaning through a renewed faith and awe of God.

- Progress in physics altered the world of science radically; Einstein theorized that scientific laws were not permanent, that time and space are relative to an observer and matter and energy are interchangeable, insights that led to the invention of the atom bomb.

- Freudian psychology believed that human behavior is determined by the pleasure-seeking unconscious "id" struggling with the rationalizing conscious "ego" and the moralizing "superego," ideas that led to a popular interpretation that encouraged growing sexual experimentation.

- A new form of writing was the stream-of-consciousness technique, used by Virginia Woolf and James Joyce in novels made up of a series of monologues telling the story from one character's point of view; other literature such as George Orwell's 1984 foretold a bleak and frightening future.

- Functionalism, such as the Bauhaus movement, decreed that art and architecture should be useful, while in painting, Dadaism and surrealism depicted abstract thoughts.

- Modern music followed the artistic trend and became dominated by emotional intensity, as ballets, operas, and music combined wild sounds and irrationality instead of traditional harmony and tonality.

After the experience of the First World War, when irrationality and violence seemed to pervade the human experience, expressionism in opera and ballet flourished. One of the most famous and powerful examples was the opera *Wozzeck*, by Alban Berg (1885–1935), first performed in Berlin in 1925. Blending a half-sung, half-spoken kind of dialogue with harsh, atonal music, *Wozzeck* is a gruesome tale of a soldier driven by Kafka-like inner terrors to murder his mistress.

Some composers turned their backs on long-established musical conventions. As abstract painters arranged lines and color but did not draw identifiable objects, so modern composers arranged sounds without creating recognizable harmonies. Led by Viennese composer Arnold Schönberg (SHON-burg) (1874–1951), they abandoned traditional harmony and tonality. The musical notes in a given piece were no longer united and organized by a key; instead they were independent and unrelated. Schönberg's twelve-tone music of the 1920s arranged all twelve notes of the scale in an abstract, mathematical pattern, or "tone row." This pattern, which sounded like no pattern at all to the ordinary listener, could be detected only by a highly trained eye studying the musical score.

Movies and Radio

In what ways did movies and radio become mainstays of popular culture?

Until after World War II at the earliest, these revolutionary changes in art and music appealed mainly to a minority of "highbrows" and not to the general public. That public was primarily and enthusiastically wrapped up in movies and radio.

Moving pictures were first shown as a popular novelty in naughty peepshows—"What the Butler Saw"—and penny arcades in the 1890s, especially in Paris. But on the eve of the First World War, filmmakers were capable of producing full-length feature films such as the Italian *Quo Vadis* (kwo VAH-dis) and the American *Birth of a Nation*. During the First World War, the United States became the dominant force in the rapidly expanding silent-film industry. Charlie Chaplin (1889–1978), an Englishman working in Hollywood, was unquestionably the king of the "silver screen" in the 1920s. In his enormously popular role as the lonely Little Tramp, complete with baggy trousers, battered derby, and an awkward, shuffling walk, Chaplin symbolized the "gay spirit of laughter in a cruel, crazy world."[5] Chaplin also demonstrated that in the hands of a genius, the new medium could combine mass entertainment and artistic accomplishment.

The early 1920s were also the great age of German films. Protected and developed during the war, the large German studios excelled in bizarre expressionist dramas, beginning with *The Cabinet of Dr. Caligari* in 1919. Unfortunately, their period of creativity was short-lived. By 1926 American money was drawing the leading German talents to Hollywood and consolidating America's international domination.

Whether foreign or domestic, motion pictures became the main entertainment of the masses until after the Second World War. In Great Britain one in every four adults went to the movies twice a week in the late 1930s, and two in five went at least once a week. The greatest appeal of motion pictures was that they offered ordinary people a temporary escape from the hard realities of everyday life. The appeal of escapist entertainment was especially strong during the Great Depression. Millions flocked to musical comedies featuring glittering stars such as Ginger Rogers and Fred Astaire and to the fanciful cartoons of Mickey Mouse and his friends.

The Great Dictator

In 1940 the renowned actor and director Charlie Chaplin abandoned the Little Tramp role to satirize the "great dictator," Adolf Hitler. Chaplin had strong political views and made a number of films with political themes as the escapist fare of the Great Depression gave way to the reality of the Second World War. (The Museum of Modern Art/Film Stills Archive)

Radio became technically possible at the turn of the century, but only in 1920 were the first major public broadcasts of special events made in Great Britain and the United States. Lord Northcliffe, who had pioneered in journalism with the inexpensive, mass-circulation *Daily Mail*, sponsored a broadcast of "only one artist . . . the world's very best, the soprano Nellie Melba."[6] Singing from London, Melba was heard simultaneously all over Europe on June 16, 1920. This historic event captured the public's imagination. The meteoric career of radio was launched.

Every major country quickly established national broadcasting networks. In the United States such networks were privately owned and financed by advertising. In Great Britain Parliament set up an independent, public corporation, the British Broadcasting Corporation (BBC), supported by licensing fees. Elsewhere in Europe the typical pattern was direct control by the government.

Radio was also well suited for political propaganda. Dictators such as Mussolini and Hitler controlled the airwaves and could reach enormous national audiences with their frequent, dramatic speeches. In democratic countries, politicians such as President Franklin Roosevelt and Prime Minister Stanley Baldwin effectively used informal "fireside chats" to bolster their support.

Motion pictures also became powerful tools of indoctrination. Lenin himself encouraged the development of Soviet film making, and the communist view of Russian history was presented in a series of epic films, the most famous of which were directed by Sergei Eisenstein (1898–1948).

In Germany Hitler turned to a young and immensely talented woman film maker, Leni Riefenstahl (REE-fuhn-shtahl) (1902–2003), for a masterpiece of documentary propaganda, *The Triumph of the Will*, based on the Nazi party rally at Nuremberg in 1934. Riefenstahl combined stunning aerial photography, joyful crowds welcoming Hitler, and mass processions of young Nazi fanatics. Her film was a brilliant and all-too-powerful documentary of Germany's "Nazi rebirth." The new media of mass culture were potentially dangerous instruments of political manipulation.

Section Review

- The revolution in the arts moved the masses in the new fields of movies and radio.

- The king of the silent film era was Charlie Chaplin, who combined humor and ingenuity to entertain, providing a way to escape the hardships of everyday life.

- Radio also took off as an inexpensive means of mass entertainment and, with movies, became a tool for political propaganda.

The Search for Peace and Political Stability

How did the democratic leaders of the 1920s deal with deep-seated instability and try to establish real peace and prosperity?

As established patterns of thought and culture were challenged and mangled by the ferocious impact of World War I, so also was the political fabric stretched and torn by the consequences of the great conflict. The Versailles settlement had established a shaky truce, not a solid peace. Thus national leaders faced a gigantic task as they struggled with uncertainty and sought to create a stable international order within the general context of intellectual crisis and revolutionary artistic experimentation.

The pursuit of real and lasting peace proved difficult for many reasons. Germany hated the Treaty of Versailles. France was fearful and isolated. Britain was undependable, and the United States had turned its back on European problems. Eastern Europe was in ferment, and no one could predict the future of communist Russia. Moreover, the international economic situation was poor and greatly complicated by war debts and disrupted patterns of trade. Yet for a time, from 1925 to late 1929, it appeared that peace and stability were within reach. When the subsequent collapse of the 1930s mocked these hopes and brought the rise of brutal dictators, the disillusionment of liberals in the democracies was intensified.

Germany and the Western Powers

Germany was the key to lasting peace. Yet to Germans, the Treaty of Versailles represented a harsh, dictated peace, to be revised or repudiated as soon as possible. The treaty had neither broken nor reduced Germany, which was potentially still the strongest country in Europe. It was too harsh for a peace of reconciliation, too soft for a peace of conquest.

Moreover, with ominous implications for the future, France and Great Britain did not agree about how to treat Germany. French politicians believed that massive reparations from Germany were a vital economic necessity, as they had to shoulder the major burden of reconstruction while also repaying war debts to the United States. Many French leaders saw strict implementation of all provisions of the Treaty of Versailles as France's best chance at curbing Germany's power and ensuring France's security.

The British, however, wanted Germany to regain its economic strength so that it would again become a major market for British goods. Indeed, many English people agreed with the analysis of the young English economist John Maynard Keynes (cainz) (1883–1946), who argued that if Germany was impoverished by war reparations and other economic measures, all of Europe would suffer. The British were also suspicious of the fact that France had the largest army in Europe and was making alliances with the newly formed states of eastern Europe. In 1921 France signed a mutual defense pact with Poland and associated itself closely with the so-called Little Entente, an alliance that joined Czechoslovakia, Romania, and Yugoslavia against defeated and bitter Hungary.

While French and British leaders drifted in different directions, the Allied reparations commission completed its work. In April 1921, it announced that Germany had to pay the enormous sum of 132 billion gold marks ($33 billion) in annual installments of 2.5 billion gold marks. Facing possible occupation of more of its territory (Versailles already authorized France to occupy the Rhineland), the young German republic—generally known as the Weimar Republic—made its first payment in 1921. Then in 1922, wracked by rapid inflation and political assassinations and motivated by hostility and arrogance as well, the Weimar Republic announced its inability to pay more. It proposed a moratorium on reparations for three years, with the clear implication that thereafter reparations would be either drastically reduced or eliminated entirely.

Led by their tough-minded prime minister, Raymond Poincaré (pwan-ka-REY) (1860–1934), the French decided they had to either call Germany's bluff or see the entire peace settlement dissolve. So, despite strong British protests, in early January

1923, armies of France and its ally Belgium moved out of the Rhineland and began to occupy the Ruhr (roor) district, the heartland of industrial Germany, creating the most serious international crisis of the 1920s. If forcible collection proved impossible, France would use occupation to paralyze Germany and force it to accept the Treaty of Versailles. Strengthened by a wave of patriotism, the German government ordered the people of the Ruhr to stop working and start passively resisting the French occupation. The coal mines and steel mills of the Ruhr grew silent, leaving 10 percent of Germany's total population in need of relief. The French answer to passive resistance was to seal off the Ruhr and the entire Rhineland from the rest of Germany, letting in only enough food to prevent starvation.

By the summer of 1923, France and Germany were engaged in a great test of wills. French armies could not collect reparations from striking workers at gunpoint. But French occupation was indeed paralyzing Germany and its economy and had turned rapid German inflation into runaway inflation. Faced with the need to support the striking Ruhr workers and their employers, the German government began to print money to pay its bills. Prices soared. People went to the store with a big bag of paper money; they returned home with a handful of groceries. German money rapidly lost all value.

Runaway inflation brought about a social revolution. The accumulated savings of many retired and middle-class people were wiped out. Catastrophic inflation cruelly mocked the old middle-class virtues of thrift, caution, and self-reliance. Many Germans felt betrayed. They hated and blamed the Western governments, their own government, big business, the Jews, the workers, and the communists for their misfortune. They were psychologically prepared to follow radical leaders in a crisis.

In August 1923, a new leader in Germany was able to diffuse the situation. Gustav Stresemann (GOOS-tahf SHTREY-zuh-mahn) (1878–1929) called off passive resistance in the Ruhr and agreed in principle to pay reparations but asked for a re-examination of Germany's ability to pay. (See the feature "Individuals in Society: Gustav Stresemann.") Poincaré accepted, recognizing that continued confrontation was a destructive, no-win situation. The British, and even the Americans, were willing to help. The first step was a reasonable agreement on the reparations question.

Hope in Foreign Affairs (1924–1929)

The reparations commission appointed an international committee of financial experts headed by American banker Charles G. Dawes to re-examine reparations from a broad perspective. The resulting **Dawes Plan** (1924) was accepted by France, Germany, and Britain. Germany's yearly reparations were reduced and depended on the level of German economic prosperity. Germany would also receive large loans from the United States to promote German recovery. In short, Germany would get private loans from the United States and pay reparations to France and Britain, thus enabling those countries to repay the large sums they owed the United States.

This circular flow of international payments was complicated and risky, but for a while it worked. The German republic experienced a spectacular economic recovery. With prosperity and large, continual inflows of American capital, Germany easily paid about $1.3 billion in reparations in 1927 and 1928, enabling France and Britain to pay the United States. In this way the Americans belatedly played a part in the general economic settlement that, though far from ideal, facilitated the worldwide recovery of the late 1920s.

Dawes Plan The product of the reparations commission headed by Charles G. Dawes that was accepted by Germany, France, and Britain, and reduced Germany's yearly reparations, made payment dependant on German economic prosperity, and granted Germany large loans from the United States to promote recovery.

Gustav Stresemann

The German foreign minister Gustav Stresemann (1878–1929) is a controversial historical figure. Hailed by many as a hero of peace, he was denounced as a traitor by radical German nationalists and then by Hitler's Nazis. After World War II, revisionist historians stressed Stresemann's persistent nationalism and cast doubt on his peaceful intentions. Weimar Germany's most renowned leader is a fascinating example of the restless quest for convincing historical interpretation.

Stresemann's origins were modest. His parents were Berlin innkeepers and retailers of bottled beer, and only Gustav of their five children was able to attend high school. Attracted first to literature and history, Stresemann later turned to economics, earned a doctoral degree, and quickly reached the top as a manager and director

Foreign Minister Gustav Stresemann of Germany *(right)* leaves a meeting with Aristide Briand, his French counterpart. (Corbis)

of German trade associations. A highly intelligent extrovert with a knack for negotiation, Stresemann entered the Reichstag in 1907 as a business-oriented liberal and nationalist. When World War I erupted, he believed, like most Germans, that Germany had acted defensively and was not at fault. He emerged as a strident nationalist and urged German annexation of conquered foreign territories. Germany's collapse in defeat and revolution devastated Stresemann. He seemed a prime candidate for the hateful extremism of the far right.

Yet although Stresemann opposed the Treaty of Versailles as an unjust and unrealistic imposition, he turned back toward the center. He accepted the new Weimar Republic and played a growing role in the Reichstag as the leader of his own small probusiness party. His hour came in the Ruhr crisis, when French and Belgian troops occupied the district. Named chancellor in August 1923, he called off passive resistance and began talks with the French. His government also quelled communist uprisings; put down rebellions in Bavaria, including Hitler's attempted coup; and ended runaway inflation with a new currency. Stresemann fought to preserve German unity, and he succeeded.

Voted out as chancellor in November 1923, Stresemann remained as foreign minister in every government until his death in 1929. Proclaiming a policy of peace and agreeing to pay reparations, he achieved his greatest triumph in the Locarno agreements of 1925 (see page 741). But the interlocking guarantees of existing French and German borders (and the related agreements to resolve peacefully all disputes with Poland and Czechoslovakia) did not lead the French to make any further concessions that might have disarmed Stresemann's extremist foes. Working himself to death, he made little additional progress in achieving international reconciliation and sovereign equality for Germany.

Stresemann was no fuzzy pacifist. Historians debunking his "legend" are right in seeing an enduring love of nation in his defense of German interests. But Stresemann, like his French counterpart Aristide Briand, was a statesman of goodwill who wanted peace through mutually advantageous compromise. A realist trained by business and politics in the art of the possible, Stresemann also reasoned that Germany had to be a satisfied and equal partner if peace was to be secure. His unwillingness to guarantee Germany's eastern borders (see Map 27.4 on page 718), which is often criticized, reflects his conviction that keeping some Germans under Polish and Czechoslovak rule created a ticking time bomb in Europe. Stresemann was no less convinced that war on Poland would almost certainly re-create the Allied coalition that had crushed Germany in 1918.[*] His insistence on the necessity of peace in the east as well as the west was prophetic. Hitler's 1939 invasion of Poland resulted in an even mightier coalition that almost annihilated Germany in 1945.

Questions for Analysis

1. What did Gustav Stresemann do to promote reconciliation in Europe? How did his policy toward France differ from that toward Poland and Czechoslovakia?

2. What is your interpretation of Stresemann? Does he arouse your sympathy or your suspicion and hostility? Why?

[*] Robert Grathwol, "Stresemann: Reflections on His Foreign Policy," *Journal of Modern History* 45 (March 1973): 52–70.

This economic settlement was matched by a political settlement. In 1925 the leaders of Europe signed a number of agreements at Locarno, Switzerland. Germany and France solemnly pledged to accept their common border, and both Britain and Italy agreed to fight either France or Germany if one invaded the other. Stresemann also agreed to settle boundary disputes with Poland and Czechoslovakia by peaceful means, and France promised those countries military aid if Germany attacked them. For years, a "spirit of Locarno" gave Europeans a sense of growing security and stability in international affairs.

Other developments also strengthened hopes. In 1926 Germany joined the League of Nations, where Stresemann continued his "peace offensive." In 1928 fifteen countries signed the Kellogg-Briand Pact, initiated by French prime minister Aristide Briand and U.S. secretary of state Frank B. Kellogg. This multinational pact "condemned and renounced war as an instrument of national policy." The signing states agreed to settle international disputes peacefully. Often seen as idealistic nonsense because it made no provisions for action in case war actually occurred, the pact was still a positive step. It fostered the cautious optimism of the late 1920s and also encouraged the hope that the United States would accept its responsibilities as a great world power and contribute to European stability.

Hope in Democratic Government

Domestic politics also offered reason to hope. During the occupation of the Ruhr and the great inflation, republican government in Germany had appeared on the verge of collapse. In 1923 communists momentarily entered provincial governments, and in November an obscure nobody named Adolf Hitler leaped onto a table in a beer hall in Munich and proclaimed a "national socialist revolution." But Hitler's plot to seize control of the government was poorly organized and easily crushed, and Hitler was sentenced to prison, where he outlined his theories and program in his book *Mein Kampf* (mine kompf) (My Struggle). Throughout the 1920s, Hitler's National Socialist Party attracted support only from a few fanatical anti-Semites, ultranationalists, and disgruntled ex-servicemen. In 1928 his party had an insignificant twelve seats in the Reichstag. Indeed, after 1923 democracy seemed to take root in Weimar Germany. A new currency was established, the economy boomed, and elections were held regularly.

Mein Kampf A book written by Adolf Hitler, in which he outlines his theories and program for a national socialist revolution.

There were, however, sharp political divisions in the country, with nationalists and monarchists on the right and newly formed Communist Party members on the left. The working classes were divided politically, but a majority supported the moderate socialist Social Democrats.

The situation in France had numerous similarities to that in Germany. Communists and Socialists battled for the support of the workers. After 1924 the democratically elected government rested mainly in the hands of coalitions of moderates, and business interests were well represented. France's great accomplishment was rapid rebuilding of its war-torn northern region. The expense of this undertaking led, however, to a large deficit and substantial inflation, which reached a crisis point in early 1926. The government restored confidence in the economy by slashing spending and raising taxes, and good times prevailed until 1930. France also became a locus of cultural energy, attracting artists and writers from all over the world. As writer Gertrude Stein (stine) (1874–1946), a leader of the large colony of American expatriates living in Paris, later recalled, "Paris was where the twentieth century was."[7]

Britain, too, faced challenges after 1920. The wartime trend toward greater social equality continued, however, helping maintain social harmony. Many of

American Jazz in Paris

This woodcut from a 1928 French book on cafés and nightclubs suggests how black musicians took Europe by storm, although the blacks are represented stereotypically. One French critic concluded that American blacks had attained a "pre-eminent" place in music since the war, "for they have impressed the entire world with their vibrating or melancholy rhythms." (akg-images)

Britain's best markets had been lost during the war, and companies laid off massive numbers of workers in response. Yet the state provided unemployment benefits of equal size to all those without jobs and supplemented those payments with subsidized housing, medical aid, and increased old-age pensions. These and other measures kept living standards from seriously declining, defused class tensions, and pointed the way toward the welfare state Britain established after World War II. Relative social harmony was accompanied by the rise of the Labour party as a determined champion of the working classes and of greater social equality. Committed to the kind of moderate, "revisionist" socialism that had emerged before World War I (see pages 668–669), the Labour Party replaced the Liberal Party as the main opposition to the Conservatives. The new prominence of the Labour Party reflected the decline of old liberal ideals of competitive capitalism, limited government control, and individual responsibility. In 1924 and 1929, the Labour Party under Ramsay MacDonald (1866–1937) governed the country with the support of the smaller Liberal Party. Yet Labour moved toward socialism gradually and democratically, so that the middle classes were not overly frightened as the working classes won new benefits.

The Conservatives under Stanley Baldwin (1867–1947) showed the same compromising spirit on social issues. The last line of Baldwin's greatest speech in March 1925 summarized his international and domestic programs: "Give us peace in our time, O Lord." In spite of such conflicts as the 1926 strike by hard-pressed coal miners, which ended in an unsuccessful general strike, social unrest in Britain was limited in the 1920s and in the 1930s as well. In 1922 Britain granted southern, Catholic Ireland full autonomy after a bitter guerrilla war, thereby removing another source of prewar friction. Thus developments in both international relations and the domestic politics of the leading democracies gave cause for optimism in the late 1920s.

Section Review

- Conflicts remained over how to treat Germany after the Treaty of Versailles; Germans thought it was too harsh, the French wanted to enforce it fully to curb Germany's power, while the British wanted Germany to regain its strength and become an important market for British goods.

- The Allied reparations commission left Germany with an enormous sum that it could not repay and led to a stalemate, with France occupying Germany in the Ruhr district until Gustav Stresemann was able to call in the British and the Americans for help in reassessing the debt.

- The Dawes Plan allowed Germany to get private loans from the United States to pay reparations to France and Britain, who then repaid their own war debt to the United States; politically all agreed to settle international disputes peacefully.

- In Germany, democracy seemed to be taking root, but division remained with nationalists and monarchists on the right and communists and socialists on the left; in France the communists and the socialists battled for support of the workers while culture thrived.

- In Great Britain, the moderate "revisionist" socialism of the Labour party led the country gradually toward socialism while Catholic Ireland finally gained full autonomy in 1922 after a bitter guerrilla war.

The Great Depression (1929–1939)

What caused the Great Depression, and how did the Western democracies respond to this challenge?

Like the Great War, the **Great Depression** must be spelled with capital letters. Economic depression was nothing new. Depressions occurred throughout the nineteenth century with predictable regularity, as they recur in the form of recessions and slumps to this day. What was new about this depression was its severity and duration. It struck the entire world with ever-greater intensity from 1929 to 1933, and recovery was uneven and slow. Only with the Second World War did the depression disappear in much of the world.

The social and political consequences of prolonged economic collapse were enormous. Mass unemployment and failing farms made insecurity a reality for millions of ordinary people, who looked in desperation for leaders who would "do something."

Great Depression A world wide economic depression from 1929 through 1933, unique in its severity and duration and with slow and uneven recovery.

The Economic Crisis

There is no agreement among historians and economists about why the Great Depression was so deep and lasted so long. Thus it is best to trace the course of the great collapse before trying to identify what caused it.

The Great Depression was triggered by developments in the United States that culminated in the stock market crash of 1929. The American economy had prospered in the late 1920s, but there was a serious imbalance between "real" investment and stock market speculation. Thus net investment—in factories, farms, equipment, and the like—actually fell from $3.5 billion in 1925 to $3.2 billion in 1929. In the same years, as money flooded into stocks, the value of shares traded on the exchanges soared from $27 billion to $87 billion. Although it was not clear to people at the time, a crash was inevitable.

The American stock market boom was built on borrowed money. Many wealthy investors, speculators, and people of modest means had bought stocks by paying only a small fraction of the total purchase price and borrowing the remainder from their stockbrokers. Such buying "on margin" was extremely dangerous. When prices started falling, the hard-pressed margin buyers either had to put up more money, which was often impossible, or sell their shares to pay off their brokers. Thus thousands of people started selling all at once. The result was a financial panic. Countless investors and speculators were wiped out in a matter of days or weeks.

The financial panic in the United States triggered a worldwide financial crisis. Throughout the 1920s, American bankers and investors had lent large amounts of capital to many countries. Many of these loans were short-term, and once panic broke, New York bankers began recalling them. Gold reserves thus began to flow out of European countries, particularly Germany and Austria, toward the United States. It became very hard for European business people to borrow money, and the panicky public began to withdraw its savings from the banks. These banking problems eventually led to the crash of the largest bank in Austria in 1931 and then to general financial chaos. The recall of private loans by American bankers also accelerated the collapse in world prices, as business people around the world dumped industrial goods and agricultural commodities in a frantic attempt to get cash to pay what they owed.

The financial crisis led to a general crisis of production: between 1929 and 1933, world output of goods fell by an estimated 38 percent. As this happened, each country turned inward and tried to go it alone. More than twenty nations, including Britain and the United States, went off the gold standard in order to price their goods more attractively in foreign markets, with no real advantage gained. Similarly, country after country followed the example of the United States when in 1930 it raised protective tariffs to their highest levels ever and tried to seal off shrinking national markets for American producers only. Within this context of fragmented and destructive economic nationalism, recovery finally began in 1933.

Although opinions differ, two factors probably best explain the relentless slide to the bottom from 1929 to early 1933. First, no country came forward to coordinate a response to the international economic situation. Second, almost every country suffered from poor national economic policy. Governments generally cut their budgets and reduced spending when they should have run large deficits in an attempt to stimulate their economies. After World War II, such a "counter-cyclical policy," advocated by John Maynard Keynes, became a well-established weapon against downturn and depression. But in the 1930s, Keynes's prescription was generally dismissed.

Mass Unemployment

The financial crisis led to cuts in production, and in turn workers all across Europe and the United States lost their jobs and had little money to buy goods (see Map 28.1). Along with economic effects, mass unemployment posed a great social problem. Poverty increased dramatically, although in most countries unemployed workers generally received some kind of meager unemployment benefits or public aid that prevented starvation. (See the feature "Listening to the Past: Life on the Dole in Great Britain" on pages 750–751.) Homes and ways of life were disrupted in millions of personal tragedies. Young people postponed marriages, and birthrates fell sharply. There was an increase in suicide and mental illness. Poverty or the threat of poverty became a grinding reality. Only strong government action could deal with mass unemployment, a social powder keg preparing to explode.

The New Deal in the United States

Of all the major industrial countries, only Germany was harder hit by the Great Depression, or reacted more radically to it, than the United States (see Chapter 29). Depression was so traumatic in the United States because the "Roaring Twenties" had been a period of great optimism. The Great Depression and the response to it marked a major turning point in American history.

MAPPING THE PAST

MAP 28.1   The Great Depression in the United States, Britain, and Europe

These maps show that unemployment was high almost everywhere, but that national and regional differences were also substantial. With this in mind: **[1]** In the United States, what in 1934 were the main channels of migration for workers? **[2]** In Britain, locate the areas with the highest levels of unemployment, which were generally dependent on traditional basic industries such as steel, coal, and textiles. What large area has the lowest unemployment? Why? **[3]** Which European countries in 1932 had the highest rate of unemployment, usually considered a good indicator of the level of economic hardship?

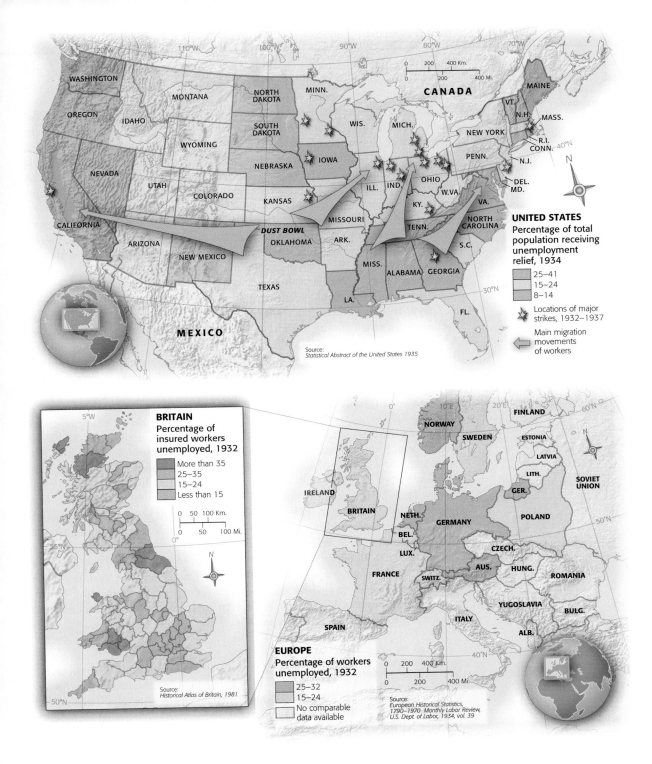

UNITED STATES
Percentage of total population receiving unemployment relief, 1934

- 25–41
- 15–24
- 8–14

★ Locations of major strikes, 1932–1937

◀ Main migration movements of workers

Source:
Statistical Abstract of the United States 1935

BRITAIN
Percentage of insured workers unemployed, 1932

- More than 35
- 25–35
- 15–24
- Less than 15

Source:
Historical Atlas of Britain, 1981

EUROPE
Percentage of workers unemployed, 1932

- 25–32
- 15–24
- No comparable data available

Source:
European Historical Statistics, 1790–1970 Monthly Labor Review, U.S. Dept. of Labor, 1934, vol. 39

President Herbert Hoover (1895–1972) and his administration initially reacted to the stock market crash and economic decline with hope for recovery and limited action. But when the full force of the financial crisis struck Europe in the summer of 1931 and boomeranged back to the United States, people's worst fears became reality. Banks failed; unemployment soared. Between 1929 and 1932, industrial production fell by about 50 percent.

New Deal Franklin Delano Roosevelt's plan to reform capitalism through forceful government intervention in the economy.

In these tragic circumstances, Franklin Delano Roosevelt (1882–1945) won a landslide presidential victory in 1932 with grand but vague promises of a "**New Deal** for the forgotten man."

Roosevelt's basic goal was to reform capitalism in order to preserve it. Roosevelt rejected socialism and government ownership of industry in 1933. To right the situation, he chose forceful government intervention in the economy. In this choice, Roosevelt was flexible, pragmatic, and willing to experiment. He and his "brain trust" of advisers adopted policies echoing the American experience in World War I, when the American economy had been thoroughly planned and regulated.

Innovative programs promoted agricultural recovery, a top priority. The Agricultural Adjustment Act of 1933 also aimed at raising prices and farm income by limiting production. These planning measures worked for a while, and farmers repaid Roosevelt in 1936 with overwhelming support.

Roosevelt and his advisers then attacked the key problem of mass unemployment directly. The federal government accepted the responsibility of employing directly as many people as financially possible. New agencies were created to undertake a vast range of projects. The most famous of these was the Works Progress Administration, or **WPA,** set up in 1935. One-fifth of the entire labor force worked for the WPA at some point in the 1930s, constructing public buildings, bridges, and highways. The WPA was enormously popular, and the hope of a government job helped check the threat of social revolution in the United States.

WPA The Works Progress Administration, set up in 1935. The most famous of Roosevelt's New Deal programs, it employed one-fifth of the entire labor force at some point in the 1930s, constructing public buildings, bridges, and highways.

Government relief programs like the WPA marked a profound shift from the traditional stress on family support and community responsibility. Other social measures aimed in the same direction. In 1935 the government established a national Social Security system, with old-age pensions and unemployment benefits, to protect many workers against some of life's uncertainties. The National Labor Relations Act of 1935 gave union organizers the green light by declaring collective bargaining to be the policy of the United States. Union membership more than doubled, from 4 million in 1935 to 9 million in 1940. In general, between 1935 and 1938 government rulings and social reforms chipped away at the privileges of the wealthy and tried to help ordinary people.

Yet despite undeniable accomplishments in social reform, the New Deal was only partly successful as a response to the Great Depression. A recession hit the United States in 1937 and 1938, and unemployment was still a staggering 10 million when war broke out in Europe in September 1939. The New Deal never did pull the United States out of the depression.

The Scandinavian Response to the Depression

Social Democrats A flexible and nonrevolutionary socialist government in Scandinavia that grew out of a strong tradition of cooperative community action. In the 1920s, it passed important social reform legislation for both peasants and workers, gained practical administrative experience, and developed a unique kind of socialism.

Of all the Western democracies, the Scandinavian countries under Social Democratic leadership responded most successfully to the challenge of the Great Depression. In the 1920s, the **Social Democrats** developed a unique kind of socialism. Flexible and nonrevolutionary, Scandinavian socialism grew out of a strong tradition of cooperative action in peasant communities. Labor leaders and capitalists had also been inclined to work together.

When the economic crisis struck in 1929, socialist governments in Scandinavia built on this pattern of cooperative social action. Sweden in particular pioneered in the use of large-scale deficits to finance public works and thereby maintain production and employment. Scandinavian governments also increased social welfare benefits, from old-age pensions and unemployment insurance to subsidized housing and maternity allowances. All this spending required a large

Oslo Breakfast

Scandinavian socialism championed cooperation and practical welfare measures, playing down strident rhetoric and theories of class conflict. The Oslo Breakfast exemplified the Scandinavian approach. It provided every schoolchild in the Norwegian capital with a good breakfast free of charge. (Courtesy, Directorate for Health and Social Affairs, Oslo)

bureaucracy and high taxes, first on the rich and then on practically everyone. Yet both private and cooperative enterprise thrived, as did democracy. Some observers saw Scandinavia's welfare socialism as an appealing "middle way" between sick capitalism and cruel communism or fascism.

Recovery and Reform in Britain and France   In Britain, MacDonald's Labour government and then, after 1931, the Conservative-dominated coalition government followed orthodox economic theory. The budget was balanced, but unemployed workers received barely enough welfare to live. Yet the economy recovered considerably after 1932 and even improved somewhat on the 1920s economy, quite the opposite of the situation in the United States and France.

This good but by no means brilliant performance reflected the gradual reorientation of the British economy toward the domestic market. New industries, such as automobiles and electrical appliances, grew in response to British home demand. Moreover, low interest rates encouraged a housing boom. These developments encouraged Britain to look inward and avoid unpleasant foreign questions.

Because France was relatively less industrialized and more isolated from the world economy, the Great Depression came late. But once the depression hit France, it was long-lived. Economic stagnation both reflected and heightened an ongoing political crisis. There was no stability in government. As before 1914, the French parliament was made up of many political parties, which could never cooperate for very long. The difference this time was that the vital center of moderate republicanism was sapped from both sides. New Fascist-type organizations agitated against parliamentary democracy and looked to Mussolini's Italy and Hitler's Germany for inspiration (see Chapter 29). At the same time, the Communist party and many workers opposed to the existing system were looking to Stalin's Russia for guidance.

Frightened by the growing strength of the fascists at home and abroad, the Communists, the Socialists, and the Radicals formed an alliance—the **Popular Front**—for the national elections of May 1936. Their clear victory reflected the trend toward polarization. The number of Communists in the parliament jumped dramatically, while the Socialists, led by Léon Blum, became the strongest party in France. The really quite moderate Radicals slipped badly, and the conservatives lost ground to the semifascists.

In the next few months, Blum's Popular Front government made the first and only real attempt to deal with France's social and economic problems. Inspired by Roosevelt's New Deal, the Popular Front encouraged the union movement and launched a far-reaching program of social reform, complete with paid vacations and a forty-hour workweek. Popular with workers and the lower middle class, these measures were quickly sabotaged by rapid inflation and cries of revolution from fascists and frightened conservatives. Wealthy people sneaked their money out of the country, labor unrest grew, and France entered a severe financial crisis. Blum was forced to announce a "breathing spell" in social reform.

The fires of political dissension were also fanned by civil war in Spain. Communists demanded that France support the Spanish republicans, while many French conservatives would gladly have joined Hitler and Mussolini in aiding the attack of Spanish fascists. Extremism grew, and France itself was within sight of civil war. Blum was forced to resign in June 1937, and the Popular Front quickly collapsed. An anxious and divided France drifted aimlessly once again, preoccupied by Hitler and German rearmament.

Popular Front A New Deal–inspired party in France led by Leon Blum that encouraged the union movement and launched a far-reaching program of social reform, complete with paid vacations and a forty-hour workweek.

Section Review

- The economic crisis that began with the crash of the American stock market in 1929 spread across the world as American bankers recalled their loans, collapsing the world market and decreasing the output of goods; countries attempted to recover by raising tariffs and going off the gold standard.
- Cuts in production caused mass unemployment and a widespread social crisis as the poor received little government aid.
- In the United States, Franklin Roosevelt reformed capitalism through the forceful government intervention of the New Deal, enacting programs to boost agriculture and employment rates, setting up a Social Security system, and allowing collective bargaining.
- The Social Democrats in Scandinavia responded most successfully to the depression by using large-scale deficits to fund public works and increasing social welfare benefits, taxing the wealthy first and then almost everyone.
- Britain weathered the depression and recovered as new automobile and electrical appliance industries grew along with a housing boom; France, on the other hand, was caught in a political crossfire between political parties and the strength of the Popular Front, unable to pull the country out of crisis.

Chapter Review

In what ways did new and disturbing ideas in philosophy, physics, psychology, and the arts reflect the general crisis in Western thought? (page 727)

After the First World War, Western intellectual life underwent a general crisis marked by pessimism, uncertainty, and fascination with irrational forces. Philosophers, building on the prewar writings of Nietzsche, rejected the traditional philosophical questions, focusing instead on the rules of language or an existential morality. Einstein's theories reordered the universe and overturned Newtonian physics; Freudian psychology privileged the power of the irrational in human thought. Ceaseless experimentation and rejection of old forms characterized literature, painting, and music. In short, almost every field of Western thought and art experienced revolutionary change.

In what ways did movies and radio become mainstays of popular culture? (page 736)

Motion pictures and radio provided entertainment and relaxation for the masses. They were enormously popular, offering escape from the hard realities of everyday life. Dictatorial governments used the new media for political propaganda.

Key Terms
logical empiricism (p. 728)
existentialism (p. 728)
neutron (p. 730)
id, ego, and superego (p. 730)
stream-of-consciousness technique (p. 731)
functionalism (p. 732)
Bauhaus (p. 732)
Dadaism (p. 733)
Dawes Plan (p. 739)
Mein Kampf (p. 741)
Great Depression (p. 743)

How did the democratic leaders of the 1920s deal with deep-seated instability and try to establish real peace and prosperity? (page 737)

The Treaty of Versailles left defeated Germany and the victorious Allies bitterly divided. The question of Germany reparations soon led to political stalemate, French occupation of Germany's Ruhr district, runaway German inflation, and the prospect of a general European collapse. In 1923, courageous new leaders turned to compromise. Led by Stresemann in Germany and Briand in France and backed by Great Britain and the United States, the new leaders worked out a complicated financial and political settlement that led to economic recovery and fragile political stability. Germany boomed, France rebuilt its war-ravaged areas, and Britain's Labour Party expanded social services.

What caused the Great Depression, and how did the Western democracies respond to this challenge? (page 743)

The Great Depression grew out of the fragile international financial system and the speculative boom in the U.S. stock market in the 1920s. The stock market crash in 1929 shattered international banking and triggered a disastrous downward spiral in prices and production, bringing massive unemployment to millions of workers. Turning inward to cope with the economic crisis and the related social problems, the Western democracies responded with relief measures, extended unemployment benefits, labor reforms, and social concern. These measures eased distress and prevented revolutions in the leading nations, but with significant exception of the Scandinavian countries the Western democracies failed to restore prosperity, eliminate high unemployment, and prevent widespread disillusionment. The old liberal ideals of individual rights and responsibilities, elected government, and economic freedom declined and appeared outmoded to many citizens. And in many countries of central and eastern Europe, these ideas were abandoned completely, as we shall see in the next chapter.

New Deal (p. 746)
WPA (p. 746)
Social Democrats (p. 746)
Popular Front (p. 748)

Notes

1. G. Greene, *Another Mexico* (New York: Viking Press, 1939), p. 3.
2. G. Orwell, *1984* (New York: New American Library, 1950), p. 220.
3. C. E. Jeanneret-Gris (Le Corbusier), *Towards a New Architecture* (London: J. Rodker, 1931), p. 15.
4. Quoted in A. H. Barr, Jr., *What Is Modern Painting?*, 9th ed. (New York: Museum of Modern Art, 1966), p. 25.
5. R. Graves and A. Hodge, *The Long Week End: A Social History of Great Britain, 1918–1939* (New York: Macmillan, 1941), p. 131.
6. Quoted in A. Briggs, *The Birth of Broadcasting*, vol. 1 (London: Oxford University Press, 1961), p. 47.
7. Quoted in R. J. Sontag, *A Broken World, 1919–1939* (New York: Harper & Row, 1971), p. 129.

To assess your mastery of this chapter, go to **bedfordstmartins.com/mckaywestbrief**

Listening to the Past

Life on the Dole in Great Britain

Periodic surges in unemployment were an old story in capitalist economies, but the long-term joblessness of millions in the Great Depression was something new and unexpected. In Britain especially, where the depression followed a weak postwar recovery, large numbers suffered involuntary idleness for years at a time. Whole families lived "on the dole," the weekly welfare benefits paid by the government.

One of the most insightful accounts of unemployed workers was written by the British journalist and novelist George Orwell (1903–1950), who studied the conditions in northern England and wrote The Road to Wigan Pier *(1937).*

Poster used in the election campaign of 1931, when unemployment rose to a new record high. (Conservative Research Department/ The Bridgeman Art Library)

When people live on the dole for years at a time they grow used to it, and drawing the dole, though it remains unpleasant, ceases to be shameful. Thus the old, independent, workhouse-fearing tradition is undermined. . . .

So you have whole populations settling down, as it were, to a lifetime of the P.A.C. . . . Take, for instance, the fact that the working class think nothing of getting married on the dole. . . . Life is still fairly normal, more normal than one really has the right to expect. Families are impoverished, but the family-system has not broken up. The people are in effect living a reduced version of their former lives. Instead of raging against their destiny they have made things tolerable by lowering their standards.

But they don't necessarily lower their standards by cutting out luxuries and concentrating on necessities; more often it is the other way about—the more natural way, if you come to think of it. Hence the fact that in a decade of unparalleled depression, the consumption of all cheap luxuries has increased. The two things that have probably made the greatest difference of all are the movies and the mass-production of cheap smart clothes since the war. The youth who leaves school at fourteen and gets a blind-alley job is out of work at twenty, probably for life; but for two pounds ten on the hire-purchase system he can buy himself a suit which, for a little while and at a little distance, looks as though it had been tailored in Savile Row. The girl can look like a fashion plate at an even lower price. . . . You can stand on the street corner, indulging in a private daydream of yourself as Clark Gable or Greta Garbo, which compensates you for a great deal. . . .

Trade since the war has had to adjust itself to meet the demands of underpaid, underfed people, with the result that a luxury is nowadays almost always cheaper than a necessity. One pair of plain solid shoes costs as much as two ultra-smart pairs. . . . And above all there is gambling, the cheapest of all luxuries. Even people on the verge of starvation can buy a few days' hope ("Something to live for," as they call it) by having a penny on a sweepstake. . . . Twenty million people are underfed but literally everyone in England has access to a radio. What we have lost in food we have gained in electricity. Whole sections of the working class who have been plundered of all they really need are being compensated, in part, by cheap luxuries which mitigate the surface of life.

Do you consider all this desirable? No, I don't. But it may be that the psychological adjustment which the working class are visibly making is the best they could make in the circumstances. They have neither turned revolutionary nor lost their self-respect; merely they have kept their tempers and settled down to make the best of things on a fish-and-chip standard. The alternative would be God knows what continued agonies of despair; or it might be attempted insurrections which, in a strongly governed country like England, could only lead to futile massacres and a régime of savage repression.

Questions for Analysis

1. What were the consequences of long-term unemployment for English workers? Were some of the consequences surprising?

2. Judging from Orwell's description, did radical revolution seem likely in England in the Great Depression? Why?

Source: Excerpts from Chapter V in *The Road to Wigan Pier* by George Orwell, copyright © 1958 and renewed 1986 by the Estate of Sonia B. Orwell. Reprinted by permission of Houghton Mifflin Harcourt Publishing Company.

CHAPTER 29

Dictatorships and the Second World War

1919–1945

Chapter Preview

Hugo Jager's photograph of a crowd of enthusiastic Hitler supporters. (Time Life Pictures/Getty Images)

The period following the First World War also saw the rise of political dictatorships. On the eve of the Second World War, liberal democratic governments were surviving only in Great Britain, France, the Low Countries, the Scandinavian nations, and Switzerland. Elsewhere in Europe, various kinds of "strongmen" ruled. Dictatorship seemed the wave of the future. Thus the intellectual and economic crisis discussed in Chapter 28 and the rise of dictatorship to be considered in this chapter were interrelated elements in the general crisis of European civilization.

The key development in the era of dictatorship was the rise of a particularly ruthless and dynamic tyranny. This new kind of tyranny reached its full realization in the Soviet Union and Nazi Germany in the 1930s. Stalin and Hitler mobilized their peoples for enormous undertakings and ruled with unprecedented severity. Both made an unprecedented "total claim" on the belief and behavior of their respective citizens, as a noted scholar has recently concluded.[1] While Stalin's aggression was directed within his state, Hitler wanted greater territory as well as the eradication of entire peoples whom he despised. His moves against Germany's neighbors sparked another great war that divided the world into two opposing forces and introduced new methods of mass destruction. Historians continue to ponder what led an entire society to rally behind a leader whose name has become synonymous with human evil. The question remains vital as state-sponsored atrocities and acts of genocide continue to plague our world.

Stalin's Soviet Union

How did Stalin and the Communist Party build a modern totalitarian state in the Soviet Union?

Lenin's harshest critics claim that he established the basic outlines of a modern totalitarian dictatorship after the Bolshevik Revolution and during the Russian civil war. If this is so, then Joseph Stalin (1879–1953) certainly finished the job. A master of political infighting, Stalin cautiously consolidated his power and eliminated his enemies in the mid-1920s. Then in 1928, as undisputed leader of the ruling Communist Party, he launched the first **five-year plan**—the "revolution from above," as he so aptly termed it.

The five-year plans marked the beginning of a renewed attempt to mobilize and transform Soviet society along socialist lines. They were achieved through propaganda, enormous sacrifice by the people, and the concentration of all power in party hands. Thus the Soviet Union in the 1930s became a dynamic, modern totalitarian state.

five-year plan A plan launched by Stalin in 1928 and termed the "revolution from above," the ultimate goal of which was to generate new attitudes, new loyalties, and a new socialist humanity.

From Lenin to Stalin

By spring 1921, Lenin and the Bolsheviks had won the civil war, but they ruled a shattered and devastated land. Many farms were in ruins, and food supplies were exhausted. In southern Russia, drought combined with the ravages of war to produce the worst famine in generations. Industrial production also broke down completely. The Bolsheviks had destroyed the economy as well as their foes.

Lenin's solution was to change course. In March 1921, he announced the **New Economic Policy (NEP)**, which re-established limited economic freedom in an attempt to rebuild agriculture and industry. Peasant producers were permitted

New Economic Policy (NEP) Lenin's 1921 policy to re-establish limited economic freedom in an attempt to rebuild agriculture and industry in the face of economic disintegration.

to sell their surpluses in free markets, and private traders and small handicraft manufacturers were allowed to reappear. Heavy industry, railroads, and banks, however, remained wholly nationalized.

The NEP represented a deal with the only force capable of overturning the government—the peasant majority. Economically, it brought rapid recovery. In 1926 industrial output surpassed the level of 1913, and Soviet peasants were producing almost as much grain as before the war.

As the economy recovered and the government partially relaxed its censorship and repression, an intense struggle for power began in the inner circles of the Communist Party, for Lenin had left no chosen successor when he died in 1924. The principal contenders were the stolid Stalin and the flamboyant Trotsky.

Joseph Stalin, born Joseph Dzhugashvili (joo-guhsh-VEE-lee), was a good organizer but a poor speaker and writer, with no experience outside of Russia. Leon Trotsky, an inspiring leader who had planned the 1917 takeover (see page 714) and then created the victorious Red Army, appeared to have all the advantages. Yet it was Stalin who succeeded Lenin. Stalin won because he was more effective at gaining the all-important support of the party, the only genuine source of power in the one-party state. Rising to general secretary of the party's Central Committee just before Lenin's first stroke in 1922, Stalin used his office to win friends and allies with jobs and promises.

The practical Stalin also won because he appeared better able to relate Marxian teaching to Soviet realities in the 1920s. Stalin developed a theory of "socialism in one country" that was more appealing to the majority of communists than Trotsky's doctrine of "permanent revolution." Stalin argued that the Russian-dominated Soviet Union had the ability to build socialism on its own. Trotsky maintained that socialism in the Soviet Union could succeed only if revolution occurred quickly throughout Europe. To many Russian communists, Trotsky's views seemed to sell their country short and to promise risky conflicts with capitalist countries.

With cunning skill, Stalin gradually achieved supreme power between 1922 and 1927. His final triumph came at the party congress of December 1927, which condemned all "deviation from the general party line" formulated by Stalin. The dictator and his followers were then ready to launch the revolution from above—the real revolution for millions of ordinary citizens.

The Five-Year Plans

The party congress of 1927, which ratified Stalin's consolidation of power, marked the end of the NEP. In its place Stalin rolled out the first in a series of five-year plans designed to catch up with the industrialized west and bring the country closer to having a true socialist economy. Building on planning models developed by Soviet economists in the 1920s, the first five-year plan had staggering economic objectives. In just five years, total industrial output was to increase by 250 percent. Heavy industry, the preferred sector, was to grow even faster. Agricultural production was slated to increase by 150 percent, and one-fifth of the peasants in the Soviet Union were scheduled to give up their private plots and join socialist collective farms. By 1930 economic and social change was sweeping the country. (See the feature "Listening to the Past: Stalin Justifies the Five-Year Plan" on pages 779–780.)

A major aspect of the second revolution was **collectivization**—the forcible consolidation of individual peasant farms into large, state-controlled enterprises. Beginning in 1929, peasants all over the Soviet Union were ordered to give up their land and animals and become members of collective farms, although they continued to live in their own homes. As for the **kulaks** (COO-lox), the better-off peas-

collectivization The forcible consolidation of individual peasant farms into large, state-controlled enterprises.

kulaks The better-off peasants who were stripped of land and livestock under Stalin and were generally not permitted to join the collective farms; many of them starved or were deported to forced-labor camps for "re-education."

ants, Stalin instructed party workers to "liquidate them as a class." Stripped of land and livestock, the kulaks were generally not even permitted to join the collective farms. Many starved or were deported to forced-labor camps for "re-education."

Since almost all peasants were in fact poor, the term *kulak* soon meant any peasant who opposed the new system. Whole villages were often attacked. One conscience-stricken colonel in the secret police confessed to a foreign journalist,

> I am an old Bolshevik. I worked in the underground against the Tsar and then I fought in the Civil War. Did I do all that in order that I should now surround villages with machine guns and order my men to fire indiscriminately into crowds of peasants? Oh, no, no![2]

Forced collectivization of the peasants led to economic and human disaster. Peasants, who had wanted to own their own land for centuries, slaughtered their animals and burned their crops in protest. Between 1929 and 1933, the number of horses, cattle, sheep, and goats in the Soviet Union fell by at least half. Nor were the state-controlled collective farms more productive. The output of grain barely increased between 1928 and 1938. Collectivized agriculture was unable to make any substantial financial contribution to Soviet industrial development in the first five-year plan.

The human dimension of the tragedy was absolutely staggering. As one leading historian writes in outrage, "The number dying in Stalin's war against the peasants was higher than the total deaths of all the countries in World War I." Yet, he notes, in Stalin's war only one side was armed and the other side bore almost all the casualties, many of whom were women, children, and the old.[3]

The Communists won the battle to collectivize farms, but their victory did not bring them the agricultural gains they had expected. Peasants fought back with indirect daily opposition until the government agreed to limit a family's labor on the state-run farms and gave them the right to cultivate tiny family plots. In 1938 these family plots grew 22 percent of all Soviet agricultural produce on only 4 percent of all cultivated land.

The industrial side of the five-year plans was more successful—indeed, quite spectacular. Soviet industry produced about four times as much in 1937 as it had in 1928. No other major country had ever achieved such rapid industrial growth. Heavy industry led the way; consumer industry grew quite slowly. A new heavy industrial complex was built almost from scratch in western Siberia. Industrial growth also went hand in hand with urban development, and more than 25 million people migrated to cities during the 1930s.

The great industrialization drive, concentrated between 1928 and 1937, was an awe-inspiring achievement purchased at enormous sacrifice. The money for investment in dozens of new factories was collected from the people by means of heavy, hidden sales taxes. The workers for the new factories were assigned by the government, which could force people to move to any job anywhere in the country. When factory managers needed more hands, they called on their counterparts on

Year	Event
1921	New Economic Policy (NEP) in U.S.S.R.
1922	Mussolini seizes power in Italy
1924–1929	Buildup of Nazi Party in Germany
1927	Stalin comes to power in U.S.S.R.
1928	Stalin's first five-year plan
1929	Lateran Agreement; start of collectivization in Soviet Union
1931	Japan invades Manchuria
1929–1939	Great Depression
1932–1933	Famine in Ukraine
1933	Hitler appointed chancellor in Germany; Nazis begin to control intellectual life and blacklist authors
1935	Mussolini invades Ethiopia; Hitler announces German rearmament
1936	Start of great purges under Stalin; German armies move into Rhineland; civil war begins in Spain
1938	Germany annexes Austria and Sudetenland
1939	Germany occupies Czech lands; Germany invades Poland; Britain and France declare war on Germany
1941	SS stops Jewish emigration from Europe; Germany invades Soviet Union; bombing of Pearl Harbor; U.S. enters war
1941–1945	Six million Jews killed in death camps
1944	Allied invasion at Normandy
1945	Germany surrenders; atomic bombs dropped on Japan; end of war

Life in a Forced-Labor Camp

This rare photo from about 1933 shows the reality of deported peasants and other political prisoners building the Stalin–White Sea Canal in far northern Russia, with their bare hands and under the most dehumanizing conditions. In books and plays Stalin's followers praised the project as a model for the regeneration of "reactionaries" and "kulak exploiters" through the joys of socialist work. (David King Collection)

the collective farms, who sent them millions of "unneeded" peasants over the years. Individuals, meanwhile, could not move without the permission of the police.

| **Life and Culture in Soviet Society** | The aim of Stalin's five-year plans was to create a new society as well as a stronger economy and army. Once everything was owned by the state, the Stalinists be- |

lieved, a utopian brotherhood of individuals with socialist values would inevitably emerge. The society that the Stalinists created, whose broad outlines existed into the mid-1980s, was far from utopian. It had both good and bad aspects.

Because consumption was reduced to pay for investment, there was no improvement in the average standard of living. Indeed, wages could buy significantly less than they had before the revolution. The masses of people lived primarily on black bread and wore old, shabby clothing. There were constant shortages in the stores, although very heavily taxed vodka was always readily available. A shortage of housing was a particularly serious problem. Millions were moving into the cities, but the government built few new apartments. A relatively lucky family received one room for all its members and shared both a kitchen and a toilet with others on the floor.

Life was hard but by no means hopeless. Idealism and ideology had real appeal for many communists, who saw themselves heroically building the world's first socialist society while capitalism crumbled in a worldwide depression and degenerated into fascism in the West. This optimistic belief in the future of the Soviet Union also attracted many disillusioned Westerners to communism in the 1930s.

On a more practical level, Soviet workers did receive some important social benefits, such as old-age pensions, free medical services, free education, and day-care centers for children. Unemployment was almost unknown. Finally, there was the possibility of personal advancement.

The keys to improving one's position were specialized skills and technical education. Rapid industrialization required massive numbers of trained experts, such as skilled workers, engineers, and plant managers. Thus the Stalinist state broke with the egalitarian policies of the 1920s and dangled high salaries and many special privileges before its growing technical and managerial elite. This elite joined with the political and artistic elites in a new upper class of the rich and powerful. The Stalinist state gave women access to higher education and the ranks of the better-paid specialists in industry and science. Medicine practically became a woman's profession. By 1950, 75 percent of all doctors in the Soviet Union were women. Women were expected to toil in factories and in heavy construction as the equals of men as well. The massive mobilization of women was a striking characteristic of the Soviet state.

Popular culture became a vehicle of the state, as newspapers, films, and radio broadcasts endlessly recounted socialist achievements and capitalist plots. Whereas the 1920s had seen considerable experimentation in modern art and theater, intellectuals were ordered by Stalin to become "engineers of human minds." It became increasingly important for the successful writer and artist to glorify Russian nationalism. Russian history was rewritten so that early tsars such as Ivan the Terrible and Peter the Great became worthy forerunners of the greatest Russian leader of all—Stalin.

Stalin seldom appeared in public, but his presence was everywhere—in portraits, statues, books, and quotations from his "sacred" writings. Although the government persecuted religion and turned churches into "museums of atheism," the state had both an earthly religion and a high priest: Marxism-Leninism and Joseph Stalin.

"Let's All Get to Work, Comrades!"

Art in the Stalinist era generally followed the official doctrine of socialist realism, representing objects in a literal style and celebrating Soviet achievements. Characteristically, this poster glorifies the working class, women's equality (in hard labor at least), mammoth factories, and the Communist Party (represented by the hammer and sickle by the woman's foot). Assailed by propaganda, Soviet citizens often found refuge in personal relations and deep friendships. (From *Art of the October Revolution*, Mikhail Guerman [Leningrad: Aurora Publishers.] Permission, Professor Guerman, Department of Education, St. Petersburg State University)

Stalinist Terror and the Great Purges

In the mid-1930s, the great effort to engineer a socialist state culminated in ruthless police terror and a massive purging of the Communist Party. The party and government elite publicly supported Stalin's initiatives, but in private there was grumbling. At a small gathering in November 1932, even Stalin's wife complained bitterly about the misery of the people and the horrible famine in Ukraine. Stalin showered her with insults, and she died that same night, apparently by her own hand. In late 1934, Stalin's number-two man, Sergei Kirov (KEER-awf), was mysteriously murdered. Although Stalin himself probably ordered Kirov's murder, he used the incident to launch a reign of terror.

- After Lenin's death, Stalin and Trotsky vied for control of the Soviet Union, but Stalin won out due to his connections within the Communist Party; he then set out to launch his revolution from above.

- The five-year plans set up by Stalin began with collectivization of agriculture, forcing peasants to give up ownership of land and animals by force, with disastrous results and enormous casualties in purges of any who dissented; growth of heavy industry and urban development were more successful.

- Although the average Soviet citizen lived in crowded conditions and food shortages were common, many had high, idealistic hopes for communism and received educational, medical, and pension benefits and enjoyed career advancement within a gender-equal workplace, while the state-controlled media espoused the wonders of socialism, vilified capitalism, and glorified Russian nationalism.

- In an effort to reorganize a socialist state, Stalin ordered purges of the Communist Party by the secret police with public show trials and confessions, sending millions to labor camps, prisons, or execution, replacing them with new party members who would serve the party and Stalin faithfully.

In August 1936, sixteen prominent Old Bolsheviks confessed to all manner of plots against Stalin in spectacular public trials in Moscow. Then in 1937 the secret police arrested a mass of lesser party officials and newer members, also torturing them and extracting more confessions for more show trials. In addition to the party faithful, union officials, managers, intellectuals, army officers, and countless ordinary citizens were struck down. In all, at least 8 million people were probably arrested, and millions of these were executed or never returned from prisons and forced-labor camps.

Stalin and the remaining party leadership recruited 1.5 million new members to take the place of those purged. Thus more than half of all Communist Party members in 1941 had joined since the purges. Often the upwardly mobile sons (and daughters) of workers, they had usually studied in the new technical schools, and they soon proved capable of managing the government and large-scale production. A product of the great purges, this new generation of Stalin-formed communists would serve the leader effectively until his death in 1953, and they would govern the Soviet Union until the early 1980s.

Stalin's mass purges remain baffling, for almost all historians believe that those purged posed no threat and confessed to crimes they had not committed. Certainly the highly publicized purges sent a warning to the people: no one was secure, and everyone had to serve the party and its leader with redoubled devotion. Some Western scholars have also argued that the terror reflected a fully developed totalitarian state, which must always be fighting real or imaginary enemies.

The long-standing Western interpretation that puts the blame for the great purges on Stalin, which became very popular in Russia after the fall of communism, has nevertheless been challenged. Some historians argue that Stalin's fears were exaggerated but real. Moreover, these fears and suspicions were shared by many in the party and in the general population. Bombarded with ideology and political slogans, the population responded energetically to Stalin's directives. Investigations and trials snowballed into a mass hysteria, a new witch-hunt that claimed millions of victims.[4] In short, in this view of the 1930s, a deluded Stalin found large numbers of willing collaborators for crime as well as for achievement.

Mussolini and Fascism in Italy

How did Mussolini's dictatorship come to power and govern in Italy?

Mussolini, like Stalin, began as a revolutionary socialist, but in his rise to power he found it necessary to turn against the working class and seek the support of conservatives. Mussolini's fascist party was the first to establish a dictatorship in western Europe. Yet few scholars today would argue that Mussolini succeeded in establishing a totalitarian state that completely reshaped and dominated the economic, social, intellectual, and cultural aspects of people's lives. Membership in the Fascist Party was more a sign of an Italian's respectability than a commitment to radical change, and the fascist experiment was relatively short-lived.

The Seizure of Power

In the early twentieth century, Italy was a liberal state with civil rights and a constitutional monarchy. On the eve of the First World War, the parliamentary regime finally granted universal male suffrage, and Italy appeared to be moving toward democracy. But there were serious tensions. Many Italians were more attached to their villages and local interests than to the national state. Relations between church and state were often strained. Class differences were also extreme, and a powerful revolutionary socialist movement had developed.

The war worsened the political situation. Having fought on the side of the Allies almost exclusively for purposes of territorial expansion, the parliamentary government bitterly disappointed Italian nationalists with Italy's modest gains at Versailles. Workers and peasants also felt cheated: to win their support during the war, the government had promised social and land reform, which it did not deliver.

The Russian Revolution inspired and energized Italy's revolutionary socialist movement. The Socialist Party quickly lined up with the Bolsheviks, and radical workers and peasants began occupying factories and seizing land in 1920. These actions scared and mobilized the property-owning classes. Moreover, after the war the pope lifted his ban on participation by Catholics in Italian politics, and a strong Catholic Party quickly emerged. Thus by 1921 revolutionary social-ists, antiliberal conservatives, and frightened property owners were all opposed— though for different reasons—to the liberal parliamentary government.

Into these crosscurrents of unrest and fear stepped the blustering, bullying Benito Mussolini (buh-NEE-toh moos-uh-LEE-nee) (1883–1945). Son of a village schoolteacher and a poor blacksmith, Mussolini began his political career as a Socialist Party leader and radical newspaper editor before World War I. In 1914, powerfully influenced by antidemocratic cults of violent action, the young Mus-solini urged that Italy join the Allies, a stand for which he was expelled from the Italian Socialist Party. Later Mussolini fought at the front and was wounded in

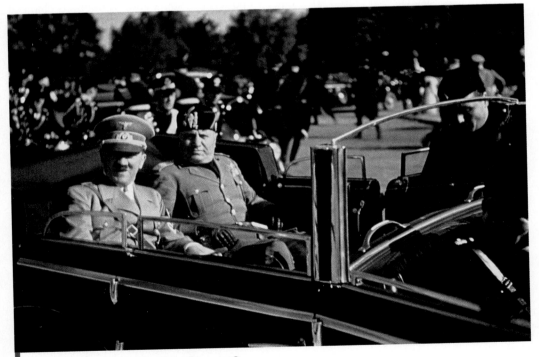

Hitler and Mussolini in Italy, May 1938
At first Mussolini distrusted Hitler, but Mussolini's conquest of Ethiopia in 1936 and Hitler's occupation of the Rhineland brought the two dictators together in a close alliance. State visits by Mussolini to Berlin in 1937 and by Hitler to Rome in 1938 included gigantic military reviews, which were filmed to impress the whole world. Uniformed Italian fascists accompany this motorcade. (Time Life Pictures/Getty Images)

fascists The members of a movement characterized by extreme, often expansionist nationalism, an antisocialism aimed at destroying working-class movements, alliances with powerful capitalists and landowners, a dynamic and violent leader, and glorification of war and the military.

Black Shirts A private army under Mussolini that destroyed socialist newspapers, union halls, and Socialist Party headquarters, eventually pushing Socialists out of the city governments of Northern Italy.

1917. Returning home, he began organizing bitter war veterans like himself into a band of **fascists**—from the Italian word for "a union of forces."

At first Mussolini's program was too similar to that of the well-organized Socialist Party, and it failed to rally people behind him. When Mussolini saw that his verbal assaults on rival Socialists won him growing support from conservatives and the frightened middle classes, he shifted gears in 1920. He and his growing private army of **Black Shirts** began to use brute force against the socialists. Typically, a band of fascist toughs would roar off in trucks at night and swoop down on a few isolated organizers, beating them up and force-feeding them almost deadly doses of castor oil. Few people were killed, but socialist newspapers, union halls, and local Socialist Party headquarters were destroyed. Mussolini convinced his followers that they were not just opposing the "Reds" but also making a real revolution of their own.

His next step was to position himself publicly as the champion of order and property against the socialists and the ineffectual liberal parliamentary government. Striking a conservative note in his speeches and gaining the sympathetic neutrality of army leaders, Mussolini demanded the resignation of the existing government and his own appointment by the king. In October 1922, to force matters, a large group of fascists marched on Rome. The threat worked. Victor Emmanuel III (r. 1900–1946), who had no love for the old liberal politicians, asked Mussolini to form a new cabinet. He was immediately granted dictatorial authority for one year by the king and the parliament.

The Regime in Action Once in power, Mussolini and his ministers changed the election laws so that the party that won the most votes was given two-thirds of the representatives in the parliament. This change allowed the Fascist Party and its allies to win an overwhelming majority in 1924. Shortly thereafter, five of Mussolini's thugs kidnapped and murdered Giacomo Matteotti (JAH-kaw-moh mat-te-AWT-tee), the leader of the Socialists in the parliament. In the face of this outrage, the opposition demanded that Mussolini's armed squads be dissolved and all violence be banned.

Although Mussolini may or may not have ordered Matteotti's murder, he stood at the crossroads of a severe political crisis. After some hesitation, he charged forward. Declaring his desire to "make the nation Fascist," he imposed a series of repressive measures. Freedom of the press was abolished, elections were fixed, and the government ruled by decree. Mussolini arrested his political opponents, disbanded all independent labor unions, and put dedicated Fascists in control of Italy's schools. Moreover, he created a fascist youth movement, fascist labor unions, and many other fascist organizations. Mussolini trumpeted his goal in a famous slogan of 1926: "Everything in the state, nothing outside the state, nothing against the state." By the end of that year, Italy was a one-party dictatorship under Mussolini's unquestioned leadership.

Mussolini, however, never destroyed the old power structure, as the Communists did in the Soviet Union, or succeeded in dominating it, as the Nazis did in Germany. Interested primarily in personal power, Mussolini was content to compromise with the old conservative classes that controlled the army, the economy, and the state. He controlled and propagandized labor but left big business to regulate itself, profitably and securely. There was no land reform.

Mussolini also drew increasing support from the Catholic Church. In the **Lateran** (LAT-er-uhn) **Agreement** of 1929, he recognized the Vatican as a tiny inde-

Lateran Agreement A 1929 agreement that recognized the Vatican as a tiny independent state, with Mussolini agreeing to give the church heavy financial support. In turn, the pope expressed his satisfaction and urged Italians to support Mussolini's government.

pendent state, and he agreed to give the church heavy financial support. The pope expressed his satisfaction and urged Italians to support Mussolini's government.

Mussolini's conservative values are evident in his treatment of women. Rather than encouraging women to participate in the building of a new society, he abolished divorce and told women to stay at home and produce children. In 1938 women were limited by law to a maximum of 10 percent of the better-paying jobs in industry and government.

Mussolini's fascist Italy was repressive and undemocratic, and he insisted on the spectacle of mass obedience in rallies and salutes. Yet in spite of his posing, his fascist Italy was never really totalitarian. Indeed, he allowed Victor Emmanuel III to remain king, and it was Victor Emmanuel who dismissed him as leader after his own party refused further support of his war policy in 1943.

Hitler and Nazism in Germany

How did Hitler gain power, what policies did totalitarian Nazi Germany pursue, and why did they lead to World War II?

The most frightening dictatorship developed in Germany. There the Nazi movement, which was a form of fascism, smashed or took over most independent organizations, mobilized the economy, and violently persecuted the Jewish population. Thus Nazism asserted an unlimited claim over German society and proclaimed the ultimate power of its endlessly aggressive leader—Adolf Hitler. Truly totalitarian in its aspirations, the dynamism of Hitler and the Nazi elite was ultimately directed to war, territorial expansion, and racial aggression.

Hitler's Road to Power

Nazism grew out of many complex developments, of which the most influential were extreme nationalism and racism. These two ideas captured the mind of the young Hitler, and it was he who dominated Nazism for as long as it lasted.

The child of a customs official, Adolf Hitler (1889–1945) spent his youth in small towns in Austria. He dropped out of high school at age fourteen following the death of his father and eventually left home for Vienna, where he became deeply impressed by the mayor, Karl Lueger (1844–1910). From Lueger and others, Hitler absorbed virulent anti-Semitism, racism, and hatred of Slavs. He developed an unshakable belief in the crudest, most exaggerated distortions of the Darwinian theory of survival, the superiority of Germanic races, and the inevitability of racial conflict. Anti-Semitism and racism became Hitler's most passionate convictions, his explanation for everything. The Jews, he claimed, directed an international conspiracy of finance capitalism and Marxian socialism against German culture, German unity, and the German race. Hitler's belief was totally irrational, but he never doubted it.

Hitler served as a dispatch carrier in the First World War, finding that the struggle and disciple of war gave life meaning. Crushed by Germany's defeat, he joined a tiny extremist group in Munich called the German Workers' Party, and by 1921 he had gained absolute control of this small but growing party. He was already a master of mass propaganda and political showmanship. His most effective tool was the mass rally, where he often worked his audience into a frenzy with

Nazism A movement born of extreme nationalism and racism and dominated by Adolf Hitler for as long as it lasted.

wild, demagogic attacks on the Versailles treaty, the Jews, Marxists, the war profiteers, and Germany's Weimar Republic.

Membership in Hitler's party multiplied tenfold after early 1922. In late 1923, the Weimar Republic seemed on the verge of collapse, and Hitler, inspired by Mussolini's recent easy victory, decided on an armed uprising in Munich. Despite the failure of the poorly organized plot and Hitler's arrest, Nazism had been born.

Hitler concluded from his unsuccessful revolt that he had to undermine, rather than overthrow, the government and come to power legally through electoral competition. He forced his more violent supporters to accept his new strategy. He also used his brief prison term to dictate his autobiography, *Mein Kampf*. There he expounded on his basic themes: "race," with a stress on anti-Semitism; "living space," with a sweeping vision of war and conquered territory; and the leader-dictator, or **Führer** (FYUR-rer), with unlimited, arbitrary power.

Führer A leader-dictator with unlimited, arbitrary power, this name was bestowed upon Adolf Hitler.

In the years of prosperity and relative stability between 1924 and 1929, Hitler concentrated on building his National Socialist German Workers' Party, or Nazi Party. While his party boasted 100,000 loyal followers by 1928, it received only 2.6 percent of the vote in the general elections. The Great Depression, shattering economic prosperity from 1929 on, presented Hitler with a new opportunity to gain votes. Chancellor (chief minister) Heinrich Brüning (BREW-ning) and President von Hindenburg inadvertently intensified the economic collapse with their economic measures, convincing many that the country's republican leaders were stupid. Never very interested in economics before, Hitler began promising German voters economic as well as political and international salvation.

Above all, Hitler rejected free-market capitalism and advocated government programs to bring recovery. Seized by panic as bankruptcies increased, unemployment soared, and the Communists made dramatic election gains, great numbers of middle- and lower-middle-class people "voted their pocketbooks"[5] and deserted the conservative and moderate parties for the Nazis. By 1932 the Nazis had became the largest party in the Reichstag.

The appeal to pocketbook interests was particularly effective in the early 1930s because Hitler appeared more mainstream, playing down his anti-Jewish hatred and racist nationalism. A master of propaganda, he had written in *Mein Kampf* that the masses were driven by fanaticism and not by knowledge. To arouse such hysterical fanaticism, he believed that all propaganda had to be limited to a few simple, endlessly repeated slogans. But now when he harangued vast audiences with wild oratory and simple slogans, he featured "national rebirth" and the "crimes" of the Versailles treaty. And many uncertain individuals, surrounded by thousands of enthralled listeners, found a sense of belonging as well as hope for better times.

Reaching a National Audience

This poster ad promotes the VE-301 receiver, "the world's cheapest radio," and claims that "All Germany listens to the Führer on the people's receiver." Constantly broadcasting official views and attitudes, the state-controlled media also put the Nazis' favorite entertainment—gigantic mass meetings that climaxed with Hitler's violent theatrical speeches—on an invisible stage for millions. (Bundesarchiv Koblenz Plak 003-022-025)

Hitler and the Nazis also appealed strongly to German youth. Indeed, in some ways the Nazi movement was a mass movement of young Germans. Hitler himself was only forty in 1929, and he and most of his top aides were much younger than other leading German politicians. "National Socialism is the organized will of the youth," proclaimed the official Nazi slogan. National recovery, exciting and rapid change, and personal advancement were the appeals of Nazism to millions of German youths.

Disunity on the left was another factor in Hitler's rise to power. The Communists refused to cooperate with the Social Democrats, even though the two parties together outnumbered the Nazis in the Reichstag, even after the elections of 1932. The Communists saw themselves as eventual victors, believing that a communist revolution would follow in the aftermath of Hitler's eventual destruction.

Finally, Hitler excelled in the dirty, backroom politics of the decaying Weimar Republic. That, in fact, brought him to power. In complicated infighting in 1932, he cleverly succeeded in gaining additional support from key people in the army and big business, who thought Hitler would advance their interests. When Hitler demanded the role of chancellor, those in power reasoned that with nine solid conservatives as ministers and only two other National Socialists, he could be controlled. On January 30, 1933, Adolf Hitler, leader of the largest party in Germany, was legally appointed chancellor by Hindenburg.

The Nazi State and Society

Hitler moved rapidly to gain total control of Germany. Continuing to maintain legal appearances, he immediately called for new elections. In the midst of a violent electoral campaign, the Reichstag building was partly destroyed by fire, and Hitler blamed the Communists. Fearing further violence, President Hindenburg agreed to emergency acts that practically abolished freedom of speech and assembly as well as most personal liberties. The Nazis in the Reichstag then gave Hitler absolute power for four years when they pushed through the so-called **Enabling Act** on March 23, 1933. President Hindenburg died the next year, and Hitler consolidated president and chancellor in the role of Führer.

Enabling Act An act pushed through the Reichstag by the Nazis that gave Hitler absolute dictatorial power for four years.

Germany soon became a one-party state. Only the Nazi Party was legal. The Reichstag was jokingly referred to as the most expensive glee club in the country, for its only function was to sing hymns of praise to the Führer. Hitler and the Nazis took over the government bureaucracy intact, installing many Nazis in top positions. At the same time, they created a series of overlapping Nazi Party organizations responsible solely to Hitler.

As research in recent years shows, the resulting system of dual government was riddled with rivalries, contradictions, and inefficiencies. Thus the Nazi state was sloppy and often disorganized, lacking the all-encompassing unity that its propagandists claimed. Yet this fractured system suited Hitler and his purposes. He could play the established bureaucracy against his private, personal "party government" and maintain his freedom of action. Hitler could concentrate on general principles and the big decisions, which he always made.

In the economic sphere, strikes were outlawed, and independent labor unions and professional organizations were replaced by Nazi associations. Publishing houses were put under Nazi control, and universities and writers were quickly brought into line. Democratic, socialist, and Jewish literature was blacklisted; banned books were burned in public squares. Modern art and architecture were ruthlessly prohibited. Life became violently anti-intellectual. By 1934 a brutal dictatorship characterized by frightening dynamism and obedience to Hitler was already largely in place.

Only the army retained independence, and Hitler moved brutally and skillfully to establish his control there, too. The Nazi storm troopers (the SA), the quasi-military band of 3 million toughs in brown shirts who had fought communists and beaten up Jews before the Nazis took power, expected top positions in the army and even talked of a "second revolution" against capitalism. Hitler decided that the SA leaders had to be eliminated. Needing to preserve good relations with the army as well as with big business, he struck on the night of June 30, 1934. Hitler's elite personal guard—the SS—arrested and shot without trial roughly a thousand SA leaders and assorted political enemies. Shortly thereafter army leaders swore a binding oath of "unquestioning obedience . . . to the Leader of the German State and People, Adolf Hitler." The SS grew rapidly. Under its methodical, inhuman leader, Heinrich Himmler (1900–1945), the SS joined with the political police, the Gestapo, to expand its network of special courts and concentration camps. Nobody was safe.

From the beginning, Jews were a special object of Nazi persecution, although Slavs, Roma (Gypsies), Jehovah's Witnesses, Communists, and homosexuals were also targets. By the end of 1934, most Jewish lawyers, doctors, professors, civil servants, and musicians had lost their jobs and the right to practice their professions. In 1935 the infamous Nuremberg Laws deprived Jews of all rights of citizenship. By 1938 roughly 150,000 of Germany's half a million Jews had emigrated, sacrificing almost all their property in order to leave Germany.

In late 1938, the attack on the Jews accelerated. In a well-organized wave of violence, known to history as "Kristallnacht," mobs smashed windows, looted shops, and destroyed homes and synagogues. German Jews were then rounded up and made to pay for the damage. Another 150,000 Jews fled Germany. Some Germans privately opposed these outrages, but most went along or looked the other way.

Hitler's Popularity

Hitler had promised the masses economic recovery—"work and bread"—and he delivered. Breaking with Brüning's do-nothing policies, Hitler launched a large public works program to help pull Germany out of the depression. Work began on superhighways, offices, gigantic sports stadiums, and public housing, and then shifted in 1936 toward rearmament and preparation for war. As a result of these policies (and plain good luck), unemployment dropped steadily and the standard of living for the average employed worker increased moderately. The profits of business rose sharply. For millions of people, economic recovery was tangible evidence that Nazi promises were more than show and propaganda.

Millions of modest middle-class and lower-middle-class people *felt* that Germany was becoming more open and equal, as Nazi propagandists constantly claimed. But quantitative studies show that the well-educated classes held on to most of their advantages and that only a modest social leveling occurred in the Nazi years. It is significant that the Nazis shared with the Italian fascists the stereotypic view of women as housewives and mothers. Only under the relentless pressure of war did they reluctantly mobilize large numbers of German women for work in offices and factories.

Not all Germans supported Hitler, however, and a number of German groups actively resisted him after 1933. Tens of thousands of political enemies were imprisoned, and thousands were executed. But opponents of the Nazis pursued various goals, and they were never unified, a fact that helps account for their ultimate lack of success. In the first years of Hitler's rule, the principal resisters were the communists and the socialists in the trade unions. But the expansion of the SS system of terror after 1935 smashed most of these leftists. A second group of opponents arose in the Catholic and Protestant churches. However, their efforts were directed primarily at preserving genuine religious life, not at overthrowing Hitler. Finally in 1938 (and again from 1942 to 1944), some high-ranking army officers, who feared the consequences of Hitler's reckless aggression, plotted against him, unsuccessfully.

Aggression and Appeasement (1933–1939)

Although economic recovery and somewhat greater opportunity for social advancement won Hitler support, they were only byproducts of the Nazi regime. The guiding and unique concepts of Nazism remained space and race—the territorial expansion of the superior German race. As we shall see, German expansion was facilitated by the uncertain and divided Western democracies, which tried to appease Hitler to avoid war.

Hitler realized that his aggressive policies had to be carefully camouflaged at first, for Germany's army was limited by the Treaty of Versailles to only one hundred thousand men. As he told a group of army commanders in February 1933, the early stages of his policy of "conquest of new living space in the East and its ruthless Germanization" had serious dangers. If France had real leaders, Hitler said, it would "not give us time but attack us, presumably with its eastern satellites."[6] Thus, Hitler loudly proclaimed his peaceful intentions, while signaling otherwise by withdrawing from the League of Nations.

Following this action, Hitler sought to incorporate independent Austria into a greater Germany. But a worried Mussolini threatened to fight, and Hitler backed down. When in March 1935 Hitler repudiated the Treaty of Versailles by establishing a general military draft and declaring Germany's right to rearm, other countries appeared to understand the danger. With France taking the lead, Italy and Great Britain protested strongly and warned against future aggressive actions.

Yet the emerging united front against Hitler quickly collapsed. Of crucial importance, Britain adopted a policy of **appeasement**, granting Hitler everything he could reasonably want (and more) in order to avoid another horrific war. The first step was an Anglo-German naval agreement in June 1935 that broke Germany's isolation. The second step came in March 1936 when Hitler suddenly marched his armies into the demilitarized Rhineland, brazenly violating the Treaties of Versailles and Locarno. This was the last good chance to stop the Nazis, but an uncertain France would not move without British support, and Britain refused to act (Map 29.1).

As the Great Powers stood on the sidelines, Hitler found allies in Italy and Japan. He supported their wars of aggression—Italy against Ethiopia and Japan against China—and they agreed to join the Axis alliance.

The fascist leaders of Germany and Italy came to the aid of another fascist power in the Spanish civil war (1936–1939). Their support eventually helped General Francisco Franco's fascist movement defeat republican Spain. Only the Soviet Union offered official support for the Spanish government, as public opinion in Britain and especially in France was hopelessly divided on the Spanish question.

In late 1937 Hitler moved forward with plans to crush Austria and Czechoslovakia at the earliest possible moment as the first step in his long-contemplated drive to the east. Threatening invasion, he forced the Austrian chancellor in March 1938 to put local Nazis in control of the government. The next day, German armies moved in unopposed, and Austria became part of Greater Germany (see Map 29.1).

appeasement The British policy toward Germany prior to World War II that aimed at granting Hitler whatever he wanted, including western Czechoslovakia, in order to avoid war.

MAP 29.1   The Growth of Nazi Germany, 1933–1939

Until March 1939, Hitler brought ethnic Germans into the Nazi state; then he turned on the Slavic peoples he had always hated. He stripped Czechoslovakia of its independence and prepared for an attack on Poland in September 1939.

Simultaneously, Hitler began demanding that the pro-Nazi, German-speaking minority of western Czechoslovakia—the Sudetenland—be turned over to Germany. Yet democratic Czechoslovakia was prepared to resist, and it counted on France, its ally since 1924, and the Soviet Union, France's ally. War appeared inevitable, but appeasement triumphed again. In September 1938, Britain's prime minister Chamberlain flew to Germany three times in fourteen days. In these negotiations, to which the U.S.S.R. (Union of Soviet Socialist Republics) was deliberately not invited, Chamberlain and the French agreed with Hitler that the Sudetenland should be ceded to Germany immediately. Returning to London from the Munich Conference, Chamberlain told cheering crowds that he had secured "peace with honor . . . peace for our time." Sold out by the Western powers, Czechoslovakia gave in.

Appeasement confirmed Hitler's belief that the Western democracies were weak and unwilling to fight. He accelerated his eastern expansion, moving into the remaining Czech lands in March 1939. The Western public now recognized Hitler's moves as acts of aggression since he was seizing Czechs and Slovaks as captive peoples. Thus when Hitler used the question of German minorities in Danzig as a pretext to claim Poland, a suddenly militant Chamberlain declared that Britain and France would fight if Hitler attacked his eastern neighbor. Hitler did not take Chamberlain's warning seriously, but he was concerned about the possible response from Poland's Soviet neighbor.

In a stunning about-face, Hitler and Stalin signed a ten-year Nazi-Soviet non-aggression pact in August 1939. Each dictator promised to remain neutral if the other became involved in war. In secret they agreed to divide eastern Europe into German and Soviet zones, "in the event of a political territorial reorganization." The nonaggression pact itself was enough to make Britain and France cry treachery, for they, too, had been negotiating with Stalin. But Stalin had remained distrustful of Western intentions, and Hitler had offered immediate territorial gain.

For Hitler, everything was set. He told his generals on the day of the nonaggression pact, "My only fear is that at the last moment some dirty dog will come up with a mediation plan." On September 1, 1939, German armies and warplanes smashed into Poland from three sides. Two days later, Britain and France, finally true to their word, declared war on Germany. The Second World War had begun.

The Second World War

How did Germany and Japan create enormous empires that were defeated by the Allies—Britain, the Soviet Union, and the United States?

War broke out in both western and eastern Europe because Hitler's ambitions were essentially unlimited. On both war fronts, Nazi soldiers scored enormous successes until late 1942, establishing a vast empire of death and destruction. Hitler's victories increased tensions in Asia between Japan and the United States and prompted Japan to attack the United States and overrun much of Southeast Asia. Yet reckless aggression by Germany and Japan also raised a mighty coalition determined to smash the aggressors. Led by Britain, the United States, and the Soviet Union, the Grand Alliance—to use Winston Churchill's favorite name for it—functioned quite effectively in military terms. Thus the Nazi and Japanese empires proved short-lived.

Hitler's Empire (1939–1942)

Using planes, tanks, and trucks in the first example of a **blitzkrieg** (BLITS-kreeg), or "lightning war," Hitler's armies crushed Poland in four weeks. While the Soviet Union quickly took its part of the booty—the eastern half of Poland and the independent Baltic states of Lithuania, Estonia, and Latvia—French and British armies dug in in the west. They expected another war of attrition and economic blockade.

In spring 1940, the lightning war struck again. After occupying Denmark, Norway, and Holland, German motorized columns broke through southern Belgium, split the Franco-British forces, and trapped the entire British army on the beaches of Dunkirk. By heroic efforts, the British withdrew their troops but not their equipment.

- Hitler honed his ideas of anti-Semitism, the superiority of the German race, a vision of conquered territory, and a leader-dictator (Führer), and he used his oratory skills to convince the masses of his economic and political plans for recovery.

- Hitler appealed to the youth by promoting national recovery, exciting change, and personal advancement, and he succeeded in winning the support of key figures in big business and the army to have himself legally declared chancellor in 1933.

- Hitler established himself as Führer and placed Nazis in key political positions, using his personal SS troops to eliminate the SA storm troopers, rivals of the regular German army, and implementing programs that discriminated against Jews and other enemies.

- The public generally supported Hitler as he delivered a large public works program that improved living conditions and employment rates, but resistance existed in the Communist and Socialist parties, the churches, and some high-ranking officials, all of whom were unable to remove Hitler from power.

- Hitler's plan for Germany was to expand the German race and territory, and he was able to do so by making an Axis alliance with Italy and Japan, annexing Austria, and helping Franco win the Spanish civil war.

- Hitler was able to gain the Sudetenland region of Czechoslovakia without a fight as France and Britain wanted to avoid another war at all costs, but when he tried to take Poland, France and Britain finally declared war.

- Hitler and Stalin signed a ten-year Nazi-Soviet nonaggression pact in August 1939, right before the outbreak of the war.

blitzkrieg A "lightning war" that used planes, tanks, and trucks; Hitler first used this method to crush Poland in four weeks.

London, 1940

Hitler believed that his relentless terror bombing of London—the "blitz"—could break the will of the British people. He was wrong. The blitz caused enormous destruction, but Londoners went about their business with courage and calm determination, as this unforgettable image of a milkman in the rubble suggests. (Corbis)

France was taken by the Nazis. Aging marshal Henri-Philippe Pétain formed a new French government—the so-called Vichy (**VISH-ee**) government—to accept defeat, and German armies occupied most of France. By July 1940, Hitler ruled practically all of western continental Europe; Italy was an ally, and the Soviet Union and Spain were friendly neutrals. Only Britain, led by the uncompromising Winston Churchill (1874–1965), remained unconquered.

Germany sought to gain control of the air, the necessary first step toward an amphibious invasion of Britain. In the Battle of Britain, up to a thousand German planes attacked British airfields and key factories in a single day, dueling with British defenders high in the skies. Losses were heavy on both sides. Then in September Hitler angrily turned from military objectives to indiscriminate bombing of British cities in an attempt to break British morale. British aircraft factories increased production, and the heavily bombed people of London defiantly dug in. In September and October 1940, Britain was beating Germany three to one in the air war. There was no possibility of an immediate German invasion of Britain.

Turning from Britain and moving into the Balkans by April 1941, Hitler now allowed his lifetime obsession with a vast eastern European empire for the "master race" to dictate policy. In June 1941, German armies suddenly attacked the Soviet Union along a vast front (see Map 29.2, p. 774). By October, Leningrad (St. Petersburg) was practically surrounded, Moscow was besieged, and most of Ukraine had been conquered. But the Soviets did not collapse, and when a severe winter struck German armies outfitted in summer uniforms, the invaders were stopped.

Stalled in Russia, Hitler ruled over a vast European empire stretching from the outskirts of Moscow to the English Channel. Hitler, the Nazi leadership, and the loyal German army were positioned to greatly accelerate construction of their "New Order" in Europe, and they continued their efforts until their final collapse in 1945. In doing so, they showed what Nazi victory would have meant.

Hitler's **New Order** was based firmly on racial imperialism, the guiding principle of Nazi **totalitarianism**. Within this New Order, the Nordic peoples—the Dutch, Norwegians, and Danes—received preferential treatment, for they were racially related to the master race, the Germans. The French, an "inferior" Latin people, occupied a middle position. All the occupied territories of western and northern Europe were exploited with increasing intensity. Material shortages and both mental and physical suffering afflicted millions of people.

Slavs in the conquered territories to the east were treated with harsh hatred as "subhumans." At the height of his success in 1941 and 1942, Hitler set the tone. He painted for his intimate circle the fantastic vision of a vast eastern colonial empire where Poles, Ukrainians, and Russians would be enslaved and forced to die out, while Germanic peasants resettled the resulting abandoned lands. But he needed countless helpers and many ambitious initiators to turn his dreams into reality. These accomplices came forth.

Himmler and the elite corps of SS volunteers shared Hitler's ideology of barbarous racial imperialism, and they rarely wavered in their efforts to realize his goals.[7] Supported (or condoned) by military commanders and German policemen in the occupied territories, the SS corps pressed relentlessly to implement the program of destruction and to create a "mass settlement space" for Germans. Many Poles, Communists, Roma, and Jehovah's Witnesses were murdered in cold blood.

> **New Order** Hitler's program based on the guiding principle of racial imperialism, which gave preferential treatment to the Nordic peoples while the French, an "inferior" Latin people, occupied a middle position. Slavs in the conquered territories to the east were treated harshly, as "subhumans."

> **totalitarianism** A dictatorship that exercises unprecedented control over the masses and seeks to mobilize them for action.

The Holocaust

Nazi racism culminated in the **Holocaust,** the systematic, state-sponsored effort to annihilate all the Jews of Europe. After the fall of Warsaw, the Nazis stepped up their expulsion campaign and began deporting all German Jews to occupied Poland. There they and Jews from all over Europe were concentrated in ghettos, compelled to wear the Jewish star, and turned into slave laborers.

In 1941, following the invasion of the Soviet Union, the large-scale "extermination" of Jews began. On the Russian front, Himmler's special SS killing squads and also regular army units forced Soviet Jews to dig giant pits, which became mass graves as the victims were lined up on the edge and cut down by machine guns. Then in late 1941, Hitler and the Nazi leadership, in some still-debated combination, ordered the SS to stop all Jewish emigration from Europe and speeded up planning for mass murder. As one German diplomat put it, "The Jewish Question must be resolved in the course of the war, for only so can it be solved without a worldwide outcry."[8] The "final solution of the Jewish question"—the murder of every single Jew—had begun. Jews were systematically arrested, packed like cattle onto freight trains, and dispatched to extermination camps. Many Jews could hardly imagine the enormity of the crime that lay before them.

Arriving at their destination, small numbers of Jews were sent to nearby slave labor camps, where they were starved and systematically worked to death. But most of the victims were moved immediately to the death camps, where they were taken by force or deception to "shower rooms" that were actually gas chambers. These gas chambers, first perfected in the quiet, efficient execution of seventy

> **Holocaust** The systematic effort of the Nazi state to exterminate all European Jews, which resulted in the murder of six million Jews.

Prelude to Murder
This photo captures the terrible inhumanity of Nazi racism and the Holocaust. Frightened and bewildered families from the soon-to-be-destroyed Warsaw Ghetto are being forced out of their homes by German soldiers for deportation to concentration camps. There they face murder in the gas chambers. (Hulton Archive/Getty Images)

thousand mentally ill Germans between 1938 and 1941, permitted rapid, hideous, and thoroughly bureaucratized mass murder. For fifteen to twenty minutes came the terrible screams and gasping sobs of men, women, and children choking to death on poison gas. Then, only silence. Special camp workers quickly yanked the victims' gold teeth from their jaws, and the bodies were then cremated or sometimes boiled for oil to make soap. At Auschwitz-Birkenau (OUSH-vits beer-ken-OW), the most infamous of the Nazi death factories, as many as twelve thousand human beings were slaughtered each day. The extermination of European Jews was the ultimate monstrosity of Nazi racism and racial imperialism. By 1945, 6 million Jews had been murdered. (See the feature "Individuals in Society: Primo Levi.")

Who was responsible for this terrible crime? An earlier generation of historians usually laid most of the guilt on Hitler and the Nazi leadership. Ordinary Germans had little knowledge of the extermination camps, it was argued, and those who cooperated had no alternative given the brutality of Nazi terror and totalitarian control. But in recent years, many studies have revealed a much broader participation of German people in the Holocaust and popular indifference (or worse) to the fate of the Jews.

The reasons for the active participation or complacency of Germans and others in the Holocaust are debated. The American historian Daniel Goldhagen has made the provocative claim that the extreme anti-Semitism of "ordinary Germans" led them to respond to Hitler and to become his "willing executioners" in World War II.[9] Yet in most occupied countries, local non-German officials also cooperated in the arrest and deportation of Jews to a large extent. As in Germany, only a

Individuals in Society

Primo Levi

Most Jews deported to Auschwitz were murdered as soon as they arrived, but the Nazis made some prisoners into slave laborers and a few of these survived. Primo Levi (1919–1987), an Italian Jew, became one of the most influential witnesses to the Holocaust and its death camps.

Like much of Italy's small Jewish community, Levi's family belonged to the urban professional classes. The young Primo graduated in 1941 from the University of Turin with highest honors in chemistry. But since 1938, when Italy introduced racial laws, he had faced growing discrimination, and two years after graduation he joined the antifascist resistance movement. Quickly captured, he was deported to Auschwitz with 650 Italian Jews in February 1944. Stone-faced SS men picked only ninety-six men and twenty-nine women to work in their respective labor camps. Primo was one of them.

Nothing prepared Levi for what he encountered. The Jewish prisoners were kicked, punched, stripped, branded with tattoos, crammed into huts, and worked unmercifully. Hoping for some sign of prisoner solidarity in this terrible environment, Levi found only a desperate struggle of each against all and enormous status differences among prisoners. Many stunned and bewildered newcomers, beaten and demoralized by their bosses—the most privileged prisoners—simply collapsed and died. Others struggled to secure their own privileges, however small, because food rations and working conditions were so abominable that ordinary Jewish prisoners perished in two to three months.

Sensitive and noncombative, Levi found himself sinking into oblivion. But instead of joining the mass of the "drowned," he became one of the "saved"—a complicated surprise with moral implications that he would ponder all his life. As Levi explained in *Survival in Auschwitz* (1947), the usual road to salvation in the camps was some kind of collaboration with German power.* Savage German criminals were released from prison to become brutal camp guards; non-Jewish political prisoners competed for jobs entitling them to better conditions, and, especially troubling for Levi, a small number of Jewish men plotted and struggled for the power of life

and death over other Jewish prisoners. Though not one of these Jewish bosses, Levi believed that he himself, like almost all survivors, had entered the "gray zone" of moral compromise. Only a very few superior individuals, "the stuff of saints and martyrs," survived the death camps without shifting their moral stance.

For Levi, compromise and salvation came from his profession. Interviewed by a German technocrat for the camp's synthetic rubber program, Levi performed brilliantly in scientific German and savored his triumph as a Jew over Nazi racism. Work in the warm camp laboratory offered Levi opportunities to pilfer equipment that could then be traded for food and necessities with other prisoners. Levi also gained critical support from three saintly prisoners, who refused to do wicked and hateful acts. And he counted "luck" as essential for his survival: in the camp infirmary with scarlet fever in February 1945 as advancing Russian armies prepared to liberate the camp, Levi was not evacuated by the Nazis and shot to death like most Jewish prisoners.

Primo Levi, who never stopped thinking, writing, and speaking about the Holocaust. (Giansanti/Corbis Sygma)

After the war Primo Levi was forever haunted by the nightmare that the Holocaust would be ignored or forgotten. Always ashamed that so many people whom he considered better than himself had perished, he wrote and lectured tirelessly to preserve the memory of Jewish victims and guilty Nazis. Wanting the world to understand the Jewish genocide in all its complexity so that never again would people tolerate such atrocities, he grappled tirelessly with his vision of individual choice and moral compromise in a hell designed to make the victims collaborate and persecute each other.

Questions for Analysis

1. Describe Levi's experience at Auschwitz. How did camp prisoners treat each other? Why?

2. What does Levi mean by the "gray zone"? How is this concept central to his thinking?

3. Will a vivid historical memory of the Holocaust help to prevent future genocide?

---

* Primo Levi, *Survival in Auschwitz: The Nazi Assault on Humanity*, rev. ed. 1958 (London: Collier Books, 1961), pp. 79–84, and *The Drowned and the Saved* (New York: Summit Books, 1988). These powerful testimonies are highly recommended.

few exceptional bystanders did not turn a blind eye. Thus some scholars have concluded that the key for most Germans (and most people in occupied countries) was that they felt no personal responsibility for Jews and therefore were not prepared to help them. This meant that many individuals, conditioned by Nazi racist propaganda but also influenced by peer pressure and brutalizing wartime violence, were psychologically prepared to join the SS ideologues and perpetrate ever-greater crimes. They were ready to plumb the depths of evil and to spiral downward from mistreatment to arrest to mass murder.

Japan's Empire in Asia

By late 1938, 1.5 million Japanese troops were bogged down in China, holding a great swath of territory but unable to defeat the Nationalists and the Communists (see Map 29.3). Nor had Japan succeeded in building a large, self-sufficient Asian economic zone, for it still depended on oil and scrap metal from the Netherlands East Indies and the United States. Thus Japanese leaders followed events in Europe closely, looking for alliances and actions that might improve their position in Asia. At home they gave free reign to the anti-Western ultranationalism that had risen in the 1920s and 1930s. In speeches, schools, and newspapers ultranationalists proclaimed Japan's liberating mission in Asia, glorified the warrior virtues of honor and sacrifice, and demanded absolute devotion to the semidivine emperor.

The outbreak of war in Europe in 1939 and Hitler's early victories opened up opportunities for the Japanese in Southeast Asia, where European empires appeared vulnerable. Expanding the war in China, the Japanese also pressured the Dutch to surrender control of the Netherlands East Indies and its rich oil fields, but Dutch colonial officials, backed by the British and the Americans, refused. The United States had repeatedly condemned Japanese aggression in China, and it now feared that embattled Britain would collapse if it lost the support of its Asian colonies.

Japan's invasion of southern Indochina in July 1941 further worsened relations with the United States. President Franklin Roosevelt demanded that Japan withdraw from China, and they refused. The United States responded by cutting off the sale of U.S. oil to Japan and thereby reducing Japan's oil supplies by 90 percent. Japanese leaders believed increasingly that war with the United States was inevitable, for Japan's battle fleet would run out of fuel in eighteen months, and its industry would be crippled. After much debate, Japanese leaders decided to launch a surprise attack on the United States. They hoped to cripple their Pacific rival, gain time to build a defensible Asian empire while getting oil from Indonesia, and eventually win an ill-defined compromise peace.

The Japanese attack on the U.S. naval base at Pearl Harbor in the Hawaiian Islands was a complete surprise but a limited success. On December 7, 1941, the Japanese sank or crippled every American battleship, but by chance all the all-important American aircraft carriers were at sea and escaped unharmed. More important, Pearl Harbor united Americans in a spirit of anger and revenge.

Hitler immediately declared war on the United States. Simultaneously, Japanese armies successfully attacked European and American colonies in Southeast Asia. Japanese armies were small (because most soldiers remained in China), but they were well trained, highly motivated, and very successful. By May 1942 Japan held a vast empire in Southeast Asia and the western Pacific (see Map 29.3, p. 776).

The Grand Alliance

Facing war across both the Pacific and the Atlantic, the United States agreed with its allies Great Britain and the Soviet Union on a policy of **Europe first**. Only after Hitler was defeated would the Allies turn toward the Pacific for an all-out attack on Japan, the lesser threat. The Allies agreed to wage war until the "unconditional surrender" of both Germany and Japan.

Europe first The Allied policy to defeat Hitler in Europe before turning their attack on Japan.

The military resources of the Grand Alliance were awesome. The strengths of the United States were its mighty industry, its large population, and its national unity. Gearing up rapidly for all-out war in 1942, the United States acquired a unique capacity to wage global war. In 1943 it outproduced not only Germany, Italy, and Japan but also all of the rest of the world combined.

Britain continued to make a great contribution as well. The British economy was totally and effectively mobilized, and the sharing of burdens through rationing and heavy taxes on war profits maintained social harmony. By early 1943 the Americans and the British were combining small aircraft carriers with radar-guided bombers to rid the Atlantic of German submarines. Britain, the impregnable floating fortress, became a gigantic frontline staging area for the decisive blow to the heart of Germany.

As for the Soviet Union, so great was its strength that it might well have defeated Germany without Western help. In the face of the German advance, whole factories and populations were successfully evacuated to eastern Russia and Siberia. There war production was reorganized and expanded, and the Red Army was increasingly well supplied and well led. Above all, Stalin drew on the massive support and heroic determination of the Soviet people, especially those in the central Russian heartland. Broad-based Russian nationalism, as opposed to narrow communist ideology, became the powerful unifying force in what the Soviet people appropriately called the "Great Patriotic War of the Fatherland."

Finally, the United States, Britain, and the Soviet Union had the resources of much of the world at their command. They were also aided by a growing resistance movement against the Nazis throughout Europe, even in Germany. After the Soviet Union was invaded in June 1941, communists throughout Europe took the lead in the underground resistance, joined by a growing number of patriots, Christians, and agents sent by governments-in-exile in London.

The War in Europe (1942–1945)

Barely halted at the gates of Moscow and Leningrad in 1941, the Germans renewed their offensive against the Soviet Union in July 1942, driving toward the southern city of Stalingrad and occupying most of the city in a month of incredibly savage house-to-house fighting.

Then, in November 1942, Soviet armies counterattacked. They rolled over Romanian and Italian troops to the north and south of Stalingrad, quickly closing the trap and surrounding the entire German Sixth Army of 300,000 men. The surrounded Germans were systematically destroyed, until by the end of January 1943 only 123,000 soldiers were left to surrender. Hitler, who had refused to allow a retreat, had suffered a catastrophic defeat. In summer 1943, the larger, better-equipped Soviet armies took the offensive and began moving forward (Map 29.2).

Not yet prepared to attack Germany directly through France, the Western Allies saw heavy fighting in North Africa from 1940 onward. In May 1942, combined German and Italian armies were finally defeated by British forces only seventy miles from Alexandria at the Battle of El Alamein (al-uh-MAYN). Almost immediately thereafter, an Anglo-American force landed in Morocco and Algeria. These

MAPPING THE PAST

MAP 29.2   World War II in Europe

The map shows the extent of Hitler's empire before the Battle of Stalingrad in late 1942 and the subsequent advances of the Allies until Germany surrendered on May 7, 1945. This map, combined with Map 29.1 on page 766, can be used to trace the rise and fall of the Nazi empire over time. **[1]** First, using Map 29.1 on page 766, what was the first country to be conquered by Hitler (and divided with the Soviet Union)? **[2]** Second, locate Germany's advance and retreat on the Russian front at different dates: December 1941, November 1942, Spring 1944, and February 1945. Locate the position of British and American forces on the battlefield at similar points in time, and then compare the respective Russian and British-American positions. What implications might the battle lines on February 1945 have for the postwar settlement in Europe?

Legend:
- Hitler's Greater Germany
- Allied with Germany
- Occupied by Germany and its allies
- Grand Alliance
- Neutral nations
- ★ Major battle

Siege of Leningrad, Sept. 1941–Jan. 1944

Siege of Stalingrad, Aug. 21, 1942–Jan. 31, 1943

German surrender: Reims, May 7, 1945; Berlin, May 8, 1945

Battle of Britain, fall 1940

Rhine Crossing, March 7, 1945

Battle of the Bulge, Dec. 1944

Invasion of Normandy, June 6, 1944

Axis troops occupy Vichy France, Nov. 10 and 11, 1942

Allies land in Provence, Aug. 15, 1944

Italian front, Feb. 1945

Monte Cassino, May 1944

Salerno, Sept. 1943

Allies invade Sicily and Italy, July–Sept. 1943

Sicily, July 1943

Casablanca, Nov. 1942

Rommel defeated in Tunisia; Axis troops evacuated, May 1943

El Alamein, summer 1942

Russian front, Spring 1944
Russian front, Nov. 1942
Russian front, Dec. 1941
Russian front, Feb. 1945
Western front, Feb. 1945

French possessions, which were under the control of Pétain's Vichy government, quickly went over to the side of the Allies.

Having driven the Axis powers from North Africa by spring 1943, Allied forces maintained the initiative by invading Sicily and then mainland Italy. Mussolini was deposed by a war-weary people, and the new Italian government publicly accepted unconditional surrender in September 1943. Italy, it seemed, was liberated. Yet German commandos rescued Mussolini in a daring raid and put him at the head of a puppet government. German armies seized Rome and all of northern Italy. Fighting continued in Italy.

Indeed, bitter fighting continued in Europe for almost two years. Germany, less fully mobilized for war than Britain in 1941, applied itself to total war in 1942 and enlisted millions of German women and millions of prisoners of war and slave laborers from all across occupied Europe in that effort. Between early 1942 and July 1944, German war production actually tripled in spite of heavy bombing by the British and American air forces. German resistance against Hitler also failed. After an unsuccessful attempt on Hitler's life in July 1944, SS fanatics brutally liquidated thousands of Germans. Terrorized at home and frightened by the prospect of unconditional surrender, the Germans fought on with suicidal stoicism.

On June 6, 1944, American and British forces under General Dwight Eisenhower landed on the beaches of Normandy, France, in history's greatest naval invasion. In a hundred dramatic days, more than 2 million men and almost half a million vehicles pushed inland and broke through German lines. Rejecting proposals to strike straight at Berlin in a massive attack, Eisenhower moved forward cautiously on a broad front. Not until March 1945 did American troops cross the Rhine and enter Germany.

The Soviets, who had been advancing steadily since July 1943, reached the outskirts of Warsaw by August 1944. For the next six months, they moved southward into Romania, Hungary, and Yugoslavia. In January 1945, the Red Army again moved westward through Poland, and on April 26 it met American forces on the Elbe River. The Allies had closed their vise on Nazi Germany and overrun Europe. As Soviet forces fought their way into Berlin, Hitler committed suicide in his bunker, and on May 7 the remaining German commanders capitulated.

The War in the Pacific (1942–1945)

In Asia, as gigantic armies clashed in Europe, the greatest naval battles in history decided the fate of warring nations (see Map 29.3). First, in the Battle of the Coral Sea in May 1942, an American carrier force fought its Japanese counterpart to a draw, thereby stopping the Japanese advance on Port Moresby and relieving Australia from the threat of invasion. This engagement was followed in June 1942 by the Battle of Midway, in which American carrier-based pilots sank all four of the attacking Japanese aircraft carriers and established overall naval equality with Japan in the Pacific. In August 1942 American marines attacked and took Guadalcanal in the Solomon Islands in heavy fighting.

Hampered by the policy of "Europe first," the United States gradually won control of the sea and air as it geared up massive production of aircraft carriers, submarines, and fighter planes. By 1943 the United States was producing one hundred thousand aircraft a year, almost twice as many as Japan produced in the entire war. In July 1943 the Americans and their Australian allies opened an "island hopping" campaign toward Japan. Pounding Japanese forces on a given island with saturation bombing, American army and marine units would then hit the beaches with rifles and flame throwers and secure victory in hand-to-hand

MAP 29.3   World War II in the Pacific

Japanese forces overran an enormous amount of territory in 1942, which the Allies slowly recaptured in a long, bitter struggle. As this map shows, Japan still held a large Asian empire in August 1945, when the unprecedented devastation of atomic warfare suddenly forced it to surrender.

combat. Many islands were bypassed, and their Japanese defenders were blockaded and left to starve.

The war in the Pacific was extremely brutal—a "war without mercy," in the words of a leading American scholar—and atrocities were committed on both sides.[10] Knowing of Japanese atrocities in China and the Philippines, the U.S. Marines and Army troops seldom took Japanese prisoners after the Battle of Guadalcanal, killing even those rare Japanese soldiers who offered to surrender. A product of spiraling violence, mutual hatred, and dehumanizing racial stereotypes, the war without mercy intensified as it moved toward Japan.

In June 1944 giant U.S. bombers began a relentless bombing campaign that intensified steadily until the end of the war. In October 1944, as Allied advances in the Pacific paralleled those in Europe, American forces won a great victory in the four-day Battle of Leyte (LEY-tee) Gulf, the greatest battle in naval history, with 282 ships involved. The Japanese navy was practically finished.

In spite of all their defeats, Japanese troops continued to fight with enormous courage and determination. Indeed, the bloodiest battles of the Pacific war took place on Iwo Jima in February 1945 and on Okinawa (oh-kee-NAH-wah) in June 1945. American commanders believed the conquest of Japan might cost a million American casualties and claim 10 to 20 million Japanese lives. In fact, Japan was almost helpless, its industry and dense, fragile wooden cities largely destroyed by incendiary bombing and uncontrollable hurricanes of fire. Yet the Japanese seemed determined to fight on, ever ready to die for a hopeless cause.

On August 6 and 9, 1945, the United States dropped atomic bombs on Hiroshima (heer-oh-SHEE-muh) and Nagasaki (nah-gah-SAH-kee) in Japan. Mass bombing of cities and civilians, one of the terrible new practices of World War II, had ended in the final nightmare—unprecedented human destruction in a single blinding flash. On August 14, 1945, the Japanese announced their surrender. The Second World War, which had claimed the lives of more than 50 million soldiers and civilians, was over.

Section Review

- The Germans used a blitzkrieg to crush Poland and most of western continental Europe except Britain, turning next to the Soviet Union, where they gained vast amounts of territory; their aim was to have Germanic peoples occupy and populate the conquered territories, enslaving and eliminating the "inferior" races there.

- Hitler's ultimate horror was his goal of racial imperialism, including the deportations to concentration camps and slave labor camps, culminating in the outright mass murder of millions of Jews and other "undesirables" in the Holocaust.

- Japan tried to expand into Southeast Asia, angering the United States, who cut off the sale of oil to Japan, which responded with a surprise attack on Pearl Harbor in Hawaii and European and American colonies in Southeast Asia, sparking Hitler's declaration of war against the United States.

- The Allied powers agreed to liberate Europe first and then to take on Japan in the Pacific; they effectively mobilized for war, with the United States out-producing every other country while Britain and the Soviet Union also fielded well-organized war machines.

- The Germans pursued their attack on the Soviet Union but suffered defeat while the Soviets went on the offensive, and with the western Allies, closed the noose, surrounding and finally entering Germany where Hitler committed suicide and the remaining Germans surrendered.

- The brutal war in the Pacific, a "war without mercy," involved an Allied "island hopping" campaign on the way to Japan; intense fighting pressed Japan to the limit, but the United States dealt the final catastrophic blow by dropping two atomic bombs to end the war.

Chapter Review

How did Stalin and the Communist Party build a modern totalitarian state in the Soviet Union? (page 753)

The crafty Stalin consolidated his power in the 1920s, and in 1928 he launched the five-year plans. In doing so, Stalin's Soviet Union asserted a total claim on the lives of its citizens. It posed ambitious goals in the form of rapid state-directed industrialization and savage collectivization of agriculture. And it found enthusiastic supporters who believed that Stalin and the Communist Party were building their kind of socialism and a new socialist personality at home. Relentless propaganda and the great purges reinforced the Party's claims of unlimited control of its citizens.

How did Mussolini's dictatorship come to power and govern in Italy? (page 758)

Mussolini began as a socialist but he turned to the right when he received growing support from conservatives. Coming to power with the king's help, Mussolini proclaimed the revolutionary, "totalitarian" character of his one-party rule. In fact, Mussolini's government retained many elements of conservative authoritarianism, such as compromising with the Catholic Church and keeping women in traditional roles.

Key Terms

five-year plan (p. 753)

New Economic Policy (NEP) (p. 753)

collectivization (p. 754)

kulaks (p. 754)

fascists (p. 760)

Black Shirts (p. 760)

Lateran Agreement (p. 760)

Nazism (p. 761)

Führer (p. 762)

Enabling Act (p. 763)

(continued)

How did Hitler gain power, what policies did totalitarian Nazi Germany pursue, and why did they lead to World War II? (page 761)

Failing to overthrow the government in 1923 in an attempted coup, Hitler came to power legally in 1933 by promising voters national renewal and economic recovery from the Great Depression. His policies appeared to help the economy and he quickly established a one-party totalitarian regime with ambitious goals and widespread popular support. But whereas Stalin concentrated on building socialism at home, Hitler and the Nazi elite aimed at unlimited territorial and racial aggression on behalf of a master race. He proceeded gradually at first, and Britain and France sought to "appease" Hitler with various diplomatic concessions. Only Hitler's unprovoked attack on Poland in 1939 brought a military response from Britain and France and the beginning of World War II.

How did Germany and Japan create enormous empires that were defeated by the Allies—Britain, the Soviet Union, and the United States? (page 767)

Nazi racism and unlimited aggression made war inevitable, first with the western European democracies, then with hated eastern neighbors, and finally with the United States. Joined by Japan after Pearl Harbor, Hitler's forces overran much of western and eastern Europe, annihilated millions of Jews, and plunged Europe into the ultimate nightmare. But unlimited aggression unwittingly forged a mighty coalition led by Britain, the Soviet Union, and the United States. This Grand Alliance held together and smashed the racist Nazi empire and its leader. The United States also destroyed Japan's vast, overextended empire in the Pacific, thus bringing to a close history's most destructive war.

appeasement (p. 765)
blitzkrieg (p. 767)
New Order (p. 769)
totalitarianism (p. 769)
Holocaust (p. 769)
Europe first (p. 773)

Notes

1. I. Kershaw, *The Nazi Dictatorship: Problems and Perspectives of Interpretation*, 2d ed. (London: Edward Arnold, 1989), p. 34.
2. Quoted in I. Deutscher, *Stalin: A Political Biography*, 2d ed. (New York: Oxford University Press, 1967), p. 325.
3. R. Conquest, *The Harvest of Sorrow: Soviet Collectivization and the Terror-Famine* (New York: Oxford University Press, 1986), pp. 4, 303.
4. R. Thurston, *Life and Terror in Stalin's Russia, 1934–1941* (New Haven, Conn.: Yale University Press, 1996), esp. pp. 16–106; also Malia, *The Soviet Tragedy*, pp. 227–270.
5. W. Brustein, *The Logic of Evil: The Social Origins of the Nazi Party, 1925–1933* (New Haven, Conn.: Yale University Press, 1996), pp. 52, 182.
6. Quoted in K. D. Bracher, *The German Dictatorship: The Origins, Structure and Effects of National Socialism* (New York: Praeger, 1970), p. 289.
7. R. Allen, *The Business of Genocide: The SS, Slave Labor, and the Concentration Camps* (Chapel Hill: University of North Carolina Press, 2002), pp. 270–285.
8. Quoted in M. Marrus, *The Holocaust in History* (Hanover, N.H.: University Press of New England, 1987), p. 28.
9. D. Goldhagen, *Hitler's Willing Executioners: Ordinary Germans and the Holocaust* (New York: Vintage Books, 1997).
10. J. Dower, *War Without Mercy: Race and Power in the Pacific War* (New York: Pantheon, 1986).

To assess your mastery of this chapter, go to **bedfordstmartins.com/mckaywestbrief**

Listening to the Past

Stalin Justifies the Five-Year Plan

On February 4, 1931, Joseph Stalin delivered the following address, entitled "No Slowdown in Tempo!," to the First Conference of Soviet Industrial Managers. Published the following day in Pravda, the newspaper of the Communist Party, and widely publicized at home and abroad, Stalin's speech sought to rally the people and generate support for the Party's program. His address captures the spirit of Soviet public discourse in the early 1930s.

"Our program is realistic," Stalin proclaims on this poster, "because it is you and me working together." (David King Collection)

It is sometimes asked whether it is not possible to slow down the tempo somewhat, to put a check on the movement. No, comrades, it is not possible! The tempo must not be reduced! On the contrary, we must increase it as much as is within our powers and possibilities. This is dictated to us by our obligations to the workers and peasants of the U.S.S.R. This is dictated to us by our obligations to the working class of the whole world.

To slacken the tempo would mean falling behind. And those who fall behind get beaten. But we do not want to be beaten. No, we refuse to be beaten! One feature of the history of old Russia was the continual beatings she suffered because of her backwardness. She was beaten by the Mongol khans, . . . the Turkish beys, . . . and the Japanese barons. All beat her—because of her backwardness, cultural backwardness, political backwardness, industrial backwardness, agricultural backwardness. They beat her because to do so was profitable and could be done with impunity. . . . Such is the law of the exploiters—to beat the backward and the weak. It is the jungle law of capitalism. You are backward, you are weak—therefore you are wrong; hence you can be beaten and enslaved. You are mighty—therefore you are right; hence we must be wary of you.

That is why we must no longer lag behind. . . .

But we have yet other, more serious and more important, obligations. They are our obligations to the world proletariat. . . . We must march forward in such a way that the working class of the whole world, looking at us, may say: There you have my advanced detachment, my shock brigade, my working-class state power, my fatherland; they are engaged on their cause, *our* cause, and they are working well; let us support them against the capitalists and promote the cause of the world revolution. Must we not justify the hopes of the world's working class, must we not fulfill our obligations to them? Yes, we must if we do not want to utterly disgrace ourselves.

Such are our obligations, internal and international.

As you see, they dictate to us a Bolshevik tempo of development.

I will not say that we have accomplished nothing in regard to management of production during these years. In fact, we have accomplished a good deal. . . . But we could have accomplished still more if we had tried during this period really to master production, the technique of production, the financial and economic side of it. . . .

It is said that it is hard to master technique. That is not true! There are no fortresses that Bolsheviks cannot capture. We have solved a number of most difficult problems. We have overthrown capitalism. We have assumed power. We have built up a huge socialist industry. We have transferred the middle peasants on the path of socialism. We have already accomplished what is most important from the point of view of construction. What remains to be done is not so much: to study technique, to master science. And when we have done that we shall develop a tempo of which we dare not even dream at present.

And we shall do it if we really want to.

Questions for Analysis

1. What reasons does Stalin give to justify an unrelenting "Bolshevik" tempo of industrial and social change? In the light of history, which reason seems most convincing? Why?

2. Imagine that the year is 1931 and you are a Soviet student reading Stalin's speech. Would Stalin's determination inspire you, frighten you, or leave you cold? Why?

3. Some historians argue that Soviet socialism was a kind of utopianism—that zealots believed that the economy, the society, and even human beings could be completely remade and perfected. What utopian elements do you see in Stalin's declaration?

Source: From Joseph Stalin, "No Slowdown in Tempo!" *Pravda*, February 5, 1931.

CHAPTER 30

Cold War Conflicts and Social Transformations

1945–1985

The youth revolution. London, ca. 1980. (Anthea Sieveking/Wellcome Images)

Chapter Preview

The Division of Europe
What were the causes of the cold war?

The Western Renaissance (1945–1968)
Why did western Europe recover so successfully? How did colonial peoples win political independence and American blacks triumph in the civil rights movement?

Soviet Eastern Europe (1945–1968)
What was the pattern of postwar rebuilding and development in the Soviet Union and communist eastern Europe?

Postwar Social Transformations (1945–1968)
How did changing patterns in technology, class relations, women's work, and youth culture bring major social transformations?

Conflict and Challenge in the Late Cold War (1968–1985)
What were the key aspects of political conflict, economic stagnation, and the feminist movement in the late cold war?

INDIVIDUALS IN SOCIETY: Margaret Thatcher

LISTENING TO THE PAST: A Feminist Critique of Marriage

The total defeat of the Nazis and their allies in 1945 laid the basis for one of Western civilization's most remarkable recoveries, as Europe dug itself out from under the rubble and fashioned a great renaissance. Yet there was also a tragic setback. The Grand Alliance against Hitler gave way to an apparently endless cold war in which tension between East and West threatened world peace.

In the late 1960s and early 1970s, three major changes marked the end of the era of postwar Western renaissance. First, as cold war competition again turned very hot in Vietnam, postwar certainties such as domestic political stability and social harmony evaporated, and several countries experienced major crises. Second, the astonishing postwar economic advance came to a halt, and this had serious social consequences. Third, new roles for women after World War II led to a powerful "second wave" of feminist thought and action in the 1970s, resulting in major changes for women and gender relations. Thus the long cold war created an underlying unity for the years 1945–1985, but the first half of the cold war era was quite different from the second.

The Division of Europe

What were the causes of the cold war?

In 1945 triumphant American and Russian soldiers came together and embraced on the banks of the Elbe River in the heart of vanquished Germany. At home, in the United States and in the Soviet Union, the soldiers' loved ones erupted in joyous celebration. Yet victory was flawed. The Allies could not cooperate politically in peacemaking. Motivated by different goals and hounded by misunderstandings, the United States and the Soviet Union soon found themselves at loggerheads. By the end of 1947, Europe was rigidly divided. It was West versus East in a cold war that was waged around the world for forty years.

The Origins of the Cold War

The most powerful allies in the wartime coalition—the Soviet Union and the United States—began to quarrel almost as soon as the threat of Nazi Germany disappeared. This hostility between the Eastern and Western superpowers was the sad but logical outgrowth of military developments, wartime agreements, and long-standing political and ideological differences.

In the early phases of the Second World War, the Americans and the British chose to avoid discussing with Stalin the shape of the eventual peace settlement. They feared that hard bargaining would encourage Stalin to consider making a separate peace with Hitler. They focused instead on the policy of unconditional surrender to solidify the alliance.

By late 1943, discussion about the shape of the postwar world could no longer be postponed. The conference that Stalin, Roosevelt, and Churchill held in the Iranian capital of Teheran in November 1943 thus proved of crucial importance in determining subsequent events. There, the **Big Three** searched for the appropriate military strategy to crush Germany. Roosevelt chose to meet Stalin's wartime demands whenever possible and so supported Stalin's plan for an American-British frontal assault through France. This strategy meant that the Soviet and the American-British armies would come together in defeated Germany along a north-

Big Three Russia, the United States, and England.

south line and that only Soviet troops would liberate eastern Europe. Thus the basic shape of postwar Europe was emerging even as the fighting continued.

When the Big Three met again in February 1945 at Yalta on the Black Sea in southern Russia, advancing Soviet armies were within a hundred miles of Berlin. The Red Army had occupied not only Poland but also Bulgaria, Romania, Hungary, part of Yugoslavia, and much of Czechoslovakia. The temporarily stalled American-British forces had yet to cross the Rhine into Germany. Moreover, the United States was far from defeating Japan. In short, the Soviet Union's position was strong and America's weak.

It was agreed at Yalta that Germany would be divided into zones of occupation and would pay heavy reparations to the Soviet Union. At American insistence, Stalin agreed to declare war on Japan after Germany was defeated. An ambiguous compromise was reached on Poland and eastern Europe: their governments were to be freely elected but pro-Russian.

The Yalta compromise over eastern Europe broke down almost immediately. Even before the Yalta Conference, Bulgaria and Poland were controlled by communists who arrived home with the Red Army. Elsewhere in eastern Europe, pro-Soviet "coalition" governments of several parties were formed, but the key ministerial posts were reserved for Moscow-trained communists.

At the postwar Potsdam Conference of July 1945, differences over eastern Europe finally surged to the fore. The new American president, Harry Truman, demanded immediate free elections throughout eastern Europe. Stalin refused point-blank. "A freely elected government in any of these East European countries would be anti-Soviet," he admitted simply, "and that we cannot allow."[1]

Here, then, is the key to the much-debated origins of the cold war. American ideals, pumped up by the crusade against Hitler, and American politics, heavily influenced by millions of voters from eastern Europe, demanded free elections in Soviet-occupied eastern Europe. Stalin, who

The Big Three

In 1945 a triumphant Winston Churchill, an ailing Franklin Roosevelt, and a determined Joseph Stalin met at Yalta in southern Russia to plan for peace. Cooperation soon gave way to bitter hostility. (Franklin Delano Roosevelt Library)

had lived through two enormously destructive German invasions, wanted absolute military security in relation to Germany and its potential Eastern allies. Suspicious by nature, he believed that only communist states could be truly dependable allies, and he realized that free elections would result in independent and possibly hostile governments on his western border. Moreover, by the middle of 1945, there was no way short of war that the United States could control political developments in eastern Europe, and war was out of the question. Stalin was bound to have his way.

West Versus East

The American response to Stalin's refusal to allow elections was to "get tough." In May 1945, Truman abruptly cut off all aid to the U.S.S.R. In October he declared that the United States would never recognize any government established by force against the free will of its people. In March 1946, former British prime minister Churchill ominously informed an American audience that an "iron curtain" had fallen across the continent, dividing Germany and all of Europe into two antagonistic camps. Emotional, moralistic denunciations of Stalin and communist Russia emerged as part of American political life. Yet the United States also responded to the popular desire to "bring the boys home" and demobilized its troops with great speed. Some historians have argued that American leaders believed that the atomic bomb gave the United States all the power it needed, but "getting tough" really meant "talking tough."

Stalin's agents quickly reheated what they viewed as the "ideological struggle against capitalist imperialism." The large, well-organized Communist Parties of France and Italy obediently started to uncover "American plots" to take over Europe and challenged their own governments with violent criticisms and large strikes. The Soviet Union also put pressure on Iran, Turkey, and Greece, while a bitter civil war raged in China. By the spring of 1947, it appeared to many Americans that Stalin was determined to export communism by subversion throughout Europe and around the world.

The United States responded to this challenge with the Truman Doctrine, which was aimed at "containing" communism to areas already occupied by the Red Army and supporting governments facing a communist threat. To begin, Truman asked Congress for military aid to Greece and Turkey, countries that Britain, weakened by war and financially overextended, could no longer protect. Then, in June, Secretary of State George C. Marshall offered Europe economic aid—the **Marshall Plan**—to help it rebuild.

Stalin refused Marshall Plan assistance for all of eastern Europe and attempted unsuccessfully to add West Berlin to the Soviet bloc. In 1949, intent on containment, the United States formed an anti-Soviet military alliance of Western governments: the North Atlantic Treaty Organization, or **NATO**. Stalin countered by tightening his hold on his satellites, later united in the Warsaw Pact. Europe was divided into two hostile blocs and the bitter **cold war** was begun (see Map 30.1, page 786).

In late 1949, the communists triumphed in China, which many Americans perceived as new evidence of a powerful worldwide communist conspiracy. When the Russian-backed communist army of North Korea invaded South Korea in 1950, President Truman acted swiftly. American-led United Nations forces under General Douglas MacArthur intervened. The bitter, bloody contest seesawed back and forth, but President Truman rejected General MacArthur's call to attack China and fired him instead. In 1953 a fragile truce was negotiated, and the fight-

Marshall Plan Secretary of State George C. Marshall's plan of economic aid to Europe to help it rebuild, which Stalin refused for all of eastern Europe.

NATO The North Atlantic Treaty Organization, an anti-Soviet military alliance of Western governments.

cold war The long period after World War II during which Europe and the United States were divided between East and West into two hostile military alliances and the tension threatened world peace.

ing stopped. Thus the United States extended its policy of containment to Asia but drew back from an attack on communist China and possible nuclear war.

The Western Renaissance (1945–1968)

Why did western Europe recover so successfully? How did colonial peoples win political independence and American blacks triumph in the civil rights movement?

As the cold war divided Europe into two blocs, the future appeared bleak on both sides of the iron curtain. European economic conditions were the worst in generations, and the overseas empires of western Europe were crumbling in the face of nationalism in Asia and Africa. Yet in less than a generation, western Europe and the United States achieved unprecedented economic prosperity and social transformation. It was an amazing rebirth—a true renaissance.

The Postwar Challenge

After the war, the people of western Europe faced severe shortages and hardships. Suffering was most intense in defeated Germany. The major territorial change of the war had moved the Soviet Union's border far to the west. Poland was in turn compensated for this loss to the Soviets with land taken from Germany. To solidify these changes in boundaries, 13 million Germans were driven from their homes and forced to resettle in a greatly reduced Germany. The Russians were also seizing factories and equipment as reparations in their zone, even tearing up railroad tracks and sending the rails to the Soviet Union.

In 1945 and 1946, conditions were not much better in the Western zones, for the Western allies also treated the German population with severity at first. Countless Germans sold prized possessions to American soldiers to buy food. By the spring of 1947, Germany was on the verge of total collapse and threatening to drag down the rest of Europe. Yet the seeds of recovery were also planted, for the people had had enough of old ideas, and new leaders were coming to the fore to guide these aspirations for change. In Italy, France, and the Federal Republic of Germany (as Western Germany was officially known), the **Christian Democrats** and Catholic Party offered strong leaders. They steadfastly rejected authoritarianism and narrow nationalism and placed their faith in democracy and cooperation. The socialists and the communists, active in the resistance against Hitler, also emerged from the war with increased power and prestige, especially in France and Italy. They, too, provided fresh leadership and pushed for social change and economic reform. In the immediate postwar years, welfare measures such as family allowances, health insurance, and increased public housing were enacted throughout continental Europe. Britain followed the same trend, as the newly elected socialist Labour Party established a "welfare state." Many British industries were nationalized, and the government provided free medical service. Thus all across Europe, social reform complemented political transformation, creating solid foundations for a great European renaissance.

Massive economic aid and ongoing military protection from the United States was also essential to rebuilding Europe. As Marshall Plan aid poured in, the battered economies of western Europe began to turn the corner in 1948. The outbreak of the Korean War in 1950 further stimulated economic activity, and Europe entered a period of rapid economic progress that lasted into the late 1960s. Never

Section Review

- Stalin and the Western Allies could not agree on a post-war settlement: Stalin argued for communist states in eastern Europe as dependable allies and the west pushed for free elections; Stalin, in a stronger position militarily, got his way.

- The Americans responded by cutting off aid to the U.S.S.R., issuing the Truman Doctrine to "contain" communism; negative propaganda was pursued by both sides; the United States formed the anti-Soviet military alliance, NATO, while Stalin formed the Warsaw pact, dividing Europe into two hostile zones, initiating the cold war.

- When China fell to the communists and North Korea attacked South Korea, the United States defended the Truman Doctrine by sending troops to intervene in Korea, but held short of invading China.

Christian Democrats Progressive Catholics and revitalized Catholic political parties that became influential after the Second World War.

ATLANTIC OCEAN

Participants in the Marshall Plan.*

Member of NATO,*
formed in 1949

Member of COMECON,** formed in
1949, and the Warsaw Pact,
organized in 1955

Member of the European
Common Market, formed in 1958

Iron Curtain

* North Atlantic Treaty Organization
** Council for Mutual Economic Assistance

400 Mi.

400 Km.

200

200

0

0

UNION OF SOVIET SOCIALIST REPUBLICS

Caspian Sea

Volga R.

Don R.

Dnieper R.

Moscow

Exploded first atomic bomb, 1949

60N

40E

60N

40N

Black Sea

TURKEY

Ankara

*Truman Doctrine, 1947
Joined NATO, 1952*

CYPRUS • Nicosia

FINLAND
• Helsinki

• Stockholm

SWEDEN

Baltic Sea

• Warsaw

POLAND

*Communist coup, 1948
U.S.S.R. invasion, 1968*

CZECHOSLOVAKIA

Prague •

ROMANIA

Bucharest •

Danube R.

BULGARIA

Sofia •

*Truman Doctrine, 1947
Joined NATO, 1952
Joined Common Market, 1981*

GREECE

Athens •

20E

Copenhagen •

NORWAY

Oslo •

DENMARK

*Berlin blockade,
1948–1949*

West Berlin

East Berlin

EAST GERMANY

Vienna •

AUSTRIA

Joined NATO, 1955

Budapest •

HUNGARY

Revolution, 1956

Belgrade •

YUGOSLAVIA

Tito-Stalin schism, 1948

Tiranë •

ALBANIA

*Zones of occupation
ended, 1955*

*Joined Common
Market, 1973*

WEST GERMANY

Bonn •

Amsterdam •

NETHERLANDS

Brussels •

BELGIUM

LUX.

Paris •

SWITZ.

Bern •

Rome •

ITALY

*Left COMECON, 1961
Withdrew from WP, 1968*

Corsica

Sardinia

Sicily

*U.S. loan of $3.5 billion, 1946
Exploded first atomic bomb, 1952
Joined Common Market, 1973*

UNITED KINGDOM

London •

North Sea

20W

IRELAND

Dublin •

*Exploded first atomic bomb, 1960
Withdrew from NATO, 1966*

FRANCE

Balearic Is.

Mediterranean Sea

Arctic Circle

ICELAND

Reykjavík •

*Joined Common
Market, 1973*

Joined Common Market, 1986

SPAIN

Madrid •

*Joined NATO, 1982
Joined Common Market, 1986*

PORTUGAL

Lisbon •

Joined Common Market, 1986

N

MAPPING THE PAST

MAP 30.1   European Alliance Systems, 1949–1989

After the cold war divided Europe into two hostile military alliances, six western European countries formed the Common Market in 1957. The Common Market grew later to include most of western Europe. The communist states organized their own economic association—COMECON. **[1]** Identify the countries that were the original members of the Common Market. What do they have in common? **[2]** Identify the members of COMECON. What communist country or countries did not join COMECON? Why? **[3]** Which non-allied nations had joined the Common Market by 1989?

before had the European economy grown so fast. In most countries, there were many people ready to work hard for low wages and the hope of a better future. Moreover, although many consumer products had been invented or perfected since the late 1920s, few Europeans had been able to buy them. In 1945 the electric refrigerator, the washing machine, and the automobile were rare luxuries. There was a great potential demand, which the economic system moved to satisfy. Finally, western European nations abandoned protectionism and gradually created a large unified market known as the **Common Market** (see Map 30.1). This historic action, which certainly stimulated the economy, was part of a larger search for European unity.

The development of the Common Market fired imaginations and encouraged hopes of rapid progress toward political as well as economic union. In the 1960s, however, these hopes were frustrated by a resurgence of more traditional nationalism. France took the lead. Mired in a bitter colonial war in Algeria, the French turned in 1958 to General de Gaulle (duh GOHL), who established the Fifth Republic and ruled as its president until 1969. Charles de Gaulle (1890–1970) was at heart a romantic nationalist, and he viewed the United States as the main threat to genuine French (and European) independence. He withdrew all French military forces from the "American-controlled" NATO, developed France's own nuclear weapons, and vetoed the scheduled advent of majority rule within the Common Market. Thus throughout the 1960s, the Common Market thrived economically but remained a union of sovereign states.

Common Market The European Economic Community, created by six western European nations in 1957 as part of a larger search for European unity.

Decolonization in East Asia

In the postwar era, Europe's long-standing overseas expansion was dramatically reversed. Future generations will almost certainly see this rolling back of Western expansion as one of world history's great turning points.

The most basic cause of imperial collapse—what Europeans called **decolonization**—was the rising demand of Asian and African peoples for national self-determination, racial equality, and personal dignity. This demand spread from intellectuals to the masses in nearly every colonial territory after the First World War. As a result, colonial empires had already been shaken by 1939, and the way was prepared for the eventual triumph of independence movements.

European empires had been based on an enormous power differential between the rulers and the ruled, a difference that had greatly declined after western Europe was battered by war. In addition, strong nationalist movements continued to develop under the Japanese occupation of European colonies in Southeast Asia. With their political power and moral authority in tatters in 1945, many Europeans had little taste for bloody colonial wars and wanted to concentrate on rebuilding at home.

decolonization The reversal of Europe's overseas expansion caused by the rising demand of Asian and African peoples for national self-determination, racial equality, and personal dignity.

Gandhi Arrives in Delhi, October 1939
A small and frail man, Gandhi possessed enormous courage and determination. His campaign of nonviolent resistance to British rule inspired the Indian masses and nurtured national identity and self-confidence. Here he arrives for talks with the British viceroy after the outbreak of World War II. (Corbis)

India, Britain's oldest, largest, and most lucrative nonwhite possession, played a key role in decolonization. Nationalist opposition to British rule coalesced after the First World War under the leadership of British-educated lawyer Mohandas "Mahatma" Gandhi (GAHN-dee) (1869–1948), one of the twentieth century's most significant and influential figures. In the 1920s and 1930s Gandhi built a mass movement preaching nonviolent "noncooperation" with the British. In 1935 the British agreed to a new constitution that was practically a blueprint for independence. When the Labour party came to power in Great Britain in 1945, it was ready to relinquish sovereignty.

If Indian nationalism drew on Western parliamentary liberalism, Chinese nationalism developed and triumphed in the framework of Marxist-Leninist ideology. In the turbulent early 1920s, a broad alliance of nationalist forces within the Soviet-supported Guomindang (Kuomintang) (kwoh-min-TANG), or National People's party, was dedicated to unifying China and abolishing European concessions. But in 1927 Chiang Kai-shek (chang kie-SHEK) (1887–1975), successor to Sun Yat-sen (see page 693) and leader of the Guomindang, broke with his more radical communist allies, headed by Mao Zedong (Mao Tse-tung) (maow dzuh-DONG), and tried to destroy them.

In the civil war that ensued, Mao's Soviet-backed forces defeated Chiang's American-backed forces, with the crucial support of the Chinese peasantry. Chiang's nationalists withdrew to the island of Taiwan in 1949. Mao (1893–1976) and the communists united China's 550 million inhabitants in a strong centralized state, expelled foreigners, and began building a new society along Soviet lines, collectivizing the peasants and implementing five-year plans to expand heavy industry.

Most Asian countries followed the pattern of either India or China. In 1946 the Philippines achieved independence peacefully from the United States. Britain quickly granted Sri Lanka (Ceylon) and Burma independence in 1948. However, Indonesian nationalists had to beat off attempts by the Dutch to reconquer the Dutch East Indies before Indonesia emerged in 1949 as a sovereign state.

The French also tried their best to re-establish colonial rule in Indochina, but despite American aid, they were defeated in 1954 by forces under the communist and nationalist guerrilla leader Ho Chi Minh (hoh chee min) (1890–1969), who was supported by the Soviet Union and China. But Indochina was not unified, and two independent Vietnamese states came into being, which led to civil war and subsequent intervention by the United States (see pages 800–801).

Decolonization in the Middle East and Africa

In the Middle East, the movement toward political independence continued after World War II. In 1944 the French gave up their League of Nations mandates in Syria and Lebanon. In British-mandated Palestine, where after 1918 the British government established a Jewish homeland alongside the Arab population, violence and terrorism mounted on both sides. In 1947 the frustrated British decided to leave Palestine, and the United Nations then voted in a nonbinding resolution to divide Palestine into two states—one Arab and one Jewish, which became Israel. The Jews accepted the plan but the Arabs did not, and in 1948 they attacked the Jewish state as soon as it was proclaimed. The Israelis drove off the invaders and conquered more territory, as roughly 900,000 Arabs fled or were expelled. Holocaust survivors from Europe streamed into Israel, as Theodor Herzl's (HER-tsuhl) Zionist dream came true (see page 665). The next fifty years saw four more wars between the Israelis and the Arab states and innumerable clashes between the Israelis and the Palestinians.

The Arab defeat in 1948 triggered a powerful nationalist revolution in Egypt in 1952, where a young army officer named Gamal Abdel Nasser (gah-MAHL AHB-dal NAH-suhr) (1918–1970) drove out the pro-Western king. In 1956 Nasser abruptly nationalized the foreign-owned Suez Canal Company, the last symbol and substance of Western power in the Middle East. Infuriated, the British and the French, along with the Israelis, invaded Egypt. This was, however, the dying gasp of traditional imperial power: the Americans joined with the Soviets to force the British, French, and Israelis to withdraw. Nasser and anti-Western Egyptian nationalism triumphed.

The failure of Britain and France to unseat Nasser in 1956 encouraged Arab nationalists in Algeria. Although they met tough resistance from the country's large French population, the Algerians won their independence in 1962. South of the Sahara, decolonization proceeded with little or no bloodshed. Beginning in 1957, Britain's colonies achieved independence and then entered a very loose association with Britain as members of the British Commonwealth of Nations. In 1958 the clever de Gaulle offered the leaders of French black Africa the choice of a total break with France or immediate independence within a kind of French commonwealth. All but one of the new states chose association with France. In exchange for aid from France, the African countries granted the French access to untapped markets for their industrial goods, raw materials for their factories, outlets for profitable investment, and good temporary jobs for their engineers and teachers. The British acted somewhat similarly.

As a result, western European countries actually managed to increase their economic and cultural ties with their former African colonies in the 1960s and 1970s. Above all, they used the lure of special trading privileges and heavy investment in French- and English-language education to enhance a powerful Western presence in the new African states. This situation led a variety of leaders and scholars to charge that western Europe (and the United States) had imposed a system of neocolonialism on the former colonies. According to this view, **neocolonialism** was a system designed to perpetuate Western economic domination and undermine the promise of political independence, thereby extending to Africa (and much of Asia) the economic subordination that the United States had established in Latin America in the nineteenth century. At the very least, enduring influence in sub-Saharan Africa testified to western Europe's resurgent economic and political power in international relations.

neocolonialism A system designed to perpetuate Western economic domination and undermine the promise of political independence, thereby extending to Africa (and much of Asia) the economic subordination that the United States had established in Latin America in the nineteenth century.

America's Civil Rights Revolution

The Second World War cured the depression in the United States and brought about an economic boom. In the postwar years, America experienced a genuine social revolution. The civil rights movement threw off a deeply entrenched system of segregation, discrimination, and repression of African Americans. As civil rights leader Martin Luther King, Jr. (1929–1968), told the white power structure, "We will not hate you, but we will not obey your evil laws."[2] Through civil disobedience and court challenges, separate schools and facilities for African Americans were deemed illegal, as were job discrimination and obstacles to voting

The March on Washington, August 1963
The march marked a dramatic climax in the civil rights struggle. More than 200,000 people gathered at the Lincoln Memorial to hear the young Martin Luther King, Jr., deliver his greatest address, the "I have a dream" speech. (Time Life Pictures/Getty Images)

rights. By the 1970s, substantial numbers of blacks had been elected to public and private office throughout the southern states, a sign of dramatic changes in American race relations.

President Lyndon Johnson (1908–1973) also declared "unconditional war on poverty," and Congress and the administration created a host of antipoverty programs intended to aid all poor Americans and bring greater economic equality. Thus the United States promoted in the mid-1960s the kind of fundamental social reform that western Europe had embraced immediately after the Second World War. The United States became more of a welfare state, as government spending for social benefits rose dramatically and approached European levels.

Soviet Eastern Europe (1945–1968)

What was the pattern of postwar rebuilding and development in the Soviet Union and communist eastern Europe?

While western Europe surged ahead economically after the Second World War and increased its political power as American influence in Europe gradually waned, eastern Europe followed a different path. The Soviet Union first tightened its grip on the "liberated" nations of eastern Europe under Stalin and then refused to let go. Thus postwar economic recovery in eastern Europe proceeded along Soviet lines, and political and social developments were strongly influenced by changes in the Soviet Union.

Stalin's Last Years (1945–1953)

The "Great Patriotic War of the Fatherland" had fostered Russian nationalism and had unified the Russian people under their leaders. Having made a heroic war effort, many people hoped in 1945 that a grateful party and government would grant greater freedom and democracy. Such hopes were soon crushed.

Stalin's new foreign foe in the West provided an excuse for re-establishing a harsh dictatorship. Many returning soldiers and ordinary citizens were purged in 1945 and 1946, as Stalin revived the terrible forced-labor camps of the 1930s. Artists who did not promote anti-Western ideology were denounced, and Soviet Jews were accused of being pro-Western and antisocialist.

Five-year plans were reintroduced to cope with the enormous task of economic reconstruction. Once again, heavy industry and the military were given top priority, and consumer goods, housing, and collectivized agriculture were neglected. Everyday life was very hard. In short, it was the 1930s all over again in the Soviet Union, although police terror was less intense.

Stalin's prime postwar innovation was to export the Stalinist system to the countries of eastern Europe. One-party states were established by 1948 and the middle class was stripped of its possessions. Forced industrialization lurched forward, and the collectivization of agriculture began.

Only Josip Broz Tito (TEE-toh) (1892–1980), the resistance leader and Communist chief of Yugoslavia, was able to resist Soviet domination successfully. Tito stood up to Stalin in 1948, and since there was no Russian army in Yugoslavia, he got away with it. Yugoslavia prospered as a multiethnic state until it began to break apart in the 1980s. Tito's proclamation of independence infuriated Stalin. Elsewhere Stalin sought obedient leaders and purged those who had the potential to challenge him.

Sergei Eisenstein: Ivan the Terrible

Eisenstein's final masterpiece—one of the greatest films ever—was filmed during the Second World War and released in two parts in 1946. In this chilling scene, the crafty paranoid tyrant, who has saved Russia from foreign invaders, invites the unsuspecting Prince Vladimir to a midnight revel that will lead to his murder. The increasingly demonic Ivan seemed to resemble Stalin, and Eisenstein was censored and purged. (David King Collection)

de-Stalinization The liberalization of the post-Stalin Soviet Union, led by reformer Nikita Khrushchev.

Reform and De-Stalinization (1953–1964)

By the time of Stalin's death in 1953, it was apparent that support for the system was eroding and reforms were needed. However, the Communist leadership was badly split on the extent of changes needed. Conservatives wanted to make as few changes as possible. Reformers, who were led by Nikita Khrushchev (**KROOSH-chof**), argued for major innovations. Khrushchev (1894–1971), who had joined the party as an uneducated coal miner in 1918 and risen to a high-level position in the 1930s, emerged as the new ruler in 1955.

To strengthen his position and that of his fellow reformers within the party, Khrushchev launched an all-out attack on Stalin and his crimes at a closed session of the Twentieth Party Congress in 1956. In gory detail, he described to the startled Communist delegates how Stalin had tortured and murdered thousands of loyal Communists, how he had trusted Hitler completely and bungled the country's defense, and how he had "supported the glorification of his own person with all conceivable methods." Khrushchev's "secret speech" was read at Communist Party meetings held throughout the country, and it strengthened the reform movement.

The liberalization—or **de-Stalinization,** as it was called in the West—of the Soviet Union was genuine. While the Communist Party maintained its monopoly on political power, Khrushchev brought in new members with new ideas. Some resources were shifted from heavy industry and the military toward consumer goods and agriculture, and Stalinist controls over workers were relaxed. The Soviet Union's very low standard of living finally began to improve and continued to rise substantially throughout the booming 1960s.

De-Stalinization created great ferment among writers and intellectuals who hungered for cultural freedom. The writer Aleksandr Solzhenitsyn (**sol-zhuh-NEET-sin**) (b. 1918) created a sensation when his *One Day in the Life of Ivan Denisovich* was published in the Soviet Union in 1962. Solzhenitsyn's novel portrays in grim detail life in a Stalinist concentration camp—a life to which Solzhenitsyn himself had been unjustly condemned—and is a damning indictment of the Stalinist past.

Khrushchev also de-Stalinized Soviet foreign policy. "Peaceful coexistence" with capitalism was possible, he argued, and great wars were not inevitable.

Khrushchev even made concessions, agreeing in 1955 to real independence for a neutral Austria after ten long years of Allied occupation. Thus there was considerable relaxation of cold war tensions between 1955 and 1957. At the same time, Khrushchev began wooing the new nations of Asia and Africa—even if they were not communist—with promises and aid.

De-Stalinization stimulated rebelliousness in the eastern European satellites. Poland took the lead in 1956, when extensive rioting brought a new government that managed to win greater autonomy. In Hungary, revolution brought tragic results. Soviet troops were forced out and a new liberal communist leader was made chief in October 1956. But after the new government promised free elections and renounced Hungary's military alliance with Moscow, the Russian leaders ordered an invasion and crushed the national and democratic revolution. Fighting was bitter until the end, for the Hungarians hoped that the United States would come to their aid. When this did not occur, most people in eastern Europe concluded that their only hope was to strive for small domestic gains while following Russia obediently in foreign affairs.

The End of Reform

By late 1962, opposition in party circles to Khrushchev's policies was strong, and in 1964 Leonid Brezhnev (BREZH-nef) (1906–1982) took control. Under Brezhnev, the Soviet Union began a period of stagnation and limited "re-Stalinization." The basic reason for this development was that Khrushchev's communist colleagues saw de-Stalinization as a dangerous threat to the dictatorial authority of the party.

Another reason for conservative opposition was that Khrushchev's policy toward the West was erratic and ultimately unsuccessful. In 1958 he ordered the Western allies to evacuate West Berlin within six months. In response, the allies reaffirmed their unity in West Berlin, and Khrushchev backed down. Then in 1961, as relations with communist China deteriorated dramatically, Khrushchev ordered the East Germans to build a wall between East and West Berlin, thereby sealing off West Berlin in clear violation of existing access agreements between the Great Powers. The recently elected U.S. president, John F. Kennedy, acquiesced to the construction of the Berlin Wall. Emboldened and seeing a chance to change the balance of military power decisively, Khrushchev ordered missiles with nuclear warheads installed in Fidel Castro's communist Cuba in 1962. President Kennedy countered with a naval blockade of Cuba. After a tense diplomatic crisis, Khrushchev agreed to remove the Soviet missiles in return for American pledges not to disturb Castro's regime. Khrushchev looked like a bumbling buffoon; his influence, already slipping, declined rapidly after the Cuban fiasco.

When Brezhnev and his supporters took over, they launched a massive arms buildup to counter American nuclear superiority. Yet Brezhnev and company avoided direct confrontation with the United States. They were, however, willing to act as aggressor against any Soviet bloc country moving toward liberalization. The 1968 invasion of Czechoslovakia exemplified the **Brezhnev Doctrine** regarding the Soviet Union's right to intervene in any socialist country whenever they saw the need.

In January 1968, the reform elements in the Czechoslovak Communist Party had gained a majority and voted out the long-time Stalinist leader in favor of Alexander Dubček (DOOB-chek) (1921–1992), whose new government aimed to build what they called "socialism with a human face." Local decision making by trade unions, managers, and consumers replaced rigid bureaucratic planning, and censorship was relaxed. Hardliners in Poland and East Germany were afraid that

Brezhnev Doctrine The doctrine created by Leonid Brezhnev and exemplified by the Soviet invasion of Czechoslovakia in 1968, according to which the Soviet Union had the right to intervene in any socialist country whenever it saw the need.

The Invasion of Czechoslovakia
Armed with Czechoslovakian flags, courageous Czechs in downtown Prague try to stop a Soviet tank and repel the invasion and occupation of their country by the Soviet Union and its eastern European allies. This dramatic confrontation marked a high point, because the Czechs and the Slovaks realized that military resistance would be suicidal. (AP/Wide World Photos)

the reform movement would spread and push them out of power, while Moscow feared that a liberalized Czechoslovakia would eventually be drawn to neutrality or even to the democratic West. Thus the Eastern bloc countries launched a concerted campaign of intimidation against the Czechoslovak leaders, and in August 1968, 500,000 Russian and allied eastern European troops suddenly occupied Czechoslovakia. The arrested leaders surrendered to Soviet demands, and the reform program was abandoned.

The 1968 invasion of Czechoslovakia was the crucial event of the Brezhnev era, which really lasted beyond the aging leader's death in 1982 until the emergence in 1985 of Mikhail Gorbachev (GORE-beh-chof). The invasion demonstrated the determination of the ruling elite to maintain the status quo throughout the Soviet bloc. Only in the 1980s, with Poland taking the lead, would a strong current of reform and opposition develop again to challenge Communist Party rule.

The Soviet Union to 1985

Determined to maintain firm control of eastern Europe, Soviet leaders set the example at home. There was a certain **re-Stalinization** of the U.S.S.R., but now dictatorship was collective rather than personal, and coercion replaced terror. This compromise seemed to suit the leaders and a majority of the people.

re-Stalinization An attempt by Soviet leaders to maintain firm control of eastern Europe.

A slowly rising standard of living for ordinary people contributed to the apparent stability in the Soviet Union, although long food lines and innumerable shortages persisted. Ambitious individuals had a tremendous incentive to do as the state wished in order to gain access to special, well-stocked stores, to attend special schools, and to travel abroad.

The strength of the government was expressed in the re-Stalinization of culture and art. Acts of open nonconformity and public protest were often punished by blacklisting, leaving the dissident unable to find a decent job. More determined protesters were quietly imprisoned, while celebrated nonconformists such as Aleksandr Solzhenitsyn were permanently expelled from the country.

Eliminating the worst aspects of Stalin's dictatorship strengthened the regime, and almost all Western experts concluded that rule by a self-perpetuating Communist Party elite in the Soviet Union appeared to be quite solid in the 1970s and early 1980s. Yet Soviet life was changing profoundly in the Brezhnev era, laying the groundwork for the revolution to come under Gorbachev. The urban population grew rapidly in the 1960s and 1970s, and these city dwellers were better educated and more sophisticated than the peasants of earlier generations. Many of them were highly trained scientists, managers, and specialists. Educated people read, discussed, and formed definite ideas on important issues, many of which could be approached and debated in "nonpolitical" terms. Developing ideas on such questions as environmental pollution and urban transportation, educated urban people increasingly saw themselves as worthy of having a voice in society's decisions, even its political decisions.

Postwar Social Transformations (1945–1968)

How did changing patterns in technology, class relations, women's work, and youth culture bring major social transformations?

During the postwar period, the patterns of everyday life and the structure of Western society were changing along with the economy and politics. New inventions and technologies profoundly affected human existence. The structure of women's lives changed dramatically. An international youth culture took shape and rose to challenge established lifestyles and even governments.

Science and Technology

With the advent of the Second World War, most leading university scientists went to work on top-secret government projects. British scientists, for example, developed radar to detect enemy aircraft, which was key to Britain's victory in the battle for air supremacy in 1940. The air war also greatly stimulated the development of jet aircraft and spurred further research on electronic computers, which calculated the complex mathematical relationships between fast-moving planes and anti-aircraft shells to increase the likelihood of a hit. However, it was the atomic bomb, the product of three years of intensive research, that showed the world both the awesome power and the heavy moral responsibilities of modern science.

The spectacular results of directed research during World War II inspired a new model for science—**Big Science.** By combining theoretical work with sophisticated engineering in a large organization, Big Science could attack extremely difficult problems, from better products for consumers to new and improved

Section Review

- Stalin's post-war programs were harsh, building up industry and the military at the expense of consumer goods, housing, and agriculture; in eastern Europe, Soviet-backed countries, with the exception of Yugoslavia, set up similar programs.

- Stalin's successor Khrushchev brought to light the horrors of Stalin's regime and began de-Stalinizing the country, bringing reforms that improved the standard of living; he also relaxed Soviet foreign policy, albeit erratically, easing cold war tensions.

- Khrushchev's successor Brezhnev went back to a Stalinist type of rule, ending reform and implementing strict control of Eastern bloc countries, putting down a progressive new government in Czechoslovakia in 1968 and launching an arms buildup to counter American superiority.

- The Soviet dictatorship was collective and domestic conditions improved, but personal advancement was based on loyalty to the party, which punished dissenters, although an increasingly educated public began to gain interest in influencing political decisions.

weapons for the military. Big Science was extremely expensive, requiring large-scale financing from governments and large corporations.

Populous, victorious, and wealthy, the United States took the lead in Big Science after World War II. Between 1945 and 1965, spending on scientific research and development in the United States grew five times as fast as the national income, and by 1965 such spending took 3 percent of all U.S. income. It was generally accepted that government should finance science heavily in both the "capitalist" United States and the "socialist" Soviet Union. In both countries a large portion of all postwar scientific research went for "defense." New weapons such as rockets, nuclear submarines, and spy satellites demanded breakthroughs no less remarkable than those of radar and the first atomic bomb. Sophisticated science, lavish government spending, and military needs all came together in the space race of the 1960s. In 1957 the Soviets put a satellite in orbit, and in 1961 they sent the world's first cosmonaut circling the globe. The United States raced to catch up with the Soviets and landed a crewed spacecraft on the moon in 1969. Four more moon landings followed by 1972.

The rise of Big Science and of close ties between science and technology greatly altered the lives of scientists. The scientific community grew much larger than ever before. There were about four times as many scientists in Europe and North America in 1975 as in 1945. With increased specialization, modern scientists and technologists normally had to work as members of a team, typically in large bureaucratic organizations. There the individual was very often a small cog in a great machine. Modern science also became highly, even brutally, competitive. James Watson, who worked with Francis Crick to discover the structure of DNA, exemplified the competitive spirit in his race to crack the molecule of heredity before another research team. With so many thousands of like-minded researchers in the wealthy countries of the world, scientific and technical knowledge rushed forward in the postwar era.

The Changing Class Structure

Scientists and engineers were not the only people to experience a transformation of the workplace in the postwar years. For both the middle and lower classes, the new economy brought new opportunities for making and spending money.

A new breed of managers and experts replaced traditional property owners as the leaders of the middle class. Well paid and highly trained, often with backgrounds in engineering or accounting, these experts increasingly came from all social classes, even the working class. The ability to serve the needs of a big organization largely replaced inherited property and family connections in determining an individual's social position. This new middle class was more open, democratic, and insecure than the old propertied middle class. At the same time, the middle class grew massively and became harder to define.

The lower classes were also transformed, as many people abandoned the traditional, rooted life of the farm for a more mobile urban existence. Meanwhile, the number of factory jobs ceased to expand and began to decline, and the remaining industrial workers became better educated and more specialized. Job opportunities for white-collar and service employees grew rapidly.

European governments were reducing class tensions with a series of social security reforms. Many of these reforms—such as increased unemployment benefits and more extensive old-age pensions—simply strengthened social security measures first pioneered in Bismarck's Germany before the First World War (see page 661). Other programs were new, like comprehensive national health systems directed by the state. Most countries introduced family allow-ances—direct government grants to parents to help them raise their children. Most European governments also gave mater-nity grants and built inexpensive public housing. These and other social reforms provided a humane floor of well-being. Reforms also promoted greater equality because they were paid for in part by higher taxes on the rich.

The rising standard of living and the availability of credit made consumer goods such as washing machines, refrigera-tors, vacuum cleaners, radios, TVs, and even automobiles more accessible to workers. With the expansion of social secu-rity safeguards for hard times and old age, ordinary people were increasingly willing to take on debt. This change had far-reaching consequences.

Leisure and recreation occupied an important place in consumer societies. The most astonishing leisure-time devel-opment was the blossoming of mass travel and tourism. With month-long paid vacations required by law in most European countries and widespread automobile ownership, beaches and ski resorts came within the reach of the middle class and much of the working class. By the late 1960s, packaged tours with cheap group flights and bargain hotel accommodations had made even distant lands easily accessible. Truly, consum-erism had come of age.

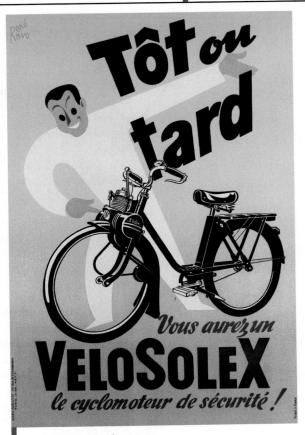

Consumers on the Move
In the early postwar years the Italians had their motor scooters and the French their motorbikes. This ad promises young people that "sooner or later" they will have a "Velo," and it subtly assures housewives that the bike is safe. In small towns and villages the slow-moving motorbike could be a godsend for errands and daily shopping. (Roger Perrin/The Bridgeman Art Library)

New Roles for Women

The postwar era saw significant transformations in the lives of women, preparing the way for the success of a new generation of feminist thinkers and a militant women's movement in the 1970s and 1980s (see pages 802–803). Building on trends that had developed with the Indus-trial Revolution, this period was one of early marriage, early childbearing, and small family size in wealthy urban areas. By the early 1970s, about half of Western women were having their last baby by the age of twenty-six or twenty-seven. When the youngest child trooped off to kindergarten, the average mother had more than forty years of life in front of her.

This was a momentous change. Throughout history male-dominated society insisted on defining most women as mothers or potential mothers, and mother-hood was very demanding. In the postwar years, however, motherhood no longer absorbed the energies of a lifetime, and more and more married women looked for new roles in the world of work outside the family (see Figure 30.1).

Three major forces helped women searching for jobs. First, the economy boomed from about 1950 to 1973 and created a strong demand for labor. Second, the economy continued its gradual shift away from the old, male-dominated heavy industries, such as coal, steel, and shipbuilding, to the more dynamic, "white-collar" service industries, such as government, education, trade, and health care. Some women had always worked in these service fields. Third, young Western women shared fully in the postwar education revolution and could take advantage of the growing need for office workers and well-trained professionals. Thus more and more married women became full-time and part-time wage earners.

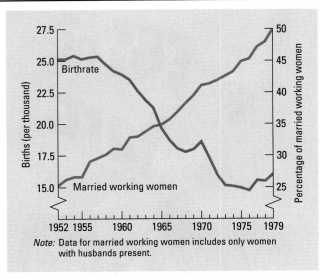

FIGURE 30.1   The Decline of the Birthrate and the Increase of Married Working Women in the United States, 1952–1979
The challenge of working away from home encouraged American wives to prefer fewer children and helped lower the birthrate.

Note: Data for married working women includes only women with husbands present.

The trend went the furthest in communist eastern Europe, where women accounted for almost half of all employed persons. In noncommunist western Europe and North America, there was a good deal of variation, with the percentage of married women in the workforce rising from a range of roughly 20 to 25 percent in 1950 to a range of 40 to 70 percent in the early 1980s.

Married women entering (or re-entering) the labor force faced widespread, long-established discrimination in pay, advancement, and occupational choice in comparison to men. Moreover, many women could find only part-time work. As the divorce rate rose in the 1960s, part-time work, with its low pay and scanty benefits, meant poverty for many women with teenage children. Finally, in the best of circumstances, married working women still carried most of the child-raising and housekeeping responsibilities. A reason for many to accept part-time employment, this gendered imbalance meant an exhausting "double day"—on the job and at home—for the full-time worker.

The injustices that married women encountered as wage earners contributed greatly to the subsequent movement for women's equality and emancipation. A young unmarried woman of a hundred years ago was more likely to accept such problems as temporary nuisances because she looked forward to marriage and motherhood for fulfillment. In the postwar era, a married wage earner in her thirties gradually developed a very different perspective. She saw employment as a permanent condition within which she, like her male counterpart, sought not only income but also psychological satisfaction. Sexism and discrimination in the workplace—and in the home—grew loathsome and evoked the sense of injustice that drives revolutions and reforms. When powerful voices arose to challenge the system, they found widespread support among working women.

Youth and the Counterculture

The "baby boom" generation born after World War II developed a distinctive and very international youth culture, which eventually became a "counterculture" of social rebellion.

Young people in the United States took the lead. By the late 1950s the "beat" movement was stoking the fires of revolt in selected urban enclaves, such as the Near North Side of Chicago. There the young (and the not-so-young) fashioned a highly publicized subculture that blended radical politics, unbridled personal experimentation (with drugs and communal living, for example), and new artistic styles. This subculture quickly spread to major American and western European cities. In the words of folksinger Bob Dylan, "the times they are a'changing."[3]

Certainly the sexual behavior of young people appeared to change dramatically in the 1960s and into the 1970s. More young people engaged in sexual intercourse, and they did so at an earlier age, in part because the discovery of safe and effective contraceptive pills could eliminate the risk of unwanted pregnancy. Perhaps even more significant was the growing tendency of young unmarried people to live together in a separate household on a semipermanent basis, demonstrating in effect that the long-standing monopoly of married couples on legitimate sexual unions was dead.

Several factors contributed to the emergence of the international youth culture in the 1960s. First, mass communications and youth travel linked countries and continents together. Second, the postwar baby boom meant that young people became an unusually large part of the population and could therefore exercise exceptional influence on society as a whole. Third, postwar prosperity and greater equality gave young people more purchasing power than ever before. This enabled them to set their own trends and patterns of consumption, which fostered generational loyalty. Finally, prosperity meant that good jobs were readily available, and employers might be more willing to hire unconventional young people. The youth culture practically fused with the counterculture in opposition to the established order in the late 1960s. Student protesters saw the materialistic West as hopelessly rotten but believed that better societies were being built in the newly independent countries of Asia and Africa. Thus the Vietnam War was perceived by young radicals as an immoral and imperialistic war against a small and heroic people. As the war intensified, so did worldwide student opposition to it.

Student protests in western Europe were also a response to the negative consequences of the rapid expansion of higher education. Classes were badly overcrowded and competition for grades became intense. Moreover, although more practical areas of study were gradually added, many students felt that they were not getting the kind of education they needed for jobs in the modern world. At the same time, some reflective students feared that universities would soon do nothing but turn out docile technocrats both to stock and to serve "the establishment."

Student Rebellion in Paris
These rock-throwing students in the Latin Quarter of Paris are trying to force education reforms and even to topple de Gaulle's government. Throughout May 1968 students clashed repeatedly with France's tough riot police in bloody street fighting. De Gaulle remained in power, but a major reform of French education did follow. (Bruno Barbey/Magnum Photos)

The many tensions within the exploding university population came to a head in the late 1960s and early 1970s, most famously in France in May 1968. Students occupied buildings and took over the University of Paris, which led to violent clashes with police. In defiance of union officials, many workers across France joined the protest by going on strike. It seemed certain that President de Gaulle's Fifth Republic would collapse.

In fact, de Gaulle stiffened, like an old-fashioned irate father. He moved troops toward Paris and called for new elections. The masses of France, fearing an eventual communist takeover, voted overwhelmingly for de Gaulle's party and a return to law and order. Workers went back to work, and the mini-revolution collapsed. Yet within a year de Gaulle resigned. Growing out of the counterculture and youthful idealism, the student rebellion of 1968 signaled the end of an era and the return of unrest and uncertainty in the 1970s and early 1980s.

Conflict and Challenge in the Late Cold War (1968–1985)

What were the key aspects of political conflict, economic stagnation, and the feminist movement in the late cold war?

The Vietnam War also marked the beginning of a new era of challenges and uncertainties in the late 1960s. The war and its aftermath divided the people of the United States, shook the ideology of containment, and weakened the Western alliance. A second challenge affecting the whole world appeared when the great postwar economic boom came to a close in 1973, opening a long period of economic stagnation, widespread unemployment, and social dislocation. The era also saw the birth of new liberation movements, including the women's movement for gender equality.

The United States and Vietnam

President Johnson wanted his legacy to be as the champion of civil rights and the leader of the "war on poverty." Instead, his presidency is better known for having drafted thousands of young American men for a foreign war that divided the nation.

American involvement in Vietnam was primarily a product of the cold war and the policy of containing the spread of communism. As western Europe began to revive and China established a communist government in 1949, efforts to contain communism shifted to Asia. The bloody Korean War (1950–1953) ended in stalemate, but the United States did succeed in preventing a communist victory in South Korea. After the Vietnamese won their independence from France in 1954, the United States refused to sign the Geneva Accords that temporarily divided Vietnam into two zones pending national unification by means of free elections. (Ho Chi Minh led a socialist state in the northern zone.) When the anticommunist South Vietnamese government declined to hold elections, President Eisenhower supported it with military aid. President Kennedy greatly increased the number of American "military advisers" in South Vietnam to sixteen thousand.

After winning the 1964 election on a peace platform, President Johnson greatly expanded the American role in the Vietnam conflict. The United States gave South Vietnam massive military aid, American forces in the South gradually grew to half a million men, and the United States bombed North Vietnam with ever-greater intensity.

The undeclared war in Vietnam, fought nightly on American television, eventually divided the nation. In October 1965, student protesters joined forces with old-line socialists, New Left intellectuals, and pacifists in antiwar demonstrations in fifty American cities. By 1967 a growing number of critics denounced the war as a criminal intrusion into a complex and distant civil war. Criticism reached a crescendo in January 1968, after the Tet Offensive, the first comprehensive attack by the Vietcong on major cities in South Vietnam. Although the Vietcong suffered heavy losses, the Tet Offensive signaled that the war was not close to ending, as Washington had claimed. President Johnson called for negotiations with North Vietnam and announced that he would not stand for re-election.

The new president, Richard Nixon (1913–1994), promised "peace with honor." In his second term in office, Nixon and Secretary of State Henry Kissinger finally reached a peace agreement with North Vietnam. The 1973 agreement allowed American forces, which had been withdrawing since 1971, to complete their withdrawal, and the United States reserved the right to resume bombing if the accords were broken. Fighting declined markedly in South Vietnam, where the South Vietnamese army appeared to hold its own against the Vietcong. But in early 1974, when North Vietnam launched a general invasion against South Vietnamese armies, the United States Congress refused to permit a military response. At this point Nixon had resigned as a result of the **Watergate** scandal, in which he and others were exposed in lies about the illegal break-in of the Democratic Party headquarters. The belated fall of South Vietnam in the wake of Watergate shook America's postwar confidence and left the country divided and uncertain about its proper role in world affairs.

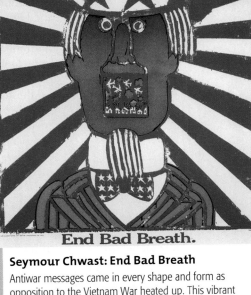

End Bad Breath.

Seymour Chwast: End Bad Breath
Antiwar messages came in every shape and form as opposition to the Vietnam War heated up. This vibrant poster assumes, quite reasonably, that the American viewer is steeped in the popular culture of the mass media. It ridicules American military involvement with a sarcastic parody of familiar television commercials. (Courtesy, Seymore Chwast/PushPin Group)

Watergate The scandal in which Nixon's assistants broke into the Democratic Party headquarters in July 1972 and the administration attempted to cover it up.

détente The progressive relaxation of cold war tensions.

Détente or Cold War?

One alternative to the badly damaged policy of containing communism was the policy of **détente** (dey-TAHNT), or the easing of cold war tensions. Thus while the cold war continued to define superpower relations between the Soviet Union and the United States, West Germany took a major step toward genuine peace in Europe.

West German leader Willy Brandt (1913–1992) aimed at nothing less than a comprehensive peace settlement for central Europe and the two German states established after 1945. Winning the chancellorship in 1969, Brandt negotiated treaties with the Soviet Union, Poland, and Czechoslovakia that formally accepted existing state boundaries in return for a mutual renunciation of force or the threat of force. Using the imaginative formula of "two German states within one German nation," Brandt's government also broke decisively with the past policy of refusing to recognize the legitimacy of East Germany and entered into direct relations with that state. He aimed for modest practical improvements rather than reunification, which at that point was inconceivable.

The policy of détente reached its high point when all European nations (except Albania), the United States, Canada, and the Soviet Union signed the Final Act of the Helsinki Conference in 1975. The thirty-five nations participating agreed that Europe's existing political frontiers could not be changed by force. They also solemnly accepted numerous provisions guaranteeing the human rights and political freedoms of their citizens.

Hopes for détente in international relations gradually faded in the later 1970s. Many Americans became convinced that the Soviet Union was steadily building up its military might and pushing for political gains and revolutions in Africa, Asia, and Latin America. The Soviet invasion of Afghanistan in December 1979, which was designed to save an increasingly unpopular Marxist regime, was especially alarming. Fearing that the oil-rich states of the Persian Gulf would be next, Americans looked to the Atlantic alliance to thwart communist expansion and hold Brezhnev to the human rights provisions of the Helsinki Agreement.

President Jimmy Carter (b. 1924), elected in 1976, tried to lead the Atlantic alliance beyond verbal condemnation and urged economic sanctions against the Soviet Union. Yet only Great Britain among the European allies supported the American initiative. The alliance showed the same lack of concerted action when the Solidarity movement rose in Poland. Some observers concluded that the alliance had lost the will to think and act decisively in dealing with the Soviet bloc.

The Atlantic alliance endured, however. The U.S. military buildup launched by Carter in his last years in office was greatly accelerated by President Ronald Reagan (1911–2004), who referred to the Soviet Union as the "evil empire." Increasing defense spending enormously, the Reagan administration concentrated on nuclear arms and an expanded navy as keys to American power in the post-Vietnam age.

A broad swing in the pendulum toward greater conservatism in the 1980s gave Reagan invaluable allies in western Europe. In Great Britain, Margaret Thatcher worked well with Reagan and was a forceful advocate for a revitalized Atlantic alliance. In West Germany, Helmut Kohl worked with the United States to coordinate military and political policy toward the Soviet bloc. In maintaining the alliance, the Western nations gave indirect support to ongoing efforts to liberalize authoritarian communist eastern Europe.

The Women's Movement

The 1970s marked the birth of a broad-based feminist movement devoted to securing genuine gender equality and promoting the general interests of women. Three basic reasons accounted for this major development. First, ongoing changes in underlying patterns of motherhood and paid work created novel conditions and new demands (see pages 797–798). Second, a vanguard of feminist intellectuals articulated a powerful critique of gender relations, which stimulated many women to rethink their assumptions and challenge the status quo. Third, taking a lesson from the civil rights movement in the United States and worldwide student protest against the Vietnam War, dissatisfied individuals recognized that they had to band together if they were to influence politics and secure fundamental reforms.

One of the most influential written works produced by this new feminist wave was *The Second Sex* (1949) by the French writer and philosopher Simone de Beauvoir (1908–1986). Beauvoir analyzed the position of women within the framework of existential thought (see pages 728–729). She argued that women had almost always been trapped by particularly inflexible and limiting conditions. (See the feature "Listening to the Past: A Feminist Critique of Marriage" on pages 808–809.) Only by courageously embracing her freedom could a woman escape the role of the inferior "other." Drawing on history, philosophy, psychology, biology, and literature, Beauvoir's massive investigation inspired a generation of female intellectuals.

Celebrating Women's History

Judy Chicago's multimedia creation *The Dinner Party* features thirty-nine handcrafted placemats and ceramic plates, each embellished with a painted motif associated with the woman being honored. Begun in 1974 and completed in 1978 with the participation of more than one hundred women, *The Dinner Party* was intended to represent the "historic struggle of women to participate in all the aspects of society." It attracted enormous crowds. (© Judy Chicago, 1979/Artists Rights Society [ARS], New York)

One such woman was the American writer and organizer Betty Friedan (**fri-DAN**) (1921–2006). In *The Feminine Mystique* (1963), Friedan concluded that many well-educated women shared her growing dissatisfaction with a life devoted to the service of husbands and children. According to Friedan, women faced a crisis of identity because they were not permitted to become mature adults and genuine human beings. In short, women faced what feminists would soon call *sexism*, a pervasive social problem that required drastic reforms.

Friedan took the lead in 1966 in founding the National Organization for Women (NOW) to press for women's rights. NOW flourished, growing from seven hundred members in 1967 to forty thousand in 1974. Many other women's organizations took root in Europe and the United States. Throughout the 1970s, a proliferation of publications, conferences, and institutions devoted to women's issues reinforced the emerging international movement.

This movement generally shared the common strategy of pushing for new statutes in the workplace: laws against discrimination, "equal pay for equal work," and supportive measures such as maternal leave and affordable day care. In addition, the movement concentrated on gender and family questions, including the right to divorce (in some Catholic countries), legalized abortion, the needs of single mothers, and protection from rape and physical violence. In almost every country, the effort to decriminalize abortion served as a catalyst in mobilizing an effective, self-conscious women's movement (and in creating an opposition to it, as in the United States). The sharply focused women's movement of the 1970s was successful in winning new rights for women. Subsequently, the movement became more diffuse, a victim of both its successes and the resurgence of an antifeminist opposition.

The accomplishments of the women's movement encouraged mobilization by many other groups. Gay men and lesbian women pressed their own demands, organizing politically and calling for an end to legal discrimination and social harassment. People with physical disabilities joined together to promote their interests. Thus many subordinate groups challenged the dominant majorities, and the expansion and redefinition of human liberty—one of the great themes of modern Western and world history—continued.

Society in a Time of Economic Uncertainty

The 1970s and early 1980s witnessed the worst economic decline since the Great Depression. The great postwar boom had been fueled by cheap oil from the Middle East, which permitted energy-intensive industries—automobiles, chemicals,

OPEC The Arab-led Organization of Petroleum Exporting Countries.

and electric power—to expand rapidly and lead other sectors of the economy forward. By 1971 the Arab-led Organization of Petroleum Exporting Countries (**OPEC**) was no longer satisfied to see the price of oil decline as the price of manufactured goods rose, and they presented a united front against the oil companies. When OPEC declared an embargo on oil shipments to the United States, during the fourth Arab-Israeli war in October 1973, oil prices quadrupled within the year. Governments, industry, and individuals had no other choice than to deal piecemeal with the so-called oil shock—a "shock" that turned out to be an earthquake.

The energy-intensive industries that had driven the economy upward in the 1950s and 1960s now dragged it down. Unemployment rose; productivity and living standards declined. By 1976 a modest recovery was in progress. But when a fundamentalist Islamic revolution struck Iran and oil production collapsed in that country, the price of crude oil doubled in 1979 and the world economy succumbed to its second oil shock. Unemployment and inflation rose dramatically before another uneven recovery began in 1982. In 1985 the unemployment rate in western Europe rose to its highest level since the Great Depression. Nineteen million people were unemployed.

Throughout the 1970s and 1980s, anxious observers, recalling the disastrous consequences of the Great Depression, worried that the Common Market would disintegrate in the face of severe economic dislocation and that economic nationalism would halt steps toward European unity. Yet the Common Market—now officially known as the European Economic Community—continued to attract new members. In 1973 Denmark and Iceland, in addition to Britain, finally joined. Greece joined in 1981, and Portugal and Spain entered in 1986. The nations of the European Economic Community also cooperated more closely in international undertakings, and the movement toward unity for western Europe stayed alive.

As a consequence of the economic stagnation of the 1970s and early 1980s, optimism gave way to pessimism; romantic utopianism yielded to sober realism. This drastic change in mood—a complete surprise only to those who had never studied history—affected states, institutions, and individuals in countless ways.

Governments responded with social programs to prevent mass suffering and degradation. Indeed, government spending increased sharply in most countries during the 1970s and early 1980s. In all countries, however, people were much more willing to see their governments increase spending than raise taxes. This imbalance contributed to the rapid growth of budget deficits, national debts, and inflation. By the late 1970s, a powerful reaction against government's ever-increasing role had set in, however, and Western governments were gradually forced to introduce austerity measures to slow the growth of public spending and the welfare state.

This conservative backlash helped bring Margaret Thatcher (b. 1925) to power in Britain in 1979. Thatcher was determined to scale back the role of government in Britain, and in the 1980s—the "Thatcher years"—she pushed through a series of controversial "free market" policies that transformed postwar Britain. In one of its most popular actions, Thatcher's Conservative government encouraged low- and moderate-income renters in state-owned housing projects to buy their apartments at rock-bottom prices. This initiative, part of Thatcher's broader privatization campaign, created a whole new class of property owners, thereby eroding the electoral base of Britain's socialist Labour Party. (See the feature "Individuals in Society: Margaret Thatcher.")

President Ronald Reagan's success in the United States was more limited. With widespread support, Reagan in 1981 pushed through major cuts in income taxes all across the board. But Reagan and Congress failed to cut government spending, which increased as a percentage of national income in the course of his

Individuals in Society

Margaret Thatcher

Margaret Thatcher (b. 1925), the first woman elected to lead a major European state, stands as one of the most significant leaders of the late twentieth century. The controversial "Iron Lady" attacked socialism, promoted capitalism, and changed the face of modern Britain.

Born Margaret Roberts in a small city in southeastern England, her father was a small shopkeeper who instilled in his daughter the classic lower-middle-class virtues—hard work, personal responsibility, and practical education. A scholarship student at a local girls school, she entered Oxford in 1943 to study chemistry but soon found that politics was her passion. Elected president of the student Conservatives, she ran in 1950 for Parliament in a solidly Labour district to gain experience. Articulate and attractive, she also gained the attention of Denis Thatcher, a wealthy businessman who drove her to campaign appearances in his Jaguar. Married a year later, the new Mrs. Thatcher abandoned chemistry, went to law school, gave birth to twins, and practiced as a tax attorney. In 1959, she returned to politics and won a seat in the Conservative triumph.

For the next fifteen years Mrs. Thatcher served in Parliament and held various ministerial posts when the Conservatives governed. In 1974, as the economy soured and the Conservatives lost two close elections, a rebellious Margaret Thatcher adroitly ran for the leadership position of the Conservative Party and won. In the 1979 election, as the Labour government faced rampant inflation and crippling strikes, Mrs. Thatcher promised to reduce union power, lower taxes, and promote free markets. Attracting swing votes from skilled workers, she won and became prime minister.

A self-described "conviction politician," Thatcher rejected postwar Keynesian efforts to manage the economy, arguing that governments had created inflation by printing too much money. Thus her government reduced the supply of money and credit, and it refused to retreat as interest rates and unemployment soared. Her popularity plummeted. But Thatcher was saved by good luck—and courage. In 1982, the generals ruling Argentina suddenly seized the Falkland Islands off the Argentine coast, the home of 1,800 British citizens. Ever a staunch nationalist, Thatcher detached a naval armada that recaptured the Falklands without a hitch. Britain loved Thatcher's determination, and the "Iron Lady" was reelected in 1983.

Thatcher's second term was the high point of her success and influence. Her whole hearted commitment to privatization changed the face of British industry. More than fifty state-owned companies, ranging from the state telephone monopoly to the nationalized steel trust, were sold to private investors. Small investors were offered shares at bargain prices to promote "people's capitalism." Thatcher also curbed the power of British labor unions with various laws and actions. Most spectacularly, when in 1984 the once mighty coal miners rejected more mine closings and doggedly struck for a year, Thatcher stood firm and beat them. This outcome had a profound psychological impact on the public.

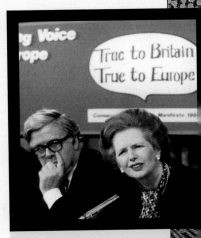

Margaret Thatcher as prime minister. (AP Images/Staff-Caulkin)

Elected again in 1987, Thatcher became increasingly stubborn, overconfident, and uncaring. Working well with her ideological soul mate, U.S. president Ronald Reagan, she opposed greater political and economic unity within the European Community. This, coupled with an unpopular effort to assert financial control over city governments, proved her undoing. In 1990, as in 1974, party stalwarts suddenly revolted and elected a new Conservative leader. Raised to the peerage by Queen Elizabeth II, the new Lady Thatcher then sat in the largely ceremonial House of Lords. The transformational changes of the Thatcher years endured, consolidated by her Conservative successor and largely accepted by the "New Labour" prime minister, the moderate Tony Blair.

Questions for Analysis

1. Why did Margaret Thatcher want to change Britain, and how did she do it?

2. Historians have often debated whether great leaders determine the course of history, or whether they only ride successfully the major forces of their time. Which view of history is supported by Thatcher's achievements? Why?

Section Review

- The United States backed the anti-communist South Vietnamese militarily, gradually expanding the American presence in Vietnam until protests at home led to a peace agreement with North Vietnam and fighting subsided, but when the North invaded the South, the United States did not respond and the South fell to the communists.

- The Helsinki conference gave hope that political and human rights for European countries was ensured, but the Soviets invaded Afghanistan and the United States revitalized NATO to contain the Soviet "evil empire."

- Feminist leaders founded the National Organization for Women, pressing for an end to sexual discrimination, giving strength to other subordinate group movements such as gays and lesbians, but also creating an anti-feminist movement, mostly angered by the abortion issue.

- Economic decline and a sharp rise in unemployment followed increasing oil prices; governments responded by increasing social welfare programs and going into debt; the new austerity sparked a trend toward environmentalism and health consciousness.

presidency. Reagan's massive military buildup was partly responsible, but spending on social programs also grew rapidly as more people needed unemployment and welfare benefits. Thus the budget deficit soared and the U.S. government debt tripled in a decade.

Individuals felt the impact of austerity at an early date, for unlike governments, they could not pay their bills by printing money and going ever further into debt. The energy crisis of the 1970s forced them to re-examine not only their fuel bills but also the whole pattern of self-indulgent materialism in the postwar years. A growing number of experts and citizens concluded that the world was running out of resources and decried wasteful industrial practices and environmental pollution. In West Germany young activists known as the Greens in 1979 founded a political party to fight for environmental causes. The German Green movement elected some national and local representatives, and similar parties developed throughout Europe as environmentalism became a leading societal concern.

Another consequence of austerity in both Europe and North America was a self-improvement movement that focused on strict diet and exercise routines as a means to longevity. In addition, men and women were encouraged to postpone marriage until they had put their careers on a firm foundation, so the age of marriage rose sharply for both sexes in many Western countries. Indeed, career planning became important to a generation faced with the very real threat of unemployment or "underemployment" in a dead-end job.

Harder times also help explain why ever more women entered or remained in the workforce after they did marry. Although attitudes related to personal fulfillment were one reason for the continuing increase—especially for well-educated, upper-middle-class women—many wives in poor and middle-class families simply had to work outside the home because of economic necessity. As in preindustrial Europe, the wife's earnings provided the margin of survival for millions of hard-pressed families.

Chapter Review

What were the causes of the cold war? (page 782)

The Cold War grew out of the way World War II was fought in Europe. American and British forces met Stalin's armies in the middle of Germany and central Europe, so that the war-torn continent was already divided militarily in 1945. Extremely suspicious of the West and well aware that democratic governments in eastern Europe would be opposed to the Soviet Union, Stalin gradually established dependent Communist dictatorships in eastern Europe to ensure the security of the Soviet Union. Stalin's action in Eastern Europe, together with bitter disagreements between the wartime allies over the treatment of Germany, then led to a spiraling ideological confrontation between East and West. The Cold War match-up in Europe was institutionalized and extended to Asia, Africa, and Latin America for a long generation.

Why did western Europe recover so successfully? How did colonial peoples win political independence and American blacks triumph in the civil rights movement? (page 785)

Western Europe's success was due to a combination of political recovery, fundamental social changes, and unprecedented economic expansion. Political recovery included the establishment of democratic governments, the NATO alliance for military security, and the movement toward European unity. A whole series of social reforms provided

Key Terms

Big Three (p. 782)

Marshall Plan (p. 784)

NATO (p. 784)

cold war (p. 784)

Christian Democrats (p. 785)

Common Market (p. 787)

decolonization (p. 787)

neocolonialism (p. 790)

de-Stalinization (p. 792)

Brezhnev Doctrine (p. 793)

re-Stalinization (p. 794)

Big Science (p. 795)

Watergate (p. 801)

the citizens of the welfare state with national health systems, family allowances, paid vacations, and shorter workweeks. In about 1950 economic growth took off for a generation, fueled by Marshall Plan aid, a consumer revolution, and the liberal trade policies of the new Common Market. The transition from imperialism to decolonization proceeded rapidly, surprisingly smoothly, and without serious damage to western Europe. American blacks won victories in the struggle for civil rights because of their courageous determination and the inspired leadership of Martin Luther King, Jr.

What was the pattern of postwar rebuilding and development in the Soviet Union and communist eastern Europe? (page 791)

Postwar developments in the Soviet Union and communist eastern Europe displayed both similarities to and differences from developments in western Europe and North America. Perhaps the biggest difference was that Stalin imposed harsh one-party rule in the lands occupied by his armies, which led to the bitter cold war. Stalin also reimposed rigid central planning in the Soviet Union after the war and made satellite countries follow his lead. Nevertheless, the Soviet Union became less dictatorial under Khrushchev, and the standard of living in the Soviet Union improved markedly in the 1950s and 1960s.

How did changing patterns in technology, class relations, women's work, and youth culture bring major social transformations? (page 795)

In the years after 1945 pure science combined with applied technology to achieve remarkable success. The triumphs of applied science contributed not only to economic expansion but also to a more fluid, less antagonistic class structure, in which specialized education was the high road to advancement for men and women. Married women entered the labor force in growing numbers. The growing prosperity of the postwar era gave young people confidence and money, spurring the development of a distinct youth culture in the 1960s.

What were the key aspects of political conflict, economic stagnation, and the feminist movement in the late cold war? (page 800)

In the late 1960s and early 1970s, Europe and North America entered a time of crisis and rapid change. Many nations, from France to Czechoslovakia to the United States, experienced major political difficulties, as cold war conflicts and ideological battles divided peoples and shook governments. Beginning with the oil shocks of the 1970s, severe economic problems added to the turmoil and brought real hardship to millions of people. Yet in western Europe and North America, the welfare system held firm, and both democracy and the movement toward European unity successfully passed through the storm. The women's movement mobilized effectively and won expanded rights in the best tradition of Western civilization. Finally, efforts to achieve détente in central Europe while still maintaining a strong Atlantic alliance met some success. This modest progress helped lay the foundations for the sudden end of the cold war and the opening of a new era.

Notes

1. Quoted in N. Graebner, *Cold War Diplomacy, 1945–1960* (Princeton, N.J.: Van Nostrand, 1962), p. 17.
2. Quoted in S. E. Morison et al., *A Concise History of the American Republic* (New York: Oxford University Press, 1977), p. 697.
3. Quoted in N. Cantor, *Twentieth-Century Culture: Modernism to Deconstruction* (New York: Peter Lang, 1988), p. 252.

To assess your mastery of this chapter, go to **bedfordstmartins.com/mckaywestbrief**

Listening to the Past

A Feminist Critique of Marriage

*T*he existentialist writer Simone de Beauvoir (1908–1986) turned increasingly to feminist concerns after World War II. Her most influential work was The Second Sex (1949), a massive declaration of independence for contemporary women. Beauvoir argued that men had generally used education and social conditioning to create a dependent "other," a negative nonman who was not permitted to grow and strive for freedom.

Marriage—on men's terms—was part of this unjust and undesirable process. Beauvoir's conclusion that some couples could establish free and equal unions was based in part on her experience with philosopher Jean-Paul Sartre, Beauvoir's encouraging companion and sometime lover.

Simone de Beauvoir as a teacher in 1947, when she was writing *The Second Sex*. (Hulton-Deutsch Collection/Corbis)

In domestic work, with or without the aid of servants, woman makes her home her own, finds social justification, and provides herself with an occupation, an activity, that deals usefully and satisfyingly with material objects—shining stoves, fresh, clean clothes, bright copper, polished furniture—but provides no escape from immanence and little affirmation of individuality. . . . Few tasks are more like the torture of Sisyphus than housework, with its endless repetition: the clean becomes soiled, the soiled is made clean, over and over, day after day. The housewife wears herself out marking time: she makes nothing, simply perpetuates the present. She never senses conquest of a positive Good, but rather indefinite struggle against negative Evil. . . . Washing, ironing, sweeping, ferreting out rolls of lint from under wardrobes—all this halting of decay is also the denial of life; for time simultaneously creates and destroys, and only its negative aspect concerns the housekeeper. . . .

Thus woman's work within the home gives her no autonomy; it is not directly useful to society, it does not open out on the future, it produces nothing. It takes on meaning and dignity only as it is linked with existent beings who reach out beyond themselves, transcend themselves, toward society in production and action. That is, far from freeing

the matron, her occupation makes her dependent upon husband and children; she is justified through them; but in their lives she is only an inessential intermediary. . . .

The tragedy of marriage is not that it fails to assure woman the promised happiness—there is no such thing as assurance in regard to happiness—but that it mutilates her; it dooms her to repetition and routine. The first twenty years of woman's life are extraordinarily rich, as we have seen; she discovers the world and her destiny. At twenty or thereabouts mistress of a home, bound permanently to a man, a child in her arms, she stands with her life virtually finished forever. Real activities, real work, are the prerogative of her man: she has mere things to occupy her which are sometimes tiring but never fully satisfying. . . .

Marriage should be a combining of two whole, independent existences, not a retreat, an annexation, a flight, a remedy. . . . The couple should not be regarded as a unit, a closed cell; rather each individual should be integrated as such in society at large, where each (whether male or female) could flourish without aid; then attachments could be formed in pure generosity with another individual equally adapted to the group, attachments that would be founded upon the acknowledgment that both are free. This balanced couple is not a utopian fancy: such couples do exist, sometimes even within the frame of marriage, most often outside it. Some mates are united by a strong sexual love that leaves them free in their friendships and in their work; others are held together by a friendship that does not preclude sexual liberty; more rare are those who are at once lovers and friends but do not seek in each other their sole reasons for living. Many nuances are possible in the relations between a man and a woman: in comradeship, pleasure, trust, fondness, co-operation, and love, they can be for each other the most abundant source of joy, richness, and power available to human beings.

Questions for Analysis

1. Do you agree with Beauvoir's assertion that domestic work is neither creative nor fully satisfying? How is domestic work depicted in current popular culture?

2. What was Beauvoir's solution to the situation she described? Was her solution desirable? Realistic?

3. What have you learned about the history of women that supports or challenges Beauvoir's analysis? Include developments since World War II and your own reflections.

Source: The Second Sex by Simone de Beauvoir, translated by H. M. Parshley, copyright © 1952 and renewed 1980 by Alfred A. Knopf, a division of Random House, Inc. Used by permission of Alfred A. Knopf, a division of Random House, Inc.

CHAPTER 31

Revolution, Rebuilding, and New Challenges

1985 to the Present

Chapter Preview

The Collapse of Communism in Eastern Europe and the Soviet Union
How did Mikhail Gorbachev try to revitalize communism in the Soviet Union? What were the radical consequences of his policies?

Building a New Europe in the 1990s
How, in the 1990s, did the different parts of a reunifying Europe meet the challenges of postcommunist reconstruction, resurgent nationalism, and economic union?

New Challenges in the Twenty-first Century
Why did the prospect of population decline, the reality of large-scale immigration, and concern for human rights emerge as critical issues in contemporary Europe?

The West and the Islamic World
How and why did relations between the West and the Islamic world deteriorate dramatically in the early twenty-first century?

INDIVIDUALS IN SOCIETY: Tariq Ramadan

LISTENING TO THE PAST: The French Riots: Will They Change Anything?

Italians protesting government economic policies gather in front of the Roman Coliseum during a nationwide strike in October 2003.

(Philippe Desmazes/AFP/Getty Images)

In the late twentieth century, massive changes swept through eastern Europe and opened a new era in human history. In the 1980s a broad movement to transform the communist system took root in Poland, and efforts to reform and revitalize the communist system in the Soviet Union snowballed out of control. In 1989 revolutions swept away communist rule throughout the entire Soviet bloc. The cold war came to a spectacular end, West Germany absorbed East Germany, and the Soviet Union broke into fifteen independent countries. Thus after forty years of cold war division, Europe regained an underlying unity, as faith in democratic government and some kind of market economy became the common European creed. In 1991 hopes for peaceful democratic progress throughout Europe were almost universal.

The post–cold war years saw the realization of some of these hopes, but the new era brought its own problems and tragedies. The cold war division of Europe had kept a lid on ethnic conflicts and nationalism, which suddenly burst into the open and led to a disastrous civil war in the former Yugoslavia. Moreover, most western European economies were plagued by high unemployment and were struggling to adapt to the global economy. In eastern Europe, the process of re-building shattered societies was more difficult than optimists had envisioned in 1991, and in western Europe, the road toward greater unity and eastward expansion proved bumpy. Nevertheless, the will to undo the cold war division prevailed, and in 2004 eight former communist countries as well as the islands of Cyprus and Malta joined the European Union—a historic achievement.

The twenty-first century brought a growing awareness of a new set of fundamental challenges, which were related to the prospect of population decline, the reality of large-scale immigration, and the promotion of human rights. These challenges promise to preoccupy Western society for years to come.

More dramatically, the old, often contentious question of relations with the Islamic world suddenly reemerged as a critical issue after the attack on New York's World Trade Center and the Pentagon in 2001. Although the West united in a quick response against al Qaeda (al-KIGHduh) and the Taliban in Afghanistan, the subsequent war in Iraq divided western Europe and threatened the future of Western cooperation in world affairs. The war in Iraq also complicated the ongoing integration of Europe's rapidly growing Muslim population.

The Collapse of Communism in Eastern Europe and the Soviet Union

How did Mikhail Gorbachev try to revitalize communism in the Soviet Union? What were the radical consequences of his policies?

Following the 1968 invasion of Czechoslovakia (pages 793–794), the Soviet Union repeatedly demonstrated that it was determined to uphold its rule throughout eastern Europe. Periodic efforts to achieve fundamental political change were doomed to failure sooner or later—or so it seemed to most Western experts into the mid-1980s.

And then Mikhail Gorbachev burst on the scene. The new Soviet leader opened an era of reform that was as sweeping as it was unexpected. His reforms rapidly transformed Soviet culture and politics, and they drastically reduced cold war tensions. But communism, which Gorbachev wanted so desperately to revitalize in order to save it, continued to decline as a functioning system throughout the Soviet bloc. In 1989 Gorbachev's plan to reform communism snowballed out of control. A series of largely peaceful revolutions swept across eastern Europe, overturning existing communist regimes and ending the communists' monopoly of power.

The revolutions of 1989 had momentous consequences. First, the countries of eastern and western Europe were no longer separate, and a new European Union slowly emerged. Second, an anticommunist revolution swept through the Soviet Union, which broke into a large Russia and fourteen other independent states. Third, West Germany quickly absorbed its East German rival and emerged as the most influential country in Europe. Finally, the long cold war came to an abrupt end, and the United States suddenly stood as the world's only superpower.

Gorbachev's Reforms in the Soviet Union

Fundamental change in Russian history has often come in short, intensive spurts, which contrast vividly with long periods of immobility. The era of reform launched by Mikhail Gorbachev in 1985 was one such decisive transformation. Gorbachev's initiatives brought political and cultural liberalization to the Soviet Union, and they then permitted democracy and national self-determination to triumph spectacularly in the old satellite empire and eventually in the Soviet Union itself, although this was certainly not Gorbachev's original intention.

As we have seen, the Soviet Union's Communist Party elite seemed secure in the early 1980s as far as any challenge from below was concerned. The long-established system of administrative controls continued to stretch downward from the central ministries and state committees to provincial cities, and from there to factories, neighborhoods, and villages. At each level of this massive state bureaucracy, the overlapping hierarchy of the Communist Party, with its 17.5 million members, continued to manage every aspect of national life. Yet the massive state and party bureaucracy was a mixed blessing. It safeguarded the elite, but it promoted apathy in the masses. Therefore, when the ailing Brezhnev finally died in 1982, his successor Yuri Andropov (**YOOR-ee an-DROH-pawf**) (1914–1984) tried to invigorate the system. Relatively little came of these efforts, but they combined with a sharply worsening economic situation to set the stage for the emergence in 1985 of Mikhail Gorbachev (b. 1931), the most vigorous Soviet leader in a generation.

Gorbachev believed in communism, but he realized it was failing to keep up with Western capitalism and technology. This was eroding the Soviet Union's status as a superpower.

Mikhail Gorbachev

In his acceptance speech before the Supreme Soviet (the U.S.S.R.'s parliament), newly elected president Mikhail Gorbachev vowed to assume "all responsibility" for the success or failure of perestroika. Previous parliaments were no more than tools of the Communist party, but this one actively debated and even opposed some government programs. (Vlastimir Shone/Gamma Presse/EYEDEA)

CHRONOLOGY

Thus Gorbachev (and his wife, Raisa, a professor of Marxist-Leninist thought) wanted to save the Soviet system by revitalizing it with fundamental reforms. In his first year in office, Gorbachev attacked corruption and incompetence in the bureaucracy, and alcoholism and drunkenness in Soviet society. He consolidated his power and elaborated his ambitious reform program.

The first set of reform policies was designed to transform and restructure the economy, in order to provide for the real needs of the Soviet population. To accomplish this economic "restructuring," or **perestroika** (per-ih-STROY-kuh), Gorbachev and his supporters permitted an easing of government price controls on some goods, more independence for state enterprises, and the setting up of profit-seeking private cooperatives to provide personal services for consumers. While these reforms produced a few improvements, the economy stalled at an intermediate point between central planning and free-market mechanisms. By late 1988, widespread shortages threatened the entire reform program.

Gorbachev's bold and far-reaching campaign "to tell it like it is" was much more successful. Very popular in a country where censorship, dull uniformity, and outright lies had long characterized public discourse, the newfound "openness," or **glasnost** (GLAZ-nost), of the government and the media marked an astonishing break with the past. Long-banned writers sold millions of copies of their works in new editions, while denunciations of Stalin and his terror became standard fare in plays and movies. Thus initial openness in government pronouncements quickly went much further than Gorbachev intended and led to something approaching free speech and free expression, a veritable cultural revolution.

Democratization was the third element of reform. Beginning as an attack on corruption in the Communist Party, it led to the first free elections in the Soviet Union since 1917. Gorbachev and the party remained in control, but a minority of critical independents was elected in April 1989 to a revitalized Congress of People's Deputies. Millions of Soviets then watched the new congress for hours on television as Gorbachev and his ministers saw their proposals debated and even rejected. The result was a new political culture at odds with the Communist Party's monopoly of power and control.

The Soviet leader also brought "new political thinking" to the field of foreign affairs. He withdrew Soviet troops from Afghanistan and pledged to respect the political choices of the peoples of eastern Europe, repudiating the Brezhnev Doctrine. Of enormous importance, he sought to halt the arms race with the United

1985	Glasnost leads to greater freedom of speech and expression in the Soviet Union
1985–	Decline in birthrate in industrialized nations continues
1986	Single European Act lays groundwork for single currency
August 1989	Solidarity gains power in Poland
November 1989	Collapse of the Berlin Wall
November–December 1989	Velvet Revolution ends communism in Czechoslovakia
October 1990	Reunification of Germany
1990–1991	First war with Iraq
July 1991	Failed coup against Gorbachev in Russia
November–December 1991	Dissolution of the Soviet Union
1991	Maastricht treaty sets financial criteria for European monetary union
1991–2000	Resurgence of nationalism and ethnic conflict in eastern Europe
1991–2001	Civil war in Yugoslavia
1992–1997	"Shock therapy" in Russia causes decline of the economy
1993	Creation of the European Union; growth of illegal immigration in Europe
1998–	Growing support for global human rights in Europe
1999	Russian economy booms
2000	Controversy over Muslim headscarves in French schools begins
September 2001	Terrorist attack on the United States
2001	War in Afghanistan
January 2002	New euro currency goes into effect in the European Union
2003	Second war with Iraq begins
2004	Ten new states join European Union

perestroika Economic restructuring and reform implemented by Gorbachev that permitted an easing of government price controls on some goods, more independence for state enterprises, and the setting up of profit-seeking private cooperatives to provide personal services for consumers.

glasnost Openness, part of Gorbachev's campaign to tell it like it is, marked a break from the past; long-banned writers sold millions of copies of their works, and denunciations of Stalin and his terror were standard public discourse.

States and convinced President Ronald Reagan of his sincerity. In December 1987, the two leaders agreed in a Washington summit to eliminate all land-based intermediate-range missiles in Europe, setting the stage for more arms reductions. Both leaders saw the opportunity to ease the strains on their national budgets that the arms race had created.

The Revolutions of 1989

Gorbachev's reforms interacted with a resurgence of popular protest in the Soviet Union's satellite empire. Developments in Poland were the most striking and significant.

Poland had been an unruly satellite from the beginning. Stalin said that introducing communism to Poland was like putting a saddle on a cow. As a result of widespread riots in 1956, Polish Communists dropped their efforts to impose Soviet-style collectivization on the peasants and to break the Roman Catholic Church. Yet they were determined to plan the economy, with poor results. Even the booming 1960s saw little economic improvement.

In 1970 Poland's working class rose again in angry protest. A new Communist leader came to power, and he wagered that massive inflows of Western capital and technology, especially from rich and now-friendly West Germany (see pages 801–802), could produce a Polish "economic miracle." Instead, bureaucratic incompetence and the first oil shock in 1973 put the economy into a nosedive. Then the real Polish miracle occurred: Cardinal Karol Wojtyla (KAH-rol voy-TIL-ah), archbishop of Cracow, was elected pope in 1978. The following year, now as Pope John Paul II, he returned from Rome and electrified the Polish nation with talk of the "inalienable rights of man." The economic crisis became a moral and spiritual crisis as well.

In August 1980, the sixteen thousand workers at the gigantic Lenin Shipyards in Gdansk (gdahynsk) (formerly known as Danzig) laid down their tools and occupied the plant. As other workers joined "in solidarity," the strikers advanced revolutionary demands, including the right to form free trade unions, freedom of speech, release of political prisoners, and economic reforms.

Led by Lenin Shipyards electrician Lech Walesa (leck wah-LENS-ah) (b. 1943), the workers proceeded to organize their free and democratic trade union. They called it **Solidarity.** Joined by intellectuals and supported by the Catholic Church, Solidarity became the union of a nation. By March 1981, it had 9.5 million union members. Yet as the economic situation worsened and some members of Solidarity became more radical, the Polish Communist leadership shrewdly denounced Solidarity for promoting economic collapse and provoking the Soviet Union. In December 1981, Communist leader General Wojciech Jaruzelski (VOI-chekh yah-roo-ZEL-skee) suddenly struck, proclaiming martial law, arresting Solidarity's leaders, and "saving" the nation.

Although it was driven underground, Solidarity maintained its organization and continued to voice the aspirations of the Polish masses after 1981. Part of the reason for the union's survival was the government's unwillingness (and probably its inability) to impose full-scale terror. Moreover, millions of Poles decided to continue acting as if they were free, even though they were not. Cultural and intellectual life remained extremely vigorous as the faltering Polish economy continued to deteriorate. Thus popular support for outlawed Solidarity remained strong under martial law in the 1980s, preparing the way for the union's political rebirth during the Gorbachev era at the end of the decade.

Solidarity Led by Lech Walesa, this group of workers in Poland organized their free and democratic trade union and quickly became the union of a nation with a full-time staff of 40,000 and 9.5 million union members by March 1981.

Lech Walesa and Solidarity
An inspiration for fellow workers at the Lenin Shipyards in the dramatic and successful strike against the Communist bosses in August 1980, Walesa played a key role in Solidarity before and after it was outlawed. Speaking here to old comrades at the Lenin Shipyards after Solidarity was again legalized in 1988, Walesa personified an enduring opposition to Communist rule in eastern Europe. (G. Merrillon/Gamma Presse/EYEDEA)

In early 1989, on the brink of economic collapse and political stalemate, Poland became the first eastern European country to experience revolution. Solidarity skillfully pressured Poland's frustrated Communist leaders into legalizing Solidarity and declaring that a large minority of representatives to the Polish parliament would be chosen by free elections in June 1989. Still guaranteed a parliamentary majority and expecting to win many of the contested seats, the Communists believed that the status quo could be maintained.

Instead the Communists were roundly defeated. Solidarity mobilized the country and won most of the contested seats in an overwhelming victory. Moreover, many angry voters crossed off the names of unopposed party candidates, so that the Communist Party failed to win the majority its leaders had anticipated. Solidarity members jubilantly entered the Polish parliament, and a dangerous stalemate quickly developed. But Solidarity's gifted leader Lech Walesa adroitly obtained a majority as two minor procommunist parties that had been part of the coalition government after World War II now joined forces with Walesa. In August 1989, the editor of Solidarity's weekly newspaper was sworn in as Poland's new noncommunist leader.

In its first year and a half, the new Solidarity government eliminated the hated secret police, the Communist ministers in the government, and finally Jaruzelski himself, but it did so step by step in order to avoid confrontation with the army or the Soviet Union. However, in economic affairs, the Solidarity-led government was radical from the beginning. It applied **shock therapy** designed to make a clean

shock therapy The Solidarity-led government's radical take on economic affairs that were designed to make a clean break with state planning and move to market mechanisms and private property.

break with state planning and move quickly to market mechanisms and private property. Thus the Solidarity government abolished controls on many prices on January 1, 1990, and reformed the monetary system with a "big bang."

Hungary followed Poland. Hungary's Communist Party boss, János Kádár (KAH-dahr), had permitted liberalization of the rigid planned economy after the 1956 uprising in exchange for political obedience and continued Communist control. In May 1988, in an effort to retain power by granting modest political concessions, the party replaced Kádár with a reform communist. But opposition groups rejected piecemeal progress, and in the summer of 1989 the Hungarian Communist Party agreed to hold free elections in early 1990. Welcoming Western investment and moving rapidly toward multiparty democracy, Hungary's Communists now enjoyed considerable popular support, and they believed, quite mistakenly it turned out, that they could defeat the opposition in the upcoming elections. In an effort to strengthen their support at home and also put pressure on East Germany's hard-line Communist regime, the Hungarians opened their border to East Germans and tore down the barbed-wire "iron curtain" with Austria. Thus tens of thousands of dissatisfied East German "vacationers" began pouring into Hungary, crossed into Austria as refugees, and continued on to immediate resettlement in thriving West Germany.

The flight of East Germans led to the rapid growth of a homegrown protest movement in East Germany. Intellectuals, environmentalists, and Protestant ministers took the lead, organizing huge candlelight demonstrations and arguing that a democratic but still socialist East Germany was both possible and desirable. These "stayers" failed to convince the "leavers," however, who continued to flee the country en masse. In a desperate attempt to stabilize the situation, the East German government opened the Berlin Wall in November 1989, and people danced for joy atop that grim symbol of the prison state. East Germany's aging Communist leaders were swept aside, and a reform government took power and scheduled free elections. In March 1990, the East German **Alliance for Germany**, which was closely tied to Kohl's West German Christian Democrats, won almost 50 percent of the votes in an East German parliamentary election. The Alliance for Germany quickly negotiated an economic union on favorable terms with Chancellor Kohl.

Finally, in the summer of 1990, the crucial international aspect of German unification was successfully resolved. In a historic agreement signed by Gorbachev and Kohl in July 1990, Germany solemnly affirmed its peaceful intentions and pledged never to develop nuclear, biological, or chemical weapons. In October 1990, East Germany merged into West Germany, forming henceforth a single nation under the West German laws and constitution.

In Czechoslovakia, communism died in December 1989 in only ten days. This so-called **Velvet Revolution** grew out of popular demonstrations led by students, intellectuals, and a dissident playwright turned moral revolutionary named Václav Havel (VAH-slav HAH-vel). The protesters practically took control of the streets and forced the Communists into a power-sharing arrangement, which quickly resulted in the resignation of the Communist government. As 1989 ended, the Czechoslovakian assembly elected Havel president.

Only in Romania was revolution violent and bloody. There, ironfisted Communist dictator Nicolae Ceauşescu (chow-CHES-ku) (1918–1989) had long combined Stalinist brutality with stubborn independence from Moscow. Faced with mass protests in December, Ceauşescu, alone among eastern European bosses, ordered his ruthless security forces to slaughter thousands, thereby sparking a classic armed uprising. After Ceauşescu's forces were defeated, the tyrant and his wife

Alliance for Germany A political party that was set up in East Germany, calling for the unification of East and West Germany, which they felt would lead to an economic bonanza in East Germany. In March 1990 they won almost 50 percent of the votes in the East German parliamentary election, thereby beating out the Socialist party.

Velvet Revolution The moment when communism died in 1989 with an ousting of Communist bosses in only ten days; it grew out of popular demonstrations led by students, intellectuals, and a dissident playwright.

The Fall of the Berlin Wall
The sudden opening of the Berlin Wall in November 1989 dramatized the spectacular collapse of communism throughout eastern Europe. Built by the Soviet leader Nikita Khrushchev in 1961, the hated barrier had stopped the flow of refugees from East Germany to West Germany. (Patrick Piel/Gamma Presse/EYEDEA)

were captured and executed by a military court. A coalition government emerged from the fighting, although the legacy of Ceaușescu's oppression left a very troubled country.

The breakdown of barriers between western and eastern Europe, with the peaceful reunification of Germany as a key element, led to agreements liquidating the cold war. In November 1990, delegates from twenty-two European countries joined those from the United States and the Soviet Union in Paris and agreed to a scaling down of all their armed forces. The delegates also solemnly affirmed that all existing borders in Europe—from unified Germany to the newly independent Baltic republics—were legal and valid. The **Paris Accord** was for all practical purposes a general peace treaty, bringing an end to World War II and the cold war.

In the months that followed, the United States and the Soviet Union agreed to scrap a significant portion of their nuclear weapons. In September 1991, the leaders of both countries canceled the around-the-clock alert status for bombers outfitted with atomic bombs. For the first time in four decades, Soviet and American nuclear weapons were no longer standing ready to destroy capitalism, communism, and life itself.

Paris Accord A general peace treaty that brought an end to World War II and the cold war that followed; it called for a scaling down of all armed forces and the acceptance of all existing borders as legal and valid.

The Disintegration of the Soviet Union

As 1990 began, revolutionary changes had triumphed in all but two eastern European states—tiny Albania and the vast Soviet Union. The great question now became whether reform communism would give way to a popular anticommunist revolution.

The elections of February 1990 provided the first indication that reform communism would not survive. As in the eastern European satellites, democrats and anticommunists won clear majorities in the leading cities of the Russian Federation. Moreover, in Lithuania the people elected an uncompromising nationalist as president, and the newly chosen parliament declared Lithuania an independent state. Gorbachev responded by placing an economic embargo on Lithuania, but he refused to use the army to crush the separatist government. The result was a tense political stalemate, which undermined popular support for Gorbachev. Separating himself further from Communist hard-liners, Gorbachev asked Soviet citizens to ratify a new constitution, which formally abolished the Communist Party's monopoly of political power and expanded the Power of the Congress of People's Deputies. Retaining his post as party secretary, Gorbachev convinced a majority of deputies to elect him president of the Soviet Union.

Gorbachev's eroding power and his unwillingness to risk a universal suffrage election for the presidency strengthened his great rival, Boris Yeltsin (1931–2007). A radical reform communist who had been purged by party conservatives in 1987, Yeltsin embraced the democratic movement, and in May 1990 he was elected leader of the Russian Federation's parliament. He boldly announced that Russia would put its interests first and declare its independence from the Soviet Union. Gorbachev tried to save the Soviet Union with a new treaty that would link the member republics in a looser, freely accepted confederation, but six of the fifteen Soviet republics rejected Gorbachev's pleas.

Opposed by democrats and nationalists, Gorbachev was also challenged again by the Communist old guard. A gang of hard-liners kidnapped a vacationing Gorbachev and his family in the Caucasus and tried to seize the Soviet government in August 1991. But the attempted coup collapsed in the face of massive popular resistance, which rallied around Yeltsin. As the world watched spellbound on television, Yeltsin defiantly denounced the hard-liners from atop a stalled tank in central Moscow and declared the "rebirth of Russia." The army supported Yeltsin, and Gorbachev returned to power as head of the Soviet Union.

The leaders of the coup wanted to preserve Communist power, state ownership, and the multinational Soviet Union, but they succeeded only in destroying all three. An anticommunist revolution swept the Russian Federation as Yeltsin and his supporters outlawed the Communist Party and confiscated its property. Locked in a personal and political duel with Gorbachev, Yeltsin and his democratic allies declared Russia independent and withdrew from the Soviet Union. All the other Soviet republics also left. The Soviet Union—and Gorbachev's job—ceased to exist on December 25, 1991 (see Map 31.1). The independent republics of the old Soviet Union then established a loose confederation, the Commonwealth of Independent States, which played only a minor role in the 1990s.

The Gulf War of 1991

As the Soviet Union collapsed, losing both the will and the means to intervene in global conflicts, the United States emerged rather suddenly as the world's only surviving superpower. In 1991 the United States used its military superiority to chal-

MAP 31.1   Russia and the Successor States

After the attempt in August 1991 to depose Gorbachev failed, an anticommunist revolution swept the Soviet Union. Led by Russia and Boris Yeltsin, the republics that formed the Soviet Union declared their sovereignty and independence. Eleven of the fifteen republics then formed a loose confederation called the Commonwealth of Independent States, but the integrated economy of the Soviet Union dissolved into separate national economies, each with its own goals and policies.

lenge Iraq's August 1990 invasion and annexation of its oil-rich southern neighbor, Kuwait.

Reacting vigorously to free Kuwait, the United States mobilized the U.N. Security Council, which in August 1990 imposed a strict naval blockade on Iraq. Receiving the support of some Arab states, as well as of Great Britain and France, the United States also landed 500,000 American soldiers in Saudi Arabia near the border of Kuwait. When the defiant Iraqi leader Saddam Hussein (sah-DAHM who-SANE) (1937–2006) refused to withdraw from Kuwait, the Security Council authorized the U.S.-led military coalition to attack Iraq. The American army and air force then smashed Iraqi forces in a lightning-quick desert campaign, although the United States stopped short of toppling Saddam because it feared a sudden disintegration of Iraq.

The defeat of Iraqi armies in the Gulf War demonstrated the awesome power of the U.S. military, rebuilt and revitalized by the spending and patriotism of the 1980s. Little wonder that in the flush of yet another victory, the first President Bush spoke of a **"new world order,"** an order that would apparently feature the

"new world order" President George H. W. Bush's vision after the U.S. defeat of Iraqi armies in the Gulf War that would feature the United States and a cooperative United Nations working together to impose peace and stability throughout the world.

- Gorbachev attempted to save communism through perestroika (restructuring), easing government control of economic markets; glasnost (openness), easing censorship of the media; democratization, allowing free elections; and by easing foreign policy and the arms race with the United States.

- Poland experienced a revolution led by the Solidarity movement that won free elections and control of the government, defeating the communists, eliminating the secret police, and abolishing state controls.

- Hungary followed Poland in its bid for free elections, ousting the communists and opening the border for East Germans to leave, which promoted protests, the fall of the Berlin Wall, and the rejoining of East and West Germany.

- Czechoslovakia's Velvet Revolution ended communism there; only in Romania was revolution accompanied by fighting, as Eastern European countries joined the West at the Paris Accord, ending the cold war.

- Political unrest plagued the Soviet Union, with Gorbachev trying to save reformed communism while Yeltsin declared independence for the Russian Federation along with the other Soviet republics, forming a loose confederation, the Commonwealth of Independent States.

- The United States challenged Iraq's invasion of Kuwait in 1991 and then, authorized by the United Nations' Security Council, attacked and defeated Iraqi forces in a quick desert campaign.

United States and a cooperative United Nations working together to impose stability throughout the world.

Building a New Europe in the 1990s

How, in the 1990s, did the different parts of a reunifying Europe meet the challenges of postcommunist reconstruction, resurgent nationalism, and economic union?

The fall of communism, the end of the cold war, and the collapse of the Soviet Union opened a new era in European and world history. The dimensions and significance of this new era, opening suddenly and unexpectedly, are subject to debate. We are so close to what is going on that we lack vital perspective. Yet the historian must take a stand.

First, we shall focus on three of the most important trends: the pressure on national economies increasingly caught up in global capitalism; the defense of social achievements under attack; and a resurgence of nationalism and ethnic conflict. Second, with these common themes providing an organizational framework, we shall examine the course of development in the three overlapping but still distinct regions of contemporary Europe. These are Russia and the western states of the old Soviet Union, previously communist eastern Europe, and western Europe.

Common Patterns and Problems

The end of the cold war and the disintegration of the Soviet Union ended the division of Europe into two opposing camps with two different political and economic systems. Thus, although Europe in the 1990s was a collage of diverse peoples, the entire continent shared an underlying network of common developments and challenges (see Map 31.2).

Of critical importance, in economic affairs European leaders embraced, or at least accepted, a large part of the neoliberal, free-market vision of capitalist development. Postcommunist governments in eastern Europe freed prices, turned state enterprises over to private owners, and sought to move toward strong currencies and balanced budgets. In western Europe, new free-market initiatives produced changes in western Europe's still-dominant welfare capitalism, which featured government intervention, high taxes, and high levels of social benefits.

Two factors were particularly important in accounting for this ongoing shift from welfare state activism to tough-minded capitalism. First, western Europeans

MAPPING THE PAST

MAP 31.2   Contemporary Europe

No longer divided by ideological competition and the cold war, today's Europe features a large number of independent states. Several of these states were previously part of the Soviet Union and Yugoslavia, both of which broke into many different countries. Czechoslovakia also divided on ethnic lines, while a reunited Germany emerged, once again, as the dominant nation in central Europe. **[1]** Which countries shown here were previously part of the Soviet Union? **[2]** Which countries were part of Yugoslavia? **[3]** Where did the old "iron curtain" run? (See Map 30.1, page 786, if necessary.)

looked to the stronger U.S. economy and borrowed the practices and ideologies instituted there and in Great Britain in the 1980s (see page 804). Second, eastern Europeans wanting to compete in the global economy were compelled to follow the rules of Western governments, multinational corporations, and international financial organizations such as the International Monetary Fund (IMF). These rules called for the free movement of capital and goods and services, as well as low inflation and limited government deficits.

The ongoing computer and electronics revolution strengthened the move toward a global economy. The computer revolution reduced the costs of distance, speeding up communications and helping businesses tap cheaper labor overseas. Reducing the friction of distance made threats of moving factories abroad ring true and helped hold down wages at home.

globalization The emergence of a freer global economy; it also refers to the exchange of cultural, political, and religious ideas throughout the world.

Globalization, the emergence of a freer global economy, probably did speed up world economic growth as enthusiasts invariably claimed, but it also had powerful and quite negative social consequences. Millions of ordinary citizens in western Europe believed that global capitalism and freer markets were undermining hard-won social achievements. As in the United States and Great Britain in the 1980s, the public in other countries generally associated globalization with the increased unemployment that accompanied corporate downsizing, the efforts to reduce the power of labor unions, and, above all, government plans to reduce social benefits. The reaction was particularly intense in France and Germany, where unions remained strong and socialists championed a minimum of change in social policies.

Indeed, the broad movement toward neoliberal global development sparked a powerful counterattack as the 1990s ended. Critics insisted that globalization hurt the world's poor, because multinational corporations destroyed local industries and paid pitiful wages, and because international financial organizations demanded harsh balanced budgets and deep cuts in government social programs. These attacks shook global neoliberalism, but it remained dominant.

In politics, European countries embraced genuine electoral competition, with elected presidents and legislatures and the outward manifestations of representative liberal governments. With some notable exceptions, such as discrimination against Roma (Gypsies), countries also guaranteed basic civil liberties. Thus, for the first time since before the French Revolution, almost all of Europe followed the same general political model of liberal democracy, although with variations.

Recasting Russia

Politics and economics were closely intertwined in Russia after the attempted Communist coup in 1991 and the dissolution of the Soviet Union. President Boris Yeltsin and his economic ministers listened to those Western advisers who argued that private economies were always best and opted in January 1992 for breakneck liberalization. Their "shock therapy" freed prices on 90 percent of all Russian goods, with the exception of bread, vodka, oil, and public transportation. The government also launched a rapid privatization of industry and turned thousands of factories and mines over to new private companies. Each citizen received a voucher worth 10,000 rubles (about $22) to buy stock in private companies, but control of the privatized companies usually remained in the hands of the old bosses—the managers and government officials from the communist era.

President Yeltsin and his economic reformers believed that shock therapy would revive production and bring prosperity after a brief period of hardship. The results of the reforms were in fact quite different. Prices increased 250 percent on the very first day, and they kept on soaring, increasing twenty-six times in the course of 1992. At the same time, Russian production fell a staggering 20 percent. Nor did the situation stabilize quickly. Throughout 1995 rapid but gradually slowing inflation raged, and output continued to fall. Only in 1997 did the economy stop declining, before crashing yet again in 1998 in the wake of Asia's financial crisis.

Runaway inflation and poorly executed privatization brought a profound social revolution to Russia. A new capitalist elite acquired great wealth and power, while large numbers of people fell into abject poverty, and the majority struggled in the midst of decline to make ends meet.

Rapid economic decline in 1992 and 1993 and rising popular dissatisfaction encouraged a majority of communists, nationalists, and populists in the Russian parliament to oppose Yeltsin and his coalition of democratic reformers and big-business interests. The erratic, increasingly hard-drinking Yeltsin would accept no compromise and insisted on a strong presidential system. Winning in April 1993 the support of 58 percent of the population in a referendum on his proposed constitution, Yeltsin then brought in tanks to crush a parliamentary mutiny in October 1993 and literally blew away the opposition. Subsequently, Yeltsin consolidated his power, and in 1996 he used his big-business cronies in the media to win an impressive come-from-behind victory. But effective representative government failed to develop, and many Russians came to equate "democracy" with the corruption, poverty, and national decline they experienced throughout the 1990s.

This widespread disillusionment set the stage for the "managed democracy" of Vladimir Putin (VLAD-ih-mir POO-tin), first elected president as Yeltsin's chosen successor in 2000 and re-elected in a landslide in March 2004. An officer in the secret police in the communist era, Putin maintained relatively free markets in the economic sphere but gradually re-established semi-authoritarian political rule. Aided greatly by high prices for oil, Russia's most important export, this combination worked well and seemed to suit most Russians. In 2007, the Russian economy had been growing rapidly for eight years, the Russian middle class was expanding, and the elected parliament supported Putin overwhelmingly. Proponents of liberal democracy were in retreat, while conservative Russian intellectuals were on the offensive, arguing that free markets and capitalism required strong political rule to control corruption and prevent chaos. Historians saw a reassertion of Russia's long authoritarian tradition. In March 2008 Putin's ally and hand-picked successor, Dmitry Medvedev, was elected president in a landslide.

Putin's forceful, competent image in world affairs also soothed the country's injured pride and symbolized its national resurgence. Nor did the government permit any negative television reports on the civil war in Chechnya (CHECH-nee-ah), the tiny republic of one million Muslims on Russia's southern border, which in 1991 had declared its independence from the Russian Federation (see Map 31.1). The savage conflict in Chechnya continued, largely unreported, with numerous atrocities on both sides.

Progress in Eastern Europe

Developments in eastern Europe shared important similarities with those in Russia, as many of the problems were the same. Thus the postcommunist states of the former satellite empire worked to replace state planning and socialism with market mechanisms and private property. Western-style electoral politics also took hold, and as in Russia, these politics were marked by intense battles between presidents and parliaments and by weak political parties. The social consequences of these revolutionary changes were similar to those in Russia. Ordinary citizens and the elderly were once again the big losers, while the young and the ex-Communists were the big winners. Inequalities between richer and poorer regions also increased. Capital cities such as Warsaw, Prague, and Budapest concentrated wealth, power, and opportunity as never before, while provincial centers stagnated and old industrial areas declined. Crime and gangsterism increased in the streets and in the executive suites.

Yet the 1990s saw more than a difficult transition, with high social costs, to market economies and freely elected governments in eastern Europe. Many citizens had never fully accepted communism, which they equated with Russian imperialism and the loss of national independence. The joyous crowds that toppled communist regimes in 1989 believed that they were liberating the nation as well as the individual. Thus communism died and nationalism was reborn.

The surge of nationalism in eastern Europe recalled a similar surge of state creation after World War I. Then, too, authoritarian multinational empires had come crashing down in defeat and revolution. Then, too, nationalities with long histories and rich cultures had drawn upon ideologies of popular sovereignty and national self-determination to throw off foreign rule and found new democratic states.

The response to this opportunity in the former communist countries was quite varied in the 1990s, but most observers agreed that Poland, the Czech Republic, and Hungary were the most successful (see Map 31.2, page 821). Each of these three countries met the critical challenge of economic reconstruction more successfully than Russia, and each could claim to be the economic leader in eastern Europe, depending on the criteria selected. The reasons for these successes included considerable experience with limited market reforms before 1989, flexibility and lack of dogmatism in government policy, and an enthusiastic embrace of capitalism by a new entrepreneurial class. In the first five years of reform, Poland created twice as many new businesses as Russia, with a total population only one-fourth as large.

The three northern countries in the former Soviet bloc also did far better than Russia in creating new civic institutions, legal systems, and independent broadcasting networks that reinforced political freedom and national revival. Lech Walesa in Poland and Václav Havel in Czechoslovakia were elected presidents of their countries and proved as remarkable in power as in opposition. After Czechoslovakia's "Velvet Revolution" in 1989, Havel and the Czech parliament accepted a "velvet divorce" in 1993 when Slovakian nationalists wanted to break off and form their own state. All three northern countries managed to control national and ethnic tensions that might have destroyed their postcommunist reconstruction.

Above all, and in sharp contrast to Russia, the popular goal of "rejoining the West" reinforced political moderation and compromise. Seeing themselves as heirs to medieval Christendom and liberal democratic values of the 1920s, Poles, Hungarians, and Czechs hoped to find security in NATO membership and economic prosperity in western Europe's ever-tighter **European Union** (the former Common Market or EEC, see page 787). Membership required many proofs of character and stability, however. Providing these proofs and endorsed by the Clinton administration, Poland, Hungary, and the Czech Republic were accepted into the NATO alliance in 1997. Gaining admission to the European Union (EU) proved more difficult, because candidates also had to accept and be ready to apply all the rules and regulations that the EU had developed since 1956—an awesome task.

Romania and Bulgaria were the eastern European laggards in the postcommunist transition. Western traditions were much weaker there, and both countries were much poorer than neighbors to the north. In 1993 Bulgaria and Romania had per capita national incomes of $1,140, in contrast to Hungary ($3,830) and

European Union The new name as of 1993 for the European Community.

the Czech Republic ($2,710). Although Romania and Bulgaria eventually made progress in the late 1990s, full membership for both countries in either NATO or the EU still lay far in the future.

Tragedy in Yugoslavia

The great postcommunist tragedy was Yugoslavia, which under Josip Tito had been a federation of republics and regions under strict communist rule. Yugoslavia had the most ethnically diverse population of Europe (see Map 31.3), and the different ethnic groups held historic grievances against one another. After Tito's death in 1980, power passed increasingly to the sister republics. Tensions among the republics mounted throughout the decade as they desired greater autonomy.

The revolutions of 1989 accelerated the breakup of Yugoslavia. Serbian president Slobodan Milosevic (SLOH-buh-dain muh-LOH-suh-vich) (1941–2006) pushed to unite all Serbs, including those living outside the existing borders of Serbia, into a "greater Serbia." The republics of Slovenia, Croatia, Bosnia-Herzegovina, and Macedonia rejected this idea while advocating for separation. In June 1991 Slovenia and Croatia declared their independence from Yugoslavia.

MAP 31.3   The Ethnic Composition of Yugoslavia, 1991
Yugoslavia had the most ethnically diverse population in eastern Europe. The Republic of Croatia had substantial Serbian and Muslim minorities. Bosnia-Herzegovina had large Muslim, Serbian, and Croatian populations, none of which had a majority. In June 1991, Serbia's brutal effort to seize territory and unite all Serbs in a single state brought a tragic civil war.

Milosevic, who controlled the Yugoslavian army and intended to maintain a united Yugoslavia under Serbian domination, sent forces to the break-off republics. Slovenia repulsed this attack, but Milosevic's armies managed to take about 30 percent of Croatia.

In 1992 the conflict spread to Bosnia-Herzegovina, which was home to Catholic Croats, Orthodox Serbs, and Muslim Slavs. When the republic voted for independence, the Serbian minority rebelled. They shared the goal of their military ally Milosevic—a "greater Serbia" composed of all Serbian-held lands. The resulting civil war between the three ethnic groups unleashed ruthless brutality, with murder, rape, destruction, and the herding of refugees into concentration camps. In 1994, the Muslims and Croats called a truce and formed an alliance. The turning point came in July 1995, when Bosnian Serbs overran Srebrenica—a Muslim city previously declared a United Nations "safe area"—and killed several thousand civilians. World outrage prompted NATO to bomb Bosnian Serb military targets intensively, and the Croatian army drove all the Serbs from Croatia. In November 1995, President Bill Clinton helped the warring sides agree to a complicated accord dividing the country between the Serbs and Muslim-Croats. Troops from NATO countries patrolled Bosnia to try to keep the peace.

Violence then flared in Kosovo, a province within Serbia that was stripped of self-rule by Milosevic in 1989. Most Kosovars were Muslim ethnic Albanians. In early 1998, frustrated Kosovar militants formed the **Kosovo Liberation Army (KLA)** to fight for independence. Serbian repression of the Kosovars increased, and in 1998 Serbian forces attacked both KLA guerrillas and unarmed villagers, displacing 250,000 people within Kosovo. By January 1999, the Western powers, led by the United States, were threatening Milosevic with heavy air raids if he did not withdraw Serbian armies from Kosovo and accept self-government (but not independence) for Kosovo. Milosevic refused, and in March 1999 NATO began bombing Yugoslavia (now reduced to Serbia and Montenegro). Serbian paramilitary forces responded by driving about 780,000 Kosovars into exile. NATO redoubled its highly destructive bombing campaign, which eventually forced Milosevic to withdraw and allowed the joyous Kosovars to regain their homeland. The impoverished Serbs eventually voted the still-defiant Milosevic out of office, and in July 2001 a new pro-Western Serbian government turned him over to the war crimes tribunal in the Netherlands. Milosevic died while standing trial for crimes against humanity.

Kosovo Liberation Army (KLA)
Formed in 1998 by frustrated Kosovar militants who sought to fight for their independence.

Unity and Identity in Western Europe

The movement toward a European identity that transcended destructive national rivalries was revitalized in the 1980s and 1990s as European leaders put forth new proposals for economic and political unity. Implementing a 1986 agreement, the European Union went to a single market in 1993 through which labor, capital, services, and goods could travel freely. The next step, a monetary union and single currency, the euro, went into effect on January 1, 2002, after more than a decade of planning and debate. Then on May 1, 2004, the European Union added 70 million people and expanded to include 455 million citizens in twenty-five different countries. The largest newcomer by far was Poland, followed in descending size by the Czech Republic, Hungary, Slovenia, Slovakia, Estonia, Lithuania, Latvia, Malta, and Cyprus.

In June 2004, more than two years after charging a special commission to write "a new constitution for European citizens," the leaders of the European Union reached agreement on the final document. Above all, the new constitution, with

Turkey's Struggle for EU Membership
Turkish elites and the general population want to "join Europe," but the road to EU membership is proving long and difficult. The EU has required Turkey to make many constitutional reforms and give greater autonomy to Turkish Kurds. Yet the Turks face ever more demands, and many now believe that the real roadblock is Europe's anti-Muslim feeling. (CartoonStock Limited)

almost 350 articles, established a single rulebook to replace the complex network of treaties concluded by the member states since the 1957 creation of the European Economic Community. The EU constitution created a president, a foreign minister, and a voting system weighted to reflect the number of people in the different states. The result of intense debate and many compromises, the constitution moved toward a more centralized federal system in several fields, but each state retained veto power in the most sensitive areas, such as taxation, social policy, and foreign affairs. In order for the constitution to take effect, each and every EU country needed to ratify it.

Nine countries, led by Germany, Italy, and seven east European members, soon ratified the constitution by parliamentary action, while seven states planned to go beyond the political elites and let the voters decide. The referendum campaigns were noisy and contentious, as generally well-informed citizens debated whether the new constitution surrendered too much national sovereignty to an emerging central European government in Brussels. British voters were considered most likely to vote no, but both the French and the Dutch beat them to it, rejecting the new constitution by clear majorities. Nationalist fears about losing sovereignty were matched by fears that an unwieldy European Union would grow to include Ukraine, Georgia, and Muslim Turkey—countries with cultures and histories that were very different from those in western Europe. Thus the long postwar march toward ever-greater European unity stopped,

Section Review

- Most European countries adopted free-market capitalism but as neoliberal global development emerged, critics argued that it hurt the poor and undermined social welfare programs.

- Yeltsin's rapid privatization of industry was successful only for the new elite, while the masses struggled; Putin re-established semi-authoritarian rule while maintaining free markets and managed some economic recovery and a resurgence of nationalism.

- Poland, Hungary, and the Czech Republic were able to make the transition from communism to capitalism and regain prosperity far better than Russia, Romania, or Bulgaria due to their leadership, flexibility, and ability to control ethnic and national tensions.

- Ethnic tensions within Yugoslavia led to civil war, with the Serbian president Milosevic pushing for a "greater Serbia" and other republics wanting independence, before NATO intervened and replaced Milosevic with a pro-Western Serbian government.

- The European Union reworked itself and expanded to include more countries, redrafting its constitution, although not all countries ratified it because they feared losing their national sovereignty.

or at least stalled, and the European Union concentrated on fully integrating the new eastern European members and redrafting the constitution.

New Challenges in the Twenty-first Century

Why did the prospect of population decline, the reality of large-scale immigration, and concern for human rights emerge as critical issues in contemporary Europe?

baby bust Falling European birthrates at the opening to the twenty-first century, that seemed to promise a shrinking and aging population in the future.

As the twenty-first century opened, European society faced new uncertainties. Of great significance, Europe continued to experience a remarkable **baby bust,** as birthrates fell to levels that seemed to promise a shrinking and aging population in the future. At the same time, the peaceful, wealthy European Union attracted rapidly growing numbers of refugees and illegal immigrants from the former Soviet Union, the Middle East, Africa, and Asia. The unexpected arrival of so many newcomers raised many perplexing questions and prompted serious thinking about European identity, Europe's humanitarian mission, and its place in the world.

The Prospect of Population Decline

Population is still growing rapidly in many poor countries, but this is not the case in the world's industrialized nations. In 2000 women in developed countries had only 1.6 children on average; only in the United States did women have, almost exactly, the 2.1 children necessary to maintain a stable population. In European countries, where women had been steadily having fewer babies since the 1950s, national fertility rates ranged from 1.2 to 1.8 children per woman.

If the current baby bust continues, the long-term consequences could be dramatic, though hardly predictable. At the least, Europe's population would decline and age. Projections for Germany are illustrative. Total German population, barring much greater immigration, would gradually decline from 82 million in 2001 to only 62 million around 2050. The number of people of working age would drop by a third, and almost half of the population would be over sixty. Social security taxes paid by the shrinking labor force would need to soar for the skyrocketing costs of pensions and health care for seniors to be met—a recipe for generational tension and conflict.

Why, in time of peace, were birthrates falling? Certainly the uneven, uninspiring European economic conditions of the 1980s and much of the 1990s played some role. But in our view, the ongoing impact of careers for married women and the related drive for gender equality remained the decisive factors in the long-term decline of postwar birthrates. Research showed that European women (and men) in their twenties, thirties, and early forties still wanted to have two or even three children—about the same number as their parents had wanted. But unlike their parents, young couples did not realize their ideal family size. Many women postponed the birth of their first child into their thirties in order to finish their education and establish themselves in their careers. Then, finding that raising even one child was more difficult and time-consuming than anticipated, new mothers tended to postpone and eventually forgo a second child. This was especially true of professional women.

By 2005 some population experts believed that European women were no longer postponing having children. At the least, birthrates appeared to have stabilized. Moreover, the frightening implications of dramatic population decline had emerged as a major public issue. Opinion leaders, politicians, and the media started to press the case for more support for families with children.

The Growth of Immigration

While the European birthrates declined in the 1990s, population numbers got a push from the surge in immigration. The collapse of communism in the East and savage civil wars in Yugoslavia sent hundreds of thousands of refugees fleeing westward. Equally brutal conflicts in Afghanistan, Iraq, Somalia, and Rwanda—to name only four countries—brought thousands more from Asia and Africa. Illegal immigration into the European Union also exploded, rising from an estimated 50,000 people in 1993 to perhaps 500,000 a decade later. This movement exceeded the estimated 300,000 unauthorized foreigners entering the United States each year.

In the early twenty-first century, many migrants still applied for political asylum and refugee status, but most were eventually rejected and classified as illegal job-seekers. Certainly, greater economic opportunities exerted a powerful pull. Germans earned on average five times more than neighboring Poles, who in turn earned much more than people farther east and in North Africa.

Illegal immigration also soared because powerful criminal gangs turned to "people smuggling" for big, low-risk profits. A large portion of the illegal immigrants were young women from eastern Europe, especially Russia and Ukraine. Often lured by criminals promising jobs as maids or waitresses and sometimes simply kidnapped and sold like slaves from hand to hand for a few thousand

Illegal Immigrants from Eritrea

Italian police have just rescued these young immigrants from an overloaded boat off the coast of Italy. Fleeing civil war and desperate for work, the immigrants are weary because of the long and dangerous voyage from Libya. Every year thousands of illegal immigrants try to reach Italy and Spain from North Africa. Many are found dead on the shoreline. (Mimi Mollica/Corbis) dollars, these women were smuggled into the most prosperous parts of central Europe and into the European Union and forced into prostitution or slavery.

Illegal immigration generated intense discussion and controversy in western Europe. A majority opposed the newcomers, who were accused of taking jobs from the unemployed and somehow undermining national unity. The idea that cultural and ethnic diversity could be a force for vitality and creativity ran counter to deep-seated beliefs. Concern about illegal migration in general often fused with fears of Muslim immigrants and Muslim residents who had grown up in Europe. As busy mosques came to outnumber dying churches in parts of some European cities, rightist politicians especially tried to exploit widespread doubts that immigrant populations from Muslim countries would ever assimilate to the different national cultures. These doubts increased after the attack on New York's World Trade Center, as we shall see later in the chapter.

An articulate minority challenged the anti-immigrant campaign and its racist overtones. They argued that Europe badly needed newcomers—preferably talented newcomers—to limit the impending population decline and provide valuable technical skills. European leaders also focused on improved policing of EU borders and tougher common procedures to combat people smuggling and punish international crime. Above all, growing illegal immigration pushed Europeans to examine the whys of this dramatic human movement and to consider how it related to Europe's proper role in world affairs.

Promoting Human Rights

The tide of refugees and illegal job-seekers, the ethnic violence of Yugoslavia, and western Europe's relative prosperity were some of the factors prompting European visionaries to seek a leadership role in promoting human rights.

In practical terms, western Europe's evolving human rights mission meant, first of all, humanitarian interventions to stop civil wars and to prevent tyrannical governments from slaughtering their own people. Thus the European Union joined with the United States to intervene militarily to stop the killing in Bosnia, Kosovo, and Macedonia and to protect the rights of embattled minorities. The states of the EU also vigorously supported U.N.-sponsored conferences and treaties that sought to verify the compliance of anti–germ warfare conventions, outlawed the use of hideously destructive land mines, and established a new international court to prosecute war criminals.

Europeans also pushed for broader definitions of individual rights. Abolishing the death penalty in the European Union, for example, they condemned its continued use in China, the United States, Saudi Arabia, and some other countries as inhumane and uncivilized. Rights for Europeans in their personal relations also continued to expand. In the pacesetting Netherlands, for example, a growing network of laws gave prostitutes (legally recognized since 1917) pensions and full workers' rights and legalized gay and lesbian marriages, the smoking of pot in licensed coffee shops, and assisted suicide (euthanasia) for the terminally ill.

As the twenty-first century opened, western Europeans also pushed as best they could to extend their broad-based concept of social and economic rights to the world's poor countries. For example, Europe's moderate social democrats combined with human rights campaigners in 2001 to help African governments secure drastic price cuts from the big international drug companies on the drug cocktails needed to combat Africa's AIDS crisis. Strong advocates of greater social equality and state-funded health care, European socialists embraced morality as a basis for action and the global expansion of human rights as a primary goal.

The West and the Islamic World

How and why did relations between the West and the Islamic world deteriorate dramatically in the early twenty-first century?

A hundred years from now, when historians assess developments in the early twenty-first century, they will almost certainly highlight the dramatic deterioration in the long, rich, up-and-down relationship between the West and the Islamic world. They will examine the reasons that the peaceful conclusion of the cold war and the joyful reunification of a divided continent gave way to spectacular terrorist attacks, Western invasions of Muslim countries, and new concern about Muslims living in the West. Unfortunately, we lack the perspective and the full range of source materials that future historians will have at their disposal. Yet we are deeply involved in this momentous historical drama, and we must try to find insight and understanding.

The al-Qaeda Attack of September 11, 2001

On the morning of September 11, 2001, two hijacked passenger planes from Boston crashed into and destroyed the World Trade Center towers in New York City. Shortly thereafter a third plane crashed into the Pentagon, and a fourth, believed to be headed for Washington, crashed into a field in rural Pennsylvania. These terrorist attacks took the lives of more than three thousand people from many countries.

The United States, led by President George W. Bush, launched a military campaign to destroy the perpetrators of the crime—Osama bin Laden's al-Qaeda network of terrorists and Afghanistan's reactionary Muslim government, the Taliban. With the support of an international coalition, the United States joined its tremendous airpower with the faltering Northern Alliance in Afghanistan, which had been fighting the Taliban for years. In mid-November the Taliban collapsed, and Afghan opposition leaders and United Nations mediators worked out plans for a new broad-based government. The hunt for bin Laden, however, was unsuccessful.

The use of terrorist tactics by organized groups against governments has its roots in the early twentieth century. Beginning in the 1920s and peaking in the 1960s, many nationalist movements used terrorism in their battles to achieve political independence and decolonization. This was the case in several new states, including Algeria, Cyprus, Ireland, Israel, and Yemen.[1] In the Vietnam War era, a second wave of terrorism saw some far-left supporters of the communist Vietcong, such as the American Weathermen, the German Red Army Faction, and the Italian Red Brigade, practicing "revolutionary terror." They added airplane hijacking to the earlier tactics of bombings, assassinations, and kidnappings. More than one hundred passenger planes a year were hijacked in the 1970s, as terrorists used civilian hostages to achieve the release of fellow terrorists or other demands. Some terrorists trained in the facilities of the PLO (the Palestine Liberation Organization) operated international networks and targeted Israel and U.S. installations abroad. This second wave receded in the 1980s as painstaking police work and international cooperation defeated these "revolutionaries" in country after country.

Scholars of the contemporary wave of terrorism have avoided the media's tendency to focus almost exclusively on extreme Islamic fundamentalism as the motivation for attacks. They have noted that recent deadly attacks had been committed by terrorists inspired by several religious faiths and religious sects and

al-Qaeda A terrorist organization led by Osama bin Laden that is committed to jihadist revolution in Muslim countries, violently anti-Western, and responsible for the September 11, 2001, attack on New York's World Trade Center.

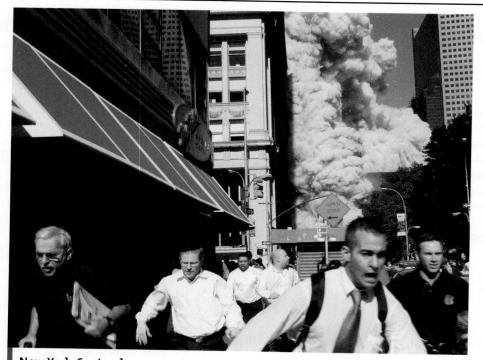

New York, September 11, 2001
Pedestrians race for safety as the World Trade Center towers collapse after being hit by jet airliners.
Al-Qaeda terrorists with box cutters hijacked four aircraft and used three of them as suicide missiles
to perpetrate their unthinkable crime. Heroic passengers on the fourth plane realized what was
happening and forced their hijackers to crash in a field. (AP Images/Suzanne Plunkett)

were by no means limited to Islamic extremists.[2] Instead they trace the terrorists'
roots to political conflicts and civil wars.

In the case of Osama bin Laden and al-Qaeda members, two stages stand out.
First, bin Laden and like-minded "holy warriors" developed terrorist skills and a
fanatical Islamic puritanism over years of fighting against the Soviet Union and
local communists in Afghanistan. They also developed a hatred of most existing
Arab governments, which they viewed as corrupt, un-Islamic, and unresponsive to
the needs of ordinary Muslims. The objects of their hostility included Egypt, Iraq,
and bin Laden's native country, Saudi Arabia. Second, when al-Qaeda members
returned home from Afghanistan and began to organize, they were usually jailed
or forced into exile, often in tolerant Europe. There they blamed the United States
for being the supporter and corrupter of existing Arab governments, and they
organized murderous plots against the United States—a despised proxy for the
Arab rulers they could not reach.

The War in Iraq

Unfortunately, Western unity in Afghanistan soon
turned into bitter quarreling and international crisis
over the prospect of war with Iraq. Many in the Bush
administration believed that the United States could create a democratic, pro-
American Iraq, an Iraq that would transform the Middle East, make peace with
Israel, and ensure access to the world's second-largest oil reserves. They publicly

argued that Saddam Hussein was still developing weapons of mass destruction in flagrant disregard of his promise to end all such programs following the first war with Iraq, in 1991.

Iraq declared that it had destroyed all prohibited weapons, and it allowed United Nations weapons inspectors to return to the country. As 2003 opened, the inspectors operated freely in Iraq and found no weapons of mass destruction. However, the United States and Britain said Iraq was hiding prohibited weapons, moved armies to the Middle East, and lobbied for a new United Nations resolution authorizing immediate military action against Iraq. France, Russia, China, Germany, and a majority of the smaller states argued for continued weapons inspections. Western governments became bitterly divided, and the Security Council deadlocked and failed to act.

In March 2003 the United States and Britain invaded Iraq from bases in Kuwait and quickly toppled Saddam's dictatorship. The allies found no weapons of mass destruction, which raised many questions about a prewar manipulation of intelligence data.

American efforts to establish a stable, pro-American Iraq proved difficult if not impossible. Poor postwar planning and management by President Bush, Defense Secretary Donald Rumsfeld, and other top aides was one factor, but there were others. Modern Iraq, a creation of Western imperialism after World War I (see page 720), is a fragile state with three distinct groups: non-Arab Kurds, and Sunnis and Shi'ites—Arab Muslims who were forever divided by a great schism in the seventh century. Saddam's dictatorship preached Arab and Iraqi nationalism, but it relied heavily on the Sunni minority—20 percent of the population—and repressed the Shi'ites, who made up 60 percent of the population. Jailed or ousted from their positions by American forces for having supported Saddam, top Sunnis quickly turned against the occupation, rallied their supporters, and launched an armed insurgency. By late 2004, radical Sunnis and al-Qaeda converts were

The Golden Mosque of Samara: Before and After

Built to commemorate two of Shi'ite Islam's most revered saints, the Golden Mosque drew countless Shi'ite pilgrims. Then, on June 13, 2006, insurgents dressed as Iraqi policemen entered the mosque, overwhelmed the guards, and detonated two bombs that collapsed the golden dome and destroyed the mosque. Sectarian conflict exploded. (A second terrorist bombing in June 2007 leveled the two minarets seen on the right.) (AP Images/Khalid Mohammed, Hameed Rasheed) slipping into Iraq, where they directed horrendous suicide bombings at American soldiers, Iraqi security forces, and defenseless Shi'ite civilians.

Believing in democracy and representative institutions, the Americans restored Iraqi sovereignty in July 2004, formed a provisional government, and held relatively free national elections in January 2005. Boycotted by the Sunnis, these elections brought the Shi'ite majority to power and marked the high point of Iraqi and American hopes for security and a gradual reconciliation with the Sunni population. Instead, Sunni fighters and jihadist (ji-HAHD-ist) extremists stepped up their deadly campaign. Then, in February 2005 in a carefully planned operation, they blew up the beautiful Golden Mosque of Samarra, one of the most sacred shrines of Shi'ite Islam. This outrage touched off violent retaliation. Shi'ite militias became death squads, killing Sunnis and driving them from their homes. By 2006 a deadly sectarian conflict had taken hold of Baghdad. American solders, loyally continuing to do their duty, were increasingly caught in the crossfire.

In 2007, in the face of widespread American opposition to the war, President Bush ordered more troops to Iraq in an attempt to quell the growing chaos. American commanders on the ground succeeded in forming a critical alliance with some Sunni tribal leaders, who accepted American money and arms and agreed to fight against rather than for the al-Qaeda–led Sunni extremists. As 2008 opened, the military situation in some Sunni provinces and in Baghdad had improved, but Iraq was still very far from peace, stable government, and American withdrawal.

The West and Its Muslim Citizens

After the attacks of September 11, the people of the United States braced for further terrorist acts. But instead Europe was next to receive the extremists' blows. In May 2004 Moroccan Muslims living in Spain exploded bombs planted on morning trains for Madrid and killed 252 commuters. A year later a similar attack was carried out in London by British citizens of Pakistani descent, young men who had grown up in Britain. The brutal murder of filmmaker Theo van Gogh (van GOH) by a young Dutch Muslim avenging van Gogh's satirical depiction of Muhammad seemed to illustrate the depths of Muslim intolerance.

These spectacular attacks and lesser actions by Islamic militants led a shrill chorus to warn that Europe's rapidly growing Muslim population threatened the West's entire Enlightenment tradition of freedom of thought, representative government, toleration, separation of church and state, and, more recently, equal rights for women and gays. Muslim clerics were believed to turn their followers into anti-Western radicals, and even those who urged assimilation were viewed with suspicion. (See the feature "Individuals in Society: Tariq Ramadan.") And time was on the side of Euro-Islam. Europe's Muslim population, estimated at 15 million in 2006, appeared likely to double to 30 million by 2025, and it would increase rapidly thereafter as the percentage of non-Muslim Europeans plummeted because of their baby bust.

Admitting that Islamic extremism could pose a serious challenge, many mainstream observers focused instead on the problem of immigrant integration. Whereas the first generation of Muslim immigrants had found jobs as unskilled workers in Europe's great postwar boom, many Muslims of the second and third generations were finding themselves locked out of work in their adopted countries. This argument was strengthened by widespread rioting in France in November 2005 that saw hundreds of young second- and third-generation Muslim men torch automobiles night after night in Paris suburbs and large cities. (See the feature "Listening to the Past: The French Riots: Will They Change Anything?" on pages

Tariq Ramadan

Religious teacher, activist professor, and media star, Tariq Ramadan (b. 1962), is Europe's most famous Muslim intellectual. He is also a controversial figure, praised by many as a moderate bridge-builder and denounced by others as an Islamic militant in clever disguise.

Born in Switzerland of Egyptian ancestry, Ramadan is the grandson of Hassan al-Banna, the charismatic founder of the powerful Muslim Brotherhood. Al-Banna fought to reshape Arab nationalism within a framework of Islamic religious orthodoxy and anti-British terrorism until he himself was assassinated in 1949. Growing up in Geneva, where his father sought refuge in 1954 after Nasser's anti-Islamic crackdown in Egypt, the young Tariq attended mainstream public schools, played soccer, and absorbed a wide-ranging Islamic heritage. For example, growing up fluent in French and Arabic, he learned English mainly from listening to Pakistani Muslims discuss issues with his father, who represented the Muslim Brotherhood and its ideology in Europe.

Ramadan studied philosophy and French literature as an undergraduate at the University of Geneva, and he then earned a doctorate in Arabic and Islamic Studies. Marrying a Swiss woman who converted to Islam, Ramadan moved his family to Cairo in 1991 to study Islamic law and philosophy. It proved to be a pivotal experience. Eagerly anticipating the return to his Muslim roots, Ramadan gradually realized that only in Europe did he feel truly "at home." In his personal experience he found his message: that Western Muslims should feel equally "at home" and that they should participate fully as active citizens in their adopted countries.

In developing his message, Ramadan left the classroom and focused on creating non-scholarly books, audio cassettes that sell in the tens of thousands, and media events. Slim and elegant in well-tailored suits and open collars, Ramadan is a brilliant speaker. His public lectures in French and English draw hundreds of Muslims (and curious non-Muslims).

Ramadan argues that Western Muslims basically live in security, have fundamental legal rights, and can freely practice their religion. He notes that Muslims in the West are often more secure than are believers in the Muslim world, where governments are frequently repressive and arbitrary. According to Ramadan, Islamic teaching requires Western Muslims to obey Western laws, although in rare cases they may need to plead "conscientious objection" and disobey on religious grounds. Becoming full citizens and refusing to live in parallel as the foreign Other, Muslims should work with non-Muslims on matters of common concern, such as mutual respect, better schools, and economic justice.* Ramadan is most effective with second- or third-generation college graduates. He urges them to think for themselves and distinguish the sacred revelation of Islam from the nonessential cultural aspects that their parents brought from African and Asian villages.

Tariq Ramadan.
(AP Images/Keystone/
Salvatore Di Nolfi)

With growing fame has come growing controversy. In 2004, preparing to take up a professorship in the United States, he was denied an entry visa on the grounds that he had contributed to a Palestinian charity with ties to terrorists. Defenders disputed the facts and charged that his criticism of Israeli policies and the invasion of Iraq were the real reasons. Ramadan's critics also claim that he says different things to different groups: hard-edged criticism of the West found on tapes for Muslims belies the reasoned moderation of his books. Some critics also argue that his recent condemnation of Western capitalism and globalization is an opportunistic attempt to win favor with European leftists, and does not reflect a self-proclaimed Islamic passion for justice. Yet, on balance, Ramadan's reputation remains intact.† An innovative bridge-builder, he symbolizes the growing importance of Europe's Muslim citizens.

Questions for Analysis

1. What is Ramadan's message to Western Muslims? How did he reach his conclusions?
2. Do you think Ramadan's ideas are realistic? Why?

*See, especially, Tariq Ramadan, *Western Muslims and the Future of Islam* (Oxford: Oxford University Press, 2004).
†See Ian Buruma, *The New York Times Magazine*, February 4, 2007.

Section Review

- The terrorist attacks on the United States on September 11, 2001, motivated by al-Qaeda's hatred of Arab governments supported by the West, inspired a U.S. military campaign against Osama bin Laden's al-Qaeda network and Afghanistan's Muslim government, the Taliban.

- The United States and Britain invaded Iraq without United Nations sanction under the pretense of finding weapons of mass destruction, which they failed to find, and in their attempt at setting up a pro-Western government, touched off a civil war between opposing Muslim groups, with American soldiers caught in the middle.

- Discrimination and fear of Muslims increased as the war in Iraq waged, while Muslim immigrant populations in Europe grew and complained of unfair treatment; acceptance of European Muslims is the way to mutual understanding and the prevention of future violence.

838–839.) The rioters complained bitterly of very high unemployment, systematic discrimination, and exclusion. Religious ideology appeared almost nonexistent in their thinking. Studies sparked by the rioting in France found poor, alienated Muslims in unwholesome ghettos throughout western Europe.

Finally, as Europe has become more secular, western Europeans have tended to find all traditional religious belief irrational and out-of-date. The renowned French scholar Olivier Roy argues that Europe must recognize that Islam is now a European religion and a vital part of European life. This recognition, he argues, will open the way to eventual full acceptance of European Muslims in both political and cultural terms. It will head off the resentment that can drive Europe's Muslim believers to separatism and acts of terror.

Chapter Review

How did Mikhail Gorbachev try to revitalize communism in the Soviet Union? What were the radical consequences of his policies? (page 811)

Gorbachev was an idealist who wanted to reform communism in order to save it. His initiatives sought to restructure the stagnant economy, provide accurate information, have meaningful elections, and improve relations with the West. When he refused to use Soviet armies in eastern Europe, the peoples of the satellite nations revolted. Led by Solidarity in Poland, they overturned communist rule in the spectacular, peaceful revolutions of 1989. The democratic movement then triumphed in the Soviet Union, East Germany was reunited with West Germany, and the cold war ended. Emerging as the only superpower, the United States defeated Iraq in the first Gulf war.

How, in the 1990s, did the different parts of a reunifying Europe meet the challenges of postcommunist reconstruction, resurgent nationalism, and economic union? (page 820)

In the 1990s, post–cold war Europe grappled with neoliberal market economies, welfare systems under continuing attack, and globalization. Post-communist reconstruction in Russia was less successful than it was in the newly independent countries of eastern Europe. The former Yugoslavia, tragically destroyed by resurgent ethnic nationalism and civil war, was the glaring exception. Eastern Europe's rebuilding and its determination to "rejoin Europe" stimulated the long postwar movement toward European unity, and the newly named European Union expanded to include almost all of Europe west of Russia, Ukraine, and the Caucasus. This expansion was the shining achievement of the post–cold war era.

Key Terms
perestroika (p. 813)
glasnost (p. 813)
Solidarity (p. 814)
shock therapy (p. 815)
Alliance for Germany (p. 816)
Velvet Revolution (p. 816)
Paris Accord (p. 817)
"new world order" (p. 819)
globalization (p. 822)
European Union (p. 824)
Kosovo Liberation Army (KLA) (p. 826)
baby bust (p. 828)
al-Qaeda (p. 831)

Why did the prospect of population decline, the reality of large-scale immigration, and concern for human rights emerge as critical issues in contemporary Europe? (page 828)

The failure of Europeans to reproduce themselves posed a multitude of serious long-term problems related to pensions, health care, and social vitality. Immigrants fleeing civil war and poverty in Africa and Asia offered a possible solution to Europe's "baby bust," but most Europeans were not prepared to accept large numbers of illegal immigrants from very different cultures. Forced to examine their consciences, Europeans concentrated on promoting human rights around the world, agreeing to humanitarian intervention in civil wars, promoting international courts of justice, and offering help to African nations for the AIDS crisis.

How and why did relations between the West and the Islamic world deteriorate dramatically in the early twenty-first century? (page 831)

The most disturbing development in the early twenty-first century was the renewed hostility between the West and the Islamic world, which was marked indelibly by the al-Qaeda attack of 2001, the American campaign to punish Afghanistan, and the American and British invasion of Iraq. The Anglo-American occupation of Iraq began as a confident effort to remake Iraq (and the Arab world) along Western lines, but early optimism quickly faded. American soldiers in Iraq ran up against a potent combination of Arab nationalism, Islamic extremism, and sectarian conflict between Sunnis, Shi'ites, and Kurds. In western Europe, war in the Middle East encouraged shrill cries about an ominous Muslin threat from immigrants living in western Europe, but a thoughtful consideration of Tariq Ramadan and his audience suggests that these fears were greatly exaggerated.

Notes

1. D. Rappaport, "The Fourth Wave: September 11 in the History of Terrorism," *Current History*, December 2001, pp. 419–424.
2. Ibid.

To assess your mastery of this chapter, go to **bedfordstmartins.com/mckaywestbrief**

Listening to the Past

The French Riots: Will They Change Anything?

In late November 2005, young Muslim males rioted for several nights in the suburbs of Paris and other French cities. Intensely reported, this explosion of car-burning and arson ignited controversy and debate throughout France and across Europe. What caused the riots? What could, what should, be done? How did the conditions of second- and third-generation Muslims in France compare with conditions of Muslims in other Western countries? One penetrating commentary, aimed at an American audience and reprinted here, came from William Pfaff, a noted author and political columnist with many years of European experience.

French police face off with young rioters, silhouetted against the frames of burning automobiles. (Reuters/Corbis)

The rioting in France's ghetto suburbs is a phenomenon of futility—but a revelation nonetheless. It has no ideology and no purpose other than to make a statement of distress and anger. It is beyond politics. It broke out spontaneously and spread in the same way, communicated by televised example, ratified by the huge attention it won from the press and television and the politicians, none of whom had any idea what to do. . . .

[The rioters'] grandfathers came to France, mostly from North Africa, to do the hard labor in France's industrial reconstruction after the Second World War. Their fathers saw the work gradually dry up as Europe's economies slowed, following the first oil shock in the early 1970s. After that came unemployment. The unemployment rate in the zones where there has been the most violence is nearly 40 percent and among young people it is higher. Many of the young men in these places have never been offered a job. When they applied, their names often excluded them.

Their grandfathers were hard-working men. Their fathers saw their manhood undermined by unemployment. These young men are doomed to be boys. They often take their frustration out on their sisters and girlfriends, who are more likely to have done well in school and found jobs—and frequently a new life—outside the ghetto. . . .

The Muslim mothers and wives of the French ghetto are often confined in the home. Drugs are big business in the American ghetto; they are not that big in France. The crimes of the French ghetto are robbery and shoplifting, stealing mobile phones, stealing cars for joyrides, burning them afterward to eliminate fingerprints, or burning cars just for the hell of it, as well as robbing middle-class students in the city and making trouble on suburban trains, looking for excitement.

Religion is important . . . in the French ghetto, it provides the shell that protects against the France that excludes Muslims. To the European Muslim, it seems that all of the powerful in the world are in collusion to exclude Muslims—or are at war with them. The war in Iraq, on television, is the constant backdrop to Muslim life in Europe. There are itinerant imams who can put the young ghetto Muslim on the road to danger and adventure in Afghanistan, Pakistan, Iraq—or elsewhere. There are plenty more who preach a still deeper ghettoization: a retreat inside Islamic fundamentalism, totally shutting out a diabolized secular world.

One would think there would be a revolutionary potential in these ghettos, vulnerability to a mobilizing ideology. This seems not to be so. We may be living in a religious age, but it is not one at political ideology. In any case, it is difficult to imagine how the marginalized, thirteen- to twenty-three-year-old children of the Muslim immigration could change France other than by what they are doing, which is to demonstrate that the French model of assimilating immigrants as citizens, and not as members of religious or ethnic groups, has failed for them. It has failed because it has not seriously been tried.

The ghettoization of immigrant youth in France is the consequence of negligence. It has been as bad as the ghettoization through political correctness of Muslims in Britain and the Netherlands, where many people who thought of themselves as enlightened said that assimilation efforts were acts of cultural aggression. The immigrant in France is told that he or she is a citizen just like everyone else, with all the rights and privileges of citizenship—including the right to be unemployed.

Questions for Analysis

1. Describe the situation of young Muslims in France. What elements of their situation strike you most forcefully? Why?

2. France has maintained that, since all citizens are equal, they should all be treated the same way. Why has this policy failed for French Muslims? What alternatives would you suggest? Why?

Source: William Pfaff, "The French Riots: Will They Change Anything?" Reprinted with permission from *The New York Review of Books*, December 15, 2005, pp. 88–89.

Index